Financial Informatics

An Information-Based Approach to Asset Pricing

Financial Informatics

An Information-Based Approach to Asset Pricing

Editors

Dorje Brody
Department of Mathematics
University of Surrey

Lane Hughston
Department of Computing
Goldsmiths University of London

Andrea Macrina
Department of Mathematics
University College London

World Scientific

NEW JERSEY • LONDON • SINGAPORE • BEIJING • SHANGHAI • HONG KONG • TAIPEI • CHENNAI • TOKYO

Published by

World Scientific Publishing Co. Pte. Ltd.
5 Toh Tuck Link, Singapore 596224
USA office: 27 Warren Street, Suite 401-402, Hackensack, NJ 07601
UK office: 57 Shelton Street, Covent Garden, London WC2H 9HE

Library of Congress Cataloging-in-Publication Data
Names: Brody, Dorje, editor. | Hughston, L. P., 1951– editor. | Macrina, Andrea, editor.
Title: Financial informatics : an information-based approach to asset pricing / editors,
Dorje Brody, Department of Mathematics, University of Surrey,
Lane Hughston, Department of Computing, Goldsmiths University of London,
Andrea Macrina, Department of Mathematics, University College London.
Description: New Jersey : World Scientific, [2022] | Includes bibliographical references and index.
Identifiers: LCCN 2021040753 | ISBN 9789811246487 (hardcover) |
ISBN 9789811246494 (ebook) | ISBN 9789811246500 (ebook other)
Subjects: LCSH: Information theory in finance. | Finance--Mathematical models. |
Investments--Mathematical models. | Valuation.
Classification: LCC HG4515.7 .F56 2022 | DDC 330.01/154--dc23
LC record available at https://lccn.loc.gov/2021040753

British Library Cataloguing-in-Publication Data
A catalogue record for this book is available from the British Library.

For any available supplementary material, please visit
https://www.worldscientific.com/worldscibooks/10.1142/12533#t=suppl

Desk Editors: Soundararajan Raghuraman/Lai Ann

Typeset by Stallion Press
Email: enquiries@stallionpress.com

Preface

For readers new to financial informatics, we offer here a few words of introduction. The importance of the role of information in finance has been recognized for a long time, dating back to the works of the Nobel laureate economist Friedrich Hayek. In the approach that we have adopted, the idea is that the flow of information to market participants has to be modelled explicitly. In this respect, we differ from the classical outlook of mathematical finance, in which the information flow is typically fixed in advance of any specific modelling constructions. We would argue that this is wrong-headed, that first one needs to model the random cash flows generated by a financial asset, and then one needs to model the imperfect information known to market participants concerning these cash flows; and only then, one makes use of this information to generate the market filtration used for pricing. Finally, for practical modelling, we require a particular class of processes designed to carry the imperfect cash-flow information in a mathematically tractable way. This is not to say that actual information is carried in precisely this way—that would be hoping for too much—rather, we merely claim that the use of such processes leads to useful models that are at once both simple and highly suggestive. The first such model that we developed for the carriage of information is what we term the Brownian bridge information process, the details of which are laid out in the first two articles in the collection presented in this book. Next comes the so-called gamma bridge information process, laid out in the third article. Since then, many other examples have followed.

Let us discuss these points in a little more detail. In financial markets, price movements are induced by transactions—investors buying or selling financial assets. When an investor makes a decision to buy or sell such an asset, they are primarily concerned with the question, "What's in it for me?" In other words, the cash flows associated with the asset are the keys, and investment decisions are made in accordance with the information that investors hold concerning these cash flows. Indeed, the fundamental theorem of asset pricing tells us that the price of an asset that pays a single cash flow is the conditional expectation (under a suitable measure and with appropriate discounting) of that cash flow, given the information available. When there are multiple cash flows, the value of an asset is given by the sum of the values of its components. Thus, the *inputs* in the fundamental theorem of asset pricing are the cash flows and information, whereas the price processes are the *outputs*. Now, this transformation from the cash flows and the available information to the price process via conditional expectation is a highly nonlinear one—that is, the price processes are nonlinear functionals of the available information. It follows that if one attempts to model the output (the asset price) from the outset, then one loses its connection to the actual cash flows and the information underlying the market. In other words, any attempt to model the output price process directly—as is commonly done in financial modelling—will necessarily have little connection to the actual, real-world price process of the asset concerned; this is simply because one cannot disentangle this nonlinear relationship. It follows that the conventional approach of directly modelling prices is methodologically doomed. Is there a way forward that will allow one to deduce more realistic models of price processes? A view that is often put forward in this respect is that the real world is so complicated that any attempt at such an endeavour is futile. Information-based asset pricing theory challenges this defeatist attitude. For sure, there has to be some trade-off of realism for analytical or numerical tractability; for, at the end of the day, one has to come up with prices, hedging positions, portfolio weightings, and so on. However, our view is that this trade-off should occur at the modelling of the inputs, not the outputs. That is, even if our models for the cash flows and the information flows are somewhat idealized and simplistic, so long as one attempts to model the "inputs" alluded to above, one *deduces* more realistic models for price processes—in other words, models for which the resulting behavioural characteristics are more consistent with intuition and more in line, one hopes, with the data.

But how can this be carried out in practice? After all, price processes are daily observed quantitatively, whereas information is amassed qualitatively and is not very easy to quantify—it seems difficult, for instance, to assign numerical values to the flow of information. This is where ideas from communication theory come to the rescue. In communication theory, we have a signal, or message, being transmitted, but observations of the signal are obscured by noise. One attempts to estimate the signal as best as possible from the noisy observations. The situation is entirely similar in financial markets, if one interprets the "signal" as representing a future cash flow. For sure, unlike a conventional communication channel, where there is a sender who actively transmits the signal, in financial markets no one is actively transmitting the actual values of future cash flows. We are not in a science fiction scenario where your future self can somehow send signals back to you in the past to enable you to become rich. Nevertheless, future cash flows do exist, and based on imperfect information about these signals, market participants try to come up with their best estimates for these cash flows, resulting in transactions and hence price dynamics. This is why the idea of modelling the flow of information, which might at first appear to be merely an abstraction, yields more realistic financial models for price dynamics.

Our theory of financial informatics came into existence in its present form in April 2005. The Isaac Newton Institute in Cambridge was hosting a six-month program called "Developments in Quantitative Finance". It was in this highly stimulating environment that the theory was formulated. Initially, the framework was constructed with applications to credit theory in mind. One has to recall that at this stage, the great financial crisis of 2007 and 2008 was still in the future. Nevertheless, there were dark clouds on the horizon and it was already recognized by finance theorists that the large investment banks were manufacturing and trading credit products that were so intricate and so *ad hoc* in their structure, so far removed from the Platonic ideal of mathematical objectivity, that it was highly unlikely that any of the big financial institutions had the resources available to value and risk-manage these products reliably.

The situation was a familiar one, where the trading in credit products had advanced in a largely unregulated way well ahead of the intellectual developments, computational facilities, and data requirements necessary for the risk management of these products, even supposing that this would be possible in principle. It was thus viewed as a challenge to the academic community to put forward credit models of a sufficiently advanced and nuanced character to be applicable in the context of this burgeoning line of business, and it was in this setting that our first information-based models for credit pricing were put forward.

In the years leading up to 2005, models for credit risk management and, in particular, for the pricing of credit derivatives, were usually classified into two types: structural and reduced-form. The latter were more commonly used in practice on account of their tractability and on account of the fact that fewer assumptions are required about the nature of the debt obligations involved and the circumstances that might lead to default. Most of the reduced-form models that had been developed so far at that time had been based on the introduction of a random time of default, where the default time was modelled as the time at which the integral of a random intensity process first hits a certain critical level, this level itself being a random variable.

An unsatisfactory feature of such "hazard-rate" models is that they do not take into account the fact that defaults are typically associated with a failure in the delivery of a specific promised cash flow—e.g., a missed coupon payment in the case of a bond or a missed mortgage payment in the case of a home loan. Another drawback of the hazard-rate approach is that it is not very well adapted to situations where one wishes to model the rise and fall of credit spreads—which can in practice be due in part to changes in the level of investor confidence, which in turn may arise as fickle crises of conscience occurring quite independently of any real propensity towards default on the part of the debt under consideration.

In April 2005, we proposed a new class of reduced-form credit models in which these problems were addressed. The outcome of this investigation forms the content of the first article in the present book. For simplicity, we assume that the underlying default-free interest rate system is deterministic. The cash flows of the debt obligation (in the case of a coupon bond, the coupon payments and the principal repayment) are modelled by a collection of random variables—default being identified as the event of the first such payment that fails to achieve the required level specified in the contract of the instrument under consideration. We assume that partial information about each cash flow is available at earlier times to the market—the actual value of the cash flow being obscured by a Gaussian noise process that is conditioned to vanish once the time of the required cash flow is reached. We derive an exact expression for the resulting bond price process and simulate its trajectories. In the case of a defaultable discount bond admitting two possible payouts (e.g., either the full principal or some fixed partial recovery payment), we derive an exact expression for the value of an option on the bond.

Remarkably, this turns out to be a formula of the Black–Scholes type, which can be readily dealt with and intuitively interpreted in a straightforward way. In particular, the parameter that governs the rate at which the true value of the impending cash flow is revealed to market participants, against the background of the obscuring noise process, turns out to play the role of a volatility parameter in the associated option pricing formula. This interpretation is reinforced with the observation that the call option price can be shown to be an increasing function of this market information flow-rate parameter. The paper concludes with a discussion of applications to the aforementioned complex debt instruments, including both single-name products and multi-name products such as first-to-default swaps and collateralized debt obligations.

Such results and many others were all in place by the end of April 2005 and were presented in a seminar at the Isaac Newton Institute on 3 May 2005. At that point we had put together a substantial draft paper, circulated at the seminar, entitled "A Class of Exactly Solvable Credit Models". We recall that many of those present in the audience were enthusiastic about the new work, particularly T. Bielecki, T. R. Hurd, and M. Rutkowski. We had some critics as well, as one usually has (and indeed needs, in any viable scientific enquiry) when new ideas are presented—in this case, notably L. C. G. Rogers, who was concerned with the fact that defaults are "predictable" in our model, rather than abrupt and out-of-the-blue, and would occur (if they did occur) only on a cash-flow date and not at the random times implicit in hazard-rate models. These were valid concerns, of course, but stemmed, in our view, from the perspective of default being a kind of corporate heart attack, coming on suddenly and without notice. We took the view, rather, that corporate default occurred, when it did, mainly at pre-determined times, namely those at which certain key flows of cash were due. We were able to show, for example, that for a suitably low value of the information flow-rate parameter (corresponding to a low rate of transmission of information regarding the possible default of a high credit quality zero-coupon bond, with a low but nonzero *a priori* default probability) default, although strictly speaking predictable, would occur for all practical purposes without announcement. In other words, one could capture within the information-based approach various phenomena that had hitherto thought to be exclusively the consequence of hazard-rate models. Our models were semi-structural in character and hence could be applied to complex instruments, namely those that had a good deal of structure.

Following our seminar, Marek Rutkowski scrutinized the mathematical foundations of the theory, concluded that they were sound, and proceeded to formulate a generalization (in collaboration with N. Yu) that relaxed the deterministic interest rate condition, published in 2007. Our work was presented at a number of different venues in the ensuing weeks and months, including talks at the WBS Workshop on Collateralized Debt Obligations in London and the Global Derivatives Conference in Paris, both in May 2005; at the Bank of Japan in Tokyo in June 2005; and at Union Bank of Switzerland in London and the closing workshop of the Isaac Newton Institute program in Cambridge in July 2005. Further talks followed at the Kruger Park Mathematics in Finance Conference and at the University of the Witwatersrand in August 2005; at the Risk conference in London in September 2005; at CEMFI (Centro de Estudios Monetarios y Financieros) in Madrid in October 2005; at King's College London in November 2005; at Herriot Watt University in Edinburgh, at Nomura in Tokyo, and at the Bank of Japan again in Tokyo, in December 2005; at the Winter School in Financial Mathematics at Lunteren in the Netherlands in January 2006; at the 16th Annual Derivative Securities and Risk Management Conference,

Federal Deposit Insurance Corporation (FDIC), Arlington, Virginia, in April 2006; at the first AMaMeF (Advanced Mathematical Methods for Finance) conference at Side, Antalya, in Turkey, also in April 2006; at Columbia University, New York, and at Bloomberg, New York, in May 2006; at Humbolt University, Berlin, in July 2006; at the Fourth World Congress of the Bachelier Finance Society, Tokyo, and at Nomura, Tokyo, in August 2006; and at the Mathematical Finance Conference in honor of Dilip Madan's 60th birthday at the University of Maryland in September 2006. By this time, the title of the talk had become "Beyond Hazard Rates: A New Framework for Credit Risk Modelling". It was with this title that the paper was published in the Festschrift volume for Dilip Madan, reproduced here as the first article in our collection. In the meantime, we had extended the scope of the theory to equity pricing, allowing also for time dependence in the flow-rate parameter. These generalizations were discussed at length in our second paper on the subject, which showed the applicability of the theory to a wider range of financial assets.

Those who were present at Dilip Madan's birthday conference in September 2006 will recall that Marc Yor gave two highly engaging talks on topics relating to gamma processes. In the discussion following the presentation of our work on information-based asset pricing, Marc then suggested, with his usual good-natured mathematical enthusiasm, that we should look to see if our theory might be applicable in the case of gamma bridges. We followed up on this idea, and eventually a beautiful new manifestation of information-based pricing did indeed present itself, in this case with applications to insurance. The theory was worked out in 2007 and published in 2008. The curious title "Dam Rain and Cumulative Gain" refers to work in the 1950s by J. Gani, D. C. Kendall[1] and others, using gamma processes to model the accumulation of water behind a dam, and the relation of this hydrological model to the problem of claims reserving in non-life insurance. The gamma bridge model for information-based pricing led the way to a wide range of interesting research into Lévy bridge models and various extensions thereof, several examples of the outputs of which we include in the present volume.

At the end of this preface, we provide a bibliography of articles and theses written over the last fifteen years or so on topics relating to or further developing our theory. We have no doubt that there will be other applications to come. One might ask if there is scope for the theory to be applicable in some form outside of asset pricing as such. We have seen hints

[1]J. Gani (1957) Problems in the probability theory of storage systems, *Journal of the Royal Statistical Society B*, **19**(2), 181–206; D. C. Kendall (1957) Some problems in the theory of dams, *Journal of the Royal Statistical Society B*, **19**(2), 207–233.

of this already. There is the paper by Cartea, Jaimungal & Kinzebulatov (2016) on algorithmic trading with learning; there is an application to greenhouse gas emissions in the context of climate risk securitization in the work of Macrina & Sekine (2021); and there are the papers of Brody (2019) and Brody & Meier (2022) on electioneering, disinformation, and fake news. Further afield, there is an interesting application of some of the mathematical elements of the theory to solve a problem in quantum mechanics concerning stochastic models for the collapse of the wave function (Brody & Hughston 2005, 2006) that ought to be pursued further. One line of enquiry that may be promising for future research is in psychology. One envisages a living creature—either a simple automaton or a more complex organism—and we consider a situation where the creature is faced with alternatives, whether to make an effort, at some cost, to seek a resource (food, shelter, reproduction), but only imperfect information is available to the organism about the extent to which the efforts will be rewarded if pursued. Many such situations can be envisaged. Based on the information available, the organism must assign a value in the present to the presently unknown eventual outcome and decide on that basis whether to pursue the given opportunity. It may be that arbitrage opportunities tend to close up rapidly in nature, once they arise, and hence a kind of equilibrium prevails over time. Nevertheless, as a part of this equilibrium, the automata are constantly seeking to maximize advantage, given the data available. An animal hears a rustling somewhere nearby in the woods—is it predator or prey? Or was that merely a dead branch falling from a tree? The animal will instinctively calculate the values associated with its possible responses, based on the limited information available, and will act accordingly. Such scenarios are not too different from our information-based market models—certainly at the level of large intelligent creatures, but also perhaps at a microbiological level, wherever there is scope for valuation and choice in the face of information flows with results achieved over finite time horizons.

We leave these thoughts for future speculation. In the present, in today's financial markets, one might take the view that derivatives have been tamed. The regulators have stepped in and measures have been taken—perhaps somewhat clumsily, and not altogether effectively—but the worst of the excesses have been abated. At least, that is what one would hope for. But one only has to open one's eyes to see that although derivatives may belong to the past, new challenges lie ahead, ripe with parallel opportunities for exploitation and scope for damaging consequence. High frequency trading . . . algorithms . . . machine learning . . . block chain finance . . . cryptocurrencies. Who does not know at least someone among their associates who has lost a bundle in crypto trading? Or has been misrepresented by an algorithm that has taken advantage? Perhaps we all can be of sufficiently cold heart to tolerate an element of private misery in others, but what happens when similar phenomena threaten to bring down trusted institutions, large corporations, and sovereign states? And aren't we already seeing this? Are not those same dark clouds gathering once more? It is of the nature of finance to be constantly reinventing itself, and for the practice to be forever slipping from the constraining hands of regulation for reasons valid or otherwise. The domains of applicability shift but the problems remain. As Wotan says in Act II of Wagner's *Die Walküre*, "Der alte Sturm, die alte Müh'! Doch Stand muss ich hier halten." (The same old storm, the same old trouble! But here I must stand firm!) Thus we see a forward path, and the old fight continues.

Our work on information-based asset pricing and related topics has benefitted from discussions with many friends, colleagues and students over the years, and we thank them all for their valuable contributions. We mention in particular our coauthors J. Akahori, G. Andruszkiewicz, S. Crépey, M. H. A. Davis, D. Filipović, R. L. Friedman, U. Horst, A. E. V. Hoyle, M. Kupper, Y. T. Law, C. Mainberger, D. M. Meier, B. K. Meister, L. A. Mengütürk, T. M. Nguyen, P. A. Parbhoo, M. F. Parry, L. G. Sánchez-Betancourt, J. Sekine, D. Skovmand and X. Yang, many of whom are represented in the papers collected in the present volume.

We are grateful to the publishers of the articles appearing in this compilation for their kind permission to include these works. We also wish to recognize T. R. Soundararajan, Ann Lai, Yubing Zhai and other colleagues at World Scientific for their valuable assistance in the production of this volume.

We dedicate this book to the memory of three giants in our subject: Tomas Björk (1947–2021), Mark H. A. Davis (1945–2020), and Marc Yor (1949–2014).

Dorje C. Brody
Lane P. Hughston
Andrea Macrina

Bibliography

Here we collect a sample of articles and theses on topics related to financial informatics. Articles included in the present volume are marked with an asterisk.

D. C. Brody & L. P. Hughston (2005) Finite-time stochastic reduction models, *Journal of Mathematical Physics* **46**, 082101:1–7.

D. C. Brody & L. P. Hughston (2006) Quantum noise and stochastic reduction, *Journal of Physics* A **39**, 833–876.

A. Macrina (2006) *An Information-Based Framework for Asset Pricing: X-Factor Theory and its Applications.* PhD thesis, Department of Mathematics, King's College London.

*D. C. Brody, L. P. Hughston & A. Macrina (2007) Beyond hazard rates: a new framework for credit-risk modelling. In: *Advances in Mathematical Finance*, Festschrift Volume in Honour of Dilip Madan. M. Fu, R. Jarrow, Ju-Yi Yen & R. Elliott (Eds.), pp. 231–257. Basel: Birkhauser.

N. Çaliskan (2007) *Asset Pricing Models: Stochastic Volatility and Information-Based Approaches.* MSc thesis, Graduate School of Applied Mathematics, Middle East Technical University.

M. Rutkowski & N. Yu (2007) An extension of the Brody-Hughston-Macrina approach to modelling of defaultable bonds. *International Journal of Theoretical and Applied Finance* **10**(3), 557–589.

*D. C. Brody, L. P. Hughston & A. Macrina (2008) Information-based asset pricing. *International Journal of Theoretical and Applied Finance* **11**(1), 107–142.

*D. C. Brody, L. P. Hughston & A. Macrina (2008) Dam rain and cumulative gain. *Proceedings of the Royal Society* A **464**, 1801–1822.

L. P. Hughston & A. Macrina (2008) Information, inflation, and interest. *Banach Center Publications* **83**, 117–138.

M. Bošel'a (2009) *Credit Risk Modelling.* MSc thesis, Department of Probability and Mathematical Statistics, Charles University in Prague.

*D. C. Brody, M. H. A. Davis, R. L. Friedman & L. P. Hughston (2009) Informed traders. *Proceedings of the Royal Society* A **465**, 1103–1122.

*D. C. Brody & R. L. Friedman (2009) Information of interest. *Risk Magazine*, December 2009 issue, 105–110. Reprinted in *Life & Pensions Magazine*, February 2010 issue, 35–40.

D. C. Brody (2010) Information and asset pricing. In: Progress in Analysis and Its Applications – *Proceedings of the 7th International ISAAC Congress.* M. Ruzhansky & J. Wirth (Eds.), pp. 381–388. Singapore: World Scientific Publishing Company.

*D. C. Brody, L. P. Hughston & A. Macrina (2010) Credit risk, market sentiment and randomly-timed default. In: *Stochastic Analysis in 2010*, D. Crisan (Ed.), pp. 267–280. Berlin, Heidelberg: Springer-Verlag.

P. V. Gapeev & M. Jeanblanc (2010) Pricing and filtering in a two-dimensional dividend switching model. *International Journal of Theoretical and Applied Finance* **13**(7), 1001–1017.

A. E. V. Hoyle (2010) *Information-Based Models for Finance and Insurance.* PhD thesis, Department of Mathematics, Imperial College London.

A. Macrina & P. A. Parbhoo (2010) Security pricing with information-sensitive discounting. In: *Recent Advances in Financial Engineering 2009,* M. Kijima, C. Hara, K. Tanaka & Y. Muromachi (Eds.), pp. 157–180. Singapore: World Scientific Publishing Company.

G. Andruszkiewicz & D. C. Brody (2011) *Noise, Premium, and Bubble.* ArXiv: 1103.3206.

*D. C. Brody, L. P. Hughston & A. Macrina (2011) Modelling information flows in financial markets. In: *Advanced Mathematical Methods for Finance,* G. Di Nunno & B. Øksendal (Eds.), pp. 133–153. Berlin, Heidelberg: Springer-Verlag.

*E. Hoyle, L. P. Hughston & A. Macrina (2011) Lévy random bridges and the modelling of financial information. *Stochastic Processes and Their Applications* **121**, 856–884.

*J. Akahori & A. Macrina (2012) Heat kernel interest rate models with time-inhomogeneous Markov processes. *International Journal of Theoretical and Applied Finance* **15**(1), 1–15.

M. L. Bedini (2012) *Information on a Default Time: Brownian Bridges on Stochastic Intervals and Enlargement of Filtrations.* PhD thesis, Friedrich-Schiller-Universität, Jena.

D. C. Brody, B. K. Meister & M. F. Parry (2012) Informational inefficiencies in financial markets. *Mathematics and Financial Economics* **6**, 249–259.

D. Filipović, L. P. Hughston & A. Macrina (2012) Conditional density models for asset pricing. *International Journal of Theoretical and Applied Finance* **15**(1), 1250002:1–24.

L. P Hughston & A. Macrina (2012) Pricing fixed-income securities in an information-based Framework. *Applied Mathematical Finance* **19**(4), 361–379.

Y. T. Law (2012) *Pricing under Random Information Flow and the Theory of Information Pricing.* PhD thesis, Department of Mathematics, Imperial College London.

*D. C. Brody & L. P. Hughston (2013) Lévy information and the aggregation of risk aversion. *Proceedings of the Royal Society A*, **469**, 20130024:1–19.

*D. C. Brody, L. P. Hughston & X. Yang (2013) Signal processing with Lévy information. *Proceedings of the Royal Society* A **469**, 20120433:1–23.

U. Horst, M. Kupper, A. Macrina & C. Mainberger (2013) Continuous equilibrium in affine and information-based capital asset pricing models. *Annals of Finance* **9**(4), 725–755.

E. Hoyle & L. A. Mengütürk (2013) Archimedian survival processes. *Journal of Multivariate Analysis* **115**, 1–15.

C. Mainberger (2013) *Essays on Supersolutions of BSDEs and Equilibrium Pricing in Generalized Capital Asset Pricing Models.* PhD thesis, Mathematische-Naturwissenschaftliche Fakultät II, Humboldt-Universität zu Berlin.

L. A. Mengütürk (2013) *Information-Based Jumps, Asymmetry and Dependence in Financial Modelling.* PhD thesis, Department of Mathematics, Imperial College London.

P. A. Parbhoo (2013) *Information-Driven Pricing Kernel Models.* PhD thesis, School of Computational and Applied Mathematics, University of the Witwatersrand.

X. Yang (2013) *Information-Based Commodity Pricing and the Theory of Signal Processing with Lévy Information.* PhD thesis, Department of Mathematics, Imperial College London.

G. Andruszkiewicz (2014) *Modelling Animal Spirits in Financial Markets.* PhD Thesis, Department of Mathematics, Imperial College London.

D. Ikpe, S. Mataramvura & R. Becker (2014) Modelling financial information by conditioning. *Communications on Stochastic Analysis* **8**(1), 99–110.

*A. Macrina (2014) Heat kernel models for asset pricing. *International Journal of Theoretical and Applied Finance* **17**(7), 1–34.

*A. Macrina & P. A. Parbhoo (2014) Randomized mixture models for pricing kernels. *Asia-Pacific Financial Markets* **21**(4), 281–315.

M. Pohl (2014) *Further Studies on the Aggregation of Risk Aversion.* MSc thesis, Department of Mathematics, Brunel University London.

D. C. Brody & Y. T. Law (2015) Pricing of defaultable bonds with random information flow. *Applied Mathematical Finance* **22**, 399–420.

E. Hoyle, L. P. Hughston & A. Macrina (2015) Stable-1/2 bridges and insurance. *Banach Center Publications* **104**, 95–120.

N. S. Aydin (2016) *Financial Modelling with Random Bridge Signals and Forward Information.* PhD thesis, The Graduate School of Applied Mathematics, Middle East Technical University.

Á. Cartea, S. Jaimungal & D. Kinzebulatov (2016) Algorithmic trading with learning. *International Journal of Theoretical and Applied Finance* **19**(4), 1650028:1–30.

S. Crépey, A. Macrina, T. M. Nguyen & D. Skovmand (2016) Rational multi-curve models with counterparty-risk valuation adjustments. *Quantitative Finance* **16**(6), 847–866.

D. C. Ikpe (2016) *Compound Lévy Random Bridges and Credit Risky Asset Pricing.* PhD thesis, AIFMRM and Department of Mathematics and Applied Mathematics, University of Cape Town.

A. Shmatko (2016) *Implied Dynamical Market Price of Risk.* MSc thesis, Department of Mathematics, Brunel University London.

N. S. Aydin (2017) *Financial Modelling with Forward-Looking Information.* Cham, Switzerland: Springer International Publishing.

P. A. Bebbington (2017) *Studies in Informational Price Formation, Prediction Markets, and Trading.* PhD thesis, Department of Physics and Astronomy, University College London.

M. L. Bedini, R. Buckdahn & H.-L. Engelbert (2017) Brownian bridges on random intervals. *Theory of Probability & Its Applications* **61**(1), 15–39.

T. Leung, J. Li & X. Li (2018) Optimal timing to trade along a randomized Brownian bridge. *International Journal of Financial Studies* **6**(75), 1–23.

L. A. Mengütürk (2018) Gaussian random bridges and a geometric model for information equilibrium. *Physica* A **494**, 465–483.
K. Thoednithi (2018) Information-based model with noisy anticipation and its application in finance. *Asia-Pacific Financial Markets* **25**, 125–177.
D. C. Brody (2019) Modelling election dynamics and the impact of disinformation. *Information Geometry* **2**, 209–230.
K. Fukuda, K. Kondo & H. Takada (2019) Price dynamics under the information-based dealer model. *Journal of Mathematical Finance* **9**, 726–746.
C. Ikamari, P. Ngare & P. Weke (2019) Discretizing the information based asset price dynamics. *Journal of Finance and Economics* **7**(2), 68–74.
M. Erraoui, A. Hilbert & M. Louriki (2020) Bridges with random length: Gamma case. *Journal of Theoretical Probability* **33**, 931–953.
*E. Hoyle, A. Macrina & L. Mengütürk (2020) Modulated information flows in financial markets. *International Journal of Theoretical and Applied Finance* **23**(4) 2050026.
*L. P. Hughston & L. Sánchez-Betancourt (2020) Pricing with variance gamma information. *Risks* **8**, 105:1–22.
C. Ikamari, P. Ngare & P. Weke (2020) Multi-asset option pricing using an information-based model. *Scientific African* **10**, e00564, 1–13.
L. A. Mengütürk & M. C. Mengütürk (2020) Captive diffusions and their applications to order-preserving dynamics. *Proceedings of the Royal Society A* **476**, 20200294.
H. Nakagawa & H. Takada (2020) A default contagion model for pricing defaultable bonds from an information based perspective. *HUB-FS Working Paper Series*, FS-2020-E-001, 1–38.
M. Erraoui, A. Hilbert & M. Louriki (2021) On an extension of the Brownian bridge with applications in finance. ArXiv:2110.0131.
*A. Macrina & J. Sekine (2021) Stochastic modelling with randomized Markov bridges. *Stochastics* **93**(1), 29–55. Published online 18 December 2019.
*D. C. Brody, L. P. Hughston & X. Yang (2022) On the pricing of storable commodities. In: *Financial Informatics: An Information-Based Approach to Asset Pricing,* D. C. Brody, L. P. Hughston & A. Macrina (Eds.). Singapore: World Scientific Publishing Company.
*D. C. Brody & D. M. Meier (2022) How to model fake news. In: *Financial Informatics: An Information-Based Approach to Asset Pricing,* D. C. Brody, L. P. Hughston & A. Macrina (Eds.). Singapore: World Scientific Publishing Company.

About the Editors

Dorje Brody is Professor of Mathematics in the Department of Mathematics at the University of Surrey. He was born in Hong Kong, and later lived in Japan, obtaining a BSc at the University of Niigata. He took his PhD at Imperial College London. Dorje has been a visiting professor at Imperial College since 2011, and at St Petersburg National Research University of Information Technologies, Mechanics and Optics since 2013. Previously, he has held a Royal Society University Research Fellowship at Imperial College, a Research Fellowship of the Particle Physics and Astronomy Research Council at Cambridge University, and a Junior Research Fellowship at Churchill College Cambridge. In 2004, he was selected as an Outstanding Young Person to meet the Emperor of Japan. Dorje is a member of the London Mathematical Society, a Fellow of the Institute of Physics, and a Lifetime Fellow of the Cambridge Philosophical Society. He works on a wide range of foundational problems in applied mathematics, theoretical physics, and mathematical finance.

Lane Hughston is Professor of Mathematics in the Department of Computing at Goldsmiths University of London. His DPhil in Mathematics is from the University of Oxford. Lane has previously held positions at Lincoln College Oxford, King's College London, and Imperial College London. He has held visiting appointments at the University of Texas at Austin, University College London, and St Petersburg National Research University of Information

Technologies, Mechanics and Optics. He belongs to the American Finance Association, the American Physical Society, the London Mathematical Society, and the Society for Industrial and Applied Mathematics. He is a lifetime member of the American Mathematical Society, the Bachelier Finance Society, and the International Society for General Relativity and Gravitation, and he is a Fellow of the Institute of Mathematics and its Applications. Lane has a number of years of experience in the banking industry to his credit, and has for many years served as Editor-in-Chief of *International Journal of Theoretical and Applied Finance.*

Andrea Macrina is Reader in Mathematics in the Department of Mathematics at University College London (UCL) and Adjunct Professor in the African Institute of Financial Markets and Risk Management at the University of Cape Town (UCT). His PhD in Mathematics is from King's College London. Andrea has previously held appointments as Lecturer in Financial Mathematics at King's College London, as Visiting Associate Professor in the Kyoto Institute of Economic Research, and as Research Fellow at ETH Zürich. He has been Director of the Financial Mathematics MSc at UCL since its inception in 2012 and is co-founder of the Financial Mathematics Team Challenge, initiated at UCT in 2014. Andrea belongs to the London Mathematical Society, the American Mathematical Society, the Society for Industrial and Applied Mathematics, the Bachelier Finance Society, and the Bernoulli Society for Mathematical Statistics and Probability. His research in applied probability and stochastic modelling, with applications to problems in financial mathematics and insurance, has benefitted from fruitful collaborations with industry practitioners.

Contents

Chapter 1

Beyond Hazard Rates: A New Framework for Credit-Risk Modelling*

Dorje C. Brody,[1] Lane P. Hughston,[2] and Andrea Macrina[2]

[1] Department of Mathematics
Imperial College
London SW7 2BZ, United Kingdom
dorje@imperial.ac.uk

[2] Department of Mathematics
King's College London
The Strand, London WC2R 2LS, United Kingdom
lane.hughston@kcl.ac.uk, andrea.macrina@kcl.ac.uk

Summary. A new approach to credit risk modelling is introduced that avoids the use of inaccessible stopping times. Default events are associated directly with the failure of obligors to make contractually agreed payments. Noisy information about impending cash flows is available to market participants. In this framework, the market filtration is modelled explicitly, and is assumed to be generated by one or more independent market information processes. Each such information process carries partial information about the values of the market factors that determine future cash flows. For each market factor, the rate at which true information is provided to market participants concerning the eventual value of the factor is a parameter of the model. Analytical expressions that can be readily used for simulation are presented for the price processes of defaultable bonds with stochastic recovery. Similar expressions can be formulated for other debt instruments, including multi-name products. An explicit formula is derived for the value of an option on a defaultable discount bond. It is shown that the value of such an option is an increasing function of the rate at which true information is provided about the terminal payoff of the bond. One notable feature of the framework is that it satisfies an overall dynamic consistency condition that makes it suitable as a basis for practical modelling situations where frequent recalibration may be necessary.

Key words: Credit risk; credit derivatives; incomplete information; information-based asset pricing; market filtration; Bayesian inference; Brownian bridge process.

1 Introduction and Summary

Models for credit risk management and, in particular, for the pricing of credit derivatives are usually classified into two types: structural and reduced-form.

*This chapter was originally published as: D. C. Brody, L. P. Hughston & A. Macrina (2007) Beyond Hazard Rates: A New Framework for Credit-Risk Modelling. In: *Advances in Mathematical Finance* (M. Fu, R. Jarrow, Ju-Yi Yen & R. Elliott, editors), Birkhauser, pp. 231–257. Reprinted with kind permission from Birkhäuser Boston.

For general overviews of these approaches, see, for example, Jeanblanc and Rutkowski [25], Hughston and Turnbull [18], Bielecki and Rutkowski [4], Duffie and Singleton [12], Schönbucher [35], Bielecki et al. [3], Lando [29], and Elizalde [13].

There is a divergence of opinion in the literature as to the relative merits of the structural and reduced-form methodologies. Both approaches have strengths, but there are also shortcomings. Structural models attempt to account at some level of detail for the events leading to default (see, e.g., Merton [33], Black and Cox [5], Leland and Toft [30], Hilberink and Rogers [17], Jarrow et al. [23], and Hull and White [19]). One general problem of the structural approach is that it is difficult in a structural model to deal systematically with the multiplicity of situations that can lead to default. For this reason, structural models are sometimes viewed as unsatisfactory as a basis for a practical modelling framework, particularly when multi-name products such as nth-to-default swaps and collateralised debt obligations (CDOs) are involved.

Reduced-form models are more commonly used in practice, on account of their tractability and because fewer assumptions are required about the nature of the debt obligations involved and the circumstances that might lead to default (see, e.g., Flesaker et al. [14], Jarrow and Turnbull [22], Duffie et al. [10], Jarrow et al. [20], Lando [28], Madan and Unal [31], [32], Duffie and Singleton [11], and Jarrow and Yu [24]). Most reduced-form models are based on the introduction of a random time of default, modelled as the time at which the integral of a random intensity process first hits a certain critical level, this level itself being an independent random variable. An unsatisfactory feature of such intensity models is that they do not adequately take into account the fact that defaults are typically associated directly with a failure in the delivery of a contractually agreed cash flow—for example, a missed coupon payment. Another drawback of the intensity approach is that it is not well adapted to the situation where one wants to model the rise and fall of credit spreads, which can in reality be due in part to changes in the level of investor confidence.

The purpose of this paper is to introduce a new class of reduced-form credit models in which these problems are addressed. The modelling framework that we develop is broadly in the spirit of the incomplete-information approaches of Kusuoka [27], Duffie and Lando [9], Cetin et al. [6], Gieseke [15], Gieseke and Goldberg [16], Jarrow and Protter [21], and others. In our approach, no attempt is made as such to bridge the gap between the structural and the intensity-based models; rather, by abandoning the need for the intensity-based approach, we are able to formulate a class of reduced-form models that exhibit a high degree of intuitively natural behaviour and analytic tractability. Our approach is to build an economic model for the information that market participants have about future cash flows.

For simplicity, we assume that the underlying default-free interest rate system is deterministic. The cash flows of the debt obligation—in the case of a coupon bond, the coupon payments and the principal repayment—are modelled by a collection of random variables, and default is identified as the event of the first such payment that fails to achieve the terms specified in the contract. We assume that partial information about each such cash flow is available at earlier times to market participants; however, the information of the actual value of the payout is obscured by a Gaussian noise process that is conditioned to vanish once the time of the required cash flow is reached. We proceed under these assumptions to derive an exact expression for the bond price process.

In the case of a defaultable discount bond admitting two possible payouts (either the full principal, or some partial recovery payment), we derive an exact expression for the value of an option on the bond. Remarkably, this turns out to be a formula of the Black–Scholes–Merton type. In particular, the parameter σ that governs the rate at which the true value of the impending cash flow is revealed to market participants, against the background of the obscuring noise process, turns out to play the role of a volatility parameter in the associated option pricing formula; this interpretation is reinforced with the observation that the option price is an increasing function of this parameter.

The structure of the paper is as follows. In Section 2, we introduce the notion of an 'information process' as a mechanism for modelling the market filtration. In the case of a credit-risky discount bond, the information process carries partial information about the terminal payoff, and it is assumed that the market filtration is generated by this process. The price process of the bond is obtained by taking the conditional expectation of the payout, and the properties of the resulting formula are analysed in the case of a binary payout. In Section 3, these results are extended to the situation of a defaultable discount bond with stochastic recovery, and a proof is given for the Markov property of the information process. In Section 4, we work out the dynamics of the price of a defaultable bond, and we show that the bond price process satisfies a diffusion equation. An explicit construction is presented for the Brownian motion that drives this process. This is given in Equation (20). We also work out an expression for the volatility of the bond price, given in Equation (28). In Section 5, we simulate the resulting price processes and show that for suitable values of the information flow-rate parameter introduced in Equation (4) the default of a credit-risky discount bond occurs in effect as a 'surprise.' In Section 6, we establish a decomposition formula similar to that obtained by Lando [28] in the case of a bond with partial recovery. In Section 7, we show that the framework has a general 'dynamical consistency' property. This has important implications for applications of the resulting models. In deriving these results we make use of special orthogonality properties of the Brownian bridge process (see, e.g., Yor [36; 37]). In Sections 8 and 9, we consider options on defaultable bonds and work out explicit formulae for the price processes of such options. In doing so, we introduce a novel change-of-measure technique that enables us to calculate explicitly various expectations involving Brownian bridge processes. This technique is of some interest in its own right. One of the consequences of the fact that the bond price process is a diffusion in this framework is that explicit formulae can be worked out for the delta-hedging of option positions. In Section 10, we extend the general theory to the situation where there are multiple cash flows. We look in particular at the case of a coupon bond and derive an explicit formula for the price process of such a bond. In Sections 11, 12 and 13, we consider complex debt instruments, and construct appropriate information-based valuation formulae for credit default swaps (CDSs) and portfolios of credit-risky instruments.

2 The Information-Based Approach

The object of this paper is to build an elementary modelling framework in which matters related to credit are brought to the forefront. Accordingly, we assume that the background default-free interest-rate system is deterministic: this assumption allows us to focus attention on credit-related issues; it also permits us to derive explicit expressions for certain types of credit derivative prices. The general philosophy is that we should try to sort out credit-related matters first, before attempting to incorporate a stochastic default-free system of interest rates.

As a further simplifying feature we take the view that default events are directly linked with anomalous cash flows. Thus default is not something that happens 'in the abstract,' but rather is associated with the failure of an agreed cash flow to materialise at the required time. In this way we improve the theory by eradicating the superfluous use of inaccessible stopping times.

Our theory is based on modelling the flow of partial information to market participants about impending debt payments. As usual, we model the financial markets with the specification of a probability space $(\Omega, \mathcal{F}, Q)$ with filtration $\{\mathcal{F}_t\}_{0\leq t<\infty}$. The probability measure Q is understood to be the risk-neutral measure, and $\{\mathcal{F}_t\}$ is understood to be the market filtration. All asset-price processes and other information-providing processes accessible to market participants are adapted to $\{\mathcal{F}_t\}$. Contrary to the usual practice, we shall model $\{\mathcal{F}_t\}$ explicitly, rather than simply regarding it as being given.

The real probability measure does not enter into the present investigation. We assume the absence of arbitrage and the existence of a pricing kernel (cf. Cochrane [8], and references cited therein). With these conditions the existence of a unique risk-neutral measure is ensured, even though the market may be incomplete. We assume further that the default-free discount-bond system, denoted $\{P_{tT}\}_{0\leq t\leq T<\infty}$, can be written in the form $P_{tT} = P_{0T}/P_{0t}$, where the function $\{P_{0t}\}_{0\leq t<\infty}$ is differentiable and strictly decreasing, and satisfies $0 < P_{0t} \leq 1$ and $\lim_{t\to\infty} P_{0t} = 0$. Under these assumptions it follows that if the integrable random variable H_T represents a cash flow occurring at T, then its value H_t at any earlier time t is given by

$$H_t = P_{tT} E\left[H_T|\mathcal{F}_t\right]. \tag{1}$$

Now let us consider, as a first example, the case of a simple credit-risky discount bond that matures at time T to pay a principal of h_1 dollars, if there is no default. In the event of default, the bond pays h_0 dollars, where $h_0 < h_1$. When two such payoffs are possible we call the resulting structure a 'binary' discount bond. In the case given by $h_1 = 1$ and $h_0 = 0$ we call the resulting defaultable debt obligation a 'digital' bond.

Let us write p_0 for the probability that the bond will pay h_0, and p_1 for the probability that the bond will pay h_1. The probabilities are risk-neutral, and hence build in any risk adjustments required in expectations needed in order to deduce prices. Thus if we write B_{0T} for the price at time 0 of the credit-risky discount bond we have

$$B_{0T} = P_{0T}(p_0 h_0 + p_1 h_1). \tag{2}$$

It follows that, providing we know the market data B_{0T} and P_{0T}, we can infer the *a priori* probabilities p_0 and p_1:

$$p_0 = \frac{1}{h_1 - h_0}\left(h_1 - \frac{B_{0T}}{P_{0T}}\right), \qquad p_1 = \frac{1}{h_1 - h_0}\left(\frac{B_{0T}}{P_{0T}} - h_0\right). \tag{3}$$

Given this setup we proceed to model the bond-price process $\{B_{tT}\}_{0\le t\le T}$. We suppose that the true value of H_T is not fully accessible until time T; that is, we assume H_T is $\mathcal{F}_T$-measurable, but not $\mathcal{F}_t$-measurable for $t < T$. We assume, nevertheless, that partial information regarding the value of the principal repayment H_T is available at earlier times. This information will in general be imperfect; one is looking into a crystal ball, so to speak, but the image is cloudy. Our model for such cloudy information is of a simple type that allows for analytic tractability. More precisely, we assume that the following $\{\mathcal{F}_t\}$-adapted process is accessible to market participants:

$$\xi_t = \sigma H_T t + \beta_{tT}. \tag{4}$$

We call $\{\xi_t\}$ a *market information process*. The process $\{\beta_{tT}\}_{0\le t\le T}$ appearing here is a standard Brownian bridge on the time interval $[0, T]$. Thus $\{\beta_{tT}\}$ is a Gaussian process satisfying $\beta_{0T} = 0$ and $\beta_{TT} = 0$, such that $E[\beta_{tT}] = 0$ and $E[\beta_{sT}\beta_{tT}] = s(T-t)/T$ for all s, t satisfying $0 \le s \le t \le T$. We assume that $\{\beta_{tT}\}$ is independent of H_T, and thus represents pure noise. Market participants do not have direct access to $\{\beta_{tT}\}$; that is to say, $\{\beta_{tT}\}$ is not assumed to be adapted to $\{\mathcal{F}_t\}$. We can think of $\{\beta_{tT}\}$ as representing the rumour, speculation, misrepresentation, overreaction, and general disinformation often occurring, in one form or another, in connection with financial activity.

Clearly the choice (4) can be generalised to include a wider class of models enjoying similar qualitative features. The present analysis sticks with (4) for the sake of definiteness and tractability. Indeed, the choice of $\{\xi_t\}$ defined by (4) has many attractive features, and can be regarded as a convenient 'standard' model for an information process. The motivation for the use of a bridge process to represent the noise is intuitively as follows. We assume that initially all available market information is taken into account in the determination of the price; in the case of a credit-risky discount bond, the relevant information is embodied in the *a priori* probabilities. After the passage of time, new rumours and stories start circulating, and we model this by taking into account that the variance of the Brownian bridge steadily increases for the first half of its trajectory. Eventually, however, the variance falls to zero at the maturity of the bond, when the 'moment of truth' arrives.

The parameter σ in this model represents the rate at which the true value of H_T is 'revealed' as time progresses. Thus, if σ is low, then the value of H_T is effectively hidden until very near the maturity date of the bond; on the other hand, if σ is high, then we can think of H_T as being revealed quickly. The parameter σ has the units $\sigma \sim [\text{time}]^{-1/2}[\text{price}]^{-1}$. A rough measure for the timescale τ_D over which information is revealed is $\tau_D = 1/\sigma^2(h_1 - h_0)^2$. In particular, if $\tau_D \ll T$, then the value of H_T will be revealed rather early in the history of the bond, for example, after the passage of a few multiples of τ_D. In this situation, if default is 'destined' to occur, even though the initial value of the bond is high, then this will be signalled by a rapid decline in the bond price. On the other hand, if $\tau_D \gg T$, then H_T will only be revealed at the last minute, so to speak, and the default will come as a surprise. It is by virtue of this feature of the framework that the use of inaccessible stopping times can be avoided.

To make a closer inspection of the default timescale, we proceed as follows. For simplicity, we assume that the only market information available about H_T at times earlier than T comes from observations of $\{\xi_t\}$. Specifically, if we denote $\mathcal{F}_t^\xi$ the subalgebra of $\mathcal{F}_t$ generated by $\{\xi_s\}_{0\le s\le t}$, then our simplifying assumption is that $\{\mathcal{F}_t\} = \{\mathcal{F}_t^\xi\}$. That is to say, we assume that the market filtration is generated by the information process.

Now we are in a position to determine the price-process $\{B_{tT}\}_{0\le t\le T}$ for a credit-risky bond with payout H_T. In particular, the bond price is given by

$$B_{tT} = P_{tT} H_{tT}, \tag{5}$$

where H_{tT} denotes the conditional expectation of the bond payout:

$$H_{tT} = E\left[H_T \,\middle|\, \mathcal{F}_t^\xi\right]. \tag{6}$$

It turns out that this conditional expectation can be worked out explicitly. The result is given by the following expression:

$$H_{tT} = \frac{p_0 h_0 \exp\left[\frac{T}{T-t}\left(\sigma h_0 \xi_t - \frac{1}{2}\sigma^2 h_0^2 t\right)\right] + p_1 h_1 \exp\left[\frac{T}{T-t}\left(\sigma h_1 \xi_t - \frac{1}{2}\sigma^2 h_1^2 t\right)\right]}{p_0 \exp\left[\frac{T}{T-t}\left(\sigma h_0 \xi_t - \frac{1}{2}\sigma^2 h_0^2 t\right)\right] + p_1 \exp\left[\frac{T}{T-t}\left(\sigma h_1 \xi_t - \frac{1}{2}\sigma^2 h_1^2 t\right)\right]}. \tag{7}$$

Thus we see that there exists a function $H(x, y)$ of two variables such that $H_{tT} = H(\xi_t, t)$, and as a consequence that the bond price can be expressed as a function of the market information.

Because $\{\xi_t\}$ is given by a combination of the random bond payout and an independent Brownian bridge, it is straightforward to simulate trajectories for $\{B_{tT}\}$. The bond price trajectories rise and fall randomly in line with the fluctuating information about the likely final payoff: in this respect, the resulting model is more satisfactory than an intensity-based model, where the only basis for shifts in credit spreads is through a random change in the default intensity.

The details of the derivation of the formula presented above are given in the next section. First, however, let us verify that the expression in (7) converges, as t approaches T, to the 'actual' value of H_T. The proof is as follows. Suppose that the actual value of the payout is $H_T = h_0$. In that case the information process takes the form

$$\xi_t = \sigma h_0 t + \beta_{tT} \tag{8}$$

Inserting this expression into (7), we divide the numerator and the denominator by the coefficient of $p_0 h_0$. As a consequence we obtain

$$H_{tT} = \frac{p_0 h_0 + p_1 h_1 \exp\left[-\frac{T}{T-t}\left(\frac{1}{2}\sigma^2(h_1 - h_0)^2 t - \sigma(h_1 - h_0)\beta_{tT}\right)\right]}{p_0 + p_1 \exp\left[-\frac{T}{T-t}\left(\frac{1}{2}\sigma^2(h_1 - h_0)^2 t - \sigma(h_1 - h_0)\beta_{tT}\right)\right]}. \tag{9}$$

We observe that as t approaches T the bond price converges to h_0, as required. A similar argument shows that if $H_T = h_1$, then the bond price converges to h_1. We note, in line with our heuristic arguments concerning the characteristic timescale τ_D, that the parameter $\sigma^2(h_1 - h_0)^2$ governs the speed at which H_{tT} converges to its terminal value. In particular, if the *a priori* probability of no default is high (say, $p_1 \approx 1$), and if σ is very small, and if in fact $H_T = h_0$, then it will only be when t is near T that serious decay in the bond price will set in.

3 Defaultable Discount Bond Price Processes

Let us now consider the more general situation where the discount bond pays the value $H_T = h_i$ $(i = 0, 1, \ldots, n)$ with *a priori* probability $Q(H_T = h_i) = p_i$. For convenience we assume $h_n > h_{n-1} > \cdots > h_1 > h_0$. The case $n = 1$ corresponds to the binary bond we have just considered. In the general situation we think of $H_T = h_n$ as the case of no default, and the other cases as various possible degrees of recovery.

Although for simplicity we work with a discrete payout spectrum for H_T, the continuous case can be formulated analogously. In that situation we assign a fixed *a priori* probability p_1 to the case of no default, and a continuous probability distribution function $p_0(x) = Q(H_T < x)$ for values of x less than or equal to h, satisfying $p_1 + p_0(h) = 1$.

Now defining the information process $\{\xi_t\}$ as before, we want to find the conditional expectation (6). It follows from the Markovian property of $\{\xi_t\}$, which is established below, that to compute (6), it suffices to take the conditional expectation of H_T with respect to the subalgebra generated by the random variable ξ_t alone. Therefore, writing $H_{tT} = E[H_T|\xi_t]$ we have

$$H_{tT} = \sum_i h_i \pi_{it}, \tag{10}$$

where $\pi_{it} = Q(H_T = h_i|\xi_t)$ is the conditional probability that the credit-risky bond pays out h_i. That is to say, $\pi_{it} = E[\mathbf{1}_{\{H_T=h_i\}}|\xi_t]$.

To show that the information process satisfies the Markov property, we need to verify that

$$Q(\xi_t \le x|\mathcal{F}_s^\xi) = Q(\xi_t \le x|\xi_s) \tag{11}$$

for all $x \in \mathbb{R}$ and all s, t such that $0 \le s \le t \le T$. It suffices to show that

$$Q\left(\xi_t \le x|\xi_s, \xi_{s_1}, \xi_{s_2}, \ldots, \xi_{s_k}\right) = Q\left(\xi_t \le x|\xi_s\right) \tag{12}$$

for any collection of times $t, s, s_1, s_2, \ldots, s_k$ such that $T \ge t > s > s_1 > s_2 > \cdots > s_k > 0$. First, we remark that for any times t, s, s_1 satisfying $t > s > s_1$ the Gaussian random variables β_{tT} and $\beta_{sT}/s - \beta_{s_1T}/s_1$ have vanishing covariance, and thus are independent. More generally, for $s > s_1 > s_2 > s_3$ the random variables $\beta_{sT}/s - \beta_{s_1T}/s_1$ and $\beta_{s_2T}/s_2 - \beta_{s_3T}/s_3$ are independent. Next, we note that $\xi_s/s - \xi_{s_1}/s_1 = \beta_{sT}/s - \beta_{s_1T}/s_1$. It follows that

$$\begin{aligned} &Q\left(\xi_t \le x|\xi_s, \xi_{s_1}, \xi_{s_2}, \ldots, \xi_{s_k}\right) \\ &= Q\left(\xi_t \le x\left|\xi_s, \frac{\xi_s}{s} - \frac{\xi_{s_1}}{s_1}, \frac{\xi_{s_1}}{s_1} - \frac{\xi_{s_2}}{s_2}, \ldots, \frac{\xi_{s_{k-1}}}{s_{k-1}} - \frac{\xi_{s_k}}{s_k}\right.\right) \\ &= Q\left(\xi_t \le x\left|\xi_s, \frac{\beta_{sT}}{s} - \frac{\beta_{s_1T}}{s_1}, \frac{\beta_{s_1T}}{s_1} - \frac{\beta_{s_2T}}{s_2}, \ldots, \frac{\beta_{s_{k-1}T}}{s_{k-1}} - \frac{\beta_{s_kT}}{s_k}\right.\right). \end{aligned} \tag{13}$$

However, because ξ_s and ξ_t are independent of the remaining random variables $\beta_{sT}/s - \beta_{s_1T}/s_1$, $\beta_{s_1T}/s_1 - \beta_{s_2T}/s_2$, $\ldots$, $\beta_{s_{k-1}T}/s_{k-1} - \beta_{s_kT}/s_k$, the desired Markov property follows immediately.

Next we observe that the *a priori* probability p_i and the *a posteriori* probability π_{it} are related by the following version of the Bayes formula:

$$Q(H_T = h_i|\xi_t) = \frac{p_i \rho(\xi_t|H_T = h_i)}{\sum_i p_i \rho(\xi_t|H_T = h_i)}. \tag{14}$$

Here the conditional density function $\rho(\xi|H_T = h_i)$, $\xi \in \mathbb{R}$, for the random variable ξ_t is defined by the relation

$$Q\left(\xi_t \le x|H_T = h_i\right) = \int_{-\infty}^{x} \rho(\xi|H_T = h_i)\, d\xi, \tag{15}$$

and is given explicitly by

$$\rho(\xi|H_T = h_i) = \frac{1}{\sqrt{2\pi t(T-t)/T}} \exp\left(-\tfrac{1}{2}\frac{(\xi - \sigma h_i t)^2}{t(T-t)/T}\right). \tag{16}$$

This expression can be deduced from the fact that conditional on $H_T = h_i$ the random variable ξ_t is normally distributed with mean $\sigma h_i t$ and variance $t(T-t)/T$. As a consequence of (14) and (16), we see that

$$\pi_{it} = \frac{p_i \exp\left[\frac{T}{T-t}(\sigma h_i \xi_t - \frac{1}{2}\sigma^2 h_i^2 t)\right]}{\sum_i p_i \exp\left[\frac{T}{T-t}(\sigma h_i \xi_t - \frac{1}{2}\sigma^2 h_i^2 t)\right]}. \tag{17}$$

It follows then, on account of (10), that

$$H_{tT} = \frac{\sum_i p_i h_i \exp\left[\frac{T}{T-t}\left(\sigma h_i \xi_t - \frac{1}{2}\sigma^2 h_i^2 t\right)\right]}{\sum_i p_i \exp\left[\frac{T}{T-t}\left(\sigma h_i \xi_t - \frac{1}{2}\sigma^2 h_i^2 t\right)\right]}. \tag{18}$$

This is the desired expression for the conditional expectation of the bond payoff. In particular, for the binary case $i = 0, 1$ we recover formula (7). The discount-bond price B_{tT} is then given by (5), with H_{tT} defined as in (18).

4 Defaultable Discount Bond Dynamics

In this section we analyse the dynamics of the defaultable bond price process $\{B_{tT}\}$ determined in Section 3. The key relation we need for working out the dynamics of the bond price is that the conditional probability $\{\pi_{it}\}$ satisfies a diffusion equation of the form

$$d\pi_{it} = \frac{\sigma T}{T-t}(h_i - H_{tT})\pi_{it}\, dW_t. \tag{19}$$

In particular, we can show that the process $\{W_t\}_{0\le t<T}$ arising here, defined by the expression

$$W_t = \xi_t + \int_0^t \frac{1}{T-s}\,\xi_s\, ds - \sigma T \int_0^t \frac{1}{T-s} H_{sT}\, ds, \tag{20}$$

is an $\{\mathcal{F}_t\}$-Brownian motion. The fact that $\{\pi_{it}\}$ satisfies (19) with $\{W_t\}$ defined as in (20) can be obtained directly from (17) by an application of Itô's lemma. We need to use the relation $(d\xi_t)^2 = dt$, which follows from the relation $(d\beta_{tT})^2 = dt$. The fact that $\{W_t\}$ is an $\{\mathcal{F}_t\}$-Brownian motion can then be verified by showing that $\{W_t\}$ is an $\{\mathcal{F}_t\}$-martingale and that $(dW_t)^2 = dt$. We proceed as follows.

To prove that $\{W_t\}$ is an $\{\mathcal{F}_t\}$-martingale, we need to show that $E[W_u|\mathcal{F}_t] = W_t$ for $0 \le t \le u < T$. First we note that it follows from (20) and the Markov property of $\{\xi_t\}$ that

$$E[W_u|\mathcal{F}_t] = W_t + E\left[(\xi_u - \xi_t)|\xi_t\right] + E\left[\int_t^u \frac{1}{T-s}\,\xi_s\,ds\,\middle|\,\xi_t\right] - \sigma T\,E\left[\int_t^u \frac{1}{T-s}\,H_{sT}\,ds\,\middle|\,\xi_t\right]. \tag{21}$$

Formula (21) can be simplified if we recall that $H_{sT} = E[H_T|\xi_s]$ and use the tower property in the last term on the right. Inserting the definition (4) into the second and third terms on the right in (21), we then have:

$$\begin{aligned} E[W_u|\mathcal{F}_t] = W_t &+ E[\sigma H_T u + \beta_{uT}|\xi_t] - E[\sigma H_T t + \beta_{tT}|\xi_t] \\ &+ \sigma E[H_T|\xi_t]\int_t^u \frac{s}{T-s}\,ds + E\left[\int_t^u \frac{1}{T-s}\,\beta_{sT}\,ds\,\middle|\,\xi_t\right] \\ &- \sigma E[H_T|\xi_t]\int_t^u \frac{T}{T-s}\,ds. \end{aligned} \tag{22}$$

It follows immediately that all of the terms involving the random variable H_T cancel each other in (22). This leads us to the following relation:

$$E[W_u|\mathcal{F}_t] = W_t + E[\beta_{uT}|\xi_t] - E[\beta_{tT}|\xi_t] + \int_t^u \frac{1}{T-s}\,E[\beta_{sT}|\xi_t]\,ds. \tag{23}$$

Next we use the tower property and the independence of $\{\beta_{tT}\}$ and H_T to deduce that

$$E[\beta_{uT}|\xi_t] = E[E[\beta_{uT}|H_T,\beta_{tT}]|\xi_t] = E[E\,[\beta_{uT}|\beta_{tT}]|\xi_t]\,. \tag{24}$$

To calculate the inner expectation $E[\beta_{uT}|\beta_{tT}]$, we use the fact that the random variable $\beta_{uT}/(T-u) - \beta_{tT}/(T-t)$ is independent of the random variable β_{tT}. This can be established by calculating their covariance, and using the relation $E[\beta_{uT}\beta_{tT}] = t(T-u)/T$. We conclude after a short calculation that

$$E[\beta_{uT}|\beta_{tT}] = \frac{T-u}{T-t}\,\beta_{tT}. \tag{25}$$

Inserting this result into (24), we obtain the following formula:

$$E[\beta_{uT}|\xi_t] = \frac{T-u}{T-t}\,E[\beta_{tT}|\xi_t]. \tag{26}$$

Applying this formula to the second and fourth terms on the right side of (23), we immediately deduce that $E[W_u|\mathcal{F}_t] = W_t$. That establishes that $\{W_t\}$ is an $\{\mathcal{F}_t\}$-martingale. Now we need to show that $(dW_t)^2 = dt$. This follows if we insert (4) into the definition of $\{W_t\}$ above and use again the fact that $(d\beta_{tT})^2 = dt$. Hence, by virtue of Lévy's criterion (see, e.g., Karatzas and Shreve [26]), we conclude that $\{W_t\}$ is an $\{\mathcal{F}_t\}$-Brownian motion.

The Brownian motion $\{W_t\}$, the existence of which we have just established, can be regarded as part of the information accessible to market participants. Unlike β_{tT}, the value of W_t contains 'real' information relevant to the bond payoff. It follows from (10) and (19) that for the discount bond dynamics, we have

$$dB_{tT} = r_t B_{tT}\, dt + \Sigma_{tT}\, dW_t. \tag{27}$$

Here $r_t = -\partial \ln P_{0t}/\partial t$ is the short rate, and the absolute bond volatility Σ_{tT} is given by

$$\Sigma_{tT} = \frac{\sigma T}{T-t} P_{tT} V_{tT}, \tag{28}$$

where V_{tT} is the conditional variance of the terminal payoff H_T, defined by

$$V_{tT} = \sum_i (h_i - H_{tT})^2 \pi_{it}. \tag{29}$$

We observe that as the maturity date is approached the absolute discount bond volatility will be high unless the conditional probability has most of its mass concentrated around the 'true' outcome; this ensures that the correct level can be eventually reached.

It follows as a consequence of (20) that $\{\xi_t\}$ satisfies the following stochastic differential equation:

$$d\xi_t = \frac{1}{T-t}\big(\sigma T H(\xi_t, t) - \xi_t\big)dt + dW_t. \tag{30}$$

We see that $\{\xi_t\}$ is a diffusion process; and because $H(\xi_t, t)$ is monotonic in its dependence on ξ_t, we deduce that $\{B_{tT}\}$ is also a diffusion process. To establish that B_{tT} is increasing in ξ_t, we note that $P_{tT} H'(\xi_t, t) = \Sigma_{tT}$, where $H'(\xi, t) = \partial H(\xi, t)/\partial \xi$. It is interesting to observe that, in principle, instead of 'deducing' the dynamics of $\{B_{tT}\}$ from the information-based arguments of the previous sections, we might have simply 'proposed' on an *ad hoc* basis the one-factor diffusion process (30), noting that it leads to the correct default dynamics. This reasoning shows that our framework can be viewed, if desired, as leading to purely 'classical' financial models, based on observable price processes.

5 Simulation of Bond Price Processes

The present framework allows for a highly efficient simulation methodology for the dynamics of defaultable bonds. In the case of a defaultable discount bond, all we need to do is to simulate the dynamics of $\{\xi_t\}$. For each run of the simulation, we choose at random a value for H_T (in accordance with the *a priori* probabilities), and a sample path for the Brownian bridge. That is to say, each simulation corresponds to a choice of $\omega \in \Omega$, and for each such choice we simulate the path $\xi_t(\omega) = \sigma t H_T(\omega) + \beta_{tT}(\omega)$ for $t \in [0, T]$. One way to simulate a Brownian bridge is to write $\beta_{tT} = B_t - (t/T)B_T$, where $\{B_t\}$ is a standard Brownian motion. It is straightforward to verify that if $\{\beta_{tT}\}$ is defined in this way then it has the correct mean and covariance. Because the bond price at t is expressed directly as a function of the random variable ξ_t, this means that pathwise simulation of the bond price trajectory is feasible for any number of recovery levels.

In Figure 1 we present some sample trajectories of the defaultable bond price process for various values of σ. These illustrations are fascinating inasmuch as they show that for small values of σ the default comes almost as a 'surprise' near the maturity date of the bond; whereas for large values of σ the default, if it occurs, effectively takes place early in the life of bond.

6 Digital Bonds and Binary Bonds with Partial Recovery

It is interesting to ask whether in the case of a binary bond with partial recovery, with possible payoffs $\{h_0, h_1\}$, the bond-price process admits the representation

$$B_{tT} = P_{tT}h_0 + D_{tT}(h_1 - h_0). \tag{31}$$

Here D_{tT} denotes the value of a digital credit-risky bond that at maturity pays a unit of currency with probability p_1 and zero with probability $p_0 = 1 - p_1$. Thus h_0 is the amount that is guaranteed, whereas $h_1 - h_0$ is the part that is 'at risk.' It is well known that such a relation can be deduced in intensity-based models. The problem now is to find a process $\{D_{tT}\}$ consistent with our scheme such that (31) holds. It turns out that this can be achieved.

Suppose we consider a digital payoff structure $D_T \in \{0, 1\}$ for which the information-flow parameter σ is replaced by $\bar{\sigma} = \sigma(h_1 - h_0)$. In other words, in establishing the appropriate dynamics for $\{D_{tT}\}$ we 'renormalise' σ by replacing it with $\bar{\sigma}$. The information available to market participants in the case of the digital bond is represented by the process $\{\bar{\xi}_t\}$ defined by

$$\bar{\xi}_t = \bar{\sigma} D_T t + \beta_{tT}. \tag{32}$$

It follows from (18) that the corresponding digital bond price is given by

$$D_{tT} = P_{tT} \frac{p_1 \exp\left[\frac{T}{T-t}\left(\bar{\sigma}\bar{\xi}_t - \frac{1}{2}\bar{\sigma}^2 t\right)\right]}{p_0 + p_1 \exp\left[\frac{T}{T-t}\left(\bar{\sigma}\bar{\xi}_t - \frac{1}{2}\bar{\sigma}^2 t\right)\right]}. \tag{33}$$

A calculation making use of (7) then allows us to confirm that (31) holds, where D_{tT} is given by (33). Thus even though *prima facie* the general binary bond process (7) does not appear to admit a decomposition of the form (31), we see that it does, once a suitably renormalised value for the market information flow-rate parameter has been introduced.

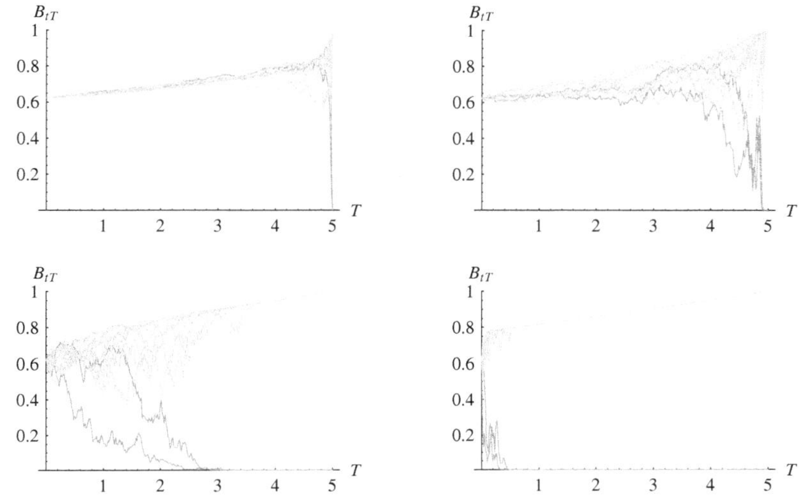

Fig. 1. Bond price processes for various information flow rates. The parameter σ governs the rate at which information is released to market participants concerning the payout of a defaultable discount bond. Four values of σ are illustrated, given by .04, .2, 1, and 5. The bond has a maturity of five years, and the default-free interest-rate system has a constant short rate given by $r = 5\%$. The *a priori* probability of default is taken to be 20%. For low values of σ, collapse of the bond price, if it occurs, takes place only 'at the last minute.'

More generally, if the bond has a number of recovery levels, so the random variable H_T can take the values $\{h_0, h_1, \ldots, h_n\}$, then h_0 can be regarded as the 'risk-free' component of the bond. The bond price process admits an additive decomposition into two parts, namely, a default-free discount bond that pays h_0, and a credit-risky discount bond that pays $\bar{h}_i = h_i - h_0$ with *a priori* probability p_i. This decomposition is given by

$$B_{tT} = P_{tT}h_0 + P_{tT}\frac{\sum_{i=1}^{n} p_i\bar{h}_i \exp\left[\frac{T}{T-t}\left(\sigma\bar{h}_i\bar{\xi}_t - \frac{1}{2}\sigma^2\bar{h}_i^2 t\right)\right]}{p_0 + \sum_{i=1}^{n} p_i \exp\left[\frac{T}{T-t}\left(\sigma\bar{h}_i\bar{\xi}_t - \frac{1}{2}\sigma^2\bar{h}_i^2 t\right)\right]}, \tag{34}$$

where $\bar{\xi}_t = \sigma(H_T - h_0)t + \beta_{tT}$ is the resulting price-shifted information process. Note that $\bar{h}_0 = 0$, which makes the summation in the numerator begin from $i = 1$; thus the second term in the right-hand side of (34) is the multiple-recovery-level analogue of formula (33) above.

7 Dynamic Consistency and Model Calibration

The technique of renormalising the information flow rate has another useful application. It turns out that the information-based framework exhibits a property that might appropriately be called 'dynamic consistency.' Loosely speaking, the question is: if the information process is given as described, but then we reinitialise the model at some specified intermediate time, is it still the case that the dynamics of the model moving forward from that intermediate time can be consistently represented by an information process?

To answer this question we proceed as follows. First we define a standard Brownian bridge over the interval $[t, T]$ to be a Gaussian process $\{\gamma_{uT}\}_{t\leq u\leq T}$ satisfying $\gamma_{tT} = 0$, $\gamma_{TT} = 0$, $E[\gamma_{uT}] = 0$ for all $u \in [t, T]$, and $E[\gamma_{uT}\gamma_{vT}] = (u-t)(T-v)/(T-t)$ for all u, v such that $t \leq u \leq v \leq T$. We make note of the following observation.

Let $\{\beta_{tT}\}_{0\leq t\leq T}$ be a standard Brownian bridge over the interval $[0, T]$, and define the process $\{\gamma_{uT}\}_{t\leq u\leq T}$ by

$$\gamma_{uT} = \beta_{uT} - \frac{T-u}{T-t}\,\beta_{tT}. \tag{35}$$

Then $\{\gamma_{uT}\}_{t\leq u\leq T}$ is a standard Brownian bridge over the interval $[t, T]$, and is independent of $\{\beta_{sT}\}_{0\leq s\leq t}$.

The result is easily proved by use of the covariance relation $E[\beta_{tT}\beta_{uT}] = t(T-u)/T$. We need to recall also that a necessary and sufficient condition for a pair of Gaussian random variables to be independent is that their covariance should vanish. Now let the information process $\{\xi_s\}_{0\leq s\leq T}$ be given, and fix an intermediate time $t \in (0, T)$. Then for all $u \in [t, T]$, let us define a process $\{\eta_u\}$ by

$$\eta_u = \xi_u - \frac{T-u}{T-t}\,\xi_t. \tag{36}$$

We claim that $\{\eta_u\}$ is an information process over the time interval $[t, T]$. In fact, a short calculation establishes that

$$\eta_u = \tilde{\sigma} H_T (u-t) + \gamma_{uT}, \tag{37}$$

where $\{\gamma_{uT}\}_{t\leq u\leq T}$ is a standard Brownian bridge over the interval $[t, T]$, independent of H_T, and the new information flow rate is given by $\tilde{\sigma} = \sigma T/(T-t)$. The interpretation of these results is as follows. The 'original' information process proceeds from time 0 up to time t. At that time we can recalibrate the model by taking note of the value of the random variable ξ_t, and introducing the reinitialised information process $\{\eta_u\}$. The new information process depends on H_T; but because the value of ξ_t is supplied, the *a priori* probability distribution for H_T now changes to the appropriate *a posteriori* distribution consistent with the information gained from the knowledge of ξ_t at time t.

These interpretive remarks can be put into a more precise form as follows. Let $0 \leq t \leq u < T$. What we want is a formula for the conditional probability π_{iu} expressed in terms of the information η_u and the 'new' *a priori* probability π_{it}. Such a formula exists, and is given as follows:

$$\pi_{iu} = \frac{\pi_{it}\exp\left[\frac{T-t}{T-u}\left(\tilde{\sigma}h_i\eta_u - \frac{1}{2}\tilde{\sigma}^2 h_i^2(u-t)\right)\right]}{\sum_i \pi_{it}\exp\left[\frac{T-t}{T-u}\left(\tilde{\sigma}h_i\eta_u - \frac{1}{2}\tilde{\sigma}^2 h_i^2(u-t)\right)\right]}. \tag{38}$$

This remarkable relation can be verified by substituting the given expressions for π_{it}, η_u, and $\tilde{\sigma}$ into the right-hand side of (38). But (38) has the same structure as the original formula (17) for π_{it}, and thus we see that the model exhibits manifest dynamic consistency.

8 Options on Credit-Risky Bonds

We now turn to consider the pricing of options on credit-risky bonds. As we demonstrate shortly, in the case of a binary bond there is an exact solution for the valuation of European-style vanilla options. The resulting expression for the option price exhibits a structure that is strikingly analogous to that of the Black–Scholes–Merton option pricing formula.

We consider the value at time 0 of an option that is exercisable at a fixed time $t > 0$ on a credit-risky discount bond that matures at time $T > t$. The value C_0 of a call option is

$$C_0 = P_{0t}E\left[(B_{tT} - K)^+\right], \tag{39}$$

where K is the strike price. Inserting formula (5) for B_{tT} into the valuation formula (39) for the option, we obtain

$$\begin{aligned} C_0 &= P_{0t}\, E\left[(P_{tT}H_{tT} - K)^+\right] \\ &= P_{0t}\, E\left[\left(\sum_{i=0}^{n} P_{tT}\pi_{it}h_i - K\right)^+\right] \\ &= P_{0t}\, E\left[\left(\frac{1}{\Phi_t}\sum_{i=0}^{n} P_{tT}p_{it}h_i - K\right)^+\right] \\ &= P_{0t}\, E\left[\frac{1}{\Phi_t}\left(\sum_{i=0}^{n}\Big(P_{tT}h_i - K\Big)p_{it}\right)^+\right]. \end{aligned} \tag{40}$$

Here the random variables p_{it}, $i = 0, 1, \ldots, n$, are the 'unnormalised' conditional probabilities, defined by

$$p_{it} = p_i\exp\left[\frac{T}{T-t}\left(\sigma h_i\xi_t - \tfrac{1}{2}\sigma^2 h_i^2 t\right)\right]. \tag{41}$$

Then $\pi_{it} = p_{it}/\Phi_t$ where $\Phi_t = \sum_i p_{it}$, or, more explicitly,

$$\Phi_t = \sum_{i=0}^{n} p_i \exp\left[\frac{T}{T-t}\left(\sigma h_i \xi_t - \tfrac{1}{2}\sigma^2 h_i^2 t\right)\right]. \tag{42}$$

Our plan now is to use the factor $1/\Phi_t$ appearing in (40) to make a change of probability measure on $(\Omega, \mathcal{F}_t)$. To this end, we fix a time horizon u at or beyond the option expiration but before the bond maturity, so $t \le u < T$. We define a process $\{\Phi_t\}_{0 \le t \le u}$ by use of the expression (42), where now we let t vary in the range $[0, u]$. It is a straightforward exercise in Itô calculus, making use of (30), to verify that

$$d\Phi_t = \sigma^2 \left(\frac{T}{T-t}\right)^2 H_{tT}^2 \Phi_t \, dt + \sigma \frac{T}{T-t} H_{tT} \Phi_t \, dW_t. \tag{43}$$

It follows then that

$$d\Phi_t^{-1} = -\sigma \frac{T}{T-t} H_{tT} \Phi_t^{-1} dW_t, \tag{44}$$

and hence that

$$\Phi_t^{-1} = \exp\left(-\sigma \int_0^t \frac{T}{T-s} H_{sT} \, dW_s - \tfrac{1}{2}\sigma^2 \int_0^t \frac{T^2}{(T-s)^2} H_{sT}^2 \, ds\right). \tag{45}$$

Because $\{H_{sT}\}$ is bounded, and $s \le u < T$, we see that the process $\{\Phi_s^{-1}\}_{0 \le s \le u}$ is a martingale. In particular, because $\Phi_0 = 1$, we deduce that $E^Q[\Phi_t^{-1}] = 1$, where t is the option maturity date, and hence that the factor $1/\Phi_t$ in (40) can be used to effect a change of measure on $(\Omega, \mathcal{F}_t)$. Writing B for the new probability measure thus defined, we have

$$C_0 = P_{0t} \, E^B\left[\left(\sum_{i=0}^{n}\left(P_{tT} h_i - K\right) p_{it}\right)^+\right]. \tag{46}$$

We call B the 'bridge' measure because it has the special property that it makes $\{\xi_s\}_{0 \le s \le t}$ a B-Gaussian process with mean zero and covariance $E^B[\xi_r \xi_s] = r(T-s)/T$ for $0 \le r \le s \le t$. In other words, with respect to the measure B, and over the interval $[0, t]$, the information process has the law of a standard Brownian bridge over the interval $[0, T]$. Armed with this fact, we proceed to calculate the expectation in (46).

The proof that $\{\xi_s\}_{0 \le s \le t}$ has the claimed properties under the measure B is as follows. For convenience we introduce a process $\{W_t^*\}_{0 \le t \le u}$ which we define as the following Brownian motion with drift in the Q-measure:

$$W_t^* = W_t + \sigma \int_0^t \frac{T}{T-s} H_{sT} \, ds. \tag{47}$$

It is straightforward to check that on $(\Omega, \mathcal{F}_t)$ the process $\{W_t^*\}_{0\le t\le u}$ is a Brownian motion with respect to the measure defined by use of the density martingale $\{\Phi_t^{-1}\}_{0\le t\le u}$ given by (45). It then follows from the definition of $\{W_t\}$, given in (20), that

$$W_t^* = \xi_t + \int_0^t \frac{1}{T-s}\,\xi_s\,ds. \tag{48}$$

Taking the stochastic differential of each side of this relation, we deduce that

$$d\xi_t = -\frac{1}{T-t}\,\xi_t\,dt + dW_t^*. \tag{49}$$

We note, however, that (49) is the stochastic differential equation satisfied by a Brownian bridge (see, e.g., Karatzas and Shreve [26], Yor [37], and Protter [34]) over the interval $[0,T]$. Thus we see that in the measure B defined on $(\Omega, \mathcal{F}_t)$, the process $\{\xi_s\}_{0\le s\le t}$ has the properties of a standard Brownian bridge over $[0,T]$, albeit restricted to the interval $[0,t]$.

For the transformation back from B to Q on $(\Omega, \mathcal{F}_t)$, the appropriate density martingale $\{\Phi_t\}_{0\le t\le u}$ with respect to B is given by

$$\Phi_t = \exp\left(\sigma\int_0^t \frac{T}{T-s}\,H_{sT}\,dW_s^* - \tfrac{1}{2}\sigma^2\int_0^t \frac{T^2}{(T-s)^2}\,H_{sT}^2\,ds\right). \tag{50}$$

The crucial point that follows from this analysis is that the random variable ξ_t is B-Gaussian. In the case of a binary discount bond, therefore, the relevant expectation for determining the option price can be carried out by standard techniques, and we are led to a formula of the Black–Scholes–Merton type. In particular, for a binary bond, (46) reads

$$C_0 = P_{0t}E^B\left[\Big((P_{tT}h_1 - K)p_{1t} + (P_{tT}h_0 - K)p_{0t}\Big)^+\right], \tag{51}$$

where p_{0t} and p_{1t} are given by

$$\begin{aligned} p_{0t} &= p_0\exp\Big[\tfrac{T}{T-t}\left(\sigma h_0\xi_t - \tfrac{1}{2}\sigma^2 h_0^2 t\right)\Big], \\ p_{1t} &= p_1\exp\Big[\tfrac{T}{T-t}\left(\sigma h_1\xi_t - \tfrac{1}{2}\sigma^2 h_1^2 t\right)\Big]. \end{aligned} \tag{52}$$

To compute the value of (51), there are essentially three different cases that have to be considered: (i) $P_{tT}h_1 > P_{tT}h_0 > K$, (ii) $K > P_{tT}h_1 > P_{tT}h_0$, and (iii) $P_{tT}h_1 > K > P_{tT}h_0$. In case (i) the option is certain to expire in the money. Thus, making use of the fact that ξ_t is B-Gaussian with mean zero and variance $t(T-t)/T$, we see that $E^B[p_{it}] = p_i$; hence in case (i) we have $C_0 = B_{0T} - P_{0t}K$. In case (ii) the option expires out of the money, and thus $C_0 = 0$. In case (iii) the option can expire in or out of the money, and there is a 'critical' value of ξ_t above which the argument of (51) is positive. This is obtained by setting the argument of (51) to zero and solving for ξ_t. Writing $\bar{\xi}_t$ for the critical value, we find that $\bar{\xi}_t$ is determined by the relation

$$\frac{T}{T-t}\sigma(h_1-h_0)\bar{\xi}_t = \ln\left[\frac{p_0(P_{tT}h_0-K)}{p_1(K-P_{tT}h_1)}\right] + \tfrac{1}{2}\sigma^2(h_1^2-h_0^2)\tau, \tag{53}$$

where $\tau = tT/(T-t)$. Next we note that inasmuch as ξ_t is B-Gaussian with mean zero and variance $t(T-t)/T$, for the purpose of computing the expectation in (51) we can set $\xi_t = Z\sqrt{t(T-t)/T}$, where Z is B-Gaussian with zero mean and unit variance. Then writing $\bar{Z}$ for the corresponding critical value of Z, we obtain

$$\bar{Z} = \frac{\ln\left[\frac{p_0(P_{tT}h_0-K)}{p_1(K-P_{tT}h_1)}\right] + \frac{1}{2}\sigma^2(h_1^2-h_0^2)\tau}{\sigma\sqrt{\tau}(h_1-h_0)}. \tag{54}$$

With this expression at hand, we can work out the expectation in (51). We are thus led to the following option pricing formula:

$$C_0 = P_{0t}\Big[p_1(P_{tT}h_1-K)N(d^+) - p_0(K-P_{tT}h_0)N(d^-)\Big]. \tag{55}$$

Here d^+ and d^- are defined by

$$d^{\pm} = \frac{\ln\left[\frac{p_1(P_{tT}h_1-K)}{p_0(K-P_{tT}h_0)}\right] \pm \frac{1}{2}\sigma^2(h_1-h_0)^2\tau}{\sigma\sqrt{\tau}(h_1-h_0)}. \tag{56}$$

A short calculation shows that the corresponding option delta, defined by $\Delta = \partial C_0/\partial B_{0T}$, is given by

$$\Delta = \frac{(P_{tT}h_1-K)N(d^+) + (K-P_{tT}h_0)N(d^-)}{P_{tT}(h_1-h_0)}. \tag{57}$$

This can be verified by using (3) to determine the dependency of the option price C_0 on the initial bond price B_{0T}.

It is interesting to note that the parameter σ plays a role like that of the volatility parameter in the Black–Scholes–Merton model. The more rapidly information is 'leaked out' about the true value of the bond repayment, the higher the volatility. It is straightforward to verify that the option price has a positive vega, that is, C_0 is an increasing function of σ. This means that we can use bond option prices (or, equivalently, caps and floors) to back out an implied value for σ, and hence to calibrate the model. Writing $\mathcal{V} = \partial C_0/\partial\sigma$ for the corresponding option vega, we obtain the following positive expression:

$$\mathcal{V} = \frac{1}{\sqrt{2\pi}}\mathrm{e}^{-rt-(1/2)A}(h_1-h_0)\sqrt{\tau p_0 p_1(P_{tT}h_1-K)(K-P_{tT}h_0)}, \tag{58}$$

where

$$A=\frac{1}{\sigma^2\tau(h_1-h_0)^2}\left(\ln\left[\frac{p_1(P_{tT}h_1-K)}{p_0(K-P_{tT}h_0)}\right]\right)^2+\tfrac{1}{4}\sigma^2\tau(h_1-h_0)^2. \tag{59}$$

We remark that in the more general case of a stochastic recovery, a semi-analytic option pricing formula can be obtained that, for practical purposes, can be regarded as fully tractable. In particular, starting from (46), we consider the case where the strike price K lies in the range $P_{tT}h_{k+1}>K>P_{tT}h_k$ for some value of $k\in\{0,1,\ldots,n\}$. It is an exercise to verify that there exists a unique critical value of ξ_t such that the summation appearing in the argument of the $\max(x,0)$ function in (46) vanishes. Writing $\bar{\xi}_t$ for the critical value, which can be obtained by numerical methods, we define the scaled critical value $\bar{Z}$ as before, by setting $\bar{\xi}_t=\bar{Z}\sqrt{t(T-t)/T}$. A calculation then shows that the option price is given by the following expression:

$$C_0=P_{0t}\sum_{i=0}^{n}p_i\,(P_{tT}h_i-K)\;N(\sigma h_i\sqrt{\tau}-\bar{Z}). \tag{60}$$

9 Bond Option Price Processes

In the previous section we obtained the initial value C_0 of an option on a binary credit-risky bond. In the present section we determine the price process $\{C_s\}_{0\le s\le t}$ of such an option. We fix the bond maturity T and the option maturity t. Then the price C_s of a call option at time $s\le t$ is given by

$$\begin{aligned}C_s&=P_{st}\,E\left[(B_{tT}-K)^+|\mathcal{F}_s\right]\\&=\frac{P_{st}}{\Phi_s}\,E^B\left[\Phi_t(B_{tT}-K)^+|\mathcal{F}_s\right]\\&=\frac{P_{st}}{\Phi_s}\,E^B\left[\left(\sum_{i=0}^{n}\Big(P_{tT}h_i-K\Big)p_{it}\right)^+\Bigg|\,\mathcal{F}_s\right].\end{aligned} \tag{61}$$

We recall that p_{it}, defined in (41), is a function of ξ_t. The calculation can thus be simplified by use of the fact that $\{\xi_t\}$ is a B-Brownian bridge. To determine the conditional expectation (61) we note that the B-Gaussian random variable Z_{st} defined by

$$Z_{st}=\frac{\xi_t}{T-t}-\frac{\xi_s}{T-s} \tag{62}$$

is independent of $\{\xi_u\}_{0\le u\le s}$. We can then express $\{p_{it}\}$ in terms of ξ_s and Z_{st} by writing

$$p_{it}=p_i\exp\left[\frac{T}{T-s}\sigma h_i T\xi_s-\tfrac{1}{2}\frac{T}{T-t}\sigma^2h_i^2t+\sigma h_i Z_{st}T\right]. \tag{63}$$

Substituting (63) into (61), we find that C_s can be calculated by taking an expectation involving the random variable Z_{st}, which has mean zero and variance v_{st}^2, given by

$$v_{st}^2 = \frac{t-s}{(T-t)(T-s)}. \tag{64}$$

In the case of a call option on a binary discount bond that pays h_0 or h_1, we can obtain a closed-form expression for (61). In that case the option price is given as follows:

$$C_s = \frac{P_{st}}{\Phi_s} E^B \left[\left((P_{tT}h_0 - K)p_{0t} + (P_{tT}h_1 - K)p_{1t} \right)^+ \middle| \mathcal{F}_t \right]. \tag{65}$$

Substituting (63) in (65) we find that the expression in the expectation is positive only if the inequality $Z_{st} > \bar{Z}$ is satisfied, where

$$\bar{Z} = \frac{\ln\left[\frac{\pi_{0s}(K-P_{tT}h_0)}{\pi_{1s}(P_{tT}h_1-K)}\right] + \frac{1}{2}\sigma^2(h_1^2 - h_0^2)v_{st}^2 T}{\sigma v_{st} T(h_1 - h_0)}. \tag{66}$$

It is convenient to set $Z_{st} = v_{st}Z$, where Z is a B-Gaussian random variable with zero mean and unit variance. The computation of the expectation in (65) then reduces to a pair of Gaussian integrals, and we obtain

$$C_s = P_{st}\Big[\pi_{1s}\,(P_{tT}h_1 - K)\,N(d_s^+) - \pi_{0s}\,(K - P_{tT}h_0)\,N(d_s^-)\Big], \tag{67}$$

where the conditional probabilities $\{\pi_{is}\}$ are as defined in (17), and

$$d_s^\pm = \frac{\ln\left[\frac{\pi_{1s}(P_{tT}h_1-K)}{\pi_{0s}(K-P_{tT}h_0)}\right] \pm \frac{1}{2}\sigma^2 v_{st}^2 T^2(h_1 - h_0)^2}{\sigma v_{st} T(h_1 - h_0)}. \tag{68}$$

We note that $d_s^+ = d_s^- + \sigma v_{st} T(h_1 - h_0)$, and that $d_0^\pm = d^\pm$.

One important feature of the model worth pointing out in the present context is that a position in a bond option can be hedged with a position in the underlying bond. This is because the option price process and the underlying bond price process are one-dimensional diffusions driven by the same Brownian motion. Because C_t and B_{tT} are both monotonic in their dependence on ξ_t, it follows that C_t can be expressed as a function of B_{tT}; the delta of the option can then be obtained in the conventional way as the derivative of the option price with respect to the underlying. In the case of a binary bond, the resulting hedge ratio process $\{\Delta_s\}_{0\le s\le t}$ is given by

$$\Delta_s = \frac{(P_{tT}h_1 - K)N(d_s^+) + (K - P_{tT}h_0)N(d_s^-)}{P_{tT}(h_1 - h_0)}. \tag{69}$$

This brings us to another interesting point. For certain types of instruments, it may be desirable to model the occurrence of credit events (e.g., credit-rating downgrades) taking place at some time preceding a cash-flow date. In particular, we may wish to consider contingent claims based on such events. In the present framework we can regard such contingent claims as derivative structures for which the payoff is triggered by the level of $\{\xi_t\}$. For example, it may be that a credit event is established if B_{tT} drops below some specific level, or if the credit spread widens beyond some threshold. As a consequence, a number of different types of contingent claims can be valued by use of barrier option methods in this framework (cf. Albanese et al. [1], Chen and Filipović [7], and Albanese and Chen [2]).

10 Coupon Bonds: The X-Factor Approach

The discussion so far has focused on simple structures, such as discount bonds and options on discount bonds. One of the advantages of the present approach, however, is that its tractability extends to situations of a more complex nature. In this section we consider the case of a credit-risky coupon bond. One should regard a coupon bond as being a rather complicated instrument from the point of view of credit risk management, because default can occur at any of the coupon dates. The market will in general possess partial information concerning all of the future coupon payments, as well as the principal payment.

As an illustration, we consider a bond with two payments remaining: a coupon H_{T_1} at time T_1, and a coupon plus the principal totalling H_{T_2} at time T_2. We assume that if default occurs at T_1, then no further payment is made at T_2. On the other hand, if the T_1-coupon is paid, default may still occur at T_2. We model this by setting

$$H_{T_1} = \mathbf{c}X_{T_1} \quad \text{and} \quad H_{T_2} = (\mathbf{c}+\mathbf{p})X_{T_1}X_{T_2}, \tag{70}$$

where X_{T_1} and X_{T_2} are independent random variables each taking the values $\{0, 1\}$, and the constants $\mathbf{c}$ and $\mathbf{p}$ denote the coupon and principal. Let us write $\{p_0^{(1)}, p_1^{(1)}\}$ for the *a priori* probabilities that $X_{T_1} = \{0, 1\}$, and $\{p_0^{(2)}, p_1^{(2)}\}$ for the *a priori* probabilities that $X_{T_2} = \{0, 1\}$. We introduce a pair of information processes

$$\xi_t^{(1)} = \sigma_1 X_{T_1} t + \beta_{tT_1}^{(1)} \quad \text{and} \quad \xi_t^{(2)} = \sigma_2 X_{T_2} t + \beta_{tT_2}^{(2)}, \tag{71}$$

where $\{\beta_{tT_1}^{(1)}\}$ and $\{\beta_{tT_2}^{(2)}\}$ are independent Brownian bridges, and σ_1 and σ_2 are parameters. Then for the credit-risky coupon-bond price process we have

$$S_t = \mathbf{c}P_{tT_1} E\left[X_{T_1}|\xi_t^{(1)}\right] + (\mathbf{c}+\mathbf{p})P_{tT_2} E\left[X_{T_1}|\xi_t^{(1)}\right] E\left[X_{T_2}|\xi_t^{(2)}\right]. \tag{72}$$

The two conditional expectations appearing in this formula can be worked out explicitly using the techniques already described. The result is

$$E\left[X_{T_i}|\xi_t^{(i)}\right] = \frac{p_1^{(i)}\exp\left[\frac{T_i}{T_i-t}\left(\sigma_i\xi_t^{(i)}-\frac{1}{2}\sigma_i^2 t\right)\right]}{p_0^{(i)}+p_1^{(i)}\exp\left[\frac{T_i}{T_i-t}\left(\sigma_i\xi_t^{(i)}-\frac{1}{2}\sigma_i^2 t\right)\right]}, \tag{73}$$

for $i = 1, 2$. It should be evident that in the case of a bond with two payments remaining we obtain a natural 'two-factor' model, the factors being the two independent Brownian motions arising in connection with the information processes $\{\xi_t^{(i)}\}_{i=1,2}$. Similarly, if there are n outstanding coupons, we model the payments by $H_{T_k} = \mathbf{c}X_{T_1}\cdots X_{T_k}$ for $k \leq n-1$ and $H_{T_n} = (\mathbf{c}+\mathbf{p})X_{T_1}\cdots X_{T_n}$, and introduce the information processes

$$\xi_t^{(i)} = \sigma_i X_{T_i} t + \beta_{tT_i}^{(i)} \qquad (i = 1, 2, \ldots, n). \tag{74}$$

The case of n outstanding payments leads to an n-factor model. The independence of the random variables $\{X_{T_i}\}_{i=1,2,\ldots,n}$ implies that the price of a credit-risky coupon bond admits a closed-form expression analogous to (72).

With a slight modification of these expressions, we can consider the case when there is partial recovery in the event of default. In the two-coupon example discussed above, for instance, we can extend the model by saying that in the event of default on the first coupon the effective recovery rate (as a percentage of coupon plus principal) is R_1, whereas in the case of default on the final payment, the recovery rate is R_2. Then $H_{T_1} = \mathbf{c}X_{T_1} + R_1(\mathbf{c}+\mathbf{p})(1 - X_{T_1})$ and $H_{T_2} = \mathbf{c} + \mathbf{p}X_{T_1}X_{T_2} + R_2(\mathbf{c}+\mathbf{p})X_{T_1}(1 - X_{T_2})$. A further extension of this reasoning allows for the introduction of a stochastic recovery rate.

11 Credit Default Swaps

Swap-like structures can also be readily treated. For example, in the case of a basic credit default swap (CDS), we have a series of premium payments, each of the amount $\mathbf{g}$, made to the seller of protection. The payments continue until the failure of a coupon payment in the reference bond, at which point a payment $\mathbf{n}$ is made to the buyer of protection.

As an illustration, we consider two reference coupons, letting X_{T_1} and X_{T_2} be the associated independent market factors, following the pattern of the previous example. We assume for simplicity that the default-swap premium payments are made immediately after the coupon dates. Then the value of the default swap, from the point of view of the seller of protection, is

$$\begin{aligned} V_t = {} & \mathbf{g}P_{tT_1}E\left[X_{T_1}|\xi_t^{(1)}\right] - \mathbf{n}P_{tT_1}E\left[1 - X_{T_1}|\xi_t^{(1)}\right] \\ & + \mathbf{g}P_{tT_2}E\left[X_{T_1}|\xi_t^{(1)}\right]E\left[X_{T_2}|\xi_t^{(2)}\right] \\ & - \mathbf{n}P_{tT_2}E\left[X_{T_1}|\xi_t^{(1)}\right]E\left[1 - X_{T_2}|\xi_t^{(2)}\right]. \end{aligned} \tag{75}$$

After some rearrangement of terms, this can be expressed more compactly as follows:

$$\begin{aligned} V_t = & -\mathbf{n}P_{tT_1} + [(\mathbf{g}+\mathbf{n})P_{tT_1} - \mathbf{n}P_{tT_2}]\, E\left[X_{T_1}|\xi_t^{(1)}\right] \\ & + (\mathbf{g}+\mathbf{n})P_{tT_2} E\left[X_{T_1}|\xi_t^{(1)}\right] E\left[X_{T_2}|\xi_t^{(2)}\right], \end{aligned} \tag{76}$$

which can then be written explicitly in terms of the expressions given in (73). A similar approach can be adapted in the multi-name credit situation. The point that we would like to emphasise is that there is a good deal of flexibility available in the manner in which the various cash flows can be modelled to depend on one another, and in many situations tractable expressions emerge that can be used as the basis for the modelling of complex credit instruments.

12 Baskets of Credit-Risky Bonds

We consider now the valuation problem for a basket of bonds where there are correlations in the payoffs. We shall obtain a closed-form expression for the value of a basket of defaultable bonds with various maturities.

For definiteness we consider a set of digital bonds. It is convenient to label the bonds in chronological order with respect to maturity. We let H_{T_1} denote the payoff of the bond that expires first; we let H_{T_2} ($T_2 \geq T_1$) denote the payoff of the first bond that matures after T_1; and so on. In general, the various bond payouts will not be independent. We propose to model this set of dependent random variables in terms of an underlying set of independent market factors. To achieve this, we let X denote the random variable associated with the payoff of the first bond: $H_{T_1} = X$. The random variable X takes on the values $\{1, 0\}$ with *a priori* probabilities $\{p, 1-p\}$. The payoff of the second bond H_{T_2} can then be represented in terms of three independent random variables: $H_{T_2} = XX_1 + (1-X)X_0$. Here X_0 takes the values $\{1, 0\}$ with the probabilities $\{p_0, 1-p_0\}$, and X_1 takes the values $\{1, 0\}$ with the probabilities $\{p_1, 1-p_1\}$. Clearly, the payoff of the second bond is unity if and only if the random variables (X, X_0, X_1) take the values $(0,1,0)$, $(0,1,1)$, $(1,0,1)$, or $(1,1,1)$. Because these random variables are independent, the *a priori* probability that the second bond does not default is $p_0 + p(p_1 - p_0)$, where p is the *a priori* probability that the first bond does not default. To represent the payoff of the third bond, we introduce four additional independent random variables:

$$\begin{aligned} H_{T_3} = & \, XX_1X_{11} + X(1-X_1)X_{10} + (1-X)X_0X_{01} \\ & + (1-X)(1-X_0)X_{00}. \end{aligned} \tag{77}$$

The market factors $\{X_{ij}\}_{i,j=0,1}$ here take the values $\{1, 0\}$ with probabilities $\{p_{ij}, 1-p_{ij}\}$. It is a matter of elementary combinatorics to determine the *a priori* probability that $H_{T_3} = 1$ in terms of p, $\{p_i\}$, and $\{p_{ij}\}$.

The scheme above can be extended to represent the payoff of a generic bond in the basket, with an expression of the following form:

$$H_{T_{n+1}} = \sum_{\{k_j\}=1,0} X^{\omega(k_1)} X_{k_1}^{\omega(k_2)} X_{k_1 k_2}^{\omega(k_3)} \cdots X_{k_1 k_2 \cdots k_{n-1}}^{\omega(k_n)} X_{k_1 k_2 \cdots k_{n-1} k_n}. \quad (78)$$

Here, for any random variable X we define $X^{\omega(0)} = 1-X$ and $X^{\omega(1)} = X$. The point to observe is that if we have a basket of N digital bonds with arbitrary *a priori* default probabilities and correlations, then we can introduce $2^N - 1$ independent digital random variables to represent the N correlated random variables associated with the bond payoffs.

One advantage of the decomposition into independent market factors is that we retain analytical tractability for the pricing of the basket. In particular, because the random variables $\{X_{k_1 k_2 \cdots k_n}\}$ are independent, it is natural to introduce $2^N - 1$ independent Brownian bridges to represent the noise that veils the values of the independent market factors:

$$\xi_t^{k_1 k_2 \cdots k_n} = \sigma_{k_1 k_2 \cdots k_n} X_{k_1 k_2 \cdots k_n} t + \beta_{tT_{n+1}}^{k_1 k_2 \cdots k_n}. \quad (79)$$

The number of independent factors grows rapidly with the number of bonds in the portfolio. As a consequence, a market that consists of correlated bonds is in general highly incomplete. This fact provides an economic justification for the creation of products such as CDSs and CDOs that enhance the 'hedgeability' of such portfolios.

13 Homogeneous Baskets

In the case of a 'homogeneous' basket, the number of independent factors determining the payoff of the portfolio can be reduced. We assume now that the basket contains n defaultable discount bonds, each maturing at time T, and each paying 0 or 1, with the same *a priori* probability of default. This situation is of interest as a first step in the analysis of the more general setup. Our goal is to model default correlations in the portfolio, and in particular to model the flow of market information concerning default correlation. Let us write H_T for the payoff at time T of the homogeneous portfolio, and set

$$H_T = n - X_1 - X_1X_2 - X_1X_2X_3 - \cdots - X_1X_2 \ldots X_n, \quad (80)$$

where the random variables $\{X_j\}_{j=1,2,\ldots,n}$, each taking the values $\{0, 1\}$, are assumed to be independent. Thus if $X_1 = 0$, then $H_T = n$; if $X_1 = 1$ and $X_2 = 0$, then $H_T = n - 1$; if $X_1 = 1$, $X_2 = 1$, and $X_3 = 0$, then $H_T = n - 2$; and so on. Now suppose we write $p_j = Q(X_j = 1)$ and $q_j = Q(X_j = 0)$ for $j = 1, 2, \ldots, n$. Then $Q(H_T = n) = q_1$, $Q(H_T = n - 1) = p_1 q_2$, $Q(H_T = n - 2) = p_1 p_2 q_3$, and so on. More generally, we have $Q(H_T = n - k) = p_1 p_2 \ldots p_k q_{k+1}$. Thus, for example, if $p_1 \ll 1$ but $p_2, p_3, \ldots, p_k$ are large, then we are in a situation of low default probability and high default correlation; that is to say, the probability of a default occurring in the portfolio is small, but conditional on at least one default occurring, the probability of several defaults is high.

The market will take a view on the likelihood of various numbers of defaults occurring in the portfolio. We model this by introducing a set of independent information processes $\{\eta_t^j\}$ defined by

$$\eta_t^j = \sigma_j X_j t + \beta_{tT}^j, \tag{81}$$

where $\{\sigma_j\}_{j=1,2,\ldots,n}$ are parameters, and $\{\beta_{tT}^j\}_{j=1,2,\ldots,n}$ are independent Brownian bridges. The market filtration $\{\mathcal{F}_t\}$ is generated collectively by $\{\eta_t^j\}_{j=1,2,\ldots,n}$, and for the portfolio value $H_t = P_{tT} E\left[H_T|\mathcal{F}_t\right]$, we have

$$H_t = P_{tT}\Big[n - E_t[X_1] - E_t[X_1]E_t[X_2] - \cdots - E_t[X_1]E_t[X_2]\ldots E_t[X_n]\Big]. \tag{82}$$

The conditional expectations appearing here can be calculated by means of formulae established earlier in the paper. The resulting dynamics for $\{H_t\}$ can then be used to describe the evolution of correlations in the portfolio. For example, if $E_t[X_1]$ is low and $E_t[X_2]$ is high, then the conditional probability at time t of a default at time T is small, whereas if $E_t[X_1]$ were to increase suddenly, then the conditional probability of two or more defaults at T would rise as a consequence. Thus, the model is sufficiently rich to admit a detailed account of the correlation dynamics of the portfolio. The losses associated with individual tranches can be identified, and derivative structures associated with such tranches can be defined. For example, a digital option that pays out in the event that there are three or more defaults has the payoff structure $H_T^{(3)} = X_1X_2X_3$. The homogeneous portfolio model has the property that the dynamics of equity-level and mezzanine-level tranches involve a relatively small number of factors. The market prices of tranches can be used to determine the *a priori* probabilities, and the market prices of options on tranches can be used to fix the information-flow parameters.

Acknowledgments

The authors are grateful to T. Bielecki, I. Buckley, T. Dean, G. Di Graziano, A. Elizalde, B. Flesaker, T. Hurd, M. Jeanblanc, B. Meister, C. Rogers, M. Rutkowski, and M. Zervos, for helpful comments.

We are grateful to seminar participants at the Isaac Newton Institute, Cambridge, 3 May, 19 June, and 8 July 2005; at the Mathematics in Finance Conference, Kruger Park, RSA, 9 August 2005; at the Imperial College Workshop on Mathematical Finance and Stochastic Analysis, 23 August 2005; at CEMFI (Centro de Estudios Monetarios y Financieros), Madrid, 3 October 2005; at the Winter School in Financial Mathematics, Lunteren, the Netherlands, 24 January 2006; at the First Conference on Advanced Mathematical Methods for Finance, Side, Antalya, Turkey, 26–29 April 2006; and at the

Bachelier Finance Society Fourth World Congress, Tokyo, Japan, 17–19 August 2006, where drafts of this paper have been presented, for their comments.

This work was carried out in part while Lane Hughston and Andrea Macrina were participants in the Isaac Newton Institute's Developments in Quantitative Finance programme (April–July 2005). We thank I. Buckley for assistance with the figures. Dorje Brody and Lane Hughston acknowledge support from The Royal Society; Lane Hughston and Andrea Macrina acknowledge support from EPSRC grant number GR/S22998/01; Andrea Macrina thanks the Public Education Authority of the Canton of Bern, Switzerland, and the UK Universities ORS scheme.

Finally, it is our pleasure to dedicate this paper to Dilip Madan on the occasion of his sixtieth birthday, in acknowledgment of his numerous significant contributions to mathematical finance and in recognition of the inspiration and encouragement he has so often and so generously given to others working in the subject.

References

1. C. Albanese, J. Campolieti, O. Chen, and A. Zavidonov. Credit barrier models. *Risk*, 16:109–113, 2003.
2. C. Albanese and O. Chen. Implied migration rates from credit barrier models. *J. Banking and Finance*, 30:607–626, 2006.
3. T.R. Bielecki, M. Jeanblanc, and M. Rutkowski. Modelling and valuation of credit risk. In *Stochastic Methods in Finance*, Bressanone Lectures 2003, eds. M. Fritelli and W. Runggaldier, LNM 1856, Springer, 2004.
4. T.R. Bielecki and M. Rutkowski. *Credit Risk: Modelling, Valuation and Hedging.* Springer, 2002.
5. F. Black and J.C. Cox. Valuing corporate securities: Some effects of bond indenture provisions. *J. Finance*, 31:351–367, 1976.
6. U. Cetin, R. Jarrow, P. Protter, and Y. Yildrim. Modelling credit risk with partial information. *Ann. Appl. Prob.*, 14:1167–1172, 2004.
7. L. Chen and D. Filipović. A simple model for credit migration and spread curves. *Finance and Stochastics*, 9:211–231, 2005.
8. J.H. Cochrane. *Asset Pricing.* Princeton University Press, 2005.
9. D. Duffie and D. Lando. Term structure of credit spreads with incomplete accounting information. *Econometrica*, 69:633–664, 2001.
10. D. Duffie, M. Schroder, and C. Skiadas. Recursive valuation of defaultable securities and the timing of resolution of uncertainty. *Ann. Appl. Prob.*, 6:1075–1090, 1996.
11. D. Duffie and K.J. Singleton. Modelling term structures of defaultable bonds. *Rev. Financial Studies*, 12:687–720, 1999.
12. D. Duffie and K.J. Singleton. *Credit Risk: Pricing, Measurement and Management.* Princeton University Press, 2003.
13. A. Elizalde. Credit risk models: I Default correlation in intensity models, II Structural models, III Reconciliation structural-reduced models, IV Understanding and pricing CDOs. `www.abelelizalde.com`, 2005.

14. B. Flesaker, L.P. Hughston, L. Schreiber, and L. Sprung. Taking all the credit. *Risk*, 7:104–108, 1994.
15. K. Giesecke. Correlated default with incomplete information. *J. Banking and Finance*, 28:1521–1545, 2004.
16. K. Giesecke and L.R. Goldberg. Sequential default and incomplete information. *J. Risk*, 7:1–26, 2004.
17. B. Hilberink and L.C.G. Rogers. Optimal capital structure and endogenous default. *Finance and Stochastics*, 6:237–263, 2002.
18. L.P. Hughston and S. Turnbull. Credit risk: Constructing the basic building blocks. *Economic Notes*, 30:281–292, 2001.
19. J. Hull and A. White. Merton's model, credit risk and volatility skews. *J. Credit Risk*, 1:1–27, 2004.
20. R.A. Jarrow, D. Lando, and S.M. Turnbull. A Markov model for the term structure of credit risk spreads. *Rev. Financial Stud.*, 10:481–528, 1997.
21. R.A. Jarrow and P. Protter. Structural versus reduced form models: A new information based perspective. *J. Invest. Management*, 2:1–10, 2004.
22. R.A. Jarrow and S.M. Turnbull. Pricing derivatives on financial securities subject to credit risk. *J. Finance*, 50:53–85, 1995.
23. R.A. Jarrow, D. van Deventer, and X. Wang. A robust test of Merton's structural model for credit risk. *J. Risk*, 6:39–58, 2003.
24. R.A. Jarrow and F. Yu. Counterparty risk and the pricing of defaultable securities. *J. Finance*, 56:1765–1799, 2001.
25. M. Jeanblanc and M. Rutkowski. Modelling of default risk: An overview. In *Mathematical Finance: Theory and Practice*, Higher Education Press, 2000.
26. I. Karatzas and S. Shreve. *Brownian Motion and Stochastic Calculus*, 2nd edition. Springer, 1991.
27. S. Kusuoka. A remark on default risk models. *Advances Math. Economics*, 1:69-82, 1999.
28. D. Lando. On Cox processes and credit risky securities. *Rev. Derivatives Research*, 2:99-120, 1998.
29. D. Lando. *Credit Risk Modelling.* Princeton University Press, 2004.
30. H.E. Leland and K.B. Toft. Optimal capital structure, endogenous bankruptcy and the term structure of credit spreads. *J. Finance*, 50:789–819, 1996.
31. D. Madan and H. Unal. Pricing the risks of default. *Rev. Derivatives Research*, 2:121–160, 1998.
32. D. Madan and H. Unal. A two-factor hazard-rate model for pricing risky debt and the term structure of credit spreads. *J. Financial and Quantitative Analysis*, 35:43–65, 2000.
33. R. Merton. On the pricing of corporate debt: The risk structure of interest rates. *J. Finance*, 29:449–470, 1974.
34. P.E. Protter. *Stochastic Integration and Differential Equations.* Springer, 2004.
35. P.J. Schönbucher. *Credit Derivatives Pricing Models.* John Wiley & Sons, 2003.
36. M. Yor. *Some Aspects of Brownian Motion, Part I: Some Special Functionals.* Birkhäuser Verlag, 1992.
37. M. Yor. *Some Aspects of Brownian Motion, Part II: Some Recent Martingale Problems.* Birkhäuser Verlag, 1996.

Chapter 2

INFORMATION-BASED ASSET PRICING[#]

DORJE C. BRODY*
Department of Mathematics, Imperial College London
London SW7 2AZ, UK
d.brody@imperial.ac.uk

LANE P. HUGHSTON[†] and ANDREA MACRINA[‡]
Department of Mathematics, King's College London
London WC2R 2LS, UK
[†]*lane.hughston@kcl.ac.uk*
[‡]*andrea.macrina@kcl.ac.uk*

Received 17 April 2007
Accepted 31 October 2007

A new framework for asset price dynamics is introduced in which the concept of noisy information about future cash flows is used to derive the corresponding price processes. In this framework an asset is defined by its cash-flow structure. Each cash flow is modelled by a random variable that can be expressed as a function of a collection of independent random variables called market factors. With each such "X-factor" we associate a market information process, the values of which we assume are accessible to market participants. Each information process consists of a sum of two terms; one contains true information about the value of the associated market factor, and the other represents "noise". The noise term is modelled by an independent Brownian bridge that spans the interval from the present to the time at which the value of the factor is revealed. The market filtration is assumed to be that generated by the aggregate of the independent information processes. The price of an asset is given by the expectation of the discounted cash flows in the risk-neutral measure, conditional on the information provided by the market filtration. In the case where the cash flows are the dividend payments associated with equities, an explicit model is obtained for the share-price process. Dividend growth is taken into account by introducing appropriate structure on the market factors. The prices of options on dividend-paying assets are derived. Remarkably, the resulting formula for the price of a European-style call option is of the Black–Scholes–Merton type. We consider the case where the rate at which information is revealed to the market is constant, and the case where the information rate varies in time. Option pricing formulae are obtained for both cases. The information-based framework generates a natural explanation for the origin of stochastic volatility in financial markets, without the need for specifying on an *ad hoc* basis the dynamics of the volatility.

Keywords: Asset pricing; partial information; stochastic volatility; correlation; dividend growth; Brownian bridge; nonlinear filtering; market microstructure.

*Corresponding author.

[#]This chapter was originally published as: D. C. Brody, L. P. Hughston & A. Macrina (2008) Information-Based Asset Pricing. *International Journal of Theoretical and Applied Finance* **11** (1), 107–142.

1. Introduction

In derivative pricing, the starting point is usually the specification of a model for the price process of the underlying asset. Such models tend to be of an *ad hoc* nature. For example, in the Black–Scholes–Merton theory, the underlying asset has a geometric Brownian motion as its price process. More generally, the economy is often modelled by a probability space equipped with the filtration generated by a multi-dimensional Brownian motion, and it is assumed that asset prices are adapted to this filtration. This example is of course the "standard" model within which a great deal of financial engineering has been carried out. The basic problem with the standard model (and the same applies to various generalisations thereof) is that the market filtration is fixed, and no comment is offered on the issue of "where it comes from". In other words, the filtration, which represents the revelation of information to market participants, is modelled first, in an *ad hoc* manner, and then it is assumed that price processes are adapted to it. But no indication is given about the nature of this "information", and it is not obvious, *a priori*, why the Brownian filtration, for example, should be regarded as providing information rather than noise.

In a complete market there is a sense in which the Brownian filtration provides no irrelevant information. That is to say, in a complete market based on a Brownian filtration the asset price movements reflect the information content of the filtration. Nevertheless, the notion that the market filtration should be "prespecified" is an unsatisfactory one in financial modelling. The intuition behind the "prespecified-filtration" approach is that the filtration represents the unfolding in time of a succession of random events that "influence" the markets, causing prices to change. For example, bad weather in South America results in a decrease in the supply of coffee beans and hence an increase in the price of coffee. Or, say, a spate of bad derivative deals causes a drop in confidence in banks, and hence a downgrade in earnings projections, and thus a drop in their prices. The idea is that one "abstractifies" these influences in the form of a prespecified filtration to which price processes are adapted. What is unsatisfactory about this is that little structure is given to the filtration: price movements behave as though they were spontaneous. In reality, we expect the price-formation process to exhibit more structure.

It would be out of place in the present context to attempt an account of the process of price formation. Nevertheless, we can improve on the "prespecified" approach. In that spirit we proceed as follows. We note that price changes arise from two sources. The first is that resulting from changes in agent preferences—that is to say, changes in the pricing kernel. Movements in the pricing kernel are associated with (a) changes in investor attitudes towards risk, and (b) changes in investor "impatience", the subjective discounting of future cash flows. Equally important are changes in price resulting from the revelation of information about the future cash flows derivable from a given asset. When a market agent decides to buy or sell an asset, the decision is made in accordance with the information available to the agent concerning the likely future cash flows associated with the asset. A change in the information available to the agent about a future cash flow will typically have an effect on the price at which they are willing to buy or sell, even if the agent's preferences remain unchanged. Consider the situation where one is thinking of purchasing an item at a price that seems attractive. But then, one reads an article pointing out an undesirable feature of the product. After reflection, one decides that the price is too high, given the deficiencies that one is now aware of. As a result, one decides not to buy, not at that price, and eventually—because other individuals will have read the same report—the price drops.

The movement of the price of an asset should, therefore, be regarded as *an emergent phenomenon*. To put the matter another way, the price process of an asset should be viewed as the output of (rather than an input into) the decisions made relating to possible transactions in the asset, and these decisions should be understood as being induced primarily by the flow of information to market participants. Taking into account this observation we propose in this paper a new framework for asset pricing based on *modelling of the flow of market information*. The information is that concerning the values of the future cash flows associated with the given assets. For example, if the asset represents a share in a firm that will make a single distribution at some agreed date, then there is a single cash flow. If the asset is a credit-risky discount bond, then the future cash flow is the payout of the bond at maturity. In each case, based on the information available relating to the likely payouts of the given financial instrument, market participants determine estimates for the value of the right to the impending cash flows. These estimates lead to the decisions concerning transactions that trigger movements in the price.

In this paper we present a class of models capturing the essence of the scenario described above. In building the framework we have several criteria in mind that we would like to see satisfied. The first of these is that our model for the flow of market information should be intuitively appealing, and should allow for a reasonably sophisticated account of aggregate investor behaviour. At the same time, the model should be simple enough to allow one to derive explicit expressions for the asset price processes thus induced, in a suitably rich range of examples, as well as for various associated derivative price processes. The framework should also be flexible enough to allow for the modelling of assets having complex cash-flow structures. Furthermore, it should be suitable for practical implementation. The framework should be mathematically sound, and manifestly arbitrage-free. In what follows we show how our modelling framework goes a long way towards satisfying these criteria.

The role of information in financial modelling has long been appreciated, particularly in the theory of market microstructure (see, e.g., Back [1], Back and Baruch [2], O'Hara [21], and references cited therein). The present framework is perhaps most closely related to the line of investigation represented, e.g., in Cetin *et al.* [5], Duffie and Lando [8], Geman *et al.* [10], Giesecke [11], Giesecke and Goldberg [12], and Jarrow and Protter [14]. The work in this paper, in particular, develops that described in Brody *et al.* [3] and Macrina [20], where preliminary accounts of some of this material appear (see also Rutkowski and Yu [23]).

The paper is organised as follows. In Secs. 2, 3, and 4 we illustrate the framework for information-based pricing by considering the scenario in which there is a single random cash flow. An elementary model for market information is presented, based on the specification of a process composed of two parts: a "signal" component containing true information about the upcoming cash flow, and an independent "noise" component which we model in a specific way. A closed-form expression for the asset price is obtained in terms of the market information available at the time the price is being specified. This result is summarised in Proposition 4.1. In Sec. 5 we show that the resulting asset price process is driven by a Brownian motion, an expression for which can be obtained in terms of the market information process: this construction indicates in explicit terms the sense in which the price process can be viewed as an "emergent" phenomenon. In Sec. 6 we show that the value of a European-style call option, in the case of an asset with a single cash flow, admits a simple formula analogous to that of the Black–Scholes–Merton model. In Sec. 7 we derive pricing formulae for the situation when the random variable associated with the single cash flow has an exponential distribution or, more generally, a gamma distribution.

The extension of the framework to assets associated with multiple cash flows is established in Sec. 8. We show that once the relevant cash flows are decomposed in terms of a collection of independent market factors, then a closed-form expression for the asset price associated with a complex cash-flow structure can be obtained. In Sec. 9 we show how the standard geometric Brownian motion model can be derived in an information-based setting. This remarkable result motivates the specific choice of information process given in Eq. (4.1). In Sec. 10 we present a simple model for dividend growth. In Sec. 11 we show that by allowing distinct assets to share one or more common market factors in the determination of one or more of their respective cash flows we obtain a natural correlation structure for the associated asset price processes. This method for introducing correlation in asset price movements contrasts with the *ad hoc* approach adopted in most financial modelling. In Sec. 12 we demonstrate that if two or more market factors affect the future cash flows of an asset, then the corresponding price process will exhibit unhedgeable stochastic volatility. This result is noteworthy since even for the class of relatively simple models considered here it is possible to identify a candidate for *the origin of stochasticity in price volatility*, as well as the form it should take, which is given in Proposition 12.1.

In the remaining sections of the paper we consider the case where the rate at which the information concerning the true value of an impending cash flow is revealed is time dependent. The introduction of a time-dependent information rate adds additional flexibility to the modelling framework, and opens the door to the possibility of calibrating the model to the market prices of options. We consider the single-factor case first, and obtain a closed-form expression for the conditional expectation of the cash flow. The result is stated first in Sec. 13 as Proposition 13.1, and the derivation is then given in the two sections that follow. In Sec. 14 we introduce a new measure appropriate for the consideration of a Brownian bridge with a random drift, which is used in Sec. 15 to obtain an expression for the conditional density of the random cash flow. The consistency of the resulting price process is established in Sec. 16. We show, in particular, that, for the given information process, if we re-initialise the model at some specified future time, the dynamics of the model moving forward from that time can be represented by a suitably re-initialised information process. This result is given in Proposition 16.1. The dynamical equation satisfied by the price is analysed in Sec. 17, where we demonstrate in Proposition 17.1 that the driving process is a Brownian motion, just as in the constant parameter case. In Sec. 18 we derive the price of a European-style call option in the case for which the information rate is time dependent.

Our approach is based on the idea that first one models the cash flows, then the information processes, then the filtration, and finally the prices. In Sec. 19, we solve the corresponding "inverse" problem. The result is stated in Proposition 19.1. Starting from the dynamics of the conditional distribution of the impending payoff, which is driven by a Brownian motion adapted to the market filtration, we construct (a) the random variable that represents the relevant market factor, and (b) an independent Brownian bridge representing irrelevant information. These two combine to generate the market filtration. We conclude in Sec. 20 with a general multi-factor extension of the time-dependent setup, for which the dynamics of the resulting price processes are given in Propositions 20.1 and 20.2.

2. The Modelling Framework

In asset pricing we require three ingredients: (a) the cash flows, (b) the investor preferences, and (c) the flow of information to market participants. Translated into a mathematical language, these ingredients amount to the following: (a′) cash flows are modelled as random variables; (b′) investor preferences are modelled with the determination of a pricing kernel; and (c′) the market information flow is modelled with the specification of a filtration. As we have indicated above, asset pricing theory conventionally attaches more weight to (a) and (b) than to (c). In this paper we emphasise the importance of ingredient (c).

Our theory will be based on modelling the flow of information accessible to market participants concerning the future cash flows associated with a position in a financial asset. We start by introducing the notation and assumptions employed in this paper. We model the financial markets with the specification of a probability space $(\Omega, \mathcal{F}, \mathbb{Q})$ on which a filtration $\{\mathcal{F}_t\}_{0\leq t<\infty}$ will be constructed. The probability measure $\mathbb{Q}$ is understood to be the risk-neutral measure, and $\{\mathcal{F}_t\}$ is understood to be the market filtration. All asset-price processes and other information-providing processes accessible to market participants will be adapted to $\{\mathcal{F}_t\}$.

Several simplifying assumptions will be made that will enable us to concentrate our efforts on the problems associated with the flow of market information. The first of these assumptions is the use of the risk-neutral measure. The "real" probability measure does not enter into the present investigation. Expectation in the measure $\mathbb{Q}$ will be denoted by $\mathbb{E}[-]$. Our second assumption is that we take the default-free system of interest rates to be deterministic. The absence of arbitrage then implies that the corresponding system of discount functions $\{P_{tT}\}_{0\leq t\leq T<\infty}$ can be written in the form $P_{tT} = P_{0T}/P_{0t}$ for $t \leq T$, where $\{P_{0t}\}_{0\leq t<\infty}$ is the initial discount function, which we take to be part of the initial data of the model. The function $\{P_{0t}\}_{0\leq t<\infty}$ is assumed to be differentiable and strictly decreasing, and to satisfy $0 < P_{0t} \leq 1$ and $\lim_{t\to\infty} P_{0t} = 0$.

We also assume, for simplicity, that cash flows occur at pre-determined dates. Now clearly for some purposes we would like to allow for cash flows occurring effectively at random times—in particular, at stopping times associated with the market filtration. But in the present exposition we want to avoid the idea of a "prespecified" filtration with respect to which stopping times are defined. We take the view that the market filtration is a "derived" notion, generated by information about upcoming cash flows, and by the values of cash flows when they occur. We shall therefore regard a "randomly-timed" cash flow as being a *set* of random cash flows occurring at various times, and with a joint distribution function that ensures only one of these flows is non-zero. Hence in our view the ontological status of a cash flow is that its timing is definite, only the amount is random—and that cash flows occurring at different times are, by their nature, different cash flows.

3. Modelling the Cash Flows

First we consider the case of an asset that provides a single isolated cash flow occurring at time T, represented by a random variable D_T. We assume that $D_T \geq 0$. The value S_t of the cash flow at any earlier time t in the interval $0 \leq t < T$ is then given by the discounted conditional expectation of D_T:

$$S_t = P_{tT}\mathbb{E}\left[D_T|\mathcal{F}_t\right]. \tag{3.1}$$

In this way we model the price process $\{S_t\}_{0\leq t<T}$ of a limited-liability asset that pays a single dividend D_T at time T. The construction of the price process here is carried out in such a way as to guarantee an arbitrage-free market if other assets are priced by the same method (see Davis [6] for a closely related point of view). We shall use the terms "cash flow" and "dividend" more or less interchangeably. If a more specific use of one of these terms is needed, then this will be evident from the context. We adopt the convention that when the dividend is paid the asset price goes "ex-dividend" immediately. Hence in the example above we have $\lim_{t\to T} S_t = D_T$ and $S_T = 0$.

In the case where the asset pays a sequence of dividends D_{T_k} $(k = 1, 2, \ldots, n)$ on the dates T_k the price (for $t < T_1$) is given by

$$S_t = \sum_{k=1}^{n} P_{tT_k}\mathbb{E}\left[D_{T_k}|\mathcal{F}_t\right]. \tag{3.2}$$

More generally, for all $t \geq 0$, and taking into account the ex-dividend behaviour, we have

$$S_t = \sum_{k=1}^{n} \mathbb{1}_{\{t<T_k\}} P_{tT_k} \mathbb{E}\left[D_{T_k}|\mathcal{F}_t\right]. \tag{3.3}$$

It will be useful if we adopt the convention that a discount bond also goes ex-dividend on its maturity date. Thus in the case of a discount bond we assume that the price of the bond is given, for dates earlier than the maturity date, by the product of the principal and the relevant discount factor. But at maturity (when the principal is paid) the value of the bond drops to zero. In the case of a coupon bond, there is a downward jump in the price of the bond at the time a coupon is paid (the value lost may be captured back in the form of an "accrued interest" payment). In this way we obtain a consistent treatment of the "ex-dividend" behaviour of all of the asset price processes under consideration. With this convention it follows that price processes are right continuous with left limits.

4. Modelling the Information Flow

Now we present a simple model for the flow of market information, following Brody *et al.* [3]. We consider first the case of a single distribution, occurring at time T, and assume that market participants have only partial information about the upcoming cash flow D_T. The information available in the market about the cash flow is assumed to be contained in a process $\{\xi_t\}_{0\leq t\leq T}$ defined by

$$\xi_t = \sigma t D_T + \beta_{tT}. \tag{4.1}$$

We call $\{\xi_t\}$ the *market information process.* This process is composed of two parts. The term $\sigma t D_T$ contains the "true information" about the dividend, and grows in magnitude as t increases. The process $\{\beta_{tT}\}_{0\leq t\leq T}$ is a standard Brownian bridge over the time interval $[0,T]$. Thus $\{\beta_{tT}\}$ is Gaussian, $\beta_{0T}=0$, $\beta_{TT}=0$, the random variable β_{tT} has mean zero, and the covariance of β_{sT} and β_{tT} for $s\leq t$ is $s(T-t)/T$. We assume that D_T and $\{\beta_{tT}\}$ are independent. Thus the information contained in the bridge process is "pure noise".

We assume that the market filtration $\{\mathcal{F}_t\}$ is generated by the market information process: $\mathcal{F}_t=\sigma(\{\xi_s\}_{0\leq s\leq t})$. The dividend D_T is therefore $\mathcal{F}_T$-measurable, but is not $\mathcal{F}_t$-measurable for $t<T$. Thus the value of D_T becomes "known" at time T, but not earlier. The bridge process $\{\beta_{tT}\}$ is not adapted to $\{\mathcal{F}_t\}$ and thus is not directly accessible to market participants. This reflects the fact that until the dividend is paid the market participants cannot distinguish the "true information" from the "noise" in the market. The introduction of the Brownian bridge models the fact that market perceptions, whether valid or not, play a role in determining asset prices. Initially, all available information is used to determine the *a priori* probability distribution for D_T. The parameter σ represents the rate at which information about the true value of D_T is revealed as time progresses. If σ is low, the value of

D_T is effectively hidden until very near the time of the dividend payment; whereas if σ is high, then the value of the cash flow is for all practical purposes revealed quickly.

In the example under consideration we have made some simplifying assumptions concerning the information structure. For instance, we assume that σ is constant. In Sec. 13, however, we consider a time-dependent information flow rate. We have also assumed that the random dividend D_T enters directly into the structure of the information process, and enters linearly. As we shall indicate later, a more general and natural setup is to let the information process depend on a random variable X_T which we call a "market factor"; then the dividend is regarded as a function of the market factor. This arrangement has the advantage that it easily generalises to the situation where a cash flow might depend on several independent market factors, or indeed where cash flows associated with different financial instruments have one or more factors in common.

Given the market information structure described above for a single cash flow, we proceed to construct the associated price dynamics. The price process $\{S_t\}$ for a share in the firm paying the specified dividend is given by formula (3.1). It is assumed that the *a priori* probability distribution of the dividend D_T is known. This distribution is regarded as part of the initial data of the problem, which in some cases can be calibrated from knowledge of the initial price of the asset along with other price data. The general problem of how the *a priori* distribution is obtained is an important one—any asset pricing model has to confront this issue—which we defer for later consideration. The initial distribution is not to be understood as being "absolutely" determined, but rather represents the "best estimate" for the distribution given the data available at that time, in accordance with what one might call a Bayesian point of view. We note the fact that the information process $\{\xi_t\}$ is Markovian (see Brody *et al.* [3], and Rutkowski and Yu [23]). Making use of this property together with the fact that D_T is $\mathcal{F}_T$-measurable we deduce that

$$S_t = \mathbb{1}_{\{t<T\}} P_{tT} \mathbb{E}\left[D_T | \xi_t\right]. \tag{4.2}$$

If the random variable D_T that represents the payoff has a continuous distribution, then the conditional expectation in (4.2) can be expressed in the form

$$\mathbb{E}\left[D_T | \xi_t\right] = \int_0^\infty x \pi_t(x)\, \mathrm{d}x. \tag{4.3}$$

Here $\pi_t(x)$ is the conditional probability density for the random variable D_T:

$$\pi_t(x) = \frac{\mathrm{d}}{\mathrm{d}x} \mathbb{Q}(D_T \le x | \xi_t). \tag{4.4}$$

We implicitly assume appropriate technical conditions on the distribution of the dividend that will suffice to ensure the existence of the expressions under consideration. Also, for convenience we use a notation appropriate for continuous distributions, though corresponding results can be inferred for discrete distributions, or more general distributions, by slightly modifying the stated assumptions and conclusions.

Bearing in mind these points, we note that the conditional probability density process for the dividend can be worked out by use of a form of the Bayes formula:

$$\pi_t(x) = \frac{p(x)\rho(\xi_t|D_T = x)}{\int_0^\infty p(x)\rho(\xi_t|D_T = x)\mathrm{d}x}. \tag{4.5}$$

Here $p(x)$ denotes the *a priori* density for D_T, which we assume is known as an initial condition, and $\rho(\xi_t|D_T = x)$ denotes the conditional density for the random variable ξ_t given that $D_T = x$. Since β_{tT} is a Gaussian random variable with mean zero and variance $t(T-t)/T$, we deduce that the conditional density for ξ_t is

$$\rho(\xi_t|D_T = x) = \sqrt{\frac{T}{2\pi t(T-t)}}\exp\left(-\frac{(\xi_t - \sigma t x)^2 T}{2t(T-t)}\right). \tag{4.6}$$

Inserting this expression into the Bayes formula we get

$$\pi_t(x) = \frac{p(x)\exp\left[\frac{T}{T-t}(\sigma x\xi_t - \frac{1}{2}\sigma^2x^2t)\right]}{\int_0^\infty p(x)\exp\left[\frac{T}{T-t}(\sigma x\xi_t - \frac{1}{2}\sigma^2x^2t)\right]\mathrm{d}x}. \tag{4.7}$$

We thus obtain the following result for the asset price:

Proposition 4.1. *The information-based price process* $\{S_t\}_{0\le t\le T}$ *of a limited-liability asset that pays a single dividend* D_T *at time* T *with a priori distribution*

$$\mathbb{Q}(D_T \le y) = \int_0^y p(x)\,\mathrm{d}x \tag{4.8}$$

is given by

$$S_t = \mathbb{1}_{\{t<T\}}P_{tT}\frac{\int_0^\infty xp(x)\exp\left[\frac{T}{T-t}(\sigma x\xi_t - \frac{1}{2}\sigma^2x^2t)\right]\mathrm{d}x}{\int_0^\infty p(x)\exp\left[\frac{T}{T-t}(\sigma x\xi_t - \frac{1}{2}\sigma^2x^2t)\right]\mathrm{d}x}, \tag{4.9}$$

where $\xi_t = \sigma t D_T + \beta_{tT}$ *is the market information.*

5. Asset Price Dynamics in the Case of a Single Cash Flow

In order to analyse the properties of the price process deduced above, and to be able to compare it with other models, we need to work out the dynamics of $\{S_t\}$. One of the advantages of the model under consideration is that we have an explicit expression for the price at our disposal. Thus in obtaining the dynamics we need to find the stochastic differential equation of which $\{S_t\}$ is the solution. This turns out to be an interesting exercise because it offers some insights into what we mean by the assertion that market price dynamics should be regarded as an "emergent phenomenon". To obtain the dynamics associated with the price process $\{S_t\}$ of a single-dividend paying asset let us write

$$D_{tT} = \mathbb{E}[D_T|\xi_t]. \tag{5.1}$$

Evidently, D_{tT} can be expressed in the form $D_{tT} = D(\xi_t, t)$, where

$$D(\xi,t) = \frac{\int_0^\infty xp(x)\exp\left[\frac{T}{T-t}(\sigma x\xi - \frac{1}{2}\sigma^2x^2t)\right]\mathrm{d}x}{\int_0^\infty p(x)\exp\left[\frac{T}{T-t}(\sigma x\xi - \frac{1}{2}\sigma^2x^2t)\right]\mathrm{d}x}. \tag{5.2}$$

A straightforward calculation making use of the Ito rules shows that the dynamical equation for $\{D_{tT}\}$ is given by

$$\mathrm{d}D_{tT} = \frac{\sigma T}{T-t}V_t\left[\frac{1}{T-t}\Big(\xi_t - \sigma T D_{tT}\Big)\mathrm{d}t + \mathrm{d}\xi_t\right]. \tag{5.3}$$

Here V_t is the conditional variance of the dividend:

$$V_t = \mathbb{E}_t[(D_T - \mathbb{E}_t[D_T])^2] = \int_0^\infty x^2\pi_t(x)\,\mathrm{d}x - \left(\int_0^\infty x\pi_t(x)\,\mathrm{d}x\right)^2. \tag{5.4}$$

Therefore, if we define a new process $\{W_t\}_{0\leq t<T}$ by setting

$$W_t = \xi_t - \int_0^t \frac{1}{T-s}(\sigma T D_{tT} - \xi_s)\mathrm{d}s, \tag{5.5}$$

we find, after some rearrangement, that

$$\mathrm{d}D_{tT} = \frac{\sigma T}{T-t}V_t\mathrm{d}W_t. \tag{5.6}$$

For the dynamics of the asset price we thus have

$$\mathrm{d}S_t = r_tS_t\mathrm{d}t + \Gamma_{tT}\mathrm{d}W_t, \tag{5.7}$$

where $r_t = -\mathrm{d}\ln P_{0t}/\mathrm{d}t$ is the short rate, and the absolute price volatility Γ_{tT} is

$$\Gamma_{tT} = P_{tT}\frac{\sigma T}{T-t}V_t. \tag{5.8}$$

A slightly different way of arriving at this result is as follows. We start with the conditional probability $\pi_t(x)$. Then, using the notation above, for its dynamics we obtain

$$\mathrm{d}\pi_t(x) = \frac{\sigma T}{T-t}(x - D_{tT})\pi_t(x)\,\mathrm{d}W_t. \tag{5.9}$$

Since according to (4.2) the asset price is given by

$$S_t = \mathbb{1}_{\{t<T\}}P_{tT}\int_0^\infty x\pi_t(x)\,\mathrm{d}x, \tag{5.10}$$

we can infer the dynamics of $\{S_t\}$ from the dynamics of the conditional probability $\{\pi_t(x)\}$, once we take into account formula (5.4) for the conditional variance.

As we shall demonstrate later, the process $\{W_t\}$ defined in (5.5) is an $\{\mathcal{F}_t\}$-Brownian motion. Hence *from the point of view of the market it is the process* $\{W_t\}$ *that drives the asset price dynamics.* In this way our framework resolves the paradoxical point of view usually adopted in financial modelling in which $\{W_t\}$ is regarded on the one hand as "noise", and yet on the other hand also generates the market information flow. And thus, instead of hypothesising the existence of a driving process for the dynamics of the markets, we are able from the information-based perspective to *deduce* the existence of such a process.

The information-flow parameter σ determines the overall magnitude of the volatility. In fact, σ plays a role analogous to the similarly-labelled parameter in the Black–Scholes–Merton theory. Thus, we can say that the rate at which information is revealed in the market determines the magnitude of the volatility. Everything else being the same, if we increase the information-flow rate, then the market volatility will increase as well. According to this point of view, those mechanisms that one might have thought were destined to make markets more efficient—e.g., globalisation of the financial markets, reduction of trade barriers, improved communications, a robust regulatory environment, and so on—can have the effect of increasing market volatility, and hence market risk, rather than reducing it.

6. European-Style Call Options

Before we turn to the consideration of more general cash flows and market information structures, let us consider the pricing of a derivative on an asset for which the price process is governed by (5.7). Specifically, we consider the valuation of a European call option on such an asset, with strike price K, and exercisable at a fixed date t. The option is written on an asset that pays a single dividend D_T at time $T > t$. The initial value of the option is

$$C_0 = P_{0t}\mathbb{E}\left[(S_t - K)^+\right]. \tag{6.1}$$

Inserting the expression for S_t derived in the previous section, we obtain

$$C_0 = P_{0t}\,\mathbb{E}\left[\left(P_{tT}\int_0^\infty x\,\pi_t(x)\mathrm{d}x - K\right)^+\right]. \tag{6.2}$$

For convenience we write the conditional probability $\pi_t(x)$ in the form

$$\pi_t(x) = \frac{p_t(x)}{\int_0^\infty p_t(x)\mathrm{d}x}, \tag{6.3}$$

where the "unnormalised" density $p_t(x)$ is defined by

$$p_t(x) = p(x)\exp\left[\frac{T}{T-t}\left(\sigma x\xi_t - \tfrac{1}{2}\sigma^2x^2t\right)\right]. \tag{6.4}$$

Substituting (6.4) into (6.2) we find that the value of the option is

$$C_0 = P_{0t}\mathbb{E}\left[\frac{1}{\Phi_t}\left(\int_0^\infty (P_{tT}x - K)\,p_t(x)\mathrm{d}x\right)^+\right], \tag{6.5}$$

where

$$\Phi_t = \int_0^\infty p_t(x)\mathrm{d}x. \tag{6.6}$$

The random variable $1/\Phi_t$ can be used to introduce a measure $\mathbb{B}$ on $(\Omega, \mathcal{F}_t)$, which we call the "bridge measure". The option price can then be written:

$$C_0 = P_{0t}\mathbb{E}^{\mathbb{B}}\left[\left(\int_0^\infty (P_{tT}x - K)\, p_t(x)\mathrm{d}x\right)^+\right]. \tag{6.7}$$

The special feature of the bridge measure, as we establish in Sec. 14 in a more general context, is that the random variable ξ_t is Gaussian under $\mathbb{B}$. In particular, under $\mathbb{B}$ we find that ξ_t has mean 0 and variance $t(T-t)/T$. Since $p_t(x)$ can be expressed as a function of ξ_t, when we calculate the expectation in (6.7) we obtain a tractable formula for C_0.

To determine the value of the option we define a constant ξ^* (the critical value) by the following condition:

$$\int_0^\infty (P_{tT}x - K)\, p(x)\exp\left[\frac{T}{T-t}\left(\sigma x\xi^* - \frac{1}{2}\sigma^2x^2t\right)\right]\mathrm{d}x = 0. \tag{6.8}$$

Then the expectation in (6.7) can be performed and we find that the option price is given by

$$C_0 = P_{0T}\int_0^\infty x\, p(x)\, N(-z^* + \sigma x\sqrt{\tau})\mathrm{d}x - P_{0t}K\int_0^\infty p(x)\, N(-z^* + \sigma x\sqrt{\tau})\mathrm{d}x, \tag{6.9}$$

where $N(x)$ is the standard normal distribution function, and

$$\tau = \frac{tT}{T-t}, \quad z^* = \xi^*\sqrt{\frac{T}{t(T-t)}}. \tag{6.10}$$

We see that a tractable expression of the Black–Scholes–Merton type is obtained. The option pricing problem, even for general $p(x)$, reduces to an elementary numerical problem. It is interesting to note that although the probability distribution for the price S_t is not of a "standard" type, nevertheless the option valuation problem remains a solvable one.

7. Examples of Specific Dividend Structures

In this section we consider the dynamics of assets with various dividend structures. First we look at a simple asset for which the cash flow is exponentially distributed. The *a priori* probability density for D_T is thus of the form

$$p(x) = \frac{1}{\delta}\exp(-x/\delta), \tag{7.1}$$

where δ is a constant. We can regard an exponentially distributed payout as a model for the situation where little is known about the distribution of the dividend, apart from its mean. Then from formula (4.9) we find that the price is:

$$S_t = \mathbb{1}_{\{t<T\}} P_{tT} \frac{\int_0^\infty x \exp(-x/\delta) \exp\left[\frac{T}{T-t}(\sigma x \xi_t - \frac{1}{2}\sigma^2 x^2 t)\right] \mathrm{d}x}{\int_0^\infty \exp(-x/\delta) \exp\left[\frac{T}{T-t}(\sigma x \xi_t - \frac{1}{2}\sigma^2 x^2 t)\right] \mathrm{d}x}. \tag{7.2}$$

We note that $S_0 = P_{0T}\delta$, so we can calibrate δ by use of the initial price. The integrals in the numerator and denominator in the expression above can be worked out explicitly. Hence, we obtain a closed-form expression for the price in the case of a simple asset with an exponentially-distributed cash flow:

$$S_t = \mathbb{1}_{\{t<T\}} P_{tT} \left[\frac{\exp(-\frac{1}{2}B_t^2/A_t)}{\sqrt{2\pi A_t}\; N(B_t/\sqrt{A_t})} + \frac{B_t}{A_t} \right], \tag{7.3}$$

where $A_t = \sigma^2 tT/(T-t)$ and $B_t = \sigma T \xi_t/(T-t) - \delta^{-1}$.

Next we consider the case of an asset for which the single dividend paid at T is gamma-distributed. More specifically, we assume the density is of the form

$$p(x) = \frac{\delta^n}{(n-1)!}\, x^{n-1} \exp(-\delta x), \tag{7.4}$$

where δ is a positive real number and n is a positive integer. This choice for the density also leads to a closed-form expression for the share price. We find that

$$S_t = \mathbb{1}_{\{t<T\}} P_{tT} \frac{\sum_{k=0}^{n} \binom{n}{k} A_t^{\frac{1}{2}k-n} B_t^{n-k} F_k(-B_t/\sqrt{A_t})}{\sum_{k=0}^{n-1} \binom{n-1}{k} A_t^{\frac{1}{2}k-n+1} B_t^{n-k-1} F_k(-B_t/\sqrt{A_t})}, \tag{7.5}$$

where A_t and B_t are as above, and

$$F_k(x) = \int_x^\infty z^k \exp\left(-\frac{1}{2}z^2\right) dz. \tag{7.6}$$

A recursion formula can be worked out for the function $F_k(x)$. This is given by

$$(k+1)F_k(x) = F_{k+2}(x) - x^{k+1} \exp\left(-\frac{1}{2}x^2\right), \tag{7.7}$$

from which it follows that $F_0(x) = \sqrt{2\pi}N(-x)$, $F_1(x) = \mathrm{e}^{-\frac{1}{2}x^2}$, $F_2(x) = x\mathrm{e}^{-\frac{1}{2}x^2} + \sqrt{2\pi}N(-x)$, $F_3(x) = (x^2+2)\mathrm{e}^{-\frac{1}{2}x^2}$, and so on. In general, the polynomial parts of $\{F_k(x)\}_{k=0,1,2,\ldots}$ are related to the Legendre polynomials.

8. Market Factors and Multiple Cash Flows

We proceed to consider the more general situation where the asset pays multiple dividends. This will allow us to consider a wider range of financial instruments. Let us write D_{T_k} $(k = 1, \ldots, n)$ for a set of random dividends paid at the pre-designated dates T_k $(k = 1, \ldots, n)$. Possession of the asset at time t entitles the bearer to the cash flows occurring at times $T_k > t$. For simplicity we assume n is finite. For each value of k we introduce a set of independent random variables $X_{T_k}^{\alpha}$ $(\alpha = 1, \ldots, m_k)$, which we call market factors or X-factors. For each value of α we assume that the market factor $X^{\alpha}_{T_k}$ is $\mathcal{F}_{T_k}$-measurable, where $\{\mathcal{F}_t\}$ is the market filtration.

For each value of k, the market factors $\{X^{\alpha}_{T_j}\}_{j\leq k}$ represent the independent elements that determine the cash flow occurring at time T_k. Thus the cash flow D_{T_k} is assumed to have the following structure:

$$D_{T_k} = \Delta_{T_k}(X^{\alpha}_{T_1}, X^{\alpha}_{T_2}, \ldots, X^{\alpha}_{T_k}), \tag{8.1}$$

where $\Delta_{T_k}(X^{\alpha}_{T_1}, X^{\alpha}_{T_2}, \ldots, X^{\alpha}_{T_k})$ is a function of $\sum_{j=1}^{k} m_j$ variables. For each cash flow it is, so to speak, the job of the financial analyst (or actuary) to determine the relevant independent market factors, and the form of the cash-flow function Δ_{T_k}. With each market factor $X^{\alpha}_{T_k}$ we associate an information process $\{\xi^{\alpha}_{tT_k}\}_{0\leq t\leq T_k}$ of the form

$$\xi^{\alpha}_{tT_k} = \sigma^{\alpha}_{T_k} X^{\alpha}_{T_k} t + \beta^{\alpha}_{tT_k}. \tag{8.2}$$

Here $\sigma^{\alpha}_{T_k}$ is a parameter, and $\{\beta^{\alpha}_{tT_k}\}$ is a standard Brownian bridge over the interval $[0, T_k]$. We assume that the X-factors and the Brownian bridge processes are independent. The parameter $\sigma^{\alpha}_{T_k}$ determines the rate at which the market factor $X^{\alpha}_{T_k}$ is revealed. The Brownian bridge represents the associated noise. We assume that the market filtration $\{\mathcal{F}_t\}$ is generated by the totality of the independent information processes $\{\xi^{\alpha}_{tT_k}\}_{0\leq t\leq T_k}$ for $k = 1, 2, \ldots, n$ and $\alpha = 1, 2, \ldots, m_k$. Hence, the price of the asset is given by

$$S_t = \sum_{k=1}^{n} \mathbb{1}_{\{t<T_k\}} P_{tT_k} \mathbb{E}_t\left[D_{T_k}\right]. \tag{8.3}$$

9. Geometric Brownian Motion Model

The simplest application of the X-factor technique arises in the case of geometric Brownian motion models. We consider a limited-liability asset that makes a single cash distribution S_T at time T. We assume that S_T has a log-normal distribution under $\mathbb{Q}$, and can be written in the form

$$S_T = S_0 \exp\left(rT + \nu\sqrt{T}X_T - \frac{1}{2}\nu^2 T\right), \tag{9.1}$$

where the market factor X_T is normally distributed with mean zero and variance one, and $r > 0$ and $\nu > 0$ are constants. The information process $\{\xi_t\}$ is taken to be of the form

$$\xi_t = \sigma t X_T + \beta_{tT}, \tag{9.2}$$

where the Brownian bridge $\{\beta_{tT}\}$ is independent of X_T, and where the information flow rate is of the special form

$$\sigma = \frac{1}{\sqrt{T}}. \tag{9.3}$$

By use of the Bayes formula we find that the conditional probability density is of the Gaussian form

$$\pi_t(x) = \sqrt{\frac{T}{2\pi(T-t)}}\,\exp\!\left(-\frac{1}{2(T-t)}(\sqrt{T}x - \xi_t)^2\right), \tag{9.4}$$

and has the following dynamics:

$$\mathrm{d}\pi_t(x) = \frac{1}{T-t}\,(\sqrt{T}x - \xi_t)\pi_t(x)\mathrm{d}\xi_t. \tag{9.5}$$

A short calculation then shows that the value of the asset at time $t < T$ is given by

$$\begin{aligned} S_t &= \mathrm{e}^{-r(T-t)}\mathbb{E}_t[S_T] \\ &= \mathrm{e}^{-r(T-t)}\int_{-\infty}^{\infty} S_0\mathrm{e}^{rT+\nu\sqrt{T}x-\frac{1}{2}\nu^2T}\pi_t(x)\mathrm{d}x \\ &= S_0\exp\left(rt + \nu\xi_t - \frac{1}{2}\nu^2 t\right). \end{aligned} \tag{9.6}$$

The surprising fact in this example is that $\{\xi_t\}$ itself turns out to be the innovation process. Indeed, it is not too difficult to verify that $\{\xi_t\}$ is an $\{\mathcal{F}_t\}$-Brownian motion. Hence, setting $W_t = \xi_t$ for $0 \le t < T$ we obtain the standard geometric Brownian motion model:

$$S_t = S_0\exp\!\left(rt + \nu W_t - \frac{1}{2}\nu^2 t\right). \tag{9.7}$$

We see therefore that starting with an information process of the form (9.2) we are able to recover the familiar asset price dynamics given by (9.7).

An important point to note here is that the Brownian bridge process $\{\beta_{tT}\}$ appears quite naturally in this context. In fact, if we start with (9.7) then we can make use of the following orthogonal decomposition of the Brownian motion (see, e.g., Yor [24]):

$$W_t = \frac{t}{T}\,W_T + \left(W_t - \frac{t}{T}\,W_T\right). \tag{9.8}$$

The second term in the right, independent of the first term on the right, is a standard representation for a Brownian bridge process:

$$\beta_{tT} = W_t - \frac{t}{T}\,W_T. \tag{9.9}$$

Thus by writing $X_T = W_T/\sqrt{T}$ and $\sigma = 1/\sqrt{T}$ we find that the right side of (9.8) is indeed the market information. In other words, formulated in the information-based framework, the standard Black–Scholes–Merton theory can be expressed in terms of a normally distributed X-factor and an independent Brownian bridge noise process.

10. Dividend Growth

As an elementary example of a multi-dividend structure, we shall look at a simple growth model for dividends in the equity markets. We consider an asset that pays a sequence of dividends D_{T_k}, where each dividend date has an associated X-factor. Let $\{X_{T_k}\}_{k=1,\ldots,n}$ be a set of independent, identically-distributed X-factors, each with mean $1+g$. The dividend structure is assumed to be of the form

$$D_{T_k} = D_0 \prod_{j=1}^{k} X_{T_j}, \tag{10.1}$$

where D_0 is a constant. The parameter g can be interpreted as the dividend growth factor, and D_0 can be understood as representing the most recent dividend before time zero. For the price of the asset we have:

$$S_t = D_0 \sum_{k=1}^{n} \mathbb{1}_{\{t<T_k\}} P_{tT_k} \mathbb{E}_t \left[\prod_{j=1}^{k} X_{T_j} \right]. \tag{10.2}$$

Since the X-factors are independent, the conditional expectation of the product appearing in this expression factorises into a product of conditional expectations, and each such conditional expectation can be written in the form of an expression of the type we have already considered. As a consequence we are led to a tractable family of dividend growth models.

11. Assets with Common Factors

The multiple-dividend asset pricing model introduced in Sec. 8 can be extended in a very natural way to the situation where two or more assets are being priced. In this case we consider a collection of N assets with price processes $\{S_t^{(i)}\}_{i=1,2,\ldots,N}$. With asset number (i) we associate the cash flows $\{D_{T_k}^{(i)}\}$ paid at the dates $\{T_k\}_{k=1,2,\ldots,n}$. We note that the dates $\{T_k\}_{k=1,2,\ldots,n}$ are not tied to any specific asset, but rather represent the totality of possible cash-flow dates of any of the given assets. If a particular asset has no cash flow on one of the dates, then it is assigned a zero cash-flow for that date. From this point, the theory proceeds exactly as in the single asset case. That is to say, with each value of k we associate a set of X-factors $X_{T_k}^{\alpha}$ ($\alpha = 1, 2, \ldots, m_k$), and a system of market information processes $\{\xi_{tT_k}^{\alpha}\}$. The X-factors and the information processes are not tied to any particular asset. The cash flow $D_{T_k}^{(i)}$ occurring at time T_k for asset number (i) is given by a cash flow function of the form

$$D_{T_k}^{(i)} = \Delta_{T_k}^{(i)}(X_{T_1}^{\alpha}, X_{T_2}^{\alpha}, \ldots, X_{T_k}^{\alpha}). \tag{11.1}$$

In other words, for each asset each cash flow can depend on all of the X-factors that have been "activated" at that point. Thus for the general multi-asset model we have the following price process system:

$$S_t^{(i)} = \sum_{k=1}^{n} \mathbb{1}_{\{t<T_k\}} P_{tT_k} \mathbb{E}_t [D_{T_k}^{(i)}]. \tag{11.2}$$

It is possible in general for two or more assets to "share" an X-factor in association with one or more of the cash flows of each of the assets. This in turn implies that the various assets will have at least one Brownian motion in common in the dynamics of their price processes. We thus obtain a natural model for the correlation structures in the prices of these assets. The intuition is that as new information comes in (whether "true" or "bogus") there will be several different assets all affected by the news, and as a consequence there will be a correlated movement in their prices.

12. Origin of Unhedgeable Stochastic Volatility

Based on the general model introduced in the previous sections, we are now in a position to make an observation concerning the nature of stochastic volatility in the equity markets. In particular, we shall show how a natural framework for *stochastic volatility* arises in the information-based framework. This is achieved without the need for any *ad hoc* assumptions concerning the dynamics of the stochastic volatility. In fact, a very specific dynamical model for stochastic volatility is obtained—thus leading to a possible means by which the theory proposed here might be tested.

We shall work out the volatility associated with the dynamics of the asset price process $\{S_t\}$ given by (8.3). The result is given in Proposition 12.1 below. First, as an example, we consider the dynamics of an asset that pays a single dividend D_T at T. We assume that the dividend depends on the market factors $\{X_T^\alpha\}_{\alpha=1,\ldots,m}$. For $t < T$ we then have:

$$\begin{aligned} S_t &= P_{tT}\mathbb{E}^{\mathbb{Q}}[\Delta_T(X_T^1,\ldots,X_T^m)|\xi_{tT}^1,\ldots,\xi_{tT}^m] \\ &= P_{tT}\int\cdots\int \Delta_T(x^1,\ldots,x^m)\,\pi_{tT}^1(x_1)\cdots\pi_{tT}^m(x_m)\,\mathrm{d}x_1\cdots\mathrm{d}x_m. \end{aligned} \tag{12.1}$$

Here the conditional density functions $\pi_{tT}^\alpha(x)$ for $\alpha = 1,\ldots,m$ are given by

$$\pi_{tT}^\alpha(x) = \frac{p^\alpha(x)\exp\left[\frac{T}{T-t}\left(\sigma^\alpha x\,\xi_{tT}^\alpha - \frac{1}{2}(\sigma^\alpha)^2x^2t\right)\right]}{\int_0^\infty p^\alpha(x)\exp\left[\frac{T}{T-t}\left(\sigma^\alpha x\,\xi_{tT}^\alpha - \frac{1}{2}(\sigma^\alpha)^2x^2t\right)\right]\mathrm{d}x}, \tag{12.2}$$

where $p^\alpha(x)$ denotes the *a priori* probability density function for the factor X_T^α. The drift of $\{S_t\}_{0\le t<T}$ is given by the short rate. This is because $\mathbb{Q}$ is the risk-neutral measure, and no dividend is paid before T. Thus, we are left with the problem of determining the volatility of $\{S_t\}$. We find that for $t < T$ the dynamical equation of $\{S_t\}$ assumes the form:

$$\mathrm{d}S_t = r_tS_t\mathrm{d}t + \sum_{\alpha=1}^m \Gamma_{tT}^\alpha\mathrm{d}W_t^\alpha. \tag{12.3}$$

Here the volatility term associated with factor number α is given by

$$\Gamma_{tT}^\alpha = \sigma^\alpha\frac{T}{T-t}P_{tT}\,\mathrm{Cov}[\Delta_T(X_T^1,\ldots,X_T^m),X_T^\alpha|\mathcal{F}_t], \tag{12.4}$$

and $\{W_t^\alpha\}$ denotes the Brownian motion associated with the information process $\{\xi_t^\alpha\}$, defined as in (5.5). The absolute volatility of $\{S_t\}$ is of the form

$$\Gamma_t = \left(\sum_{\alpha=1}^{m} (\Gamma_{tT}^\alpha)^2 \right)^{1/2}. \tag{12.5}$$

For the dynamics of a multi-factor single-dividend paying asset we can thus write $\mathrm{d}S_t = r_t S_t \mathrm{d}t + \Gamma_t \mathrm{d}Z_t$, where the $\{\mathcal{F}_t\}$-Brownian motion $\{Z_t\}$ that drives the asset-price process is

$$Z_t = \int_0^t \frac{1}{\Gamma_s} \sum_{\alpha=1}^{m} \Gamma_{sT}^\alpha \, \mathrm{d}W_s^\alpha. \tag{12.6}$$

The point to note here is that in the case of a multi-factor model we obtain an unhedgeable stochastic volatility. That is to say, although the asset price is in effect driven by a single Brownian motion, its volatility in general depends on a multiplicity of Brownian motions. This means that in general an option position cannot be hedged with a position in the underlying asset. The components of the volatility vector are given by the covariances of the cash flow and the independent market factors. Unhedgeable stochastic volatility thus emerges from the multiplicity of uncertain elements in the market that affect the value of the future cash flow. As a consequence we see that *in this framework we obtain a natural explanation for the origin of stochastic volatility.*

This result can be contrasted with, say, the Heston model [13], which despite its popularity suffers from the fact that it is *ad hoc* in nature. Much the same can be said for the various generalisations of the Heston model used in commercial applications. The approach to stochastic volatility proposed in the present paper is thus of a new character. Expression (12.3) generalises to the case for which the asset pays a set of dividends D_{T_k} $(k = 1, \ldots, n)$, and for each k the dividend depends on the X-factors $\{\{X_{T_j}^\alpha\}_{j=1,\ldots,k}^{\alpha=1,\ldots,m_j}\}$. The result can be summarised as follows.

Proposition 12.1. *The price process of a multi-dividend asset has the following dynamics*:

$$\mathrm{d}S_t = r_t \, S_t \, \mathrm{d}t + \sum_{k=1}^{n} \sum_{j=1}^{k} \sum_{\alpha=1}^{m_j} \mathbb{1}_{\{t<T_k\}} P_{tT_k} \frac{\sigma_j^\alpha T_j}{T_j - t} \, \mathrm{Cov}[D_{T_k}, X_{T_j}^\alpha | \mathcal{F}_t] \mathrm{d}W_t^{\alpha j}$$
$$+ \sum_{k=1}^{n} D_{T_k} \mathrm{d}\mathbb{1}_{\{t<T_k\}}, \tag{12.7}$$

where $D_{T_k} = \Delta_{T_k}(X_{T_1}^\alpha, X_{T_2}^\alpha, \cdots, X_{T_k}^\alpha)$ *is the dividend at time* T_k $(k = 1, 2, \ldots, n)$.

13. Time-Dependent Information Flow

We consider now a generalisation of the foregoing material to the situation in which the information-flow rate varies in time. The time-dependent problem is of relevance to many circumstances. For example, there will typically be more activity in a market during the day than at night—such a consideration is important for short-term investments. Alternatively, it may be that the annual report of a firm is going to be published on a specified day—in this case much more information concerning the future of the firm may be made available on that day than normal.

We begin our analysis of the time-dependent case by considering the situation where there is a single cash flow D_T occurring at T, and the associated market factor is the cash flow itself. In this way we can focus our attention on mathematical issues arising from the time dependence of the information flow rate. Once these issues have been dealt with, we shall consider more complicated cash-flow structures. For the market information process we propose an expression of the form

$$\xi_t = D_T \int_0^t \sigma_s \mathrm{d}s + \beta_{tT}, \tag{13.1}$$

where the function $\{\sigma_s\}_{o \le s \le T}$ is taken to be deterministic and nonnegative. We assume that $0 < \int_0^T \sigma_s^2 ds < \infty$. The price process $\{S_t\}$ of the asset is then given by

$$S_t = \mathbb{1}_{\{t<T\}} P_{tT} \mathbb{E}[D_T | \mathcal{F}_t], \tag{13.2}$$

where the market filtration is, as in the previous sections, assumed to be generated by the information process.

Our first task is to work out the conditional expectation in (13.2). This can be achieved by use of a change-of-measure technique, which will be outlined in Sec. 14. It will be useful, however, to state the result first. We define the conditional probability density process $\{\pi_t(x)\}$ by setting

$$\pi_t(x) = \frac{\mathrm{d}}{\mathrm{d}x} \mathbb{Q}(D_T \le x | \mathcal{F}_t). \tag{13.3}$$

The following result is obtained:

Proposition 13.1. *Let the information process $\{\xi_t\}$ be given by* (13.1). *Then the conditional probability density process $\{\pi_t(x)\}$ for the random variable D_T is*

$$\pi_t(x) = \frac{p(x)\, \mathrm{e}^{x\left(\frac{1}{T-t}\xi_t \int_0^t \sigma_s \mathrm{d}s + \int_0^t \sigma_s \mathrm{d}\xi_s\right) - \frac{1}{2}x^2\left(\frac{1}{T-t}\left(\int_0^t \sigma_s \mathrm{d}s\right)^2 + \int_0^t \sigma_s^2 \mathrm{d}s\right)}}{\int_0^\infty p(x)\, \mathrm{e}^{x\left(\frac{1}{T-t}\xi_t \int_0^t \sigma_s \mathrm{d}s + \int_0^t \sigma_s \mathrm{d}\xi_s\right) - \frac{1}{2}x^2\left(\frac{1}{T-t}\left(\int_0^t \sigma_s \mathrm{d}s\right)^2 + \int_0^t \sigma_s^2 \mathrm{d}s\right)} \mathrm{d}x}. \tag{13.4}$$

We deduce at once from Proposition 3 that the conditional expectation of the random variable D_T is

$$D_{tT} = \frac{\int_0^\infty x p(x)\, \mathrm{e}^{x\left(\frac{1}{T-t}\xi_t \int_0^t \sigma_s \mathrm{d}s + \int_0^t \sigma_s \mathrm{d}\xi_s\right) - \frac{1}{2}x^2\left(\frac{1}{T-t}\left(\int_0^t \sigma_s \mathrm{d}s\right)^2 + \int_0^t \sigma_s^2 \mathrm{d}s\right)} \mathrm{d}x}{\int_0^\infty p(x)\, \mathrm{e}^{x\left(\frac{1}{T-t}\xi_t \int_0^t \sigma_s \mathrm{d}s + \int_0^t \sigma_s \mathrm{d}\xi_s\right) - \frac{1}{2}x^2\left(\frac{1}{T-t}\left(\int_0^t \sigma_s \mathrm{d}s\right)^2 + \int_0^t \sigma_s^2 \mathrm{d}s\right)} \mathrm{d}x}. \tag{13.5}$$

The associated price process $\{S_t\}$ is then given by $S_t = \mathbb{1}_{\{t<T\}} P_{tT} D_{tT}$.

14. Changes of Measure for Brownian Bridges

Since the information process is a Brownian bridge with a random drift, we shall require formulae relating a Brownian bridge with drift in one measure to a standard Brownian bridge in another measure to establish Proposition 13.1. We proceed as follows. First we recall a well-known integral representation for the Brownian bridge. Let the probability space $(\Omega, \mathcal{F}, \mathbb{Q})$ be given, with a filtration $\{\mathcal{G}_t\}_{0\leq t<\infty}$, and let $\{B_t\}$ be a standard $\{\mathcal{G}_t\}$-Brownian motion. Then the process $\{\beta_{tT}\}$, defined by

$$\beta_{tT} = (T-t)\int_0^t \frac{1}{T-s}\,\mathrm{d}B_s, \tag{14.1}$$

for $0 \leq t < T$, and by $\beta_{tT} = 0$ for $t = T$, is a standard Brownian bridge over the interval $[0, T]$. Expression (14.1) converges to zero as $t \to T$; see, e.g., Karatzas and Shreve [17], Protter [22]. The filtration $\{\mathcal{G}_t\}$ is larger than the market filtration $\{\mathcal{F}_t\}$. In particular, since $\{\beta_{tT}\}$ is adapted to $\{\mathcal{G}_t\}$ we can think of $\{\mathcal{G}_t\}$ as the filtration describing the information available to an "insider" who can distinguish between what is noise and what is not.

Let D_T be a random variable on $(\Omega, \mathcal{F}, \mathbb{Q})$. We assume that D_T is $\mathcal{G}_0$-measurable and that D_T is independent of $\{\beta_{tT}\}$. Thus the value of D_T is known "all along" to the insider, but not to the typical market participant. For simplicity in what follows we assume that D_T is bounded; this condition can be relaxed with the introduction of an appropriate Novikov-type condition; but we will not pursue the more general situation here. Define the deterministic nonnegative process $\{\nu_t\}_{0\leq t\leq T}$ by

$$\nu_t = \sigma_t + \frac{1}{T-t}\int_0^t \sigma_s \mathrm{d}s, \tag{14.2}$$

and let $\{\xi_t\}$ be defined as in (13.1). We define the process $\{\Lambda_t\}_{0\leq t<T}$ by the relation

$$\frac{1}{\Lambda_t} = \exp\left(-D_T\int_0^t \nu_s \mathrm{d}B_s - \frac{1}{2}D_T^2\int_0^t \nu_s^2 \mathrm{d}s\right). \tag{14.3}$$

With these elements in hand, we fix a time horizon $U \in (0, T)$ and introduce a probability measure $\mathbb{B}$ on $\mathcal{G}_U$ by the relation

$$\mathrm{d}\mathbb{B} = \Lambda_U^{-1}\mathrm{d}\mathbb{Q}. \tag{14.4}$$

Then we have the following facts: (i) The process $\{W_t^*\}_{0\leq t<U}$ defined by

$$W_t^* = D_T\int_0^t \nu_s \mathrm{d}s + B_t \tag{14.5}$$

is a $\mathbb{B}$-Brownian motion. (ii) The process $\{\xi_t\}$ defined by (13.1) is a $\mathbb{B}$-Brownian bridge and is independent of D_T. (iii) The random variable D_T has the same probability law with respect to $\mathbb{B}$ and $\mathbb{Q}$. (iv) The conditional expectation for any integrable function $f(D_T)$ of the random variable D_T can be expressed in the form

$$\mathbb{E}^{\mathbb{Q}}[f(D_T)|\mathcal{F}_t^{\xi}] = \frac{\mathbb{E}^{\mathbb{B}}[f(D_T)\Lambda_t|\mathcal{F}_t^{\xi}]}{\mathbb{E}^{\mathbb{B}}[\Lambda_t|\mathcal{F}_t^{\xi}]}. \tag{14.6}$$

We note that the measure $\mathbb{B}$ is independent of the specific choice of the time horizon U in the sense that if $\mathbb{B}$ is defined on $\mathcal{G}_{U'}$ for some $U' > U$, then the restriction of that measure to $\mathcal{G}_U$ agrees with the measure $\mathbb{B}$ as already defined.

When we say that $\{\xi_t\}$ is a $\mathbb{B}$-Brownian bridge what we mean, more precisely, is that $\xi_0 = 0$, that $\{\xi_t\}$ is $\mathbb{B}$-Gaussian, that $\mathbb{E}^{\mathbb{B}}[\xi_t] = 0$, and that

$$\mathbb{E}^{\mathbb{B}}[\xi_s\xi_t] = \frac{s(T-t)}{T} \tag{14.7}$$

for $0 \leq s \leq t \leq U$. Thus with respect to the measure $\mathbb{B}$ the process $\{\xi_t\}_{0\leq t\leq U}$ has the properties of a standard $[0,T]$-Brownian bridge that has been truncated at time U. The fact that $\{\xi_t\}$ is a $\mathbb{B}$-Brownian bridge can be verified as follows. By (13.1), (14.1), and (14.5) we have

$$\begin{aligned}
\xi_t &= D_T \int_0^t \sigma_s \mathrm{d}s + (T-t)\int_0^t \frac{1}{T-s}\,\mathrm{d}B_s \\
&= D_T \int_0^t \sigma_s \mathrm{d}s + (T-t)\int_0^t \frac{1}{T-s}\,(\mathrm{d}W_s^* - D_T\nu_s \mathrm{d}s) \\
&= D_T \left(\int_0^t \sigma_s \mathrm{d}s - (T-t)\int_0^t \frac{1}{T-s}\,\nu_s \mathrm{d}s\right) + (T-t)\int_0^t \frac{1}{T-s}\,\mathrm{d}W_s^* \\
&= (T-t)\int_0^t \frac{1}{T-s}\,\mathrm{d}W_s^*,
\end{aligned} \tag{14.8}$$

where in the final step we used the relation

$$\int_0^t \frac{1}{T-s}\,\nu_s \mathrm{d}s = \frac{1}{T-t}\int_0^t \sigma_s \mathrm{d}s. \tag{14.9}$$

This formula can be verified by differentiation, which gives (14.2). In (14.8) we see that $\{\xi_t\}$ has been given the standard integral representation of a Brownian bridge.

We remark, incidentally, that (14.6) can be thought of a variation of the Kallianpur-Striebel formula appearing in the literature of nonlinear filtering (see, for example, Bucy and Joseph [4], Davis and Marcus [7], Fujisaki *et al.* [9], Kailath [15], Kallianpur and Striebel [16], Krishnan [18], and Liptser and Shiryaev [19]).

15. Derivation of the Conditional Density

We have introduced the idea of measure changes associated with Brownian bridges in order to introduce formula (14.6), which involves the density process $\{\Lambda_t\}$, which in (14.3) is defined in terms of the $\mathbb{Q}$-Brownian motion $\{B_t\}$. On the other hand, the expectations in (14.6) are conditional with respect to the information generated by $\{\xi_t\}$. Therefore, it will be convenient to express $\{\Lambda_t\}$ in terms of $\{\xi_t\}$. To do this we substitute (14.5) in (14.3) to obtain

$$\Lambda_t = \exp\left(D_T \int_0^t \nu_s \mathrm{d}W_s^* - \frac{1}{2} D_T^2 \int_0^t \nu_s^2 \mathrm{d}s \right). \tag{15.1}$$

We then observe, by differentiating (14.8), that

$$\mathrm{d}\xi_t = -\frac{\xi_t}{T-t}\,\mathrm{d}t + \mathrm{d}W_t^*. \tag{15.2}$$

Substituting this relation in (15.1) we obtain

$$\Lambda_t = \exp\left[D_T \left(\int_0^t \nu_s \mathrm{d}\xi_s + \int_0^t \frac{1}{T-s} \nu_s \xi_s \mathrm{d}s \right) - \frac{1}{2} D_T^2 \int_0^t \nu_s^2 \mathrm{d}s \right]. \tag{15.3}$$

In principle at this point all we need to do is to substitute (14.2) into (15.3) to obtain the result for $\{\Lambda_t\}$. In practice, further simplification can be achieved. To this end, we note that by taking the differential of the coefficient of D_T in the exponent of (15.3) we get

$$\begin{aligned} \mathrm{d}\left(\int_0^t \nu_s \mathrm{d}\xi_s + \int_0^t \frac{1}{T-s} \nu_s \xi_s \mathrm{d}s \right) &= \nu_t \left(\mathrm{d}\xi_t + \frac{1}{T-t}\,\xi_t \mathrm{d}t \right) \\ &= \left(\sigma_t + \frac{1}{T-t} \int_0^t \sigma_s \mathrm{d}s \right) \left(\mathrm{d}\xi_t + \frac{1}{T-t}\,\xi_t \mathrm{d}t \right) \\ &= \mathrm{d}\left(\frac{1}{T-t}\,\xi_t \int_0^t \sigma_s \mathrm{d}s + \int_0^t \sigma_s \mathrm{d}\xi_s \right). \end{aligned} \tag{15.4}$$

Then integrating both sides of (15.4) we obtain:

$$\int_0^t \nu_s \mathrm{d}\xi_s + \int_0^t \frac{1}{T-s} \nu_s \xi_s \mathrm{d}s = \frac{1}{T-t}\,\xi_t \int_0^t \sigma_s \mathrm{d}s + \int_0^t \sigma_s \mathrm{d}\xi_s. \tag{15.5}$$

Similarly, by taking the differential of the coefficient of $-\frac{1}{2}D_T^2$ in the exponent of (15.3) and making use of (14.2), we find

$$\begin{aligned} \nu_t^2 \mathrm{d}t &= \left[\sigma_t^2 + 2\frac{1}{T-t} \sigma_t \int_0^t \sigma_s \mathrm{d}s + \frac{1}{(T-t)^2} \left(\int_0^t \sigma_s \mathrm{d}s \right)^2 \right] \mathrm{d}t \\ &= \mathrm{d}\left[\frac{1}{T-t} \left(\int_0^t \sigma_s \mathrm{d}s \right)^2 + \int_0^t \sigma_s^2 \mathrm{d}s \right]. \end{aligned} \tag{15.6}$$

Therefore, by integrating both sides of (15.6) we obtain an identity for the coefficient of the term $-\frac{1}{2}D_T^2$.

It follows by virtue of the two identities just obtained that $\{\Lambda_t\}$ can be expressed in terms of $\{\xi_t\}$. More explicitly, we have

$$\Lambda_t = \exp\left[D_T\left(\frac{1}{T-t}\,\xi_t\int_0^t \sigma_s \mathrm{d}s + \int_0^t \sigma_s \mathrm{d}\xi_s\right) - \frac{1}{2}D_T^2\left(\frac{1}{T-t}\left(\int_0^t \sigma_s \mathrm{d}s\right)^2 + \int_0^t \sigma_s^2 \mathrm{d}s\right)\right]. \tag{15.7}$$

Note that by transforming (15.3) into (15.7) we have eliminated a term having $\{\xi_t\}$ in the integrand, thus achieving a considerable simplification. Proposition 13.1 can then be deduced if we use equation (14.9) and the basic relation

$$\mathbb{Q}(D_T \leq x|\mathcal{F}_t) = \mathbb{E}^{\mathbb{Q}}[\mathbb{1}_{\{D_T\leq x\}}|\mathcal{F}_t]. \tag{15.8}$$

In particular, since D_T and $\{\xi_t\}$ are independent under the bridge measure, by virtue of (14.6), (15.7), and (15.8) we obtain

$$\mathbb{Q}(D_T \leq x|\mathcal{F}_t) = \frac{\int_0^x p(y)\,\mathrm{e}^{y\left(\frac{1}{T-t}\xi_t\int_0^t\sigma_s\mathrm{d}s + \int_0^t\sigma_s\mathrm{d}\xi_s\right) - \frac{1}{2}y^2\left(\frac{1}{T-t}\left(\int_0^t\sigma_s\mathrm{d}s\right)^2 + \int_0^t\sigma_s^2\mathrm{d}s\right)}\mathrm{d}y}{\int_0^\infty p(y)\,\mathrm{e}^{y\left(\frac{1}{T-t}\xi_t\int_0^t\sigma_s\mathrm{d}s + \int_0^t\sigma_s\mathrm{d}\xi_s\right) - \frac{1}{2}y^2\left(\frac{1}{T-t}\left(\int_0^t\sigma_s\mathrm{d}s\right)^2 + \int_0^t\sigma_s^2\mathrm{d}s\right)}\mathrm{d}y}, \tag{15.9}$$

from which we infer Proposition 13.1 by differentiation with respect to x.

We conclude this section by noting that an alternative expression for $\{\pi_t(x)\}$, written in terms of $\{W_t^*\}$, is given by

$$\pi_t(x) = \frac{p(x)\,\exp\left(x\int_0^t \nu_u \mathrm{d}W_u^* - \frac{1}{2}x^2\int_0^t \nu_u^2 \mathrm{d}u\right)}{\int_0^\infty p(x)\,\exp\left(x\int_0^t \nu_u \mathrm{d}W_u^* - \frac{1}{2}x^2\int_0^t \nu_u^2 \mathrm{d}u\right)\mathrm{d}x}. \tag{15.10}$$

16. Consistency Relations

Before we proceed to analyse in detail the dynamics of the price process $\{S_t\}$, first we shall establish a useful *dynamical consistency* relation satisfied by prices obtained in the information-based framework. By "consistency" we have in mind the following. Suppose that we re-initialise the information process at an intermediate time $s \in (0, T)$ by specifying the value ξ_s of the information at that time. For the framework to be dynamically consistent, we require that the remainder of the period $[s, T]$ admits a representation in terms of a suitably "renormalised" information process. Specifically, we have:

Proposition 16.1. *Let $0 \leq s \leq t \leq T$. The conditional probability $\pi_t(x)$ can be written in terms of the intermediate conditional probability $\pi_s(x)$ in the form*

$$\pi_t(x) = \frac{\pi_s(x)\,\mathrm{e}^{x\left(\frac{1}{T-t}\eta_t\int_s^t\tilde{\sigma}_u\mathrm{d}u+\int_s^t\tilde{\sigma}_u\mathrm{d}\eta_u\right)-\frac{1}{2}x^2\left(\frac{1}{T-t}\left(\int_s^t\tilde{\sigma}_u\mathrm{d}u\right)^2+\int_s^t\tilde{\sigma}_u^2\mathrm{d}u\right)}}{\int_0^\infty\pi_s(x)\,\mathrm{e}^{x\left(\frac{1}{T-t}\eta_t\int_s^t\tilde{\sigma}_u\mathrm{d}u+\int_s^t\tilde{\sigma}_u\mathrm{d}\eta_u\right)-\frac{1}{2}x^2\left(\frac{1}{T-t}\left(\int_s^t\tilde{\sigma}_u\mathrm{d}u\right)^2+\int_s^t\tilde{\sigma}_u^2\mathrm{d}u\right)}\mathrm{d}x}, \tag{16.1}$$

where

$$\tilde{\sigma}_u = \sigma_u + \frac{1}{T-s}\int_0^s \sigma_v \mathrm{d}v \tag{16.2}$$

is the re-initialised market information-flow rate, and

$$\eta_t = \xi_t - \frac{T-t}{T-s}\xi_s \tag{16.3}$$

is the re-initialised information process.

The fact that $\{\eta_t\}_{s\leq t\leq T}$ represents the updated information process bridging the interval $[s, T]$ can be seen as follows. First, we note that $\eta_s = 0$ and that $\eta_T = \xi_T$. Substituting (13.1) in (16.3) we find that

$$\eta_t = D_T \int_s^t \tilde{\sigma}_u \mathrm{d}u + \gamma_{tT}, \tag{16.4}$$

where $\tilde{\sigma}_u$ is as defined in (16.2), and

$$\gamma_{tT} = \beta_{tT} - \frac{T-t}{T-s}\beta_{sT}. \tag{16.5}$$

A calculation making use of the covariance of $\{\beta_{tT}\}$ shows that the Gaussian process $\{\gamma_{tT}\}_{s\leq t\leq T}$ is a standard Brownian bridge over the interval $[s, T]$. It follows that $\{\eta_t\}$ is the information bridge interpolating the interval $[s, T]$.

To verify (16.1) we note that (15.10) can be written in the form

$$\pi_t(x) = \frac{\pi_s(x)\,\exp\left(x\int_s^t \nu_u \mathrm{d}W_u^* - \frac{1}{2}x^2\int_s^t \nu_u^2\mathrm{d}u\right)}{\int_0^\infty \pi_s(x)\,\exp\left(x\int_s^t \nu_u \mathrm{d}W_u^* - \frac{1}{2}x^2\int_s^t \nu_u^2\mathrm{d}u\right)\mathrm{d}x}. \tag{16.6}$$

The identity (15.4) then implies that

$$\begin{aligned}\int_s^t \nu_u \mathrm{d}W_u^* &= \frac{1}{T-t}\xi_t\int_s^t \sigma_u\mathrm{d}u + \int_s^t \sigma_u \mathrm{d}\xi_u + \left(\frac{\xi_t}{T-t} - \frac{\xi_s}{T-s}\right)\int_0^s \sigma_u \mathrm{d}u \\ &= \frac{1}{T-t}\eta_t\int_s^t \tilde{\sigma}_u\mathrm{d}u + \int_s^t \tilde{\sigma}_u\mathrm{d}\eta_u, \end{aligned} \tag{16.7}$$

where we have made use of (16.2) and (16.3). Similarly, (15.5) implies that

$$\int_s^t \nu_u^2 \mathrm{d}u = \frac{1}{T-t}\left(\int_0^t \sigma_u \mathrm{d}u\right)^2 - \frac{1}{T-s}\left(\int_0^s \sigma_u \mathrm{d}u\right)^2 + \int_s^t \sigma_u^2 \mathrm{d}u$$

$$= \frac{1}{T-t}\left(\int_s^t \tilde{\sigma}_u \mathrm{d}u\right)^2 + \int_s^t \tilde{\sigma}_u^2 \mathrm{d}u. \tag{16.8}$$

Substitution of (16.7) and (16.8) into (16.6) establishes (16.1). In particular, the form of (16.1) is identical to the original formula (13.4), modulo the indicated renormalisation of the information process and the associated information flow rate.

17. Expected Dividend

The goal of Secs. 13, 14, and 15 was to obtain an expression for the conditional expectation (5.1) in the case of a single-dividend asset when one has a time-dependent information-flow rate. In the analysis of the price process it will be useful to work out the dynamics of the conditional expectation of the dividend. In particular, an application of Ito's rule to (13.5), after some rearrangement, shows that

$$\mathrm{d}D_{tT} = \nu_t V_t \left(\frac{1}{T-t}\,\xi_t - \nu_t D_{tT}\right)\mathrm{d}t + \nu_t V_t \mathrm{d}\xi_t, \tag{17.1}$$

where $\{V_t\}$ is the conditional variance of the random variable D_T, given by (5.4). Let us define a new process $\{W_t\}$ by

$$W_t = \xi_t + \int_0^t \frac{1}{T-s}\,\xi_s \mathrm{d}s - \int_0^t \nu_s D_{sT} \mathrm{d}s. \tag{17.2}$$

We refer to $\{W_t\}$ as the "innovation process". It follows from the definition of $\{W_t\}$ that

$$\mathrm{d}D_{tT} = \nu_t V_t \,\mathrm{d}W_t. \tag{17.3}$$

Since $\{D_{tT}\}$ is an $\{\mathcal{F}_t\}$-martingale we are thus led to conjecture that $\{W_t\}$ must also be an $\{\mathcal{F}_t\}$-martingale. In fact, we have the following result:

Proposition 17.1. *The process $\{W_t\}$ defined by (17.2) is an $\{\mathcal{F}_t\}$-Brownian motion under $\mathbb{Q}$.*

Proof. We need to establish that (i) $\{W_t\}$ is an $\{\mathcal{F}_t\}$-martingale, and that (ii) $(\mathrm{d}W_t)^2 = \mathrm{d}t$. Writing $\mathbb{E}_t[-] = \mathbb{E}^{\mathbb{Q}}[-|\mathcal{F}_t]$ and letting $t \le u$ we have

$$\mathbb{E}_t[W_u] = \mathbb{E}_t[\xi_u] + \mathbb{E}_t\left[\int_0^u \frac{1}{T-s}\,\xi_s \mathrm{d}s\right] - \mathbb{E}_t\left[\int_0^u \nu_s D_{sT} \mathrm{d}s\right]. \tag{17.4}$$

Splitting the second two terms on the right into integrals between 0 and t, and between t and u, we obtain

$$\mathbb{E}_t[W_u] = \mathbb{E}_t[\xi_u] + \int_0^t \frac{1}{T-s}\,\xi_s \mathrm{d}s - \int_0^t \nu_s D_{sT} \mathrm{d}s + \int_t^u \frac{1}{T-s}\,\mathbb{E}_t[\xi_s]\mathrm{d}s - \int_t^u \nu_s \mathbb{E}_t[D_{sT}]\mathrm{d}s. \tag{17.5}$$

The martingale property of the conditional expectation implies that $\mathbb{E}_t[D_{sT}] = D_{tT}$ for $t \leq s$, which allows us to simplify the last term. To simplify the expression for the expectation $\mathbb{E}_t[\xi_s]$ for $t \leq s$ we use the tower property:

$$\mathbb{E}_t[\beta_{sT}] = \mathbb{E}_t[\mathbb{E}[\beta_{sT}|H_T, \beta_{tT}]] = \mathbb{E}_t[\mathbb{E}[\beta_{sT}|\beta_{tT}]]. \tag{17.6}$$

To calculate the inner expectation $\mathbb{E}[\beta_{sT}|\beta_{tT}]$ we use the fact that the random variable $\beta_{sT}/(T-s) - \beta_{tT}/(T-t)$ is independent of β_{tT} and deduce that

$$\mathbb{E}[\beta_{sT}|\beta_{tT}] = \frac{T-s}{T-t}\,\beta_{tT}, \tag{17.7}$$

from which it follows that

$$\mathbb{E}_t[\beta_{sT}] = \frac{T-s}{T-t}\,\mathbb{E}_t[\beta_{tT}]. \tag{17.8}$$

As a result we obtain

$$\mathbb{E}_t[\xi_s] = D_{tT}\int_0^s \sigma_v \mathrm{d}v + \frac{T-s}{T-t}\,\mathbb{E}_t[\beta_{tT}]. \tag{17.9}$$

We also recall the definition of $\{W_t\}$ given by (17.2), which implies that

$$\int_0^t \frac{1}{T-s}\,\xi_s \mathrm{d}s - \int_0^t \nu_s D_{sT}\mathrm{d}s = W_t - \xi_t. \tag{17.10}$$

Therefore, substituting (17.9) and (17.10) into (17.5) we obtain

$$\mathbb{E}_t[W_u] = D_{tT}\int_0^u \sigma_s \mathrm{d}s + W_t - \xi_t + D_{tT}\int_t^u \frac{1}{T-s}\left(\int_0^s \sigma_v \mathrm{d}v\right)\mathrm{d}s - D_{tT}\int_t^u \nu_s \mathrm{d}s + \mathbb{E}_t[\beta_{tT}]. \tag{17.11}$$

Next we split the first term into an integral from 0 to t and an integral from t to u, and we insert the definition (14.2) of $\{\nu_t\}$ into the fifth term. The result is:

$$\mathbb{E}_t[W_u] = W_t + D_{tT}\int_0^t \sigma_s \mathrm{d}s + \mathbb{E}_t[\beta_{tT}] - \xi_t. \tag{17.12}$$

Finally, if we make use of the fact that $\xi_t = \mathbb{E}_t[\xi_t]$, and hence that

$$\xi_t = D_{tT}\int_0^t \sigma_s \mathrm{d}s + \mathbb{E}_t[\beta_{tT}], \tag{17.13}$$

we see that $\{W_t\}$ satisfies the martingale condition. On the other hand, by virtue of (17.2) we have $(\mathrm{d}W_t)^2 = \mathrm{d}t$. We conclude that $\{W_t\}$ is an $\{\mathcal{F}_t\}$-Brownian motion under the measure $\mathbb{Q}$. □

18. Asset Prices and Derivative Prices

We are now in a position to consider in more detail the dynamics of the price process of an asset paying a single dividend D_T in the case of a time-dependent information flow. For $\{S_t\}$ we have $S_t = \mathbb{1}_{\{t<T\}} P_{tT} D_{tT}$, or equivalently

$$S_t = \mathbb{1}_{\{t<T\}} P_{tT} \frac{\int_0^\infty x p(x)\, e^{x\left(\frac{1}{T-t}\xi_t \int_0^t \sigma_s \mathrm{d}s + \int_0^t \sigma_s \mathrm{d}\xi_s\right) - \frac{1}{2}x^2\left(\frac{1}{T-t}\left(\int_0^t \sigma_s \mathrm{d}s\right)^2 + \int_0^t \sigma_s^2 \mathrm{d}s\right)} \mathrm{d}x}{\int_0^\infty p(x)\, e^{x\left(\frac{1}{T-t}\xi_t \int_0^t \sigma_s \mathrm{d}s + \int_0^t \sigma_s \mathrm{d}\xi_s\right) - \frac{1}{2}x^2\left(\frac{1}{T-t}\left(\int_0^t \sigma_s \mathrm{d}s\right)^2 + \int_0^t \sigma_s^2 \mathrm{d}s\right)} \mathrm{d}x}. \tag{18.1}$$

A calculation making use of (17.3) shows that for the dynamics of the price we have

$$\mathrm{d}S_t = r_t S_t \mathrm{d}t + \Gamma_{tT} \mathrm{d}W_t, \tag{18.2}$$

where the asset price volatility is given by $\Gamma_{tT} = \nu_t P_{tT} V_t$, and V_t is the conditional variance of the dividend, given by (5.4). It should be evident by virtue of its definition that $\{V_t\}$ is a supermartingale. More specifically, for the dynamics of $\{V_t\}$ we obtain

$$\mathrm{d}V_t = -\nu_t^2 V_t^2 \mathrm{d}t + \nu_t \kappa_t \mathrm{d}W_t, \tag{18.3}$$

where κ_t denotes the third conditional moment of the random variable D_T, given by the expression $\kappa_t = \mathbb{E}_t\left[(D_T - D_{tT})^3\right]$.

Although we have derived (18.1) by assuming that the price process is induced by the market information $\{\xi_t\}$, the result to be shown in Sec. 19 demonstrates that we can regard the dynamical equation (18.2) for the price process as given, and then deduce the structure of the underlying information. The information-based interpretation of the modelling framework, however, is more appealing. According to this interpretation there is a flow of market information, which is available to all market participants and is represented by the filtration generated by $\{\xi_t\}$. Given this information, each participant will "act", in our interpretation, so as to minimise the risk adjusted future P&L variance associated with the cash flow under consideration. The future P&L is determined by the value of D_T, and the estimate of D_T that minimises its variance is indeed given by the conditional expectation (5.1). By discounting this expectation with P_{tT} we recover the price process $\{S_t\}$.

We note that $\{\Gamma_{tT}\}$ is "infinitely stochastic" in the sense that all of the higher-order volatilities (the volatility of the volatility, and so on) are stochastic. These higher-order volatilities have a natural interpretation: the volatility of the asset price is determined by the variance of the random cash flow; the volatility of the volatility is determined by the skewness of D_T; its volatility is determined by the kurtosis of D_T; and so on.

The fact that the asset price in the bridge measure is given by a function of a Gaussian random variable means that the pricing of derivatives is numerically straightforward. We have seen this in the case of a constant information-flow rate, but the result holds in the time-dependent case as well. For example, consider a

European-style call option with strike K and maturity t, where $t \leq T$, for which the value is (6.1). If we express the asset price S_t on the option maturity date in terms of the $\mathbb{B}$-Brownian motion $\{W_t^*\}$ we find

$$C_0 = P_{0t}\mathbb{E}^{\mathbb{Q}}\left[\frac{1}{\Phi_t}\left\{\int_0^\infty (P_{tT}x - K)p(x)\,\exp\left(x\int_0^t \nu_s \mathrm{d}W_s^* - \frac{1}{2}x^2\int_0^t \nu_s^2 \mathrm{d}s\right)\mathrm{d}x\right\}^+\right], \tag{18.4}$$

where

$$\Phi_t = \int_0^\infty p(x)\exp\left(x\int_0^t \nu_s \mathrm{d}W_s^* - \frac{1}{2}x^2\int_0^t \nu_s^2 \mathrm{d}s\right)\mathrm{d}x. \tag{18.5}$$

To proceed we shall use the factor $1/\Phi_t$ in (18.4) to make a change of measure on $(\Omega, \mathcal{F}_t)$. The idea is as follows. We fix a time horizon u at or beyond the option expiration but before the bond maturity, so $t \leq u < T$, and define a process $\{\Phi_t\}_{0 \leq t \leq u}$ by use of the expression (18.5), where now we let t vary in the range $[0, u]$. By an application of Ito calculus on (18.5) we see that $\mathrm{d}\Phi_t = \nu_t D_{tT}\Phi_t\,\mathrm{d}W_t^*$. On the other hand, it follows from (15.2) and (17.2) that the $\mathbb{B}$-Brownian motion $\{W_t^*\}$ and the $\mathbb{Q}$-Brownian motion $\{W_t\}$ are related by

$$\mathrm{d}W_t^* = \mathrm{d}W_t + \nu_t D_{tT}\mathrm{d}t. \tag{18.6}$$

Therefore, in terms of $\{W_t\}$ we have

$$\mathrm{d}\Phi_t = \nu_t^2 D_{tT}^2 \Phi_t \mathrm{d}t + \nu_t D_{tT}\Phi_t\,\mathrm{d}W_t, \tag{18.7}$$

from which it follows that

$$\mathrm{d}\Phi_t^{-1} = -\nu_t D_{tT}\Phi_t^{-1}\mathrm{d}W_t. \tag{18.8}$$

Upon integration we deduce

$$\Phi_t^{-1} = \exp\left(-\int_0^t \nu_s D_{sT}\,\mathrm{d}W_s - \frac{1}{2}\int_0^t \nu_s^2 D_{sT}^2\,\mathrm{d}s\right). \tag{18.9}$$

Since $\{\nu_s D_{sT}\}$ is bounded, and $s \leq u < T$, we see that $\{\Phi_s^{-1}\}_{0 \leq s \leq u}$ is a $\mathbb{Q}$-martingale with $\mathbb{E}^{\mathbb{Q}}[\Phi_t^{-1}] = 1$, where t is the option maturity date. Therefore, the factor $1/\Phi_t$ in (18.4) can be used to effect a change of measure $\mathbb{Q} \to \mathbb{B}$ on $(\Omega, \mathcal{F}_t)$. We note that while on the space $(\Omega, \mathcal{G}_t)$ it is the process $\{\Lambda_t\}$ introduced in (14.3) that defines the measure change from $\mathbb{B}$ and $\mathbb{Q}$, on $(\Omega, \mathcal{F}_t)$ it is $\Phi_t = \mathbb{E}^{\mathbb{Q}}[\Lambda_t | \mathcal{F}_t]$ that defines the relevant measure change. As a consequence, by changing the measure in (18.4) we obtain

$$C_0 = P_{0t}\mathbb{E}^{\mathbb{B}}\left[\left\{\int_0^\infty (P_{tT}x - K)p(x)\exp\left(x\int_0^t \nu_s \mathrm{d}W_s^* - \frac{1}{2}x^2\int_0^t \nu_s^2 \mathrm{d}s\right)\,\mathrm{d}x\right\}^+\right]. \tag{18.10}$$

This result should be compared with (6.5). We note that in the bridge measure the expression $\int_0^t \nu_s \mathrm{d}W_s^*$ is a Gaussian random variable with mean zero and variance

$$\omega_t^2 = \int_0^t \nu_s^2 \mathrm{d}s = \frac{1}{T-t}\left(\int_0^t \sigma_s \mathrm{d}s\right)^2 + \int_0^t \sigma_s^2 \mathrm{d}s. \tag{18.11}$$

Here we have used the relation (15.6). Therefore, if we set

$$Y = \omega_t^{-1} \int_0^t \nu_s \mathrm{d}W_s^*, \tag{18.12}$$

it follows that Y is $\mathbb{B}$-Gaussian. For the call price we thus have

$$C_0 = P_{0t}\mathbb{E}^{\mathbb{B}}\left[\left\{\int_0^\infty (P_{tT}x - K)p(x)\mathrm{e}^{\omega_t x Y - \frac{1}{2}\omega_t^2 x^2}\mathrm{d}x\right\}^+\right], \tag{18.13}$$

and hence

$$C_0 = P_{0t}\frac{1}{\sqrt{2\pi}}\int_{y=-\infty}^\infty \mathrm{e}^{-\frac{1}{2}y^2}\left(\int_{x=0}^\infty (P_{tT}x - K)p(x)\mathrm{e}^{\omega_t x y - \frac{1}{2}\omega_t^2 x^2}\mathrm{d}x\right)^+ \mathrm{d}y. \tag{18.14}$$

We observe that there exists a critical value $y = y^*$ such that the argument of the "plus" function vanishes in the expression above. Thus y^* is given by

$$\int_0^\infty (P_{tT}x - K)p(x)\,\mathrm{e}^{\omega_t x y^* - \frac{1}{2}\omega_t^2 x^2}\mathrm{d}x = 0. \tag{18.15}$$

As a consequence the call price can be written

$$C_0 = P_{0t}\frac{1}{\sqrt{2\pi}}\int_{y=y^*}^\infty \mathrm{e}^{-\frac{1}{2}y^2}\left(\int_{x=0}^\infty (P_{tT}x - K)p(x)\mathrm{e}^{\omega_t x y - \frac{1}{2}\omega_t^2 x^2}\mathrm{d}x\right) \mathrm{d}y. \tag{18.16}$$

The integration in the y variable can be performed, and we deduce the following representation for the call price:

$$C_0 = P_{0t}\int_0^\infty (P_{tT}x - K)p(x)N(\omega_t x - y^*)\mathrm{d}x. \tag{18.17}$$

When the cash flow is represented by a discrete random variable and the information-flow rate is constant, this result reduces to an expression equivalent to the option pricing formula derived in Brody *et al.* [3]. If the cash flow is a continuous random variable and the information flow rate is constant then we recover the expression (6.9) given in Sec. IV (see also Rutkowski and Yu [23]).

We conclude this section with the remark that the simulation of $\{S_t\}$ is straightforward. First, we generate a Brownian trajectory, and form the associated Brownian bridge $\{\beta_{tT}(\omega)\}$. We then select a value for D_T by a method consistent with the *a priori* probability density $p(x)$, and substitute these in the formula $\xi_t(\omega) = D_T(\omega)\int_0^t \sigma_s \mathrm{d}s + \beta_{tT}(\omega)$ for some choice of $\{\sigma_t\}$. Finally, substitution of $\{\xi_t(\omega)\}$ in (18.1) gives us a simulated path $\{S_t(\omega)\}$. The statistics of the process $\{S_t\}$ are obtained by repeating this procedure, the results of which can be used to price derivatives, or to calibrate the information-flow rate $\{\sigma_t\}$.

19. Existence of the Information Process

We consider now what might be called the "inverse problem" for information-based asset pricing. The idea is to begin with the conditional density process $\{\pi_t(x)\}$ and to construct from it the independent degrees of freedom represented by the X-factor D_T and the noise $\{\beta_{tT}\}$. The setup is as follows. On the probability space $(\Omega, \mathcal{F}, \mathbb{Q})$ let $\{W_t\}$ be a Brownian motion and let $\{\mathcal{F}_t\}$ be the filtration generated by $\{W_t\}$. Let D_T be $\mathcal{F}_T$-measurable, and let $\{\pi_t(x)\}$ denote the associated conditional probability density process. We assume that $\{\pi_t(x)\}$ satisfies the stochastic differential equation

$$\mathrm{d}\pi_t(x) = \nu_t(x - D_{tT})\pi_t(x)\,\mathrm{d}W_t, \tag{19.1}$$

with the initial condition $\pi_0(x) = p(x)$, where $\{\nu_t\}$ is given by (14.2), and where

$$D_{tT} = \int_0^\infty x\pi_t(x)\,\mathrm{d}x. \tag{19.2}$$

We define the process $\{\xi_t\}$ as follows:

$$\xi_t = (T-t)\int_0^t \frac{1}{T-s}(\mathrm{d}W_s + \nu_s D_{sT}\mathrm{d}s). \tag{19.3}$$

Then we have the following result:

Proposition 19.1. *The random variables D_T and $\beta_{tT} = \xi_t - D_T\int_0^t \sigma_s \mathrm{d}s$ are $\mathbb{Q}$-independent for $t \in [0,T]$. Furthermore, the process $\{\beta_{tT}\}$ is a $\mathbb{Q}$-Brownian bridge.*

Proof. To establish the independence of D_T and β_{tT} it suffices to verify that

$$\mathbb{E}^{\mathbb{Q}}[\mathrm{e}^{x\beta_{tT}+yD_T}] = \mathbb{E}^{\mathbb{Q}}[\mathrm{e}^{x\beta_{tT}}]\,\mathbb{E}^{\mathbb{Q}}[\mathrm{e}^{yD_T}] \tag{19.4}$$

for arbitrary x, y. Using the tower property we have

$$\mathbb{E}^{\mathbb{Q}}[\mathrm{e}^{x\beta_{tT}+yD_T}] = \mathbb{E}^{\mathbb{Q}}[\mathrm{e}^{x\xi_t}\,\mathbb{E}_t^{\mathbb{Q}}[\mathrm{e}^{(y-x\int_0^t\sigma_s\mathrm{d}s)D_T}]], \tag{19.5}$$

where we have inserted the definition of β_{tT} given in the statement of the Proposition. We consider the inner expectation first. From equation (14.6) for the conditional expectation of a function of D_T we deduce that

$$\mathbb{E}_t^{\mathbb{Q}}[\mathrm{e}^{(y-x\int_0^t\sigma_s\mathrm{d}s)D_T}] = \Phi_t^{-1}\int_0^\infty p(z)\,\mathrm{e}^{(y-x\int_0^t\sigma_s\mathrm{d}s)z}\,\mathrm{e}^{z\int_0^t\nu_u\mathrm{d}W_u^*-\frac{1}{2}z^2\int_0^t\nu_u^2\mathrm{d}u}\mathrm{d}z, \tag{19.6}$$

where the process $\{\Phi_t\}$ is defined by (18.5). We now change the probability measure from $\mathbb{Q}$ to $\mathbb{B}$, so that the term Φ_t^{-1} appearing in (19.6) drops out to give us

$$
\begin{aligned}
&\mathbb{E}^{\mathbb{Q}}[\mathrm{e}^{x\xi_t}\,\mathbb{E}_t^{\mathbb{Q}}[\mathrm{e}^{(y-x\int_0^t\sigma_s\mathrm{d}s)D_T}]] \\
&\quad = \mathbb{E}^{\mathbb{B}}\left[\mathrm{e}^{x\xi_t}\int_0^\infty p(z)\,\mathrm{e}^{(y-x\int_0^t\sigma_s\mathrm{d}s)z}\,\mathrm{e}^{z\int_0^t\nu_u\mathrm{d}W_u^*-\frac{1}{2}z^2\int_0^t\nu_u^2\mathrm{d}u}\mathrm{d}z\right] \\
&\quad = \int_0^\infty p(z)\,\mathbb{E}^{\mathbb{B}}\left[\mathrm{e}^{x(T-t)\int_0^t\frac{1}{T-s}\mathrm{d}W_s^*+(y-x\int_0^t\sigma_s\mathrm{d}s)z+z\int_0^t\nu_s\mathrm{d}W_s^*-\frac{1}{2}z^2\int_0^t\nu_s^2\mathrm{d}s}\right]\mathrm{d}z \\
&\quad = \int_0^\infty p(z)\,\mathrm{e}^{(y-x\int_0^t\sigma_s\mathrm{d}s)z-\frac{1}{2}z^2\int_0^t\nu_s^2\mathrm{d}s+\frac{1}{2}\int_0^t\alpha_s^2\mathrm{d}s}\,\mathbb{E}^{\mathbb{B}}\left[\mathrm{e}^{\int_0^t\alpha_s\mathrm{d}W_s^*-\frac{1}{2}\int_0^t\alpha_s^2\mathrm{d}s}\right]\mathrm{d}z,
\end{aligned}
\tag{19.7}
$$

where $\alpha_s = x(T-t)/(T-s) + z\nu_s$, and therefore

$$
\mathbb{E}^{\mathbb{Q}}[\mathrm{e}^{x\beta_{tT}+yD_T}] = \int_0^\infty p(z)\,\mathrm{e}^{(y-x\int_0^t\sigma_s\mathrm{d}s)z-\frac{1}{2}z^2\int_0^t\nu_s^2\mathrm{d}s+\frac{1}{2}\int_0^t\alpha_s^2\mathrm{d}s}\mathrm{d}z. \tag{19.8}
$$

Furthermore, making use of relation (14.9) we have

$$
\exp\left(-xz\int_0^t\sigma_s\mathrm{d}s-\frac{1}{2}z^2\int_0^t\nu_s^2\mathrm{d}s+\frac{1}{2}\int_0^t\alpha_s^2\mathrm{d}s\right)=\exp\left(\frac{t(T-t)}{2T}\,x^2\right). \tag{19.9}
$$

As a consequence, it follows from (19.8) that

$$
\mathbb{E}^{\mathbb{Q}}[\mathrm{e}^{x\beta_{tT}+yD_T}] = \left(\int_0^\infty p(z)\,\mathrm{e}^{yz}\mathrm{d}z\right)\exp\left(\frac{t(T-t)}{2T}x^2\right). \tag{19.10}
$$

This establishes the independence of $\{\beta_{tT}\}$ and D_T.

The factorisation (19.10) also shows that the process $\{\beta_{tT}\}$ is $\mathbb{Q}$-Gaussian, with mean zero and variance $t(T-t)/T$. To establish that $\{\beta_{tT}\}$ is a Brownian bridge, we must show that for $s \le t$ the covariance of β_{sT} and β_{tT} is given by $s(T-t)/T$. Alternatively, it suffices to analyse the moment generating function $\mathbb{E}[\mathrm{e}^{x\beta_{sT}+y\beta_{tT}}]$. We proceed as follows. First, using the tower property we have

$$
\begin{aligned}
\mathbb{E}^{\mathbb{Q}}[\mathrm{e}^{x\beta_{sT}+y\beta_{tT}}] &= \mathbb{E}[\mathrm{e}^{x\xi_s+y\xi_t-(x\int_0^s\sigma_u\mathrm{d}u+y\int_0^t\sigma_u\mathrm{d}u)D_T}] \\
&= \mathbb{E}[\mathrm{e}^{x\xi_s+y\xi_t}\mathbb{E}_t^{\mathbb{Q}}[\mathrm{e}^{-(x\int_0^s\sigma_u\mathrm{d}u+y\int_0^t\sigma_u\mathrm{d}u)D_T}]].
\end{aligned}
\tag{19.11}
$$

Next, by use of formula (14.6), the inner expectation can be carried out to give

$$
\begin{aligned}
&\mathbb{E}^{\mathbb{Q}}[\mathrm{e}^{x\beta_{sT}+y\beta_{tT}}] \\
&\quad = \mathbb{E}\left[\mathrm{e}^{x\xi_s+y\xi_t}\Phi_t^{-1}\int_0^\infty p(z)\,\mathrm{e}^{-(x\int_0^s\sigma_u\mathrm{d}u+y\int_0^t\sigma_u\mathrm{d}u)z}\,\mathrm{e}^{z\int_0^t\nu_u\mathrm{d}W_u^*-\frac{1}{2}z^2\int_0^t\nu_u^2\mathrm{d}u}\mathrm{d}z\right].
\end{aligned}
\tag{19.12}
$$

If we change the probability measure to $\mathbb{B}$ the random variable Φ_t in the denominator drops out, and we have

$$\mathbb{E}^{\mathbb{Q}}[\mathrm{e}^{x\beta_{sT}+y\beta_{tT}}]$$
$$= \int_0^\infty p(z)\,\mathrm{e}^{-(x\int_0^s \sigma_u \mathrm{d}u + y\int_0^t \sigma_u \mathrm{d}u)z - \frac{1}{2}z^2\int_0^t \nu_u^2 \mathrm{d}u}\,\mathbb{E}^{\mathbb{B}}[\mathrm{e}^{x\xi_s+y\xi_t+z\int_0^t \nu_s \mathrm{d}W_s^*}]\mathrm{d}z. \tag{19.13}$$

Let us consider the inner expectation first. By defining $a_u = x(T-s)/(T-u)$ and $b_u = y(T-t)/(T-u) + z\nu_u$ we can write

$$\mathbb{E}^{\mathbb{B}}[\mathrm{e}^{x\xi_s+y\xi_t+z\int_0^t \nu_s \mathrm{d}W_s^*}] = \mathbb{E}^{\mathbb{B}}[\mathrm{e}^{\int_0^s a_u \mathrm{d}W_u^* + \int_0^t b_u \mathrm{d}W_u^*}]. \tag{19.14}$$

However, since $\{W_t^*\}$ is a $\mathbb{B}$-Brownian motion, using the properties of Gaussian random variable we find that

$$\mathbb{E}^{\mathbb{B}}[\mathrm{e}^{\int_0^s a_u \mathrm{d}W_u^* + \int_0^t b_u \mathrm{d}W_u^*}] = \exp\left\{\frac{1}{2}\left(\int_0^s a_u^2 \mathrm{d}u + \int_0^t b_u^2 \mathrm{d}u + 2\int_0^s a_u b_u \mathrm{d}u\right)\right\}. \tag{19.15}$$

Substituting the definitions of $\{a_u\}$ and $\{b_u\}$ into the right side of (19.15) and combining the result with the remaining terms in the exponent of the right side of (19.13) we find that the terms involving the integration variable z drop out, and we are left with the integral of the density function $p(z)$, which is unity. Gathering the remaining terms we obtain

$$\mathbb{E}^{\mathbb{Q}}[\mathrm{e}^{x\beta_{sT}+y\beta_{tT}}] = \exp\left\{\frac{1}{2}\left(x^2\,\frac{s(T-s)}{T} + y^2\,\frac{t(T-t)}{T} + 2xy\,\frac{s(T-t)}{T}\right)\right\}. \tag{19.16}$$

It follows that the covariance of β_{sT} and β_{tT} for $s \leq t$ is given by

$$\left.\frac{\partial^2}{\partial x \partial y}\mathbb{E}^{\mathbb{Q}}\left[\mathrm{e}^x \beta_{sT} + y\beta_{tT}\right]\right|_{x=y=0} = \frac{s(T-t)}{T}. \tag{19.17}$$

This establishes the assertion that $\{\beta_{tT}\}$ is a $\mathbb{Q}$-Brownian bridge. □

The result above shows that, for the class of price processes we are considering, even if at the outset we take the "usual" point of view in financial modelling, and regard the price process of the asset as being adapted to some "prespecified" filtration, nevertheless it is possible to *deduce* the structure of the underlying information-based model.

20. Multi-Factor Models with a Time-Dependent Information Flow Rate

Let us now turn to consider the case of a single cash flow D_T that depends on a *multiplicity* of market factors $\{X_{T_k}^{\alpha}\}_{k=1,\ldots,n}^{\alpha=1,\ldots,m_k}$, where we have the n pre-designated information dates $\{T_k\}_{k=1,2,\ldots,n}$, and where for each value of k we have a set of m_k

market factors. For simplicity we set $T = T_n$. Each market factor $X^{\alpha}_{T_k}$ is associated with an information process

$$\xi^{\alpha}_{tT_k} = X^{\alpha}_{T_k} \int_0^t \sigma^{\alpha}_{sT_k} \mathrm{d}s + \beta^{\alpha}_{tT_k}, \tag{20.1}$$

where $X^{\alpha}_{T_k}$ and $\{\beta^{\alpha}_{tT_k}\}$ are independent. It should be evident that although the random variable D_T representing the cash flow is $\mathcal{F}_T$-measurable, the values of some of the X-factors upon which it depends may be revealed at earlier times. That is to say, the uncertainties arising from some of the economic elements affecting the value of the cash flow at time T may be resolved before that time.

Since the X-factors are independent, it follows that for each market factor the associated conditional density process $\pi^{\alpha}_{tT_k}(x)$ takes the form given in (13.4), and the corresponding dynamical equation is given by

$$\mathrm{d}\pi^{\alpha}_{tT_k} = \nu^{\alpha}_{tT_k}(x^{\alpha}_k - \mathbb{E}^{\mathbb{Q}}[X^{\alpha}_{T_k}|\mathcal{F}_t])\pi^{\alpha}_{tT_k} \,\mathrm{d}W^{\alpha k}_t. \tag{20.2}$$

The function $\nu^{\alpha}_{tT_k}$ appearing here is given by an expression of the form (14.2):

$$\nu^{\alpha}_{tT_k} = \sigma^{\alpha}_{tT_k} + \frac{1}{T_k - t}\int_0^t \sigma^{\alpha}_{sT_k} \mathrm{d}s. \tag{20.3}$$

The innovation process $\{W^{\alpha k}_t\}$ is defined in terms of $\{\xi^{\alpha}_{tT_k}\}$ via the relation

$$W^{\alpha k}_t = \xi^{\alpha}_{tT_k} + \int_0^t \frac{1}{T_k - s}\xi^{\alpha}_{sT_k} \mathrm{d}s - \int_0^t \nu^{\alpha}_{sT_k} X^{\alpha}_{T_k} \mathrm{d}s. \tag{20.4}$$

The expectation $\mathbb{E}^{\mathbb{Q}}[D_T|\mathcal{F}_t]$ is thus given by the multi-dimensional integral

$$\begin{aligned} D_{tT} = &\int_0^\infty \cdots \int_0^\infty \Delta_T(x^1_1, \ldots, x^{m_1}_1, \ldots, x^1_n, \ldots, x^{m_n}_n) \\ &\times \pi_{t1}(x^1_1)\cdots\pi_{t1}(x^{m_1}_1)\cdots\pi_{tn}(x^1_n)\cdots\pi_{tn}(x^{m_n}_n)\,\mathrm{d}x^1_1\cdots\mathrm{d}x^{m_1}_1\cdots\mathrm{d}x^1_n\cdots\mathrm{d}x^{m_n}_n, \end{aligned} \tag{20.5}$$

and the price of the asset for $t < T$ is $S_t = P_{tT}D_{tT}$. A straightforward application of Ito's rule then establishes the following result:

Proposition 20.1. *The price process $\{S_t\}_{0\le t<T}$ of an asset that pays a single dividend D_T at time $T(= T_n)$ depending on the market factors $\{X^{\alpha}_{T_k}\}^{\alpha=1,2,\ldots,m_k}_{k=1,2,\ldots n}$, satisfies the dynamical equation*

$$\mathrm{d}S_t = r_t S_t \mathrm{d}t + \sum_{k=1}^{n}\sum_{\alpha=1}^{m_k} \nu^{\alpha}_{tT_k} \mathrm{Cov}_t[D_T, X^{\alpha}_{T_k}]\,\mathrm{d}W^{\alpha k}_t, \tag{20.6}$$

where

$$D_T = \Delta_T(X^{\alpha}_{T_1}, \ldots, X^{\alpha}_{T_n}). \tag{20.7}$$

Here $\mathrm{Cov}_t[D_T, X^{\alpha}_{T_k}]$ denotes the covariance between the cash-flow D_T and the market factor $X^{\alpha}_{T_k}$, conditional on the information $\mathcal{F}_t$ generated by the information processes $\{\xi^{\alpha}_{sT_k}\}_{0\le s\le t}$, for $k = 1, 2, \ldots, n$ and $\alpha = 1, 2, \ldots, m_k$.

In the more general case of an asset that pays multiple dividends (see Sec. 8) the price is given by

$$S_t = \sum_{k=1}^{n} \mathbb{1}_{\{t<T_k\}} P_{tT_k} \mathbb{E}^{\mathbb{Q}}[\Delta_{T_k}(\{X_{T_j}^{\alpha}\}_{j=1,\ldots,k}^{\alpha=1,2,\ldots,m_j})|\mathcal{F}_t]. \tag{20.8}$$

Proposition 20.2. *The price process* $\{S_t\}$ *of an asset that pays the random dividends* D_{T_k} *on the dates* T_k $(k = 1, \ldots, n)$ *satisfies the dynamical equation*

$$\mathrm{d}S_t = r_t S_t \mathrm{d}t + \sum_{k=1}^{n}\sum_{j=1}^{k}\sum_{\alpha=1}^{m_j} \mathbb{1}_{\{t<T_k\}} P_t T_k \nu_{tT_j}^{\alpha} \mathrm{Cov}_t[D_{T_k}, X_{T_j}^{\alpha}]\mathrm{d}W_t^{\alpha j} + \sum_{k=1}^{n} D_{T_k} \mathrm{d}\mathbb{1}_{\{t<T_k\}}, \tag{20.9}$$

where

$$D_{T_k} = \Delta_{T_k}(\{X_{T_j}^{\alpha}\}_{j=1,\ldots,k}^{\alpha=1,\ldots,m_j}). \tag{20.10}$$

Here $\mathrm{Cov}_t[D_{T_k}, X_{T_j}^{\alpha}]$ *denotes the covariance between the dividend* D_{T_k} *and the market factor* $X_{T_j}^{\alpha}$*, conditional on the market information* $\mathcal{F}_t$.

We conclude that the multi-factor, multi-dividend situation is fully tractable when the information-flow rates associated with the various market factors are time dependent. A straightforward extension of Proposition 20.2 allows us to formulate the joint price dynamics of a system of assets, the associated dividend flows of which may depend on common market factors. As a consequence, a specific model for stochastic volatility and correlation emerges for such a system of assets, and it is one of the main conclusions of this paper that such a model can be formulated. The information-based "X-factor" approach presented here thus offers a new insights into the nature of volatility and correlation, and as such may find applications in a number of different areas of financial risk analysis. We have in mind, in particular, applications to equity portfolios, credit portfolios, and insurance, all of which exhibit intertemporal market correlation effects. We also have in mind the problem of firm-wide risk management and optimal capital allocation for banking institutions.

Acknowledgments

The authors thank T. Bielecki, T. Björk, I. Buckley, H. Bühlmann, S. Carter, I. Constantinou, M. Davis, J. Dear, A. Elizalde, B. Flesaker, H. Geman, V. Henderson, D. Hobson, T. Hurd, M. Jeanblanc, A. Lokka, J. Mao, B. Meister, M. Monoyios, M. Pistorius, M. Rutkowski, D. Taylor, and M. Zervos for stimulating discussions. The authors are grateful for comments made by seminar participants at meetings where parts of this work have been presented, including: the Developments in Quantitative Finance conference, July 2005, Isaac Newton Institute, Cambridge; the Mathematics in Finance conference, August 2005, Kruger National Park; University of the Witwatersrand, August 2005; Centro de Estudios Monetarios y Financieros (CEMFI), Madrid, October 2005; Heriot-Watt University, December 2005; King's

College London, December 2005; Bank of Japan, Tokyo, December 2005; Nomura, Tokyo, December 2005; the 16th Annual Derivatives Securities and Risk Management Conference, Federal Deposit Insurance Corporation, Virginia, April 2006; and ETH Zurich, June 2006. DCB acknowledges support from The Royal Society; LPH and AM acknowledge support from EPSRC (grant number GR/S22998/01); AM thanks the Public Education Authority of the Canton of Bern, Switzerland, and the UK Universities ORS scheme, for support.

References

[1] K. Back, Insider trading in continuous time, *Review of Financial Studies* **5** (1992) 387–407.
[2] K. Back and S. Baruch, Information in securities markets: Kyle meets Glosten and Milgrom, *Econometrica* **72** (2004) 433–465.
[3] D. C. Brody, L. P. Hughston and A. Macrina, Beyond hazard rates: A new framework for credit-risk modelling, in *Advances in Mathematical Finance: Festschrift Volume in Honour of Dilip Madan*, M. Fu, J.-Y. Yen, R. Jarrow and R. Elliott, eds. (Birkhäuser, Basel, 2007).
[4] R. S. Bucy and P. D. Joseph, *Filtering for Stochastic Processes with Applications to Guidance* (Interscience Publishers, New York, 1968).
[5] U. Cetin, R. Jarrow, P. Protter and Y. Yildrim, Modelling credit risk with partial information, *Annals of Applied Probability* **14** (2004) 1167–1172.
[6] M. H. A. Davis, Complete-market models of stochastic volatility, *Proceedings of the Royal Society London A* **460** (2004) 11–26.
[7] M. H. A. Davis and S. I. Marcus, An introduction to nonlinear filtering, in *Stochastic Systems: The Mathematics of Filtering and Identification and Application*, M. Hazewinkel and J. C. Willems, eds. (D. Reidel, Dordrecht, 1981).
[8] D. Duffie and D. Lando, Term structure of credit spreads with incomplete accounting information, *Econometrica* **69** (2001) 633–664.
[9] M. Fujisaki, G. Kallianpur and H. Kunita Stochastic differential equations for the non linear filtering problem, *Osaka Journal of Mathematics* **9** (1972) 19–40.
[10] H. Geman, D. B. Madan and M. Yor, Probing option prices for information, *Methodology and Computing in Applied Probability* **9** (2007) 115–131.
[11] K. Giesecke, Correlated default with incomplete information, *Journal of Banking and Finance* **28** (2004) 1521–1545.
[12] K. Giesecke and L. R. Goldberg, Sequential default and incomplete information, *Journal of Risk* **7** (2004) 1–26.
[13] S. L. Heston, A closed-form solution for options with stochastic volatility with applications to bond and currency options, *Review of Financial Studies* **6** (1993) 327–343.
[14] R. A. Jarrow and P. Protter, Structural versus reduced form models: A new information based perspective, *Journal of Investment Management* **2** (2004) 34–43.
[15] T. Kailath, A view of three decades of linear filtering theory, *IEEE Transactions on Information Theory* **IT-20** (1974) 146–181.
[16] G. Kallianpur and C. Striebel, Estimation of stochastic systems: Arbitrary system process with additive white noise observation errors, *Annals of Mathematical Statisics* **39** (1968) 785–801.
[17] I. Karatzas and S. E. Shreve, *Brownian Motion and Stochastic Calculus* (Springer, Berlin, 1997).
[18] V. Krishnan, *Nonlinear Filtering and Smoothing* (Dover, New York, 2005).

[19] R. S. Liptser and A. N. Shiryaev, *Statistics of Random Processes*, Vols. I and II, 2nd ed. (Springer, Berlin, 2000).

[20] A. Macrina, An information-based framework for asset pricing: X-factor theory and its applications, PhD thesis, King's College London (2006).

[21] M. O'Hara, *Market Microstructure Theory* (Blackwell, Cambridge, Massachusetts, 1995).

[22] P. Protter *Stochastic Integration and Differential Equations: A New Approach*, 2nd ed. (Springer, Berlin, 2003).

[23] M. Rutkowski and N. Yu, An extension of the Brody–Hughston–Macrina approach to modelling of defaultable bonds, *International Journal of Theoretical and Applied Finance* **10** (2007) 557–589.

[24] M. Yor, *Some Aspects of Brownian Motion, Part I: Some Special Functionals* (Birkhäuser, Basel, 1992).

Chapter 3

Dam rain and cumulative gain†

By Dorje C. Brody[1,*], Lane P. Hughston[2,3] and Andrea Macrina[2,4]

[1]*Department of Mathematics, Imperial College London, London SW7 2BZ, UK*
[2]*Department of Mathematics, King's College London, London WC2R 2LS, UK*
[3]*Perimeter Institute for Theoretical Physics, Waterloo, Ontario N2L 2YS, Canada*
[4]*Department of Mathematics, ETH Zürich, 8092 Zürich, Switzerland*

We consider a financial contract that delivers a single cash flow given by the terminal value of a cumulative gains process. The problem of modelling such an asset and associated derivatives is important, for example, in the determination of optimal insurance claims reserve policies, and in the pricing of reinsurance contracts. In the insurance setting, aggregate claims play the role of cumulative gains, and the terminal cash flow represents the totality of the claims payable for the given accounting period. A similar example arises when we consider the accumulation of losses in a credit portfolio, and value a contract that pays an amount equal to the totality of the losses over a given time interval. An expression for the value process of such an asset is derived as follows. We fix a probability space, together with a pricing measure, and model the terminal cash flow by a random variable; next, we model the cumulative gains process by the product of the terminal cash flow and an independent gamma bridge; finally, we take the filtration to be that generated by the cumulative gains process. An explicit expression for the value process is obtained by taking the discounted expectation of the future cash flow, conditional on the relevant market information. The price of an Arrow–Debreu security on the cumulative gains process is determined, and is used to obtain a closed-form expression for the price of a European-style option on the value of the asset at the given intermediate time. The results obtained make use of remarkable properties of the gamma bridge process, and are applicable to a wide variety of financial products based on cumulative gains processes such as aggregate claims, credit portfolio losses, defined benefit pension schemes, emissions and rainfall.

Keywords: asset pricing; insurance claim reserves; credit portfolio risk; gamma bridge process; beta distribution; reinsurance

1. Introduction

There are a number of problems in finance and insurance that involve the analysis of processes representing cumulative gains or losses. The typical setup is as follows. We fix an accounting period $[0, T]$, where time 0 is the present. At time T a contract pays a random cash flow X_T, which is assumed to be positive and given by the terminal value of a process of accumulation. In the case of an insurance contract, for example, we consider the situation where claims are made

* Author for correspondence (dorje@imperial.ac.uk).

Received 16 October 2007
Accepted 19 February 2008

†This chapter was originally published as: D. C. Brody, L. P. Hughston & A. Macrina (2008) Dam Rain and Cumulative Gain. *Proceedings of the Royal Society A* **464**, 1801–1822. Reprinted with kind permission from The Royal Society.

over the accounting period, and are then paid at T. The variable X_T represents the totality of the payments made at T in settlement of claims arising over $[0, T]$. Let us write $\{S_t\}$ for the value process of the contract that pays X_T at T, $\{\mathcal{F}_t\}$ for the filtration representing the flow of information available to market participants, and $\mathbb{Q}$ for the pricing measure. Then the value at t of the contract that pays X_T at T is $S_t = P_{tT}\mathbb{E}[X_T|\mathcal{F}_t]$, where $\mathbb{E}[\cdot]$ denotes expectation with respect to $\mathbb{Q}$, and P_{tT} denotes the discount factor, which for simplicity we take to be deterministic. One can interpret S_t as the reserve the insurance firm requires at t to ensure that X_T will be payable at T. Alternatively, one can view S_t as the amount that would have to be paid at t for the insurance firm to relieve itself of the obligation to pay X_T, that is, to commute the relevant claims. Similarly, the cost C_{tT} at t of a stop-loss reinsurance contract that pays $(X_T - K)^+$ at T for some fixed threshold K is given by $C_{tT} = P_{tT}\mathbb{E}[(X_T - K)^+|\mathcal{F}_t]$. We assume that $\{\mathcal{F}_t\}$ is generated by an aggregate claims process $\{\xi_t\}$, where for each t the variable ξ_t represents the totality of claims known at t to be payable at T. The problem can then be stated as follows: given the history of claims over the interval $[0, t]$, what is the appropriate reserve to allocate for settlement of these and any future claims arising in the accounting period? To obtain a solution we need to specify $\{\xi_t\}$, then work out the reserve process $\{S_t\}$. Once we have the reserve process, we can value reinsurance contracts.

Another example of an accumulation process comes from credit risk management. We consider a large credit portfolio and let X_T denote the accumulated losses at T. For instance, at time 0 a credit card firm has a large number of customers, each with an outstanding balance payable in the accounting period. If a customer does not pay the balance by the required date, they will be deemed to be in default, and a loss will be registered. The random variable X_T will denote the totality of such losses. We assume that once a customer is in default, no further payments are made by that customer (this assumption can be relaxed in a more sophisticated model). The problem facing the firm is to determine what reserve policy to maintain, and what premium to charge over the base interest rate, to ensure that funds will be in hand to cover the default losses.

The purpose of this paper is to present a modelling framework for accumulation processes, and to establish explicit formulae for the associated valuation processes. We shall assume that $\{\xi_t\}$ takes the form

$$\xi_t = X_T \gamma_{tT}, \tag{1.1}$$

where $\{\gamma_{tT}\}$ is a gamma bridge over $[0, T]$, independent of X_T. The idea that the gamma process might be used for describing the losses associated with insurance claims dates to the work of Hammersley (1955), Moran (1956), Gani (1957), Kendall (1957), Kingman (1963) and others (see, for example, Bingham 1975; Basawa & Brockwell 1978), in connection with the theory of storage and dams. Moran (1956), in particular, observed that the amount of rainfall accumulating in a dam can be modelled by a gamma process, and Gani (1957) pointed out the relevance to insurance, that if the portfolio of events insured is large, one can think of the arrival of claims as analogous to the accumulation of dam rain. The gamma process has since then been investigated by Dufresne *et al.* (1991), Dickson & Waters (1993), Norberg (1999) and others as a model for aggregate claims. Let us therefore consider in more detail what results if we model the aggregate claims as a $\mathbb{Q}$-gamma process. In other words, suppose we set $\xi_t = \kappa\gamma_t$, where κ is a constant and $\{\gamma_t\}$ is a standard gamma process under $\mathbb{Q}$, with mean and variance mt (see §2 for definitions). It follows that $\xi_t = X_T\gamma_{tT}$, where $X_T = \kappa\gamma_T$ and the process $\{\gamma_{tT}\}$, defined by $\gamma_{tT} = \gamma_t/\gamma_T$, is a gamma bridge. Moreover, by virtue of the special properties of the gamma process, we find that X_T is independent of $\{\gamma_{tT}\}$. In the $\mathbb{Q}$-gamma model the aggregate claims process is thus the product of a gamma-distributed terminal cash flow and an independent gamma bridge. One can think of the gamma bridge as representing that part of the aggregate claims process that has no bearing on the terminal result. We are thus led to a multiplicative decomposition of the claims process into the product of a 'signal' X_T and an independent 'noise' $\{\gamma_{tT}\}$.

For such processes we are able to apply the techniques of information-based asset pricing developed in Macrina (2006), Brody *et al.* (2007, 2008), Rutkowski & Yu (2007) and Hughston & Macrina (2008). Through this line of enquiry one is led to consider the situation where the terminal cash flow has a generic *a priori* distribution and the claims process takes the form (1.1). The additive decomposition of the information process in the case of the Brownian bridge noise considered in the references cited above is natural from the viewpoint of nonlinear filtering theory. The product representation of the gamma information process is also natural, since many properties of the Brownian bridge that hold additively have multiplicative analogues for gamma bridges (Yor & Émery 2004; Yor 2007). The resulting model for aggregate claims is remarkably tractable, and we are able to derive explicit formulae both for the claims reserve process and for the valuation of reinsurance contracts. These insurance products have analogues in various other financial markets, for which the same modelling techniques are applicable.

The paper is organized as follows. In §§2 and 3 we review the properties of the gamma process and the gamma bridge. At the same time, we establish our notation and some techniques that will be applied later. In §4 we derive an expression for the value process of a contract that delivers the cash flow X_T at time T, when the market filtration is generated by the accumulation process (1.1). We show in proposition 4.1 that $\{\xi_t\}$ has the Markov property, then use the Bayes theorem to determine the conditional density of X_T, and finally the value process, which is given in proposition 4.2. By use of the conditional density we are also able to obtain an expression for the value process of a simple stop-loss reinsurance contract. In §5 we consider the valuation of general reinsurance contracts. We derive a formula for the value at time 0 of a contract that at some fixed time t gives the contract holder the option to commute the claim X_T by paying a fixed amount K at t. Such a contract takes the form of a European call option on the value of the reserve at t. An Arrow–Debreu method is introduced to perform the calculations. The resulting formula for the option value is expressed in terms of the cumulative beta distribution. In §6 we examine the case where X_T takes discrete values. When X_T is a binary random variable, the problem of option pricing can be solved completely. In §7 the material of §5 is extended to determine the price process of an option on the value of an aggregate claim. This result allows one to value various types of reinsurance instruments. In §8 we conclude by returning to the case where X_T has a $\mathbb{Q}$-gamma distribution.

The key results of the paper include: (i) the valuation of an aggregate claim, given by (4.4), (ii) the valuation of a stop-loss reinsurance policy, given by (4.11), (iii) the price of an Arrow–Debreu security based on the level of the cumulative gains at some intermediate time, given by (5.7), (iv) the price of a general reinsurance policy, given by (5.14) and (7.8), and (v) the price of the Arrow–Debreu security in the case of a gamma-distributed cumulative gain, given by (8.4).

2. Gamma processes and associated martingales

We fix a probability space $(\Omega, \mathcal{F}, \mathbb{Q})$. In our applications $\mathbb{Q}$ will always denote the pricing (risk-neutral) measure, but the material in this section, and the next, does not depend on this interpretation. Equalities and inequalities among random variables are to be understood as holding except possibly on sets of measure zero. By a *standard gamma process* $\{\gamma_t\}_{0\leq t<\infty}$ on $(\Omega, \mathcal{F}, \mathbb{Q})$ with growth rate m, we mean a process with independent increments such that $\gamma_0=0$ and such that the random variable γ_t has a gamma distribution with mean and variance mt. More precisely, writing $\mathbb{Q}[\gamma_t\in \mathrm{d}x]=g(x)\mathrm{d}x$, we have

$$g(x) = \mathbb{1}_{\{x>0\}}\frac{x^{mt-1}\mathrm{e}^{-x}}{\Gamma[mt]} \tag{2.1}$$

for the density of γ_t. Here, $\Gamma[a]$ is the gamma function, which for $a>0$ has the Eulerian representation $\Gamma[a]=\int_0^\infty x^{a-1}\mathrm{e}^{-x}\,\mathrm{d}x$. The identity $\Gamma[a+1]=a\Gamma[a]$ implies that $\mathbb{E}[\gamma_t]=mt$, justifying the interpretation of m as the *mean growth rate.*

A straightforward calculation shows that the characteristic function for the gamma process is given by

$$\mathbb{E}[\mathrm{e}^{\mathrm{i}\lambda\gamma_t}] = \frac{1}{(1-\mathrm{i}\lambda)^{mt}}, \tag{2.2}$$

valid for $t\geq 0$ and for $\lambda\in\mathbb{C}$ such that $\mathrm{Im}(\lambda)>-1$, from which the higher moments of γ_t can be deduced. Writing $(a)_0=1$ and $(a)_k=a(a+1)(a+2)\cdots(a+k-1)$ for the Pochhammer symbol, we find that $\mathbb{E}[\gamma_t^n]=(mt)_n$. We note that $\mathbb{E}[\gamma_t^2]=mt+m^2t^2$, and hence $\mathrm{var}[\gamma_t]=mt$. It follows from the independent increments property that $\mathrm{cov}[\gamma_t,\gamma_u]=mt$ for $u\geq t$.

An alternative expression for the characteristic function is given by the Lévy–Khintchine representation $\mathbb{E}[\mathrm{e}^{\mathrm{i}\lambda\gamma_t}]=\mathrm{e}^{-t\psi(\lambda)}$ for $\mathrm{Im}(\lambda)>-1$, where

$$\psi(\lambda) = m\ln(1-\mathrm{i}\lambda) = \int_0^\infty mx^{-1}\mathrm{e}^{-x}(1-\mathrm{e}^{\mathrm{i}\lambda x})\,\mathrm{d}x, \tag{2.3}$$

which shows that the Lévy density associated with the gamma process is given by $mx^{-1}\mathrm{e}^{-x}$ for $x>0$ (see, for example, Protter 2005).

By use of the independent increments property we deduce that for $u\geq t\geq 0$ and for $a,b\in\mathbb{C}$ with $\mathrm{Im}(a+b)>-1$ and $\mathrm{Im}(b)>-1$ we have

$$\begin{aligned}\mathbb{E}[\exp(\mathrm{i}a\gamma_t+\mathrm{i}b\gamma_u)] &= \mathbb{E}[\exp(\mathrm{i}(a+b)\gamma_t+\mathrm{i}b(\gamma_u-\gamma_t))]\\ &= \mathbb{E}[\exp(\mathrm{i}(a+b)\gamma_t)]\mathbb{E}[\exp(\mathrm{i}b(\gamma_u-\gamma_t))]\\ &= \frac{1}{[1-\mathrm{i}(a+b)]^{mt}}\frac{1}{(1-\mathrm{i}b)^{m(u-t)}}.\end{aligned} \tag{2.4}$$

In particular, if we set $-a=b=\lambda$ we see that $\gamma_u-\gamma_t$ is gamma distributed with parameter $m(u-t)$. It follows that the increments of $\{\gamma_t\}$ have a stationary probability law in the sense that $\gamma_{u+h}-\gamma_{t+h}$ has the same distribution as $\gamma_u-\gamma_t$.

It is straightforward to deduce that $\{\gamma_t-mt\}$ and $\{(\gamma_t-mt)^2-mt\}$ are martingales. More generally, for $\alpha>-1$ the process $\{L_t\}$ defined by

$$L_t = (1+\alpha)^{mt}\mathrm{e}^{-\alpha\gamma_t} \tag{2.5}$$

is a martingale, which can be verified by use of (2.4). We refer to this process as the exponential gamma martingale. It follows, by consideration of the corresponding power series in α, that for each term we obtain a martingale involving a polynomial expression in the gamma process. Suppose for $n\in\mathbb{N}$ and $k\in\mathbb{R}$ we define the so-called associated Laguerre polynomials $\{L_n^k(z)\}$ by setting

$$L_n^k(z) = \frac{z^{-k}\mathrm{e}^z}{n!}\frac{\mathrm{d}^n}{\mathrm{d}z^n}(z^{n+k}\mathrm{e}^{-z}). \tag{2.6}$$

The standard Laguerre polynomials $L_n(z)=L_n^0(z)$ have the property that if Z is a standard exponentially distributed random variable then $\mathbb{E}[L_n(Z)L_{n'}(Z)]=0$ for $n\neq n'$ (cf. Wiener 1949). More generally, if Z has a gamma distribution with parameter $k+1$, i.e. such that $\mathbb{Q}[Z<z]=\int_0^z x^k\mathrm{e}^{-x}\,\mathrm{d}x/\Gamma[k+1]$ for $k>-1$, then $\mathbb{E}[L_n^k(Z)L_{n'}^k(Z)]=0$ for $n\neq n'$. The significance of the associated Laguerre polynomials arises from the identity

$$(1+\alpha)^h\mathrm{e}^{-z\alpha} = \sum_{n=0}^{\infty} L_n^{h-n}(z)\alpha^n, \tag{2.7}$$

for $|\alpha|<1$ and $h\geq 0$ (Erdélyi 1953), which gives us the required series expansion. By setting $h=mt$ and $z=\gamma_t$ in equation (2.7), we deduce that for each n the process $\{L_n^{mt-n}(\gamma_t)\}$, $t\geq 0$, is a martingale (cf. Schoutens 2000). For example, we have $L_1^{mt-1}(\gamma_t)=-(\gamma_t-mt)$ and $L_2^{mt-2}(\gamma_t)=[(\gamma_t-mt)^2-mt]/2$.

So far we have considered the case of the 'standard' gamma process, for which $\mathbb{E}[\gamma_t]=mt$ and $\mathrm{var}[\gamma_t]=mt$, for some m. We note that $(\mathbb{E}[\gamma_t])^2/\mathrm{var}[\gamma_t]$ is dimensionless, and hence that m has the units of inverse time. For fixed m, we can choose the units of time so that $m=1$ in those units (this is done implicitly, e.g., in Yor 2007). We shall take the units of time as fixed, and m as a model parameter.

For many applications it is useful to consider a broader family of processes, labelled by two parameters, which we shall call 'scaled' gamma processes. By a scaled gamma process with growth rate μ and spread σ we mean a process $\{\Gamma_t\}_{0\leq t<\infty}$ with independent increments such that $\Gamma_0=0$ and such that Γ_t has a gamma distribution with mean μt and variance $\sigma^2 t$, where μ and σ are parameters. Defining $m=\mu^2/\sigma^2$ and $\kappa=\sigma^2/\mu$, we have $\mu=\kappa m$ and $\sigma^2=\kappa^2 m$. One can think of m as a 'standardized' growth rate, and κ as a scale. The density of Γ_t is given by

$$\mathbb{Q}[\Gamma_t\in\mathrm{d}x] = \mathbb{1}_{\{x>0\}}\frac{\kappa^{-mt}x^{mt-1}\mathrm{e}^{-x/\kappa}}{\Gamma[mt]}\mathrm{d}x. \tag{2.8}$$

One can check that if $\{\Gamma_t\}$ is a scaled gamma process with standardized growth rate m and scale κ, then $\{\kappa^{-1}\Gamma_t\}$ is a gamma process with growth rate m.

Now suppose that $\{\gamma_t\}$ is a standard gamma process on $(\Omega, \mathcal{F}, \mathbb{Q})$, let $\{\mathcal{G}_t\}$ denote the filtration generated by $\{\gamma_t\}$, and let $\mathbb{Q}^*$ denote the measure on $(\Omega, \mathcal{G}_T)$, for some fixed T, defined by the likelihood ratio

$$\left.\frac{\mathrm{d}\mathbb{Q}^*}{\mathrm{d}\mathbb{Q}}\right|_T = \kappa^{-mT}\exp\left(\frac{1-\kappa}{\kappa}\gamma_T\right) \tag{2.9}$$

for some $\kappa>0$. Then $\{\gamma_t\}_{0\le t\le T}$ is a scaled gamma process on $(\Omega, \mathcal{G}_T, \mathbb{Q}^*)$, with scale parameter κ. Thus, $\mathbb{E}[\gamma_t]=mt$, $\mathrm{var}[\gamma_t]=mt$, $\mathbb{E}^*[\gamma_t]=\kappa mt$ and $\mathrm{var}^*[\gamma_t]=\kappa^2 mt$. This can be established by working out the joint characteristic function under $\mathbb{Q}^*$ of the increments $\gamma_t-\gamma_s$, $\gamma_s-\gamma_{s_1}$, ..., $\gamma_{s_{n-1}}-\gamma_{s_n}$ for $T\ge t\ge s\ge s_1\ge\cdots\ge s_n$ for each $n\in\mathbb{N}$. The change-of-measure density martingale arising in this example is obtained by taking the process (2.5) and setting $\alpha=(1-\kappa)/\kappa$.

The gamma process has been used as the basis of a number of different asset pricing models; see, for example, Madan & Seneta (1990), Madan & Milne (1991), Heston (1995), Carr *et al.* (2002) and Baxter (2007*a*,*b*).

3. Properties of gamma bridge processes

Let $\{\gamma_t\}_{0\le t<\infty}$ be a standard gamma process with growth rate m, and for fixed T define the process $\{\gamma_{tT}\}_{0\le t\le T}$ by setting $\gamma_{tT}=\gamma_t/\gamma_T$. Then clearly $\gamma_{0T}=0$ and $\gamma_{TT}=1$. We refer to $\{\gamma_{tT}\}$ as the standard gamma bridge over $[0,T]$ associated with $\{\gamma_t\}$. More generally, we refer to any process having the law of $\{\gamma_{tT}\}$ as a standard gamma bridge over $[0,T]$. It can be shown that the random variable γ_{tT} has a beta distribution.

Proposition 3.1. *Let* $\mathbb{Q}[\gamma_{tT}\in \mathrm{d}y]=f(y)\mathrm{d}y$. *Then*

$$f(y) = \mathbb{1}_{\{0<y<1\}}\frac{y^{mt-1}(1-y)^{m(T-t)-1}}{B[mt, m(T-t)]}, \tag{3.1}$$

where $B[a,b]=\Gamma[a]\Gamma[b]/\Gamma[a+b]$.

Proof. Since γ_t and $\gamma_T-\gamma_t$ are independent, we see that

$$\begin{aligned}\mathbb{Q}\left[\frac{\gamma_t}{\gamma_T}\le y\right] &= \mathbb{Q}\left[\gamma_t\le\frac{y}{1-y}(\gamma_T-\gamma_t)\right]\\ &= \mathbb{E}\left[\mathbb{Q}\left[\gamma_t\le\frac{y}{1-y}(\gamma_T-\gamma_t)\middle|\gamma_T-\gamma_t\right]\right]\\ &= \frac{1}{\Gamma[mt]}\mathbb{E}\left[\int_0^{y(\gamma_T-\gamma_t)/(1-y)} x^{mt-1}\mathrm{e}^{-x}\,\mathrm{d}x\right].\end{aligned} \tag{3.2}$$

The corresponding density is therefore given by

$$f(y) = \mathbb{1}_{\{0<y<1\}}\frac{y^{mt-1}(1-y)^{-mt-1}}{\Gamma[mt]}\mathbb{E}\left[(\gamma_T-\gamma_t)^{mt}\exp\left(-\frac{y}{1-y}(\gamma_T-\gamma_t)\right)\right]. \tag{3.3}$$

Now, since $\gamma_T - \gamma_t$ has a gamma distribution with parameter $m(T-t)$, for the expectation appearing in the line above we obtain

$$\mathbb{E}\left[(\gamma_T-\gamma_t)^{mt}\exp\left(-\frac{y}{1-y}(\gamma_T-\gamma_t)\right)\right]=\frac{\Gamma[mT]}{\Gamma[m(T-t)]}(1-y)^{mT}. \tag{3.4}$$

Putting this result back into (3.3), we obtain (3.1). ■

Recalling that $B[a,b]=\int_0^1 y^{a-1}(1-y)^{b-1}\,\mathrm{d}y$, we deduce for $n\in\mathbb{N}$ that $\mathbb{E}[\gamma_{tT}^n]=B[mt+n,m(T-t)]/B[mt,m(T-t)]=(mt)_n/(mT)_n$. We see that $\mathbb{E}[\gamma_{tT}]=t/T$ and $\mathbb{E}[\gamma_{tT}^2]=t(mt+1)/T(mT+1)$, and hence $\mathrm{var}[\gamma_{tT}]=t(T-t)/T^2(1+mT)$. Note that the expectation of γ_{tT} does not depend on the growth rate m, and the variance of γ_{tT} decreases with increasing m.

Proposition 3.2. *Let $\{\gamma_t\}_{0\le t<\infty}$ be a standard gamma process. Then for $T\ge t\ge 0$ the random variables γ_t/γ_T and γ_T are independent.*

Proof. Writing $F(y,z)$ for the joint distribution of γ_t/γ_T and γ_T, we have

$$\begin{aligned}F(y,z)&=\mathbb{Q}\left[\frac{\gamma_t}{\gamma_T}\le y\cap\gamma_T\le z\right]\\&=\mathbb{Q}\left[\gamma_t\le\frac{y}{1-y}(\gamma_T-\gamma_t)\cap\gamma_t\le z-(\gamma_T-\gamma_t)\right].\end{aligned} \tag{3.5}$$

Conditioning with respect to $\gamma_T-\gamma_t$, we use the independence of γ_t and $\gamma_T-\gamma_t$ to deduce that

$$F(y,z)=\frac{1}{\Gamma[mt]}\mathbb{E}\left[\int_0^\infty \mathbb{1}_{\{x\le y(\gamma_T-\gamma_t)/(1-y)\}}\mathbb{1}_{\{x\le z-(\gamma_T-\gamma_t)\}}x^{mt-1}\mathrm{e}^{-x}\,\mathrm{d}x\right], \tag{3.6}$$

and hence the following expression for the joint density:

$$\begin{aligned}f(y,z)=\frac{1}{\Gamma[mt]}\mathbb{E}\bigg[\int_0^\infty&\frac{\gamma_T-\gamma_t}{(1-y)^2}\delta\left(x-\frac{y}{1-y}(\gamma_T-\gamma_t)\right)\\&\times\delta(x-[z-(\gamma_T-\gamma_t)])x^{mt-1}\mathrm{e}^{-x}\,\mathrm{d}x\bigg].\end{aligned} \tag{3.7}$$

Here we have used the relation $\partial_x\mathbb{1}_{\{x\le a\}}=-\delta(x-a)$, where $\delta(z)$ denotes the Dirac distribution. Integrating out the first delta function we have, for $0<y<1$ and $z>0$,

$$\begin{aligned}f(y,z)&=\frac{1}{\Gamma[mt]}\mathbb{E}\bigg[\frac{\gamma_T-\gamma_t}{(1-y)^2}\delta\left(\frac{y}{1-y}(\gamma_T-\gamma_t)-[z-(\gamma_T-\gamma_t)]\right)\\&\qquad\times\left(\frac{y}{1-y}(\gamma_T-\gamma_t)\right)^{mt-1}\exp\left(-\frac{y}{1-y}(\gamma_T-\gamma_t)\right)\bigg]\\&=\frac{y^{mt-1}(1-y)^{-mt-1}}{\Gamma[mt]}\mathbb{E}\bigg[(\gamma_T-\gamma_t)^{mt}\exp\left(-\frac{y}{1-y}(\gamma_T-\gamma_t)\right)\\&\qquad\times\delta\left(\frac{\gamma_T-\gamma_t}{1-y}-z\right)\bigg].\end{aligned} \tag{3.8}$$

Now we introduce the Fourier representation $\delta(x)=(2\pi)^{-1}\int_{-\infty}^{\infty}\mathrm{e}^{\mathrm{i}\lambda x}\,\mathrm{d}\lambda$ for the delta function, interpreted as a distribution, from which we deduce that

$$f(y,z)=\frac{y^{mt-1}(1-y)^{-mt-1}}{\Gamma[mt]}\frac{1}{2\pi}\int_{-\infty}^{\infty}\mathrm{e}^{-\mathrm{i}\lambda z}\mathbb{E}\left[(\gamma_T-\gamma_t)^{mt}\exp\left(-\frac{y}{1-y}(\gamma_T-\gamma_t)\right)\times\exp\left(\mathrm{i}\lambda\frac{1}{1-y}(\gamma_T-\gamma_t)\right)\right]\mathrm{d}\lambda. \quad (3.9)$$

When one works out the expectation appearing in the integrand above the result is

$$\frac{\Gamma[mT]}{\Gamma[m(T-t)]}\frac{(1-y)^{mT}}{(1-\lambda)^{mT}}.$$

Substituting this expression into (3.9) we see that

$$\begin{aligned}f(y,z)&=\frac{\Gamma[mT]}{\Gamma[mt]\Gamma[m(T-t)]}y^{mt-1}(1-y)^{m(T-t)-1}\frac{1}{2\pi}\int_{-\infty}^{\infty}\frac{\mathrm{e}^{-\mathrm{i}\lambda z}}{(1-\mathrm{i}\lambda)^{mT}}\,\mathrm{d}\lambda\\&=\frac{y^{mt-1}(1-y)^{m(T-t)-1}}{B[mt,m(T-t)]}\frac{z^{mT-1}\mathrm{e}^{-z}}{\Gamma[mT]}\end{aligned} \quad (3.10)$$

for $0<y<1$ and $z>0$. Thus, the joint density for γ_t/γ_T and γ_T factorizes into the product of a beta density for γ_t/γ_T and a gamma density for γ_T. ■

More generally, it follows from proposition 3.2 and the independent increments property of the gamma process that $\{\gamma_u\}_{u\geq T}$ and $\{\gamma_{tT}\}_{0\leq t\leq T}$ are independent. This allows us to verify that $\{\gamma_t\}$ has the Markov property (which one knows is the case, since $\{\gamma_t\}$ is a Lévy process). We need to check for $a>0$ that

$$\mathbb{Q}[\gamma_t<a|\gamma_s,\gamma_{s_1},\gamma_{s_2},\ldots,\gamma_{s_n}]=\mathbb{Q}[\gamma_t<a|\gamma_s] \quad (3.11)$$

for all $t\geq s\geq s_1\geq s_2\geq\cdots\geq s_n\geq 0$ and for all $n\geq 1$. But clearly,

$$\mathbb{Q}[\gamma_t<a|\gamma_s,\gamma_{s_1},\gamma_{s_2},\ldots,\gamma_{s_n}]=\mathbb{Q}\left[\gamma_t<a\left|\gamma_s,\frac{\gamma_{s_1}}{\gamma_s},\frac{\gamma_{s_2}}{\gamma_{s_1}},\ldots\right.\right]=\mathbb{Q}[\gamma_t<a|\gamma_s], \quad (3.12)$$

since γ_{s_1}/γ_s, $\gamma_{s_2}/\gamma_{s_1}$, ... are independent of γ_s and γ_t. A similar argument shows that the gamma bridge is Markovian. In particular, we see that

$$\begin{aligned}\mathbb{Q}\left[\frac{\gamma_t}{\gamma_T}<a\left|\frac{\gamma_s}{\gamma_T},\frac{\gamma_{s_1}}{\gamma_T},\frac{\gamma_{s_2}}{\gamma_T},\ldots\right.\right]&=\mathbb{Q}\left[\frac{\gamma_t}{\gamma_T}<a\left|\frac{\gamma_s}{\gamma_T},\frac{\gamma_{s_1}}{\gamma_s},\frac{\gamma_{s_2}}{\gamma_{s_1}},\ldots\right.\right]\\&=\mathbb{Q}\left[\frac{\gamma_t}{\gamma_T}<a\left|\frac{\gamma_s}{\gamma_T}\right.\right],\end{aligned} \quad (3.13)$$

since the random variables γ_{s_1}/γ_s, $\gamma_{s_2}/\gamma_{s_1}$, ... are independent of γ_t/γ_T and γ_s/γ_T.

The following lemma is a classical result (Lukacs 1955) which can be used as the basis of an alternative proof of proposition 3.2.

Lemma 3.3. *Let A and B be independent gamma variables with parameters p and q, respectively. Then $A/(A+B)$ and $A+B$ are independent, $A/(A+B)$ has a* beta(p, q) *distribution and $A+B$ has a* gamma$(p+q)$ *distribution.*

Proof. It suffices to show that the joint Laplace transform of $A/(A+B)$ and $A+B$ factorizes. In particular, for positive constants α and β we have

$$\mathbb{E}\left[\exp\left(-\alpha\frac{A}{A+B}-\beta(A+B)\right)\right]$$
$$=\int_0^\infty\int_0^\infty \frac{a^{p-1}\mathrm{e}^{-a}}{\Gamma[p]}\frac{b^{q-1}\mathrm{e}^{-b}}{\Gamma[q]}\exp\left(-\alpha\frac{a}{a+b}-\beta(a+b)\right)\mathrm{d}a\,\mathrm{d}b. \tag{3.14}$$

Setting $x=a/(a+b)$ and $y=a+b$, we have $a=xy$ and $b=(1-x)y$, and hence $\mathrm{d}a\,\mathrm{d}b=y\,\mathrm{d}x\,\mathrm{d}y$. We see that

$$\mathbb{E}\left[\exp\left(-\alpha\frac{A}{A+B}-\beta(A+B)\right)\right]$$
$$=\int_0^1\frac{x^{p-1}(1-x)^{q-1}}{B[p,q]}\mathrm{e}^{-\alpha x}\,\mathrm{d}x\int_0^\infty\frac{y^{p+q-1}\mathrm{e}^{-y}}{\Gamma[p+q]}\mathrm{e}^{-\beta y}\,\mathrm{d}y$$
$$=\mathbb{E}\left[\exp\left(-\alpha\frac{A}{A+B}\right)\right]\mathbb{E}[\exp(-\beta(A+B))]. \tag{3.15}$$

Proposition 3.2 follows if we set $A=\gamma_t$ and $B=\gamma_T-\gamma_t$. More generally, if we set $A=\gamma_u-\gamma_t$ and $B=\gamma_T-\gamma_u$ for $0\le t\le u\le T$, we deduce that $(\gamma_u-\gamma_t)/(\gamma_T-\gamma_t)$ and $\gamma_T-\gamma_t$ are independent. A straightforward extension of lemma 3.3 establishes that for $n\ge1$ and $T\ge t\ge s\ge s_1\ge\cdots\ge s_n$ the variables γ_T, γ_{tT}, γ_{st}, $\gamma_{s_1s},\ldots,\gamma_{s_ns_{n-1}}$ are independent. ■

4. Valuation of aggregate claims

Our objective is to calculate the value at t of a contract that pays X_T at T. We assume that X_T is strictly positive and integrable. For simplicity of exposition, in this section we take X_T to be a continuous random variable; the adjustments required for the more general situation are straightforward (a discrete example follows in §7). We assume that the default-free interest rate system is deterministic, that $\mathbb{Q}$ is the risk-neutral measure, and that the market filtration is generated by an aggregate claims process $\{\xi_t\}_{0\le t\le T}$ of the form $\xi_t=X_T\gamma_{tT}$, where $\{\gamma_{tT}\}$ is a standard gamma bridge under $\mathbb{Q}$, with parameter m, which we take to be independent of X_T. The value S_t of the contract at $t\le T$ is given under these assumptions by $S_t=P_{tT}\mathbb{E}[X_T|\mathcal{F}_t]$, where $\mathcal{F}_t=\sigma(\{\xi_s\}_{0\le s\le t})$. In our modelling considerations we are to some extent looking towards the future, where we may presume a rich range of insurance-related derivative products will be trading in liquid financial markets; it is then reasonable to assume that $\mathbb{Q}$ will be established. In contrast to the actuarial approach (Arjas 1989; Dickson & Waters 1993; Norberg 1999), we are concerned with valuation rather than prediction or estimation. The assumptions that interest rates are deterministic, that the gains process is of the specific simple form (1.1) and that the filtration is generated by a single information process, are model simplifications that can be relaxed in various ways, and are not essential.

Proposition 4.1. *The aggregate claims process* $\{\xi_t\}_{0\le t\le T}$ *has the Markov property.*

Proof. For the Markov property we must verify that $\mathbb{Q}[\xi_t < a|\mathcal{F}_s] = \mathbb{Q}[\xi_t < a|\xi_s]$ for all s, t such that $0\le s\le t\le T$. It suffices to establish that

$$\mathbb{Q}\left[\xi_t < a|\xi_s, \xi_{s_1}, \xi_{s_2}, \ldots, \xi_{s_n}\right] = \mathbb{Q}[\xi_t < a|\xi_s] \tag{4.1}$$

for all $t\ge s\ge s_1\ge s_2\ge\cdots\ge s_n$ and for all $n\ge 1$. We use the representation $\{\gamma_{tT}\} = \{\gamma_t/\gamma_T\}$, where $\{\gamma_t\}$ is a standard gamma process with rate m. Then,

$$\begin{aligned}\mathbb{Q}\left[\xi_t < a|\xi_s, \xi_{s_1}, \xi_{s_2}, \ldots\right] &= \mathbb{Q}\left[\xi_t < a\left|X_T\frac{\gamma_s}{\gamma_T}, X_T\frac{\gamma_{s_1}}{\gamma_T}, X_T\frac{\gamma_{s_2}}{\gamma_T}, \ldots\right.\right]\\ &= \mathbb{Q}\left[\xi_t < a\left|X_T\frac{\gamma_s}{\gamma_T}, \frac{\gamma_{s_1}}{\gamma_s}, \frac{\gamma_{s_2}}{\gamma_{s_1}}, \ldots\right.\right].\end{aligned} \tag{4.2}$$

But $\gamma_{s_1}/\gamma_s, \gamma_{s_2}/\gamma_{s_1}, \ldots$ are independent of ξ_t and ξ_s, which gives the result. ■

By virtue of the fact that $\{\xi_t\}$ has the Markov property and that X_T is $\mathcal{F}_T$-measurable, we are able to simplify the expression for S_t so that it takes the form

$$S_t = P_{tT}\mathbb{E}[X_T|\xi_t]. \tag{4.3}$$

The conditional expectation appearing here can be carried out in closed form, leading to the following pricing formula.

Proposition 4.2. *The value* S_t *at time* $t< T$ *of the aggregate claim that pays the continuous random variable* $X_T>0$ *at time* T *is given by*

$$S_t = P_{tT}\frac{\int_{\xi_t}^{\infty} p(x)x^{2-mT}(x-\xi_t)^{m(T-t)-1}\,\mathrm{d}x}{\int_{\xi_t}^{\infty} p(x)x^{1-mT}(x-\xi_t)^{m(T-t)-1}\,\mathrm{d}x}, \tag{4.4}$$

where $p(x)$ *is the density of* X_T.

Proof. The conditional expectation (4.3) can be written in the form

$$\mathbb{E}[X_T|\xi_t] = \int_0^{\infty} x\pi_t(x)\,\mathrm{d}x, \tag{4.5}$$

where $\{\pi_t(x)\}$ is the conditional density process for X_T, which by virtue of the Markov property of $\{\xi_t\}$ is given by $\pi_t(x)\,\mathrm{d}x = \mathrm{d}\mathbb{Q}[X_T\le x|\xi_t]$. We can compute $\pi_t(x)$ by use of the following form of the Bayes formula:

$$\pi_t(x) = \frac{p(x)\rho(\xi_t|X_T = x)}{\int_0^{\infty} p(x)\rho(\xi_t|X_T = x)\,\mathrm{d}x}, \tag{4.6}$$

where $\rho(\xi_t|X_T = x)$ is the conditional density for ξ_t, valued at ξ_t, given by

$$\rho(\xi|X_T = x) = \frac{\mathrm{d}}{\mathrm{d}\xi}\mathbb{Q}[\xi_t\le\xi|X_T = x] = \frac{\mathrm{d}}{\mathrm{d}\xi}\mathbb{Q}\left[\gamma_{tT}\le\frac{\xi}{x}\right]. \tag{4.7}$$

Therefore, writing $f(y)$ for the density of γ_{tT}, we find

$$\rho(\xi|X_T = x) = \frac{\mathrm{d}}{\mathrm{d}\xi}\int_0^{\xi/x} f(y)\,\mathrm{d}y = \frac{1}{x}f\left(\frac{\xi}{x}\right). \tag{4.8}$$

Hence by proposition 3.1 we have

$$\rho(\xi|X_T = x) = \mathbb{1}_{\{x>\xi\}}\xi^{mt-1}\frac{x^{1-mT}(x-\xi)^{m(T-t)-1}}{B[mt, m(T-t)]}. \tag{4.9}$$

The conditional density is thus given by

$$\pi_t(x) = \mathbb{1}_{\{x>\xi_t\}}\frac{p(x)x^{1-mT}(x-\xi_t)^{m(T-t)-1}}{\int_{\xi_t}^{\infty} p(x)x^{1-mT}(x-\xi_t)^{m(T-t)-1}\,\mathrm{d}x}, \tag{4.10}$$

from which (4.4) follows at once. ∎

With these results at hand, we are also in a position to price a simple stop-loss reinsurance policy. For such a policy the value process is given by

$$\begin{aligned} C_{tT} &= P_{tT}\int_0^{\infty}(x-K)^{+}\pi_t(x)\,\mathrm{d}x \\ &= P_{tT}\frac{\int_{\xi_t}^{\infty}(x-K)^{+}p(x)x^{1-mT}(x-\xi_t)^{m(T-t)-1}\,\mathrm{d}x}{\int_{\xi_t}^{\infty}p(x)x^{1-mT}(x-\xi_t)^{m(T-t)-1}\,\mathrm{d}x} \end{aligned} \tag{4.11}$$

for $t<T$, and $C_{TT}=(X_T-K)^{+}$. Once a time t has been reached such that $\xi_t\geq K$, then $C_{uT}=S_u-P_{uT}K$ for $t\leq u\leq T$; that is, when a sufficient number of claims have accumulated, the option is sure to expire in-the-money. It should be evident that although the language of the results of this section, and those following, is mainly that of insurance, the relevant concepts are equally applicable to a variety of financial products. In the case of a large credit portfolio, for example, C_{tT} has the interpretation of being the value at t of a contract that pays at T an amount equal to the total loss incurred by the portfolio, in excess of some threshold K. It is then straightforward to see that the pay-off function can be adjusted to accommodate a segregation of the loss allocation into tranches.

5. Valuation of general reinsurance contracts

In §4 we showed how one works out the reserve process for an aggregate claim that pays X_T at T, and we were also able to determine the value process of a stop-loss reinsurance contract that pays $(X_T-K)^{+}$ at T. In this section we consider the more general situation of a contract that at a fixed time $t<T$ allows the firm the option of commuting the claim X_T in exchange for a pre-fixed settlement K. Let us write C_{0t} for the value at time 0 of such an option; then clearly we have

$$C_{0t} = P_{0t}\mathbb{E}\left[(S_t-K)^{+}\right], \tag{5.1}$$

where S_t is the value at t of the claim that pays X_T at T. In the context of a credit portfolio, S_t represents the value at t of a contract that pays an amount equal to the accumulated losses in the portfolio at time T; then C_{0t} is the price at time 0 of a contract that pays at time t the excess of S_t over K. With reference to proposition 4.2, we introduce a function $S(t,y)$ for $t<T$ and $y\geq 0$ by setting

$$S(t,\,y) = P_{tT}\frac{\int_y^{\infty}p(x)x^{2-mT}(x-y)^{m(T-t)-1}\,\mathrm{d}x}{\int_y^{\infty}p(x)x^{1-mT}(x-y)^{m(T-t)-1}\,\mathrm{d}x}. \tag{5.2}$$

Then the value of the claim is $S_t = S(t, \xi_t)$, and the value of the option is

$$C_{0t} = P_{0t}\mathbb{E}\big[(S(t,\xi_t) - K)^+\big]. \tag{5.3}$$

Before proceeding with the calculation of this expectation let us check that the integrals in (5.2) converge. Let $T > t > 0$ and $y > 0$ be given, set $a = mt$ and $b = m(T-t)$, fix a constant $z > y$, and for the numerator term in (5.2) write $I = I^+ + I^-$, where $I^+ = \int_z^\infty p(x)x^{2-(a+b)}(x-y)^{b-1}\,\mathrm{d}x$ and $I^- = \int_y^z p(x)x^{2-(a+b)}(x-y)^{b-1}\,\mathrm{d}x$. It follows that

$$I^+ = \int_z^\infty p(x)x^{1-a}(1-y/x)^{b-1}\,\mathrm{d}x \leq c\int_z^\infty p(x)x^{1-a}\,\mathrm{d}x, \tag{5.4}$$

where $c = 1$ if $b > 1$, and $c = (1-y/z)^{b-1}$ if $b \leq 1$. In either case we have $I^+ < c\int_z^\infty p(x)x\,\mathrm{d}x < \infty$, since X_T is assumed to be integrable. On the other hand, we have $I^- = b^{-1}\int_{x=y}^z p(x)x^{2-(a+b)}\mathrm{d}(x-y)^b$; writing $w = (x-y)^b$ we obtain

$$I^- = b^{-1}\int_{w=0}^{(z-y)^b} p(y + w^{1/b})(y + w^{1/b})^{2-(a+b)}\,\mathrm{d}w, \tag{5.5}$$

which is finite. Similar arguments show that the denominator in (5.2) is finite.

Since the payout of the option is a function of ξ_t, one way of working out the expectation in (5.3) is to obtain an expression for the price $A_{0t}(y)$ of an Arrow–Debreu security that pays $\delta(\xi_t - y)$ at t, where $y \geq 0$ is a parameter. Thus, we have $A_{0t}(y) = P_{0t}\mathbb{E}[\delta(\xi_t - y)]$, and for the option we can write

$$C_{0t} = \int_0^\infty A_{0t}(y)[S(t, y) - K]^+\,\mathrm{d}y. \tag{5.6}$$

We shall calculate $A_{0t}(y)$ and use the result to determine the expectation (5.3). We state the result first, the proof of which is given at the end of this section.

Proposition 5.1. *The price $A_{0t}(y)$ at time 0 of an Arrow–Debreu security that pays $\delta(\xi_t - y)$ at t is given by*

$$A_{0t}(y) = P_{0t}\frac{y^{mt-1}}{B[mt, m(T-t)]}\int_y^\infty p(x)x^{1-mT}(x-y)^{m(T-t)-1}\,\mathrm{d}x. \tag{5.7}$$

By comparing (5.2) and (5.7) we observe that the integral term in (5.7) cancels with the denominator in the expression for $S(t, y)$. We thus obtain

$$C_{0t} = \int_0^\infty \frac{P_{0t}y^{mt-1}}{B[mt, m(T-t)]}\left[\int_y^\infty p(x)(xP_{tT} - K)x^{1-mT}(x-y)^{m(T-t)-1}\,\mathrm{d}x\right]^+\mathrm{d}y. \tag{5.8}$$

We are now left with the task of finding the critical values at which the argument of the max function in (5.8) vanishes. Suppose $S(t, y)$ is monotonic in y; then there is at most a single critical value y^*, obtained by solving

$$\int_{y^*}^\infty p(x)(xP_{tT} - K)x^{1-mT}(x-y^*)^{m(T-t)-1}\,\mathrm{d}x = 0. \tag{5.9}$$

The lower limit of the outer integration in the expression for C_{0t} above can then be changed, and we have

$$C_{0t} = \int_{y^*}^\infty \frac{P_{0t}y^{mt-1}}{B[mt, m(T-t)]}\left[\int_y^\infty p(x)(xP_{tT} - K)x^{1-mT}(x-y)^{m(T-t)-1}\,\mathrm{d}x\right]\mathrm{d}y. \tag{5.10}$$

This expression simplifies further if we swap the order of integration as follows:

$$C_{0t} = \frac{P_{0t}}{B[mt, m(T-t)]} \int_{y^*}^{\infty} \int_{y^*}^{x} p(x)(xP_{tT} - K) y^{mt-1} x^{1-mT} (x-y)^{m(T-t)-1} \, \mathrm{d}y \, \mathrm{d}x. \tag{5.11}$$

Making the substitution $y = xz$, we then obtain

$$C_{0t} = \frac{P_{0t}}{B[mt, m(T-t)]} \int_{y^*}^{\infty} p(x)(xP_{tT} - K) \int_{y^*/x}^{1} z^{mt-1}(1-z)^{m(T-t)-1} \, \mathrm{d}z \, \mathrm{d}x. \tag{5.12}$$

Let us now define the complementary beta distribution function $\mathcal{B}(u)$ with parameters mt and $m(T-t)$ by the expression

$$\mathcal{B}(u) = \frac{\int_u^1 z^{mt-1}(1-z)^{m(T-t)-1} \, \mathrm{d}z}{\int_0^1 z^{mt-1}(1-z)^{m(T-t)-1} \, \mathrm{d}z}. \tag{5.13}$$

Clearly, the denominator in (5.13) is $B[mt, m(T-t)]$. We thus find that the integration over the variable z in (5.12) combines with the factor $B[mt, m(T-t)]$ to give a cumulative beta distribution function, and for the option price we have

$$C_{0t} = P_{0t} \int_{y^*}^{\infty} p(x)(xP_{tT} - K) \mathcal{B}\left(\frac{y^*}{x}\right) \mathrm{d}x. \tag{5.14}$$

We remark, incidentally, that a sufficient condition for $S(t, y)$ to be monotonic in y for fixed t is $m(T-t) > 1$. To see this, we differentiate $S(t, y)$ with respect to y, assuming the stated condition, and after some rearrangement we obtain

$$\frac{\partial S(t, y)}{\partial y} = P_{tT}[m(T-t) - 1] \left(\frac{\int_y^\infty p(x)\alpha^2(x) \, \mathrm{d}x \int_y^\infty p(x)\beta^2(x) \, \mathrm{d}x}{\left(\int_y^\infty p(x)\alpha(x)\beta(x) \, \mathrm{d}x\right)^2} - 1 \right), \tag{5.15}$$

where $\alpha^2(x) = x^{1-mT}(x-y)^{m(T-t)}$ and $\beta^2(x) = x^{1-mT}(x-y)^{m(T-t)-2}$. Then if $m(T-t) > 1$, the integrals exist, and $\partial S(t, y)/\partial y > 0$ by the Schwartz inequality.

Proof of proposition 5.1. Using the Fourier representation for the delta function we can write

$$\mathbb{E}[\delta(\xi_t - y)] = \frac{1}{2\pi} \int_{-\infty}^{\infty} \mathrm{e}^{-\mathrm{i}\lambda y} \mathbb{E}[\exp(\mathrm{i}\lambda\xi_t)] \, \mathrm{d}\lambda. \tag{5.16}$$

Since X_T and γ_{tT} are independent, it follows from the tower property that

$$\begin{aligned} \mathbb{E}\left[\mathrm{e}^{\mathrm{i}\lambda\xi_t}\right] &= \mathbb{E}[\mathbb{E}[\exp(\mathrm{i}\lambda X_T \gamma_{tT}) | X_T]] = \int_0^\infty p(x) \mathbb{E}[\exp(\mathrm{i}\lambda x \gamma_{tT})] \, \mathrm{d}x \\ &= \int_0^\infty p(x)\phi(\lambda x) \, \mathrm{d}x, \end{aligned} \tag{5.17}$$

where $\phi(\nu) = \mathbb{E}[\exp(\mathrm{i}\nu\gamma_{tT})]$ is the characteristic function of γ_{tT}. We deduce that

$$\mathbb{E}[\delta(\xi_t - y)] = \frac{1}{2\pi} \int_{-\infty}^{\infty} \mathrm{e}^{-\mathrm{i}\lambda y} \int_{x=0}^{\infty} p(x)\phi(\lambda x) \, \mathrm{d}x \, \mathrm{d}\lambda. \tag{5.18}$$

Thus, by interchanging the order of integration and using the fact that the inverse Fourier transform of the characteristic function is the density function we have

$$\mathbb{E}[\delta(\xi_t - y)] = \int_{x=0}^{\infty} p(x)\left[\frac{1}{2\pi}\int_{-\infty}^{\infty} \mathrm{e}^{-\mathrm{i}\lambda y}\phi(\lambda x)\,\mathrm{d}\lambda\right]\mathrm{d}x$$

$$= \int_{x=0}^{\infty} p(x)\frac{1}{x}\left[\frac{1}{2\pi}\int_{-\infty}^{\infty} \mathrm{e}^{-\mathrm{i}\nu y/x}\phi(\nu)\,\mathrm{d}\nu\right]\mathrm{d}x$$

$$= \int_{0}^{\infty} p(x)\frac{1}{x}f\Big(\frac{y}{x}\Big)\,\mathrm{d}x, \tag{5.19}$$

where f is the density function of γ_{tT}. Substituting (3.1) into (5.19) we find that

$$\mathbb{E}[\delta(\xi_t - y)] = \int_{0}^{\infty} p(x)\frac{1}{x}\mathbb{1}_{\{x>y\}}\frac{(y/x)^{mt-1}(1-y/x)^{m(T-t)-1}}{B[mt, m(T-t)]}\,\mathrm{d}x$$

$$= \frac{y^{mt-1}}{B[mt, m(T-t)]}\int_{y}^{\infty} p(x)x^{1-mT}(x-y)^{m(T-t)-1}\,\mathrm{d}x, \tag{5.20}$$

which verifies the claim. ■

We remark that the price of the Arrow–Debreu security can be put in the form

$$A_{0t}(y) = P_{0t}\frac{\int_0^1 p(y/u)u^{mt-2}(1-u)^{m(T-t)-1}\,\mathrm{d}u}{\int_0^1 u^{mt-1}(1-u)^{m(T-t)-1}\,\mathrm{d}u}, \tag{5.21}$$

by use of which the normalization $\int_0^\infty A_{0t}(y)\,\mathrm{d}y = P_{0t}$ can be checked. It follows also from (5.21) that the characteristic function $\Phi_\xi(\lambda)$ of ξ_t is given by the beta average of the characteristic function ϕ_X of X_T:

$$\Phi_\xi(\lambda) = \frac{\int_0^1 \phi_X(\lambda u)u^{mt-1}(1-u)^{m(T-t)-1}\,\mathrm{d}u}{\int_0^1 u^{mt-1}(1-u)^{m(T-t)-1}\,\mathrm{d}u}. \tag{5.22}$$

It is worthwhile noting that $\lim_{t\to T}A_{0t}(y) = P_{0T}p(y)$, a result that is intuitively reasonable, though not immediately evident from (5.7) or (5.21). This shows that if we are given a set of call option prices with maturity T for all strikes, then the density function $p(x)$ can be constructed. It follows more generally that if we are given the values of call options for all strikes for any specific maturity date t, then the density can be constructed, and hence option prices for all other maturities.

6. Discretely distributed cash flows

In this section we consider the example for which X_T takes values in a discrete set $\{x_i\}_{i=1,\ldots,n}$. The corresponding *a priori* probabilities will be denoted $\{p_i\}$. The calculation presented in §4 holds and we obtain, instead of (4.4), the following expression for the value process:

$$S_t = P_{tT}\frac{\sum_i p_i x_i^{2-mT}(x_i - \xi_t)^{m(T-t)-1}\mathbb{1}_{\{\xi_t<x_i\}}}{\sum_i p_i x_i^{1-mT}(x_i - \xi_t)^{m(T-t)-1}\mathbb{1}_{\{\xi_t<x_i\}}}. \tag{6.1}$$

It is straightforward to verify that expression (6.1) converges to the correct terminal value as t approaches T. To see this, suppose that for some $\omega\in\Omega$ the value of X_T is x_k. Then for that choice of ω we have, after some rearrangement,

$$S_t = P_{tT}\frac{p_k x_k^{1-mt} + \sum_{i\neq k} p_i x_i^{2-mT}\left(\frac{1-\gamma_{tT}}{x_i - x_k\gamma_{tT}}\right)^{1-m(T-t)} \mathbb{1}_{\{x_i > x_k\gamma_{tT}\}}}{p_k x_k^{-mt} + \sum_{i\neq k} p_i x_i^{1-mT}\left(\frac{1-\gamma_{tT}}{x_i - x_k\gamma_{tT}}\right)^{1-m(T-t)} \mathbb{1}_{\{x_i > x_k\gamma_{tT}\}}}. \tag{6.2}$$

It follows at once that $S_T = x_k$. See figure 1 for typical sample paths of $\{S_t\}$.

We proceed now to value a reinsurance contract that pays $(S_t - K)^+$ at time t. For this purpose we need the price of an Arrow–Debreu security with pay-off $\delta(\xi_t - y)$ at t. In the discrete case the Arrow–Debreu price is given by

$$A_{0t}(y) = P_{0t}\frac{y^{mt-1}}{B[mt, m(T-t)]}\sum_{i=0}^{n} p_i x_i^{1-mT}(x_i - y)^{m(T-t)-1}\mathbb{1}_{\{x_i > y\}}. \tag{6.3}$$

Substituting (6.3) and the function

$$S(t,\, y) = P_{tT}\frac{\sum_i p_i x_i^{2-mT}(x_i - y)^{m(T-t)-1}\mathbb{1}_{\{x_i > y\}}}{\sum_i p_i x_i^{1-mT}(x_i - y)^{m(T-t)-1}\mathbb{1}_{\{x_i > y\}}} \tag{6.4}$$

into (5.6), we obtain

$$C_{0t} = \int_0^\infty \frac{P_{0t}y^{mt-1}}{B[mt, m(T-t)]}\left[\sum_{i=1}^{n} p_i x_i^{1-mT}(x_i - y)^{m(T-t)-1}\mathbb{1}_{\{x_i > y\}}(P_{tT}x_i - K)\right]^+ \mathrm{d}y. \tag{6.5}$$

A discrete version of formula (5.15) shows that $S(t, y)$ is increasing in y if $m(T-t) > 1$, and decreasing in y for $y \in (x_k, x_{k+1})$ for each $k = 1, \ldots, n-1$ if $m(T-t) < 1$. For fixed t there is at most a single critical value $y = y^*$ for which $S(t, y) = K$, when $y \neq x_k$ for all k. We thus have three scenarios to consider: (i) $S(t, y)$ is increasing in y at $y = y^*$, (ii) the critical value y^* is at $y = x_k$ for some k, and (iii) $S(t, y)$ is decreasing in y at $y = y^*$.

In case (i) the integrand in (6.5) is nonzero when $y \in (y^*, \infty)$, and for the price of the reinsurance contract we have

$$C_{0t} = P_{0t}\sum_{i=1}^{n}\frac{p_i x_i^{1-mT}(P_{tT}x_i - K)}{B[mt, m(T-t)]}\int_{y^*}^{\infty} y^{mt-1}(x_i - y)^{m(T-t)-1}\mathbb{1}_{\{x_i > y\}}\,\mathrm{d}y. \tag{6.6}$$

The y integration in (6.6) can be carried out by observing that for $x_i > y^*$ we have

$$\int_{y^*}^{\infty} y^{mt-1}(x_i - y)^{m(T-t)-1}\mathbb{1}_{\{x_i > y\}}\,\mathrm{d}y = x_i^{mT-1}\int_{y^*/x_i}^{1} z^{mt-1}(1-z)^{m(T-t)-1}\,\mathrm{d}z. \tag{6.7}$$

Therefore, the price of the reinsurance contract can be expressed in terms of the complementary beta distribution function with parameters mt and $m(T-t)$:

$$C_{0t} = P_{0t}\sum_{i=1}^{n}\mathbb{1}_{\{x_i > y^*\}}p_i(P_{tT}x_i - K)\mathcal{B}(y^*/x_i). \tag{6.8}$$

If there is no critical value in the range (x_k, x_{k+1}), then $y^* = x_k$ for some k. Hence the pricing formula in case (ii) is identical to the result obtained in (6.8), with $y^* = x_k$. In case (iii) there are two distinct regions for which the integrand in (6.5) is nonzero. These are given by $y \in [x_k, y^*)$ and $y \geq x_{k+1}$ for some k. Thus, the pricing formula is similar to that obtained in (6.8), except there are additional terms arising from the integration over the range $[x_k, y^*)$.

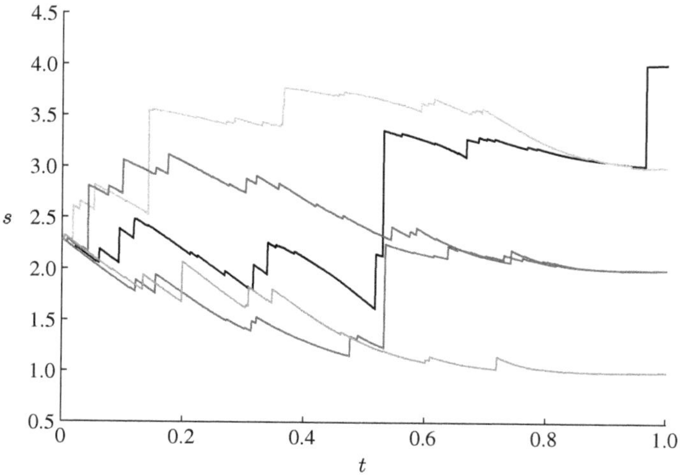

Figure 1. Five sample paths for the reserve process $\{S_t\}$ in the case of a terminal claim taking four possible values. The parameters are chosen such that m=10.0, r=5%, T=1, $\{x_1, x_2, x_3, x_4\}$= {1, 2, 3, 4}, and $\{p_1, p_2, p_3, p_4\}$={0.2, 0.4, 0.2, 0.2}.

As an example of a discrete cash flow, we consider the case where X_T can take the values x_0, x_1. The critical value $y^* < x_0$ can be worked out by solving

$$x_0^{1-mT}(x_0 - y^*)^{m(T-t)-1} = \frac{p_1(K - P_{tT}x_1)}{p_0(P_{tT}x_0 - K)} x_1^{1-mT}(x_1 - y^*)^{m(T-t)-1} \tag{6.9}$$

for y^*. A short calculation shows that

$$y^* = \frac{\theta x_1 - x_0}{\theta - 1}, \quad \text{where} \quad \theta = \left[\frac{p_1(K - P_{tT}x_1)}{p_0(P_{tT}x_0 - K)}\left(\frac{x_1}{x_0}\right)^{1-mT}\right]^{1/[m(T-t)-1]}. \tag{6.10}$$

It follows that the price of a reinsurance contract in the case of a binary pay-off is

$$C_{0t} = p_0(P_{0T}x_0 - P_{0t}K)\mathcal{B}(y^*/x_0) + p_1(P_{0T}x_1 - P_{0t}K)\mathcal{B}(y^*/x_1). \tag{6.11}$$

7. Price processes for options on reserves

We now generalize the analysis of §5 to derive the price process of a call option on the value of the reserve S_t at time t associated with the claim X_T. As before, let K be the strike. Then the value of the option at time $s \le t$ is

$$C_{st} = P_{st}\mathbb{E}\left[(S(t, \xi_t) - K)^+ | \xi_s\right]. \tag{7.1}$$

Once again we find it convenient to obtain first the price process for the Arrow–Debreu security. This is on account of the relation

$$\begin{aligned} C_{st} &= P_{st}\mathbb{E}\left[\left.\int_0^\infty \delta(\xi_t - y)(S(t, y) - K)^+ \,\mathrm{d}y\right| \xi_s\right] \\ &= P_{st}\int_0^\infty \mathbb{E}[\delta(\xi_t - y)|\xi_s](S(t, y) - K)^+ \,\mathrm{d}y = \int_0^\infty A_{st}(y)(S(t, y) - K)^+ \,\mathrm{d}y, \end{aligned} \tag{7.2}$$

where $S(t, y)$ is defined as in (5.2) and $\{A_{st}\}_{0\le s\le t\le T}$ is given by $P_{st}\mathbb{E}[\delta(\xi_t - y)|\xi_s]$. By taking the conditional expectation, we obtain the following result.

Proposition 7.1. *The price process $\{A_{st}(y)\}_{0\le s\le t\le T}$ of the Arrow–Debreu security that pays out $\delta(\xi_t - y)$ at t is*

$$A_{st}(y) = P_{st}\frac{\mathbb{1}_{\{y>\xi_s\}}(y-\xi_s)^{m(t-s)-1}}{B[m(t-s), m(T-t)]}\,\frac{\int_y^\infty p(x)x^{1-mT}(x-y)^{m(T-t)-1}\,\mathrm{d}x}{\int_{\xi_s}^\infty p(x)x^{1-mT}(x-\xi_s)^{m(T-s)-1}\,\mathrm{d}x}, \tag{7.3}$$

where $p(x)$ is the density of X_T.

This result is established later in this section. By substitution of (7.3) in (7.2) we see that the price process of the option is given by

$$C_{st} = \frac{P_{st}}{B[m(t-s), m(T-t)]\int_{\xi_s}^\infty p(x)x^{1-mT}(x-\xi_s)^{m(T-s)-1}\,\mathrm{d}x}$$
$$\times \int_{y=\xi_s}^\infty (y-\xi_s)^{m(t-s)-1}\left[\int_y^\infty p(x)x^{1-mT}(x-y)^{m(T-t)-1}(P_{tT}x-K)\,\mathrm{d}x\right]^+\mathrm{d}y. \tag{7.4}$$

Assuming that there is only one critical value y^* that solves (5.9), we find that the integration over y in (7.4) vanishes for $y<y^*$. In this case, we can lift the max function, and by interchanging the order of integration we obtain

$$C_{st} = \frac{P_{st}}{B[m(t-s), m(T-t)]\int_{\xi_s}^\infty p(x)x^{1-mT}(x-\xi_s)^{m(T-s)-1}\,\mathrm{d}x}$$
$$\times P_{tT}\int_{x=y^*}^\infty p(x)x^{1-mT}(P_{tT}x-K)\int_{y=y^*}^x (y-\xi_s)^{m(t-s)-1}(x-y)^{m(T-t)-1}\,\mathrm{d}y\,\mathrm{d}x. \tag{7.5}$$

Making the substitutions $y=z+\xi_s$ and $z=w(x-\xi_s)$ we get

$$\int_{y=y^*}^x (y-\xi_s)^{m(t-s)-1}(x-y)^{m(T-t)-1}\,\mathrm{d}y = \int_{z=y-\xi_s}^{x-\xi_s} z^{m(t-s)-1}(x-\xi_s-z)^{m(T-t)-1}\,\mathrm{d}z$$
$$= (x-\xi_s)^{m(T-s)-1}\int_{w=(y^*-\xi_s)/(x-\xi_s)}^1 w^{m(t-s)-1}(1-w)^{m(T-t)-1}\,\mathrm{d}w. \tag{7.6}$$

We see that together with the beta function in the denominator of (7.5) the integral term on the right side of (7.6) gives rise to a complementary beta distribution function. Therefore, the option price can be written in the form

$$C_{st} = P_{st}\int_{x=y^*}^\infty \frac{p(x)x^{1-mT}(x-\xi_s)^{m(T-s)-1}}{\int_{\xi_s}^\infty p(x)x^{1-mT}(x-\xi_s)^{m(T-s)-1}\,\mathrm{d}x}(P_{tT}x-K)\mathcal{B}\left(\frac{y^*-\xi_s}{x-\xi_s}\right)\mathrm{d}x. \tag{7.7}$$

Finally, we observe that the quotient in the integrand is the conditional density $\pi_s(x)$. The price at time $s\le t$ thus reduces to the following expression:

$$C_{st} = P_{st}\int_{y^*}^\infty \pi_s(x)(xP_{tT}-K)\mathcal{B}\left(\frac{y^*-\xi_s}{x-\xi_s}\right)\mathrm{d}x. \tag{7.8}$$

As in the case of the initial price, the range of integration in (7.8) must be modified if there is more than one critical value for which (5.9) is satisfied. We now proceed to derive the expression for the Arrow–Debreu price process.

Proof of proposition 7.1. Using the Fourier representation for $\delta(x)$ we have

$$\mathbb{E}[\delta(\xi_t - y)|\xi_s] = \frac{1}{2\pi}\int_{-\infty}^{\infty} \mathrm{e}^{-\mathrm{i}\lambda y}\mathbb{E}\left[\mathrm{e}^{\mathrm{i}\lambda\xi_t}|\xi_s\right] \mathrm{d}\lambda. \tag{7.9}$$

To determine the conditional expectation $\mathbb{E}[\mathrm{e}^{\mathrm{i}\lambda\xi_t}|\xi_s]$, the following result is handy.

Lemma 7.2. *Let $\{\xi_t\}_{0\le t\le T}$ be given by $\xi_t = X_T\gamma_{tT}$, where $\{\gamma_{tT}\}$ is a gamma bridge and X_T is an independent positive random variable. Then for fixed s such that $0\le s\le t\le T$ we have $\xi_t=\xi_s+Z_T\delta_{tT}$, where $Z_T=(1-\gamma_{sT})X_T$ and where the process $\delta_{tT}=(\gamma_{tT}-\gamma_{sT})/(1-\gamma_{sT})$ is a gamma bridge over the interval $t\in[s,T]$ and is independent of ξ_s and Z_T.*

By use of $\xi_t=\xi_s+Z_T\delta_{tT}$ and the tower property we find that

$$\begin{aligned}\mathbb{E}[\exp(\mathrm{i}\lambda\xi_t)|\xi_s] &= \mathbb{E}[\exp(\mathrm{i}\lambda(\xi_s + Z_T\delta_{tT}))|\xi_s] \\ &= \exp(\mathrm{i}\lambda\xi_s)\mathbb{E}[\mathbb{E}[\exp(\mathrm{i}\lambda Z_T\delta_{tT})|\xi_s,\delta_{tT}]|\xi_s].\end{aligned} \tag{7.10}$$

Since $Z_T=X_T-\xi_s$ and $\{\delta_{tT}\}$ is independent of ξ_s and X_T, the inner expectation can be carried out explicitly by use of the conditional density for X_T:

$$\mathbb{E}\left[\exp(\mathrm{i}\lambda\xi_t)\middle|\xi_s\right] = \exp(\mathrm{i}\lambda\xi_s)\mathbb{E}\left[\int_{x=\xi_s}^{\infty} \exp(\mathrm{i}\lambda(x-\xi_s)\delta_{tT})\pi_s(x)\,\mathrm{d}x\middle|\xi_s\right]. \tag{7.11}$$

By substituting (7.11) in (7.9) we deduce that

$$\begin{aligned}\mathbb{E}[\delta(\xi_t - y)|\xi_s] &= \frac{1}{2\pi}\int_{-\infty}^{\infty}\exp(-\mathrm{i}\lambda(y-\xi_s))\int_{x=\xi_s}^{\infty}\Phi_\delta[\lambda(x-\xi_s)]\pi_s(x)\,\mathrm{d}x\,\mathrm{d}\lambda \\ &= \int_{x=\xi_s}^{\infty}\left(\frac{1}{2\pi}\int_{-\infty}^{\infty}\exp(-\mathrm{i}\lambda(y-\xi_s))\Phi_\delta[\lambda(x-\xi_s)]\,\mathrm{d}\lambda\right)\pi_s(x)\,\mathrm{d}x \\ &= \int_{x=\xi_s}^{\infty}\left(\frac{1}{2\pi}\int_{-\infty}^{\infty}\exp\left(-\mathrm{i}\frac{y-\xi_s}{x-\xi_s}z\right)\Phi_\delta(z)\,\mathrm{d}z\right)\frac{1}{x-\xi_s}\pi_s(x)\,\mathrm{d}x \\ &= \int_{x=\xi_s}^{\infty}\frac{\pi_s(x)}{x-\xi_s}f_\delta\left(\frac{y-\xi_s}{x-\xi_s}\right)\mathrm{d}x,\end{aligned} \tag{7.12}$$

where Φ_δ is the characteristic function for δ_{tT} and f_δ is the density of δ_{tT}. Since δ_{tT} is beta distributed with parameters $m(t-s)$ and $m(T-t)$, we deduce expression (7.3) for the Arrow–Debreu price. ∎

Proof of lemma 7.2. The decomposition $\xi_t=\xi_s+Z_T\delta_{tT}$ can be verified if one sets $\{\gamma_{tT}\}=\{\gamma_t/\gamma_T\}$, where $\{\gamma_t\}$ is a standard gamma process. To see that $\{\delta_{tT}\}_{s\le t\le T}$ is, for fixed s, a gamma bridge over $[s,T]$, it suffices to note that $\delta_{tT}=(\gamma_t-\gamma_s)/(\gamma_T-\gamma_t)$ and that $\{\gamma_t-\gamma_s\}_{s\le t<\infty}$ is a gamma process. In particular, we observe that the independent increments property holds, and that $\gamma_t-\gamma_s$ is gamma distributed with mean $m(t-s)$. Finally, to see that $\{\delta_{tT}\}$ is independent of ξ_s and Z_T, it suffices to show that δ_{tT}, γ_s and $\gamma_T-\gamma_s$ are independent. We have

$$\begin{aligned}
&\mathbb{Q}(\{\delta_{tT}<a\}\cap\{\gamma_T-\gamma_s<b\}\cap\{\gamma_s<c\}) = \mathbb{E}[\mathbb{1}_{\{\delta_{tT}<a\}}\mathbb{1}_{\{\gamma_T-\gamma_s<b\}}\mathbb{1}_{\{\gamma_s<c\}}]\\
&\quad= \mathbb{E}[\mathbb{E}[\mathbb{1}_{\{\delta_{tT}<a\}}\mathbb{1}_{\{\gamma_T-\gamma_s<b\}}\mathbb{1}_{\{\gamma_s<c\}}|\gamma_s]] = \mathbb{E}[\mathbb{E}[\mathbb{1}_{\{\delta_{tT}<a\}}\mathbb{1}_{\{\gamma_T-\gamma_s<b\}}|\gamma_s]\mathbb{1}_{\{\gamma_s<c\}}]\\
&\quad= \mathbb{E}[\mathbb{E}[\mathbb{1}_{\{\delta_{tT}<a\}}\mathbb{1}_{\{\gamma_T-\gamma_s<b\}}]\mathbb{1}_{\{\gamma_s<c\}}] = \mathbb{E}[\mathbb{1}_{\{\delta_{tT}<a\}}\mathbb{1}_{\{\gamma_T-\gamma_s<b\}}]\mathbb{E}[\mathbb{1}_{\{\gamma_s<c\}}]\\
&\quad= \mathbb{E}[\mathbb{1}_{\{\delta_{tT}<a\}}]\mathbb{E}[\mathbb{1}_{\{\gamma_T-\gamma_s<b\}}]\mathbb{E}[\mathbb{1}_{\{\gamma_s<c\}}].
\end{aligned} \tag{7.13}$$

Here, we have used the fact that γ_s is independent of δ_{tT} and $\gamma_T-\gamma_s$, which follows from the independent increments property of $\{\gamma_t\}$. We have also used lemma 3.3, together with the fact that we can write $\delta_{tT}=B/(A+B)$ and $\gamma_T-\gamma_s=A+B$, with $A=\gamma_T-\gamma_t$ and $B=\gamma_t-\gamma_s$, from which it follows that δ_{tT} and $\gamma_T-\gamma_s$ are independent. ■

The result of lemma 7.2 leads to a remark concerning model calibration. Suppose that the aggregate claims process is given, and we reinitialize the model at a specified intermediate time. We would like the dynamics moving forward from the intermediate time to be represented by an aggregate claims process of the same type. It follows from lemma 7.2 that the process $\{\eta_t\}_{s\le t\le T}$, defined by $\eta_t=Z_T\delta_{tT}$, is an aggregate claims process spanning the interval $[s,T]$. The random variable Z_T represents the information about X_T that is 'not yet revealed' at time s. The idea is that at time s the value of ξ_s is known, and the 'new' gains process $\{\eta_t\}_{s\le t\le T}$ begins to reveal the value of Z_T in such a way that $\eta_s=0$ and $\eta_T=Z_T$.

Alternatively, at time s we can use the knowledge of ξ_s to compute the new *a priori* density for X_T. Thus, at s the *a priori* density $p(x)$ is replaced by the *a posteriori* density $\pi_s(x)$. On account of the relation $Z_T=X_T-\xi_s$ we have

$$\mathbb{Q}[Z_T<z|\xi_s] = \mathbb{Q}[X_T<\xi_s+z|\xi_s], \tag{7.14}$$

from which it follows that the conditional density of Z_T is given at time s by $\pi_s(\xi_s+z)$. We can think of $\pi_s(\xi_s+z)$ as a new *a priori* density, now for the random variable Z_T. Given this density we calculate the conditional probability $\mathbb{Q}[Z_T<z|\eta_t]$ for $t\in[s,T]$. By the method used to establish proposition 4.1 and the probability law for the gamma bridge $\{\delta_{tT}\}$ we deduce that

$$\frac{\mathrm{d}}{\mathrm{d}z}\mathbb{Q}[Z_T<z|\eta_t] = \mathbb{1}_{\{z>\eta_t\}}\frac{\pi_s(\xi_s+z)z^{1-m(T-s)}(z-\eta_t)^{m(T-t)-1}}{\int_{\eta_t}^{\infty}\pi_s(\xi_s+z)z^{1-m(T-s)}(z-\eta_t)^{m(T-t)-1}\,\mathrm{d}z}, \tag{7.15}$$

from which we see that the value process can be represented in the following form:

$$S_t = P_{tT}\left[\xi_s + \frac{\int_{\eta_t}^{\infty}\pi_s(\xi_s+z)z^{2-m(T-s)}(z-y)^{m(T-t)-1}\,\mathrm{d}z}{\int_{\eta_t}^{\infty}\pi_s(\xi_s+z)z^{1-m(T-s)}(z-y)^{m(T-t)-1}\,\mathrm{d}z}\right]. \tag{7.16}$$

Making the substitution $z=x-\xi_s$ and also substituting $\eta_t=\xi_t-\xi_s$, we see that this expression reduces to the value process obtained in (4.4).

8. Gamma-distributed terminal gains

When the terminal payout X_T of the cumulative gains process (1.1) is gamma distributed with mean κmT and variance $\kappa^2 mT$ for some κ, the value process $\{S_t\}$ has an especially simple structure, and we are led back to the $\mathbb{Q}$-gamma model discussed in §1. This can be seen as follows. Let $\{\gamma_t\}$ be a standard gamma process with rate m and let $\{\gamma_{tT}\}$ be the associated bridge. Then X_T and $\kappa\gamma_T$ have the same distribution; but since γ_T and $\{\gamma_{tT}\}$ are independent, $\{X_T\gamma_{tT}\}$ and $\{\kappa\gamma_T\gamma_{tT}\}$ have the same probability law; therefore, $\{\xi_t\}$ has the same law as $\{\kappa\gamma_t\}$ and hence is a $\mathbb{Q}$-gamma process with scale κ and standard growth rate m. The fact that ξ_t is gamma distributed can be verified directly as follows. The characteristic function of X_T is $\phi_X(\lambda)=(1-\mathrm{i}\kappa\lambda)^{-mT}$. Substituting this into (5.22) and setting $z=(1-u)/(1-\mathrm{i}\kappa\lambda u)$, we deduce that $\Phi_\xi(\lambda)=(1-\mathrm{i}\kappa\lambda)^{-mt}$, which is the characteristic function of a gamma variable with mean κmt and variance $\kappa^2 mt$.

It is interesting to note that although the $\mathbb{Q}$-gamma process has independent increments the general cumulative gains process (1.1) has dependent increments. In particular, for the covariance of ξ_s and $\xi_t-\xi_s$ in the general case we have

$$\mathrm{cov}[\xi_s,\xi_t-\xi_s]=\frac{ms(t-s)}{T(mT+1)}\mathbb{E}[X_T^2]-\frac{s(t-s)}{T^2}(\mathbb{E}[X_T])^2. \tag{8.1}$$

Hence a necessary condition for independent increments is given by $(\mathbb{E}[X_T])^2= mT\,\mathrm{var}[X_T]$.

The value processes for various claims in the $\mathbb{Q}$-gamma model can be worked out explicitly. For the density of X_T we have the expression defined by (2.8). Substituting this into (4.4) and carrying out the integration, we are led to the following linear expression for the reserve process:

$$S_t=P_{tT}(\xi_t+\kappa m(T-t)). \tag{8.2}$$

We observe that $S_0=P_{0T}\kappa mT$ and that $S_T=X_T$, as required. An alternative derivation of (8.2) is as follows. Since $\{\xi_t\}$ is a gamma process with scale parameter κ and standardized growth rate m, by the Markov property we have $S_t=P_{tT}\mathbb{E}[\xi_T|\xi_t]$, and (8.2) follows from the independent increments property of the gamma process.

These relations lead to simplifications in the valuation of contingent claims. Let us work out the value C_{tT} at time t of a stop-loss reinsurance contract that pays $\max(X_T-K,0)$ at T for some fixed threshold K. In the $\mathbb{Q}$-gamma model we have $C_{tT}=P_{tT}\mathbb{E}[(\xi_T-K)^+|\xi_t]$, and hence by use of the independent increments property we deduce that

$$\begin{aligned} C_{tT}&=P_{tT}\int_{(K-\xi_t)/\kappa}^{\infty}(\kappa z+\xi_t-K)\frac{z^{m(T-t)-1}\mathrm{e}^{-z}}{\Gamma[m(T-t)]}\,\mathrm{d}z\\ &=P_{tT}\left[\kappa\frac{\Gamma[m(T-t)+1,(K-\xi_t)/\kappa]}{\Gamma[m(T-t)]}-(K-\xi_t)\frac{\Gamma[m(T-t),(K-\xi_t)/\kappa]}{\Gamma[m(T-t)]}\right], \end{aligned} \tag{8.3}$$

where $\Gamma[a,z]=\int_z^\infty x^{a-1}\mathrm{e}^{-x}\,\mathrm{d}x$ denotes the incomplete gamma integral.

We proceed to calculate the associated Arrow–Debreu price A_{st} in this model. By substituting (8.2) in (7.3), we deduce that

$$A_{st}(y) = P_{st}\frac{\kappa^{-m(t-s)}}{\Gamma[m(t-s)]}(y-\xi_s)^{m(t-s)-1}\exp\left(-\frac{1}{\kappa}(y-\xi_s)\right). \tag{8.4}$$

Writing $R_s = P_{tT}^{-1}K - (S_s + \kappa m(t-s))$ we see by use of (8.2) that the price at time s of a reinsurance contract with payout $(S_t - K)^+$ at t is given by

$$C_{st} = P_{st}\mathbb{E}_s[(S_t-K)^+] = \int_0^\infty A_{st}(y)[P_{tT}(y+\kappa m(T-t)) - K]^+ \,\mathrm{d}y$$

$$= P_{sT}\left[\frac{\Gamma[m(t-s)+1,\kappa^{-1}R_s]}{\Gamma[m(t-s)]} - \kappa^{-1}R_s\frac{\Gamma[m(t-s),\kappa^{-1}R_s]}{\Gamma[m(t-s)]}\right]. \tag{8.5}$$

It may be surprising that the linear martingale $\{\gamma_t - mt\}$ can be used as the basis of a model for a limited liability asset, but this is consistent with the finite time horizon over which the asset is defined. In fact, for each value of n, the associated Laguerre martingale can be 'positivized' over the time interval $[0,T]$ by the addition of suitable lower order counter terms. In particular, for each $n\in\mathbb{N}$ we consider the martingale $L_n^{-m(T-t)-n}(\gamma_t)$, $t\geq 0$, where $L_n^k(z)$ is defined as in (2.6). In this way we obtain the positive martingales (i) $\{\gamma_t + m(T-t)\}$, (ii) $\{(\gamma_t+m(T-t))^2 + m(T-t)\}$, (iii) $\{(\gamma_t+m(T-t))^3 + 3m(T-t)(\gamma_t+m(T-t)) + 2m(T-t)\}$, and so on. These processes arise naturally if we take the gamma process to be the information process associated with an X-factor (as defined in the sense of Macrina 2006 and Brody *et al.* 2007, 2008) given by the terminal value of the gamma process, and let the terminal pay-off of the asset be a polynomial in the X-factor.

This example also points towards the way in which the theory put forward here can be developed further to take into account multiple cash flows, families of interdependent assets, and filtrations of greater complexity. Each asset is defined by a series of one or more cash flows, each such cash flow being dependent on a set of one or more independent market factors (X-factors). Each X-factor has an associated information process, which may be of the Brownian bridge type considered in the references cited above, or the gamma bridge type considered here, or possibly some generalization thereof; and the market filtration is taken to be generated collectively by this set of information processes.

The authors thank M. Baxter, I. Buckley, M. Davis, E. Hoyle, A. Lokka, D. Madan, M. Parry, M. Pistorius, E. Ronn and M. Yor for stimulating discussions. L.P.H. and A.M. acknowledge support from EPSRC grant number GR/S22998/01.

References

Arjas, E. 1989 The claims reserving problem in non-life insurance: some structural ideas. *ASTIN Bull.* **19**, 139–152. (doi:10.2143/AST.19.2.2014905)

Basawa, I. V. & Brockwell, P. J. 1978 Inference for gamma and stable processes. *Biometrika* **65**, 129–133. (doi:10.1093/biomet/65.1.129)

Baxter, M. 2007*a* Lévy simple structural models. *Int. J. Theor. Appl. Finance* **10**, 593–606. (doi:10.1142/S021902490700438X)

Baxter, M. 2007*b* Gamma process dynamic modelling of credit. *Risk*. October, 98–101.
Bingham, N. H. 1975 Fluctuation theory in continuous time. *Adv. Appl. Prob.* **7**, 705–766. (doi:10.2307/1426397)
Brody, D. C., Hughston, L. P. & Macrina, A. 2007 Beyond hazard rates: a new framework to credit-risk modelling. In *Advances in mathematical finance* (eds M. Fu, R. Jarrow, J.-Y. J. Yen & R. Elliott), pp. 231–257. Basel, Switzerland: Birkhäuser.
Brody, D. C., Hughston, L. P. & Macrina, A. 2008 Information-based asset pricing. *Int. J. Theor. Appl. Finance* **11**, 107–142. (doi:10.1142/S0219024908004749)
Carr, P., Geman, H., Madan, D. B. & Yor, M. 2002 The fine structure of asset returns: an empirical investigation. *J. Business* **75**, 305–332. (doi:10.1086/338705)
Dickson, D. C. M. & Waters, H. R. 1993 Gamma processes and finite time survival probabilities. *ASTIN Bull.* **23**, 259–272. (doi:10.2143/AST.23.2.2005094)
Dufresne, F., Gerber, H. U. & Shiu, E. S. 1991 Risk theory with the gamma process. *ASTIN Bull.* **21**, 177–192. (doi:10.2143/AST.21.2.2005362)
Erdélyi, A. 1953 *Higher transcendental functions.* Bateman manuscript project, vol. 2. New York, NY: McGraw-Hill.
Gani, J. 1957 Problems in the probability theory of storage systems. *J. R. Statist. Soc. B* **19**, 181–206.
Hammersley, J. M. 1955 Storage problems. *Math. Ann.* **128**, 475–478. (doi:10.1007/BF01360150)
Heston, S. L. 1995 A model of discontinuous interest rate behaviour, yield curves, and volatility. Working paper, Washington University, St Louis.
Hughston, L. P. & Macrina, A. 2008 Information, inflation, and interest. In *Advances in mathematics of finance* (ed. L. Stettner), Warsaw, Poland: Banach Centre Publications.
Kendall, D. G. 1957 Some problems in the theory of dams. *J. R. Statist. Soc. B* **19**, 207–212.
Kingman, J. F. C. 1963 On continuous time models in the theory of dams. *J. Austral. Math. Soc.* **3**, 480–487.
Lukacs, E. 1955 Characterization of the gamma distribution. *Ann. Math. Statist.* **26**, 319–324. (doi:10.1214/aoms/1177728549)
Macrina, A. 2006 An information-based framework for asset pricing: *X*-factor theory and its applications. PhD thesis, King's College, London.
Madan, D. B. & Milne, F. 1991 Option pricing with VG martingale components. *Math. Fin.* **1**, 39–55. (doi:10.1111/j.1467-9965.1991.tb00018.x)
Madan, D. B. & Seneta, E. 1990 The variance gamma (V.G.) model for share market returns. *J. Business* **63**, 511–524. (doi:10.1086/296519)
Moran, P. A. P. 1956 A probability theory of a dam with a continuous release. *Quart. J. Math. Oxf.* **7**, 130–137. (doi:10.1093/qmath/7.1.130)
Norberg, R. 1999 Prediction of outstanding liabilities II: model variations and extensions. *ASTIN Bull.* **29**, 5–25. (doi:10.2143/AST.29.1.504603)
Protter, P. 2005 *Stochastic integration and differential equations: a new approach*, 2nd edn., 3rd printing. Berlin, Germany: Springer.
Rutkowski, M. & Yu, N. 2007 An extension of the Brody–Hughston–Macrina approach to modelling of defaultable bonds. *Int. J. Theor. Appl. Finance* **10**, 557–589. (doi:10.1142/S0219024907004263)
Schoutens, W. 2000 *Stochastic processes and orthogonal polynomials.* Lecture notes in statistics 146, Berlin, Germany: Springer.
Wiener, N. 1949 *Extrapolation, interpolation, and smoothing of stationary time series.* Cambridge, MA: MIT Press.
Yor, M. 2007 Some remarkable properties of gamma processes. In *Advances in mathematical finance* (eds M. Fu, R. Jarrow, J.-Y. J. Yen & R. Elliott), pp. 37–47. Basel, Switzerland: Birkhäuser.
Yor, M. & Émery, M. 2004 A parallel between Brownian bridges and gamma bridges. *Publ. RIMS, Kyoto Univ.* **40**, 669–688. (doi:10.2977/prims/1145475488)

Chapter 4

Informed traders†

By Dorje C. Brody[1,*], Mark H. A. Davis[1], Robyn L. Friedman[1,2] and Lane P. Hughston[1]

[1]*Department of Mathematics, Imperial College London, London SW7 2BZ, UK*
[2]*Royal Bank of Scotland, 135 Bishopsgate, London EC2M 3UR, UK*

An asymmetric information model is introduced for the situation in which there is a small agent who is more susceptible to the flow of information in the market than the general market participant, and who tries to implement strategies based on the additional information. In this model market participants have access to a stream of noisy information concerning the future return of an asset, whereas the informed trader has access to a further information source which is obscured by an additional noise that may be correlated with the market noise. The informed trader uses the extraneous information source to seek statistical arbitrage opportunities, while at the same time accommodating the additional risk. The amount of information available to the general market participant concerning the asset return is measured by the mutual information of the asset price and the associated cash flow. The worth of the additional information source is then measured in terms of the difference of mutual information between the general market participant and the informed trader. This difference is shown to be non-negative when the signal-to-noise ratio of the information flow is known in advance. Explicit trading strategies leading to statistical arbitrage opportunities, taking advantage of the additional information, are constructed, illustrating how excess information can be translated into profit.

Keywords: statistical arbitrage; asymmetric information; information-based asset pricing; hedge funds; insider trading; mutual information

1. Introduction

There are many different approaches to the modelling of so-called insider trading strategies. Starting with the work of Kyle (1985) and Back (1992), a number of investigations have been carried out (to name a few, Seyhun 1988; Amendinger *et al.* 1998; Föllmer *et al.* 1999; Back *et al.* 2000; León *et al.* 2003; Corcuera *et al.* 2004; Biagini & Øksendal 2005, 2006; Ankirchner *et al.* 2006; Campi & Çetin 2007). It is sometimes assumed in the literature that the 'insider' has direct access to the values of future asset prices. While such a scenario may indeed occasionally prevail, the more common situation is that informed agents do not have advance access to the exact values of future asset prices. How, then, do agents having high information susceptibility—when compared with the average market participant—use their strengths in reality? An increasingly popular

* Author for correspondence (dorje@imperial.ac.uk).

Received 14 November 2008
Accepted 17 November 2008
1

†This chapter was originally published as: D. C. Brody, M. H. A. Davis, R. L. Friedman & L. P. Hughston (2009) Informed Traders. *Proceedings of the Royal Society A* **465**, 1103–1122. Reprinted with kind permission from The Royal Society.

strategy adopted by some large hedge funds is to make use of publicly available information in addition to the high-frequency price data. What gives these funds an edge is their significant computational power for the data and text mining, thus allowing them to extract useful information from publicly available sources *faster* than their competitors. Against this background it is natural to ask how much added information an extra source provides, how does it affect trading strategies and more generally in what way can such information-based strategies be modelled mathematically?

The purpose of the present paper is: (i) to introduce a phenomenological approach to model the agent susceptive to information, (ii) to quantify the amount of added information, and (iii) to derive trading strategies that lead to statistical arbitrage opportunities for such an agent. Our analysis is carried out within the information-based asset pricing framework of Brody, Hughston and Macrina (Macrina 2006; Brody *et al.* 2007, 2008*a*,*b*; Rutkowski & Yu 2007; Hughston & Macrina 2008). In this framework—hereafter referred to as the BHM framework—the price process of an asset is derived from the specification of (a) the future cash flows associated with the asset, and (b) the flow of information to market participants. The price is then given by the discounted risk-adjusted expectation of the cash flows conditional on the available information.

The simplest model that arises in the BHM framework is briefly reviewed in §2. In this set-up the asset is characterized by a contract that delivers a single random cash flow at a predesignated time. Such an asset can be interpreted as having the structure of a credit-risky discount bond. In §3 we consider the problem of quantifying the amount of information contained in the bond price concerning the value of the future bond payout. To this end we determine the mutual information (Yaglom & Yaglom 1983; Cover & Thomas 1991) of these two random variables. Initially the market has no information, beyond that already implicit in the asset price, concerning the value of the cash flow. However, as time goes by, the market gathers information. When the amount of information reaches the level of the initial entropy of the cash flow, the market finally 'learns' what the value of the cash flow is. The information-theoretic analysis is extended in §4, where we show that the mutual information at time t is given by the initial uncertainty, less the expected uncertainty that remains at that time.

In §5 a simple model for an informed trader is introduced. In our approach the informed trader is more susceptive to the flow of market information than other market participants, and thus on average is able to estimate the value of the impending cash flow more quickly and accurately than the other market participants. Simulation studies show a comparison of the sample paths for the market price process and the corresponding valuations made by the informed trader, revealing various intuitive as well as counter-intuitive properties of these processes. The dynamics of the valuations estimated by the informed trader are worked out in §6, where we obtain the associated innovations representation. With a basic model for an informed trader at hand we are able to quantify the amount of added information held by the trader. This is worked out in §7, where we construct an elementary trading strategy making use of the additional information, demonstrating the existence of statistical arbitrage opportunities in such circumstances.

2. Information and asset pricing

The simplest model arising in the BHM framework can be summarized thus. We fix a probability space $(\Omega, \mathcal{F}, \mathbb{Q})$, where $\mathbb{Q}$ denotes the risk-neutral measure. We write $\mathbb{E}$ for expectation with respect to $\mathbb{Q}$. The market is not assumed to be complete, but we assume the absence of arbitrage and the existence of an established pricing kernel—these assumptions ensure the existence of a preferred pricing measure (cf. Cochrane 2005). Let X_T denote the random cash flow associated with the asset and paid at time T (for example, the payout of a credit-risky discount bond). Before time T market participants do not have direct access to the value of the cash flow. We assume, nevertheless, that partial information concerning the value of X_T, obscured by market noise, can be obtained before T. This noisy 'observation' of X_T generates the market filtration $\{\mathcal{F}_t\}$, and the price at time t is given by the risk-neutral expectation of the discounted cash flow, conditional on $\mathcal{F}_t$.

We assume that the 'signal' of the noisy observation concerning X_T is revealed to the market at a constant rate σ, that the 'noise' is generated by an independent Brownian bridge process $\{\beta_{tT}\}$, and that the market filtration is generated by an information process $\{\xi_t\}$ defined for $0 \leq t \leq T$ by

$$\xi_t = \sigma t X_T + \beta_{tT}. \tag{2.1}$$

In other words, $\{\mathcal{F}_t\} = \sigma(\{\xi_s\}_{0\leq s\leq t})$. The use of a bridge process for the noise is motivated by the idea that at time 0 all the available information about X_T is incorporated into the *a priori* distribution, and that at time T the value of X_T is revealed and there is no remaining noise: the choice of a Brownian bridge is made for simplicity and tractability. If we further assume that the default-free system of interest rates is deterministic and let $\{P_{tT}\}$ denote the price at time t of a discount bond that matures at T, then the price of the credit-risky discount bond at time t is given by $B_{tT} = P_{tT}\mathbb{E}[X_T|\mathcal{F}_t]$. In the case where X_T takes the discrete values $\{x_i\}_{i=1,\dots,n}$ with the *a priori* probabilities $\{p_i\}_{i=1,\dots,n}$, a calculation shows that

$$B_{tT} = P_{tT}\frac{\sum_{i=1}^{n} p_i x_i \exp\left[\frac{T}{T-t}\left(\sigma x_i \xi_t - \frac{1}{2}\sigma^2 x_i^2 t\right)\right]}{\sum_{i=1}^{n} p_i \exp\left[\frac{T}{T-t}\left(\sigma x_i \xi_t - \frac{1}{2}\sigma^2 x_i^2 t\right)\right]}. \tag{2.2}$$

This follows from the fact that the conditional risk-neutral probability defined by $\pi_{it} = \mathbb{Q}(X_T = x_i|\mathcal{F}_t)$ takes the form

$$\pi_{it} = \frac{p_i \exp\left[\frac{T}{T-t}\left(\sigma x_i \xi_t - \frac{1}{2}\sigma^2 x_i^2 t\right)\right]}{\sum_{i=1}^{n} p_i \exp\left[\frac{T}{T-t}\left(\sigma x_i \xi_t - \frac{1}{2}\sigma^2 x_i^2 t\right)\right]}. \tag{2.3}$$

By taking the stochastic differential of (2.2) one finds that the dynamical equation satisfied by the bond price is

$$\mathrm{d}B_{tT} = r_t B_{tT}\,\mathrm{d}t + \frac{\sigma T}{T-t} P_{tT} V_{tT}\,\mathrm{d}W_t, \tag{2.4}$$

where $r_t = -\partial \ln P_{0t}/\partial t$, and where the process $\{W_t\}$ defined by the expression

$$W_t = \xi_t + \int_0^t \frac{1}{T-s}\xi_s \, ds - \sigma T \int_0^t \frac{1}{T-s}\hat{X}_s \, ds \tag{2.5}$$

turns out to be a standard $\{\mathcal{F}_t\}$-Brownian motion. Here, $\hat{X}_t = \sum_{i=1}^n x_i \pi_{it}$ denotes the conditional expectation of the cash flow X_T, and

$$V_{tT} = \sum_{i=1}^n (x_i - \hat{X}_t)^2 \pi_{it} \tag{2.6}$$

is the conditional variance of X_T (see Macrina 2006 and Brody *et al.* 2007 for derivations of the foregoing results).

We observe that in the information-based framework it is possible to *deduce* the diffusive dynamics (2.4) for the price process, starting from the specification of the cash flow X_T and the information process $\{\xi_t\}$. The theme that underlies this framework is that the market acts as a 'signal processor' for future cash flows so as to generate the dynamics of asset prices. This point of view is natural as a basis for understanding the elements of price formation, since investment decisions are often made in accordance with the perceptions of market participants concerning the future cash flows associated with a given asset.

As far as the market filtration is concerned, the information contained in $\{\xi_t\}$ is equivalent to that in $\{B_{tT}\}$: we have $\sigma(\{\xi_s\}_{0\le s\le t}) = \sigma(\{B_{sT}\}_{0\le s\le t})$. This follows from the fact that one can write $B_{tT} = B(t, \xi_t)$, where

$$B(t,x) = P_{tT} \frac{\sum_{i=1}^n p_i x_i \exp\left[\frac{T}{T-t}\left(\sigma x_i x - \frac{1}{2}\sigma^2 x_i^2 t\right)\right]}{\sum_{i=1}^n p_i \exp\left[\frac{T}{T-t}\left(\sigma x_i x - \frac{1}{2}\sigma^2 x_i^2 t\right)\right]}, \tag{2.7}$$

from which by differentiation we deduce that

$$B'(t,x) = \frac{\sigma T P_{tT}}{T-t} \frac{\sum_{i=1}^n p_i [x_i - B(t,x)/P_{tT}]^2 \exp\left[\frac{T}{T-t}\left(\sigma x_i x - \frac{1}{2}\sigma^2 x_i^2 t\right)\right]}{\sum_{i=1}^n p_i \exp\left[\frac{T}{T-t}\left(\sigma x_i x - \frac{1}{2}\sigma^2 x_i^2 t\right)\right]}, \tag{2.8}$$

which is positive. Therefore, $B(t, x)$ is monotonically increasing in x, and hence invertible. It follows that from knowledge of the trajectory $\{\xi_s\}_{0\le s\le t}$, one can construct $\{B_{sT}\}_{0\le s\le t}$; conversely from knowledge of the trajectory $\{B_{sT}\}_{0\le s\le t}$ one can construct $\{\xi_s\}_{0\le s\le t}$.

3. Amount of information about the future cash flow contained in the price process

We would like to quantify how much information regarding the value of the cash flow X_T is contained in the value at time t of the information process (2.1). A reasonable measure for such quantification is given by the mutual information $J(\xi_t, X_T)$ between the two random variables (Shannon & Weaver 1949; Gel'fand *et al.* 1956; Gel'fand & Yaglom 1957), which in the present context is given by the expression

$$J(\xi_t, X_T) = \sum_{i=1}^{n} \int_{-\infty}^{\infty} \rho_{\xi X}(x, i) \ln\left(\frac{\rho_{\xi X}(x, i)}{\rho_\xi(x)\rho_X(i)}\right) \mathrm{d}x, \tag{3.1}$$

where

$$\rho_{\xi X}(x, i) = \frac{\mathrm{d}}{\mathrm{d}x}\mathbb{Q}[(\xi_t < x) \cap (X_T = x_i)] \tag{3.2}$$

is the joint density function of the random variables (ξ_t, X_T), and where $\rho_\xi(x)$ and $\rho_X(i)$ are the respective marginal probabilities. By use of the relation

$$\mathbb{Q}[(\xi_t < x) \cap (X_T = x_i)] = \mathbb{Q}(\xi_t < x \,|\, X_T = x_i)\mathbb{Q}(X_T = x_i) \tag{3.3}$$

we deduce that

$$\rho_{\xi X}(x, i) = p_i \frac{1}{\sqrt{2\pi t(T-t)/T}} \exp\left(-\frac{1}{2}\frac{(x-\sigma x_i t)^2}{t(T-t)/T}\right), \tag{3.4}$$

since conditional on $X_T = x_i$ the random variable ξ_t is normally distributed with mean $\sigma x_i t$ and variance $t(T-t)/T$. From (3.4) the marginal densities

$$\rho_\xi(x) = \sum_{i=1}^{n} \rho_{\xi X}(x, i) \quad \text{and} \quad \rho_X(i) = \int_{-\infty}^{\infty} \rho_{\xi X}(x, i)\mathrm{d}x \tag{3.5}$$

can be deduced at once. In particular, we have $\rho_X(i) = p_i$, as it should.

An alternative way of deriving the mutual information in this context is to make use of the identity

$$J(\xi_t, X_T) = H(\xi_t) - H(\xi_t \,|\, X_T). \tag{3.6}$$

Here $H(\xi_t) = -\mathbb{E}[\ln \rho_\xi(\xi_t)]$ is the entropy of the random variable ξ_t (Wiener 1948; Khintchine 1953) and $H(\xi_t|X_T) = -\mathbb{E}[\ln \rho_\xi(\xi_t|X_T)]$ is the entropy of ξ_t conditional on X_T. The conditional density function $\rho_\xi(x|X_T)$, $x \in \mathbb{R}$, is defined by $\rho_\xi(x|X_T) = \mathrm{d}\mathbb{Q}(\xi_t < x|X_T)/\mathrm{d}x$. Since conditional on X_T both of the random variables ξ_t and β_{tT} are normally distributed, with the same variance $t(T-t)/T$, and since the entropy of a normally distributed random variable is independent of its mean, we find that $H(\xi_t|X_T) = H(\beta_{tT})$. In other words, the mutual information in the present context is given by the difference of the two entropies:

$$J(\xi_t, X_T) = H(\xi_t) - H(\beta_{tT}). \tag{3.7}$$

As a consequence, the information about the cash flow X_T contained in ξ_t can be determined (a different approach to extracting information concerning the asymptotic dividend stream from option price data is considered in Geman *et al.* 2007).

From an information-theoretic point of view, a pair of processes related through an invertible smooth function, and thus sharing the *same* filtration, in general possess *different* information content (entropy). On the other hand, since what is directly observed in the market is the price B_{tT}, which is an invertible function of ξ_t, one might argue that it is more relevant to determine the mutual information $J(B_{tT}, X_T)$, that is, the amount of information about the future cash flow contained in the market price. However, since mutual information is given

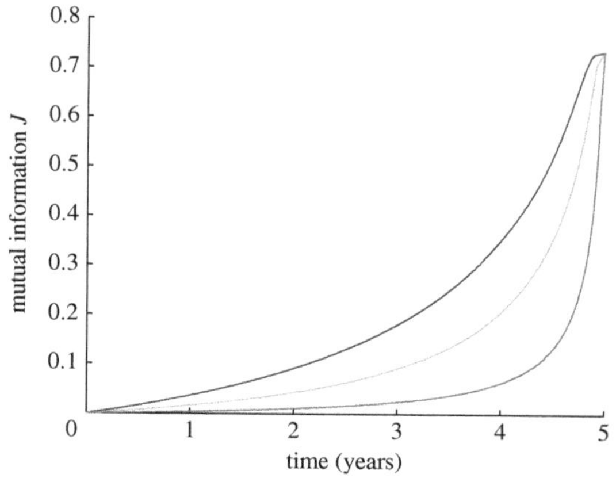

Figure 1. Mutual information J contained in the price B_{tT} concerning the value of the cash flow X_T. Early observation of the price yields little information concerning the value of X_T. As time progresses, the market extracts more information about X_T; eventually, close to the date when the value of X_T is revealed, the amount of information gained by the market reaches $-\sum_i p_i \ln p_i$. The parameters are chosen to be $h_1 = 0$, $h_2 = 0.5$, $h_3 = 1$, $p_1 = 0.1$, $p_2 = 0.15$, $p_3 = 0.75$ and $T=5$. The three plots correspond to $\sigma = 0.75$ (black curve), $\sigma = 0.5$ (grey curve) and $\sigma = 0.25$ (dark grey curve). The terminal value of J in these examples is approximately 0.73.

by a difference of entropies, and since changes in the two entropies resulting from the transform cancel, we have $J(B_{tT}, X_T) = J(\xi_t, X_T)$. Therefore, the amount of information about X_T contained in B_{tT} is given by (3.7).

In figure 1 we plot the mutual information $J(B_{tT}, X_T)$ as a function of $t \in [0, T]$ for three values of the information flow-rate parameter σ. The information gained by market participants increases more rapidly as σ is raised. On the other hand, the dynamical relation (2.4) shows that the value of σ determines the overall magnitude of the price volatility. Thus, it is possible to quantify the market information gain and to compare this with the price volatility.

To see how entropy transforms under a nonlinear invertible map, suppose that X is a random variable with density $p(x)$, and that Y is another random variable given by $Y = f(x)$, where $f(x)$ is smooth and invertible. Then the density function for Y is given by $q(y) = p(f^{-1}(y))/f'(f^{-1}(y))$. Substituting this in $H(Y) = -\int q(y) \ln q(y)\, \mathrm{d}y$ and changing variables by setting $y = f(x)$, we find that $H(Y) = H(X) + \int p(x) \ln f'(x) \mathrm{d}x$. As a consequence, we have

$$H(B_{tT}) = H(\xi_t) + \int_{-\infty}^{\infty} \rho_\xi(x) \ln B'(t, x) \mathrm{d}x, \tag{3.8}$$

where $B'(t, x) = \partial B(t, x)/\partial x$. The advantage of this expression is that we need not determine the inverse of the function $B(t, x)$ defined in (2.7) in order to calculate $H(B_{tT})$. From (2.8) it follows that

$$\int_{-\infty}^{\infty} \rho_\xi(x) \ln B'(t, x) \mathrm{d}x = \mathbb{E}\left[\ln\left(\frac{\sigma T}{T-t} P_{tT} V_{tT}\right)\right]. \tag{3.9}$$

In other words, the difference between $H(B_{tT})$ and $H(\xi_t)$ is the average log volatility of the price process at time t.

4. Analysis of information measures

We proceed in this section to consider the Shannon–Wiener entropy associated with the conditional risk-neutral probabilities. The analysis of the entropy leads to insights into the qualitative behaviour of the asset price volatility. The Shannon–Wiener entropy is defined by the expression

$$H_t = -\sum_{i=1}^{n} \pi_{it} \ln \pi_{it}. \tag{4.1}$$

We shall demonstrate that the mutual information (3.1) and the entropy (4.1) are related as follows:

$$J(\xi_t, X_T) = H_0 - \mathbb{E}[H_t]. \tag{4.2}$$

Thus, the mutual information at time t is given by the initial uncertainty, less the expected uncertainty that still remains at that time.

The derivation of (4.2) proceeds in two steps. First we shall show that

$$\mathbb{E}[H_t] = H_0 - \frac{1}{2}\mathbb{E}\left[\int_0^t \frac{\sigma^2 T^2}{(T-s)^2} V_{sT}\, \mathrm{d}s\right], \tag{4.3}$$

and then we show that

$$J(\xi_t, X_T) = \frac{1}{2}\mathbb{E}\left[\int_0^t \frac{\sigma^2 T^2}{(T-s)^2} V_{sT}\, \mathrm{d}s\right]. \tag{4.4}$$

Proof of (4.3). Let us begin by deriving the dynamical equation satisfied by the Shannon–Wiener entropy. From (2.3) and (2.5) we find that the conditional probability satisfies

$$\mathrm{d}\pi_{it} = \frac{\sigma T}{T-t}(x_i - \hat{X}_t)\pi_{it}\, \mathrm{d}W_t. \tag{4.5}$$

It follows, by an application of Ito's lemma to (4.1), that

$$H_t = H_0 - \frac{1}{2}\int_0^t \frac{\sigma^2 T^2}{(T-s)^2} V_{st}\, \mathrm{d}s - \int_0^t \frac{\sigma T}{T-s}\left(\sum_{i=1}^{n}(x_i - \hat{X}_s)\pi_{is} \ln \pi_{is}\right)\mathrm{d}W_s. \tag{4.6}$$

Taking the expectation of both sides of (4.6), we obtain (4.3), as desired. ■

Proof of (4.4). In Gel'fand & Yaglom (1957) it is shown that the mutual information can be expressed as the expectation of the log density of the joint measure $\mu_{\xi X}$ with respect to the product measure $\mu_\xi \otimes \mu_X$:

$$J(\xi_t, X_T) = \mathbb{E}\left[\ln \frac{\mathrm{d}\mu_{\xi X}}{\mathrm{d}(\mu_\xi \otimes \mu_X)}\right]. \tag{4.7}$$

We are thus required to determine the relevant Radon–Nikodym derivative. We shall follow the line of argument presented in Davis (1978); see also Duncan (1970). To proceed, we require the introduction of an auxiliary measure $\mathbb{B}$ introduced in Macrina (2006) and Brody *et al.* (2007, 2008*a*). This is the so-called bridge measure under which the information process $\{\xi_t\}$ becomes a Brownian bridge. The argument goes as follows. We fix the probability space $(\Omega,\mathcal{F},\mathbb{Q})$ with a filtration $\{\mathcal{H}_t\}_{0\leq t<\infty}$, and introduce a $\mathbb{Q}$-Brownian motion $\{B_t\}$ such that the Brownian bridge $\{\beta_{tT}\}$ appearing in (2.1) is given by

$$\beta_{tT} = (T-t)\int_0^t \frac{1}{T-s}\,\mathrm{d}B_s. \tag{4.8}$$

This is the standard integral representation for a Brownian bridge (Hida 1980; Protter 2005). Setting $\nu_t=\sigma T/(T-t)$ we define

$$\Lambda_t^{-1} = \exp\left(-\int_0^t \nu_s X_T\,\mathrm{d}B_s - \frac{1}{2}\int_0^t \nu_s^2 X_T^2\,\mathrm{d}s\right), \tag{4.9}$$

where X_T is $\mathbb{Q}$-independent of $\{B_t\}$ and is $\mathcal{H}_0$-measurable. For fixed $u<T$ we introduce the measure $\mathbb{B}$ on $\mathcal{H}_u$ by writing

$$\mathrm{d}\mathbb{B} = \Lambda_u^{-1}\,\mathrm{d}\mathbb{Q}. \tag{4.10}$$

Then the process $\{W_t^*\}_{0\leq t\leq u}$ defined by

$$W_t^* = \int_0^t \nu_s X_T\,\mathrm{d}s + B_t \tag{4.11}$$

is a $\mathbb{B}$-Brownian motion, since $\nu_s X_T$ is bounded for any $s\leq u$.

Under $\mathbb{B}$ we find that the distribution of X_T is the same as it is under $\mathbb{Q}$, that $\{\xi_t\}$ and X_T are independent, and that $\{\xi_t\}$ is a $\mathbb{B}$-Brownian bridge (cf. Brody *et al.* 2008*a*). To see these, recall that, since X_T and $\{\beta_{tT}\}$, and hence X_T and $\{B_t\}$, are independent, the probability law of $\{B_t\}$ conditional on X_T remains that of a Brownian motion. Now take a bounded function $f(x)$ and consider

$$\mathbb{E}^{\mathbb{B}}[f(X_T)] = \mathbb{E}\left[f(X_T)\mathbb{E}[\Lambda_u^{-1}\,|\,X_T]\right]. \tag{4.12}$$

Conditional on X_T, Λ_u^{-1} takes the form of a Girsanov exponential, since $\{B_t\}$ is a $\mathbb{Q}$-Brownian motion. Therefore, the inner expectation equals unity, and we find

$$\mathbb{E}^{\mathbb{B}}[f(X_T)] = \mathbb{E}[f(X_T)] \tag{4.13}$$

for every bounded function $f(x)$. In other words, X_T has the same probability law under $\mathbb{Q}$ and $\mathbb{B}$. In a similar manner, for any sequence of times $t_1,\ldots,t_n\in[0,u]$ and any bounded function $g:\mathbb{R}^n\to\mathbb{R}$, we wish to calculate

$$\mathbb{E}^{\mathbb{B}}[f(X_T)g(\xi_{t_1},\ldots,\xi_{t_n})] = \mathbb{E}\left[f(X_T)\mathbb{E}\left[g(\xi_{t_1},\ldots,\xi_{t_n})\Lambda_u^{-1}\,|\,X_T\right]\right]. \tag{4.14}$$

By the same argument as above, for each X_T the process $\{W_t^*|_{X_T}\}_{0\leq t\leq u}$ is Brownian under the measure whose density is $\Lambda_u^{-1}|_{X_T}$. Since $\{W_t^*\}_{0\leq t\leq u}$ itself is Brownian under $\mathbb{B}$, we have

$$\mathbb{E}\left[g(\xi_{t_1},\ldots,\xi_{t_n})\Lambda_u^{-1}\,|\,X_T\right] = \mathbb{E}^{\mathbb{B}}[g(\xi_{t_1},\ldots,\xi_{t_n})], \tag{4.15}$$

and hence

$$\mathbb{E}^{\mathbb{B}}[f(X_T)g(\xi_{t_1},\ldots,\xi_{t_n})] = \mathbb{E}[f(X_T)]\mathbb{E}^{\mathbb{B}}[g(\xi_{t_1},\ldots,\xi_{t_n})]. \tag{4.16}$$

However, $\mathbb{B}$ and $\mathbb{Q}$ coincide on X_T so that $\mathbb{E}^{\mathbb{B}}[f(X_T)] = \mathbb{E}[f(X_T)]$, from which it follows that X_T and $\{\xi_t\}$ are $\mathbb{B}$-independent. By combining (4.8) and (4.11) we get

$$\mathrm{d}W_t^* = \nu_t X_T \,\mathrm{d}t + \frac{1}{T-t}\beta_{tT}\,\mathrm{d}t + \mathrm{d}\beta_{tT}. \tag{4.17}$$

Eliminating β_{tT} by the use of $\beta_{tT}=\xi_t-\sigma t X_T$ we obtain the relation

$$\mathrm{d}\xi_t = -\frac{1}{T-t}\xi_t\,\mathrm{d}t + \mathrm{d}W_t^*, \tag{4.18}$$

which is the dynamical equation satisfied by a Brownian bridge in the $\mathbb{B}$-measure.

Let Ψ be the map $\omega \rightarrow \{\{\xi_t(\omega)\}_{0\le t\le u}, X_T(\omega)\}$. Then the joint sample space measure of $\{\{\xi_t(\omega)\}, X_T(\omega)\}$ is $\mu_{\xi X}(A)=\mathbb{Q}(\Psi^{-1}(A))$ for any measurable set A, and the sample space measure of X_T is $\mu_X(A')=\mathbb{Q}(X_T^{-1}(A'))$ for any measurable set A'. However, since $\{\xi_t\}$ and X_T are independent under $\mathbb{B}$, and $\{\xi_t\}$ is a $\mathbb{B}$-Brownian bridge, we have $\mu_X \otimes \mu_\beta(A)=\mathbb{B}(\Psi^{-1}(A))$. It follows from (4.9) that

$$\frac{\mathrm{d}\mathbb{Q}}{\mathrm{d}\mathbb{B}} = \exp\left(\int_0^u \nu_s X_T\,\mathrm{d}B_s + \frac{1}{2}\int_0^u \nu_s^2 X_T^2\,\mathrm{d}s\right). \tag{4.19}$$

Substituting (4.11) in here we thus deduce that

$$\frac{\mathrm{d}\mu_{\xi X}}{\mathrm{d}(\mu_X \otimes \mu_\beta)} = \exp\left(\int_0^u \nu_s X_T\,\mathrm{d}W_s^* - \frac{1}{2}\int_0^u \nu_s^2 X_T^2\,\mathrm{d}s\right). \tag{4.20}$$

Turning to the innovations representation (2.5) we find, along with (4.18), that $\{W_t\}$ and $\{W_t^*\}$ are related according to

$$\mathrm{d}W_t^* = \nu_t \hat{X}_t\,\mathrm{d}t + \mathrm{d}W_t. \tag{4.21}$$

Thus, following a similar line of argument we obtain

$$\frac{\mathrm{d}\mu_\xi}{\mathrm{d}\mu_\beta} = \exp\left(\int_0^u \nu_s \hat{X} s\,\mathrm{d}W_s^* - \frac{1}{2}\int_0^u \nu_s^2 \hat{X}_s^2\,\mathrm{d}s\right), \tag{4.22}$$

which is a version of the likelihood ratio formula of Kailath (1971). The measure μ_ξ thus corresponds to the 'signal present' situation, while the 'signal absent' case corresponds to $\{\xi_t\}$ being pure bridge noise with measure μ_β. Combining (4.20) and (4.22), and making use of (4.20), we deduce that

$$\frac{\mathrm{d}\mu_{\xi X}}{\mathrm{d}(\mu_\xi \otimes \mu_X)} = \exp\left(\int_0^u \nu_s (X_T - \hat{X}_s)\mathrm{d}B_s + \frac{1}{2}\int_0^u \nu_s^2 (X_T - \hat{X}_s)^2\,\mathrm{d}s\right). \tag{4.23}$$

Taking the expectation of the logarithm of this, bearing in mind that $\{B_t\}$ is a $\mathbb{Q}$-Brownian motion, we recover (4.4), as claimed. ■

The entropy process $\{H_t\}_{0\le t<T}$ has the property that $\lim_{t\to T} H_t=0$. This follows from the fact that the conditional probability process $\{\pi_{it}\}_{0\le t<T}$ has the limiting behaviour

$$\lim_{t\to T} \pi_{it}(\omega) = \mathbb{1}\{X_T(\omega) = x_i\} \tag{4.24}$$

for $i=1, \ldots, n$.

Proof of (4.24). Let $\omega \in \Omega$ be fixed, and suppose that $X_T(\omega) = x_k$ for some k. For this realization of ω the information process is given by $\xi_t = \sigma t x_k + \beta_{tT}$. Substituting this expression for ξ_t into (2.3) and dividing the denominator and the numerator by the exponential factor appearing in the numerator, we deduce that

$$\pi_{kt} = \frac{p_k}{p_k + \sum_{j \neq k} p_j \exp\left[\frac{T}{T-t}\left(\sigma(x_j - x_k)\beta_{tT} - \frac{1}{2}\sigma^2 t (x_j - x_k)^2\right)\right]}. \tag{4.25}$$

Observe that all of the terms in the sum in the denominator vanish as t approaches T, and therefore $\lim_{t \to T} \pi_{kt} = 1$. It follows that $\lim_{t \to T} \pi_{it} = 0$ for $i \neq k$, and thus (4.24). Finally, since $H_t = -\ln \prod_{i=1}^{n} \pi_{it}^{\pi_{it}}$ by (4.1) and since $\lim_{t \to T} \pi_{it}^{\pi_{it}} = 1$, we deduce that $\lim_{t \to T} H_t = 0$. ∎

If we let t approach T in (4.3), we find the following relation:

$$H_0 = \frac{1}{2} \mathbb{E}\left[\int_0^T \frac{\sigma^2 T^2}{(T-s)^2} V_{sT} \, \mathrm{d}s\right]. \tag{4.26}$$

Since H_0 is bounded by $\ln n$, where n is the number of values X_T can take, and since the coefficient of the conditional variance $\{V_{sT}\}$ in the integrand diverges quadratically as s approaches T, this relationship shows that the variance process has to decay sufficiently rapidly to ensure the existence of the right-hand side of (4.26). On the other hand, the conditional variance also generates the random movement of the asset price volatility in (2.4). As a consequence, we are able to obtain a crude estimate of the magnitude of the cumulative volatility. It is worth noting that in the models based on Brownian noise, the entropy and mutual information are closely related to the prices of variance or volatility derivatives. A related observation has been made by Soklakov (2008).

It should be remarked that the limiting behaviour $\lim_{t \to T} H_t = 0$ is specific to the case in which X_T takes discrete values. If X_T is a continuous random variable, then the associated entropy has the property that $\lim_{t \to T} H_t = -\infty$, which can be seen from the Hirschman inequality in Fourier analysis (Beckner 1975):

$$H_t \leq \frac{1}{2}(1 + \ln(2\pi)) + \frac{1}{2} \ln V_{tT}. \tag{4.27}$$

It follows from (4.6) that the variance process $\{V_{sT}\}$ in this case does not vanish sufficiently rapidly to ensure finiteness of the right-hand side of (4.3) as t approaches T. In other words, there is a qualitative difference in the behaviour of the volatility process, depending on whether the cash flow is a continuous or discrete random variable. In particular, the volatility products may be overpriced in models based on continuous cash flows, since the real market cash flows are not continuous.

5. A model for an informed trader

In the previous sections we have examined the BHM framework from an information-theoretic perspective. In particular, we have been able to quantify the amount of information about the future cash flow of an asset contained in its price. We turn now to consider a model for an informed trader who has access to an additional information source, apart from the price process itself, concerning the future return of an asset. We assume that the informed trader is 'small' in the sense that access to the additional information is limited, and that the actions of the informed trader will not impact the price process. In other words, the model is not for a large number of small agents; rather, it is for a single agent, or a highly restricted number of agents, who carefully execute their trading strategies, taking advantage of the additional information.

One might expect that the use of additional information gives a *definite* advantage for the trader. This, however, is not necessarily the case: additional information is in general obscured by additional noise. As a consequence, the valuation process estimated by the informed trader can entail higher volatility than the actual market price movements. It follows that any strategy making use of additional information will tend to embody additional risk. Nevertheless, on the whole such strategies are expected to outperform the market, and this is the idea behind some of the statistical arbitrage schemes adopted by hedge funds.

The BHM framework is sufficiently flexible to model this kind of scenario. Indeed, the use of this approach as a basis for the development of insider-trading models was recognized early on (Macrina 2006). Our intention here is to apply such ideas to describe the disparity in the ability of processing publicly available information, and to illustrate how statistical arbitrage opportunities can be seen to arise in a simple model. It should be emphasized that many of the simplifying assumptions—that the asset entails a single cash flow, that the information flow rates are constants, that the interest rate is deterministic, and that the noises are modelled by Brownian bridges—can be relaxed without affecting the main qualitative features of the model.

We assume the set-up for the market outlined in §2. There is additionally, however, an informed trader who has a further noisy information source represented by the information process

$$\xi'_t = \sigma' t X_T + \beta'_{tT}. \tag{5.1}$$

The noise term $\{\beta'_{tT}\}$ may or may not be correlated with the market noise $\{\beta_{tT}\}$. We let $\{B_t\}$ and $\{B'_t\}$ be a pair of Brownian motions with correlation ρ, and define the associated Brownian bridges by

$$\beta_{tT} = B_t - \frac{t}{T} B_T \quad \text{and} \quad \beta'_{tT} = B'_t - \frac{t}{T} B'_T. \tag{5.2}$$

In this way we can model the two noise terms with a fair amount of generality (we may use alternatively the integral representation (4.8) to construct the bridge processes; however, the choice (5.2) is more suitable for simulation purposes), since ρ determines the correlation of $\{\beta_{tT}\}$ and $\{\beta'_{tT}\}$. In particular, if $|\rho|=1$ then the informed trader has two linear equations (2.1) and (5.1) for the two unknowns X_T and β_{tT}; hence the value of the future cash flow X_T will become instantly accessible to the trader (assuming $|\sigma| \neq |\sigma'|$). This situation corresponds to the fully-informed insider often considered in the literature. The other extreme, for which $|\rho| \ll 1$, is of interest, since the informed trader must choose a strategy optimally to avoid being overwhelmed by the additional noise.

Let $\{\mathcal{F}'_t\}$ denote the filtration generated by $\{\xi'_t\}$. If $\sigma' > \sigma$, then knowledge of the value of X_T is revealed at a faster rate in the 'primed' filtration. This, however, does not mean that $\{\mathcal{F}_t\}$ is contained in $\{\mathcal{F}'_t\}$ even if $\rho=1$; the two filtrations are merely inequivalent. On the other hand, since the informed trader also has access to the price process, which is adapted to $\{\mathcal{F}_t\}$, it is reasonable to assume that the information source is given by $\{\mathcal{G}_t\}=\sigma(\{\xi_s,\xi'_s\}_{0\le s\le t})$. We assume that the additional information commences at time $t=0$; hence, the *a priori* probabilities $\{p_i\}$ for X_T to take the values $\{x_i\}$ remain the same. This assumption may seem limiting; however, it is not unreasonable since the 'lifetime' of the extra information, i.e. the period over which extra information has value, is often short in practice.

The informed trader will use the extra information to work out the price that the market would have made had $\{\mathcal{G}_t\}$ been accessible to general market participants. We shall now calculate the valuation process made by the informed trader on this basis. From the Markov property of the joint information process $\{\xi_t,\xi'_t\}$ we find that the informed valuation process is given by

$$\tilde{B}_{tT} = P_{tT}\sum_{i=1}^{n} x_i\tilde{\pi}_{it}, \tag{5.3}$$

where $\tilde{\pi}_{it}=\mathbb{Q}(X_T=x_i\,|\,\xi_t,\xi'_t)$. By the use of the Bayes formula

$$\tilde{\pi}_{it} = \frac{p_i\rho(\xi_t,\xi'_t\,|\,X_T=x_i)}{\sum_{i=0}^{n} p_i\rho(\xi_t,\xi'_t\,|\,X_T=x_i)}, \tag{5.4}$$

where the conditional density is given by the bivariate normal density function

$$\rho(\xi_t,\xi'_t\,|\,X_T=x_i) = \frac{T}{2\pi t(T-t)\sqrt{1-\rho^2}}\exp\Bigg[-\frac{T}{2(1-\rho^2)}$$
$$\times\left(\frac{(\xi_t-\sigma x_i t)^2}{t(T-t)}-\frac{2\rho(\xi_t-\sigma x_i t)(\xi'_t-\sigma' x_i t)}{t(T-t)}+\frac{(\xi'_t-\sigma' x_i t)^2}{t(T-t)}\right)\Bigg], \tag{5.5}$$

we deduce that

$$\tilde{B}_{tT} = P_{tT}\frac{\sum_{i=1}^{n} p_i x_i \exp\left[\frac{T}{\varrho(T-t)}\left(x_i(\sigma_1\xi_t+\sigma_2\xi'_t)-\frac{1}{2}\sigma_3^2x_i^2t\right)\right]}{\sum_{i=1}^{n} p_i \exp\left[\frac{T}{\varrho(T-t)}\left(x_i(\sigma_1\xi_t+\sigma_2\xi'_t)-\frac{1}{2}\sigma_3^2x_i^2t\right)\right]}. \tag{5.6}$$

Here we set $\sigma_1=\sigma-\rho\sigma'$, $\sigma_2=\sigma'-\rho\sigma$, $\sigma_3^2=\sigma^2-2\rho\sigma\sigma'+\sigma'^2$ and $\varrho=1-\rho^2$.

The process (5.6) is our model for the valuation made by the informed trader. It is straightforward to simulate the informed valuation process $\{\tilde{B}_{tT}\}$ and compare this against the uninformed market price process $\{B_{tT}\}$. By suitably adjusting the values for σ, σ' and ρ, we are able to confirm various intuitive aspects of the behaviour of these processes; some examples are displayed in figure 2. With respect to any given sample path, the valuation of the informed trader at time $t\in[0,T]$ may be less accurate (by 'accurate' we mean close to the true value) than the market price. However, on average the valuation determined by the informed trader converges more rapidly to the true value of the bond. This is illustrated in figure 3 where we plot the averaged sample paths conditional on the given outcome.

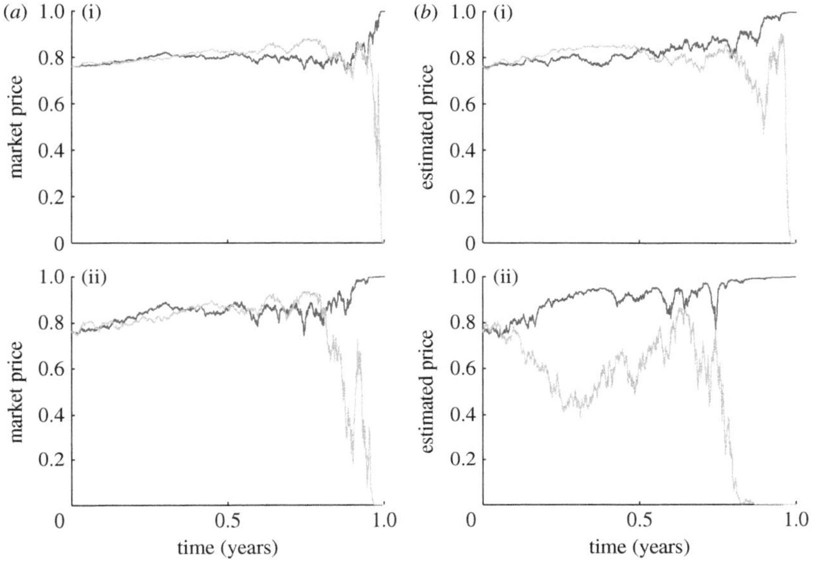

Figure 2. Sample paths comparison for a defaultable digital bond. Each plot contains a pair of sample paths: one for which the bond does not default and the other for which the bond defaults. (*a*) The market prices with (i) $\sigma=0.25$ and (ii) $\sigma=0.7$. (*b*) The market prices can be compared with the valuations estimated by the informed trader. The parameters are chosen to be (i) $\sigma'=0.4$, $\rho=0.1$ and (ii) $\sigma'=0.01$, $\rho=0.9$. In all plots, the other parameters are set to be $h_1=0$, $h_2=1$, $p_0=0.2$, $p_1=0.8$, $r=0.05$ and $T=1$.

Figure 3*b* indicates that the performance of the informed trader is high even if the signal-to-noise ratio σ' of the additional information source is set to zero (and hence $\{\xi'_t\}$ is pure noise). In fact the quality of the estimate decreases as the value of σ' is raised from zero, until it reaches the critical level $\sigma'=\rho\sigma$. Putting the matter differently, we observe that the quality of the estimate made by an informed trader is not monotonic in the signal-to-noise ratio of the additional information source. This feature may appear counter-intuitive, but it can be understood by rearrangement of (5.6) into a form analogous to (4.5):

$$\tilde{B}_{tT}=P_{tT}\frac{p_k x_k+\sum_{i\neq k}p_i x_i\exp\left[\frac{T}{\varrho(T-t)}\left((1-\rho)(\sigma+\sigma')\omega_{ik}\beta_{tT}-\frac{1}{2}\sigma_3^2\omega_{ik}^2 t\right)\right]}{p_k+\sum_{i\neq k}p_i\exp\left[\frac{T}{\varrho(T-t)}\left((1-\rho)(\sigma+\sigma')\omega_{ik}\beta_{tT}-\frac{1}{2}\sigma_3^2\omega_{ik}^2 t\right)\right]}. \tag{5.7}$$

Here we write $\omega_{ik}=x_i-x_k$. This expression shows that the exponential rate of convergence for the process $\{\tilde{B}_{tT}\}$ to approach the 'true' value x_k is governed by the ratio $\sigma_3^2 tT/[2\varrho(T-t)]$. In particular, for fixed σ and ρ this ratio takes a minimum value at $\sigma'=\rho\sigma$. When $\sigma'=\rho\sigma$, the linear equations $\xi_t=\sigma tX_T+\beta_{tT}$ and $\xi'_t=\sigma' tX_T+\beta'_{tT}$ become the closest to being degenerate, and hence the value of the additional information is minimized.

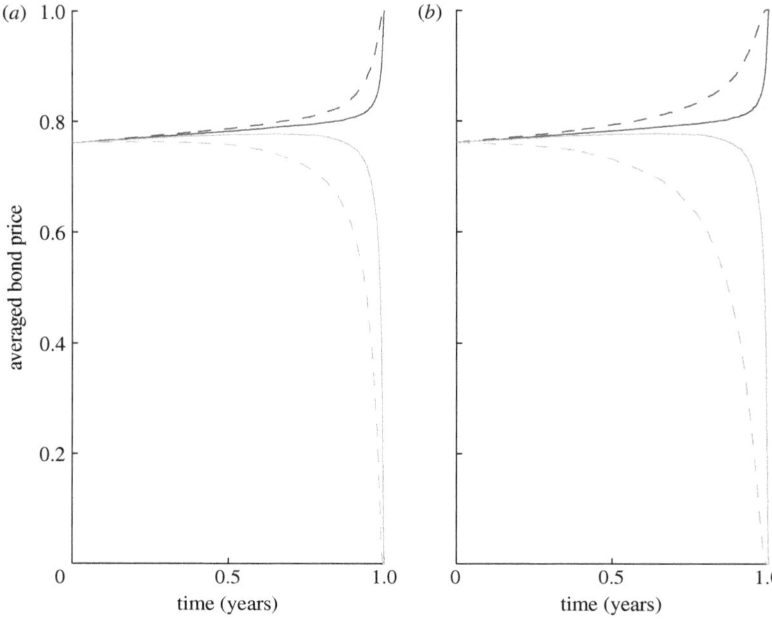

Figure 3. Comparison between the averaged market prices and the informed valuations. In both plots, the solid lines represent averaged market prices of a defaultable digital bond: one for which default does not occur and the other which the bond defaults. The parameters are chosen so that X_T takes the values 0 or 1 with *a priori* default probability 20%, $r=5\%$, $T=1$, and the market signal-to-noise ratio is $\sigma=0.2$. These are compared with the corresponding averages for the informed trader (dashed lines), with two different sets of parameters: (a) $\sigma'=0.4$ and $\rho=0.1$, and (b) $\sigma'=0$ and $\rho=0.95$.

6. Innovations and the dynamics of informed valuations

Our objective now is to obtain an innovations representation for the valuations made by the informed trader. For this purpose it suffices to derive the dynamical equation satisfied by the 'insider' valuation $\{\tilde{B}_{tT}\}$, or equivalently, by the conditional probability $\{\tilde{\pi}_{it}\}$. The calculation simplifies if we express (5.6) in the form

$$\tilde{B}_{tT} = P_{tT}\frac{\sum_{i=1}^{n} p_i x_i \exp\left[\frac{T}{T-t}\left(\hat{\sigma}x_i\hat{\xi}_t - \frac{1}{2}\hat{\sigma}^2 x_i^2 t\right)\right]}{\sum_{i=1}^{n} p_i \exp\left[\frac{T}{T-t}\left(\hat{\sigma}x_i\hat{\xi}_t - \frac{1}{2}\hat{\sigma}^2 x_i^2 t\right)\right]}. \tag{6.1}$$

Here the process

$$\hat{\xi}_t = \hat{\sigma}tX_T + \hat{\beta}_{tT}, \quad \hat{\sigma}^2 = \frac{\sigma^2 - 2\rho\sigma\sigma' + \sigma'^2}{1-\rho^2}, \tag{6.2}$$

represents the 'enhanced' information being effectively received by the informed trader, with the modified bridge noise

$$\hat{\beta}_{tT} = \sqrt{\frac{1-\rho^2}{\sigma^2 - 2\rho\sigma\sigma' + \sigma'^2}}\left[\frac{\sigma - \rho\sigma'}{1-\rho^2}\beta_{tT} + \frac{\sigma' - \rho\sigma}{1-\rho^2}\beta'_{tT}\right]. \tag{6.3}$$

Applying Ito's lemma to (5.4) and making use of (6.2), we find that

$$\frac{\mathrm{d}\tilde{\pi}_{it}}{\tilde{\pi}_{it}} = \frac{\hat{\sigma}T}{T-t}(x_i - \tilde{X}_t)\mathrm{d}Z_t, \tag{6.4}$$

where $\tilde{X}_t = \mathbb{E}[X_T \mid \mathcal{G}_t]$. The process $\{Z_t\}$ appearing in (6.4) is defined by

$$Z_t = \hat{\xi}_t + \int_0^t \frac{1}{T-s}\hat{\xi}_s \,\mathrm{d}s - \int_0^t \frac{\hat{\sigma}T}{T-s}\tilde{X}_s \,\mathrm{d}s. \tag{6.5}$$

By following a line of argument similar to that presented in Brody *et al.* (2007), it can be shown that $\{Z_t\}$ is a standard $\mathcal{G}_t$-Brownian motion. We deduce that the valuation process of the informed trader obeys the following dynamical equation:

$$\mathrm{d}\tilde{B}_{tT} = r_t\tilde{B}_{tT}\,\mathrm{d}t + \Gamma_t\,\mathrm{d}Z_t, \tag{6.6}$$

where the volatility process $\{\Gamma_t\}$ is given by

$$\Gamma_t = \frac{\hat{\sigma}T}{T-t}P_{tT}\tilde{V}_{tT}, \tag{6.7}$$

and $\tilde{V}_{tT}$ denotes the variance of X_T conditional on $\mathcal{G}_t$.

The fact that the information $\{\xi_t, \xi'_t\}$ accessible to the informed trader can be 'compactified' into a single enhanced information $\{\hat{\xi}_t\}$ can be understood as follows. Since the noise processes $\{\beta_{tT}\}$ and $\{\beta'_{tT}\}$ have correlation ρ, one can write

$$\beta'_{tT} = \rho\beta_{tT} + \sqrt{1-\rho^2}\bar{\beta}_{tT}, \tag{6.8}$$

where the Brownian bridge process $\{\bar{\beta}_{tT}\}$ is taken to be independent of $\{\beta_{tT}\}$. Similarly, we can decompose the extra information $\{\xi'_t\}$ in the form

$$\xi'_t = \rho\xi_t + \sqrt{1-\rho^2}\bar{\xi}_t, \tag{6.9}$$

where $\bar{\xi}_t = \bar{\sigma}tX_T + \bar{\beta}_{tT}$ and $\bar{\sigma} = (\sigma' - \rho\sigma)/\sqrt{1-\rho^2}$. It should be evident that the filtration generated jointly by $\{\xi_t, \xi'_t\}$ is equivalent to that generated jointly by $\{\xi_t, \bar{\xi}_t\}$. However, the information processes $\{\xi_t\}$ and $\{\bar{\xi}_t\}$ have independent noises. To proceed, we note that the process $\{\delta_t\}$ defined by

$$\delta_t = \frac{\xi_t}{\sigma} - \frac{\bar{\xi}_t}{\bar{\sigma}} = \frac{\beta_{tT}}{\sigma} - \frac{\bar{\beta}_{tT}}{\bar{\sigma}} \tag{6.10}$$

is purely noise, and is independent of X_T. We can construct a new Brownian bridge that is independent of this noise. A standard orthogonalization shows that this is given by the bridge process $\{\hat{\beta}_{tT}\}$ defined by (6.3). It follows that the enhanced information process $\{\hat{\xi}_t\}$ defined by (6.2) is independent of $\{\delta_t\}$. Furthermore, the filtration generated jointly by $\{\xi_t, \xi'_t\}$ is equivalent to that generated jointly by $\{\hat{\xi}_t, \delta_t\}$. Since $\{\delta_t\}$ provides no useful information about X_T, i.e. $J(\delta_t, X_T) = 0$, the informed trader in effect has $\{\hat{\xi}_t\}$ as the primary basis for valuation.

This line of argument, making use of the orthogonalization procedure, extends more generally to the case where there are multiple information processes relating to the cash flow X_T: starting with a family of processes $\{\xi^k_t\}_{k=1,\ldots,n}$ with signal-to-noise ratios $\{\sigma_k\}_{k=1,\ldots,n}$, one orthogonalizes the associated noises. The result is a new set of information processes $\{\bar{\xi}^k_t\}_{k=1,\ldots,n}$ with signal-to-noise ratios $\{\bar{\sigma}_k\}_{k=1,\ldots,n}$. Then the information process that the informed trader uses as a basis for valuation can be represented by a single *effective* information process $\{\hat{\xi}_t\}$ with the enhanced signal-to-noise ratio $\hat{\sigma} = (\sum_k \bar{\sigma}_k^2)^{1/2}$.

7. Additional information held by the informed trader and statistical arbitrage strategies exploiting this

We are in a position to quantify the amount of excess information held by the informed trader above that of the market. This is measured by the difference of the mutual information:

$$\Delta J = J(\hat{\xi}_t, X_T) - J(\xi_t, X_T). \tag{7.1}$$

By the argument in §3, the mutual information of the informed trader is given by an entropy difference of the form

$$J(\hat{\xi}_t, X_T) = H(\hat{\xi}_t) - H(\hat{\xi}_t \,|\, X_T). \tag{7.2}$$

The entropy $H(\hat{\xi}_t)$ of the 'insider' information is determined by the marginal density of $\hat{\xi}_t$, whereas the conditional entropy $H(\hat{\xi}_t \,|\, X_T)$ is the entropy of a Brownian bridge.

Following the line of argument presented in §4 we are able to represent the mutual information difference in terms of the expected entropy differences:

$$\Delta J = \mathbb{E}[H_t] - \mathbb{E}[\tilde{H}_t], \tag{7.3}$$

where $\tilde{H}_t = -\sum_i \tilde{\pi}_{it} \ln \tilde{\pi}_{it}$. This expression makes it apparent that ΔJ is non-negative, since the entropy characterizes the amount of uncertainty concerning the value of the cash flow X_T, and for any $t \in (0, T)$ this uncertainty is greater on average for the general market participant than for the informed trader. In figure 4 we plot an example of ΔJ, indicating the way in which the excess information held by the informed trader changes in time.

Given that the informed trader is in general 'more knowledgeable' than the general market participant, it is natural to ask how this advantage can be turned into profit. One of the issues that can be addressed in this connection is the derivation of optimal trading strategies. For such an analysis, one may need to introduce additional structure into the problem in the form of a suitable criterion for optimality and a specification of the market price of risk. In the present investigation, we confine the discussion to a demonstration, supported by simulation studies, of how even very simple strategies can yield statistical arbitrage opportunities by outperforming the market.

For example, suppose we consider a strategy such that at some designated time $t \in (0, T)$ a market trader purchases a digital bond iff at that time the bond price B_{tT} is greater than KP_{tT} for some specified threshold K. The value of K can be regarded as the risk aversion level of the trader. An informed trader

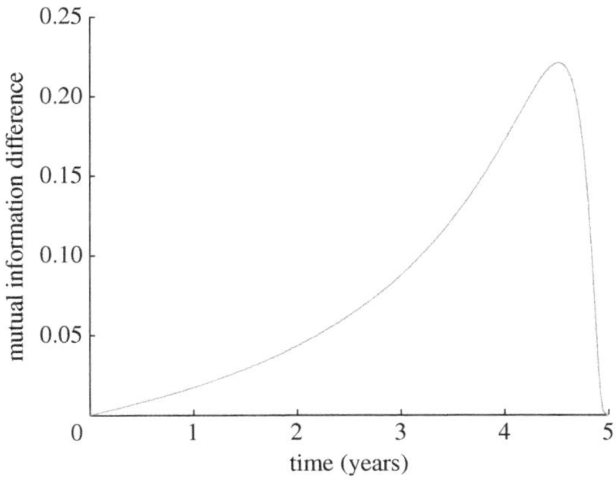

Figure 4. Mutual information difference. The additional information held by the informed trader over that of the market is non-negative. The parameters are set to be $h_1=0$, $h_2=1$, $p_1=0.2$, $p_2=0.8$, $T=1$, $\sigma=0.25$, $\sigma'=0.45$ and $\rho=0.15$.

follows the same rule, but makes a better estimate for the value of the bond, and hence purchases the bond iff $\tilde{B}_{tT} > KP_{tT}$. In either case a bond that is purchased will be held until maturity. That such a strategy leads to a statistical arbitrage opportunity for the informed trader can be seen as follows. We assume that the initial position of the trader is zero, i.e. purchase of a digital bond at t requires borrowing the amount B_{tT} at that time, and repaying the amount $P_{tT}^{-1}B_{tT}$ at T. Thus, the value of the market trader's portfolio at T is

$$V_T = \mathbb{1}\{B_{tT} > KP_{tT}\}(X_T - P_{tT}^{-1}B_{tT}), \tag{7.4}$$

whereas the terminal value of the informed trader's portfolio is

$$\tilde{V}_T = \mathbb{1}\{\tilde{B}_{tT} > KP_{tT}\}(X_T - P_{tT}^{-1}B_{tT}). \tag{7.5}$$

Consider now the present value $P_{0T}\mathbb{E}[\Delta V_T]$ of a security that delivers a cash flow equal to the excess profit and loss (P&L) $\Delta V_T = \tilde{V}_T - V_T$ generated by the strategy of the informed trader. By use of the tower property we have $\mathbb{E}[\Delta V_T] = \mathbb{E}[\mathbb{E}[\Delta V_T \,|\, \mathcal{G}_t]]$; but

$$\mathbb{E}[\Delta V_T \,|\, \mathcal{G}_t] = P_{tT}^{-1}(\mathbb{1}\{\tilde{B}_{tT} > KP_{tT}\} - \mathbb{1}\{B_{tT} > KP_{tT}\})(\tilde{B}_{tT} - B_{tT}), \tag{7.6}$$

since the random variables B_{tT} and $\tilde{B}_{tT}$ are both $\mathcal{G}_t$-measurable. If $\tilde{B}_{tT} > B_{tT}$, then $\mathbb{1}\{\tilde{B}_{tT} > KP_{tT}\} - \mathbb{1}\{B_{tT} > KP_{tT}\}$ is non-negative, whereas if $\tilde{B}_{tT} < B_{tT}$ then $\mathbb{1}\{\tilde{B}_{tT} > KP_{tT}\} - \mathbb{1}\{B_{tT} > KP_{tT}\}$ is non-positive. It follows that $\mathbb{E}[\varDelta V_T \,|\, \mathcal{G}_t]$ is a non-negative random variable, and hence $\mathbb{E}[\varDelta V_T] > 0$, since $\mathbb{E}[\varDelta V_T \,|\, \mathcal{G}_t] > 0$ with probability greater than zero. Therefore, the informed trader can execute a transaction at zero cost that has positive value, and this is what we mean by 'statistical arbitrage'.

We have examined the P&L profile, both for a general market trader and for an informed trader, resulting from the repeated application of such a strategy. The results are plotted in figure 5. In particular, we consider 2000 realizations (sample paths) for the information processes governing the bond price

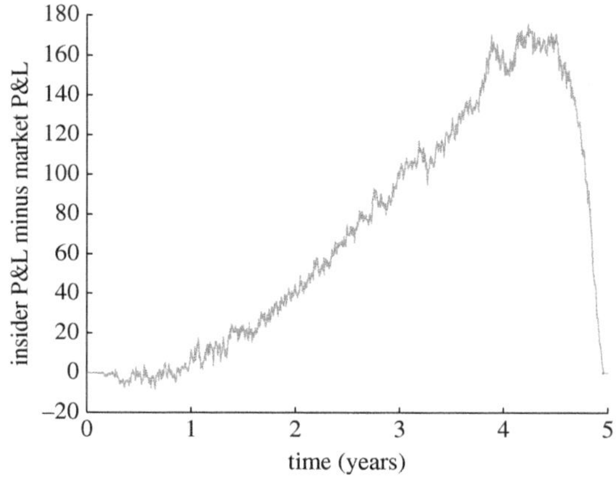

Figure 5. The P&L difference for digital bonds. At each time the traders purchase the bond if and only if the valuation of the bond is greater than a specified threshold. The general market trader buys if $B_{tT} > KP_{tT}$, whereas the informed trader uses the condition $\tilde{B}_{tT} > KP_{tT}$. The difference in P&L between the informed trader and the general market trader is plotted, based on 2000 realizations, when the *a priori* probability of the default is $p_1 = 0.2$. The other parameters are set to be $h_1 = 0$, $h_2 = 1$, $T = 5$, $\sigma = 0.25$, $\sigma' = 0.45$, $\rho = 0.15$ and $K = 0.7$.

valuations. For each fixed $t \in [0, T]$, we calculate the total P&L for the informed trader and for the market trader obtained by following the specified strategy over and over for each of the 2000 independent sample paths. For each fixed t, we chart in figure 5 the difference between the total P&L of the informed trader and that of the market trader. Providing that the strategy is executed after enough time has passed for the informed trader to gain an informational advantage, we find that the difference between the P&L of the informed trader and that of the market trader is always positive. Furthermore, the qualitative behaviour of the resulting P&L difference is in agreement with the qualitative behaviour of the magnitude of the excess information possessed by the informed trader indicated in figure 4 (we have chosen the same parameter values for these two figures to allow for direct comparison).

Our objective has been to demonstrate how statistical arbitrage strategies arise in a market characterized by heterogeneous information flow. It is interesting that a qualitatively similar behaviour for the excess information and the excess P&L is observed in the case of the rather primitive strategy we have considered. There are many ways in which one can improve upon the trading strategy examined above. An important open issue is to determine the optimal trading strategy, subject to suitable optimality criteria, that exploits the excess information. We conclude by remarking that a related approach to the modelling of insider trading within the information-based framework is suggested in Macrina (2006), where the asset return is modelled as being dependent on more than one market factor, for which only some of the associated information processes are accessible to the market. It would be of interest to examine whether the kind of hedge fund strategy considered here is also applicable in a setup involving multiple market factors.

We thank J. Z. Kelly, A. Macrina, B. K. Meister and M. F. Parry for stimulating discussions.

References

Amendinger, J., Imkeller, P. & Schweizer, M. 1998 Additional logarithmic utility of an insider. *Stoch. Process. Appl.* **75**, 263–286. (doi:10.1016/S0304-4149(98)00014-3)

Ankirchner, S., Dereich, S. & Imkeller, P. 2006 The Shannon information of filtrations and the additional logarithmic utility of insiders. *Ann. Probab.* **34**, 743–778. (doi:10.1214/009117905000000648)

Back, K. 1992 Insider trading in continuous time. *Rev. Finance Stud.* **5**, 387–409. (doi:10.1093/rfs/5.3.387)

Back, K., Cao, C. H. & Willard, G. A. 2000 Imperfect competition among informed traders. *J. Finance* **55**, 2117–2155. (doi:10.1111/0022-1082.00282)

Beckner, W. 1975 Inequalities in Fourier analysis. *Ann. Math.* **102**, 159–182. (doi:10.2307/1970980)

Biagini, F. & Øksendal, B. 2005 A general stochastic calculus approach to insider trading. *Appl. Math. Optim.* **52**, 167–181. (doi:10.1007/s00245-005-0825-2)

Biagini, F. & Øksendal, B. 2006 Minimal variance hedging for insider trading. *Int. J. Theor. Appl. Finance* **9**, 1351–1375. (doi:10.1142/S0219024906003998)

Brody, D. C., Hughston, L. P. & Macrina, A. 2007 Beyond hazard rates: a new framework to credit risk modelling. In *Advances in mathematical finance* (eds M. Fu, R. Jarrow, J.-Y. J. Yen & R. Elliott), pp. 231–257. Basel, Switzerland: Birkhäuser.

Brody, D. C., Hughston, L. P. & Macrina, A. 2008*a* Information-based asset pricing. *Int. J. Theor. Appl. Finance* **11**, 107–142. (doi:10.1142/S0219024908004749)

Brody, D. C., Hughston, L. P. & Macrina, A. 2008*b* Dam rain and cumulative gain. *Proc. R. Soc. A* **464**, 1801–1822. (doi:10.1098/rspa.2007.0273)

Campi, L. & Çetin, U. 2007 Insider trading in an equilibrium model with default: a passage from reduced-form to structural modelling. *Finance Stoch.* **11**, 591–602. (doi:10.1007/s00780-007-0038-4)

Cochrane, J. H. 2005 *Asset pricing*. Princeton, NJ: Princeton University Press.

Corcuera, J. M., Imkeller, P., Kohatsu-Higa, A. & Nualart, D. 2004 Additional utility of insiders with imperfect dynamical information. *Finance Stoch.* **8**, 437–450. (doi:10.1007/s00780-003-0119-y)

Cover, T. M. & Thomas, J. A. 1991 *Elements of information theory*. New York, NY: Wiley.

Davis, M. H. A. 1978 Detection, mutual information and feedback encoding: applications of stochastic calculus. In *Communication systems and random process theory (Proc. 2nd NATO Advanced Study Institute, Darlington, 1977)*. NATO Advanced Study Institute Series E: Applied Sciences, no. 25, pp. 705–720. Alphen aan den Rijn, The Netherlands: Sijthoff & Noordhoff.

Duncan, T. E. 1970 On the calculation of mutual information. *SIAM J. Appl. Math.* **19**, 215–220. (doi:10.1137/0119020)

Föllmer, H., Wu, C.-T. & Yor, M. 1999 Canonical decomposition of linear transformations of two independent Brownian motions motivated by models of insider trading. *Stoch. Process. Appl.* **84**, 137–164. (doi:10.1016/S0304-4149(99)00057-5)

Gel'fand, I. M. & Yaglom, A. M. 1957 Calculation of the amount of information about a random function contained in another such function. *Uspehi Mat. Nauk* **12**, 3–52.

Gel'fand, I. M., Kolmogorov, A. N. & Yaglom, A. M. 1956 On the general definition of the amount of information. *Dokl. Akad. Nauk SSSR* **111**, 745–748.

Geman, H., Madan, D. B. & Yor, M. 2007 Probing option prices for information. *Methodol. Comput. Appl. Probab.* **9**, 115–131. (doi:10.1007/s11009-006-9005-3)

Hida, T. 1980 *Brownian motion*. Berlin, Germany: Springer.

Hughston, L. P. & Macrina, A. 2008 Information, inflation, and interest. In *Advances in mathematics of finance* (ed. L. Stettner). Warsaw, Poland: Institute of Mathematics, Polish Academy of Sciences, Banach Centre Publications **83**, 117–138.

Kailath, T. 1971 The structure of Radon–Nikodým derivatives with respect to Wiener and related measures. *Ann. Math. Stat.* **42**, 1054–1067. (doi:10.1214/aoms/1177693332)

Khintchine, A. Y. 1953 The concept of entropy in the theory of probability. *Uspehi Mat. Nauk* **8**, 3–20.

Kyle, A. 1985 Continuous auctions and insider trading. *Econometrica* **53**, 1315–1335. See http://www.jstor.org/stable/1913210.

León, J. A., Navarro, R. & Nualart, D. 2003 An anticipating calculus approach to the utility maximization of an insider. *Math. Finance* **13**, 171–185. (doi:10.1111/1467-9965.00012)

Macrina, A. 2006 An information-based framework for asset pricing: *X*-factor theory and its applications. PhD thesis, King's College London. (http://arXiv:0807.2124).

Protter, P. 2005 *Stochastic integration and differential equations: a new approach*, 2nd edn. Berlin, Germany: Springer.

Rutkowski, M. & Yu, N. 2007 An extension of the Brody–Hughston–Macrina approach to modelling of defaultable bonds. *Int. J. Theor. Appl. Finance* **10**, 557–589. (doi:10.1142/S0219024907004263)

Seyhun, H. N. 1988 The information content of aggregate insider trading. *J. Business* **61**, 1–24. (doi:10.1086/296417)

Shannon, C. E. & Weaver, W. 1949 *The mathematical theory of communication.* Urbana, IL: University of Illinois Press.

Soklakov, A. 2008 Information derivatives. *Risk*, April, 90–94.

Wiener, N. 1948 *Cybernetics: or control and communication in the animal and the machine.* Cambridge, MA: MIT Press.

Yaglom, A. M. & Yaglom, I. M. 1983 Probability and information (transl. Russian by V. K. Jain. Originally published as: Вероятность и информация, 3rd revised and enlarged edn. Izdatel'stvo 'Nauka', Moscow, 1973). Delhi, India: Hindustan Publishing Corporation.

Chapter 5

Information of interest*

The flow of information in financial markets on future liquidity risk generates the rise and fall of demand for default-free bonds. Here, we present an approach to pricing these bonds and the associated derivatives, based on noisy information about the possible future liquidity crises, while deriving option pricing formulas and showing the impact of liquidity on the risk premium.

BY DORJE BRODY AND ROBYN FRIEDMAN

IN THIS ARTICLE, we present a method of generating interest rate dynamics from elementary economic considerations. There are of course numerous economic factors that affect the movement of interest rates, and causal relations that hold between these factors are often difficult to disentangle. So, rather than attempting to address a range of factors simultaneously, we will focus on one factor important in determining the interest rate term structure, namely the liquidity risk, in the narrow sense of cash demand. The interplay between liquidity and interest rates has long been discussed in economics literature (see, for example, Friedman, 1968). Our objective is to build an information-based model that reflects the market perception of future liquidity risk, and use it for the pricing and general risk management of interest rate derivatives.

In the framework of arbitrage-free pricing theory, the value of an asset is determined by the risk-adjusted expectation of the suitably discounted cashflow. In principle one can derive the price process of an asset by the specification of the random cashflow, along with the market filtration and the discounting factor. Such an idea has been applied successfully to obtain the price process of, for example, credit-risky bonds (Brody, Hughston & Macrina, 2007) or reinsurance-related products (Brody, Hughston & Macrina, 2008). When it comes to the modelling of the interest rate term structure, however, the matter is made somewhat more complicated, because the cashflow of a discount bond is not random, and thus one has to specify the discount factor to deduce the bond price. One is then led to the specification of the short rate or forward rate processes, but such an approach is undesirable if the objective is to generate from the outset the dynamics of the term structure. This forces us to take an alternative route for deriving bond prices and the associated rates.

The pricing framework outlined here, based on the consideration of liquidity risk, has several advantages: (i) it provides intuitive economic interpretations of the discount function, the associated rates and their volatilities; (ii) the initial term structure can be specified exogenously in a straightforward manner; (iii) arbitrage-free dynamics of interest rates emerge endogenously in such a manner that they are consistent with the market perception of future cash demand; (iv) semi-analytic formulas for caplets and swaptions, expressed in terms of elementary Gaussian integrations, can be obtained; and (v) risk premiums can in principle be estimated from prices of interest rate derivatives. To illustrate the role played by liquidity risk in determining interest rate systems, let us begin by examining deterministic term structures.

Deterministic term structures

Positivity of nominal rates and a common sense argument imply that a zero-coupon discount bond P_{0T} is decreasing in the maturity T, tending to zero at infinity. Hence, P_{0T} defines a right-side cumulative distribution function on the positive real line $\mathbb{R}_+$, implying the existence of a random variable X on a probability space with measure $\mathbb{Q}$ such that $P_{0T} = \mathbb{Q}(X \geq T)$. What, then, is the economic interpretation of the random variable X and the role of the probability measure $\mathbb{Q}$?

It is reasonable to regard the random variable X as representing the occurrence time of future liquidity crises, at least to first approximation. From the viewpoint of the buyer of a bond, if with high probability cash is needed before maturity T, then purchase will be made only if the bond price is sufficiently low. Likewise, the seller of a bond would be willing to offer a discount if there is a likely need for

*This chapter was originally published as: D. C. Brody & R. L. Friedman (2009) Information of Interest, *Risk Magazine*, December 2009 issue, pp. 105–110. Reprinted in *Life & Pensions Magazine*, February 2010 issue, pp. 35–40. Reprinted here with kind permission from Incisive Media.

cash before time T. The bond price therefore represents a survival function, where surviving means a liquidity crisis failing to occur. The price P_{tT} at time t of a zero-coupon bond of maturity T is the $\mathbb{Q}$-probability of survival until T, conditional on survival until t:

$$P_{tT} = \mathbb{Q}\left(X \geq T \middle| X \geq t\right) \tag{1}$$

The measure $\mathbb{Q}$ is in fact the risk-neutral measure, as will be shown later, but let us for the moment assume this is the case. The density of X is $\rho_0(T) = -\partial_T P_{0T}$, and the associated hazard rate is just the initial forward rate $f_{0T} = -\partial_T \ln P_{0T}$. For a small dT we have:

$$f_{0T}dT = \mathbb{Q}\left(X \in [T, T + dT] \middle| X \geq T\right) \tag{2}$$

In other words, $f_{0T}dT$ is the ***a priori*** risk-neutral probability of a liquidity crisis occurring in an infinitesimal interval $[T, T + dT]$, conditional upon survival until T. Based on these observations, a general arbitrage-free dynamical equation satisfied by the term structure density process $\rho_t(T) = -\partial_T P_{tT}$ was obtained by Brody & Hughston (2001). In particular, in a deterministic interest rate system, we can calibrate the initial term structure density $\rho_0(T)$ via the initial yield curve, from which the subsequent evolution is determined in accordance with (1).

Market information about future liquidity

We aim to extend the deterministic model (1) into a dynamical one without losing the economic interpretation that the bond price represents the conditional risk-neutral probability that the liquidity issue arises beyond time T. In the case of a deterministic term structure (1), the conditioning is given merely by the event $X \geq t$, but in a dynamical set-up market participants accumulate noisy information concerning future liquidity risk. It is this noisy observation of the timing X of the future cash demand that generates random movements in the bond price. If we let $\mathcal{F}_t$ denote the information generated by this observation, the price of a discount bond is given by the conditional probability:

$$P_{tT} = \mathbb{Q}\left(X \geq T \middle| \sigma(X \geq t) \cap \mathcal{F}_t\right) \tag{3}$$

where $\sigma(X \geq t)$ is the smallest sigma algebra generated by $\{X \geq t\}$. Evidently, the random variable representing the timing of cash demand itself may change in time. In the present investigation, however, we shall confine our analysis to models based on fixed X.

If we apply the Bayes formula, and use $\{X \geq T\} \subset \{X \geq t\}$, (3) can be expressed in a more intuitive form:

$$P_{tT} = \frac{\mathbb{Q}\left(X \geq T \middle| \mathcal{F}_t\right)}{\mathbb{Q}\left(X \geq t \middle| \mathcal{F}_t\right)} \tag{4}$$

An elementary model for bond pricing

We introduce a specific model for the information $\mathcal{F}_t$, involving both signal and noise portions. Because what concerns market participants is the value of X, the signal component must be generated in some form by X itself, while there is an independent noise that obscures the value of X. Motivated by the approach introduced in Macrina (2006) and Brody, Hughston & Macrina (2007) for the information-based asset pricing framework, let us consider a simple model where the information concerning the value of X is revealed to the market linearly in time at a constant rate σ, and the noise is generated by an independent $\mathbb{Q}$-Brownian motion. Hence the information-generating process is given by:

$$\xi_t = \sigma t \phi(X) + B_t \tag{5}$$

where $\phi(x)$ is an invertible function and the filtration $\mathcal{F}_t$ is the sigma algebra generated by $\{\xi_s\}_{0\leq s\leq t}$.[1] The rationale of the Brody-Hughston-Macrina (BHM) framework is that asset price dynamics are generated by the response of market participants to the unravelling of relevant information. By directly modelling the flow of information in the form of 'signal plus noise', a more realistic but nevertheless tractable model for the price process can be derived, leading to a radically new approach to both pricing and risk management. We will say more about the choice of the function $\phi(x)$ shortly, but for the moment will proceed with generality.

Since the magnitude of the signal-to-noise ratio is given by $\sigma\sqrt{t}$, the value of X will be revealed asymptotically, that is, X is $\mathcal{F}_\infty$-measurable. Along with the fact that ξ_t is Markovian, we find that the bond pricing formula simplifies in this model to:

$$P_{tT} = \frac{\mathbb{Q}\left(X \geq T \middle| \xi_t\right)}{\mathbb{Q}\left(X \geq t \middle| \xi_t\right)} \tag{6}$$

For the calculation of the bond price (6), we consider the joint probability $\mathbb{Q}(\{X \geq T\} \cap \{\xi_t \in d\xi\})$. Then, by the definition (5), we have:

$$\mathbb{Q}\left(\{X \geq T\} \cap \{\xi_t \in d\xi\}\right) = \int_T^\infty \mathbb{Q}\left(B_t \in \left[d\xi - \sigma t \phi(x)\right]\right) \rho_0(x)\, dx \tag{7}$$

where again $\rho_0(x) = -\partial_x P_{0x}$ is the initial term structure density. Using the density function for Brownian motion, we obtain the following expression:

$$P_{tT} = \frac{\int_T^\infty \rho_0(x)\, e^{\sigma\phi(x)\xi_t - \frac{1}{2}\sigma^2\phi^2(x)t} dx}{\int_t^\infty \rho_0(x)\, e^{\sigma\phi(x)\xi_t - \frac{1}{2}\sigma^2\phi^2(x)t} dx} \tag{8}$$

Sample paths for the bond price process (8) are shown in figure 1, with $\rho_0(x)$ calibrated against market data from July 2009.

As in the deterministic case, the model can be calibrated against the initial yield curve (see below). The subsequent evolution is then determined by the Markovian market information process. In this respect, the model has a feature resembling the Markov-functional models (Hunt & Kennedy, 2000), and thus falls within the Heath-Jarrow-Morton (HJM) framework, but such that interest rate positivity is ensured. The advantage is that the dynamical behaviour of the model can be understood by means of somewhat elementary economic insight.

[1] Strictly speaking we should replace the Brownian noise B_t by a 'killed' Brownian noise $\mathbb{1}\{X \geq t\}B_t$. As we are interested in events on $\{X \geq t\}$, we shall be using (5) for simplicity of exposition. This does not affect the bond pricing formula.

Figure 1 Sample paths of the discount function (8) and the associated short rate (9)

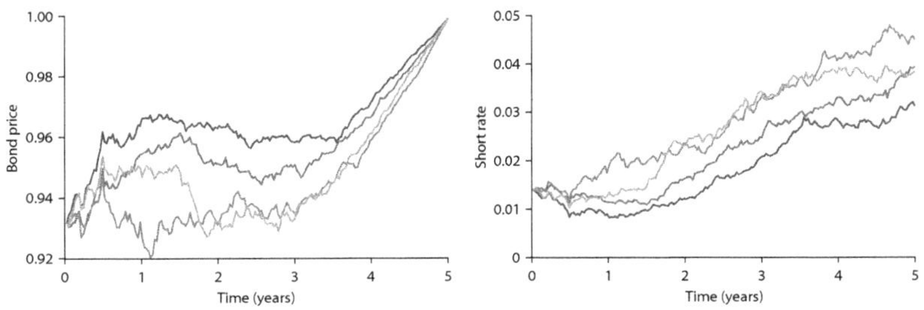

Note: the information-adjusting function is set as $\phi(x) = e^{-0.025x}$ and the initial term structure $\rho_0(x)$ is calibrated to market data using the sterling curve dated July 6, 2009. The information flow rate is set as $\sigma = 0.3$ and the bond maturity is five years

From the bond price (8), we can infer the implied short rate:

$$r_t = -\partial_T P_{tT}\big|_{T=t} = \frac{\rho_0(t)e^{\sigma\phi(t)\xi_t - \frac{1}{2}\sigma^2\phi^2(t)t}}{\int_t^\infty \rho_0(x)e^{\sigma\phi(x)\xi_t - \frac{1}{2}\sigma^2\phi^2(x)t}dx} \tag{9}$$

The instantaneous forward rate $f_{tT} = -\partial_T \ln P_{tT}$ is expressed analogously as:

$$f_{tT} = \frac{\rho_0(T)e^{\sigma\phi(T)\xi_t - \frac{1}{2}\sigma^2\phi^2(T)t}}{\int_T^\infty \rho_0(x)e^{\sigma\phi(x)\xi_t - \frac{1}{2}\sigma^2\phi^2(x)t}dx} \tag{10}$$

Example. Consider a flat initial term structure given by $P_{0T} = e^{-rT}$. The associated ***a priori*** density function is then exponential: $\rho_0(T) = re^{-rT}$. In a linear information model, we have $\phi(x) = x$. Substitution of these in (8) yields the following bond price process:

$$P_{tT} = \frac{N\left(\frac{\xi_t - r/\sigma}{\sqrt{t}} - \sigma T\sqrt{t}\right)}{N\left(\frac{\xi_t - r/\sigma}{\sqrt{t}} - \sigma t\sqrt{t}\right)} \tag{11}$$

where $N(x)$ is the normal distribution function.

Dynamics of the bond price

We now turn to the analysis of the discount bond dynamics. We introduce the following one-parameter family of processes:

$$\hat{\Phi}_{tu} = \frac{\int_u^\infty \phi(x)\rho_0(x)e^{\sigma\phi(x)\xi_t - \frac{1}{2}\sigma^2\phi^2(x)t}dx}{\int_u^\infty \rho_0(x)e^{\sigma\phi(x)\xi_t - \frac{1}{2}\sigma^2\phi^2(x)t}dx} \tag{12}$$

For $u = t$ this corresponds to the conditional expectation $\hat{\Phi}_{tt} = \mathbb{E}[\phi(X)\mathbf{1}\{X \geq t\}|X \geq t, \xi_t]$.

The bond price dynamics can be deduced by taking the stochastic differential of (8):

$$\frac{dP_{tT}}{P_{tT}} = r_t dt + \sigma\Sigma_{tT} dW_t \tag{13}$$

where we have defined:

$$\Sigma_{tT} = \hat{\Phi}_{tT} - \hat{\Phi}_{tt} \tag{14}$$

and:

$$W_t = \xi_t - \sigma\int_0^t \hat{\Phi}_{ss} ds \tag{15}$$

The key result that we shall establish below is that this W_t is a $\mathbb{Q}$-Brownian motion on $\{X \geq t\}$ with respect to the market filtration $\mathcal{G}_t$ determined jointly by $\mathcal{F}_t$ and the sigma algebra generated by $\{X \geq s\}_{0\leq s\leq t}$.[2] It follows from (13) that the probability measure $\mathbb{Q}$ can be identified with the risk-neutral measure, since the drift of the bond in this measure is given by the short rate. Following the terminology of Wiener, we shall refer to W_t as the innovations process, because it measures the arrival of new information to the market concerning future liquidity risk. Equation (13) also shows that the model is a single-factor diffusion, with a (hedgeable) stochastic volatility and stochastic rates.

We observe from (14) that the bond volatility is determined by the difference between the forward conditional expectation $\hat{\Phi}_{tT} = P_{tT}^{-1}\mathbb{E}[\phi(X)\mathbf{1}\{X \geq T\}|X \geq t, \xi_t]$ of $\phi(X)$ to time T and the conditional expectation $\hat{\Phi}_{tT} = \mathbb{E}[\phi(X)\mathbf{1}\{X \geq t\}|X \geq t, \xi_t]$ of $\phi(X)$ at time t. Therefore, if the forward expectation of the function $\phi(X)$ of the timing for future cash demand is close to the current (time t) expectation, then the bond

[2] More precisely, $\mathbf{1}\{X \geq t\}W_t$ is a killed Brownian motion

volatility is low. Conversely, if there is a large discrepancy between the forward and the current expectation of $\phi(X)$, the bond price process becomes volatile.

Example. In the case of a linear information model $\phi(X) = x$, we can assign a more direct financial interpretation to the meaning of the bond volatility, by virtue of an observation made in Brody & Hughston (2001) that the expectation $\mathbb{E}[X]$ of the random variable X is the initial price of a perpetual annuity. In the present framework, in which $\phi(x) = x$, $\hat{\Phi}_{tu}$ represents the shifted price process of the annuity. Specifically, we have the following representation:

$$\hat{\Phi}_{tt} = t + \int_t^\infty P_{tx} dx \quad \text{and} \quad \hat{\Phi}_{tT} = T + P_{tT}^{-1} \int_T^\infty P_{tx} dx \tag{16}$$

Hence the bond volatility, when $\phi(x) = x$, is given by the difference between the forward and current prices of the perpetual annuity plus the time gap $T - t$. In this way we are able to identify an elementary economic interpretation for the bond price dynamics. Furthermore, it also implies that volatility-related products for discount bonds are essentially exotic derivatives on annuities.

To show that the innovations process W_t is a Brownian motion on $\{X \geq t\}$, we note that since $(dW_t)^2 = dt$ it suffices to verify that W_t is a martingale. The proof can be sketched as follows. Writing $\mathbb{E}_t[-]$ for the conditional $\mathbb{Q}$-expectation with respect to $\mathcal{G}_t$ and restricting attention on $\{X \geq t\}$, we obtain:

$$\begin{aligned} \mathbb{E}_t[W_u] &= \mathbb{E}_t[\xi_u] - \sigma \int_0^u \mathbb{E}_t\left[\hat{\Phi}_{ss}\right] ds \\ &= \sigma u \mathbb{E}_t[\phi(X)] + \mathbb{E}_t[B_u] - \sigma \int_0^t \hat{\Phi}_{ss} ds - \sigma \int_t^u \mathbb{E}_t\left[\hat{\Phi}_{ss}\right] ds \end{aligned} \tag{17}$$

Since $\mathbf{1}\{X \geq t\}\mathbb{E}_t[\phi(X)] = \mathbf{1}\{X \geq t\}\hat{\Phi}_{tt}$ (see Bielecki & Rutkowski, 2002, chapter 5), on $\{X \geq t\}$ the random variable $\hat{\Phi}_{tt}$ is the conditional expectation of $\phi(X)$ with respect to $\mathcal{G}_t$. It follows that on $\{X \geq t\}$ we have:

$$\mathbb{E}_t[W_u] = \sigma t \mathbb{E}_t[\phi(X)] + \mathbb{E}_t[B_u] - \sigma \int_0^t \hat{\Phi}_{ss} ds \tag{18}$$

From the tower property of conditional expectation, we find $\mathbb{E}_t[B_u] = \mathbb{E}_t[\mathbb{E}[B_u|\mathcal{F}_t^B, X]] = \mathbb{E}_t[B_t]$, and since $\mathbb{E}_t[\xi_t] = \xi_t$ we deduce the martingale condition $\mathbb{E}_t[W_u] = W_t$. It follows from Lévy's characterisation that W_t is a $\mathbb{Q}$-Brownian motion on $\{X \geq t\}$.

In the event $\{X < t\}$ the bond price goes to zero and the dynamics is terminated, resulting in the killing of the Brownian motion. Such a hypothetical event corresponds to the sudden freezing of the market, when liquidity has dried up and no transferrable funds are available.

In terms of the risk-neutral Brownian motion W_t the forward rate dynamics can be expressed manifestly in the HJM form:

$$df_{tT} = \sigma^2 \Sigma_{tT}(\partial_T \Sigma_{tT})dt - \sigma(\partial_T \Sigma_{tT})dW_t \tag{19}$$

such that interest rate positivity is ensured. This follows from taking the stochastic differential of (10), and making use of expressions (12), (14) and (15). A calculation shows that the absolute volatility of the instantaneous forward rate is given by $\sigma f_{tT}(\phi(T) - \hat{\Phi}_{tT})$.

By considering the measure $\mathbb{B}$ under which ξ_t is a standard Brownian motion, one can find simple formulas for vanilla options on the bond price (see a longer version of this article in *Risk*, November 2009, pp. 101–106). A call option is given by

$$C = \int_0^\infty \rho_0(x) N(\mathrm{d}) \left(1_{[T,\infty)} - \mathrm{K} 1_{[t,\infty)} \right) dx \tag{20}$$

where $\mathrm{d} = \pm\left(\frac{\xi^*}{\sqrt{t}} - \sigma\sqrt{t}\phi(x)\right)$, the positive/negative sign depending on whether $|\phi|$ is increasing or decreasing, and ξ^* the unique value of ξ such that $P_{tT} = K$.

Calibration procedure

We now outline the calibration procedure in steps. The model for the discount bond is (8), which contains three quantities to be calibrated: $\rho_0(x)$, $\phi(x)$ and σ. Writing $R(x)$ for the initial yield curve data, we calibrate the initial term structure according to the prescription $\rho_0(x) = -\partial_x e^{-xR(x)}$. Then $\phi(x)$ provides an entire functional degrees of freedom; ideally one would like to calibrate ϕ to fit derivatives prices using (20), but this is computationally intense, so we choose a model for ϕ. Numerical studies indicate that the choice $\phi(x) = e^{-\kappa x}$ is particularly well behaved. Finally, we take the ATM option price, say, to calibrate the value of σ using (20), for a fixed value of κ. The choice of the parameter κ then provides some level of flexibility to adjust skews and smiles.

Whether the calibration of σ via the option price can always be done consistently depends on whether the option vega defined by $\mathcal{V} = \partial C/\partial \sigma$

Figure 2. Price of a call option on a discount bond

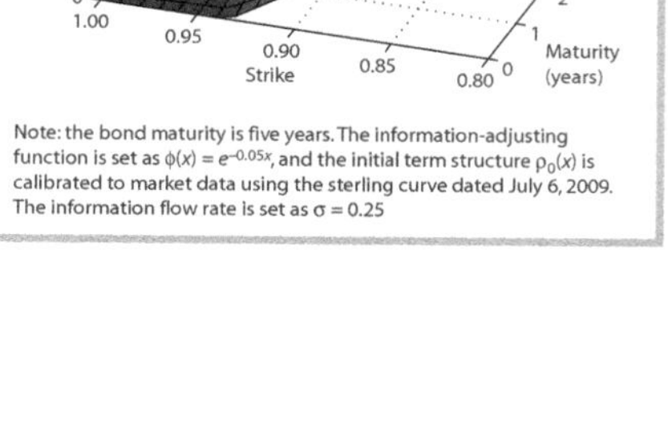

Note: the bond maturity is five years. The information-adjusting function is set as $\phi(x) = e^{-0.05x}$, and the initial term structure $\rho_0(x)$ is calibrated to market data using the sterling curve dated July 6, 2009. The information flow rate is set as $\sigma = 0.25$

changes its sign. We have considered special cases for the *a priori* density $\rho_0(x)$ and various specifications of $\phi(x)$ to confirm the positivity/negativity of $\mathcal{V}$, suggesting that either $\mathcal{V} > 0$ or $\mathcal{V} < 0$ holds for arbitrary $\rho_0(x)$ and monotonic $\phi(x)$. It seems plausible that 'implied volatility' $\sigma(K)$ in the present framework can always be determined unambiguously from option prices.

We note that once the three inputs are calibrated, the simulation for the price process and the various associated rates can be done very fast, since there is no need for solving a stochastic differential equation. Hence the model is suitable for fast numerical valuation of exotic products.

Interpretation of the auxiliary measure

The probability measure $\mathbb{B}$ introduced here somewhat artificially for the purpose of calculating derivatives prices in fact embodies an economic interpretation. This can be seen from the expression (14) for the bond price volatility Σ_{tT}, which shows that the Σ_{tT} is invariant under the shift $\phi(X) \to \phi(X) + \alpha_t$ in the drift of the information process for any α_t independent of X. This degree of freedom can be used to fix the risk premium according to $\lambda_t = -\sigma\hat{\Phi}_{tt}$ without loss of generality (see also the discussion in Brody & Hughston, 2002). Thus we find that the auxiliary measure $\mathbb{B}$ introduced for the purpose of option pricing can be identified with the market measure.

The key point to note here is that the specification of a model ξ_t for the flow of information concerning the timing of the liquidity risk fixes both the short rate process r_t and the risk premium process λ_t. As a consequence, we find that the process π_t defined by the expression:

$$\pi_t = \int_t^\infty p_t(x)dx \tag{21}$$

appearing, for example, in the denominator of the bond price (8), is the pricing kernel, where $p_t(x)$ denotes the unnormalised conditional probability density for the random variable X given $\mathcal{F}_t$:

$$\mathbb{Q}(X \geq t|\mathcal{F}_t) = \frac{\int_t^\infty p_t(x)dx}{\int_0^\infty p_t(x)dx} \tag{22}$$

In other words, $p_t(x)$ solves the Zakai equation associated with the filtering equation for $\phi(X)$. This observation is useful in considering the pricing of hybrid derivatives because if H_T represents the random payout on the maturity day T of a derivatives contract (for example, the payout $H_T = (S_T - K)^+$ of a European-style option on a stock), then the price H_{tT} of the derivative at time $t \leq T$ is given by $H_{tT} = \mathbb{E}^{\mathbb{B}}[\pi_T H_T]/\pi_t$. In particular, for $H_T = 1$ we recover the bond pricing formula. Similarly, if π_t^i is the pricing kernel calibrated to currency i and π_t^j is the pricing kernel calibrated to currency j, then the arbitrage-free and friction-free foreign exchange rate is given by the ratio π_t^i/π_t^j. In particular, it is the market perception of the random variables X_i and X_j that determines the exchange rate volatility (for a pricing-kernel approach to interest rate and foreign exchange system, see Brody & Hughston, 2004, and references cited therein).

Although in the present investigation we have closely examined a simple model (5) for the market information, many of the derived concepts are applicable to a wide range of models for $\mathcal{F}_t$. Of course, expressions for various quantities such as the bond price or forward rate volatility are dependent on the choice of the information process. For example, if the rate at which information concerning the value of $\phi(X)$ is revealed to the market is time-dependent, then the Markov information model (5) will be modified to a non-Markov process: $\xi_t = \phi(X)\int_0^t \sigma_s ds + B_t$. The price of the bond in this case can still be calculated straightforwardly, with the result:

$$P_{tT} = \frac{\int_T^\infty \rho_0(x) e^{\phi(x)\int_0^t \sigma_s d\xi_s - \frac{1}{2}\phi^2(x)\int_0^t \sigma_s^2 ds} dx}{\int_t^\infty \rho_0(x) e^{\phi(x)\int_0^t \sigma_s d\xi_s - \frac{1}{2}\phi^2(x)\int_0^t \sigma_s^2 ds} dx} \tag{23}$$

Such a model is suitable for dealing with the high-volatility environment seen recently in the market. Alternatively, we may consider an interest rate model driven by pure jump Lévy processes. An example is given by the gamma filter introduced in Brody, Hughston & Macrina (2008), whereby the information process is $\xi_t = X\gamma_t$. Here γ_t denotes a standard gamma process with rate parameter m. In this case, the expression for the bond price process reads:

$$P_{tT} = \frac{\int_T^\infty \rho_0(x) x^{-mt} e^{-\xi_t/x} dx}{\int_t^\infty \rho_0(x) x^{-mt} e^{-\xi_t/x} dx} \tag{24}$$

and the associated short rate process is:

$$r_t = \frac{\rho_0(t) t^{-mt} e^{-\xi_t/t}}{\int_t^\infty \rho_0(x) x^{-mt} e^{-\xi_t/x} dx} \tag{25}$$

Hence the present framework provides for a wide range of new interest rate models to be created that are tractable and easy to implement.

Interpretation of the function $\phi(x)$

Let us now discuss the choice of the function $\phi(x)$ introduced in the information process (5). What might appear to be the most natural candidate for $\phi(x)$ is a linear function: $\phi(x) = x$. As indicated above, in this case the bond volatility has a natural financial characterisation. We find, however, that in this model the market price of risk (the excess rate of return above the short rate) is strictly negative. From an information-theoretic point of view, such a market can be interpreted as follows. Recall that a small value of X implies that there is an acute liquidity crisis awaiting. However, according to the information process $\xi_t = \sigma t X + B_t$ there is little prior warning to the market concerning the 'smallness' of X, since ξ_t in this case is dominated by noise. As a consequence, liquidity issues arise essentially as a surprise. What the model shows is that in such a scenario the risk premium becomes negative.

Under normal market conditions we expect the risk premium to be positive. This is obtained by a function ϕ such that $|\phi|$ decreases to zero for large X. Examples of this type are $\phi(x) = \pm e^{-\kappa x}$ for a positive κ, or $\phi(x) = \pm(x - x_0)^{-1}$ for a positive x_0. For these choices, small values of X carry heavier weights in the signal component, as compared with larger values of X. As a consequence, signals of an imminent liquidity crisis reach the market ahead of time, enabling appropriate precautions to be taken, thus leading to a positive risk premium. This feature can be understood in conjunction with the fact that ξ_t is a Brownian motion in the market measure. The bond volatilities in these examples are determined by certain weighted annuity prices. For example, when $\phi(x) = e^{-\kappa x}$ we have:

$$\Sigma_{tT} = \left(e^{-\kappa T} - e^{-\kappa t}\right) - \kappa\left[P_{tT}^{-1}\int_T^\infty e^{-\kappa x} P_{tx} dx - \int_t^\infty e^{-\kappa x} P_{tx} dx\right] \qquad (26)$$

The positivity of the risk premium in the arbitrage pricing theory is an assumption that cannot be deduced from the no-arbitrage condition. Hence, it is satisfying that in the present framework we are able to deduce how the structure of the flow of information affects the signature of the risk premium. In particular, it may be possible to use the functional degree of freedom $\phi(x)$ to calibrate various derivatives prices. This is useful, because it is virtually impossible to estimate the risk premium directly from the price process of risky assets.

Conclusion

Empirical studies indicate that a persistent increase in money supply leads in the short term (up to a month or so) to a fall in nominal interest rates. This is the so-called liquidity effect (Cochrane, 1989). On the other hand, in the longer term an increase in money supply increases expected inflation, hence leading to an increase in nominal rates. This is the so-called Fisher effect. Typically, both effects coexist in that an increase in money supply reduces nominal rates but increases expected inflation so that the real rate also falls. Needless to say, interrelations between these effects are difficult to disentangle. The implication of these macroeconomic considerations for the present approach is that the random variable X, which we identified as representing the timing of a liquidity crisis in the narrow sense of cash demand, is dependent on a number of market factors and not merely on money supply.

We would like to formulate a model for real discount bonds, thus allowing us to price inflation-related products in a manner consistent with the nominal interest rate dynamics. One way of realising this within the information-based pricing framework might be through using multiple market factors (see Macrina, 2006). This would allow inflation to be modelled consistently with the interest rate term structure.

Our objective here has been the introduction of a new interest rate modelling framework that captures some important macroeconomic elements, in such a way that resulting models can be used in practice for the pricing and risk management of interest rate derivatives. The random variable X, whose existence is ensured by the positivity of nominal rates and the vanishing of infinite-maturity bond prices, has the dimension of time, and hence it has been interpreted as representing the timing of future liquidity crises. It is worth emphasising that all the results established here are, of course, independent of this particular interpretation. Nevertheless, our interpretation allows us to enhance fixed-income risk management with an intuitive economic understanding of the model being used.

Dorje Brody is a reader in mathematics at Imperial College London. Robyn Friedman is a quantitative analyst at Royal Bank of Scotland and a PhD student at Imperial College London. The opinions expressed in this article are those of the authors. Email: dorje@imperial.ac.uk, robyn.friedman@rbs.com

References

Bielecki T and M Rutkowski, 2002
Credit risk: modelling, valuation and hedging
Springer-Verlag

Brody D and L Hughston, 2001
Interest rates and information geometry
Proceedings of the Royal Society London A457, pages 1,343–1,364

Brody D and L Hughston, 2002
Entropy and information in the interest rate term structure
Quantitative Finance 2, pages 70–80

Brody D and L Hughston, 2004
Chaos and coherence: a new framework for interest rate modeling
Proceedings of the Royal Society London A460, pages 85–110

Brody D, L Hughston and A Macrina, 2007
Beyond hazard rates: a new framework for credit-risk modeling
In Advances in Mathematical Finance: Festschrift Volume in Honour of Dilip Madan, Birkhäuser

Brody D, L Hughston and A Macrina, 2008
Dam rain and cumulative gain
Proceedings of the Royal Society London A464, pages 1,801–1,822

Cochrane J, 1989
The return of the liquidity effect: a study of the short-run relation between money growth and interest rates
Journal of Business and Economic Statistics 7, pages 75–83

Friedman M, 1968
The role of monetary policy
American Economic Review 58, pages 1–17

Hunt P and J Kennedy, 2000
Financial derivatives in theory and practice
Wiley

Macrina A, 2006
An information-based framework for asset pricing: X-factor theory and its applications
PhD thesis, King's College London

Chapter 6

Credit Risk, Market Sentiment and Randomly-Timed Default*

Dorje C. Brody, Lane P. Hughston, and Andrea Macrina

Abstract We propose a model for the credit markets in which the random default times of bonds are assumed to be given as functions of one or more independent "market factors". Market participants are assumed to have partial information about each of the market factors, represented by the values of a set of market factor information processes. The market filtration is taken to be generated jointly by the various information processes and by the default indicator processes of the various bonds. The value of a discount bond is obtained by taking the discounted expectation of the value of the default indicator function at the maturity of the bond, conditional on the information provided by the market filtration. Explicit expressions are derived for the bond price processes and the associated default hazard rates. The latter are not given *a priori* as part of the model but rather are deduced and shown to be functions of the values of the information processes. Thus the "perceived" hazard rates, based on the available information, determine bond prices, and as perceptions change so do the prices. In conclusion, explicit expressions are derived for options on discount bonds, the values of which also fluctuate in line with the vicissitudes of market sentiment.

Keywords Information-based asset pricing · Credit derivatives · Random times

MSC (2010): 91G40, 93E11, 60G40, 94Axx

D.C. Brody and L.P. Hughston (✉)
Department of Mathematics, Imperial College London, London SW7 2AZ, United Kingdom
e-mail: dorje@imperial.ac.uk, l.hughston@imperial.ac.uk

A. Macrina
Department of Mathematics, King's College London, London WC2R 2LS, United Kingdom
and
Institute of Economic Research, Kyoto University, Kyoto 606-8501, Japan
e-mail: andrea.macrina@kcl.ac.uk

*This chapter was originally published as: D. C. Brody, L. P. Hughston & A. Macrina (2010) Credit Risk, Market Sentiment and Randomly-Timed Default. In: *Stochastic Analysis in 2010* (D. Crisan, editor), Springer-Verlag, pp. 267–280. Reprinted with kind permission from Springer.

1 Credit-Risk Modeling

In this paper, we consider a simple model for defaultable securities and, more generally, for a class of financial instruments for which the cash flows depend on the default times of a set of defaultable securities. For example, if τ is the time of default of a firm that has issued a simple credit-risky zero-coupon bond that matures at time T, then the bond delivers a single cash-flow H_T at T, given by

$$H_T = N\,\mathbb{1}\{\tau > T\}, \tag{1}$$

where N is the principal, and $\mathbb{1}\{\tau > T\} = 1$ if $\tau > T$ and $\mathbb{1}\{\tau > T\} = 0$ if $\tau \leq T$. By a "simple" credit-risky zero-coupon bond we mean the case of an idealised bond where there is no recovery of the principal if the firm defaults. If a fixed fraction R of the principal is paid at time T in the event of default, then we have

$$H_T = N\mathbb{1}\{\tau > T\} + RN\mathbb{1}\{\tau \leq T\}. \tag{2}$$

More realistic models can be developed by introducing random factors that determine the amount and timing of recovery levels. See, e.g., Brody, Hughston and Macrina [7, 10], and Macrina and Parbhoo [24].

As another example, let $\tau_1, \tau_2 \ldots, \tau_n$ denote the default times of a set of n discount bonds, each with maturity after T. Write $\bar{\tau}_1, \bar{\tau}_2, \ldots, \bar{\tau}_n$ for the "order statistics" of the default times. Hence $\bar{\tau}_1$ is the time of the first default (among $\tau_1, \tau_2, \ldots, \tau_n$), $\bar{\tau}_2$ is the time of the second default, and so on. Then a structured product that pays

$$H_T = K\,\mathbb{1}\{\bar{\tau}_k \leq T\} \tag{3}$$

is a kind of insurance policy that pays K at time T if there have been k or more defaults by time T.

One of the outstanding problems associated with credit-risk modeling is the following. What counts in the valuation of credit-risky products is not necessarily the "actual" or "objective" probability of default (even if this can be meaningfully determined), but rather the "perceived" probability of default. This can change over time, depending on shifts in market sentiment and the flow of relevant market information. How do we go about modeling the dynamics of such products?

2 Modeling the Market Filtration

We introduce a probability space with a measure $\mathbb{Q}$ which, for simplicity, we take to be the risk-neutral measure. Thus, the price process of any non-dividend-paying asset, when the price is expressed in units of a standard money-market account, is a $\mathbb{Q}$-martingale. We do not assume that the market is necessarily complete; rather, we merely assume that there is an established pricing kernel. We assume, again for simplicity, that the default-free interest-rate term structure is deterministic. Time 0 denotes the present, and we write P_{tT} for the price at t of a default-free discount bond that matures at T. To ensure absence of arbitrage, we require that $P_{tT} = P_{0T}/P_{0t}$, where $\{P_{0t}\}_{0\leq t<\infty}$ is the initial term structure. No attempt will be made in the present investigation to examine the case of stochastic interest rates: to keep credit-related issues in the foreground, we suppress considerations relating to the default-free interest rate term structure. See Rutkowski and Yu [25], Hughston and Macrina [20], Brody and Friedman [4], and Macrina and Parbhoo [24] for discussions of the stochastic interest rate case in an information-based setting.

The probability space comes equipped with a filtration $\{\mathcal{G}_t\}$ which we take to be the market filtration. Our first objective is to define $\{\mathcal{G}_t\}$ in such a way that market sentiments concerning the default times can be modeled explicitly. We let $\tau_1, \tau_2, \dots, \tau_n$ be a collection of non-negative random times such that $\mathbb{Q}(\tau_\alpha = 0) = 0$ and $\mathbb{Q}(\tau_\alpha > t) > 0$ for $t > 0$ and $\alpha = 1, 2, \dots, n$. We set

$$\tau_\alpha = f_\alpha(X_1, X_2, \dots, X_N), \qquad (\alpha = 1, 2, \dots, n). \tag{4}$$

Here $X_1, X_2, \dots, X_N$ are N independent, continuous, real-valued *market factors* that determine the default times, and f_α for each α is a smooth function of N variables that determines the dependence of τ_α on the market factors. We note that if two default times share an X-factor in common, then they will in general be correlated. With each τ_α, we associate a "survival" indicator process $\mathbb{1}\{\tau_\alpha > t\}$, $t \geq 0$, which takes the value unity until default occurs, at which time it drops to zero. Additionally, we introduce a set of N information processes $\{\xi_t^k\}_{t\geq 0}$ in association with the market factors, which in the present investigation we take to be of the form

$$\xi_t^k = \sigma_k t X_k + B_t^k. \tag{5}$$

Here, for each k, σ_k is a parameter ("information flow rate") and $\{B_t^k\}_{t\geq 0}$ is a Brownian motion ("market noise"). We assume that the X-factors and the market noise processes are all independent of one another.

We take the market filtration $\{\mathcal{G}_t\}_{t\geq 0}$ to be generated jointly by the information processes and the survival indicator processes. Therefore, we have:

$$\mathcal{G}_t = \sigma\left[\{\xi_s^k\}_{0\leq s\leq t}^{k=1,\dots,N}, \mathbb{1}\{\tau^\alpha > s\}_{0\leq s\leq t}^{\alpha=1,\dots,n}\right]. \tag{6}$$

It follows that at t the market knows the information generated up to t and the history of the indicator processes up to time t. For the purpose of calculations, it is useful also to introduce the filtration $\{\mathcal{F}_t\}_{t\geq 0}$ generated by the information processes:

$$\mathcal{F}_t = \sigma\left[\{\xi_s^k\}_{0\leq s\leq t}^{k=1,\dots,N}\right]. \tag{7}$$

Then clearly $\mathcal{F}_t \subset \mathcal{G}_t$. We do not require as such the notion of a "background" filtration for our theory. Indeed, we can think of the ξ's and the $\mathbb{1}$'s as providing two related but different types of information about the X's.

3 Credit-Risky Discount Bond

As an example, we study in more detail the case $n = 1$, $N = 1$. We have a single random market factor X and an associated default time $\tau = f(X)$. We assume that X is continuous and that $f(X)$ is monotonic. The market filtration $\{\mathcal{G}_t\}$ is generated jointly by an information process of the form

$$\xi_t = \sigma t X + B_t, \qquad t \geq 0, \tag{8}$$

and the indicator process $\mathbb{1}\{\tau > t\}$, $t \geq 0$. The Brownian motion $\{B_t\}_{t>0}$ is taken to be independent of X. The value of a defaultable T-maturity discount bond, when there is no recovery on default, is then given by

$$B_{tT} = P_{tT}\,\mathbb{E}\left[\mathbb{1}\{\tau > T\}\,|\,\mathcal{G}_t\right] \tag{9}$$

for $0 \leq t \leq T$. We shall write out an explicit expression for B_{tT}. First, we use the identity (see, e.g., Bielecki, Jeanblanc and Rutkowski [1]):

$$\mathbb{E}\left[\mathbb{1}\{\tau > T\}\,|\,\mathcal{G}_t\right] = \mathbb{1}\{\tau > t\}\frac{\mathbb{E}\left[\mathbb{1}\{\tau > T\}|\mathcal{F}_t\right]}{\mathbb{E}\left[\mathbb{1}\{\tau > t\}|\mathcal{F}_t\right]}, \tag{10}$$

where $\mathcal{F}_t$ is as defined in (7). It follows that

$$B_{tT} = P_{tT}\mathbb{1}\{\tau > t\}\frac{\mathbb{E}\left[\mathbb{1}\{\tau > T\}|\mathcal{F}_t\right]}{\mathbb{E}\left[\mathbb{1}\{\tau > t\}|\mathcal{F}_t\right]}. \tag{11}$$

We note that the information process $\{\xi_t\}$ has the Markov property with respect to its own filtration. To see this, it suffices to check that

$$\mathbb{Q}\left(\xi_t \leq x|\xi_s, \xi_{s_1}, \xi_{s_2}, \ldots, \xi_{s_k}\right) = \mathbb{Q}\left(\xi_t \leq x|\xi_s\right) \tag{12}$$

for any collection of times $t \geq s \geq s_1 \geq s_2 \geq \cdots \geq s_k > 0$. We observe that for $s > s_1 > s_2 > s_3 > 0$, the random variables $\{B_s/s - B_{s_1}/s_1\}$ and $\{B_{s_2}/s_2 - B_{s_3}/s_3\}$ are independent. This follows directly from a calculation of their covariance. Hence from the relation

$$\frac{\xi_s}{s} - \frac{\xi_{s_1}}{s_1} = \frac{B_s}{s} - \frac{B_{s_1}}{s_1} \tag{13}$$

we conclude that

$$\begin{aligned}\mathbb{Q}(\xi_t \leq x|\,\xi_s, \xi_{s_1}, \ldots, \xi_{s_k}) &= \mathbb{Q}\left(\xi_t \leq x\,\middle|\,\xi_s, \frac{\xi_s}{s} - \frac{\xi_{s_1}}{s_1}, \frac{\xi_{s_1}}{s_1} - \frac{\xi_{s_2}}{s_2}, \ldots, \frac{\xi_{s_{k-1}}}{s_{k-1}} - \frac{\xi_{s_k}}{s_k}\right)\\ &= \mathbb{Q}\left(\xi_t \leq x\,\middle|\,\xi_s, \frac{B_s}{s} - \frac{B_{s_1}}{s_1}, \frac{B_{s_1}}{s_1} - \frac{B_{s_2}}{s_2}, \ldots, \frac{B_{s_{k-1}}}{s_{k-1}} - \frac{B_{s_k}}{s_k}\right).\end{aligned} \tag{14}$$

However, since ξ_t and ξ_s are independent of $B_s/s - B_{s_1}/s_1$, $B_{s_1}/s_1 - B_{s_2}/s_2, \ldots,$ $B_{s_{k-1}}/s_{k-1} - B_{s_k}/s_k$, the result (12) follows.

As a consequence of the Markovian property of $\{\xi_t\}$ and the fact that X is $\mathcal{F}_\infty$-measurable, we therefore obtain

$$B_{tT} = P_{tT}\mathbb{1}\{\tau > t\}\,\frac{\mathbb{E}\left[\mathbb{1}\{\tau > T\}\,|\,\xi_t\right]}{\mathbb{E}\left[\mathbb{1}\{\tau > t\}\,|\,\xi_t\right]} \tag{15}$$

for the defaultable bond price. Thus we can write

$$B_{tT} = P_{tT}\,\mathbb{1}\{\tau > t\}\,\frac{\int_{-\infty}^{\infty}\mathbb{1}\{f(x) > T\}\rho_t(x)\mathrm{d}x}{\int_{-\infty}^{\infty}\mathbb{1}\{f(x) > t\}\rho_t(x)\mathrm{d}x}. \tag{16}$$

Here

$$\rho_t(x) = \mathbb{E}\left[\delta(X - x)\,|\,\xi_t\right] \tag{17}$$

is the conditional density for X given ξ_t, and a calculation using the Bayes law shows that:

$$\rho_t(x) = \frac{\rho_0(x)\exp\left[\sigma x\xi_t - \frac{1}{2}\sigma^2x^2t\right]}{\int_{-\infty}^{\infty}\rho_0(x)\exp\left[\sigma x\xi_t - \frac{1}{2}\sigma^2x^2t\right]\mathrm{d}x}, \tag{18}$$

where $\rho_0(x)$ is the *a priori* density of X. Thus for the bond price we obtain:

$$B_{tT} = P_{tT}\mathbb{1}\{\tau > t\}\,\frac{\int_{-\infty}^{\infty}\rho_0(x)\mathbb{1}\{f(x) > T\}\exp\left[\sigma x\xi_t - \frac{1}{2}\sigma^2x^2t\right]\mathrm{d}x}{\int_{-\infty}^{\infty}\rho_0(x)\mathbb{1}\{f(x) > t\}\exp\left[\sigma x\xi_t - \frac{1}{2}\sigma^2x^2t\right]\mathrm{d}x}. \tag{19}$$

It should be apparent that the value of the bond fluctuates as ξ_t changes. This reflects the effects of changes in market sentiment concerning the possibility of default. Indeed, if we regard τ as the default time of an obligor that has issued a number of different bonds (coupon bonds can be regarded as bundles of zero-coupon bonds), then similar formulae will apply for each of the various bond issues.

When the default times of two or more distinct obligors depend on a common market factor, the resulting bond price dynamics are correlated and so are the default times. The modelling framework presented here therefore provides a basis for a number of new constructions in credit-risk management, including explicit expressions for the volatilities and correlations of credit-risky bonds.

Our methodology is to consider models for which each independent X-factor has its own information process. Certainly, we can also consider the situation where there may be two or more distinct information processes available concerning the same X-factor. This situation is relevant to models with asymmetric information, where some traders may have access to "more" information about a given market factor than other traders; see Brody, Davis, Friedman and Hughston [3], Brody, Brody, Meister and Parry [2], and Brody, Hughston and Macrina [10].

In principle, a variety of different types of information processes can be considered. We have in (5) used for simplicity what is perhaps the most elementary type of information process, a Brownian motion with a random drift. The linearity of the drift term in the time variable ensures on the one hand that the information process has the Markov property, and on the other hand, since the Brownian term grows in magnitude on average like the square-root of time, that the drift term eventually comes to dominate the noise term, thus allowing for the release of information concerning the likely time of default. Information processes based variously on the Brownian bridge (Brody, Hughston and Macrina [7, 8]), the gamma bridge (Brody, Hughston and Macrina [9]), and the Lévy random bridge (Hoyle, Hughston and Macrina [18, 19]) have been applied to problems in finance and insurance.

Our work can be viewed in the context of the growing body of literature on the role of information in finance and its application to credit risk modeling in particular. No attempt will be made here at a systematic survey of material in this line. We refer the reader, for example, to Kusuoka [22], Föllmer, Wu and Yor [14], Duffie and Lando [13], Jarrow and Protter [21], Çetin, Jarrow, Protter and Yildirim [11], Giesecke [17], Geman, Madan and Yor [16], Coculescu, Geman and Jeanblanc [12], Frey and Schmidt [15], Bielecki, Jeanblanc and Rutkowski [1], and works cited therein.

4 Discount Bond Dynamics

Further insight into the nature of the model can be gained by working out the dynamics of the bond price. An application of Ito calculus gives the following dynamics over the time interval from 0 to T:

$$\mathrm{d}B_{tT} = (r_t + h_t)B_{tT}\mathrm{d}t + \sigma\Sigma_{tT}\, B_{tT}\mathrm{d}W_t + B_{t-T}\mathrm{d}\mathbb{1}\{\tau > t\}. \tag{20}$$

Here

$$r_t = -\partial_t \ln(P_{0t}) \tag{21}$$

is the deterministic short rate of interest, and

$$h_t = \frac{\mathbb{E}\left[\delta(f(X) - t) \mid \mathcal{F}_t\right]}{\mathbb{E}\left[\mathbb{1}\{f(X) > t\} \mid \mathcal{F}_t\right]} \tag{22}$$

is the so-called hazard rate. It should be evident that if $\tau \leq T$, then when the default time is reached the bond price drops to zero. The defaultable discount bond volatility Σ_{tT} is given by

$$\Sigma_{tT} = \frac{\mathbb{E}\left[\mathbb{1}\{f(X) > T\}X \mid \mathcal{F}_t\right]}{\mathbb{E}\left[\mathbb{1}\{f(X) > T\} \mid \mathcal{F}_t\right]} - \frac{\mathbb{E}\left[\mathbb{1}\{f(X) > t\}X \mid \mathcal{F}_t\right]}{\mathbb{E}\left[\mathbb{1}\{f(X) > t\} \mid \mathcal{F}_t\right]}. \tag{23}$$

The process $\{W_t\}$ appearing in the dynamics of $\{B_{tT}\}$ is defined by the relation:

$$W_t = \int_0^t \mathbb{1}\{f(X) > s\} \left(\mathrm{d}\xi_s - \sigma \mathbb{E}\left[X | \mathcal{G}_s\right] \mathrm{d}s\right). \tag{24}$$

To deduce the formulae above, we define a one-parameter family of $\{\mathcal{F}_t\}$-adapted processes $\{F_{tu}\}$ by setting

$$F_{tu} = \int_{-\infty}^{\infty} \rho_0(x) \mathbb{1}\{f(x) > u\} \exp\left[\sigma x \xi_t - \tfrac{1}{2}\sigma^2 x^2 t\right] \mathrm{d}x. \tag{25}$$

Then the bond price can be written in the form

$$B_{tT} = P_{tT} \mathbb{1}\{\tau > t\} \frac{F_{tT}}{F_{tt}}. \tag{26}$$

An application of Ito's lemma gives

$$\frac{\mathrm{d}F_{tT}}{F_{tT}} = \sigma \frac{\mathbb{E}\left[\mathbb{1}\{f(X) > T\} X \mid \mathcal{F}_t\right]}{\mathbb{E}\left[\mathbb{1}\{f(X) > T\} \mid \mathcal{F}_t\right]} \mathrm{d}\xi_t \tag{27}$$

and

$$\frac{\mathrm{d}F_{tt}}{F_{tt}} = -\frac{\mathbb{E}\left[\delta(f(X) - t) \mid \mathcal{F}_t\right]}{\mathbb{E}\left[\mathbb{1}\{f(X) > t\} \mid \mathcal{F}_t\right]} \mathrm{d}t + \sigma \frac{\mathbb{E}\left[\mathbb{1}\{f(X) > t\} X \mid \mathcal{F}_t\right]}{\mathbb{E}\left[\mathbb{1}\{f(X) > t\} \mid \mathcal{F}_t\right]} \mathrm{d}\xi_t. \tag{28}$$

The desired results then follow by use of the relation

$$\mathrm{d}\left(\frac{F_{tT}}{F_{tt}}\right) = \frac{F_{tT}}{F_{tt}} \left[\frac{\mathrm{d}F_{tT}}{F_{tT}} - \frac{\mathrm{d}F_{tt}}{F_{tt}} + \left(\frac{\mathrm{d}F_{tt}}{F_{tt}}\right)^2 - \frac{\mathrm{d}F_{tT}}{F_{tT}} \frac{\mathrm{d}F_{tt}}{F_{tt}}\right]. \tag{29}$$

The process $\{W_t\}_{0 \le t < \tau}$ defined by (24) is a $\{\mathcal{G}_t\}$-Brownian motion. This can be seen by use of Lévy's characterisation. Specifically, we have $\mathrm{d}W_t^2 = \mathrm{d}t$ and $\mathbb{E}[W_u \mid \mathcal{G}_t] = W_t$. To see that $\{W_t\}_{0 \le t < \tau}$ is a $\{\mathcal{G}_t\}$-martingale, we observe that

$$\begin{aligned} W_u &= \int_0^u \mathbb{1}\left\{\tau > s\right\} \left(\mathrm{d}\xi_s - \sigma \mathbb{E}\left[X \mid \mathcal{G}_s\right] \mathrm{d}s\right), \\ &= W_t + \int_t^u \mathbb{1}\{\tau > s\} \left(\mathrm{d}\xi_s - \sigma \mathbb{E}\left[X \mid \mathcal{G}_s\right] \mathrm{d}s\right), \end{aligned} \tag{30}$$

and hence

$$\mathbb{E}\left[W_u \mid \mathcal{G}_t\right] = W_t + \mathbb{E}\left[\int_t^u \mathbb{1} \left(\mathrm{d}\xi_s - \sigma \mathbb{E}[X \mid \mathcal{G}_s] \mathrm{d}s\right) \middle| \mathcal{G}_t\right]. \tag{31}$$

Then by inserting $\mathrm{d}\xi_s = \sigma X \mathrm{d}s + \mathrm{d}B_s$ and using the tower property, we find that the terms involving X cancel and we are left with

$$\begin{aligned}
\mathbb{E}\left[W_u \,|\, \mathcal{G}_t\right] &= W_t + \mathbb{E}\left[\int_t^u \mathbb{1}\{\tau > s\}\mathrm{d}B_s \,\middle|\, \mathcal{G}_t\right], \\
&= W_t + \mathbb{E}\left[\mathbb{E}\left[\int_t^u \mathbb{1}\{\tau > s\}\mathrm{d}B_s \,\middle|\, \sigma\left\{X, \mathcal{G}_t\right\}\right] \,\middle|\, \mathcal{G}_t\right], \\
&= W_t.
\end{aligned} \tag{32}$$

The Brownian motion that "drives" the defaultable bond is not adapted to a pre-specified background filtration. Rather, it is directly associated with information about the factors determining default. In this respect, the information-based approach is closer in spirit to a structural model, even though it retains the economy of a reduced-form model.

5 Hazard Rates and Forward Hazard Rates

Let us now examine more closely properties of the intensity process $\{h_t\}$ given by the expression (22). We remark first that the intensity at time t is a function of ξ_t. This shows that in the present model, the default intensity is determined by "market perceptions." Our model can thus be characterised as follows:

> The market does not know the "true" default intensity; rather, from the information available to the market a kind of "best estimate" for the default intensity is used for the pricing of bonds—but the market is "aware" of the fact that this estimate is based on perceptions, and hence as the perceptions change, so will the estimate, and so will the bond prices. Thus, in the present model (and unlike the majority of credit models hitherto proposed), there is no need for "fundamental changes" in the state of the obligor, or the underlying economic environment, as the basis for improvement or deterioration of credit quality: it suffices simply that the information about the credit quality should change—whether or not this information is actually representative of the true state of affairs.

In the present example, we can obtain a more explicit expression for the intensity by transforming variables as follows. Since f is invertible, we can introduce the inverse function $\phi(\tau) = f^{-1}(\tau) = X$ and write

$$\xi_t = \sigma t \phi(\tau) + B_t \tag{33}$$

for the information process. As before, we assume that the Brownian motion $\{B_t\}_{t\geq 0}$ is independent of the default time τ. Writing $p(u)$ for the *a priori* density of the random variable $\tau = f(X)$, we deduce from (22) that the hazard process is given by the expression

$$h_t = \frac{p(t)\,\mathrm{e}^{\sigma\phi(t)\xi_t - \frac{1}{2}\sigma^2\phi^2(t)t}}{\int_t^\infty p(u)\,\mathrm{e}^{\sigma\phi(u)\xi_t - \frac{1}{2}\sigma^2\phi^2(u)t}\mathrm{d}u}. \tag{34}$$

This expression manifestly reminds us the fact that $\{h_t\}$ is a function of the information ξ_t, and thus its value moves up and down according to the market perception of the timing of default.

In the present context, it is also natural to consider the forward hazard rate defined by the expression

$$h_{tu} = \frac{\mathbb{E}\left[\delta(f(X) - u) \,|\, \mathcal{F}_t\right]}{\mathbb{E}\left[\mathbb{1}\{f(X) > u\} \,|\, \mathcal{F}_t\right]}. \tag{35}$$

We observe that $h_{tu}du$ represents the *a posteriori* probability of default in the infinitesimal interval $[u, u + \mathrm{d}u]$, conditional on no default until time u. More explicitly, we have

$$h_{tu} = \frac{p(u)\,\mathrm{e}^{\sigma\phi(u)\xi_t - \frac{1}{2}\sigma^2\phi^2(u)t}}{\int_u^\infty p(v)\,\mathrm{e}^{\sigma\phi(v)\xi_t - \frac{1}{2}\sigma^2\phi^2(v)t}\mathrm{d}v} \tag{36}$$

for the forward hazard rate.

It is a straightforward matter to simulate the dynamics of the bond price and the associated hazard rates by Monte Carlo methods. First we simulate a value for X by use of the *a priori* density $\rho_0(x)$. From this, we deduce the corresponding value of τ. Then we simulate an independent Brownian motion $\{B_t\}$, and thereby also the information process $\{\xi_t\}$. Putting these ingredients together we have a simulation for the bond price and the associated hazard rate. In Fig. 1, we sketch several sample paths resulting from such a simulation study.

6 Options on Defaultable Bonds

We consider the problem of pricing an option on a defaultable bond with bond maturity T. Let K be the option strike price and let t $(< T)$ be the option maturity. The payoff of the option is then $(B_{tT} - K)^+$. Let us write the bond price in the form

$$B_{tT} = \mathbb{1}\{\tau > t\}B(t, \xi_t), \tag{37}$$

where the function $B(t, y)$ is defined by

$$B(t, y) = P_{tT}\frac{\int_T^\infty p(u)\exp\left[\sigma\phi(u)y - \frac{1}{2}\sigma^2\phi^2(u)t\right]\mathrm{d}u}{\int_t^\infty p(u)\exp\left[\sigma\phi(u)y - \frac{1}{2}\sigma^2\phi^2(u)t\right]\mathrm{d}u}. \tag{38}$$

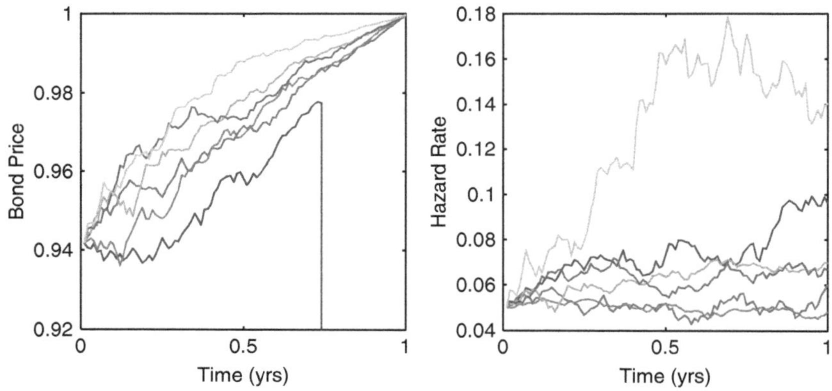

Fig. 1 Sample paths of the defaultable discount bond and the associated hazard rate. We choose $\phi(t) = \mathrm{e}^{-0.025t}$, and the initial term structure is assumed to be flat with $P_{0t} = \mathrm{e}^{-0.02t}$. The information flow rate parameter is set to be $\sigma = 0.3$, and the bond maturity is one year

We make note of the identity

$$\left(\mathbb{1}\{\tau > t\}B(t,\xi_t) - K\right)^+ = \mathbb{1}\{\tau > t\}\left(B(t,\xi_t) - K\right)^+, \tag{39}$$

satisfied by the option payoff. The price of the option is thus given by

$$C_0 = P_{0t}\,\mathbb{E}\Big[\mathbb{1}\{\tau > t\}\left(B(t,\xi_t) - K\right)^+\Big]. \tag{40}$$

We find, in particular, that the option payoff is a function of the random variables τ and ξ_t. To determine the expectation (40), we need to work out the joint density of τ and ξ_t, defined by

$$\rho(u,y) = \mathbb{E}\left[\delta(\tau - u)\delta(\xi_t - y)\right] = -\frac{\mathrm{d}}{\mathrm{d}u}\mathbb{E}\left[\mathbb{1}\{\tau > u\}\delta(\xi_t - y)\right]. \tag{41}$$

Note that the expression

$$A_0(u,y) = P_{0t}\,\mathbb{E}\left[\mathbb{1}\{\tau > u\}\delta(\xi_t - y)\right] \tag{42}$$

appearing on the right side of (41), with an additional discounting factor, can be regarded as representing the price of a "defaultable Arrow-Debreu security" based on the value at time t of the information process.

To work out the expectation appearing here we shall use the Fourier representation for the delta function:

$$\delta(\xi_t - y) = \frac{1}{2\pi}\int_{-\infty}^{\infty} \exp\left(-\mathrm{i}y\lambda + \mathrm{i}\xi_t\lambda\right)\mathrm{d}\lambda, \tag{43}$$

which of course has to be interpreted in an appropriate way with respect to integration against a class of test functions. We have

$$\mathbb{E}\left[\mathbb{1}\{\tau > u\}\delta(\xi_t - y)\right] = \frac{1}{2\pi}\int_{-\infty}^{\infty} \mathrm{e}^{-\mathrm{i}y\lambda}\mathbb{E}\left[\mathbb{1}\{\tau > u\}\mathrm{e}^{\mathrm{i}\xi_t\lambda}\right]\mathrm{d}\lambda. \tag{44}$$

The expectation appearing in the integrand is given by

$$\mathbb{E}\left[\mathbb{1}\{\tau > u\}\mathrm{e}^{\mathrm{i}\xi_t\lambda}\right] = \int_{-\infty}^{\infty} \mathbb{1}\{x > u\}\, p(x)\exp\left(\mathrm{i}\sigma\lambda t\phi(x) - \tfrac{1}{2}\lambda^2 t\right)\mathrm{d}x, \tag{45}$$

where we have made use of the fact that the random variables τ and B_t appearing in the definition of the information process (33) are independent. We insert this intermediate result in (44) and rearrange terms to obtain

$$\mathbb{E}\left[\mathbb{1}\{\tau > u\}\delta(\xi_t - y)\right] = \frac{1}{2\pi}\int_{-\infty}^{\infty} \mathbb{1}\{x > u\}\, p(x)\int_{-\infty}^{\infty} \mathrm{e}^{-\mathrm{i}y\lambda+\mathrm{i}\sigma\lambda t\phi(x)-\frac{1}{2}\lambda^2 t}\mathrm{d}\lambda\mathrm{d}x. \tag{46}$$

Performing the Gaussian integration associated with the λ variable, we deduce that the price of the defaultable Arrow–Debreu security is

$$A_0(u, y) = \frac{P_{0t}}{\sqrt{2\pi\, t}}\int_{-\infty}^{\infty} \mathbb{1}\{x > u\}p(x)\exp\left[-\frac{(\sigma t\phi(x) - y)^2}{2t}\right]\mathrm{d}x. \tag{47}$$

For the calculation of the price of a call option written on a defaultable discount bond, it is convenient to rewrite (47) in the following form:

$$A_0(y) = \frac{P_{0t}}{\sqrt{2\pi\, t}}\exp\left(-\frac{y^2}{2t}\right)\int_{u}^{\infty} p(x)\exp\left(\sigma\phi(x)y - \tfrac{1}{2}\sigma^2\phi^2(x)t\right)\mathrm{d}x. \tag{48}$$

It follows that for the joint density function we have

$$\rho(u, y) = \frac{1}{\sqrt{2\pi t}}\, p(u)\,\mathrm{e}^{-\frac{1}{2t}y^2}\,\mathrm{e}^{\sigma\phi(u)y-\frac{1}{2}\sigma^2\phi^2(u)t}. \tag{49}$$

The price of the call option can therefore be worked out as follows:

$$\begin{aligned} C_0 &= P_{0t}\int_{-\infty}^{\infty}\mathrm{d}u\int_{-\infty}^{\infty}\mathrm{d}y\,\rho(u, y)\mathbb{1}\{u > t\}(B(t, y) - K)^+ \\ &= \frac{P_{0t}}{\sqrt{2\pi t}}\int_{-\infty}^{\infty}\mathrm{d}y\,\mathrm{e}^{-\frac{1}{2t}y^2}(B(t, y)-K)^+\left[\int_t^{\infty} p(u)\mathrm{e}^{\sigma\phi(u)y-\frac{1}{2}\sigma^2\phi^2(u)t}\mathrm{d}u\right]. \end{aligned} \tag{50}$$

We notice that the term inside the square brackets is identical to the denominator of the expression for $B(t, y)$. Therefore, we have

$$C_0 = \frac{P_{0t}}{\sqrt{2\pi t}} \int_{-\infty}^{\infty} \mathrm{d}y\, \mathrm{e}^{-\frac{1}{2t}y^2} \left(P_{tT} \int_T^{\infty} p(u) \mathrm{e}^{\sigma\phi(u)y - \frac{1}{2}\sigma^2\phi^2(u)t} \mathrm{d}u \right.$$
$$\left. - K \int_t^{\infty} p(u) \mathrm{e}^{\sigma\phi(u)y - \frac{1}{2}\sigma^2\phi^2(u)t} \mathrm{d}u \right)^{+}. \quad (51)$$

An analysis similar to the one carried out in Brody and Friedman [4] shows the following result: Provided that $\phi(u)$ is a decreasing function, there exists a unique critical value y^* for y such that

$$P_{tT} \int_T^{\infty} p(u) \mathrm{e}^{\sigma\phi(u)y - \frac{1}{2}\sigma^2\phi^2(u)t} \mathrm{d}u - K \int_t^{\infty} p(u) \mathrm{e}^{\sigma\phi(u)y - \frac{1}{2}\sigma^2\phi^2(u)t} \mathrm{d}u > 0 \quad (52)$$

if $y < y^*$. On the other hand, if $\phi(u)$ is increasing, then there is likewise a unique critical value $y^\dagger$ of y such that for $y > y^\dagger$ we have

$$P_{tT} \int_T^{\infty} p(u) \mathrm{e}^{\sigma\phi(u)y - \frac{1}{2}\sigma^2\phi^2(u)t} \mathrm{d}u - K \int_t^{\infty} p(u) \mathrm{e}^{\sigma\phi(u)y - \frac{1}{2}\sigma^2\phi^2(u)t} \mathrm{d}u > 0. \quad (53)$$

Therefore, we can perform the y-integration in (51) to obtain the value

$$C_0 = P_{0T} \int_T^{\infty} p(u)\, N\left(\frac{y^* - \sigma\phi(u)t}{\sqrt{t}} \right) \mathrm{d}u$$
$$- P_{0t} K \int_t^{\infty} p(u)\, N\left(\frac{y^* - \sigma\phi(u)t}{\sqrt{t}} \right) \mathrm{d}u \quad (54)$$

when $\phi(u)$ is decreasing. If $\phi(u)$ is increasing, we have

$$C_0 = P_{0T} \int_T^{\infty} p(u)\, N\left(\frac{\sigma\phi(u)t - y^\dagger}{\sqrt{t}} \right) \mathrm{d}u$$
$$- P_{0t} K \int_t^{\infty} p(u)\, N\left(\frac{\sigma\phi(u)t - y^\dagger}{\sqrt{t}} \right) \mathrm{d}u. \quad (55)$$

The critical values $y^*_\phi(t, T, K, \sigma)$ and $y^\dagger_\phi(t, T, K, \sigma)$ can be determined numerically to value the prices of call options. An example of the call price as a function of its strike and maturity, when $\phi(u)$ is decreasing, is shown in Fig. 2. If the function $\phi(u)$ is not monotonic, then there is in general more than one critical value of y for which the argument of the max function in (51) is positive. Therefore, in this case there will be more terms in the option-valuation formula.

The case represented by a simple discount bond is merely an example and as such cannot be taken as a completely realistic model. Nevertheless, it is interesting that modelling the information available about the default time leads to a dynamical model for the bond price, in which the Brownian fluctuations driving the price process arise in a natural way as the innovations associated with the flow of

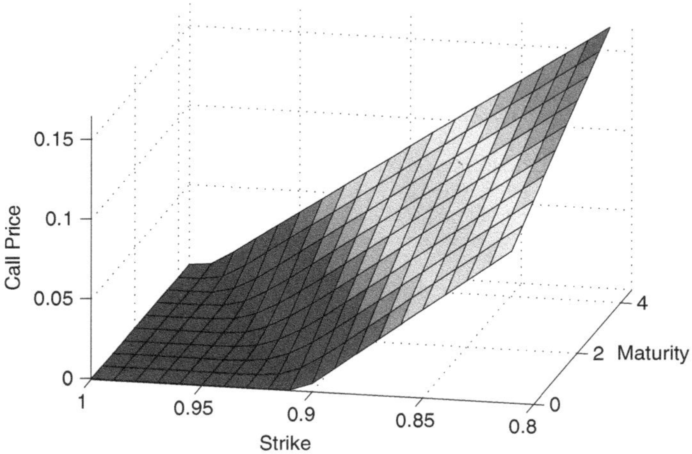

Fig. 2 Price of a call option on a defaultable discount bond. The bond maturity is five years. The information-adjusting function is set to be $\phi(t) = e^{-0.05t}$, and the initial term structure is assumed to be flat so that $P_{0t} = e^{-0.02t}$. The information flow rate is set to be $\sigma = 0.25$

information to the market concerning the default time. Thus no "background filtration" is required for the analysis of default in models here proposed. The information flow-rate parameter σ is not directly observable, but rather can be backed out from option-price data on an "implied" basis. The extension of the present investigation, which can be regarded as a synthesis of the "density" approach to interest-rate modeling proposed in Brody and Hughston [5,6] and the information-based asset pricing framework developed in Brody, Hughston and Macrina [7–9] and Macrina [23], to multiple asset situations with portfolio credit risk will be pursued elsewhere.

Acknowledgements The authors are grateful to seminar participants at the Workshop on Incomplete Information on Mathematical Finance, Chemnitz (June 2009), the Kyoto Workshop on Mathematical Finance and Related Topics in Economics and Engineering (August 2009), Quant Congress Europe, London (November 2009), King's College London (December 2009), Hitotsubashi University, Tokyo (February 2010) and Hiroshima University (February 2010) for helpful comments and suggestions. Part of this work was carried out while LPH was visiting the Aspen Center for Physics (September 2009), and Kyoto University (August and October 2009). DCB and LPH thank HSBC, Lloyds TSB, Shell International, and Yahoo Japan for research support.

References

1. Bielecki, T.R., Jeanblanc, M., Rutkowski, M.: Credit risk modelling. Osaka University Press (2009)
2. Brody, D.C., Brody, J., Meister, B.K., Parry, M.F.: Outsider trading. arXiv:1003.0764 (2010)
3. Brody, D.C., Davis, M.H.A., Friedman, R.L., Hughston, L.P.: Informed traders. Proceedings of the Royal Society London A **465**, 1103–1122 (2008)

4. Brody, D.C., Friedman, R.L.: Information of interest. Risk magazine, December 2009 issue, 101–106 (2009)
5. Brody, D.C., Hughston, L.P.: Interest rates and information geometry. Proc. R. Soc. Lond. A **457**, 1343–1364 (2001)
6. Brody, D.C., Hughston, L.P.: Entropy and information in the interest rate term structure. Quant. Finance **2**, 70–80 (2002)
7. Brody, D.C., Hughston, L.P., Macrina, A.: Beyond hazard rates: a new framework for credit-risk modelling. In: Fu, M., Jarrow, R., Yen, J.-Y., Elliott, R. (eds.) Advances in Mathematical Finance: Festschrift Volume in Honour of Dilip Madan. Birkhäuser, Basel (2007)
8. Brody, D.C., Hughston, L.P., Macrina, A.: Information-based asset pricing. Int. J. Theor. Appl. Finance **11**, 107–142 (2008)
9. Brody, D.C., Hughston, L.P., Macrina, A.: Dam rain and cumulative gain. Proc. R. Soc. Lond. A **464**, 1801–1822 (2008)
10. Brody, D.C., Hughston, L.P., Macrina, A.: Modelling information flows in financial markets. In: Di Nunno, G., Øksendal, B. (eds.) Advanced Mathematical Methods for Finance. Springer, Berlin (2011)
11. Çetin, U., Jarrow, R., Protter, P., Yildirim, Y.: Modeling credit risk with partial information. Ann. Appl. Probab. **14**, 1167–1178 (2004)
12. Coculescu, D., Geman, H., Jeanblanc, M.: Valuation of default sensitive claims under inperfect information. Finance Stoch. **12**, 195–218 (2008)
13. Duffie, D., Lando, D.: Term structures of credit spreads with incomplete accounting information. Econometrica **69**, 633–664 (2001)
14. Föllmer, H., Wu, C.-T., Yor, M.: Canonical decomposition of linear transformations of two independent Brownian motions motivated by models of insider trading. Stoch. Processes Appl. **84**, 137–164 (1999)
15. Frey, R., Schmidt, T.: Pricing corporate securities under noisy asset information. Math. Finance **19**, 403–421 (2009)
16. Geman, H., Madan, D.B., Yor, M.: Probing option prices for information. Methodology Comput. Appl. Probab. **9**, 115–131 (2007)
17. Giesecke, K.: Default and information. J. Econ. Dyn. Control **30**, 2281–2303 (2006)
18. Hoyle, E., Hughston, L.P., Macrina, A.: Lévy random bridges and the modelling of financial information. arXiv:0912.3652 (2009)
19. Hoyle, E., Hughston, L.P., Macrina, A.: Stable-1/2 bridges and insurance: a Bayesian approach to non-life reserving. arXiv:1005.0496 (2010)
20. Hughston, L.P., Macrina, A.: Pricing fixed-income securities in an information-based framework. arXiv:0911.1610 (2009)
21. Jarrow, R., Protter, P.: Structural versus reduced-form models: a new information based perspective. J. Investment Manag. **2**, 1–10 (2004)
22. Kusuoka, S.: A remark on default risk models. Adv. Math. Econ. **1**, 69–82 (1999)
23. Macrina, A.: An information-based framework for asset pricing: X-factor theory and its applications. PhD thesis, King's College, London (2006)
24. Macrina, A., Parbhoo, P.A.: Security pricing with information-sensitive discounting. In: Kijima, M., Hara, C., Tanaka, K., Muromachi, Y. (eds.) Recent Advances in Financial Engineering 2009, pp. 157–180. World Scientific (2010)
25. Rutkowski, M., Yu, N.: On the Brody–Hughston–Macrina approach to modelling of defaultable term structure. Int. J. Theor. Appl. Finance **10**, 557–589 (2007)

Chapter 7

Lévy random bridges and the modelling of financial information†

Edward Hoyle[a], Lane P. Hughston[a], Andrea Macrina[b,c,*]

[a] *Department of Mathematics, Imperial College London, London SW7 2AZ, UK*
[b] *Department of Mathematics, King's College London, London WC2R 2LS, UK*
[c] *Institute of Economic Research, Kyoto University, Kyoto 606-8501, Japan*

Received 4 June 2010; received in revised form 27 November 2010; accepted 6 December 2010
Available online 13 December 2010

Abstract

The information-based asset-pricing framework of Brody–Hughston–Macrina (BHM) is extended to include a wider class of models for market information. To model the information flow, we introduce a class of processes called Lévy random bridges (LRBs), generalising the Brownian bridge and gamma bridge information processes of BHM. Given its terminal value at T, an LRB has the law of a Lévy bridge. We consider an asset that generates a cash-flow X_T at T. The information about X_T is modelled by an LRB with terminal value X_T. The price process of the asset is worked out, along with the prices of options.

Keywords: Lévy processes; Lévy bridges; Information-based asset pricing; Option pricing; Non-linear filtering theory

---

1. Introduction

In financial markets, the information that traders and investors have about an asset is reflected in its price. The arrival of new information then leads to changes in asset prices. The 'information-based framework' (or 'X-factor theory') of Brody, Hughston and Macrina (BHM) isolates the emergence of information, and examines its role as a driver of price dynamics (see [8–10,23,25,28]). In the BHM framework, each asset is associated with a collection of random cash flows. The price of the asset is the sum of the discounted conditional expectations of the cash flows. The conditional expectations are taken with respect to (i) an appropriate measure, and

* Corresponding author at: Department of Mathematics, King's College London, London WC2R 2LS, UK.
E-mail address: andrea.macrina@kcl.ac.uk (A. Macrina).

0304-4149/$ - see front matter
doi:10.1016/j.spa.2010.12.003

†This chapter was originally published as: E. Hoyle, L. P. Hughston & A. Macrina (2011) Lévy Random Bridges and the Modelling of Financial Information. *Stochastic Processes and their Applications* **121**, 856–884. Reprinted with kind permission from Elsevier.

(ii) the filtration generated by a set of so-called information processes. The information processes carry noisy or imperfect market information about the cash flows. The present paper extends the work of BHM by introducing a wider class of information processes as a basis for the generation of the market filtration.

Qualitatively speaking, if information about an asset arrives infrequently, and in large lots, then its price process will exhibit large jumps. Conversely, if information arrives smoothly and steadily, then the impact of information arrival over short time-scales will be relatively modest. Thus, the emergence of information as the driver of price dynamics presents itself as an interesting avenue of investigation.

In a stochastic model, it is the filtration that encodes the emergence of information. Choosing an asset price process to be a geometric Brownian motion, for example, implies that the process is adapted to a Brownian filtration. Although this approach of implicitly choosing a filtration by specifying the law of a price process is common in the literature of mathematical finance, we wish to avoid it, and to specify the filtration $\{\mathcal{F}_t\}$ directly. In particular, we postulate the existence of a market information process $\{\xi_{tT}\}$ that generates $\{\mathcal{F}_t\}$. Then prices are derived by taking suitably discounted conditional expectations of cash flows with respect to this filtration. The dynamics of prices are dependent on the dynamics of the information process $\{\xi_{tT}\}$. To this end, we introduce a large class of processes, which we term Lévy random bridges (LRBs), for the modelling of $\{\xi_{tT}\}$. This class contains the Brownian and gamma information processes of BHM. The motivation for LRBs is the desire for Markov processes, defined over a fixed time interval, over which we have a distributional degree of freedom for the terminal value. We achieve this by conditioning Lévy processes on their value at some fixed future date T. We note that conditioned processes have been applied to various other problems in finance—see, for example, Back and Pedersen [1], Baudoin [3], Baudoin and Nguyen-Ngoc [4], Elliott and Jeanblanc [12], Elliott and Kopp [13], Gasbarra et al. [17], Geman et al. [18], and Madan and Yor [27]. Nevertheless, leaving the existing information-based literature aside, the present work differs considerably from earlier work in its aims and methods.

Section 2 begins with a brief introduction to Lévy processes and Lévy bridges. A Lévy bridge is a stochastic process defined over a finite time horizon, and is a Lévy process whose terminal value is known from the outset. We provide a proof of the Markov property for Lévy bridges.

In Section 3 we define Lévy random bridges. An LRB is a process defined over a finite time horizon whose bridge laws are the bridge laws of a Lévy process. It can be interpreted as being a Lévy process conditioned to have a fixed marginal law at a fixed future date. We shall see that such processes are useful for asset pricing in the information-based framework. We derive various properties of LRBs including: that LRBs are Markov processes; that the law of an LRB is equivalent to the law of a Lévy process (at least for all times up to the LRBs termination time); that LRBs have stationary increments; that the joint distribution of the increments of an LRB have a generalized multivariate Liouville distribution; and, if the path of an LRB is split into non-overlapping portions, then each portion is itself an LRB. The marginal characteristic function often proves convenient in the analysis of a Lévy process. This is not the case for an LRB. However, we are able to provide an expression for the transition law of a general LRB.

The information-based framework of Brody, Hughston & Macrina is described in Section 4. In this framework, cash flows are functions of independent X-factors. Information processes generate the market filtration, and reveal the value of the X-factors—thus, they reveal the value of the cash flows. Cash flows are priced by discounting their expected value given the market information. A general multi-factor set-up is described that allows for a rich dependency structure between cash flows. Much of the analysis is presented for a single X-factor market where the only information process is an LRB. The final value of the LRB is set to be the value of the X-factor. Using a single factor may sound restrictive, but this includes some well-known one-dimensional exponential Lévy models as special cases (the Black–Scholes model is recovered from an information-based model in Brody et al. [10] and Macrina [25]). Using Bayesian methods, we are able to derive the dynamics of the price of a cash flow. From this, we can price European call options on the cash flow price. An expression for the call price is given in a general LRB-information model.

2. Preliminaries

We fix a probability space $(\Omega, \mathbb{Q}, \mathcal{F})$, and assume that all processes and filtrations under consideration are càdlàg. Unless otherwise stated, when discussing a stochastic process we assume that the process takes values in $\mathbb{R}$, begins at time 0, and the filtration is that generated by the process itself. We work with a finite time horizon $[0, T]$.

2.1. Lévy processes

This section summarises a few well-known results about one-dimensional Lévy processes, further details of which can be found in Bertoin [5] and Sato [29]. A Lévy process is a stochastically-continuous process that starts from the value 0, and has stationary, independent increments. An increasing Lévy process is called a *subordinator*. If $\{L_t\}$ is a Lévy process, its *characteristic exponent* $\Psi : \mathbb{R} \to \mathbb{C}$ is defined by

$$\mathbb{E}[\mathrm{e}^{\mathrm{i}\lambda L_t}] = \exp(-t\,\Psi(\lambda)), \quad \lambda \in \mathbb{R}. \tag{1}$$

The characteristic exponent of a Lévy process characterises its law, and its form is prescribed by the Lévy–Khintchine formula:

$$\Psi(\lambda) = \mathrm{i}a\lambda + \frac{1}{2}\sigma^2\lambda^2 + \int_{-\infty}^{\infty} (1 - \mathrm{e}^{\mathrm{i}x\lambda} + \mathrm{i}x\lambda \mathbb{1}_{\{|x|<1\}})\Pi(\mathrm{d}x), \tag{2}$$

where $a \in \mathbb{R}$, $\sigma \geq 0$, and Π is a measure (the *Lévy measure*) on $\mathbb{R} \setminus \{0\}$ such that

$$\int_{-\infty}^{\infty} (1 \wedge |x|^2)\, \Pi(\mathrm{d}x) < \infty. \tag{3}$$

There are particular subclasses of Lévy processes that we shall consider, defined as follows:

Definition 2.1. Let $\{L_t\}_{0\leq t\leq T}$ and $\{M_t\}_{0\leq t\leq T}$ be Lévy processes. Then we write

1. $\{L_t\} \in \mathcal{C}[0, T]$ if the density of L_t exists for every $t \in (0, T]$,
2. $\{M_t\} \in \mathcal{D}$ if the marginal law of M_t is discrete for some $t > 0$.

Remark 2.2. If the marginal law of M_t is discrete for some $t > 0$, then the marginal law of M_t is discrete for all $t > 0$. The density of L_t exists if and only if its law is absolutely continuous with respect to the Lebesgue measure. In general, the absolute continuity of L_t depends on t (see [29], chapter 5); thus $\mathcal{C}[0, T_1] \supseteq \mathcal{C}[0, T_2]$ for $T_1 \leq T_2$.

We reserve the notation $f_t(x)$ to represent the density of L_t for some $\{L_t\} \in \mathcal{C}[0, T]$. Hence $f_t : \mathbb{R} \to \mathbb{R}_+$ and $\mathbb{Q}[L_t \in \mathrm{d}x] = f_t(x)\,\mathrm{d}x$. We reserve $Q_t(a)$ to represent the probability mass function of M_t for some $\{M_t\} \in \mathcal{D}$. We denote the state-space of $\{M_t\}$ by $\{a_i\} \subset \mathbb{R}$. Hence $Q_t : \{a_i\} \to [0, 1]$ and $\mathbb{Q}[M_t = a_i] = Q_t(a_i)$. We assume that the sequence $\{a_i\}$ is strictly increasing.

The transition probabilities of Lévy processes satisfy the convolution identities

$$f_t(x) = \int_{-\infty}^{\infty} f_{t-s}(x-y) f_s(y)\,\mathrm{d}y \quad \text{for } \{L_t\} \in \mathcal{C}[0,T], \tag{4}$$

and

$$Q_t(a_n) = \sum_{m=-\infty}^{\infty} Q_{t-s}(a_n - a_m) Q_s(a_m) \quad \text{for } \{M_t\} \in \mathcal{D}, \tag{5}$$

for $0 \le s < t \le T$. These are the Chapman–Kolmogorov equations for the processes $\{L_t\}$ and $\{M_t\}$.

The law of any càdlàg stochastic process is characterised by its finite-dimensional distributions. The finite-dimensional densities of $\{L_t\}_{0\le t\le T}$ exist and, with the understanding that $x_0 = t_0 = 0$, they are given by

$$\mathbb{Q}[L_{t_1} \in \mathrm{d}x_1, \ldots, L_{t_n} \in \mathrm{d}x_n] = \prod_{i=1}^{n} \left[f_{t_i - t_{i-1}}(x_i - x_{i-1})\,\mathrm{d}x_i \right], \tag{6}$$

for every $n \in \mathbb{N}_+$, every $0 < t_1 < \cdots < t_n \le T$, and every $(x_1, \ldots, x_n) \in \mathbb{R}^n$. With the understanding that $a_{k_0} = t_0 = 0$, the finite-dimensional probabilities of $\{M_t\}$ are

$$\mathbb{Q}[M_{t_1} = a_{k_1}, \ldots, M_{t_n} = a_{k_n}] = \prod_{i=1}^{n} Q_{t_i - t_{i-1}}(a_{k_i} - a_{k_{i-1}}), \tag{7}$$

for every $n \in \mathbb{N}_+$, every $0 < t_1 < \cdots < t_n$, and every $(k_1, \ldots, k_n) \in \mathbb{Z}^n$.

2.2. *Lévy bridges*

A bridge is a stochastic process that is pinned to some fixed point at a fixed future time. Bridges of Markov processes were constructed and analysed by Fitzsimmons et al. [16] in a general setting. In this section we focus on the bridges of Lévy processes in the classes $\mathcal{C}[0,T]$ and $\mathcal{D}$. In particular we have the following:

Proposition 2.3. *The bridges of processes in* $\mathcal{C}[0,T]$ *and* $\mathcal{D}$ *are Markov processes.*

Proof. We need to show that the process $\{L_t\} \in \mathcal{C}[0,T]$ is a Markov process when we know that $L_T = x$, for some constant x such that $0 < f_T(x) < \infty$. (It will be explained later why the condition that $0 < f_T(x) < \infty$ is required to ensure that the law of the bridge process is well defined.) In other words, we need to show that

$$\mathbb{Q}\left[L_t \le y \mid L_{t_1} = x_1, \ldots, L_{t_m} = x_m, L_T = x\right] = \mathbb{Q}\left[L_t \le y \mid L_{t_m} = x_m, L_T = x\right], \tag{8}$$

for all $m \in \mathbb{N}_+$, all $(x_1, \ldots, x_m, y) \in \mathbb{R}^{m+1}$, and all $0 \le t_1 < \cdots < t_m < t \le T$. The key property of $\{L_t\}$ that we use is that it has independent increments. Let us write

$$\Delta_i = L_{t_i} - L_{t_{i-1}}, \tag{9}$$
$$\delta_i = x_i - x_{i-1}, \tag{10}$$

for $1 \le i \le m$, where $t_0 = 0$ and $x_0 = 0$. Then we have:

$$\mathbb{Q}\left[L_t \le y | L_{t_1} = x_1, \ldots, L_{t_m} = x_m, L_T = x\right]$$

$$
\begin{aligned}
&= \mathbb{Q}\left[L_t - L_{t_m} \le y - x_m \middle| \Delta_1 = \delta_1, \ldots, \Delta_m = \delta_m, L_T - L_{t_m} = x - x_m\right] \\
&= \mathbb{Q}\left[L_t - L_{t_m} \le y - x_m \middle| L_T - L_{t_m} = x - x_m\right] \\
&= \mathbb{Q}\left[L_t - L_{t_m} \le y - x_m \middle| L_T - L_{t_m} = x - x_m, L_{t_m} = x_m\right] \\
&= \mathbb{Q}\left[L_t \le y \middle| L_T = x, L_{t_m} = x_m\right]. \qquad (11)
\end{aligned}
$$

The proof for processes in class $\mathcal{D}$ is similar. □

Let $\{L_t\} \in \mathcal{C}[0, T]$, and let $\{L_{tT}^{(z)}\}_{0 \le t \le T}$ be an $\{L_t\}$-bridge to the value $z \in \mathbb{R}$ at time T. For the transition probabilities of the bridge process to be well defined, we require that $0 < f_T(z) < \infty$. By the Bayes theorem we have

$$
\begin{aligned}
\mathbb{Q}\left[L_{tT}^{(z)} \in \mathrm{d}y \middle| L_{sT}^{(z)} = x\right] &= \mathbb{Q}\left[L_t \in \mathrm{d}y | L_s = x, L_T = z\right] \\
&= \frac{\mathbb{Q}[L_t \in \mathrm{d}y, L_T \in \mathrm{d}z | L_s = x]}{\mathbb{Q}[L_T \in \mathrm{d}z | L_s = x]} \\
&= \frac{f_{t-s}(y-x) f_{T-t}(z-y)}{f_{T-s}(z-x)} \,\mathrm{d}y, \qquad (12)
\end{aligned}
$$

for $0 \le s < t < T$. We define the marginal bridge density $f_{tT}(y; z)$ by

$$
f_{tT}(y; z) = \frac{f_t(y) f_{T-t}(z-y)}{f_T(z)}. \qquad (13)
$$

In this way we have

$$
\mathbb{Q}\left[L_{tT}^{(z)} \in \mathrm{d}y \middle| L_{sT}^{(z)} = x\right] = f_{t-s,T-s}(y-x; z-x)\,\mathrm{d}y. \qquad (14)
$$

The condition $0 < f_T(z) < \infty$ is enough to ensure that

$$
y \mapsto f_{t-s,T-s}(y - L_{sT}^{(z)}; z - L_{sT}^{(z)}) \qquad (15)
$$

is a well defined density for almost every value of $L_{sT}^{(z)}$. To see this, we note that

$$
\begin{aligned}
&\int_{-\infty}^{\infty} \int_{-\infty}^{\infty} f_{t-s,T-s}(y-x; z-x) \mathbb{Q}\left[L_{sT}^{(z)} \in \mathrm{d}x\right] \mathrm{d}y \\
&= \int_{-\infty}^{\infty} \int_{-\infty}^{\infty} f_{t-s,T-s}(y-x; z-x) f_{s,T}(x; z)\,\mathrm{d}x\,\mathrm{d}y \\
&= \int_{-\infty}^{\infty} \frac{f_{T-t}(z-y)}{f_T(z)} \int_{-\infty}^{\infty} f_{t-s}(y-x) f_s(x)\,\mathrm{d}x\,\mathrm{d}y \\
&= \frac{1}{f_T(z)} \int_{-\infty}^{\infty} f_{T-t}(z-y) f_t(y)\,\mathrm{d}y = 1. \qquad (16)
\end{aligned}
$$

From (16) it follows that

$$
\mathbb{Q}\left[\int_{-\infty}^{\infty} f_{t-s,T-s}(y - L_{sT}^{(z)}; z - L_{sT}^{(z)})\,\mathrm{d}y = 1\right] = 1. \qquad (17)
$$

Let $\{M_t\} \in \mathcal{D}$, and let $\{M_{tT}^{(k)}\}_{0 \le t \le T}$ be an $\{M_t\}$-bridge to the value a_k at time T, so $\mathbb{Q}[M_{TT}^{(k)} = a_k] = 1$. For the transition probabilities of the bridge to be well defined, we require that $\mathbb{Q}[M_T = a_k] = Q_T(a_k) > 0$. Then the Bayes theorem gives

$$\mathbb{Q}\left[M_{tT}^{(k)} = a_j | M_{sT}^{(k)} = a_i\right] = \mathbb{Q}\left[M_t = a_j | M_s = a_i, M_T = a_k\right]$$
$$= \frac{\mathbb{Q}\left[M_t = a_j, M_T = a_k | M_s = a_i\right]}{\mathbb{Q}\left[M_T = a_k | M_s = a_i\right]}$$
$$= \frac{Q_{t-s}(a_j - a_i)Q_{T-t}(a_k - a_j)}{Q_{T-s}(a_k - a_i)}, \tag{18}$$

for $0 \leq s < t < T$. Note that if $Q_T(a_k) = 0$, then the ratio (18) is not well defined when $s = 0$.

3. Lévy random bridges

The idea of information-based asset pricing is to model the flow of information in financial markets and hence to construct the market filtration explicitly. Let X_T be a random variable (a market factor), with a given *a priori* distribution. The value of X_T will be revealed to the market at time T. We wish to construct an information process $\{\xi_{tT}\}$ such that $\xi_{TT} = X_T$. We can then use the filtration generated by $\{\xi_{tT}\}$ to model the information that market participants have about X_T. One problem to overcome is how to ensure that the marginal law of ξ_{TT} is the *a priori* law of X_T.

Two explicit forms for the information process have been considered in the literature. The first is

$$\xi_{tT} = \frac{t}{T}X_T + \beta_{tT} \quad (0 \leq t \leq T), \tag{19}$$

where $\{\beta_{tT}\}_{0 \leq t \leq T}$ is a Brownian bridge starting and ending at the value zero ([8]; see also [7,10, 23,25,28]). The second is

$$\xi_{tT} = X_T\, \gamma_{tT} \quad (0 \leq t \leq T), \tag{20}$$

where $X_T > 0$ and $\{\gamma_{tT}\}_{0 \leq t \leq T}$ is a gamma bridge starting at the value zero and ending at the value one (see [9]). These forms share the property that each is identical in law to a Lévy process conditioned to have the *a priori* law of X_T at time T. The Brownian bridge information process is identical in law to a conditioned Brownian motion, and the gamma bridge information process is identical in law to a conditioned gamma process.

With this as motivation, in the present section we define a class of processes that we call Lévy random bridges (LRBs). An LRB is identical in law to a Lévy process conditioned to have a prespecified marginal law at T. Later we shall use LRBs as information processes in information-based models.

To make a link to the existing literature, and for simplicity of exposition, we use random bridges of Brownian motion and the gamma process as examples throughout the paper. Further examples—covering random bridges of the variance-gamma process, the normal inverse-Gaussian process, the Poisson process, the Cauchy process, and the stable-1/2 subordinator—can be found in Hoyle [21].

3.1. Defining LRBs

An LRB can be described as a process whose bridge laws are Lévy bridge laws. In the definitions below we define LRBs by reference to their finite-dimensional distributions rather than as conditioned Lévy processes. This proves convenient in future calculations.

Definition 3.1. We say that $\{L_{tT}\}_{0\le t\le T}$ has the law $LRB_{\mathcal{C}}([0,T],\{f_t\},\nu)$ if the following are satisfied:

1. L_{TT} has marginal law ν.
2. There exists a Lévy process $\{L_t\}\in\mathcal{C}[0,T]$ such that L_t has density $f_t(x)$ for all $t\in(0,T]$.
3. ν concentrates mass where $f_T(z)$ is positive and finite, i.e. $0<f_T(z)<\infty$ for ν-a.e. z.
4. For every $n\in\mathbb{N}_+$, every $0<t_1<\cdots<t_n<T$, every $(x_1,\ldots,x_n)\in\mathbb{R}^n$, and ν-a.e. z, we have

$$\mathbb{Q}\left[L_{t_1,T}\le x_1,\ldots,L_{t_n,T}\le x_n|L_{TT}=z\right]=\mathbb{Q}\left[L_{t_1}\le x_1,\ldots,L_{t_n}\le x_n|L_T=z\right].$$

Definition 3.2. We say that $\{M_{tT}\}_{0\le t\le T}$ has the law $LRB_{\mathcal{D}}([0,T],\{Q_t\},P)$ if the following are satisfied:

1. M_{TT} has probability mass function P.
2. There exists a Lévy process $\{M_t\}\in\mathcal{D}$ such that M_t has marginal probability mass function $Q_t(a)$ for all $t\in(0,T]$.
3. The law of M_{TT} is absolutely continuous with respect to the law of M_T, i.e.

   if $P(a)>0$ then $Q_T(a)>0$.
4. For every $n\in\mathbb{N}_+$, every $0<t_1<\cdots<t_n<T$, every $(k_1,\ldots,k_n)\in\mathbb{Z}^n$, and every b such that $P(b)>0$, we have

$$\begin{aligned}&\mathbb{Q}\left[M_{t_1,T}=a_{k_1},\ldots,M_{t_n,T}=a_{k_n}|M_{TT}=b\right]\\&\quad=\mathbb{Q}\left[M_{t_1}=a_{k_1},\ldots,M_{t_n}=a_{k_n}|M_T=b\right].\end{aligned}$$

Definition 3.3. For a fixed time $s<T$, if the law of the process $\{\eta_{s+t}\}_{0\le t\le T-s}$ is of the type $LRB_{\mathcal{C}}([0,T-s],\cdot,\cdot)$, resp. $LRB_{\mathcal{D}}([0,T-s],\cdot,\cdot)$, then we say that $\{\eta_t\}_{s\le t\le T}$ has law $LRB_{\mathcal{C}}([s,T],\cdot,\cdot)$, resp. $LRB_{\mathcal{D}}([s,T],\cdot,\cdot)$.

If the law of a process is one of the *LRB*-types defined above, then we say that it is a Lévy random bridge (LRB).

3.2. Finite-dimensional distributions

For the rest of this section we assume that $\{L_{tT}\}$ and $\{M_{tT}\}$ are LRBs with laws $LRB_{\mathcal{C}}([0,T],\{f_t\},\nu)$ and $LRB_{\mathcal{D}}([0,T],\{Q_t\},P)$, respectively. We also assume that $\{L_t\}$ is a Lévy process such that L_t has density $f_t(x)$ for $t\le T$, and $\{M_t\}$ is a Lévy process such that M_t has probability mass function $Q_t(a_i)$ for $t\le T$.

The finite dimensional distributions of $\{L_{tT}\}$ are given by

$$\begin{aligned}&\mathbb{Q}\left[L_{t_1,T}\in\mathrm{d}x_1,\ldots,L_{t_n,T}\in\mathrm{d}x_n,L_{TT}\in\mathrm{d}z\right]\\&\quad=\prod_{i=1}^{n}\left[f_{t_i-t_{i-1}}(x_i-x_{i-1})\,\mathrm{d}x_i\right]\psi_{t_n}(\mathrm{d}z;x_n),\end{aligned}\tag{21}$$

where the (un-normalised) measure $\psi_t(\mathrm{d}z;\xi)$ is given by

$$\psi_0(\mathrm{d}z;\xi)=\nu(\mathrm{d}z),\tag{22}$$

$$\psi_t(\mathrm{d}z;\xi)=\frac{f_{T-t}(z-\xi)}{f_T(z)}\nu(\mathrm{d}z),\tag{23}$$

for $0 < t < T$. It follows from the definition of $LRB_{\mathcal{C}}([0, T], \{f_t\}, \nu)$ and (17) that

$$f_{tT}(x; z) = \frac{f_t(x) f_{T-t}(z - x)}{f_T(z)} \tag{24}$$

is a well-defined density (as a function of x) for $t < T$ and ν-a.e. z. Then from (21) the marginal law of L_{tT} is given by

$$\begin{aligned} \mathbb{Q}[L_{tT} \in \mathrm{d}x] &= f_t(x)\psi_t(\mathbb{R}; x)\, \mathrm{d}x \\ &= \int_{z=-\infty}^{\infty} f_{tT}(x; z)\nu(\mathrm{d}z)\, \mathrm{d}x. \end{aligned} \tag{25}$$

Hence the density of L_{tT} exists for $t < T$, and

$$0 \leq \psi_t(\mathbb{R}; x) < \infty \quad \text{for Lebesgue-a.e. } x \in \text{Support}(f_t). \tag{26}$$

In particular, we have

$$0 < \psi_t(\mathbb{R}; L_{tT}) < \infty \quad \text{and} \quad 0 < f_{T-t}(x - L_{tT}) < \infty \tag{27}$$

for almost every value of L_{tT}. If $\nu(\{z\}) = 1$ for some point $z \in \mathbb{R}$, i.e. $\mathbb{Q}[L_{TT} = z] = 1$, then $\{L_{tT}\}$ is a Lévy bridge. If $\nu(\mathrm{d}z) = f_T(z)\, \mathrm{d}z$, then $\{L_{tT}\} \stackrel{\text{law}}{=} \{L_t\}$ for $t \in [0, T]$.

In the discrete case, the finite-dimensional probabilities of $\{M_{tT}\}$ are

$$\begin{aligned} &\mathbb{Q}\left[M_{t_1,T} = a_{k_1}, \ldots, M_{t_n,T} = a_{k_n}, M_{TT} = z\right] \\ &= \prod_{i=1}^{n} \left[Q_{t_i - t_{i-1}}(a_{k_i} - a_{k_{1-1}})\right] \phi_{t_n}(z; a_{k_n}), \end{aligned} \tag{28}$$

where the function $\phi_t(z; \xi)$ is given by

$$\phi_0(z; \xi) = P(z), \tag{29}$$

$$\phi_t(z; \xi) = \frac{Q_{T-t}(z - \xi)}{Q_T(z)} P(z), \tag{30}$$

for $0 < t < T$. If P is identical to Q_T, then $\{M_{tT}\} \stackrel{\text{law}}{=} \{M_t\}$ for $t \in [0, T]$.

The existing literature on information-based asset pricing exploits special properties of Brownian and gamma bridges. See Émery and Yor [14], and Yor [30] for insights into how remarkable these bridges are. The methods we use do not generally require special properties of particular Lévy bridges. We use the Brownian and gamma cases as examples, and the results we obtain agree with previous work.

Many of the results that follow are proved for the LRB $\{L_{tT}\}$, which has a continuous state-space. Analogous results are provided for the discrete state-space process $\{M_{tT}\}$; details of proofs are omitted since they are similar to the continuous case.

3.3. LRBs as conditioned Lévy processes

It is useful to interpret an LRB as a Lévy process conditioned to have a specified marginal law ν at time T. Suppose that the random variable Z has law ν; then:

$$\mathbb{Q}\left[L_{t_1} \in \mathrm{d}x_1, \ldots, L_{t_n} \in \mathrm{d}x_n, L_T \in \mathrm{d}z | L_T = Z\right]$$

$$= \mathbb{Q}\left[L_{t_1} \in \mathrm{d}x_1, \ldots, L_{t_n} \in \mathrm{d}x_n | L_T = z\right] \nu(\mathrm{d}z)$$

$$= \frac{f_{T-t_n}(z - x_{n-1})}{f_T(z)} \prod_{i=1}^{n} \left[f_{t_i - t_{i-1}}(x_i - x_{i-1})\,\mathrm{d}x_i\right] \nu(\mathrm{d}z). \tag{31}$$

Hence the conditioned Lévy process has law $LRB_{\mathcal{C}}([0, T], \{f_t\}, \nu)$.

3.4. The Markov property

In this section we show that LRBs are Markov processes. The Markov property is a key tool in the application of LRBs to information-based asset pricing. As will be seen below, the Markov property of an LRB follows from the Markov property from the associated Lévy bridge process.

3.4.1. Continuous state-space

Proposition 3.4. *The process $\{L_{tT}\}_{0 \le t \le T}$ is a Markov process with transition law*

$$\mathbb{Q}[L_{tT} \in \mathrm{d}y \mid L_{sT} = x] = \frac{\psi_t(\mathbb{R}; y)}{\psi_s(\mathbb{R}; x)} f_{t-s}(y - x)\,\mathrm{d}y,$$
$$\mathbb{Q}[L_{TT} \in \mathrm{d}y \mid L_{sT} = x] = \frac{\psi_s(\mathrm{d}y; x)}{\psi_s(\mathbb{R}; x)}, \tag{32}$$

for $0 \le s < t < T$.

Proof. To show that $\{L_{tT}\}$ is Markov, it is sufficient to show that

$$\mathbb{Q}\left[L_{tT} \le y \mid L_{t_1,T} = x_1, \ldots, L_{t_m,T} = x_m\right] = \mathbb{Q}\left[L_{tT} \le y \mid L_{t_m,T} = x_m\right], \tag{33}$$

for all $m \in \mathbb{N}_+$, all $(x_1, \ldots, x_m, y) \in \mathbb{R}^{m+1}$, and all $0 \le t_1 < \cdots < t_m < t \le T$. When $t = T$ we apply the Bayes theorem to (21) and obtain

$$\mathbb{Q}\left[L_{TT} \in \mathrm{d}y | L_{t_1,T} = x_1, \ldots, L_{t_m,T} = x_m\right] = \frac{\psi_{t_m}(\mathrm{d}y; x_m)}{\psi_{t_m}(\mathbb{R}; x_m)}. \tag{34}$$

We need now only consider the case $t < T$. Proposition 2.3 shows that Lévy bridges are Markov processes; therefore,

$$\mathbb{Q}\left[L_t \le y \mid L_{t_1} = x_1, \ldots, L_{t_m} = x_m, L_T = x\right] = \mathbb{Q}\left[L_t \le y \mid L_{t_m} = x_m, L_T = x\right]. \tag{35}$$

It is straightforward by Definition 3.1 part 4 to show that LRBs are Markov processes. Indeed we have:

$$\mathbb{Q}\left[L_{tT} \le y | L_{t_1,T} = x_1, \ldots, L_{t_m,T} = x_m\right]$$
$$= \int_{-\infty}^{\infty} \mathbb{Q}\left[L_{tT} \le y | L_{t_1,T} = x_1, \ldots, L_{t_m,T} = x_m, L_{T,T} = x\right] \nu(\mathrm{d}x)$$
$$= \int_{-\infty}^{\infty} \mathbb{Q}\left[L_t \le y | L_{t_1} = x_1, \ldots, L_{t_m} = x_m, L_T = x\right] \nu(\mathrm{d}x)$$
$$= \int_{-\infty}^{\infty} \mathbb{Q}\left[L_t \le y | L_{t_m} = x_m, L_T = x\right] \nu(\mathrm{d}x)$$
$$= \int_{-\infty}^{\infty} \mathbb{Q}\left[L_{tT} \le y | L_{t_m,T} = x_m, L_{T,T} = x\right] \nu(\mathrm{d}x)$$
$$= \mathbb{Q}\left[L_{tT} \le y | L_{t_m,T} = x_m\right]. \tag{36}$$

The form of the transition law of $\{L_{tT}\}$ appearing in (32) follows from (21). □

Example. In the Brownian case we set

$$f_t(z) = \frac{1}{\sqrt{2\pi t}} \exp\left[-\frac{z^2}{2t}\right] \tag{37}$$

for $t > 0$. Thus $f_t(x)$ is the marginal density of a standard Brownian motion at time t. Then we have

$$\mathbb{Q}[L_{tT} \in \mathrm{d}y \mid L_{sT} = x] = \sqrt{\frac{T-s}{T-t}} \frac{\int_{-\infty}^{\infty} \mathrm{e}^{-\frac{1}{2}\left[\frac{(z-y)^2}{T-t} - \frac{z^2}{T}\right]} \nu(\mathrm{d}z)}{\int_{-\infty}^{\infty} \mathrm{e}^{-\frac{1}{2}\left[\frac{(z-x)^2}{T-s} - \frac{z^2}{T}\right]} \nu(\mathrm{d}z)} \frac{\mathrm{e}^{-\frac{1}{2}\frac{(y-x)^2}{t-s}}}{\sqrt{2\pi(t-s)}} \mathrm{d}y, \tag{38}$$

and

$$\begin{aligned} \mathbb{Q}[L_{TT} \in \mathrm{d}y \mid L_{sT} = x] &= \frac{\mathrm{e}^{-\frac{1}{2}\left[\frac{(y-x)^2}{T-s} - \frac{y^2}{T}\right]} \nu(\mathrm{d}y)}{\int_{-\infty}^{\infty} \mathrm{e}^{-\frac{1}{2}\left[\frac{(z-x)^2}{T-s} - \frac{z^2}{T}\right]} \nu(\mathrm{d}z)} \\ &= \frac{\mathrm{e}^{\frac{1}{T-s}\left[xy - \frac{1}{2}\frac{s}{T}y^2\right]} \nu(\mathrm{d}y)}{\int_{-\infty}^{\infty} \mathrm{e}^{\frac{1}{T-s}\left[xz - \frac{1}{2}\frac{s}{T}z^2\right]} \nu(\mathrm{d}z)}. \end{aligned} \tag{39}$$

Example. In the gamma case we consider a one-parameter family of processes indexed by $m > 0$. We set

$$f_t(z) = \mathbb{1}_{\{z>0\}} \frac{z^{mt-1}}{\Gamma[mt]} \mathrm{e}^{-z}, \tag{40}$$

where $\Gamma[z]$ is the gamma function, defined as usual for $x > 0$ by

$$\Gamma[x] = \int_0^{\infty} u^{x-1} \mathrm{e}^{-u} \, \mathrm{d}u. \tag{41}$$

These densities are the increment densities of the gamma process with mean m and variance m at time $t = 1$ (see [9]). Then

$$\begin{aligned} &\mathbb{Q}[L_{tT} \in \mathrm{d}y \mid L_{sT} = x] \\ &= \frac{\mathbb{1}_{\{y>x\}}}{\mathrm{B}[m(T-t), m(t-s)]} \frac{\int_y^{\infty} (z-y)^{m(T-t)-1} z^{1-mT} \nu(\mathrm{d}z)}{\int_x^{\infty} (z-x)^{m(T-s)-1} z^{1-mT} \nu(\mathrm{d}z)} (y-x)^{m(t-s)-1} \, \mathrm{d}y, \end{aligned} \tag{42}$$

and

$$\mathbb{Q}[L_{TT} \in \mathrm{d}y \mid L_{sT} = x] = \frac{\mathbb{1}_{\{y>x\}} (y-x)^{m(T-s)-1} y^{1-mT} \nu(\mathrm{d}y)}{\int_x^{\infty} (z-x)^{m(T-s)-1} z^{1-mT} \nu(\mathrm{d}z)}. \tag{43}$$

Here $\mathrm{B}[\alpha, \beta]$ is the beta function, defined as usual for $\alpha > 0$ and $\beta > 0$ by

$$\mathrm{B}[\alpha, \beta] = \int_0^1 x^{\alpha-1} (1-x)^{\beta-1} \, \mathrm{d}x = \frac{\Gamma[\alpha]\Gamma[\beta]}{\Gamma[\alpha+\beta]}. \tag{44}$$

3.4.2. Discrete state-space

The analogous result to Proposition 3.4 for the discrete case is provided below—the proof is similar.

Proposition 3.5. *The process $\{M_{tT}\}_{0\le t\le T}$ has the Markov property, with transition probabilities given by*

$$\begin{aligned}\mathbb{Q}\left[M_{tT}=a_j\,|\,M_{sT}=a_i\right]&=\frac{\sum_{k=-\infty}^{\infty}\phi_t(a_k;a_j)}{\sum_{k=-\infty}^{\infty}\phi_s(a_k;a_i)}Q_{t-s}(a_j-a_i),\\ \mathbb{Q}\left[M_{TT}=a_j\,|\,M_{sT}=a_i\right]&=\frac{\phi_s(a_j;a_i)}{\sum_{k=-\infty}^{\infty}\phi_s(a_k;a_i)},\end{aligned} \tag{45}$$

for $0\le s<t<T$.

3.5. Conditional terminal distributions

Let $\{\mathcal{F}_t^L\}$ and $\{\mathcal{F}_t^M\}$ be the filtrations generated by $\{L_{tT}\}$ and $\{M_{tT}\}$, respectively.

Definition 3.6. Let ν_s be the $\mathcal{F}_s^L$-conditional law of the terminal value L_{TT}, and let P_s be the $\mathcal{F}_s^M$-conditional probability mass function of the terminal value M_{TT}.

We have $\nu_0(A)=\nu(A)$, and $P_0(a)=P(a)$. Furthermore, when $s>0$, it follows from the results of the previous section that

$$\nu_s(\mathrm{d}z)=\frac{\psi_s(\mathrm{d}z;L_{sT})}{\psi_s(\mathbb{R};L_{sT})}, \tag{46}$$

and

$$P_s(a_k)=\frac{\phi_s(a_k;M_{sT})}{\sum_{j=-\infty}^{\infty}\phi_s(a_j;M_{sT})}. \tag{47}$$

When the *a priori* qth moment of L_{TT} is finite, the $\mathcal{F}_s^L$-conditional qth moment is finite and given by

$$\int_{-\infty}^{\infty}|z|^q\,\nu_s(\mathrm{d}z). \tag{48}$$

Similarly, when the *a priori* qth moment of M_{TT} is finite, the $\mathcal{F}_s^M$-conditional qth moment is finite and given by

$$\sum_{k=-\infty}^{\infty}|a_k|^q\,P_s(a_k). \tag{49}$$

When they are finite, the quantities in (48) and (49) are martingales with respect to $\{\mathcal{F}_t^L\}$ and $\{\mathcal{F}_t^M\}$, respectively. If $q\in\mathbb{Z}$ then $\int|z|^q\nu(\mathrm{d}z)<\infty$ ensures that $\int z^q\,\nu(\mathrm{d}z)$ is a martingale, and $\sum|a_k|^q P(a_k)<\infty$ ensures that $\sum a_k^q P(a_k)$ is a martingale.

When the terminal law ν admits a density, we denote it by $p(z)$, i.e. $\nu(\mathrm{d}z) = p(z)\,\mathrm{d}z$. In this case the L_{tT}-conditional density of L_{TT} exists, and we denote it by

$$p_t(z) = \frac{\nu_t(\mathrm{d}z)}{\mathrm{d}z} = \frac{f_{T-t}(z - L_{tT})p(z)}{\psi_t(\mathbb{R}; L_{tT}) f_T(z)}. \tag{50}$$

3.6. Measure changes

In this section we assume that there exists a measure $\mathbb{L}$ under which $\{L_{tT}\}$ is a Lévy process, and that the density of L_{tT} is $f_t(x)$. Writing $\psi_t = \psi_t(\mathbb{R}; L_{tT})$, we can show that $\{\psi_t\}_{0\le t<T}$ is an $\mathbb{L}$-martingale (with respect to the filtration generated by $\{L_{tT}\}$). In particular, for times $0 \le s < t$ we have

$$\begin{aligned}
\mathbb{E}_{\mathbb{L}}\left[\psi_t | \mathcal{F}^L_s\right] &= \mathbb{E}_{\mathbb{L}}\left[\int_{-\infty}^{\infty} \frac{f_{T-t}(z - L_{tT})}{f_T(z)} \nu(\mathrm{d}z) \,\middle|\, \mathcal{F}^L_s\right] \\
&= \mathbb{E}_{\mathbb{L}}\left[\int_{-\infty}^{\infty} \frac{f_{T-t}(z - L_{sT} - (L_{tT} - L_{sT}))}{f_T(z)} \nu(\mathrm{d}z) \,\middle|\, L_{sT}\right] \\
&= \int_{y=-\infty}^{\infty}\int_{z=-\infty}^{\infty} \frac{f_{T-t}(z - L_{sT} - y)}{f_T(z)} \nu(\mathrm{d}z) f_{t-s}(y)\,\mathrm{d}y \\
&= \int_{z=-\infty}^{\infty} \frac{1}{f_T(z)} \int_{y=-\infty}^{\infty} f_{T-t}(z - L_{sT} - y) f_{t-s}(y)\,\mathrm{d}y\,\nu(\mathrm{d}z) \\
&= \int_{z=-\infty}^{\infty} \frac{f_{T-s}(z - L_{sT})}{f_T(z)} \nu(\mathrm{d}z) \\
&= \psi_s.
\end{aligned} \tag{51}$$

Since $\psi_0 = 1$, we can define a probability measure $\mathbb{L}^{\mathrm{rb}}$ by the Radon–Nikodým derivative

$$\left.\frac{\mathrm{d}\mathbb{L}^{\mathrm{rb}}}{\mathrm{d}\mathbb{L}}\right|_{\mathcal{F}^L_t} = \psi_t \quad \text{for } 0 \le t < T. \tag{52}$$

It was noted in Section 3.2 that $0 < \psi_t < \infty$, so $\mathbb{L}^{\mathrm{rb}}$ is equivalent to $\mathbb{L}$ for $t < T$. For $0 \le s < t < T$, the transition law of $\{L_{tT}\}$ under $\mathbb{L}^{\mathrm{rb}}$ is

$$\begin{aligned}
\mathbb{L}^{\mathrm{rb}}\left[L_{tT} \in \mathrm{d}y | \mathcal{F}^L_s\right] &= \mathbb{E}_{\mathbb{L}^{\mathrm{rb}}}\left[\mathbb{1}_{\{L_{tT}\in\mathrm{d}y\}} | \mathcal{F}^L_s\right] \\
&= \psi_s^{-1}\mathbb{E}_{\mathbb{L}}\left[\psi_t \mathbb{1}_{\{L_{tT}\in\mathrm{d}y\}} | L_{sT}\right] \\
&= \psi_s^{-1}\int_{-\infty}^{\infty} \frac{f_{T-t}(z - y)}{f_T(z)} \nu(\mathrm{d}z) f_{t-s}(y - L_{sT})\,\mathrm{d}y \\
&= \frac{\psi_t(\mathbb{R}; y)}{\psi_s(\mathbb{R}; L_{sT})} f_{t-s}(y - L_{sT})\,\mathrm{d}y.
\end{aligned} \tag{53}$$

We see that $\{L_{tT}\}_{0\le t<T}$ is a Markov process under the measure $\mathbb{L}^{\mathrm{rb}}$. Furthermore, by virtue of Proposition 3.4, $\{L_{tT}\}$ is an LRB with law $LRB_{\mathcal{C}}([0, T], \{f_t\}, \nu)$.

We can restate this result with reference to the measure $\mathbb{Q}$ as the following:

Proposition 3.7. *Let* $\mathbb{L}$ *be defined by*

$$\left.\frac{\mathrm{d}\mathbb{L}}{\mathrm{d}\mathbb{Q}}\right|_{\mathcal{F}_t^L} = \psi_t(\mathbb{R}; L_{tT})^{-1} \tag{54}$$

for $t \in [0, T)$. *Then* $\mathbb{L}$ *is a probability measure. Under* $\mathbb{L}$, $\{L_{tT}\}_{0\le t<T}$ *is a Lévy process, and* L_{tT} *has density* $f_t(x)$.

In the case of a discrete state space a similar result is obtained.

Proposition 3.8. *Let* $\mathbb{L}$ *be defined by*

$$\left.\frac{\mathrm{d}\mathbb{L}}{\mathrm{d}\mathbb{Q}}\right|_{\mathcal{F}_t^M} = \left[\sum_{k=-\infty}^{\infty} \phi_t(a_k; M_{tT})\right]^{-1} \tag{55}$$

for $t \in [0, T)$. *Then* $\mathbb{L}$ *is a probability measure. Under* $\mathbb{L}$, $\{M_{tT}\}_{0\le t<T}$ *is a Lévy process, and* M_{tT} *has mass function* $Q_t(a)$.

3.7. Dynamic consistency

In this section we show that LRBs possess the so-called dynamic consistency property. For $\{L_{tT}\}$, this property means the process $\{\eta_t\}$ defined by setting

$$\eta_t = L_{tT} - L_{sT} \quad (s \le t \le T) \tag{56}$$

is an LRB for fixed s and L_{sT} given. Defining the filtration $\{\mathcal{F}_t^\eta\}$ by

$$\mathcal{F}_t^\eta = \sigma\left(L_{sT}, \{\eta_u\}_{s\le u\le t}\right), \tag{57}$$

we see that

$$\mathbb{Q}\left[F\left(\{L_{uT}\}_{s\le u\le T}\right) \in B|\mathcal{F}_t^\eta\right] = \mathbb{Q}\left[F\left(\{L_{uT}\}_{s\le u\le T}\right) \in B|\mathcal{F}_t^L\right], \tag{58}$$

for $0 \le s < t < T$, and F an arbitrary measurable functional. Suppose two market participants, trader A and trader B, watch the evolution of $\{L_{tT}\}$, trader A watching from time 0 and trader B watching from time s. The filtration of trader A, $\{\mathcal{F}_t^L\}$, is larger than the filtration of trader B, $\{\mathcal{F}_t^\eta\}$, but they have a common view of the future evolution of $\{L_{tT}\}$. This is the Markov property. The dynamic consistency (or "renewability") property is stronger. It states that the filtration of trader B can be regarded as being generated by an LRB, in this case $\{\eta_t\}$, plus some information about the current state of the world, in this case L_{sT}.

Later we shall model the market filtration as being generated by a set of LRBs. Through the dynamic consistency property, we can consider each market participant's filtration to be generated by a set of LRBs, regardless of the time in which they enter the market, and without their views being inconsistent with those of other participants.

The dynamic consistency property was introduced in Brody et al. [8] with regard to Brownian random bridges, and was shown by the same authors to hold for gamma random bridges in Brody et al. [9].

Fix a time $s < T$. Given L_{sT}, we define a process $\{\eta_t\}$ by (56). We shall show that $\{\eta_t\}$ is an LRB. At time s, the law of η_T is

$$\nu^*(A) = \nu_s(A + L_{sT}) \quad \text{for all } A \in \mathcal{B}(\mathbb{R}), \tag{59}$$

where $A + y$ denotes the shifted set given by

$$A + y = \{x : x - y \in A\}. \tag{60}$$

Given the terminal value η_T, the finite-dimensional distributions of $\{\eta_t\}$ are given by

$$\begin{aligned}
&\mathbb{Q}\left[\eta_{s+t_1} \in \mathrm{d}x_1, \ldots, \eta_{s+t_n} \in \mathrm{d}x_n \,\middle|\, L_{sT}, \eta_T = z\right] \\
&= \mathbb{Q}\left[L_{s+t_1,T} - L_{sT} \in \mathrm{d}x_1, \ldots, L_{s+t_n,T} - L_{sT} \in \mathrm{d}x_n \,\middle|\, L_{sT}, L_{TT} - L_{sT} = z\right] \\
&= \mathbb{Q}\left[L_{s+t_1} - L_s \in \mathrm{d}x_1, \ldots, L_{s+t_n} - L_s \in \mathrm{d}x_n \,\middle|\, L_s, L_T - L_s = z\right] \\
&= \mathbb{Q}\left[L_{t_1} \in \mathrm{d}x_1, \ldots, L_{t_n} \in \mathrm{d}x_n \,\middle|\, L_{T-s} = z\right] \\
&= \frac{f_{T-s-t_n}(z - x_n)}{f_{T-s}(z)} \prod_{i=1}^{n} f_{t_i - t_{i-1}}(x_i - x_{i-1}),
\end{aligned} \tag{61}$$

for every $n \in \mathbb{N}_+$, every $0 = t_0 < t_1 < \cdots < t_n < T - s$, and every $(x_1, \ldots, x_n) \in \mathbb{R}^n$, where $x_0 = 0$. Then we have

$$\begin{aligned}
&\mathbb{Q}\left[\eta_{s+t_1} \in \mathrm{d}x_1, \ldots, \eta_{s+t_n} \in \mathrm{d}x_n, \eta_T \in \mathrm{d}z \,\middle|\, L_{sT}\right] \\
&= \frac{f_{T-s-t_n}(z - x_n)}{f_{T-s}(z)} \prod_{i=1}^{n} f_{t_i - t_{i-1}}(x_i - x_{i-1})\, \nu^*(\mathrm{d}z).
\end{aligned} \tag{62}$$

Comparing this expression to (21) shows that the process $\{\eta_{s+t}\}_{0\le t\le T-s}$ has the law $LRB_{\mathcal{C}}([0, T-s], \{f_t\}, \nu^*)$, and so the law of $\{\eta_t\}_{s\le t\le T}$ is $LRB_{\mathcal{C}}([s, T], \{f_t\}, \nu^*)$.

In the discrete case, we define $\{\eta_t\}$ by

$$\eta_t = M_{tT} - M_{sT} \quad (s \le t \le T). \tag{63}$$

Then, given M_{sT}, $\{\eta_t\}$ has the law $LRB_{\mathcal{D}}([s, T], \{Q_t\}, P^*)$, where P^* is defined by

$$P^*(a) = P_s(a + M_{sT}). \tag{64}$$

3.8. Increments of LRBs

The form of the transition law in Proposition 3.4 shows that in general the increments of an LRB are not independent. The special cases of LRBs with independent increments are discussed later. A result that holds for all LRBs is that they have stationary increments:

Proposition 3.9. *For s, t, u satisfying $0 \le s < u < T$ and $0 < t \le T - u$, we have*

$$\mathbb{Q}\left[L_{u+t,T} - L_{uT} \le z | L_{sT}\right] = \mathbb{Q}[L_{s+t,T} - L_{sT} \le z | L_{sT}], \tag{65}$$

and

$$\mathbb{Q}\left[M_{u+t,T} - M_{uT} \le z | M_{sT}\right] = \mathbb{Q}[M_{s+t,T} - M_{sT} \le z | M_{sT}]. \tag{66}$$

Proof. We provide the proof for $\{L_{tT}\}$. The proof for $\{M_{tT}\}$ is similar. Throughout the proof we assume that $t < T - u$. The case $t = T - u$ follows from the stochastic continuity of $\{L_{tT}\}$. First we assume that $s = 0$. From (32), we have

$$\mathbb{Q}[L_{u+t,T} \in \mathrm{d}y, L_{uT} \in \mathrm{d}x] = \psi_{u+t}(\mathbb{R}; y) f_t(y - x) f_u(x)\, \mathrm{d}x\, \mathrm{d}y. \tag{67}$$

Then we have

$$\begin{aligned}\mathbb{Q}[L_{u+t,T} - L_{uT} \in \mathrm{d}z, L_{uT} \in \mathrm{d}x] &= \psi_{u+t}(\mathbb{R}; z+x) f_t(z) f_u(x)\, \mathrm{d}x\, \mathrm{d}z \\ &= \int_{w=-\infty}^{\infty} \frac{f_{T-(u+t)}(w-z-x)}{f_T(w)} \mathrm{d}w f_t(z) f_u(x)\, \mathrm{d}x\, \mathrm{d}z. \end{aligned} \tag{68}$$

Integrating over x and changing the order of integration yields

$$\begin{aligned}\mathbb{Q}[L_{u+t,T} - L_{uT} \in \mathrm{d}z] &= \int_{w=-\infty}^{\infty} \int_{x=-\infty}^{\infty} f_{T-(u+t)}(w-z-x) f_u(x)\, \mathrm{d}x \frac{\mathrm{d}w}{f_T(w)} f_t(z)\, \mathrm{d}z \\ &= \int_{w=-\infty}^{\infty} \frac{f_{T-t}(w-z)}{f_T(w)} \mathrm{d}w f_t(z)\, \mathrm{d}z \\ &= \psi_t(\mathbb{R}, z) f_t(z)\, \mathrm{d}z \\ &= \mathbb{Q}[L_{tT} \in \mathrm{d}z]. \end{aligned} \tag{69}$$

For the case $s > 0$, we use the dynamic consistency property. For s fixed and L_{sT} given, the process $\{\eta_{uT}\}_{s\le u\le T} = \{L_{uT} - L_{sT}\}_{s\le u\le T}$ is an LRB with the law $LRB_{\mathbb{C}}([s,T], \{f_t\}, \nu^*)$, where $\nu^*(A) = \nu_s(A + L_{sT})$. We have

$$\begin{aligned}\mathbb{Q}\left[L_{u+t,T} - L_{uT} \in \mathrm{d}z | L_{sT}\right] &= \mathbb{Q}\left[\eta_{u+t,T} - \eta_{uT} \in \mathrm{d}z | L_{sT}\right] \\ &= \mathbb{Q}\left[\eta_{tT} \in \mathrm{d}z | L_{sT}\right] \\ &= \int_{-\infty}^{\infty} \frac{f_{T-t}(w-z)}{f_{T-s}(w)} \nu^*(\mathrm{d}w) f_{t-s}(z)\, \mathrm{d}z \\ &= \int_{-\infty}^{\infty} \frac{f_{T-t}(w-z+L_{sT})}{f_{T-s}(w-L_{sT})} \nu_s(\mathrm{d}w) f_{t-s}(z)\, \mathrm{d}z \\ &= \frac{1}{\psi_s(\mathbb{R}; L_{sT})} \int_{-\infty}^{\infty} \frac{f_{T-t}(w-z+L_{sT})}{f_T(w)} \nu(\mathrm{d}w) f_{t-s}(z)\, \mathrm{d}z \\ &= \frac{\psi_t(\mathbb{R}; z+L_{sT})}{\psi_s(\mathbb{R}; L_{sT})} f_{t-s}(z)\, \mathrm{d}z \\ &= \mathbb{Q}\left[L_{tT} - L_{sT} \in \mathrm{d}z | L_{sT}\right]. \quad \square \end{aligned} \tag{70}$$

When $\{L_{tT}\}$ is integrable, the stationary increments property offers enough structure to allow the calculation of the expected value of L_{tT}:

Corollary 3.10. *If* $\mathbb{E}[|L_{tT}|] < \infty$ *for all* $t \in (0, T]$ *then*

$$\mathbb{E}[L_{tT} | L_{sT}] = \frac{T-t}{T-s} L_{sT} + \frac{t-s}{T-s} \mathbb{E}[L_{TT} | L_{sT}] \quad (s < t), \tag{71}$$

and if $\mathbb{E}[|M_{tT}|] < \infty$ *for all* $t \in (0, T]$ *then*

$$\mathbb{E}[M_{tT} | M_{sT}] = \frac{T-t}{T-s} M_{sT} + \frac{t-s}{T-s} \mathbb{E}[M_{TT} | M_{sT}] \quad (s < t). \tag{72}$$

Proof. We provide the proof for $\{L_{tT}\}$. The proof for $\{M_{tT}\}$ is similar. The case $t = T$ is immediate, so we assume that $t < T$. First we consider the case $s = 0$. Suppose that $t = mT/n$, where $m, n \in \mathbb{N}_+$ and $m < n$. We wish to show that

$$\mathbb{E}[L_{tT}] = \frac{m}{n} \mathbb{E}[L_{TT}]. \tag{73}$$

Writing $L(t, T) = L_{tT}$, define the random variables $\{\Delta_i\}$ by

$$\Delta_i = L\left(\frac{i}{n}T, T\right) - L\left(\frac{(i-1)}{n}T, T\right). \tag{74}$$

It follows from Proposition 3.9 that the Δ_i's are identically distributed, and by assumption they are integrable. Hence we have

$$\mathbb{E}[\Delta_i] = \frac{1}{n}\mathbb{E}\left[\sum_{i=1}^{n} \Delta_i\right] = \frac{1}{n}\mathbb{E}[L_{TT}]. \tag{75}$$

Then, as required, we have

$$\mathbb{E}\left[L\left(\frac{m}{n}T, T\right)\right] = \mathbb{E}\left[\sum_{i=1}^{m} \Delta_i\right] = \frac{m}{n}\mathbb{E}[L_{TT}]. \tag{76}$$

For general t, the result follows from the stochastic continuity of LRBs.

For the case $s > 0$, we use the dynamic consistency property. For s fixed and L_{sT} given, the process

$$\eta_{tT} = L_{tT} - L_{sT} \quad (s \le t \le T) \tag{77}$$

is an LRB with law $LRB_C([s, T], \{f_t\}, \nu^*)$, where $\nu^*(A) = \nu_s(A + L_{sT})$. Then we have

$$\begin{aligned} \mathbb{E}[L_{tT}|L_{sT}] &= L_{sT} + \mathbb{E}[\eta_{tT}|L_{sT}] \\ &= L_{sT} + \frac{t-s}{T-s}\int_{-\infty}^{\infty} z\nu^*(dz) \\ &= L_{sT} + \frac{t-s}{T-s}\int_{-\infty}^{\infty} (z - L_{sT})\nu_s(dz) \\ &= \frac{T-s}{T-s}L_{sT} + \frac{t-s}{T-s}\mathbb{E}[L_{TT}|L_{sT}]. \quad \square \end{aligned} \tag{78}$$

We have shown that the increments of LRBs are stationary, so it is natural to ask when the increments are independent, i.e. when is an LRB a Lévy process? The answer lies in the functional form of $\psi_t(\mathbb{R}; y)$.

For $0 \le s < t < T$, the likelihood that $L_{tT} = y$ given that $L_{sT} = x$ is

$$q(t, y; s, x) = \frac{\psi_t(\mathbb{R}; y)}{\psi_s(\mathbb{R}; x)} f_{t-s}(y - x). \tag{79}$$

If $\{L_{tT}\}$ has stationary, independent increments then

$$q(t, y; s, x) = q(t - s, y - x; 0, 0). \tag{80}$$

Therefore the ratio

$$\frac{\psi_t(\mathbb{R}; y)}{\psi_s(\mathbb{R}; x)} \tag{81}$$

is a function of the differences $t - s$ and $y - x$. Thus if we have

$$\psi_t(\mathbb{R}; y) = a \exp(by + ct), \tag{82}$$

for constants a, b and c, then $\{L_{tT}\}$ is a Lévy process. There are constraints on a, b and c since (79) is a probability density. When $b = c = 0$ we have $\nu(\mathrm{d}z) = f_T(z)\,\mathrm{d}z$ which is the case where $\{L_{tT}\} \overset{\text{law}}{=} \{L_t\}$.

Example. In the Brownian case we consider a process $\{W_{tT}\}$ with law

$$LRB_{\mathcal{C}}([0,T], \{f_t\}, f_T(z-\theta T)\,\mathrm{d}z),$$

where $f_t(x)$ is the normal density with zero mean and variance t, given by (37). In other words, $\{W_{tT}\}$ is a standard Brownian motion conditioned so that W_{TT} is a normal random variable with mean θT and variance T. In this case, we have

$$\begin{aligned}\psi_t(\mathbb{R}; y) &= \int_{-\infty}^{\infty} \frac{f_{T-t}(z-y)}{f_T(z)} f_T(z-\theta T)\,\mathrm{d}z \\ &= \exp\left(\theta y - \frac{\theta}{2} t\right). \end{aligned} \tag{83}$$

Simplifying the expression for the transition densities of the process $\{W_{tT}\}$ allows one to verify that $\{W_{tT}\}$ is a Brownian motion with drift θ. It is notable, by Girsanov's theorem, that $\{\psi_t(\mathbb{R}; W_t)\}$ is the Radon–Nikodým density process that transforms a standard Brownian motion into a Brownian motion with drift θ. Hence we can alternatively deduce that $\{W_{tT}\}$ is a Brownian motion with drift θ from the analysis in Section 3.6.

Example. In the gamma case, we consider a process $\{\Gamma_{tT}\}$ with law

$$LRB_{\mathcal{C}}([0,T], \{f_t\}, \kappa^{-1} f_T(z/\kappa)\,\mathrm{d}z),$$

where $f_t(x)$ is the gamma density with mean mt and variance mt defined by (40), and $\kappa > 0$ is constant. Then $\{\Gamma_{tT}\}$ is a gamma process with mean m and variance m at $t = 1$, conditioned so that Γ_{TT} has a gamma distribution with mean $\kappa m T$ and variance $\kappa^2 m T$. We have:

$$\begin{aligned}\psi_t(\mathbb{R}; y) &= \int_{-\infty}^{\infty} \frac{f_{T-t}(z-y)}{f_T(z)} \frac{f_T(z/\kappa)}{\kappa}\,\mathrm{d}z \\ &= \kappa^{-mt} \exp\left((1-\kappa^{-1})y\right). \end{aligned} \tag{84}$$

The transition density of $\{\Gamma_{tT}\}$ is

$$\mathbb{Q}[\Gamma_{tT} \in \mathrm{d}y \mid \Gamma_{sT} = x] = \mathbb{1}_{\{y>x\}} \frac{(y-x)^{m(t-s)-1} \mathrm{e}^{-(y-x)/\kappa}}{\kappa^{m(t-s)}\Gamma(m(t-s))}\,\mathrm{d}y. \tag{85}$$

Hence $\{\Gamma_{tT}\}$ is a gamma process with mean κm and variance $\kappa^2 m$ at $t = 1$.

3.8.1. Increment distributions

For financial applications, one needs the joint distribution of n increments of an LRB. Such a situation arises, for example, if one considers the valuation of an exotic option or structured product where the payout of the product depends on the values of an underlying asset at, say, n different times, and where the underlying asset price process itself is modelled, in an LRB information-based framework, by consideration of the conditional expectation of its terminal value.

Partition the time interval $[0, T]$ by $0 = t_0 < t_1 < t_2 < \cdots < t_n = T$. Then define the increments $\{\Delta_i\}_{i=1}^n$ and $\{\alpha_i\}_{i=1}^n$ by

$$\Delta_i = L_{t_i,T} - L_{t_{i-1},T} \tag{86}$$

$$\alpha_i = t_i - t_{i-1}. \tag{87}$$

Assume that ν has no *continuous singular part* [29]. Denoting the Dirac delta function centred at z by $\delta_z(x)$, $x \in \mathbb{R}$, we can write

$$\nu(\mathrm{d}z) = \sum_{i=-\infty}^{\infty} v_i \delta_{z_i}(z)\,\mathrm{d}z + p(z)\,\mathrm{d}z, \tag{88}$$

for some $\{a_i\} \subset \mathbb{R}$, $\{z_i\} \subset \mathbb{R}_+$, and $p : \mathbb{R} \to \mathbb{R}_+$. Here $p(z)$ is the density of the continuous part of ν, and v_i is a point mass of ν located at z_i. By (21), the joint law of the random vector $(\Delta_1, \ldots, \Delta_n)^\top$ is given by

$$\mathbb{Q}[\Delta_1 \in \mathrm{d}y_1 \ldots, \Delta_n \in \mathrm{d}y_n] = \widetilde{f}\left(\sum_{i=1}^n y_i\right)\prod_{i=1}^n f_{\alpha_i}(y_i)\,\mathrm{d}y_i, \tag{89}$$

where

$$\widetilde{f}(z) = \frac{p(z) + \sum_{i=-\infty}^{\infty} v_i \delta_{z_i}(z)}{f_T(z)}. \tag{90}$$

Eq. (89) shows that $(\Delta_1, \ldots, \Delta_n)^\top$ has a generalized multivariate Liouville distribution as defined by Gupta and Richards [19]. The classical multivariate Liouville distribution is obtained when $f_t(x)$ is the density of a gamma distribution [15]. A survey of Liouville distributions can be found in Gupta and Richards [20]. Barndorff-Nielsen and Jørgensen [2] construct a generalized Liouville distribution by conditioning a vector of independent inverse-Gaussian random variables on their sum.

In the discrete case, the joint distribution of increments also has a generalized Liouville distribution. Define the increments $\{D_i\}$ by

$$D_i = M_{t_i,T} - M_{t_{i-1},T}. \tag{91}$$

Then we can write

$$\mathbb{Q}[D_1 \in \mathrm{d}y_1 \ldots, D_n \in \mathrm{d}y_n] = \widetilde{Q}\left(\sum_{i=1}^n y_i\right)\prod_{i=1}^n \mathrm{d}Q_{\alpha_i}(y_i), \tag{92}$$

where

$$\widetilde{Q}(z) = \frac{\sum_{i=-\infty}^{\infty} P(a_i)\delta_{a_i}(z)}{Q_T(z)}. \tag{93}$$

3.8.2. The reordering of increments

We are able to extend the Markov property of LRBs. If we partition the path of an LRB into increments, then the Markov property means that future increments depend on the past only through the *sum* of past increments. We shall show that for LRBs the ordering of the increments does not matter for this to hold—given the values of any set of increments of an LRB (past or future), the other increments depend on this subset only through the sum of its elements. This result can be considered a joint statement of the Markov property and the so-called "cyclic exchangeability" of LRBs. For examples of the usefulness of such results see Bertoin et al. [6] and Chaumond et al. [11].

Let π be a permutation of $\{1, 2, \ldots, n\}$. We define the partial sum S_m^π by

$$S_m^\pi = \sum_{i=1}^{m} \Delta_{\pi(i)} \quad \text{for } m = 1, 2, \ldots, n, \tag{94}$$

where the $\{\Delta_i\}$ are defined as in (86); and we define the partition $0 = t_0^\pi < t_1^\pi < \cdots < t_n^\pi = T$ by

$$t_{j+1}^\pi = \sum_{i=1}^{j} \alpha_{\pi(i)} \quad \text{for } j = 1, 2, \ldots, n-1. \tag{95}$$

Proposition 3.11. *We may extend the Markov property of* $\{L_{tT}\}$ *to the following:*

$$\begin{aligned} &\mathbb{Q}\left[\Delta_{\pi(m+1)} \le y_{m+1}, \ldots, \Delta_{\pi(n)} \le y_n \,|\, \Delta_{\pi(1)}, \ldots, \Delta_{\pi(m)}\right] \\ &\quad = \mathbb{Q}\left[\Delta_{\pi(m+1)} \le y_{m+1}, \ldots, \Delta_{\pi(n)} \le y_n \,\middle|\, S_m^\pi\right]. \end{aligned} \tag{96}$$

If ν *has no singular continuous part, then*

$$\begin{aligned} &\mathbb{Q}\left[\Delta_{\pi(m+1)} \in \mathrm{d}y_{m+1}, \ldots, \Delta_{\pi(n)} \in \mathrm{d}y_n \,\middle|\, S_m^\pi\right] \\ &\quad = \frac{\tilde{f}\left(S_m^\pi + \sum\limits_{i=m+1}^{n} y_i\right)}{\psi_{t_m^\pi}(\mathbb{R}; S_m^\pi)} \prod_{i=m+1}^{n} f_{\alpha_{\pi(i)}}(y_i)\,\mathrm{d}y_i. \end{aligned} \tag{97}$$

Proof. Define the increments $\{\Delta_i^\pi\}$ by

$$\Delta_i^\pi = L_{t_n^\pi, T} - L_{t_{n-1}^\pi, T}. \tag{98}$$

The law of the random vector $(\Delta_1^\pi, \ldots, \Delta_{n-1}^\pi, \sum_1^n \Delta_i^\pi)^\top$ is given by

$$\begin{aligned} &\mathbb{Q}\left[\Delta_1^\pi \in \mathrm{d}y_1, \ldots, \Delta_{n-1}^\pi \in \mathrm{d}y_{n-1}, \sum_{i=1}^{n} \Delta_i^\pi \in \mathrm{d}z\right] \\ &\quad = \frac{\nu(\mathrm{d}z)}{f_T(z)} f_{\alpha_{\pi(n)}}\left(z - \sum_{i=1}^{n-1} y_i\right) \prod_{i=1}^{n-1} f_{\alpha_{\pi(i)}}(y_i)\,\mathrm{d}y_i. \end{aligned} \tag{99}$$

This is also the law of $(\Delta_{\pi(1)}, \ldots, \Delta_{\pi(n-1)}, \sum_1^n \Delta_{\pi(i)})^\top$; hence

$$(\Delta_{\pi(1)}, \ldots, \Delta_{\pi(n)}) \overset{\text{law}}{=} (\Delta_1^\pi, \ldots, \Delta_n^\pi). \tag{100}$$

The Markov property of LRBs gives

$$\mathbb{Q}\left[\Delta_{m+1}^\pi \le y_{m+1}, \ldots, \Delta_n^\pi \le y_n \,\middle|\, \Delta_1^\pi, \ldots, \Delta_m^\pi\right]$$

$$= \mathbb{Q}\left[\Delta^{\pi}_{m+1} \le y_{m+1}, \ldots, \Delta^{\pi}_{n} \le y_n \,\middle|\, \sum_{i=1}^{m} \Delta^{\pi}_{i}\right], \tag{101}$$

and so we have

$$\begin{aligned} &\mathbb{Q}\left[\Delta_{\pi(m+1)} \le y_{m+1}, \ldots, \Delta_{\pi(n)} \le y_n \,\middle|\, \Delta_{\pi(1)}, \ldots, \Delta_{\pi(m)}\right] \\ &\quad = \mathbb{Q}\left[\Delta_{\pi(m+1)} \le y_{m+1}, \ldots, \Delta_{\pi(n)} \le y_n \,\middle|\, S^{\pi}_{m}\right]. \end{aligned} \tag{102}$$

This proves the first part of the proposition.

For the second part of the proof we assume that ν takes the form (88). Note that

$$L_{t^{\pi}_{m},T} = \sum_{i=1}^{m} \Delta^{\pi}_{i}, \tag{103}$$

and that the density of $L_{t^{\pi}_{m},T}$ is

$$x \mapsto f_{t^{\pi}_{m}}(x)\psi_{t^{\pi}_{m}}(\mathbb{R}; x) = \int_{z=-\infty}^{\infty} \frac{f_{t^{\pi}_{m}}(x) f_{T-t^{\pi}_{m}}(z-x)}{f_T(z)} \nu(\mathrm{d}z). \tag{104}$$

The elements of the vector $(L_{t^{\pi}_{m},T}, \Delta^{\pi}_{m+1}, \ldots, \Delta^{\pi}_{n})^{\top}$ are non-overlapping increments of $\{L_{tT}\}$, and the law of the vector is given by

$$\begin{aligned} &\mathbb{Q}\left[L_{t^{\pi}_{m},T} \in \mathrm{d}x, \Delta^{\pi}_{m+1} \in \mathrm{d}y_{m+1}, \ldots, \Delta^{\pi}_{n} \in \mathrm{d}y_n\right] \\ &\quad = \tilde{f}\left(x + \sum_{i=m+1}^{n} y_i\right) f_{t^{\pi}_{m}}(x)\,\mathrm{d}x \prod_{i=m+1}^{n} f_{\alpha_{\pi(i)}}(y_i)\,\mathrm{d}y_i. \end{aligned} \tag{105}$$

Thus we have

$$\begin{aligned} &\mathbb{Q}\left[\Delta^{\pi}_{m+1} \in \mathrm{d}y_{m+1}, \ldots, \Delta^{\pi}_{n} \in \mathrm{d}y_n \,\middle|\, L_{t^{\pi}_{m},T} = x\right] \\ &\quad = \frac{\mathbb{Q}\left[\Delta^{\pi}_{m+1} \in \mathrm{d}y_{m+1}, \ldots, \Delta^{\pi}_{n} \in \mathrm{d}y_n, L_{t^{\pi}_{m},T} \in \mathrm{d}x\right]}{\mathbb{Q}\left[L_{t^{\pi}_{m},T} \in \mathrm{d}x\right]} \\ &\quad = \frac{\tilde{f}\left(x + \sum_{i=m+1}^{n} y_i\right) \prod_{i=m+1}^{n} f_{\alpha_{\pi(i)}}(y_i)}{\psi_{t^{\pi}_{m}}(\mathbb{R}; S^{\pi}_{m})}. \quad \square \end{aligned} \tag{106}$$

We note that Gupta and Richards [19] prove that if $(\Delta_1, \Delta_2, \ldots, \Delta_n)^{\top}$ has a generalized Liouville distribution then Eq. (96) holds.

We can use Proposition 3.11 to extend the dynamic consistency property. In particular we have the following:

Corollary 3.12. (a) *Fix times s_1, T_1 satisfying $0 < T_1 \le T - s_1$. The time-shifted, space-shifted partial process*

$$\eta^{(1)}_{t,T_1} = L_{s_1+t,T} - L_{s_1,T}, \quad (0 \le t \le T_1), \tag{107}$$

is an LRB with the law $LRB_{\mathbb{C}}([0, T_1], \{f_t\}, \nu^{(1)})$, where $\nu^{(1)}$ is a probability law on $\mathbb{R}$ with density $f_{T_1}(x)\psi_{T_1}(\mathbb{R}; x)$.

(b) *Construct the partial processes* $\{\eta^{(i)}_{t,T_i}\}$, $i = 1, \dots, n$, *from non-overlapping portions of* $\{L_{tT}\}$ *in a similar way to that above. The intervals* $[s_i, s_i + T_i]$, $i = 1, \dots, n$, *are non-overlapping except possibly at the endpoints. Set* $\eta^{(i)}_{t,T_i} = \eta^{(i)}_{T_i,T_i}$ *when* $t > T_i$. *If* $u > t$, *then*

$$\mathbb{Q}\left[\eta^{(1)}_{u,T_1} - \eta^{(1)}_{t,T_1} \le x_1, \dots, \eta^{(n)}_{u,T_n} - \eta^{(n)}_{t,T_n} \le x_n \,\middle|\, \mathcal{F}^\eta_t\right]$$
$$= \mathbb{Q}\left[\eta^{(1)}_{u,T_1} - \eta^{(1)}_{t,T_1} \le x_1, \dots, \eta^{(n)}_{u,T_n} - \eta^{(n)}_{t,T_n} \le x_n \,\middle|\, \sum_{i=1}^{n} \eta^{(i)}_{t,T_i}\right], \tag{108}$$

where

$$\mathcal{F}^\eta_t = \sigma\left(\left\{\eta^{(i)}_{s,T_i}\right\}_{0\le s\le t}, i = 1, 2, \dots, n\right). \tag{109}$$

Remark 3.13. The partial processes of Corollary 3.12 are dependent, and

$$\mathbb{Q}\left[\eta^{(i)}_{tT} \in \mathrm{d}x \,\middle|\, \mathcal{F}^\eta_s\right] = \mathbb{Q}\left[\eta^{(i)}_{tT} \in \mathrm{d}x \,\middle|\, \eta^{(i)}_{sT}, \sum_{j=1}^{n} \eta^{(j)}_{sT}\right], \tag{110}$$

for $0 \le s < t \le T$.

Remark 3.14. Corollary 3.12 provides a natural way to construct dependent LRBs. Hoyle et al. [22], working with a class of stable-1/2 LRBs, present an insurance model with two cumulative loss processes using this result.

We state but do not prove a discrete analogue of Proposition 3.11, which is as follows:

Proposition 3.15. *One can extend the Markov property of* $\{M_{tT}\}$ *to the following:*

$$\mathbb{Q}\left[D_{\pi(m+1)} \le y_{m+1}, \dots, D_{\pi(n)} \le y_n \,\middle|\, D_{\pi(1)}, \dots, D_{\pi(m)}\right]$$
$$= \mathbb{Q}\left[D_{\pi(m+1)} \le y_{m+1}, \dots, D_{\pi(n)} \le y_n \,\middle|\, R^\pi_m\right], \tag{111}$$

where $R^\pi_m = \sum_{i=1}^m D_{\pi(i)}$. *Furthermore,*

$$\mathbb{Q}\left[D_{\pi(m+1)} = y_{m+1}, \dots, D_{\pi(n)} = y_n \,\middle|\, D^\pi_m\right]$$
$$= \frac{\widetilde{Q}\left(R^\pi_m + \sum_{i=m+1}^{n} y_i\right)}{\sum_{k=-\infty}^{\infty} \phi_{t^\pi_m}(a_k; R^\pi_m)} \prod_{i=m+1}^{n} Q_{\alpha_{\pi(i)}}(y_i). \tag{112}$$

Corollary 3.12 can be extended to include LRBs with discrete state-spaces.

4. Information-based asset pricing

4.1. BHM framework

We begin with a brief overview of the BHM framework. The approach was applied to credit risk in Brody et al. [8], and this was extended to include stochastic interest rates in Rutkowski and Yu [28]. A general asset pricing framework was proposed in Brody et al. [10] (see also [25]), and there have also been applications to inflation modelling [23], insider trading [7], insurance [9], and interest rate theory [24,26].

We fix a finite time horizon $[0, T]$ and a probability space $(\Omega, \mathcal{F}, \mathbb{Q})$. We assume that the risk-free rate of interest $\{r_t\}$ is deterministic, and that $r_t > 0$ and $\int_t^\infty r_u \, \mathrm{d}u = \infty$, for all $t > 0$. Then the time-s (no-arbitrage) price of a risk-free, zero-coupon bond maturing at time t (paying a nominal amount of unity) is

$$P_{st} = \exp\left(-\int_s^t r_u \, \mathrm{d}u\right) \quad (s \le t). \tag{113}$$

For $t < T$, the time-t price of a contingent cash flow H_T, due at time T, is given by an expression of the form

$$H_{tT} = P_{tT}\mathbb{E}[H_T \mid \mathcal{F}_t], \tag{114}$$

where $\{\mathcal{F}_t\}$ is the *market filtration*. The sigma-algebra $\mathcal{F}_t$ represents the information available to market participants at time t. In order for Eq. (114) to be consistent with the theory of no-arbitrage pricing, we interpret $\mathbb{Q}$ to be a risk-neutral measure.

In such a set-up, the dynamics of the price process $\{H_{tT}\}$ are implicitly determined by the evolution of the market filtration $\{\mathcal{F}_t\}$. We assume the existence of a (possibly multi-dimensional) *information process* $\{\xi_{tT}\}_{0 \le t \le T}$ such that

$$\mathcal{F}_t = \sigma\left(\{\xi_{sT}\}_{0 \le s \le t}\right). \tag{115}$$

Thus $\{\xi_{tT}\}$ is responsible for the delivery of all information to the market participants. The task of modelling the emergence of information in the market is reduced to that of specifying the law of the information process $\{\xi_{tT}\}$.

4.1.1. Single X-factor market

We assume that the cash flow H_T can be written in the form

$$H_T = h(X_T), \tag{116}$$

for some function $h(x)$, and some market factor X_T. We call X_T an X-factor. We assume that $\{\xi_{tT}\}$ is a one-dimensional process such that $\xi_{TT} = X_T$. Then we have

$$H_{tT} = P_{tT}\mathbb{E}[h(X_T) \mid \mathcal{F}_t] = P_{tT}\mathbb{E}[h(\xi_{TT}) \mid \mathcal{F}_t], \tag{117}$$

which ensures that $H_{TT} = H_T$. In the case where $\{\xi_{tT}\}$ is a Markov process, we have

$$H_{tT} = P_{tT}\mathbb{E}[h(\xi_{TT}) \mid \xi_{tT}]. \tag{118}$$

4.1.2. Multiple X-factor market

In the more general framework, we model an asset that generates N cash flows $H_{T_1}, H_{T_2}, \ldots, H_{T_N}$, which are to be received on the dates $T_1 \le T_2 \le \cdots \le T_N$, respectively. At time T_k, we assume that the vector of X-factors $X_{T_k} \in \mathbb{R}^{n_k}$ $(n_k \in \mathbb{N}_+)$ is revealed to the market, and we write

$$X_{T_k} = \left(X_{T_k}^{(1)}, X_{T_k}^{(2)}, \ldots, X_{T_k}^{(n_k)}\right)^\top. \tag{119}$$

We assume the X-factors are mutually independent, and that

$$H_{T_k} = h_k(X_{T_1}, X_{T_2}, \dots, X_{T_k}), \tag{120}$$

for some $h_k : \mathbb{R}^{n_1} \times \mathbb{R}^{n_2} \times \cdots \times \mathbb{R}^{n_k} \to \mathbb{R}$ which we call a cash-flow function. For each X-factor $X_{T_j}^{(i)}$, there is a factor information process $\{\xi_t^{(i,j)}\}$ such that $\xi_t^{(i,j)} = X_{T_j}^{(i)}$ for $t \geq T_j$, and the factor information processes are mutually independent. Setting $T = T_N$, we define the market information process $\{\xi_{tT}\}$ to be an $\mathbb{R}^{n_1+n_2+\cdots+n_N}$-valued process with each of its elements being a factor information process. The market filtration $\{\mathcal{F}_t\}$ is generated by $\{\xi_{tT}\}$. By construction, H_{T_k} is $\mathcal{F}_t$-measurable for $t \geq T_k$. The time-t price of the cash flow H_{T_k} is

$$H_{tT}^{(k)} = \begin{cases} P_{t,T_k}\mathbb{E}\left[h_k(X_{T_1}, X_{T_2}, \dots, X_{T_k}) \middle| \mathcal{F}_t\right] & \text{for } t < T_k, \\ 0 & \text{for } t \geq T_k. \end{cases} \tag{121}$$

Here we adopt the convention that cash flows have nil value at the time that they are due. In other words, prices are quoted on an ex-dividend basis. In this way the process $\{H_t^{(k)}\}$ is right-continuous at $t = T_k$. The asset price process is then

$$H_{tT} = \sum_{k=1}^{n} H_{tT}^{(k)} \quad (0 \leq t \leq T). \tag{122}$$

4.2. Lévy bridge information

We consider a market with a single factor, which we denote X_T. This X-factor is the size of a contingent cash flow to be received at time $T > 0$, so we take $h(x) = x$. For example, X_T could be the redemption amount of a credit risky bond. X_T is assumed to be integrable and to have the *a priori* probability law ν (we exclude the case where X_T is constant). Information is supplied to the market by an information process $\{\xi_{tT}\}$. The law of $\{\xi_{tT}\}$ is $LRB_{\mathcal{C}}([0,T], \{f_t\}, \nu)$, and we set $\xi_{TT} = X_T$. We assume throughout this section that the information process has a continuous state-space; the results can be extended to include LRB information processes with discrete state-spaces.

Since the information process has the Markov property, the price of the cash flow X_T is given by

$$X_{tT} = P_{tT}\mathbb{E}\left[X_T \,|\xi_{tT}\right] \quad (0 \leq t \leq T). \tag{123}$$

We note that X_T is $\mathcal{F}_T$-measurable and $X_{TT} = X_T$, but X_T is not $\mathcal{F}_t$-measurable for $t < T$ since we have excluded the case where X_T is constant. For $t \in (0,T)$, the $\mathcal{F}_t$-conditional law of X_T as given by Eq. (46) is

$$\nu_t(\mathrm{d}z) = \frac{\psi_t(\mathrm{d}z; \xi_{tT})}{\psi_t(\mathbb{R}; \xi_{tT})}, \tag{124}$$

where

$$\psi_t(\mathrm{d}z; \xi) = \frac{f_{T-t}(z-\xi)}{f_T(z)}\,\mathrm{d}z. \tag{125}$$

Then we have

$$X_{tT} = P_{tT}\int_{-\infty}^{\infty} z\nu_t(\mathrm{d}z). \tag{126}$$

When ν admits a density $p(z)$, the $\mathcal{F}_t$-conditional density of X_T exists and is given by

$$p_t(z) = \frac{f_{T-t}(z - \xi_{tT})p(z)}{\psi_t(\mathbb{R}; \xi_{tT})f_T(z)}. \tag{127}$$

Example. In the Brownian case the price is

$$X_{tT} = P_{tT} \frac{\int_{-\infty}^{\infty} z \mathrm{e}^{\frac{1}{T-t}\left[\xi_{tT} z - \frac{1}{2}\frac{t}{T}z^2\right]}\nu(\mathrm{d}z)}{\int_{-\infty}^{\infty} \mathrm{e}^{\frac{1}{T-t}\left[\xi_{tT} z - \frac{1}{2}\frac{t}{T}z^2\right]}\nu(\mathrm{d}z)}. \tag{128}$$

The following SDE can be derived for $\{X_{tT}\}$ (see [8,10,25,28]):

$$\mathrm{d}X_{tT} = r_t X_{tT}\,\mathrm{d}t + \frac{P_{tT}\mathrm{Var}[X_T \mid \xi_{tT}]}{T-t}\,\mathrm{d}W_t, \tag{129}$$

where $\{W_t\}$ is an $\{\mathcal{F}_t\}$-Brownian motion.

Example. In the gamma case we have

$$X_{tT} = P_{tT} \frac{\int_{\xi_{tT}}^{\infty} (z - \xi_{tT})^{m(T-t)-1} z^{2-mT}\,\nu(\mathrm{d}z)}{\int_{\xi_{tT}}^{\infty} (z - \xi_{tT})^{m(T-t)-1} z^{1-mT}\,\nu(\mathrm{d}z)}. \tag{130}$$

4.3. European option pricing

We consider the problem of pricing a European option on the price X_{tT} at time t. For a strike price K and $0 \le s < t < T$, the time-s price of a t-maturity call option on X_{tT} is

$$C_{st} = P_{st}\mathbb{E}\left[(X_{tT} - K)^+ \middle| \xi_{sT} \right]. \tag{131}$$

The expectation can be expanded in the form

$$\begin{aligned} \mathbb{E}_{\mathbb{Q}}\left[(X_{tT} - K)^+ \middle| \xi_{sT} \right] &= \mathbb{E}_{\mathbb{Q}}\left[\left(P_{tT}\mathbb{E}_{\mathbb{Q}}[X_T \mid \xi_{tT}] - K\right)^+ \middle| \xi_{sT} \right] \\ &= \mathbb{E}_{\mathbb{Q}}\left[\left(\int_{-\infty}^{\infty} (P_{tT}z - K)\nu_t(\mathrm{d}z) \right)^+ \middle| \xi_{sT} \right] \\ &= \mathbb{E}_{\mathbb{Q}}\left[\frac{1}{\psi_t(\mathbb{R}; \xi_{tT})} \left(\int_{-\infty}^{\infty} (P_{tT}z - K)\psi_t(\mathrm{d}z; \xi_{tT}) \right)^+ \middle| \xi_{sT} \right]. \end{aligned} \tag{132}$$

Recall that the Radon–Nikodym density process

$$\left.\frac{\mathrm{d}\mathbb{L}}{\mathrm{d}\mathbb{Q}}\right|_{\mathcal{F}_t} = \psi_t(\mathbb{R}; \xi_{tT})^{-1} \tag{133}$$

defines a measure $\mathbb{L}$ under which $\{\xi_{tT}\}_{0 \le t < T}$ is a Lévy process. By changing measure, we find that the expectation is

$$\frac{1}{\psi_s(\mathbb{R}; \xi_{sT})}\mathbb{E}_{\mathbb{L}}\left[\left(\int_{-\infty}^{\infty} (P_{tT}z - K)\psi_t(\mathrm{d}z; \xi_{tT}) \right)^+ \middle| \xi_{sT} \right]$$

$$= \frac{1}{\psi_s(\mathbb{R};\xi_{sT})}\mathbb{E}_{\mathbb{L}}\left[\left(\int_{-\infty}^{\infty}(P_{tT}z-K)\frac{f_{T-t}(z-\xi_{tT})}{f_T(z)}\nu(\mathrm{d}z)\right)^+\middle|\,\xi_{sT}\right]. \tag{134}$$

Eq. (27) states that $0 < f_{T-s}(z-\xi_{sT}) < \infty$. Thus we can write the expectation in terms of the ξ_{sT}-conditional terminal law ν_s in the form

$$\mathbb{E}_{\mathbb{L}}\left[\left(\int_{-\infty}^{\infty}(P_{tT}z-K)\frac{f_{T-t}(z-\xi_{tT})}{f_{T-s}(z-\xi_{sT})}\nu_s(\mathrm{d}z)\right)^+\middle|\,\xi_{sT}\right]$$
$$= \int_{-\infty}^{\infty}\left(\int_{-\infty}^{\infty}(P_{tT}z-K)\frac{f_{T-t}(z-x)}{f_{T-s}(z-\xi_{sT})}\nu_s(\mathrm{d}z)\right)^+ f_{t-s}(x-\xi_{sT})\,\mathrm{d}x. \tag{135}$$

We defined the (marginal) Lévy bridge density $f_{tT}(x;z)$ by

$$f_{tT}(x;z) = \frac{f_{T-t}(z-x)f_t(x)}{f_T(z)}. \tag{136}$$

From this we can define the ξ_{sT}-dependent law $\mu_{st}(\mathrm{d}x;z)$ by

$$\mu_{st}(\mathrm{d}x;z) = f_{t-s,T-s}(x-\xi_{sT}, z-\xi_{sT})\,\mathrm{d}x. \tag{137}$$

Thus $\mu_{st}(\mathrm{d}x;z)$ is the time-t marginal law of a Lévy bridge starting at the value ξ_{sT} at time s, and terminating at the value z at time T. Defining the set B_t by

$$B_t = \left\{x\in\mathbb{R} : \int_{-\infty}^{\infty}(P_{tT}z-K)\frac{f_{T-t}(z-x)}{f_T(z)}\nu(\mathrm{d}z) > 0\right\}, \tag{138}$$

one finds that the expectation reduces to

$$\int_{-\infty}^{\infty}(P_{tT}z-K)\mu_{st}(B_t;z)\nu_s(\mathrm{d}z). \tag{139}$$

The option price is then given by

$$C_{st} = P_{st}\int_{-\infty}^{\infty}(P_{tT}z-K)\mu_{st}(B_t;z)\nu_s(\mathrm{d}z). \tag{140}$$

We can write $X_{tT} = \Lambda(t,\xi_{tT})$, for Λ a deterministic function. The set B_t can then be written

$$B_t = \{\xi\in\mathbb{R} : \Lambda(t,\xi) > K\}. \tag{141}$$

We see that if Λ is increasing in its second argument then $B_t = (\xi_t^*,\infty)$ for some critical value ξ_t^* of the information process. Λ is monotonic if $\{\xi_{tT}\}$ is a Lévy process.

Example. In the Brownian case we have

$$\Lambda(t,x) = P_{tT}\frac{\int_{-\infty}^{\infty} z\,\mathrm{e}^{\frac{1}{T-t}\left[xz-\frac{1}{2}\frac{t}{T}z^2\right]}\nu(\mathrm{d}z)}{\int_{-\infty}^{\infty}\mathrm{e}^{\frac{1}{T-t}\left[xz-\frac{1}{2}\frac{t}{T}z^2\right]}\nu(\mathrm{d}z)}. \tag{142}$$

It can be shown that the function Λ is increasing in its second argument (see, for example, [10] or [28]); hence $B_t = (\xi_t^*,\infty)$ for the unique ξ_t^* satisfying $\Lambda(t,\xi_t^*) = K$. A short calculation verifies that $\mu_{st}(\mathrm{d}x; z)$ is the normal law with mean $M(z)$ and variance V given by

$$M(z) = \frac{T-t}{T-s}\xi_{sT} + \frac{t-s}{T-s}z, \qquad V = \frac{t-s}{T-s}(T-t). \tag{143}$$

This is the time-t marginal law of a Brownian bridge starting from the value ξ_{sT} at time s, and finishing at the value z at time T. We have

$$\mu_{st}(B_t; z) = 1 - \Phi\left[\frac{\xi_t^* - M(z)}{\sqrt{V}}\right] = \Phi\left[\frac{M(z) - \xi_t^*}{\sqrt{V}}\right], \tag{144}$$

where $\Phi[x]$ is the standard normal distribution function. The option price is then

$$C_{st} = P_{sT}\int_{-\infty}^{\infty} z\Phi\left[\frac{M(z) - \xi_t^*}{\sqrt{V}}\right]\nu_s(\mathrm{d}z) + P_{st}K\int_{-\infty}^{\infty} \Phi\left[\frac{M(z) - \xi_t^*}{\sqrt{V}}\right]\nu_s(\mathrm{d}z). \tag{145}$$

Example. In the gamma case we have

$$\Lambda(t, x) = P_{tT}\frac{\int_x^{\infty}(z-x)^{m(T-t)-1}z^{2-mT}\nu(\mathrm{d}z)}{\int_x^{\infty}(z-x)^{m(T-t)-1}z^{1-mT}\nu(\mathrm{d}z)}. \tag{146}$$

The monotonicity of $\Lambda(t, x)$ in x was proved for $m(T-t) > 1$ by Brody et al. [9]. The authors also give a numerical example where $\Lambda(t, x)$ was not monotonic in x for $m(T-t) < 1$. For all $t \in (0, T)$, we have

$$\mu_{st}(\mathrm{d}x; z) = \mathbb{1}_{\{\xi_{sT} < x < z\}}k(z)^{-1}\left(\frac{x-\xi_{st}}{z-\xi_{sT}}\right)^{m(t-s)-1}\left(\frac{z-y}{z-\xi_{sT}}\right)^{m(T-t)-1}\mathrm{d}x, \tag{147}$$

where $k(z)$ is the normalising constant

$$k(z) = (z-\xi_{sT})\mathrm{B}[m(t-s), m(T-t)]. \tag{148}$$

Hence $\mu_{st}(\mathrm{d}x; z)$ is an $(z-\xi_{sT})$-scaled, ξ_{sT}-shifted, beta law with parameters $\alpha = m(t-s)$ and $\beta = m(T-t)$. This is the time-t marginal law of a gamma bridge starting at the value ξ_{sT} at time s, and terminating at the value x at time T. When $m(T-t) > 1$, a critical ξ_t^* exists such that $\Lambda(t, \xi_t^*) = K$. Then $B_t = (\xi_t^*, \infty)$, and

$$\begin{aligned}\mu_{st}(B_t; z) &= 1 - I\left[\frac{\xi_t^* - \xi_{sT}}{z-\xi_{sT}}; m(t-s), m(T-t)\right]\\ &= I\left[\frac{z-\xi_t^*}{z-\xi_{sT}}; m(T-t), m(t-s)\right].\end{aligned} \tag{149}$$

Here $I[z; \alpha, \beta]$ is the regularized incomplete beta function, defined for $\alpha, \beta > 0$ by

$$I[z; \alpha, \beta] = \frac{1}{\mathrm{B}[\alpha, \beta]}\int_0^z x^{\alpha-1}(1-x)^{\beta-1}\,\mathrm{d}x. \tag{150}$$

The option price is then given by

$$\begin{aligned}C_{st} = {}& P_{sT}\int_{\xi_{sT}}^{\infty} zI\left[\frac{z-\xi_t^*}{z-\xi_{sT}}; m(T-t), m(t-s)\right]\nu_s(\mathrm{d}z)\\ &+ P_{st}K\int_{\xi_{sT}}^{\infty} I\left[\frac{z-\xi_t^*}{z-\xi_{sT}}; m(T-t), m(t-s)\right]\nu_s(\mathrm{d}z).\end{aligned} \tag{151}$$

4.4. Binary bond

The simplest non-trivial contingent cash flow is $X_T \in \{k_0, k_1\}$, for $k_0 < k_1$. This is the pay-off from a zero-coupon, credit-risky bond that has principle k_1, and a fixed recovery rate k_0/k_1 on default. Assume that, *a priori*, $\mathbb{Q}[X_T = k_0] = p > 0$ and $\mathbb{Q}[X_T = k_1] = 1 - p$. Then

$$\mathbb{Q}[X_T = k_0 \mid \xi_{tT}] = \left(1 + \frac{f_T(k_0)}{f_T(k_1)} \frac{f_{T-t}(k_1 - \xi_{tT})}{f_{T-t}(k_0 - \xi_{tT})} \frac{1-p}{p}\right)^{-1}, \tag{152}$$

and

$$\mathbb{Q}[X_T = k_1 \mid \xi_{tT}] = \left(1 + \frac{f_T(k_1)}{f_T(k_0)} \frac{f_{T-t}(k_0 - \xi_{tT})}{f_{T-t}(k_1 - \xi_{tT})} \frac{p}{1-p}\right)^{-1}. \tag{153}$$

The bond price process $\{X_{tT}\}$ associated with the given terminal cash flow is given by

$$X_{tT} = P_{tT}\left(k_0 \mathbb{Q}[X_T = k_0 \mid \xi_{tT}] + k_1 \mathbb{Q}[X_T = k_1 \mid \xi_{tT}]\right) \quad (0 \le t \le T). \tag{154}$$

Example. In the Brownian case we have

$$\mathbb{Q}[X_T = k_0 \mid \xi_{tT}] = \left(1 + \exp\left[-\frac{1}{2}\frac{k_1 - k_0}{T-t}\left(\frac{t}{T}(k_0 + k_1) - 2\xi_{tT}\right)\right]\frac{1-p}{p}\right)^{-1}, \tag{155}$$

and

$$\mathbb{Q}[X_T = k_1 \mid \xi_{tT}] = \left(1 + \exp\left[\frac{1}{2}\frac{k_1 - k_0}{T-t}\left(\frac{t}{T}(k_0 + k_1) - 2\xi_{tT}\right)\right]\frac{p}{1-p}\right)^{-1}. \tag{156}$$

Writing $\rho_i = \mathbb{Q}[X_T = k_i \mid \xi_{tT}]$, note that

$$\begin{aligned}
\mathrm{Var}[X_T \mid \xi_{tT}] &= (k_1 - k_0)^2 \rho_1 \rho_0 \\
&= -(k_0 - k_0\rho_0 - k_1\rho_1)(k_1 - k_0\rho_0 - k_1\rho_1) \\
&= -(k_0 - X_{tT})(k_1 - X_{tT}).
\end{aligned} \tag{157}$$

Thus, recalling (129), we see that the SDE of $\{X_{tT}\}$ is

$$\mathrm{d}X_{tT} = r_t X_{tT}\,\mathrm{d}t - \frac{P_{tT}(k_0 - X_{tT})(k_1 - X_{tT})}{T-t}\,\mathrm{d}W_t, \tag{158}$$

with the initial condition $X_{0T} = P_{0T}(k_0 p + k_1(1-p))$. For $K \in (P_{tT}k_0, P_{tT}k_1)$, we are able to solve the equation $\Lambda(t, x) = K$ for x. We have

$$\begin{aligned}
\Lambda(t, x) &= P_{tT}\left(k_0 \mathbb{Q}[X_T = k_0 \mid \xi_{tT} = x] + k_1 \mathbb{Q}[X_T = k_1 \mid \xi_{tT} = x]\right) \\
&= P_{tT}\left(k_1 - (k_1 - k_0)\mathbb{Q}[X_T = k_0 \mid \xi_{tT} = x]\right),
\end{aligned} \tag{159}$$

so the solution to $\Lambda(t, x) = K$ is

$$\xi_t^* = \frac{t}{2T}(k_0 + k_1) - \frac{T-t}{k_1 - k_0}\log\left[\frac{p}{1-p}\frac{K - P_{tT}k_0}{P_{tT}k_1 - K}\right]. \tag{160}$$

The price of a call option on X_{tT} is

$$C_{st} = P_{st}\sum_{i=0}^{1}(P_{tT}k - K)\Phi\left[\frac{M(k_i) - \xi_t^*}{\sqrt{V}}\right]\mathbb{Q}[X_T = k_i \mid \xi_{sT}]. \tag{161}$$

Acknowledgements

The authors are grateful to seminar participants at ETH Zürich, Switzerland, April 2008; at the Bachelier Finance Society Fifth World Congress, London, UK, June 2008; and at the Mathematics in Finance Conference, Kruger National Park, RSA, September 2008, where drafts of this paper were presented, for their comments. Edward Hoyle acknowledges the support of an EPSRC Doctoral Training Grant and a European Science Foundation research visit grant under the Advanced Mathematical Methods in Finance programme (AMaMeF). This work was undertaken in part while Edward Hoyle and Lane P. Hughston were members of the Department of Mathematics, King's College London, and while Andrea Macrina was a member of the Department of Mathematics, ETH Zürich. Lane P. Hughtson acknowledges the support of the Aspen Center for Physics where a portion of this work was carried out.

References

[1] K. Back, H. Pedersen, Long-lived information and intraday patterns, Journal of Financial Markets 1 (1998) 385–402.

[2] O. Barndorff-Nielsen, B. Jørgensen, Some parametric models on the simplex, Journal of Multivariate Analysis 39 (1991) 106–116.

[3] F. Baudoin, Conditioned stochastic differential equations: theory, examples and application to finance, Stochastic Processes and their Applications 100 (2002) 109–145.

[4] F. Baudoin, L. Nguyen-Ngoc, The financial value of a weak information on a financial market, Finance and Stochastics 8 (2004) 415–435.

[5] J. Bertoin, Lévy Processes, Cambridge University Press, Cambridge, 1996.

[6] J. Bertoin, L. Chaumont, J. Pitman, Path transformations of first passage bridges, Electronic Communications in Probability 8 (2003) 155–166.

[7] D.C. Brody, M. Davis, R. Friedman, L.P. Hughston, Informed traders, Proceedings of the Royal Society A 465 (2008) 1103–1122.

[8] D.C. Brody, L.P. Hughston, A. Macrina, Beyond hazard rates: A new framework for credit-risk modelling, in: R. Elliott, M. Fu, R. Jarrow, J.Y. Yen (Eds.), Advances in Mathematical Finance, Festschrift vol. in honour of Dilip Madan, Birkhäuser/Springer, 2007.

[9] D.C. Brody, L.P. Hughston, A. Macrina, Dam rain and cumulative gain, Proceedings of the Royal Society A 464 (2008) 1801–1822.

[10] D.C. Brody, L.P. Hughston, A. Macrina, Information-based asset pricing, International Journal of Theoretical and Applied Finance 11 (2008) 107–142.

[11] L. Chaumond, D. Hobson, M. Yor, Some consequences of the cyclic exchangeability property for exponential functionals of Lévy processes, in: Séminaire de probabilités de Strasbourg, vol. 35, Springer-Verlag, Berlin, 2001, pp. 334–347.

[12] R. Elliott, M. Jeanblanc, Incomplete markets with jumps and informed agents, Mathematical Methods in Operations Research 50 (1999) 475–492.

[13] R. Elliott, P. Kopp, Equivalent martingale measures for bridge processes, Stochastic Analysis and Applications 9 (1991) 429–444.

[14] M. Émery, M. Yor, A parallel between Brownian bridges and gamma bridges, Publications of the Research Institute for Mathematical Sciences 40 (2004) 669–688.

[15] K.T. Fang, S. Kotz, K. Ng, Symmetric Multivariate and Related Distributions, Chapman & Hall, New York, 1990.

[16] P. Fitzsimmons, J. Pitman, M. Yor, Markovian bridges: Construction, palm interpretation, and splicing, Seminar on Stochastic Processes 33 (1993) 102–133.

[17] D. Gasbarra, E. Valkeila, L. Vostrikova, Enlargement of filtration and additional information in pricing models: a Bayesian approach, in: Y. Kabanov, R. Lipster, J. Stoyanov (Eds.), From Stochastic Calculus to Mathematical Finance: The Shiryaev Festschrift, Springer, Berlin, 2006, pp. 257–285.

[18] H. Geman, D. Madan, M. Yor, Probing option prices for information, Methodology and Computing in Applied Probability 9 (2007) 115–131.

[19] R. Gupta, D.S.P. Richards, Multivariate Liouville distributions IV, Journal of Multivariate Analysis 54 (1995) 1–17.

[20] R. Gupta, D.S.P. Richards, The history of the Dirichlet and Liouville distributions, International Statistical Review 69 (2001) 433–446.
[21] E. Hoyle, Information-based models for finance and insurance, Ph.D. Thesis, Imperial College London, 2010. arXiv:1010.0829.
[22] E. Hoyle, L.P. Hughston, A. Macrina, Stable-1/2 bridges and insurance: a Bayesian approach to non-life reserving, Working Paper (2010). arXiv:1005.0496.
[23] L.P. Hughston, A. Macrina, Information, inflation, and interest, in: L. Stettner (Ed.), in: Advances in Mathematics of Finance, vol. 83, Banach Centre Publications, Institute of Mathematics, Polish Academy of Sciences, Warsaw, 2008, pp. 117–138.
[24] L.P. Hughston, A. Macrina, Pricing fixed-income securities in an information-based framework, Working Paper (2009). arXiv:0911.1610.
[25] A. Macrina, An information-based framework for asset pricing: X-factor theory and its applications, Ph.D. Thesis, King's College London, 2006. arXiv:0807.2124.
[26] A. Macrina, P.A. Parbhoo, Security pricing with information-sensitive discounting, in: M. Kijima, C. Hara, K. Tanaka (Eds.), Recent Advances in Financial Engineering 2009: Proceedings of the KIER-TMU International Workshop on Financial Engineering 2009, World Scientific Publishing Company, 2010.
[27] D. Madan, M. Yor, Making Markov martingales meet marginals: with explicit constructions, Bernouilli 8 (4) (2002) 509–536.
[28] M. Rutkowski, N. Yu, On the Brody–Hughston–Macrina approach to modelling of defaultable term structure, International Journal of Theoretical and Applied Finance 10 (2007) 557–589.
[29] K.I. Sato, Lévy Processes and Infinitely Divisible Distributions, Cambridge University Press, Cambridge, 1999.
[30] M. Yor, Some remarkable properties of gamma processes, in: R. Elliott, M. Fu, R. Jarrow, J.Y. Yen (Eds.), Advances in Mathematical Finance, Festschrift volume in honour of Dilip Madan, Birkhäuser/Springer, 2007.

Chapter 8

Chapter 5
Modelling Information Flows in Financial Markets*

Dorje C. Brody, Lane P. Hughston, and Andrea Macrina

Abstract This paper presents an overview of information-based asset pricing. In the information-based approach, an asset is defined by its cash-flow structure. The market is assumed to have access to "partial" information about future cash flows. Each cash flow is determined by a collection of independent market factors called X-factors. The market filtration is generated by a set of information processes, each of which carries information about one of the X-factors, and eventually reveals the X-factor in a way that ensures that the associated cash flows have the correct measurability properties. In the models considered each information process has two terms, one of which contains a "signal" about the associated X-factor, and the other of which represents "market noise". The existence of an established pricing kernel, adapted to the market filtration, is assumed. The price of an asset is given by the expectation of the discounted cash flows in the associated risk-neutral measure, conditional on the information provided by the market. When the market noise is modelled by a Brownian bridge, one is able to construct explicit formulae for asset prices, as well as semi-analytic expressions for the prices and greeks of options and derivatives. In particular, option price data can be used to determine the information flow-rate parameters implicit in the definitions of the information processes. One consequence of the modelling framework is a specific scheme of stochastic volatility and correlation processes. Instead of imposing a volatility and correlation model upon the dynamics of a set of assets, one is able to deduce the dynamics of the volatilities and correlations of the asset price movements from more primitive assumptions involving the associated cash flows. The paper concludes with an

D.C. Brody (✉) · L.P. Hughston
Department of Mathematics, Imperial College London, London SW7 2AZ, UK
e-mail: d.brody@imperial.ac.uk

L.P. Hughston
e-mail: l.hughston@imperial.ac.uk

A. Macrina
Department of Mathematics, King's College London, London WC2R 2LS, UK
e-mail: andrea.macrina@kcl.ac.uk

A. Macrina
Institute of Economic Research, Kyoto University, Kyoto 606-8501, Japan

G. Di Nunno, B. Øksendal (eds.), *Advanced Mathematical Methods for Finance*, 133
DOI 10.1007/978-3-642-18412-3_5,

*This chapter was originally published as: D. C. Brody, L. P. Hughston & A. Macrina (2011) Modelling Information Flows in Financial Markets. In: *Advanced Mathematical Methods for Finance* (G. Di Nunno & B. Øksendal, editors), Springer-Verlag, pp. 133–153. Reprinted with kind permission from Springer.

examination of situations involving asymmetric information. We present a simple model for informed traders and show how this can be used as a basis for so-called statistical arbitrage. Finally, we consider the problem of price formation in a heterogeneous market with multiple agents.

Keywords Information-based asset pricing · Information filter · Price formation · Statistical arbitrage

Mathematics Subject Classification (2010) 91G40 · 93E11 · 60G40 · 94Axx

5.1 Cash Flow Structures and Market Factors

In financial markets, the revelation of information is the most important factor in the determination of the price movements of financial assets. When a new piece of information (whether true, partly true, misleading, or bogus) circulates in a financial market, the prices of related assets move in response, and they move again when the information is updated. But how do we build specific models that incorporate the impact of information on asset prices? In this article we present an overview of some of the key issues involved in modelling the flow of information in financial markets and develop in some detail some elementary models for "information" in various situations. We show how information flow processes, when appropriately modelled, can be used to determine the associated price processes of financial assets. Applications to the pricing of various types of contingent claims will also be indicated. One of the contributions of the present work is to introduce a model for dynamic correlation in the situation where we consider a portfolio of assets. Rather than imposing an artificial correlation structure on the assets under consideration, we are able to infer the correlation structure from more basic assumptions. In the final section of the paper, we make some remarks about statistical arbitrage strategies and about price formation in markets characterised by inhomogeneous information flows.

When models are constructed for the pricing and risk management of complicated financial products, the price dynamics of the simpler financial assets, upon which the more complicated products are based, are often simply "assumed" (modulo some parametric or functional freedom). One can understand from a practical angle why it can be expeditious to proceed on that basis. Nevertheless, from a fundamental view we have to consider that even the basic financial assets (shares, bonds, etc.) are characterised by a number of potentially "complex" features, and so to make sense of the behaviour of such assets we need to consider what goes into the determination of their prices. To build up models for the dynamics of asset prices, it seems logical to proceed step by step along the following lines: (1) model the cash-flows arising from the asset as random variables; (2) model the market filtration (the flow of information to the market); (3) model the pricing kernel (which takes into account discounting, risk aversion, and the absence of arbitrage); and (4) work out the resulting dynamics for the price process.

We model the unfolding of chance in a financial market with the specification of a probability space $(\Omega, \mathcal{F}, \mathbb{P})$ on which we are going to construct a filtration

$\{\mathcal{F}_t\}$ representing the flow of information to market participants. Here $\mathbb{P}$ denotes the "physical" probability measure. The markets we consider will, in general, be incomplete. That is to say, although derivatives can be priced, we do not assume that they can be hedged. Since we are going to model the filtration, we say that we are working in an information-based asset pricing framework. The general approach that we describe here is that of Brody, Hughston, and Macrina [1–3].

Consider a financial instrument that delivers to its owner a set of random cash flows $\{D_{T_k}\}_{k=1,\ldots,n}$ on the dates $\{T_k\}_{k=1,\ldots,n}$. For simplicity, we assume that these dates are fixed and finite in number. The extension to random dates and to an infinite number of dates is straightforward. Let the pricing kernel be denoted $\{\pi_t\}$. At time t the value S_t of a contract that generates the cash flows $\{D_{T_k}\}_{k=1,\ldots,n}$ is given by the following *valuation formula*:

$$S_t = \frac{1}{\pi_t} \sum_{k=1}^{n} \mathbb{1}_{\{t<T_k\}} \mathbb{E}^{\mathbb{P}}[\pi_{T_k} D_{T_k} | \mathcal{F}_t]. \tag{5.1}$$

Thus, at time t, for each cash flow that has not yet occurred, we take its discounted risk-adjusted conditional expectation, and then we form the sum of such expressions to give the total value of the asset.

Sometimes it is maintained that to regard share prices as being entirely determined by expected dividends is incorrect—that other factors come into play as well, such as the value implicit in corporate control, the value of the status of being a shareholder, and so on. In our view such "implicit" dividends, to the extent that they are relevant and can be assigned a value, have to be modelled and thus enter the valuation formula alongside the tangible cash flows. Sometimes it is argued that market sentiment is also important: indeed, it clearly is; but our view is that sentiment is implicit in the imperfect information the market is receiving concerning future cash flows; that sentiment about a future share price is, in essence, information concerning cash flows (both tangible and intangible) extending beyond the date or dates to which the sentiment refers.

In order to apply the valuation formula, we need to model the market filtration $\{\mathcal{F}_t\}$ and the pricing kernel $\{\pi_t\}$. In particular, it is logical to model the filtration first since the pricing kernel has to be adapted to the filtration. To model the filtration, we proceed as follows. Let us introduce a set of independent random variables $\{X_{T_k}\}_{k=1,\ldots,n}$, which we call *market factors* or simply "X-factors". For each k, the cash flow D_{T_k} is assumed to depend on the market factors $X_{T_1}, X_{T_2}, \ldots, X_{T_k}$. Thus, in association with each date T_k, we introduce a so-called "cash-flow function" Δ_{T_k} such that

$$D_{T_k} = \Delta_{T_k}(X_{T_1}, X_{T_2}, \ldots, X_{T_k}). \tag{5.2}$$

For each asset, we need to model the X-factors, the a priori probabilities, and the cash-flow functions. In general, the X-factor associated with a given date will be a vectorial quantity. The cash-flow diagram associated with a typical asset is illustrated schematically in Fig. 5.1.

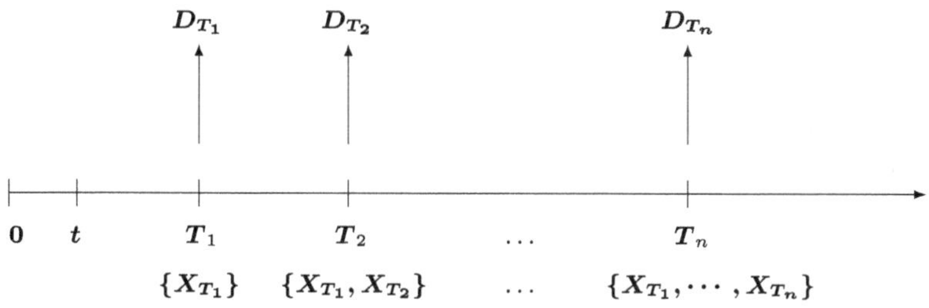

Fig. 5.1 The value S_t at time t of a security that delivers the random cash flows $D_{T_1}, D_{T_2}, \ldots$ at times $T_1, T_2, \ldots$ is determined by the valuation formula (5.1). The cash flow D_{T_1} is determined by a set of one or more independent X-factors $\{X_{T_1}\}$. Then D_{T_2} is determined by $\{X_{T_1}, X_{T_2}\}$, where X_{T_2} represents a further set of independent X-factors, and so on

5.2 X-factor Analysis

Let us look at some elementary examples of cash-flow models based on X-factors. The first example we consider is a simple credit-risky bond, with two remaining coupons to be paid and no recovery on default. Then we have the following cash-flow structure:

$$D_{T_1} = cX_{T_1}, \tag{5.3}$$

$$D_{T_2} = (c+n)X_{T_1}X_{T_2}. \tag{5.4}$$

Here c and n denote the coupon and principal, respectively, and X_{T_1} and X_{T_2} are independent digital random variables taking the values 0 or 1 with designated a priori probabilities. Evidently, if the first coupon is not paid then neither will the second. On the other hand, even if X_{T_1} takes the value unity, and the first coupon is paid, the second coupon and the principal will not be paid unless X_{T_2} also takes the value unity.

The second example is a simple model for a credit-risky coupon bond with recovery. In this case the cash-flow functions are given as follows:

$$D_{T_1} = cX_{T_1} + R_1(c+n)(1-X_{T_1}), \tag{5.5}$$

$$D_{T_2} = (c+n)X_{T_1}X_{T_2} + R_2(c+n)X_{T_1}(1-X_{T_2}). \tag{5.6}$$

Here R_1 and R_2 denote recovery rates. Thus if default occurs at the first coupon, then both the coupon and principal become immediately due, and a fixed fraction R_1 of $c+n$ is paid. But if default occurs at the second coupon date, then the recovery rate is R_2. We observe that the X-factor method allows for a rather transparent representation of the cash-flow structure of such a security and isolates the variables that underlie the various cash flows.

5.3 Information Processes

We assume that with reference to each market factor market participants will have access to information, which in general is imperfect. We model the imperfect information available to market participants concerning a typical market factor X_T with the introduction of a so-called "information process" $\{\xi_{tT}\}_{0\le t\le T}$. An information process is required to have the property

$$\xi_{TT} = f(X_T) \tag{5.7}$$

for some invertible function $f(x)$. This condition ensures that the information process "reveals" the value of the associated market factor X_T at time T. At earlier times, the value of ξ_{tT} contains "partial information" about the value of the X-factor. We shall come to some explicit examples of information processes shortly.

We are now in a position to say how we model the market filtration. In particular, we shall assume that $\{\mathcal{F}_t\}$ is generated collectively by the various market information processes $\{\xi_{tT_k}\}_{k=1,\dots,n}$. In other words, the information at time t is given by the following sigma-algebra:

$$\mathcal{F}_t = \sigma\big[\{\xi_{sT_k}\}_{0\le s\le t,\ k=1,\dots,n}\big]. \tag{5.8}$$

We thus have the following sequence of ideas: market participants are concerned with cash flows; cash flows are dependent on a set of independent market factors; market participants have partial access to the market factors; and this imperfect information generates the market filtration.

We are left with the problem of taking the conditional expectation of the risk-adjusted discounted cash flows to generate price processes; for this purpose, we have to model the pricing kernel. We assume that the pricing kernel is adapted to the market filtration. Thus from knowledge of the history of the information processes from time 0 up to time t one can work out the value of the pricing kernel at t (see, e.g., [6–9]). In a typical model the pricing kernel is given by the discounted marginal utility of consumption of a representative agent. It is reasonable to suppose that the consumption plan of the agent is adapted to the information filtration. The idea is that the filtration represents the flow of information available at each time t about the relevant market factors and that the consumption of the agent is determined by this information. In other words, the agent behaves "rationally", always acting optimally on the available information, in accordance with appropriate criteria. There may be an idiosyncratic element to any given agent's consumption plan that is not adapted to the market filtration and is essentially private. But the *representative* agent has no idiosyncratic consumption.

5.4 Brownian-Bridge Information

For the construction of explicit models, it is useful to transform to the risk-neutral measure $\mathbb{Q}$. This can be achieved by use of the pricing kernel, which we regard as specified. Thus for the present we confine the discussion to "microeconomic" issues: we take no notice of the informational notions implicit in the formulation of the pricing kernel and make the additional simplifying assumption in what follows that the default-free interest-rate system is deterministic. Then the valuation formula takes the following form:

$$S_t = \sum_{k=1}^{n} \mathbb{1}_{\{t<T_k\}} P_{tT_k} \mathbb{E}^{\mathbb{Q}}[D_{T_k}|\mathcal{F}_t]. \tag{5.9}$$

Absence of arbitrage implies that the discount bond system $\{P_{tT}\}_{0\leq t\leq T<\infty}$ is of the form $P_{tT} = P_{0T}/P_{0t}$, where $\{P_{0t}\}_{0\leq t<\infty}$ is the initial term structure.

With these assumptions in place, we are in a position to specify a model for the information flow. For each X-factor X_T, we take the associated information process to be of the form

$$\xi_{tT} = \sigma t X_T + \beta_{tT}. \tag{5.10}$$

Here $\{\beta_{tT}\}$ is a $\mathbb{Q}$-Brownian bridge over the interval $[0, T]$, satisfying $\beta_{0T} = 0$, $\beta_{TT} = 0$, $\mathbb{E}[\beta_{tT}] = 0$, and $\mathbb{E}[\beta_{sT}\beta_{tT}] = s(T-t)/T$. The X-factor and the Brownian bridge are assumed to be $\mathbb{Q}$-independent. Thus the Brownian bridge represents "market noise", and only the "market signal" term involving the X-factor contains true market information. The parameter σ can be interpreted as the "information flow rate" for the factor X_T.

In the situation where we have a multiplicity of factors X_{T_k} $(k = 1, \ldots, n)$, the information processes are taken to be of the form

$$\xi_{tT_k} = \sigma_k t X_{T_k} + \beta_{tT_k}, \tag{5.11}$$

where we assume that the X-factors and Brownian bridges are independent.

The motivation for the use of a bridge to represent noise is intuitively as follows. We assume that initially all available market information is taken into account in the determination of prices, or, equivalently, the a priori probability laws for the market factors. After the passage of time, new stories circulate, and we model this by taking into account that the variance of the Brownian bridge increases for the first half of its trajectory. Eventually, the variance falls to zero at T, when the "moment of truth" arrives. The parameter σ represents the rate at which the true value of X_T is "revealed" as time progresses. Thus, if σ is low, then X_T is effectively hidden until near the time T; on the other hand, if σ is high, then we can think of X_T as being revealed quickly. If the X-factor is "dimensionless", then σ has the units

$$\sigma \sim [\text{time}]^{-1/2}, \tag{5.12}$$

and a rough measure for the timescale τ over which information is revealed is

$$\tau = \frac{1}{\sigma^2 \operatorname{Var}[X_T]}. \tag{5.13}$$

In particular, if $\tau \ll T$, then the value of X_T will be revealed rather early, e.g., after the passage of a few multiples of τ. On the other hand, if $\tau \gg T$, then X_T will only be revealed at the last minute, as a "surprise".

We remark that the information process (5.10) has the Markov property. This feature implies simplifications in the resulting models. In particular, on account of relation (5.7) we find that the conditioning with respect to $\mathcal{F}_t$ in (5.9) can be replaced by conditioning with respect to the random variables ξ_{tT_k} $(k = 1, \ldots)$. For a proof of the Markov property, see [1, 9].

5.5 Assets Paying a Single Dividend

Consider an asset that pays single dividend $D_T \geq 0$ at time T, and assume that there is only one market factor X_T, so $D_T = f(X_T)$. For the moment, let us assume further that $f(x) = x$. Thus, we have $D_T = X_T$, where the market factor X_T is a continuous nonnegative random variable with a priori $\mathbb{Q}$-density $p(x)$ for $x > 0$. It follows by use of the Markov property of $\{\xi_{tT}\}$ that the price of such an asset can be written in the form

$$\begin{aligned} S_t &= P_{tT}\mathbb{E}[D_T|\xi_{tT}] \\ &= P_{tT}\int_0^\infty x p_t(x)\,dx, \end{aligned} \tag{5.14}$$

where $p_t(x)$ is the conditional density of X_T. Making use of the Bayes formula, one can show that $p_t(x)$ is given more explicitly by

$$p_t(x) = \frac{p(x)\exp[\frac{T}{T-t}(\sigma x\xi_{tT} - \frac{1}{2}\sigma^2x^2t)]}{\int_0^\infty p(x)\exp[\frac{T}{T-t}(\sigma x\xi_{tT} - \frac{1}{2}\sigma^2x^2t)]\,dx}. \tag{5.15}$$

Thus, at each time $t < T$ the price of the asset is determined by the random value of the information ξ_{tT} available at that time and is given by

$$S_t = P_{tT}\frac{\int_0^\infty xp(x)\exp[\frac{T}{T-t}(\sigma x\xi_{tT} - \frac{1}{2}\sigma^2x^2t)]\,dx}{\int_0^\infty p(x)\exp[\frac{T}{T-t}(\sigma x\xi_{tT} - \frac{1}{2}\sigma^2x^2t)]\,dx}. \tag{5.16}$$

The dynamics of the price process can then be obtained by an application of Ito's lemma, with the following result:

$$dS_t = r_tS_t\,dt + P_{tT}\frac{\sigma T}{T-t}\mathrm{Var}_t[X_T]\,dW_t. \tag{5.17}$$

Here

$$\mathrm{Var}_t[X_T] = \int_0^\infty x^2p_t(x)\,dx - \left(\int_0^\infty xp_t(x)\,dx\right)^2 \tag{5.18}$$

denotes the conditional variance of X_T, which by (5.15) is evidently given as a function of t and ξ_{tT}. The $\{\mathcal{F}_t\}$-adapted process $\{W_t\}$ driving the dynamics of the asset in (5.17) above is not given exogenously, but rather is defined in terms of the information process itself for $t < T$ by the following formula:

$$W_t = \xi_{tT} - \int_0^t \frac{1}{T-s}\big(\sigma T \mathbb{E}_s[X_T] - \xi_{sT}\big)\,ds. \tag{5.19}$$

Indeed, one can verify, by use of the Lévy criterion, that the process $\{W_t\}$, as thus defined, is an $\{\mathcal{F}_t\}$-Brownian motion. Hence we see that in an information-based approach we can *derive* the Brownian motions that drive the markets: they are not "inputs" to the model, but rather can be seen as arising as a "consequence" of the model.

5.6 Geometric Brownian Motion Model

A simple application of the X-factor technique arises in the case of geometric Brownian motion models. We consider a limited-liability company that makes a single cash distribution S_T at time T. Alternatively, think of a portfolio containing a single stock which will be sold off at time T for S_T, with the proceeds of the sale going to the investor. We assume that S_T has a log-normal distribution under $\mathbb{Q}$ and can be written in the form

$$S_T = S_0 \exp\Big(rT + \nu\sqrt{T}X_T - \frac{1}{2}\nu^2 T\Big), \tag{5.20}$$

where the market factor X_T is normally distributed with mean zero and variance one, and where $r > 0$ and $\nu > 0$ are constants. The information process $\{\xi_t\}$ is taken to be of the form (5.10), where in the present example the information flow rate is given by

$$\sigma = \frac{1}{\sqrt{T}}. \tag{5.21}$$

By use of the Bayes formula we find that the conditional probability density is Gaussian,

$$p_t(x) = \sqrt{\frac{T}{2\pi(T-t)}}\exp\Big(-\frac{1}{2(T-t)}\big(\sqrt{T}x - \xi_{tT}\big)^2\Big), \tag{5.22}$$

and has the following dynamics:

$$dp_t(x) = \frac{1}{T-t}\big(\sqrt{T}x - \xi_{tT}\big)p_t(x)\,d\xi_{tT}. \tag{5.23}$$

A short calculation then shows that the value of the asset in this example is given at time $t < T$ by

$$\begin{aligned} S_t &= e^{-r(T-t)}\mathbb{E}_t[S_T] \\ &= e^{-r(T-t)} \int_{-\infty}^{\infty} S_0 e^{rT+\nu\sqrt{T}x-\frac{1}{2}\nu^2 T}\, p_t(x)\, dx \\ &= S_0 \exp\left(rt + \nu\xi_{tT} - \frac{1}{2}\nu^2 t \right). \end{aligned} \tag{5.24}$$

The surprising fact is that $\{\xi_{tT}\}$ itself turns out to be an $\{\mathcal{F}_t\}$-Brownian motion. Hence, writing $W_t = \xi_{tT}$ for $0 \le t \le T$, we obtain the standard geometric Brownian motion model,

$$S_t = S_0 \exp\left(rt + \nu W_t - \frac{1}{2}\nu^2 t \right). \tag{5.25}$$

We see that starting with an information-based argument we are able to recover the familiar asset price dynamics given by (5.25). An important point to note is that the Brownian bridge process $\{\beta_{tT}\}$ arises naturally in this context. In fact, if we start with (5.25) then we can make use of the following well-known orthogonal decomposition:

$$W_t = \frac{t}{T} W_T + \left(W_t - \frac{t}{T} W_T \right). \tag{5.26}$$

The second term on the right, which is independent of the first term on the right, is a standard representation for a Brownian bridge process:

$$\beta_{tT} = W_t - \frac{t}{T} W_T. \tag{5.27}$$

Then by setting $X_T = W_T/\sqrt{T}$ and $\sigma = 1/\sqrt{T}$ we find that the right side of (5.26) is indeed the market information. In other words, when it is formulated in an information-based framework, the standard Black–Scholes–Merton theory can be expressed in terms of a normally distributed X-factor and an independent Brownian-bridge noise process.

5.7 Pricing Contingent Claims

The information-based price (5.16) of a single-dividend paying asset at first glance appears to be given by a rather complicated expression, suggesting perhaps that it would be impractical for use as a model for the pricing and hedging of contingent claims. However, there is a remarkable simplification involving a change of measure that allows one both to price and to hedge vanilla options. This can be seen as follows. Let us consider a European-style call option on the asset, with option maturity t and strike K. The value of the option at time 0 is given by

$$C_0 = P_{0t}\mathbb{E}^{\mathbb{Q}}\big[(S_t - K)^+\big]. \tag{5.28}$$

Let us define a process $\{\Phi_t\}$ by the expression appearing in the denominator of (5.16), so

$$\Phi_t = \int_0^\infty p(x)\exp\left[\frac{T}{T-t}\left(\sigma x\xi_{tT} - \frac{1}{2}\sigma^2 x^2 t\right)\right]dx. \tag{5.29}$$

Then it can be shown that $\{\Phi_t^{-1}\}$ is a positive $\mathbb{Q}$-martingale, which can be used to change the probability measure from $\mathbb{Q}$ to a new measure $\mathbb{B}$. Under the measure $\mathbb{B}$, which we call the "bridge measure", the information process itself is a Brownian bridge. More precisely, under $\mathbb{B}$ the process $\{\xi_{sT}\}_{0\le s\le t}$ has the law of a Brownian bridge spanning the interval $[0, T]$, restricted to $[0, t]$. That is to say, $\{\xi_{sT}\}_{0\le s\le t}$ is $\mathbb{B}$-Gaussian with mean zero and covariance $\mathrm{cov}[\xi_{aT}, \xi_{bT}] = a(T-b)/T$ for $0 \le a \le b \le t$. The initial value of the option is thus given by

$$C_0 = P_{0t}\mathbb{E}^{\mathbb{B}}\left[\left(P_{tT}\int_0^\infty xp(x)e^{\frac{T}{T-t}(\sigma x\xi_{tT} - \frac{1}{2}\sigma^2x^2t)}\,dx \right.\right.$$
$$\left.\left. - K\int_0^\infty p(x)e^{\frac{T}{T-t}(\sigma x\xi_{tT} - \frac{1}{2}\sigma^2x^2t)}\,dx\right)^+\right]. \tag{5.30}$$

It can be shown that the asset price is a monotonically increasing function of the value of ξ_{tT}. It follows that there is a unique critical level ξ^* for the information such that the expression inside the max-function in (5.30) is positive. It follows that the option price can be written in terms of a single integration involving the normal distribution function:

$$C_0 = P_{0t}\int_0^\infty p(x)(P_{tT}x - K)N\left(\frac{\xi^* - \sigma x t}{\sqrt{t(T-t)/T}}\right)dx. \tag{5.31}$$

As another example, we consider the following. Suppose that the single cash flow D_T is a binary random variable taking the values $\{d_0, d_1\}$ with a priori probabilities $\{p_0, p_1\}$. The asset in this case can be thought of as a simple credit-risky discount bond that pays d_1 if there is no default and d_0 if there is a default. A short calculation allows one to verify that

$$C_0 = P_{0t}\big[p_1(P_{tT}d_1 - K)N(u^+) - p_0(K - P_{tT}d_0)N(u^-)\big], \tag{5.32}$$

where u^+ and u^- are defined by

$$u^\pm = \frac{\ln\left[\frac{p_1(P_{tT}d_1 - K)}{p_0(K - P_{tT}d_0)}\right] \pm \frac{1}{2}\sigma^2(d_1 - d_0)^2\tau}{\sigma\sqrt{\tau}(d_1 - d_0)} \tag{5.33}$$

with $\tau = tT/(T-1)$. It can be shown that the option delta at time 0, defined as usual by

$$\delta_0 = \frac{\partial C_0}{\partial S_0}, \tag{5.34}$$

can be calculated explicitly, with the following result:

$$\delta_0 = \frac{(P_{tT}d_1 - K)N(u^+) + (K - P_{tT}d_0)N(u^-)}{P_{tT}(d_1 - d_0)}. \tag{5.35}$$

We see, therefore, that the apparent complexity of (5.16) does not lead to any intractability when it comes to derivatives pricing and hedging.

5.8 Volatility and Correlation

In the case of an asset that pays multiple dividends, the price is determined by the conditional expectation given in (5.9). In terms of the cash-flow functions defined by (5.2), we thus obtain the following for the dynamics of the asset price:

$$\begin{aligned} dS_t &= r_t S_t\, dt + \sum_{k=1}^{n} \Delta_{T_k}\, d\mathbb{1}_{\{t<T_k\}} \\ &\quad + \sum_{k=1}^{n} \mathbb{1}_{\{t<T_k\}} P_{tT_k} \sum_{j=1}^{k} \frac{\sigma_j T_j}{T_j - t} \mathrm{Cov}_t[\Delta_{T_k}, X_{T_j}]\, dW_t^j. \end{aligned} \tag{5.36}$$

The leading term in the drift is the short rate, as one might expect, and there is also a term representing the downward jump in the asset that occurs when a dividend is paid. The independent $\{\mathcal{F}_t\}$-adapted Brownian motions $\{W_t^j\}$ driving the price dynamics are given in terms of the corresponding information processes by

$$W_t^j = \xi_{tT_j} - \int_0^t \frac{1}{T_j - s}\left(\sigma_j T_j \mathbb{E}_s[X_{T_j}] - \xi_{sT_j}\right) ds. \tag{5.37}$$

We see that if an asset delivers one or more cash flows depending on two or more market factors, then it will exhibit "unhedgeable" stochastic volatility [2, 7]. That is to say, one would not expect to be able to hedge a position in an option by use of a position in the underlying. In general, if the asset cash flows depend on n X-factors in total, then to hedge a generic derivative based on the given asset one will need the underlying together with $n-1$ options as hedging instruments, i.e., n hedging instruments in total. One can read from (5.36) the generic form of the stochastic volatility implied for a given configuration of X-factors and cash-flow functions.

It follows likewise from (5.36) that two or more assets will exhibit dynamic correlation when they share one or more X-factors in common. As a specific example of dynamic correlation, let us consider a pair of credit-risky discount bonds. The first bond is defined by a cash flow D_{T_1} at T_1. The second is defined by a cash flow D_{T_2} at $T_2 > T_1$. The cash flow structure is taken to be

$$D_{T_1} = n_1 X_{T_1} + R_1 n_1 (1 - X_{T_1}) \tag{5.38}$$

and

$$\begin{aligned} D_{T_2} &= n_2 X_{T_1} X_{T_2} + R_2^a n_2 (1 - X_{T_1}) X_{T_2} \\ &\quad + R_2^b n_2 X_{T_1} (1 - X_{T_2}) + R_2^c n_2 (1 - X_{T_1})(1 - X_{T_2}). \end{aligned} \tag{5.39}$$

Here, n_1 and n_2 denote the bond principals, and X_{T_1} and X_{T_2} are independent digital random variables. The possible recovery rates in the case of default are denoted by R_1, R_2^a, R_2^b, and R_2^c. One can have in mind the following story. Consider a factory with debt S_t^1. Across the street there is a little restaurant with debt S_t^2. If the factory goes bust ($X_{T_1} = 0$), then so will the restaurant, because this is where the workers have their lunch. On the other hand, even if the factory is successful ($X_{T_1} = 1$), the restaurant may still go bust on account of bad management ($X_{T_2} = 0$). The recovery rates on the restaurant bond depend on the details of what goes wrong: R_2^a (restaurant fails because factory fails); R_2^b (restaurant fails on account of bad management); R_2^c (factory fails, and bad restaurant management). One might expect $R_2^b > R_2^a$, since as long as the factory continues, the restaurant facilities could be sold at a good price. The worst scenario is that of R_2^c. For the dynamics of the first bond (the "factory"), for which the price is

$$S_t^1 = P_{tT_1} \mathbb{E}_t[D_{T_1}] \quad (t < T_1), \tag{5.40}$$

we have:

$$dS_t^1 = r_t S_t^1 \, dt + P_{tT_1} \frac{\sigma_1 T_1}{T_1 - t} \alpha \, \mathrm{Var}_t[X_{T_1}] \, dW_t^1, \tag{5.41}$$

where $\alpha = n_1(1 - R_1)$. For the dynamics of the second bond (the "restaurant"), for which the price is

$$S_t^2 = P_{tT_2} \mathbb{E}_t[D_{T_2}] \quad (t < T_2), \tag{5.42}$$

we have:

$$\begin{aligned} dS_t^2 &= r_t S_t^2 \, dt + P_{tT_2} \frac{\sigma_1 T_1}{T_1 - t} \big(\beta + \delta \mathbb{E}_t[X_{T_2}]\big) \, \mathrm{Var}_t[X_{T_1}] \, dW_t^1 \\ &\quad + P_{tT_2} \frac{\sigma_2 T_2}{T_2 - t} \big(\gamma + \delta \mathbb{E}_t[X_{T_1}]\big) \, \mathrm{Var}_t[X_{T_2}] \, dW_t^2, \end{aligned} \tag{5.43}$$

where the constants β, γ, and δ are given by $\beta = n_2(R_2^b - R_2^c)$, $\gamma = n_2(R_2^a - R_2^c)$, and $\delta = n_2(1 - R_2^a - R_2^b + R_2^c)$. The filtration $\{\mathcal{F}_s\}$ is generated by the information processes $\{\xi_{sT_1}\}$ and $\{\xi_{sT_2}\}$ associated with X_{T_1} and X_{T_2}. The dynamics of the bond prices depend on a common Brownian driver $\{W_t^1\}$. The fact that the asset payoffs share a common X-factor thus gives rise to a dynamic correlation between the movements of the price processes $\{S_t^1\}$ and $\{S_t^2\}$. The instantaneous correlation between the price movements of the factory bond and the restaurant bond is given by the following expression:

$$\rho_t = \frac{dS_t^1\, dS_t^2}{\sqrt{(dS_t^1)^2 (dS_t^2)^2}}. \tag{5.44}$$

Hence, using the formulae for the dynamics of the two assets, we obtain

$$\rho_t = \frac{1}{\sqrt{\psi_t}} \frac{\sigma_1 T_1}{T_1 - t} \big(\beta + \delta \mathbb{E}_t[X_{T_1}]\big) \operatorname{Var}_t[X_{T_1}], \tag{5.45}$$

where

$$\begin{aligned} \psi_t = {} & \left(\frac{\sigma_1 T_1}{T_1 - t}\right)^2 \big(\beta + \delta \mathbb{E}_t[X_{T_2}]\big)^2 \big(\operatorname{Var}_t[X_{T_1}]\big)^2 \\ & + \left(\frac{\sigma_2 T_2}{T_2 - t}\right)^2 \big(\gamma + \delta \mathbb{E}_t[X_{T_1}]\big)^2 \big(\operatorname{Var}_t[X_{T_2}]\big)^2. \end{aligned} \tag{5.46}$$

We see from (5.45) that we are able to calculate explicitly the dynamics of the correlation between the movements of the two asset prices.

5.9 Amount of Information about the Future Cash Flow Contained in the Price Process

Since we are modelling the flow of information in an explicit manner, we are able to quantify how much information regarding the value of the cash flow D_T is contained in the value ξ_t at time t of the associated information process. For simplicity, in the discussion that follows we shall assume that the cash flow D_T takes the discrete values $\{d_i\}_{i=1,\ldots,n}$ with a priori probabilities $\{p_i\}_{i=1,\ldots,n}$. A reasonable measure for quantifying the information content is given by the mutual information $J(\xi_t, D_T)$ between the two random variables, which in the present context is given by the expression

$$J(\xi_t, D_T) = \sum_{i=1}^{n} \int_{-\infty}^{\infty} \rho(\xi, i) \ln\left(\frac{\rho(\xi, i)}{\rho(\xi)\rho(i)}\right) d\xi, \tag{5.47}$$

where

$$\rho(\xi, i) = \frac{d}{d\xi} \mathbb{Q}\big[(\xi_t < \xi) \cap (D_T = d_i)\big] \tag{5.48}$$

is the joint density of the random variables ξ_t and D_T, and $\rho(\xi)$ and $\rho(i)$ are the respective marginal probabilities. By use of the relation

$$\mathbb{Q}\big[(\xi_t < \xi) \cap (D_T = d_i)\big] = \mathbb{Q}(\xi_t < \xi | D_T = d_i)\mathbb{Q}(D_T = d_i) \tag{5.49}$$

we deduce that

$$\rho(\xi, i) = p_i \frac{1}{\sqrt{2\pi t(T-t)/T}} \exp\left(-\frac{1}{2}\frac{(x - \sigma d_i t)^2}{t(T-t)/T}\right), \tag{5.50}$$

since conditional on $D_T = d_i$ the random variable ξ_t is normally distributed with mean $\sigma t d_i$ and variance $t(T-t)/T$. From (5.50) the marginal densities

$$\rho(\xi) = \sum_{i=1}^{n} \rho(\xi, i) \quad \text{and} \quad \rho(i) = \int_{-\infty}^{\infty} \rho(\xi, i)\, d\xi \tag{5.51}$$

can be deduced. In particular, $\rho(i) = p_i$. By substituting (5.50) into (5.47), the information about the cash flow D_T contained in ξ_t can be determined.

From an information-theoretic point of view, two processes related through an invertible function, thus sharing the *same* filtration, in general possess *different* information content. On the other hand, since what is observed in the market is the price S_t, which is an invertible function of ξ_t, it is more relevant to determine the mutual information $J(S_t, D_T)$, that is, the amount of information about the future cash flow contained in the market price. It can be shown that in the present context we have $J(S_t, D_T) = J(\xi_t, D_T)$.

5.10 Information Disparity and Statistical Arbitrage

So far we have assumed that market participants have equal access to information, but one can ask what happens if some traders are more "informed" than others. Suppose that we consider a financial product that pays a single cash flow D_T at time T. We can think of this product as a kind of bond. The general market trader has access to an information process concerning D_T, but there are also "informed" traders who have access to one or more additional information processes concerning D_T. The informed trader is thus in some sense able to make a "better estimate" of the value of the asset.

To be more specific, let us suppose that while the general market trader has access to the information $\xi_t = \sigma t D_T + \beta_{tT}$, an informed trader has access in addition, say, to the information $\xi'_t = \sigma' t D_T + \beta'_{tT}$, where $\{\beta'_{tT}\}$ may or may not be correlated with the market noise $\{\beta_{tT}\}$. Thus, the information source for the informed trader is given by $\{\mathcal{G}_t\} = \sigma(\{\xi_s, \xi'_s\}_{0\le s\le t})$. The use of such extra information can, but need not, represent "insider trading" in the usual sense. That is, it may be that the informed trader merely has better access to (and better computer power for the purpose of digesting) the vast domain of publicly available information. Since we have

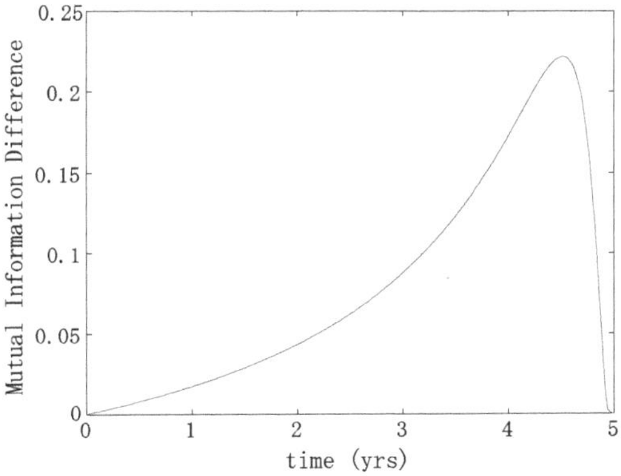

Fig. 5.2 Mutual information difference. The additional information held by an informed trader over that of the market is nonnegative. The parameters are set to be $d_1 = 0$, $d_2 = 1$, $p_1 = 0.2$, $p_2 = 0.8$, $T = 5$, $\sigma = 0.25$, $\sigma' = 0.45$, and $\rho = 0.15$ (the correlation between β_{tT} and β'_{tT})

introduced an information measure regarding impending cash flows, we can quantify the excess information held by the informed trader above that held by general market traders. This is measured by the difference of the mutual information ΔJ. In Fig. 5.2 we plot an example of ΔJ, indicating the way in which the excess information held by the informed trader changes in time.

Given that the informed trader is on average "more knowledgeable" than the general market trader, it is natural to ask how the informed trader can take advantage of the situation to seek so-called "statistical arbitrage" opportunities. We assume that the informed trader operates on a relatively small scale and that the actions of this trader do not significantly influence the market. Suppose that we consider a trading strategy such that at some designated time $t \in (0, T)$ a market trader purchases a bond if, and only if, at that time the bond price S_t is greater than the quantity $K P_{tT}$ for some specified constant K. Once a bond is purchased, it is held to maturity. The informed trader follows the same rule, but makes a better estimate of the value of the bond, and hence purchases the bond iff $\tilde{S}_t > K P_{tT}$, where

$$\tilde{S}_t = P_{tT}\mathbb{E}[D_T|\mathcal{G}_t]. \tag{5.52}$$

The significance of $\tilde{S}_t$ is that it represents the price that the informed trader knows that the market as a whole would make if the market as a whole had the same knowledge as the informed trader.

That such a strategy leads to a statistical arbitrage opportunity for the informed trader can be seen as follows [4]. We assume that the initial position of a trader is zero, i.e., purchase of a bond at t requires borrowing the amount S_t at that time and repaying the amount $P_{tT}^{-1} S_t$ at T. Thus the value of a general market trader's portfolio at T is

$$V_T = \mathbb{1}\{S_t > K P_{tT}\}\big(D_T - P_{tT}^{-1} S_t\big), \tag{5.53}$$

whereas the value of the informed trader's portfolio at T is

$$\tilde{V}_T = \mathbb{1}\{\tilde{S}_t > K P_{tT}\}\big(D_T - P_{tT}^{-1} S_{tT}\big). \tag{5.54}$$

Consider the present value $P_{0T}\mathbb{E}[\Delta V_T]$ of a security that delivers a cash flow equal to the excess profit or loss

$$\Delta V_T = \tilde{V}_T - V_T \tag{5.55}$$

generated by the strategy of the informed trader. By the tower property we have

$$\mathbb{E}[\Delta V_T] = \mathbb{E}\big[\mathbb{E}[\Delta V_T | \mathcal{G}_t]\big]. \tag{5.56}$$

However,

$$\mathbb{E}[\Delta V_T | \mathcal{G}_t] = P_{tT}^{-1}\big(\mathbb{1}\{\tilde{S}_t > K P_{tT}\} - \mathbb{1}\{S_t > K P_{tT}\}\big)(\tilde{S}_t - S_t), \tag{5.57}$$

since the random variables S_t and $\tilde{S}_t$ are $\mathcal{G}_t$-measurable. If $\tilde{S}_t > S_t$, then

$$\mathbb{1}\{\tilde{S}_t > K P_{tT}\} - \mathbb{1}\{S_t > K P_{tT}\} \geq 0; \tag{5.58}$$

whereas if $\tilde{S}_t < S_t$, then

$$\mathbb{1}\{\tilde{S}_t > K P_{tT}\} - \mathbb{1}\{S_t > K P_{tT}\} \leq 0. \tag{5.59}$$

It follows that $\mathbb{E}[\Delta V_T | \mathcal{G}_t] > 0$ with probability greater than zero, and therefore $\mathbb{E}[\Delta V_T] > 0$. We know that according to the usual no-arbitrage arguments, the present value of the payoff of the strategy of the general market trader must be zero. It follows that the informed trader can execute a transaction at zero cost that has positive value: this is what we mean by "statistical arbitrage". A simulation study of the profit arising from this trading strategy is shown in Fig. 5.3, indicating a close

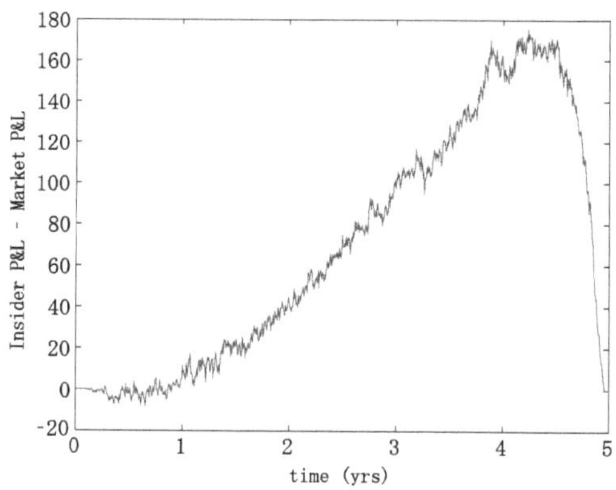

Fig. 5.3 The P&L difference for digital bonds. At each time traders purchase the bond if and only if the valuation of the bond is greater than a specified threshold. The general market trader buys if $S_t > K P_{tT}$, whereas the informed trader uses the criterion $\tilde{S}_t > K P_{tT}$. The difference in profit and loss between the informed trader and the general market trader is plotted, based on 2000 realisations, when the a priori probability of default is $p_1 = 0.2$. Other parameters are set to be $d_1 = 0$, $d_2 = 1$, $T = 5$, $\sigma = 0.25$, $\sigma' = 0.45$, $\rho = 0.15$, and $K = 0.7$

correspondence with the excess information held by the informed trader shown in Fig. 5.2.

5.11 Price Formation in Inhomogeneous Markets

The idea of "informed trading" can be extended to a market that has a number of traders operating in it, all more or less on an equal footing, but where different traders have access to different information. In other words, there is an inhomogeneous information flow in the market. This line of thinking leads naturally to the consideration of price formation in such a market, as illustrated in Fig. 5.4.

Let us consider, as an example, a market with two traders, labelled "Trader 1" and "Trader 2". As before, there is a single asset, with a single dividend D_T paid at time T. The traders have access to separate sources of information about D_T, given respectively by $\xi_t^1 = \sigma_1 t D_T + \beta_{tT}^1$ and $\xi_t^2 = \sigma_2 t D_T + \beta_{tT}^2$. Here the Brownian bridges $\{\beta_{tT}^1\}$ and $\{\beta_{tT}^2\}$ are assumed, for simplicity, to be independent. Trader 1 works out the price

$$S_t^1 = P_{tT}\mathbb{E}\left[D_T \,|\, \xi_t^1\right] \tag{5.60}$$

that he knows the market would have made had the market possessed the information generated by $\{\xi_t^1\}$. Likewise, Trader 2 works out the price

$$S_t^2 = P_{tT}\mathbb{E}\left[D_T \,|\, \xi_t^2\right] \tag{5.61}$$

that she knows the market would have made had the market possessed the information generated by $\{\xi_t^2\}$.

Traders 1 and 2 are unaware of each other's prices but can gain information by trading. The trading process works as follows. Each trader makes a spread about their price. Letting $0 < \phi^- < 1 < \phi^+$, we set

$$S_t^{1\pm} = \phi^{\pm} S_t^1 \tag{5.62}$$

for the buy price S_t^{1-} and sell price S_t^{1+} made by Trader 1 at time t. Thus Trader 1 is willing to buy at a price slightly below his information-based valuation S_t^1 and is willing to sell at a price that is slightly above that valuation. Likewise Trader 2 is willing to buy at a price slightly below her information-based valuation S_t^2 and is willing to sell at a price that is slightly above that valuation:

$$S_t^{2\pm} = \phi^{\pm} S_t^2. \tag{5.63}$$

We assume that there is an exchange that continuously monitors the prices made by the traders. The exchange effects a trade of some fixed size when the buy price of one of the traders reaches the level of the sell price of the other trader. That is to say, a trade takes place when

$$S_t^{1-} = S_t^{2+} \quad \text{or} \quad S_t^{1+} = S_t^{2-}. \tag{5.64}$$

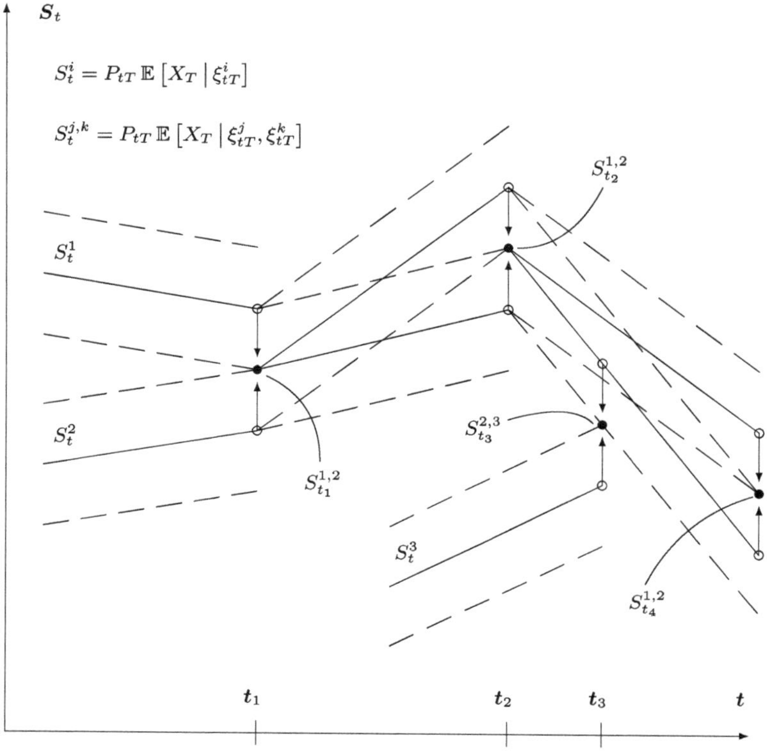

Fig. 5.4 Schematic illustration of information-based trading. An exchange executes a trade when the sell price of Trader i matches the buy price of Trader j (*dashed lines meet at filled dots*). At the execution time t_n, both traders have access to each other's valuations $S^i_{t_n}$ (*empty circles*) and thus to each other's information. As a consequence, the traders are able to update their valuations and obtain the common price $S^{j,k}_{t_n}$. After the trade has been executed and the respective asset valuations have been updated, the traders "separate" and return to their individual valuations. The respective valuations may drift in different directions. The traders will get in contact again as soon as the exchange notifies them that the respective sell and buy prices have matched again. Such an information-based trading mechanism can be extended to multiple traders, as suggested in the illustration

When a trade occurs, at that moment each trader learns the price of the other and, as a consequence, can back out the value of the corresponding information process. Therefore, when a trade occurs, the traders each briefly have access to both pieces of information and are thus in a position to make a better price, namely that given by

$$S_t^{1,2} = P_{tT}\mathbb{E}\big[D_T \,|\, \xi_t^1, \xi_t^2\big]. \tag{5.65}$$

We conclude that immediately after a trade the information-based prices made by each of the traders will jump to the same level and the a priori probability distribution for D_T will be updated correspondingly.

Once the trade is concluded, the link between the two traders is lost, and each trader again has access only to their own information source. Starting from the same price, the prices made by the two traders diverge as they receive different information going forward. A further trade will then occur when the buy price of one of the traders next hits the sell price of the other trader.

At the time the trade is executed, the joint information can be embodied in the value of an effective information process $\{\hat{\xi}_t\}_{0\leq t\leq T}$ given by

$$\hat{\xi}_t = \sqrt{(\sigma_1)^2+(\sigma_2)^2}\,t D_T + \frac{\sigma_1\beta^1_{tT}+\sigma_2\beta^2_{tT}}{\sqrt{(\sigma_1)^2+(\sigma_2)^2}}. \tag{5.66}$$

We note that $\{\hat{\xi}_t\}$ is indeed an information process, since it can be written in the form

$$\hat{\xi}_t = \hat{\sigma} t D_T + \hat{\beta}_{tT}, \tag{5.67}$$

where

$$\hat{\sigma} = \sqrt{(\sigma_1)^2+(\sigma_2)^2}, \quad \text{and} \quad \hat{\beta}_{tT} = \frac{\sigma_1\beta^1_{tT}+\sigma_2\beta^2_{tT}}{\sqrt{(\sigma_1)^2+(\sigma_2)^2}}. \tag{5.68}$$

One can show that $\{\hat{\beta}_{tT}\}$ is a Brownian bridge and is independent of D_T. Thus, immediately after the trade is executed, the price $S^{1,2}_t$ made by both traders is of the form

$$S^{1,2}_t = P_{tT}\frac{\int_0^\infty x p(x)\exp[\frac{T}{T-t}(\hat{\sigma} x\hat{\xi}_t - \frac{1}{2}\hat{\sigma}^2x^2t)]\,dx}{\int_0^\infty p(x)\exp[\frac{T}{T-t}(\hat{\sigma} x\hat{\xi}_t - \frac{1}{2}\hat{\sigma}^2x^2t)]\,dx}. \tag{5.69}$$

As an example, let us consider the case of a digital payout taking the values 0 and 1 with a priori probabilities p_0 and p_1. We consider the case in which the information flow rates are the same, so we set $\sigma_1=\sigma_2=\sigma$. Then for the valuations, we have

$$S^1_t = \frac{p_1\exp[\frac{T}{T-t}(\sigma\xi^1_t - \frac{1}{2}\sigma^2t)]}{p_0+p_1\exp[\frac{T}{T-t}(\sigma\xi^1_t - \frac{1}{2}\sigma^2t)]} \tag{5.70}$$

and

$$S^2_t = \frac{p_1\exp[\frac{T}{T-t}(\sigma\xi^2_t - \frac{1}{2}\sigma^2t)]}{p_0+p_1\exp[\frac{T}{T-t}(\sigma\xi^2_t - \frac{1}{2}\sigma^2t)]}. \tag{5.71}$$

For the spreads, we assume that $\phi^+=1+\delta$ and $\phi^-=1-\delta$, where δ is small. If Trader 1 is the buyer, then the condition for a trade is

$$(1-\delta)S^1_t = (1+\delta)S^2_t. \tag{5.72}$$

Given his knowledge ξ_t^1, Trader 1 can use the condition to work out the value of ξ_t^2. In particular, suppose that

$$\xi_t^2 = \xi_t^1 + \varepsilon_t, \tag{5.73}$$

where ε_t is small. Then a calculation shows that ε_t is given, to first order, by

$$\varepsilon_t = -\frac{2\delta(T-t)}{\sigma T(1-\mathbb{E}[X_T|\xi_t^1])}. \tag{5.74}$$

The general situation, where there are a number of traders present in the market, and where the asset cash flows depend on a number of market factors, is very rich. It is evident that in the broad picture there is no universal filtration, nor a universal pricing measure. Nevertheless, by exchanging information through trading activity, market participants can maintain a "law of reasonable price range" if not a "law of one price".

Certainly, the notion that there is a universal market filtration is unrealistic. What counts is not merely "access in principle" to information, but rather "access in practice". Perhaps some broader version of market efficiency will survive, taking into account the cost of such access (cf. [5]). A subscription to the Wall Street Journal is not free, nor is a Bloomberg terminal. Access to vast information providers such as Google and Yahoo may seem free or nearly so, but from a broader perspective this is not so—someone pays, in cash or kind. What is the market price of information? And how does this depend on the "information about the information"? For the answers to these questions, we must await the development of new models.

Acknowledgements The authors are grateful to seminar participants at the Fourth General Conference on Advanced Mathematical Methods in Finance, Alesund, Norway, May 2009, the Workshop on Incomplete Information in Mathematical Finance, Chemnitz, Germany, June 2009, the Graduate School of Management, Kyoto, October 2009, and the Kyoto Institute of Economic Research, January 2010, for helpful comments. Part of this work was carried out while LPH was visiting the Aspen Center for Physics (September 2009) and Kyoto University (August, October 2009). DCB and LPH thank HSBC, Lloyds TSB, Shell International, and Yahoo Japan for research support.

References

1. D.C. Brody, L.P. Hughston, A. Macrina, Beyond hazard rates: a new framework for credit-risk modelling, in *Advances in Mathematical Finance, Festschrift Volume in Honour of Dilip Madan*, ed. by R. Elliott, M. Fu, R. Jarrow, J.-Y. Yen (Birkhäuser, Basel, 2007)
2. D.C. Brody, L.P. Hughston, A. Macrina, Information-based asset pricing. Int. J. Theor. Appl. Finance **11**, 107–142 (2008)
3. D.C. Brody, L.P. Hughston, A. Macrina, Dam rain and cumulative gain. Proc. R. Soc. Lond. A **464**, 1801–1822 (2008)
4. D.C. Brody, M.H.A. Davis, R.L. Friedman, L.P. Hughston, Informed traders. Proc. R. Soc. Lond. A **465**, 1103–1122 (2009)
5. S.J. Grossman, J.E. Stiglitz, On the impossibility of informationally efficient markets. Am. Econ. Rev. **70**, 393–408 (1980)

6. L.P. Hughston, A. Macrina, Information, inflation, and interest, in *Advances in Mathematics of Finance*. Banach Center Publications, vol. 83 (Institute of Mathematics, Polish Academy of Sciences, Warszawa, 2008)
7. A. Macrina, An information-based framework for asset pricing: X-factor theory and its applications. Ph.D. Thesis, King's College London (2006)
8. A. Macrina, P.A. Parbhoo, Securities pricing with information-sensitive discounting, in *Recent Advances in Financial Engineering 2009. Proceedings of the KIER-TMU International Workshop on Financial Engineering 2009* (World Scientific, Singapore, 2010)
9. M. Rutkowski, N. Yu, On the Brody–Hughston–Macrina approach to modelling of defaultable term structure. Int. J. Theor. Appl. Finance **10**, 557–589 (2007)

Chapter 9

HEAT KERNEL INTEREST RATE MODELS WITH TIME-INHOMOGENEOUS MARKOV PROCESSES†

JIRÔ AKAHORI

Department of Mathematical Sciences
Ritsumeikan University
1-1-1 Nojihigashi, Kusatsu 52-8577, Shiga, Japan
akahori@se.ritsumei.ac.jp

ANDREA MACRINA*

Department of Mathematics
King's College London
Strand, London WC2R 2LS, UK
and
Institute of Economic Research, Kyoto University
Yoshida-Honmachi, Sakyo-Ku, Kyoto 606-8501, Japan
andrea.macrina@kcl.ac.uk

Received 10 December 2010
Accepted 7 March 2011

We consider a heat kernel approach for the development of stochastic pricing kernels. The kernels are constructed by positive propagators, which are driven by time-inhomogeneous Markov processes. We multiply such a propagator with a positive, time-dependent and decreasing weight function, and integrate the product over time. The result is a so-called weighted heat kernel that by construction is a supermartingale with respect to the filtration generated by the time-inhomogeneous Markov processes. As an application, we show how this framework naturally fits the information-based asset pricing framework where time-inhomogeneous Markov processes are utilized to model partial information about random economic factors. We present examples of pricing kernel models which lead to analytical formulae for bond prices along with explicit expressions for the associated interest rate and market price of risk. Furthermore, we also address the pricing of fixed-income derivatives within this framework.

Keywords: Time-inhomogeneous Markov processes; Lévy processes; heat kernels; pricing kernels; information-based pricing; interest rate models; fixed-income assets.

1. Introduction

In work by Hughston and Macrina [8], and Macrina and Parbhoo [10], the information-based asset pricing framework developed by Brody *et al.* [2, 3] is applied

*Corresponding author.

†This chapter was originally published as: J. Akahori & A. Macrina (2012) Heat Kernel Interest Rate Models with Time-Inhomogeneous Markov Processes. *International Journal of Theoretical and Applied Finance* **15** (1), 1–15.

to the modelling of the pricing kernel with the goal to price fixed-income securities. The view taken is that interest rates and market prices of risk fluctuate due to noisy information about economic factors that becomes available to investors as time passes. Another reason for proposing information-based pricing kernels is the necessity to develop stochastic discount models which naturally combine with, e.g., the equity, credit and insurance pricing models presented in Brody *et al.* [2–4] and in Hoyle *et al.* [7]. A first, albeit different, extension of information-based pricing to include stochastic discount factors can be found in Rutkowski and Yu [13]. The theory of pricing kernels is treated in, e.g., Cochrane [5] and in Duffie [6].

We briefly summarise the information-based method for the construction of pricing kernels. The financial market is modelled by a filtered probability space $(\Omega, \mathcal{F}, \{\mathcal{F}_t\}, \mathbb{P})$ where $\mathbb{P}$ is the real probability measure. The filtration $\{\mathcal{F}_t\}_{0\leq t}$ is assumed to be generated by so-called information processes which model the noisy information about economic factors that market investors may observe. An information process $\{L_{tU}\}_{0\leq t\leq U}$ is constructed such that the associated economic factor X_U is revealed at some fixed future time U. In order to ensure that the derived asset price processes are adapted to the market filtration, it is postulated that the pricing kernel $\{\pi_t\}$ be a functional of the information processes which generate $\{\mathcal{F}_t\}$.

We shall consider the simpler situation where the filtration is generated by a single information process that has the Markov property, and where the pricing kernel can be expressed by a positive function of time and the value of the information process at that time:

$$\pi_t = \pi(t, L_{tU}). \tag{1.1}$$

The function $\pi(t, L_{tU})$ needs to be specified in such a way that the resulting pricing kernel process is a positive supermartingale. To find explicit pricing kernel models, it is also necessary to specify the information process. For example one can choose $\{L_{tU}\}$ to be a Brownian bridge information process defined by

$$L_{tU} = \sigma t X_U + \beta_{tU} \tag{1.2}$$

where σ is a constant parameter and $\{\beta_{tU}\}_{0\leq t\leq U}$ is an independent standard Brownian bridge. In this case it is convenient to assume that the pricing kernel is expressed by

$$\pi_t = \pi(t, L_{tU}) = M_t f(t, L_{tU}), \tag{1.3}$$

where $\{M_t\}_{0\leq t<U}$ is a positive $\mathbb{P}$-martingale that induces a change of measure to the so-called bridge measure $\mathbb{B}$ under which $\{L_{tU}\}$ has the law of a Brownian bridge. It is then shown in Hughston and Macrina [8] that $\{\pi_t\}$ is a positive $\mathbb{P}$-supermartingale if and only if the function $f(t,x)$ is positive and it satisfies the following partial differential inequality:

$$\frac{x}{U-t}\partial_x f(t,x) - \frac{1}{2}\partial_{xx} f(t,x) - \partial_t f(t,x) > 0. \tag{1.4}$$

Heat Kernel Interest Rate Models with Time-Inhomogeneous Markov Processes

The short rate of interest $\{r_t\}$ and the market price of risk $\{\lambda_t\}$ associated with a pricing kernel of the form (1.3) are given by

$$r_t = \frac{1}{f(t,x)}\left(\frac{x}{U-t}\partial_x f(t,x) - \frac{1}{2}\partial_{xx} f(t,x) - \partial_t f(t,x)\right)\Bigg|_{x=L_{tU}}, \tag{1.5}$$

$$\lambda_t = \frac{\sigma U}{U-t}\mathbb{E}[X_U | L_{tU}] - \frac{\partial_x f(t,x)}{f(t,x)}\Bigg|_{x=L_{tU}}. \tag{1.6}$$

The condition (1.4) is equivalent to requiring that the short rate of interest be a positive process. This is evident if (1.5) is compared with (1.4). The expectation in (1.6) can be worked out analytically by utilizing the Bayes formula.

In this paper we present a method that enables us to produce pricing kernel models which by construction are supermartingales adapted to the market filtration generated by information processes. We then show, as an example, that in the case of pricing kernels driven by Brownian bridge information processes (1.2), the function $f(t,x)$ associated with the constructed pricing kernel automatically satisfies the partial differential inequality (1.4). Thus we also obtain a class of positive interest rate models which are driven by time-inhomogenous Markov processes. The heat kernel approach for the construction of supermartingales that we consider, is introduced in Akahori *et al.* [1] for the case that the pricing kernel is driven by time-homogeneous Markov processes. We point to references therein for further background on the modelling of pricing kernels, and highlight work by Rogers [12] and material in Hunt *et al.* [9]. Since we generate the market filtration by information processes which by construction are time-inhomogeneous Markov processes, we need to modify the heat kernel approach used by Akahori *et al.* [1]. We focus on the weighted heat kernel approach that for our purpose turns out to be perhaps the more natural of the heat kernel methods. The Brownian bridge information process, the gamma bridge information process introduced in Brody *et al.* [3], and more generally the Lévy random bridge information processes proposed in Hoyle *et al.* [7] are all examples of time-inhomogeneous processes that possess the Markov property with respect to their natural filtration.

We shall denote a general time-inhomogeneous Markov process by $\{X_t\}$. A Lévy random bridge is denoted by $\{L_{tU}\}_{0\le t\le U}$ where the subscript reminds us that $\{L_{tU}\}$ has a stochastic dynamics for $t \in [0, U]$, and that after time U it "freezes" at the value L_{UU} for all $t > U$. For example, the Brownian bridge information process (1.2) takes the value $L_{UU} = \sigma U X_U$ for all $t \ge U$. In Sec. 2 we present the heat kernel approach adapted for time-inhomogeneous Markov processes and introduce weighted heat kernels which will form the basis for the construction of information-based pricing kernels. In Sec. 3 we summarise the theory of Lévy random bridges and apply it to the modelling of pricing kernels by use of weighted heat kernels. Furthermore we provide the dynamics of bond prices, and show how to price fixed income vanilla options. In Sec. 4 we focus on the situation where the time-inhomogeneous Markov process is a Brownian bridge information process. This example is developed in detail, offering analytical pricing kernel models. We also provide the associated explicit stochastic interest rate and market price of risk models.

2. Heat Kernels for Supermartingales

The heat kernel approach introduced in Akahori *et al.* [1] is a systematic method for the construction of Markov functionals for interest rate models. Pricing kernel processes are modelled by assuming that they are functionals of Markov processes which generate the market filtration. The pricing kernel models give rise to the Markov functionals of the related interest rate models. Bond pricing and in general the pricing of fixed-income instruments is performed by applying the pricing kernel models. We propose the same scheme for the construction of pricing kernels driven by information processes. However, we adapt the heat kernel scheme to the case in which the driving Markov processes are time-inhomogeneous.

Let $\{X_t\}_{0\leq t}$ be a Markov process, and let $q(s,t,x,y)$ be its transition function, where $0\leq s\leq t$. Then we have:

$$\mathbb{P}[X_{t+s}\in \mathrm{d}y|X_s=x]=q(s,t,x,\mathrm{d}y). \tag{2.1}$$

A Markov process is said to be time-homogeneous (or simply homogeneous) if its transition function is independent of s; see for instance [11]. If the transition function admits the form

$$q(s,t,x,\mathrm{d}y)=p(s,t,x,y)\mathrm{d}y, \tag{2.2}$$

then the function $p(s,t,x,y)$ is often called a "heat kernel". Usually $p(s,t,x,y)$ is not defined on the set $s=t$. For the construction of pricing kernels, we consider so-called "propagators" defined as follows:

Definition 2.1. Let $\mathcal{S}$ be a Polish space, and $\mathcal{U}:=\{(u,t)\in[0,U)^2 : u+t<U, u\neq 0\}$. Let $\{X_t\}_{0\leq t<U}$ be a Markov process with state space $\mathcal{S}$. A measurable function $p:\mathcal{U}\times\mathcal{S}\to\mathbb{R}$ is a propagator if it satisfies

$$\mathbb{E}[p(u,t,X_t)|X_s=x]=p(u+t-s,s,x) \tag{2.3}$$

for arbitrary $(u,t)\in\mathcal{U}$ and $0\leq s\leq t$.

Remark 2.1. By excluding $u=0$ from $\mathcal{U}$, we allow for the class of propagators to include heat kernels.

Proposition 2.1. *Let $F:[0,U)\to\mathbb{R}^+$ be a measurable function. Set*

$$p(u,t,x):=\mathbb{E}[F(u+t,X_{u+t})|X_t=x], \tag{2.4}$$

where $x\in\mathcal{S}$ and $0\leq t$, $0\leq u$. Then $p(u,t,x)$ is a propagator.

Heat Kernel Interest Rate Models with Time-Inhomogeneous Markov Processes

Proof. We have:

$$\begin{aligned}\mathbb{E}[p(u,t,X_t)|X_s] &= \mathbb{E}[\mathbb{E}[F(u+t,X_{u+t})|X_t]|X_s],\\ &= \mathbb{E}[F(u+t,X_{u+t})|X_s],\\ &= \mathbb{E}[F((u+t-s)+s,X_{(u+t-s)+s})|X_s],\\ &= p(u+t-s,s,X_s). \end{aligned} \tag{2.5}$$

□

Remark 2.2. If we allow $u = 0$ in (2.3), then the converse of Proposition 2.1 holds. Namely, the propagator is represented by some measurable function $F : [0, U) \to \mathbb{R}^+$ as given in (2.4). More precisely, we have

$$p(u,t,X_t) = \mathbb{E}[p(0,u+t,X_{u+t})|X_t], \tag{2.6}$$

by letting $u \to 0$, $t \to u+t$ and $s \to t$. That is, $F(t,x) = p(0,t,x)$.

Definition 2.2. Let a measurable function $w : [0,U]^2 \to \mathbb{R}^+$ that satisfies

$$w(t,u-s) \le w(t-s,u) \tag{2.7}$$

for $0 < U \le \infty$ and $s \le t \wedge u$, be called a "weight function". A "weighted heat kernel" $f(t,x)$ is defined by

$$f(t,x) = \int_0^{U-t} p(u,t,x)w(t,u)\mathrm{d}u, \tag{2.8}$$

for $0 \le t < U$, $u \ne 0$, and where $p(u,t,x)$ is a propagator.

Proposition 2.2. *Consider the propagator* (2.4). *Assume that* $\mathbb{P}[f(t,X_t) < \infty] = 1$ *for all* $t \in [0,U)$, *and let* $0 \le u+t < U$. *Then*

$$f(t,X_t) = \int_0^{U-t} \mathbb{E}[F(u+t,X_{u+t})|X_t]w(t,u)\mathrm{d}u \tag{2.9}$$

is a positive supermartingale.

Proof. For $0 \le s \le t$, we have

$$\mathbb{E}[f(t,X_t)|X_s] = \int_0^{U-t} \mathbb{E}[\mathbb{E}[F(u+t,X_{u+t})|X_t]|X_s]w(t,u)\mathrm{d}u \tag{2.10}$$

where we make use of Fubini's theorem. By the propagation property and the change of variables $u = v - t + s$, we obtain

$$\mathbb{E}[f(t,X_t)|X_s] = \int_{t-s}^{U-s} \mathbb{E}[F(v+s,X_{v+s})|X_s]w(t,v-t+s)\mathrm{d}v. \tag{2.11}$$

We complete the proof by applying the property (2.7):

$$\begin{aligned}\mathbb{E}[f(t,X_t)|X_s] &\leq \int_{t-s}^{U-s} \mathbb{E}[F(v+s,X_{v+s})|X_s]w(t-(t-s),v)\mathrm{d}v \\ &\leq \int_{0}^{U-s} \mathbb{E}[F(v+s,X_{v+s})|X_s]w(s,v)\mathrm{d}v \\ &\leq f(s,X_s). \end{aligned} \tag{2.12}$$

□

Remark 2.3.

1. Let $w_1(t,u)$ and $w_2(t,u)$ be weight functions, and c be a positive constant. Then $c\,w_1(t,u)$, $w_1(t,u)+w_2(t,u)$, and $w_1(t,u)\,w_2(t,u)$ are weight functions.
2. If $w(t,u)$ is non-increasing in t and non-decreasing in u, then $w(t,u)$ is a weight function.
3. If $w(t,u)=\bar{w}(t+u)$ for some measurable function $\bar{w}:\mathbb{R}\to\mathbb{R}^+$, then $w(t,u)$ is a weight function.

The assertions 1 and 2 are obvious. The assertion 3 is shown by observing that $w(t,u-s)=\bar{w}(t+u-s)=w(t-s,u)$.

Remark 2.4. Since the state space of the time-inhomogeneous Markov processes is a Polish space, the heat kernel approach may also be applied to construct pricing kernel models which are driven by multiple information processes. The development of explicit multi-factor models is deferred to future research. We refer to Hughston and Macrina [8], and Macrina and Parbhoo [10] for further material on multi-factor interest rate models, and emphasize that multi-factor pricing kernels may have dynamics simultaneously driven by time-inhomogeneous Markov processes based, for instance, on various different Lévy processes.

3. Pricing with Time-Inhomogeneous Markov Information

Fixed-income assets can be priced by use of pricing kernel models. Let us consider a single-dividend-paying asset which, at a fixed future date T, has a random cash flow H_T. The price H_t at time $t\leq T$ of such an asset is

$$H_t=\frac{1}{\pi_t}\mathbb{E}[\pi_T H_T|\mathcal{F}_t], \tag{3.1}$$

where $\{\pi_t\}$ is the pricing kernel. For $H_T=1$ we recover the pricing formula for a discount bond with maturity T. In order to obtain specific processes for the discount bond system, we need to develop explicit pricing kernel models. Let us denote the price process of the discount bond by $\{P_{tT}\}_{0\leq t\leq T}$, and let us consider pricing kernel models of the form $\pi_t=\pi(t,X_t)$ where $\{X_t\}$ is a Markov process that generates

Heat Kernel Interest Rate Models with Time-Inhomogeneous Markov Processes

the market filtration $\{\mathcal{F}_t\}$. Hence we have

$$P_{tT} = \frac{\mathbb{E}[\pi(T, X_T)|X_t]}{\pi(t, X_t)}. \tag{3.2}$$

No-arbitrage requires the pricing kernel to be a positive supermartingale. We can thus apply Proposition 2.2 to construct these pricing kernels:

$$\pi(t, X_t) = \int_0^{U-t} \mathbb{E}[F(u+t, X_{u+t})|X_t]w(t, u)\mathrm{d}u. \tag{3.3}$$

Assuming $0 \leq t \leq T < U$, the price of the discount bond is

$$P_{tT} = \frac{\int_{T-t}^{U-t} \mathbb{E}[F(u+t, X_{u+t})|X_t]w(T, u-T+t)\mathrm{d}u}{\int_0^{U-t} \mathbb{E}[F(u+t, X_{u+t})|X_t]w(t, u)\mathrm{d}u}, \tag{3.4}$$

where (2.11) is used in order to work out the conditional expectation in (3.2).

There are three ingredients which need to be specified so that explicit pricing models can be derived: (i) the Markov process $\{X_t\}$, (ii) the positive function $F(t, x)$, and (iii) the weight function $w(t, u)$. The specification of $\{X_t\}$ is rather crucial since it also determines the model for the market filtration. As an example of a class of Markov processes which can be applied to model the market information flow, we take the Lévy random bridges proposed in Hoyle *et al.* [7]. These Markov processes are manifestly time-inhomogeneous since their transition function depends explicitly on the time variable. We shall adopt the notation in Hoyle *et al.* [7], that is also useful in making a distinction between a general Markov process $\{X_t\}$ and a Lévy random bridge denoted $\{L_{tU}\}$.

Definition 3.1. A Lévy random bridge $\{L_{tU}\}_{0\leq t\leq U}$ that takes values in a continuous state space, is a process with the following properties:

1. L_{UU} has marginal law ν.
2. There exists a Lévy process $\{L_t\}$ such that L_t has density $\rho_t(x)$ for all $t \in (0, U]$.
3. ν concentrates mass where $\rho_U(z)$ is positive and finite, i.e. $0 < \rho_U(z) < \infty$ for ν-almost every z.
4. For every $n \in \mathbb{N}_+$, every $0 < t_1 < \cdots < t_n < U$, every $(x_1, \ldots, x_n) \in \mathbb{R}^n$, and ν-almost every z, we have

$$\begin{aligned}\mathbb{P}[L_{t_1U} \leq x_1, \ldots, L_{t_nU} \leq x_n | L_{UU} = z] \\ = \mathbb{P}[L_{t_1} \leq x_1, \ldots, L_{t_n} \leq x_n | L_U = z].\end{aligned}$$

For the computation of the conditional expectation involved in (3.3) and (3.4), the following result in Hoyle *et al.* (2011) is useful: For $0 \leq s < t < U$,

$$\mathbb{P}[L_{tU} \in \mathrm{d}y | L_{sU} = x] = \frac{\psi_{tU}(\mathbb{R}; y)}{\psi_{sU}(\mathbb{R}, x)}\rho_{t-s}(y-x)\mathrm{d}y, \tag{3.5}$$

J. Akahori & A. Macrina

where

$$\psi_{tU}(\mathbb{R};y) := \int_{-\infty}^{\infty} \frac{\rho_{U-t}(z-y)}{\rho_U(z)}\nu(\mathrm{d}z), \quad \psi_{0U}(\mathrm{d}z;y) := \nu(\mathrm{d}z). \tag{3.6}$$

If we assume that the Markov process $\{X_t\}$ driving the bond price process (3.4) is a Lévy random bridge, then the conditional expectation in (3.4) is given by

$$\mathbb{E}[F(u+t, L_{u+t,U})|L_{tU}] = \int_{-\infty}^{\infty} F(u+t,y)\frac{\psi_{u+t,U}(\mathbb{R};y)}{\psi_{tU}(\mathbb{R},L_{tU})}\rho_u(y-L_{tU})\mathrm{d}y. \tag{3.7}$$

In this case, the evolution of the bond price is determined by the conditional law of ρ_t of the Lévy process $\{L_t\}$. The density ρ_t is given by a function of time t and the value of L_{tU} prevailing at t.

Before we go on to work out explicitly the price of a fixed-income security, e.g., a discount bond, by choosing a specific Lévy random bridge, we show how in this framework one can also price derivatives. In particular, we show how to calculate a bond option via (3.1). Let $\{C_{st}\}$, $0 \leq s \leq t \leq T < U$, be the price process of a European-style call bond option with maturity t and strike K. The option price at time s is

$$C_{st} = \frac{1}{\pi(s, L_{sU})}\mathbb{E}^{\mathbb{P}}\left[\pi(t,L_{tU})(P_{tT}-K)^+|L_{sU}\right], \tag{3.8}$$

where here P_{tT} is defined by (3.2) for $X_t = L_{tU}$. Since the pricing kernel is a positive process, we may take $\pi(t, L_{tU})$ inside the max-function. We obtain

$$C_{st} = \frac{1}{\pi(s, L_{sU})}\mathbb{E}^{\mathbb{P}}\left[(\mathbb{E}^{\mathbb{P}}[\pi(T,L_{TU})|L_{tU}] - K\pi(t,L_{tU}))^+|L_{sU}\right]. \tag{3.9}$$

For $\pi(t, L_{tU})$, we use formula (3.3) where $X_t = L_{tU}$. Furthermore,

$$\mathbb{E}^{\mathbb{P}}[\pi(T, L_{TU} \mid L_{tU})] = \int_{T-t}^{U-t} \mathbb{E}^{\mathbb{P}}\left[F(u+t, L_{u+t,U})|L_{tU}\right] w(T, u-T+t)\mathrm{d}u, \tag{3.10}$$

which can be simplified by (3.7). The implicit result is a function of time t and L_{tU} that we denote $I(t, L_{tU})$. We rewrite the option price in the form

$$C_{st} = \frac{1}{\pi(t, L_{sU})}\mathbb{E}^{\mathbb{P}}[(I(t,L_{tU}) - K\pi(t,L_{tU}))^+|L_{sU}]. \tag{3.11}$$

For fixed t, let z^* be the set defined by

$$z^* := \{z|I(t,z) - K\pi(t,z) > 0\}. \tag{3.12}$$

Then we have

$$C_{st} = \frac{1}{\pi(s, L_{sU})}\int_{z^*}^{\infty} (I(t,z) - K\pi(t,z))\mathbb{P}[L_{tU} \in \mathrm{d}z|L_{sU}], \tag{3.13}$$

where $\mathbb{P}[L_{tU} \in \mathrm{d}z|L_{sU}]$ is given by (3.5). We observe that the option price is determined by a function of time and the value at time s of the time-inhomogeneous Markov process $\{L_{tU}\}_{0 \leq s \leq t \leq U}$.

Heat Kernel Interest Rate Models with Time-Inhomogeneous Markov Processes

4. Explicit Pricing Kernel Models

We reconsider the case in which the Lévy random bridge is a Brownian random bridge (Brownian bridge information process) as defined in (1.2). As shown in Hoyle *et al.* [7], the conditional density (3.5) can be computed in closed form. We can thus utilize this result in order to directly write down the expression for the bond price process (3.4) driven, e.g., by Brownian random bridge information. In this case we need working out a Gaussian integral over the range of the variable u. However, we shall apply a change-of-measure technique introduced in Brody *et al.* [2, 3].

Recall that the Brownian bridge information process is a Lévy random bridge of the form

$$L_{tU} = \sigma t X_U + \beta_{tU}, \tag{4.1}$$

where $\{\beta_{tU}\}_{0\leq t\leq U}$ is a Brownian bridge that is independent of X_U. Let $\{M_t\}_{0\leq t<U}$ be defined by

$$\frac{\mathrm{d}M_t}{M_t} = -\frac{\sigma U}{U-t}\mathbb{E}[X_U|L_{tU}]\mathrm{d}W_t, \tag{4.2}$$

where

$$W_t = L_{tU} + \int_0^t \frac{L_{sU}}{U-s}\mathrm{d}s - \sigma U\int_0^t \frac{1}{U-s}\mathbb{E}[X_U|L_{sU}]\mathrm{d}s. \tag{4.3}$$

The $(\{\mathcal{F}_t\},\mathbb{P})$-martingale $\{M_t\}$ induces a change of measure from $\mathbb{P}$ to the so-called bridge measure $\mathbb{B}$ under which $\{L_{tU}\}$ has the distribution of a Brownian bridge. We emphasize that the process $\{W_t\}$ is an $(\{\mathcal{F}_t\},\mathbb{P})$-Brownian motion on $[0,U)$. The bond price is modelled by

$$P_{tT} = \frac{\mathbb{E}[\pi(T,L_{TU})|L_{tU}]}{\pi(t,L_{tU})}. \tag{4.4}$$

Next we assume, with no loss of generality, that

$$\pi(t,L_{tU}) = M_t f(t,L_{tU}), \tag{4.5}$$

and perform the change of measure $\mathbb{P}$ to $\mathbb{B}$ so that

$$P_{tT} = \frac{\mathbb{E}^{\mathbb{B}}[f(T,L_{TU})|L_{tU}]}{f(t,L_{tU})}. \tag{4.6}$$

The pricing kernel $\{\pi(t,L_{tU})\}$ is a positive $\mathbb{P}$-supermartingale if and only if $\{f(t,L_{tU})\}$ is a positive supermartingale under $\mathbb{B}$. That is, for $0\leq s\leq t$,

$$\mathbb{E}^{\mathbb{P}}[\pi_t|\mathcal{F}_s] = M_s\mathbb{E}^{\mathbb{B}}[f(t,L_{tU})|L_{sU}] \leq M_s f(s,L_{sU}) = \pi_s. \tag{4.7}$$

The positive $\mathbb{B}$-supermartingale $\{f(t,L_{tU})\}_{0\leq t<U}$ can now be constructed by positive weighted heat kernels according to Proposition 2.2, where the conditional expectation is taken with respect to the $\mathbb{B}$-measure. The price P_{tT} is thus calculated by

the formula

$$P_{tT} = \frac{\int_{T-t}^{U-t} \mathbb{E}^{\mathbb{B}}[F(u+t, L_{u+t,U})|L_{tU}]w(T, u-T+t)\mathrm{d}u}{\int_0^{U-t} \mathbb{E}^{\mathbb{B}}[F(u+t, L_{u+t,U})|L_{tU}]w(t,u)\mathrm{d}u}. \tag{4.8}$$

Since, under the $\mathbb{B}$-measure, L_{tU} has the law of a Brownian bridge, the conditional expectation involves the Gaussian density function. Explicit expressions for the bond price are obtained by specifying $F(t,x)$ and the weight function $w(t,u)$. Depending on the combination of $F(t,x)$ and $w(t,u)$, the integration with respect to u in (4.8) can be performed in closed form. Some examples follow:

Quadratic models. We consider the positive function $F(x) = x^2$, and a weight function $w(t,u) = U - t - u$. As we shall see shortly, such a combination leads to a stochastic interest model and a closed-form expression for the bond price. The propagator (3.7) that gives rise to the stochastic dynamics of the bond price is given by

$$\mathbb{E}^{\mathbb{B}}\left[(L_{u+t,U})^2|L_{tU}\right] = \frac{u(U-t-u)}{U-t} + \left(\frac{U-t-u}{U-t}\right) L_{tU}^2. \tag{4.9}$$

Here we use the property that L_{tU} has the law of a Brownian bridge over $[0,U)$ under the $\mathbb{B}$-measure. The weighted heat kernel takes the form

$$\begin{aligned} f(t, L_{tU}) &= \int_0^{U-t} \mathbb{E}^{\mathbb{B}}[F(L_{u+t,U})|L_{tU}]w(t,u)\mathrm{d}u, \\ &= \frac{1}{12}(U-t)^3 + \frac{1}{4}(U-t)^2 L_{tU}^2, \end{aligned} \tag{4.10}$$

which ensures that the pricing kernel (4.5) is, via (4.7), a positive $\mathbb{P}$-supermartingale. Inserting (4.9) and (4.10) in (4.8), we obtain the bond price

$$P_{tT} = \frac{\frac{1}{12}(U-T)^3 + \frac{1}{4}\frac{(T-t)(U-T)^3}{(U-t)} + \frac{1}{4}\frac{(U-T)^4}{(U-t)^2}L_{tU}^2}{\frac{1}{12}(U-t)^3 + \frac{1}{4}(U-t)^2 L_{tU}^2}. \tag{4.11}$$

The associated short rate of interest $\{r_t\}$ can be obtained by calculating the instantaneous forward rate associated with the bond price $\{P_{tT}\}_{0\le t\le T<U}$. Alternatively, (4.10) can be inserted in formula (1.5) for the short rate process. We get

$$r(t, L_{tU}) = \frac{L_{tU}^2}{\frac{1}{4}(U-t)\left[\frac{1}{3}(U-t) + L_{tU}^2\right]}, \tag{4.12}$$

for $0 \le t < U$. We emphasize that this is, by construction, a positive interest rate model. The market price of risk $\{\lambda_t\}$ can be obtained via (1.6). We have

$$\lambda(t, L_{tU}) = \frac{\sigma U}{U-t}\mathbb{E}^{\mathbb{P}}[X_U|L_{tU}] - \frac{\frac{1}{2}(U-t)^2 L_{tU}}{\frac{1}{12}(U-t)^3 + \frac{1}{4}(U-t)^2 L_{tU}^2}. \tag{4.13}$$

The expectation $\mathbb{E}^{\mathbb{P}}[X_U|L_{tU}]$ can be calculated in closed form by applying the Bayes formula.

Heat Kernel Interest Rate Models with Time-Inhomogeneous Markov Processes

Exponential quadratic models. We consider a positive function $F(t,x)$ that depends explicitly on time, unlike in the previous example. Let

$$F(u+t,x) = \exp\left(\frac{1}{2}\gamma_{t+u}x^2\right), \tag{4.14}$$

where γ_{t+u} is positive and deterministic. In this case the propagator takes the form

$$\mathbb{E}^{\mathbb{B}}\left[\exp\left(\frac{1}{2}\gamma_{t+u}L^2_{t+u,U}\right)\middle| L_{tU}\right] = \frac{1}{\sqrt{1-u\gamma_{t+u}a_{t+u}}}\exp\left(\frac{\gamma_{t+u}a^2_{t+u}}{2\,(1-u\gamma_{t+u}a_{t+u})}L^2_{tU}\right), \tag{4.15}$$

where $a_{t+u} = (U-t-u)/(U-t)$. By setting $\gamma_{t+u} = (U-t-u)^{-1}$, and by choosing the weight function

$$w(t,u) = (U-t-u)^{\eta-\frac{1}{2}} \quad (\eta > \tfrac{1}{2}), \tag{4.16}$$

we obtain an analytical expression for the $\mathbb{B}$-supermartingale $\{f(t,L_{tU})\}$:

$$f(t,L_{tU}) = \frac{1}{\eta-\frac{1}{2}}(U-t)^{\eta}\exp\left(\frac{L^2_{tU}}{2(U-t)}\right). \tag{4.17}$$

This supermartingale leads to a deterministic bond price, even though the related pricing kernel is stochastic. However, we can modify $\{f(t,L_{tU})\}$ slightly. Let $g_0(t)$ and $g_1(t)$ be positive, decreasing, and differentiable functions. Consider the supermartingale

$$\tilde{f}(t,L_{tU}) = g_0(t) + g_1(t)(U-t)^{\eta}\exp\left(\frac{L^2_{tU}}{2(U-t)}\right). \tag{4.18}$$

Then the associated bond price system has the following stochastic dynamics:

$$P_{tT} = \frac{g_0(T) + g_1(T)(U-T)^{\eta-1/2}(U-t)^{1/2}\exp\left(\frac{L^2_{tU}}{2(U-t)}\right)}{g_0(t)+g_1(t)(U-t)^{\eta}\exp\left(\frac{L^2_{tU}}{2(U-t)}\right)}, \tag{4.19}$$

for $t\in[0,U)$ and $u\in[0,U-t]$. By use of (1.5) we work out the short rate process, and obtain

$$r_t = \frac{g_1(t)(U-t)^{\eta}\exp\left[\frac{L^2_{tU}}{2(U-t)}\right]}{g_0(t)+g_1(t)(U-t)^{\eta}\exp\left[\frac{L^2_{tU}}{2(U-t)}\right]} \times\left[\left(\eta-\frac{1}{2}\right)(U-t)^{-1} - \frac{\partial_t g_1(t)}{g_1(t)} - \frac{\partial_t g_0(t)}{g_1(t)(U-t)^{\eta}\exp\left[\frac{L^2_{tU}}{2(U-t)}\right]}\right]. \tag{4.20}$$

Next we consider a particular choice for $g_1(t)$. If

$$g_1(t) = (U-t)^{-(\eta-\frac{1}{2})}, \tag{4.21}$$

then (4.20) reduces to

$$r_t = -\frac{\partial_t g_0(t)}{g_0(t) + (U-t)^{1/2} \exp\left[\frac{L_{tU}^2}{2(U-t)}\right]}. \tag{4.22}$$

Since $g_0(t)$ is a positive decreasing function, its derivative is negative. Thus the interest rate process (4.22) is positive. The market price of risk model can of course also be derived in closed form — e.g., via (1.6) — and it is given in terms of a function of time and L_{tU}. We conclude this section by noting that further examples can be constructed. A semi-analytic formula is obtained for the exponential linear family where, for instance, $F(x) = \exp(-\mu x)$ may be chosen.

5. Fixed-Income Derivatives with Brownian Bridge Information

In Sec. 3 we introduced formula (3.8) for the pricing of a European-style bond option with strike K and maturity t. The market information is modelled by a Lévy random bridge process, and the pricing kernel is assumed to be of the form $\pi_t = \pi(t, L_{tU})$. The price process of the bond option is then given implicitly in terms of a function of time and the Lévy random bridge.

In this section we go one step further, and price the bond option under the assumption that the market filtration is generated by a Brownian bridge information process (4.1). In order to derive an explicit price process for the option, we need to specify the price process of the underlying bond. We shall use the quadratic models as an example, and thus apply (4.11). The related pricing kernel model is

$$\pi_t = M_t f(t, L_{tU}), \tag{5.1}$$

where $\{M_t\}_{0\le t<U}$ is defined by (4.2), and $\{f(t, L_{tU})\}$ is given by (4.10). We write down equation (3.8) for the option price under the bridge measure $\mathbb{B}$, that is

$$C_{st} = \frac{1}{f(s, L_{sU})}\mathbb{E}^{\mathbb{B}}[f(t, L_{tU})(P_{tT} - K)^+ | L_{sU}]. \tag{5.2}$$

We take the positive $\mathbb{B}$-supermartingale $\{f(t, L_{tU})\}$ inside the max-function where, on one hand it cancels with the denominator of P_{tT}, and on the other hand, it is multiplied with the strike price K. We re-arrange the resulting terms, and obtain

$$\begin{aligned} C_{st} = \frac{1}{f(s, L_{sU})}\mathbb{E}^{\mathbb{B}}\Bigg[\Bigg(&\frac{1}{4}\frac{(T-t)(U-T)^3}{U-t} + \frac{1}{12}[(U-T)^3 - K(U-t)^3] \\ &+ \frac{1}{4}\left[\frac{(U-T)^4}{(U-t)^2} - K(U-t)^2\right] L_{tU}^2\Bigg)^+ \Bigg| L_{sU}\Bigg] \end{aligned} \tag{5.3}$$

In order to work out the conditional expectation, we make the substitution

$$L_{tU} = \nu_{st} Y + \frac{U-t}{U-s} L_{sU}, \tag{5.4}$$

Heat Kernel Interest Rate Models with Time-Inhomogeneous Markov Processes

where Y is a standard normally-distributed random variable that is $\mathbb{B}$-independent of L_{sU}. Furthermore,

$$\nu_{st} = \sqrt{\frac{(t-s)(U-t)}{U-s}}. \tag{5.5}$$

Due to the properties of Y, the expression for the option price reduces to the following Gaussian integral:

$$C_{st} = \frac{1}{f(s, L_{sU})} \int_{-\infty}^{\infty} \left(A + B\left(\nu_{st} y + \frac{U-t}{U-s} L_{sU}\right)^2\right)^+ \frac{1}{\sqrt{2\pi}} \exp\left(-\frac{1}{2}y^2\right) \mathrm{d}y, \tag{5.6}$$

where

$$A = \frac{1}{4}\frac{(T-t)(U-T)^3}{U-t} + \frac{1}{12}[(U-T)^3 - K(U-t)^3] \tag{5.7}$$

$$B = \frac{1}{4}\left[\frac{(U-T)^4}{(U-t)^2} - K(U-t)^2\right]. \tag{5.8}$$

Next we integrate over the range of y for which the max-function does not vanish. This can be written as follows:

$$C_{st} = \frac{1}{f(s, L_{sU})} \int_{cy^2+by+a>0}^{\infty} (cy^2 + by + a) \frac{1}{\sqrt{2\pi}} \exp\left(-\frac{1}{2}y^2\right) \mathrm{d}y, \tag{5.9}$$

where

$$a = A + B\left(\frac{U-t}{U-s}\right)^2 L_{sU}^2, \quad b = 2B\nu_{st}\frac{U-t}{U-s}L_{sU}, \quad c = B\nu_{st}^2. \tag{5.10}$$

Next we solve for the values y that satisfy the inequality $cy^2 + by + a > 0$. Let $N(x)$ denote the cumulative normal distribution function. Then:

1. Case $c = 0$. For $b > 0$ we obtain

$$C_{st} = \frac{1}{f(s, L_{sU})}\left[aN\left(\frac{a}{b}\right) + \frac{b}{\sqrt{2\pi}}\exp\left(-\frac{1}{2}\left(\frac{a}{b}\right)^2\right)\right], \tag{5.11}$$

and for $b < 0$ we have

$$C_{st} = \frac{1}{f(s, L_{sU})}\left[aN\left(-\frac{a}{b}\right) - \frac{b}{\sqrt{2\pi}}\exp\left(-\frac{1}{2}\left(\frac{a}{b}\right)^2\right)\right]. \tag{5.12}$$

2. Case $c \neq 0$ and $b^2 - 4ac = -4AB\nu_{st}^2 > 0$. For $c < 0$ we have

$$y_{\pm} = \frac{1}{2c}\left(-b \pm \sqrt{b^2 - 4ac}\right), \tag{5.13}$$

and thus

$$C_{st} = \frac{1}{f(s, L_{sU})}\left[(a+b)[N(y_+) - N(y_-)] + (b + cy_-)\exp\left(-\frac{1}{2}(y_-)^2\right)\right.$$
$$\left. - (b + cy_+)\exp\left(-\frac{1}{2}(y_+)^2\right)\right]. \tag{5.14}$$

For $c > 0$ we have either $y \leq y_-$ or $y \geq y_+$ and thus

$$C_{st} = \frac{1}{f(s, L_{sU})}\left[(a+c)[N(y_-) + N(y_+)] - (b + cy_-)\frac{1}{\sqrt{2\pi}}\exp\left(-\frac{1}{2}(y_-)^2\right)\right.$$
$$\left. + (b + cy_+)\frac{1}{\sqrt{2\pi}}\exp\left(-\frac{1}{2}(y_+)^2\right)\right]. \tag{5.15}$$

3. Case $c \neq 0$ and $b^2 - 4ac = -4AB\nu_{st}^2 \leq 0$. For $c < 0$ the probability that $cy^2 + by + a > 0$ is zero. This means that in such a case the option at time s is almost always out of the money, and we have $C_{st} = 0$. For $c > 0$ we have $cy^2 + by + a > 0$ with probability one, and thus the option is almost always in the money. Hence we have

$$C_{st} = \frac{a+c}{f(s, L_{sU})}. \tag{5.16}$$

Acknowledgments

The authors are grateful to seminar participants at the KIER-TMU International Workshop on Financial Engineering 2009, the Vienna Institute of Finance (September 2009), Hitotsubashi University (November 2009), and at the Workshop on Financial Derivatives and Risk Management at the Fields Institute in Toronto (May 2010) for helpful comments and suggestions. In particular, we thank P. A. Parbhoo and J. Sekine for stimulating and fruitful discussions. AM thanks Ritsumeikan University in Kusatsu, Japan, for their hospitality and friendly work environment.

References

[1] J. Akahori, Y. Hishida, J. Teichmann and T. Tsuchiya, A heat kernel approach to interest rate models, arXiv.org: 0910.5033 (2009).

[2] D. C. Brody, L. P. Hughston and A. Macrina, Beyond hazard rates: a new framework for credit-risk modelling, in *Advances in Mathematical Finance*, Festschrift volume in honour of D. Madan, R. Elliot, M. Fu, R. Jarrow and J. Y. Yen, eds. (Birkhäuser, Springer Verlag, 2007).

[3] D. C. Brody, L. P. Hughston and A. Macrina, Information-based asset pricing, *International Journal of Theoretical and Applied Finance* **1** (2008) 107–142.

[4] D. C. Brody, L. P. Hughston and A. Macrina, Dam rain and cumulative gain, *Proceedings of the Royal Society A* **464** (2008) 1801–1822.

Heat Kernel Interest Rate Models with Time-Inhomogeneous Markov Processes

[5] J. H. Cochrane, *Asset Pricing*, Revised edition (Princeton University Press, 2005).
[6] D. Duffie, *Dynamic Asset Pricing*, Third edition (Princeton University Press, 2001).
[7] E. Hoyle, L. P. Hughston and A. Macrina, Lévy random bridges and the modelling of financial information, *Stochastic Processes and their Applications* **121** (2011) 856–884.
[8] L. P. Hughston and A. Macrina, Pricing fixed-income securities in an information-based framework, *Applied Mathematical Finance*, DOI: 10.1080/1350486X.2011.631757 (2012).
[9] P. J. Hunt, J. E. Kennedy and A. Pelsser, Markov-functional interest rate models, *Finance and Stochastics* **4**(4) (2000) 391–408.
[10] A. Macrina and P. A. Parbhoo, Security pricing with information-sensitive discounting, in *Recent Advances in Financial Engineering 2009, Proceedings of the KIER-TMU International Workshop on Financial Engineering 2009*, M. Kijima, C. Hara, K. Tanaka, eds. (World Scientific Publishing Company, 2010).
[11] D. Revuz and M. Yor, *Continuous Martingales and Brownian Motion*, 3rd edition (Springer Verlag, 1999).
[12] L. C. G. Rogers, The potential approach to the term structure of interest rates and foreign exchange rates, *Mathematical Finance* **7**(2) (1997) 157–176.
[13] M. Rutkowski and N. Yu, On the Brody-Hughston-Macrina approach to modelling of defaultable term structure, *International Journal of Theoretical and Applied Finance* **10** (2007) 557–589.

Chapter 10

PROCEEDINGS
OF
THE ROYAL SOCIETY A

rspa.royalsocietypublishing.org

Research

Cite this article: Brody DC, Hughston LP. 2013 Lévy information and the aggregation of risk aversion. Proc R Soc A 469: 20130024.
http://dx.doi.org/10.1098/rspa.2013.0024

Received: 15 January 2013
Accepted: 5 March 2013

Subject Areas:
mathematical finance, applied mathematics

Keywords:
asset pricing, heterogeneous markets, pricing kernel, risk aversion, risk premium, jump risk

Author for correspondence:
Dorje C. Brody
e-mail: Dorje.Brody@brunel.ac.uk

Lévy information and the aggregation of risk aversion*

Dorje C. Brody[1] and Lane P. Hughston[2]

[1]Department of Mathematical Sciences, Brunel University, Uxbridge UB8 3PH, UK
[2]Department of Mathematics, University College London, London WC1E 6BT, UK

When investors have heterogeneous attitudes towards risk, it is reasonable to assume that each investor has a pricing kernel, and that these individual pricing kernels are aggregated to form a market pricing kernel. The various investors are then buyers or sellers depending on how their individual pricing kernels compare with that of the market. In Brownian-based models, we can represent such heterogeneous attitudes by letting the market price of risk be a random variable, the distribution of which corresponds to the variability of attitude across the market. If the flow of market information is determined by the movements of prices, then neither the Brownian driver nor the market price of risk are directly visible: the filtration is generated by an 'information process' given by a combination of the two. We show that the market pricing kernel is then given by the harmonic mean of the individual pricing kernels associated with the various market participants. Remarkably, with an appropriate definition of Lévy information one draws the same conclusion in the case when asset prices can jump. As a consequence, we are led to a rather general scheme for the management of investments in heterogeneous markets subject to jump risk.

1. Introduction

The importance of the flow of information in financial markets is clearly evident. As market participants we are all 'signal processors'. It is logical therefore to base our financial models as much as reasonably possible on the information available to market participants, and to try to understand the way in which market signals are processed. One has to admit from the outset that markets are complicated, not only in terms of their structure, but also in terms of the investor psychology. Nevertheless,

*This chapter was originally published as: D. C. Brody & L. P. Hughston (2013) Lévy Information and the Aggregation of Risk Aversion. *Proceedings of the Royal Society A*, **469**, 20130024:1–19. Reprinted with kind permission from The Royal Society.

we shall show that there is scope for building relatively simple but intuitively natural mathematical models that capture the effects of information flows in heterogeneous markets, thus allowing one to address a variety of practical issues arising in the general area of investment management that might otherwise seem unapproachable.

In a typical financial model, it is usual to begin with a probability space $(\Omega, \mathcal{F}, \mathbb{P})$, together with a filtration $\{\mathcal{F}_t\}_{t\geq 0}$. The so-called 'physical' probability measure $\mathbb{P}$ is meant to summarize the system of market probability assignments to various possible events, and the 'market filtration' $\{\mathcal{F}_t\}$ is meant to summarize, for each time $t \geq 0$, the totality of information available to market participants up to time t. Clearly, both of these ideas involve a good deal of idealization, and it may be taking the notion of 'market efficiency' too far to suppose that such a characterization of the market is realistic. It makes better sense perhaps to suggest that each market participant in some way implicitly builds their own version of the basic model, and then by some process all these different versions of the basic model are amalgamated to produce an overall effective model that represents the market. The individual investor then trades in a way that is consistent with the relation of their 'private' model to that of the market as a whole.

Our purpose here is to examine a particular example of such a scheme, arising in connection with the apparent variability of opinion one observes concerning the expected rates of returns on financial assets. It is plainly obvious to the investment management community that well-informed, intelligent market participants will often have significantly differing opinions on rates of return—indeed, not only with respect to their views on the expected returns associated with individual assets, but also the expected returns associated with the market as a whole. Clearly, some sort of hypothesis of 'natural variation' is needed to model such a situation. The question thus arising is the following: how one can reconcile such a view with those well-established techniques of financial engineering that entail some sort of equilibrium, or, at least, the absence of arbitrage, as part of the very basis of the modelling framework, usually coupled implicitly with the assumption of a high degree of homogeneity and uniformity across the market—some version of the *law of one price*?

Our approach will be to model the excess rate of return (above the interest rate) as a random variable, the interpretation of which reflects the spread of opinion in the market about the rate of return to be demanded in exchange for the assumption of a given level of risk. We shall assume that the investors can be modelled as having a degree of rationality, in the sense that they recognize that other investors have differing opinions, and that the collective effect of these differing opinions will have an effect on market movements.

In the context of financial modelling, we take the accepted 'modern' view that financial models are by their nature ephemeral. By that, we mean that models are always used 'in the present' for a specific purpose—pricing, hedging, asset allocation, decision-making. Once the model has been used, then it is (so to speak) thrown away, and another model is constructed for the next task. The 'new' model may be identical in structure to its predecessor—perhaps differing only slightly in the assignment of some parameter values. Nevertheless, it is different: one starts each day (or minute, or microsecond) with a fresh model. In practice, the term 'new model' is usually applied only if there is some significant structural difference involved—for example, in the sense that the Vasicek and Cox–Ingersoll–Ross interest rate models are structurally different. In casual discussion, one would not normally say that two different versions of the Vasicek model with different values of the mean reversion parameter were distinct models. But it is useful to maintain the idea that one really is in fact working with different models—perhaps a better choice of words would be to say that one is working with a parametric family of models. Then the periodic adjustment of the parameters is the 'calibration' of the model. Indeed, the pervasive need for a regular regimen of robust model recalibration is a dominant feature of much of modern banking.

How does one use a financial model? That depends on the particular type of problem one is trying to solve (pricing, hedging, asset allocation, and so on), but typically one uses the freshly calibrated model to generate (by simulation, or numerical integration, or exact solution) the trajectories of the asset prices under different outcomes of chance; and then certain functions of the trajectories are averaged, with appropriate weightings, to provide the figures needed for the particular application.

The point is that when 'averaging' is carried out in a financial model, one is typically averaging over the outcome of chance in two different senses simultaneously—the first being the usual sense of the development of the trajectory as time goes by (for example, one averages over a multitude of distinct random walks); and the second being the sense that one averages over different views or characteristics of a multiplicity of market participants. Thus, if one models the excess rate of return as a random variable, the 'randomness' of the excess rate of return is not necessarily to be interpreted—in the model—exclusively in the sense that one particular value turns out to be the 'correct' one selected by chance (as if by coin flip), but rather in the sense that if one were to select an investor at random then one could say with what probability that investor will have a view or characteristic that lies in a certain range. Thus in the model, it is the collective effect (via the weighted average) of variation in the future trajectory that determines the solution to a problem posed in the present.

In this paper, we make use of pricing kernel methods, which turn out to be particularly useful, allowing one to distinguish between pricing issues and hedging issues. See Cochrane [1] for an informal but comprehensive introduction to the application of pricing kernels in finance. The study of heterogeneous markets is still, one could probably say, in its infancy, and in a state of active development. Indeed, one can be overwhelmed by trying to contend with all the different types of heterogeneity that can arise in financial markets—heterogeneity in risk attitude, in impatience, in probability assignment, in transmission of information, in network connectivity, in information processing speed, and so on. See Brown & Rogers [2], Duffie [3], Ziegler [4], and references cited therein, for overviews of some of the issues connected to heterogeneity in financial markets currently being pursued. There is also a large literature devoted to portfolio management under partial information (see, for example, Björk *et al.* [5] and references cited therein). Our approach in what follows is novel inasmuch as it combines pricing-kernel methods with information-based pricing and elements of behavioural finance in an intuitive yet mathematically rigorous treatment aimed at problems of asset allocation and investment decision, with a view particularly on how to manage such problems in the face of issues involving jumps in asset prices, in situations where the 'hedging paradigm' for derivative pricing breaks down, and in the context of a post-crisis world-view where buy-side concerns are taken as seriously as sell-side concerns.

The structure of the paper is as follows. In §2, we consider the problem of a heterogeneous market in which investors have variegated attitudes towards risk. We specialize to the case in which asset prices are driven by Brownian motion, and we model the variation in attitude towards risk by taking the excess rate of return to be a random variable. We introduce the idea of an 'information process' as the generator of the market filtration, and derive the conditional distribution of the market price of risk. In §3, we work out the form that the pricing kernel takes in such a model and derive the remarkable result that the market pricing kernel is given by the harmonic mean of the pricing kernels attributable to the various market participants based on their attitudes towards risk. In §4, we work out the dynamics of a typical financial asset under the assumptions that we have made, and show how the dynamics can be represented in a way that is explicitly consistent with the absence of arbitrage. In particular, we are able to establish the existence of a Brownian motion adapted to the filtration generated by the information process and such that the dynamical equations of both the asset and the pricing kernel are driven by this 'market' Brownian motion. Finally, in §5 and §6, we show how the general framework that we have developed in the case of Brownian motion based models can be extended very naturally to a wide family of models admitting jumps.

2. Random risk aversion and market heterogeneity

It will be useful if one regards the market filtration $\{\mathcal{F}_t\}$ as being generated by a set of one or more 'information processes'. By an information process, we mean a process that carries noisy or imperfect information about some quantity that is of relevance to market participants. The notion is a quite general one, and a number of different situations arise in which one can model the flow of information relevant to the formation of prices. Examples include information flows concerning the market factors that determine dividends on stocks, defaults on bonds, or claims on insurance contracts. The approach that we are adopting is that of 'information-based asset pricing', as represented in Brody *et al.* [6–10], Brody & Friedman [11], Filipovic *et al.* [12], Hoyle [13], Hoyle *et al.* [14], Hughston & Macrina [15,16], Macrina [17], Macrina & Parbhoo [18], and Rutkowski & Yu [19]. An important advantage of thinking of the filtration as being generated by information processes is that the treatment of informationally heterogeneous markets can then be pursued in a relatively straightforward way. We consider a set of information processes, some of which are accessible to investor A, some to investor B, some to investor C, and so on, generally with some overlap. If the overlap is substantial for a relatively large number of investors, then we can for some purposes call this the 'market filtration'. Generally speaking, the system of filtrations has a kind of hierarchical structure that takes the form of a lattice. In what follows, we shall work with a single market filtration, since our main concern is with heterogeneous attitudes towards risk rather than heterogeneous information flows, but the set-up will be structured in such a way that the consideration of heterogeneous information flows is also feasible.

An interesting and important example of an information process arises rather naturally in the context of geometric Brownian motion (GBM) models when we try to generalize such models to situations where the rate of return on the stock is not known exactly. The GBM models are, needless to say, a little too simple as such to be taken seriously as real-world models for asset price dynamics. Nevertheless, they do capture rather succinctly certain key elements of the relation between risk and return, and it is in that context that we confine the discussion initially to the GBM class. The idea is that once one obtains some understanding of how to deal with random rates of return in the case of constant-parameter GBM models, then one might focus on how to generalize the modelling framework to incorporate more realistic features, such as stochastic volatility or the inclusion of jumps.

We begin by consideration of the case of a single risky asset in the standard GBM family of models. The discussion that follows readily generalizes to the situation where a number of risky assets are traded. For simplicity, we present the case of a single such asset, and we assume that no dividends are paid over the time horizon considered. For the price we write

$$S_t = S_0\,\mathrm{e}^{(r+\sigma\lambda)t}\mathrm{e}^{\sigma B_t - \frac{1}{2}\sigma^2 t}, \tag{2.1}$$

where S_0 is the initial price, $\{B_t\}_{t\geq 0}$ is a standard Brownian motion, $r > 0$ is the interest rate, $\sigma > 0$ is the volatility and $\lambda > 0$ is the risk aversion factor. The term $\sigma\lambda$ is called the 'risk premium' or 'excess rate of return'. For a fixed level of risk aversion, the risk premium increases if one increases the level of riskiness (as represented by the volatility), and for a fixed level of riskiness, the risk premium increases if one increases the level of risk aversion. Since $\lambda\sigma$ is linear in each factor, it follows that λ has the interpretation of being the 'excess rate of return per unit of risk', or 'market price of risk' in the GBM model. It should be evident, on the other hand, that there is no *a priori* reason why the excess rate of return should be bilinear. In fact, the case of a bilinear risk premium is quite special. For example, in a general Lévy model the excess rate of return is a nonlinear function of the risk aversion and the volatility (Brody *et al.* [20], Mackie [21]), and the notion of 'market price of risk' is inappropriate.

To complete the specification of the model, we need a pricing kernel $\{\pi_t\}_{t>0}$, which in the standard GBM model takes the form

$$\pi_t = \mathrm{e}^{-rt}\mathrm{e}^{-\lambda B_t - \frac{1}{2}\lambda^2 t}. \tag{2.2}$$

The pricing kernel in an arbitrage-free model has the property that its product with the price of any non-dividend-paying asset gives a martingale under the physical measure $\mathbb{P}$. In the present situation we have

$$\pi_t S_t = S_0\,\mathrm{e}^{(\sigma-\lambda)B_t - \frac{1}{2}(\sigma-\lambda)^2 t}, \tag{2.3}$$

and one sees that the martingale condition is indeed satisfied. It is important to observe that for the expression of the principle of no arbitrage one needs to specify both the asset price and the pricing kernel.

Thus, in summary, in the case of a single risky asset (and under the assumption that no dividends are paid over the time horizon considered), the model is given by the price process (2.1) and the pricing kernel (2.2). These processes are defined on a probability space $(\Omega, \mathcal{F}, \mathbb{P})$ with respect to which $\{B_t\}_{t\geq 0}$ is a standard Brownian motion, and we can take the market filtration $\{\mathcal{F}_t\}$ as being the standard augmented filtration generated by $\{B_t\}$. The parameters of the model are S_0, r, λ and σ. Once specified, the model can be used at time 0 to value and risk-manage certain other classes of asset. For example, if H_T represents a random cash flow (perhaps the payoff of an investment strategy) at time T determined by the trajectory of $\{S_t\}_{0\leq t\leq T}$ over the time interval $[0, T]$, then in the model constructed at time 0, the random value H_t, at any time $t \geq 0$, of the asset that delivers H_T at time T is represented by

$$H_t = \frac{1}{\pi_t}\mathbb{1}(t < T)\mathbb{E}_t[\pi_T H_T], \tag{2.4}$$

where $\mathbb{1}(\cdot)$ denotes the indicator function and $\mathbb{E}_t[\cdot]$ denotes conditional expectation with respect to $\mathcal{F}_t$. For example, if $H_T = \max(S_t - K, 0)$, then a calculation shows that H_t is given by the familiar Black–Scholes formula for the value at time t of a call option with strike K and maturity T. Note that the pricing kernel methodology gives this result rather directly, without the involvement of hedging arguments, replication portfolios, market completeness, risk neutrality, change of measure or the solution of partial differential equations—all of which, important and useful as they are in various specific contexts, are ultimately irrelevant to the determination of the price of an option once the pricing kernel has been specified.

As another example, consider the optimal investment problem for an investor with utility $U(x)$ and initial endowment H_0, who wishes to invest in such a way as to maximize the expected utility of a contract that pays H_T at time T. Assuming that $U(x)$, $x > 0$, is a standard utility function satisfying $U'(x) > 0$ and $U''(x) < 0$, and writing $I(y)$, $y > 0$, for the inverse marginal utility satisfying $I(U'(x)) = x$ for all $x > 0$, a variational argument shows that the optimal investment is in a contract that at time T pays $H_T = I(\beta\pi_T)$, where the parameter β is the (unique) solution to the budget constraint $H_0 = \mathbb{E}[\pi_T I(\beta\pi_T)]$. In the case of logarithmic utility $U(x) = \ln x$, for instance, one finds that $H_T = H_0/\pi_T$. Such results follow more or less directly from the pricing kernel methodology, without the need for consideration, for example, of the optimal portfolio strategy (if such exists) that will generate H_T. In principle the investor simply pays H_0 and buys the contract that delivers H_T, and it is up to the seller whether they prefer (i) to accept the unhedged risk of delivering the contracted payment H_T at T, or (ii) to hedge the risk by using H_0 to construct a portfolio that is then managed in such a way as to produce the required H_T at T.

One sees that derivative contracts and investment management contracts are much the same thing from the point of view of the investor, at least if we add the further provision that the derivatives should have non-negative payoffs. Perhaps the investment management paradigm has the moral advantage that at least in some sense the investor is clearly being sold a product that is optimal. Whether such well-defined optimization criteria enter into the actual decision-making processes involved in the marketing of investment opportunities and the targeting of clients is another matter—but clearly they should, to the extent that this is practically possible, if we may speak normatively, and the same goes for the marketing of investment-grade derivatives. A key point is that the optimal investment plan typically involves characteristics of the investor (as modelled, for example, with the specification of a utility function), together with the pricing kernel—but the microstructure of the market, as represented by the various stocks that are traded, and so forth, does not come into play.

Now suppose that the risk aversion factor (or excess rate of return per unit of risk) is not directly observable, and that there is uncertainty in the market as to its value. This state of affairs, as we have argued earlier, is in many ways representative of reality, and suggests a simple generalization of the GBM model. Let us therefore write X for the unknown value of the risk aversion factor, which we shall treat as a random variable. Then in our model for the typical asset price (assuming, for simplicity, that X and $\{B_t\}$ are independent, that X is positive, and that the other model parameters are constants), we have

$$S_t = S_0 \, \mathrm{e}^{(r+\sigma X)t} \mathrm{e}^{\sigma B_t - \frac{1}{2}\sigma^2 t}. \tag{2.5}$$

Thus if we introduce a so-called 'information process' $\{\xi_t\}_{t\geq 0}$ defined by

$$\xi_t = B_t + Xt, \tag{2.6}$$

we can write the price in the form

$$S_t = S_0 \, \mathrm{e}^{rt} \mathrm{e}^{\sigma \xi_t - \frac{1}{2}\sigma^2 t}. \tag{2.7}$$

Note that the asset price is monotonic in the information. It follows that the filtration generated by the asset price is the same as the filtration generated by the information process. Therefore, in our model it is rather natural to let this be the market filtration $\{\mathcal{F}_t\}$. Then the 'true' value of the market risk aversion factor X remains hidden, and at best can only be estimated by observations of the asset price (or, equivalently, the information). This is a rather satisfactory way of viewing the market, since it conforms to intuition, and allows for an embodiment of the idea that past performance is not necessarily a reliable guide to future performance. The information process has the property that for large t the value of X is revealed. In particular, we have

$$\lim_{t\to\infty} \frac{1}{t}\xi_t = X. \tag{2.8}$$

This relation follows from the fact that Brownian motion grows in magnitude like the square root of t. Thus investors do not know in advance the excess rate of return on an asset, but in the long run this is revealed.

By use of the Bayes law, taking advantage of the fact that the random variable ξ_t is conditionally Gaussian given X, one can work out the conditional distribution of the market factor X given the relevant market information up to time t. The details of the calculation leading to this result are shown in appendix A. One finds that

$$p_t(\mathrm{d}x) = \frac{\exp[x\xi_t - \frac{1}{2}x^2 t]p(\mathrm{d}x)}{\int_0^\infty \exp[z\xi_t - \frac{1}{2}z^2 t]p(\mathrm{d}z)}, \tag{2.9}$$

where the measure $p(\mathrm{d}x)$ determines the unconditional distribution of X. The conditional distribution of the risk aversion factor is then given by

$$\mathbb{P}(X < x \mid \mathcal{F}_t) = \int_0^x p_t(\mathrm{d}z), \tag{2.10}$$

with $p_t(\mathrm{d}x)$ as in (2.9), and it follows in particular that its conditional mean is

$$\mathbb{E}[X \mid \mathcal{F}_t] = \int_0^\infty x\, p_t(\mathrm{d}x). \tag{2.11}$$

The statement 'X is unknown' can be interpreted in several ways. One is that there is a 'secret' value of X which none of the market participants know but the asset somehow 'knows', and that over time this secret value of X works its way through the dynamics of the asset price to contribute to the eventual return displayed by the asset. Many people like to think in this way, even if they do not actually believe the asset 'knows' anything. It is as though the market somehow 'knows'. One sees this manner of thinking in the use of animistic language, in phrases like 'the market is always right', and also in the language of technical analysis. Another interpretation of 'X is unknown' is that there is variability of opinion in the market about the rate of return that ought to be expected for a given level of risk, and that the distribution of X represents this spread of opinion. Such variation might well be elemental, in the sense that each participant has their own private level of risk aversion, and that the distribution of X reflects this. Indeed, it is a matter of human nature that equally intelligent and well-informed individuals can and will, by choice or disposition, exhibit markedly differing levels of risk tolerance and risk aversion. This is a practical fact of life that one encounters constantly in day-to-day interactions with other people (or for that matter animals). We know from experience that even a single individual can, depending on mood and circumstance, exhibit significantly variable attitudes towards risk. It seems therefore both necessary and reasonable to suppose that an equilibrium can be established in a market where investors have widely differing attitudes towards risk, and that market prices are obtained by averaging in some sense over all these different attitudes.

Is it possible to reconcile the 'X is secret' point of view with the 'X represents variation' idea? From a modelling perspective, it would appear so. In particular, to calculate prices, one needs to form weighted averages over a large number of trajectories. One can imagine that each trajectory invoked in the averaging procedure involves some specific 'secret' value of X; or alternatively, one can think of averaging over the whole market, taking into account all of the various risk preferences: the result is the same.

3. Modelling the pricing kernel

With these thoughts in mind, we need to consider how to model the pricing kernel in a situation where heterogeneous attitudes towards risk prevail. One might be inclined simply to replace the parameter λ in the GBM pricing kernel (2.2) with the random variable X to give a tentative expression of the form

$$\pi_t \stackrel{?}{=} \mathrm{e}^{-rt}\mathrm{e}^{-XB_t-\frac{1}{2}X^2t} \tag{3.1}$$

as a candidate for the pricing kernel. Unfortunately, this will not quite work, since once we introduce ξ_t we obtain

$$\pi_t \stackrel{?}{=} \mathrm{e}^{-rt}\mathrm{e}^{-X\xi_t+\frac{1}{2}X^2t}, \tag{3.2}$$

which is clearly not $\mathcal{F}_t$-measurable, on account of the explicit appearance of X, and as a consequence the associated process $\{\pi_t\}$ is not adapted to the filtration $\{\mathcal{F}_t\}$ generated by $\{\xi_t\}$. However, if we take the conditional expectation of the expression above with respect to $\mathcal{F}_t$, this gives a better candidate for the pricing kernel, namely

$$\pi_t = \mathbb{E}_t\left[\exp\left(-rt - X\xi_t + \frac{1}{2}X^2t\right)\right] = \int_0^\infty \exp\left(-rt - x\xi_t + \frac{1}{2}x^2t\right)\,p_t(\mathrm{d}x), \tag{3.3}$$

which has the virtue of being $\mathcal{F}_t$-measurable. Then after insertion of expression (2.9) for $p_t(\mathrm{d}x)$ we obtain

$$\pi_t = \frac{1}{\int_0^\infty \exp(rt + x\xi_t - \frac{1}{2}x^2t)p(\mathrm{d}x)}. \tag{3.4}$$

This formula is perhaps most easily understood as follows. The process $\{n_t\}$ defined in terms of the pricing kernel by $n_t = 1/\pi_t$ is the so-called 'natural numeraire' or 'benchmark process' (see, for example, Flesaker & Hughston [22], Long [23]). The price process of any non-dividend-paying asset, when expressed in units of the natural numeraire, is a martingale in the market filtration. Thus in the present context we have

$$n_t = \int_0^\infty \exp\left(rt + x\xi_t - \frac{1}{2}x^2t\right)p(\mathrm{d}x). \tag{3.5}$$

We note that for each value of x the integrand corresponds to an asset with unit initial price and of the form (2.7) with volatility x. Therefore, in the case of an unknown risk aversion factor, we form a weighted portfolio of the numeraire assets obtained for various specific values of the risk aversion, and then invert this to obtain the pricing kernel $\pi_t = 1/n_t$. This leads us to the following important conclusion: *the pricing kernel associated with random risk aversion is given by the harmonic mean of the pricing kernels arising for various specific values of the risk aversion.*

We have thus obtained a nice example of the use of information processes in shedding light on a problem of considerable interest in the investment community. Indeed, in the behavioural finance literature (see [24,25], and works cited therein), a good deal of evidence has been gathered to the effect that the correct way of amalgamating risk aversion in a heterogeneous market is not by simply averaging the risk aversion parameter over the market, but rather by taking a suitable average (typically a Hölder mean) of the associated stochastic discount factors. Thus, if agent A says that the market price of risk should be x, and agent B says with equal conviction that the market price of risk should be y, then instead of naively averaging these numbers to obtain $\frac{1}{2}(x+y)$ and inserting this figure into the stochastic discount factor to express the aggregate view, the behaviouralists propose first to work out the stochastic discount factors corresponding separately to the views of A and B, and then to take a suitable average. As we have seen above, our calculations support this general line of argument, and indeed we are able to go further by deducing from first principles a specific rule for the aggregation of risk aversion.

4. Information-based estimation of market risk aversion

The following question can be posed. Is it possible to formulate the price dynamics of the risky asset in such a way that the resulting representations for $\{S_t\}$ and $\{\pi_t\}$ are expressible entirely in the language of stochastic differential equations, without explicit reference to the 'hidden' risk aversion variable X? By doing so, we would have a model formulated, so to speak, in the spirit of 'classical mathematical finance'. That is to say, the model would be proposed in the form of a closed system of dynamical equations satisfied by the asset and the pricing kernel, with appropriate initial conditions, and some parametric freedom. Only later one would discover, as it were, that the solution to this system of equations implies and admits the existence of the hidden variables X and $\{B_t\}$.

It turns out that such a programme is feasible, and indeed is rather enlightening, since it allows one to put forward a version of the theory described in the previous sections without the introduction of 'unobservable' elements, and yet with exactly the same practical conclusions. Furthermore, at the same time we are able to 'deduce' the existence of a random variable X having the characteristics already discussed, along with the associated 'true' noise $\{B_t\}$, thus allowing the theory to admit the interpretation we have given it.

We proceed as follows. As in the previous sections, we fix a probability space $(\Omega, \mathcal{F}, \mathbb{P})$ and introduce a Brownian motion $\{B_t\}$ and an independent random variable X. We introduce the information process $\{\xi_t\}$ defined by (2.6), along with the filtration $\{\mathcal{F}_t\}$ that it generates, and we define the asset price by (2.7) and the pricing kernel by (3.4). By virtue of the relation $\mathrm{d}\xi_t^2 = \mathrm{d}t$, the dynamical equation satisfied by the asset price takes the form

$$\mathrm{d}S_t = rS_t\,\mathrm{d}t + \sigma S_t\,\mathrm{d}\xi_t. \tag{4.1}$$

Our goal is to write the dynamics in a way that brings out more explicitly the fact that the price movements are being driven by Brownian motion. The only difficulty is that the Brownian motion $\{B_t\}$, in terms of which the information process $\{\xi_t\}$ is defined, is not adapted to the market filtration; and thus we cannot quite say that the asset price is 'driven' by $\{B_t\}$ in the usual sense.

To overcome this problem, we make use of an idea from filtering theory—the idea of a so-called innovations process. In particular, we define a process $\{W_t\}$ by

$$W_t = \xi_t - \int_0^t \mathbb{E}[X \mid \mathcal{F}_s]\mathrm{d}s. \tag{4.2}$$

One can show, for example, by use of the Lévy criterion (see appendix B) that $\{W_t\}$ is an $\{\mathcal{F}_t\}$-Brownian motion. Next we define a process $\{\lambda_t\}$ by setting

$$\lambda_t = \mathbb{E}[X \mid \mathcal{F}_t]. \tag{4.3}$$

By virtue of the relations (2.11), (4.2) and (4.3), the information process $\{\xi_t\}$ evidently satisfies a stochastic differential equation of the form

$$\mathrm{d}\xi_t = \lambda_t \mathrm{d}t + \mathrm{d}W_t, \tag{4.4}$$

where

$$\lambda_t = \frac{\int_0^\infty x \exp(x\xi_t - \frac{1}{2}x^2 t)p(\mathrm{d}x)}{\int_0^\infty \exp(x\xi_t - \frac{1}{2}x^2 t)p(\mathrm{d}x)}, \tag{4.5}$$

and it follows that the dynamical equation for the price can be put in the desired form

$$dS_t = (r + \lambda_t\sigma)S_t\, dt + \sigma S_t\, dW_t. \tag{4.6}$$

We note that the resulting 'effective' market price of risk $\{\lambda_t\}$ is given by the conditional expectation (4.3), and hence can be interpreted as the best estimate, given the information available, of the 'true' value of the random variable X. A little reflection shows that we can drop the adjective 'effective' and simply assert that $\{\lambda_t\}$ is indeed the market price of risk (or market risk aversion level) in this model and that X is the (unknown) *actual* excess rate of return per unit of risk. Market participants acknowledge that only 'the gods' know what the actual excess rate of return will turn out to be, or to have been, but that $\{\lambda_t\}$, which is knowable, represents the market consensus, the best estimate, the weighted opinion of market experts, the vote. *The observable drift of an asset is thus determined not by the actual risk premium, but rather by the market best estimate for the risk premium.* In particular, given the price S_t of the asset at time t, one deduces by use of (2.7) and (4.5) that the best estimate of the market price of risk is given by the following expression:

$$\lambda_t = \frac{\int_0^\infty x(S_t/S_0)^{x/\sigma} \exp[-\frac{1}{2}x^2 t + (\frac{1}{2}\sigma - r/\sigma)xt]p(dx)}{\int_0^\infty (S_t/S_0)^{x/\sigma} \exp[-\frac{1}{2}x^2 t + (\frac{1}{2}\sigma - r/\sigma)xt]p(dx)}. \tag{4.7}$$

This formula shows explicitly how the investor is able to update the *a priori* estimate for the market price of risk given the current price level of the risky asset.

It follows from (4.4) that the information process $\{\xi_t\}$ is a Brownian motion under the risk-neutral measure $\mathbb{Q}$. Furthermore, if we make use of the market price of risk to effect a change of measure, a calculation shows that (i) the random variables ξ_t and X are independent under $\mathbb{Q}$, and (ii) the probability law for X under $\mathbb{Q}$ is given by $p(dx)$; that is to say, it is the same as it is under the physical measure $\mathbb{P}$. Therefore, an 'observer' in the risk-neutral frame of reference $(\Omega, \mathcal{F}, \mathbb{Q})$ detects the 'message' $\{\xi_t\}$, or equivalently the price $\{S_t\}$, but finds that it contains no information about the level of risk aversion—this is the sense in which the level of risk aversion cannot be inferred *a priori* from derivative prices in the context of Brownian-motion-based models. If stronger modelling assumptions are made about the structure of the pricing kernel in a Brownian model, then in some contexts it is possible to infer information about the risk aversion level from derivative prices [20,26–28]. The approach that we are taking is, perhaps, more practically oriented, inasmuch as an explicit estimation formula for the risk premium, such as that given by (4.7), can be obtained in a direct and transparent manner without any reference to the risk-neutral measure.

The $\{\mathcal{F}_t\}$-dynamics of the pricing kernel can be pursued similarly. In fact, it is more convenient first to work out the dynamics of the natural numeraire. Starting with equation (3.5), by a direct application of Ito calculus we obtain

$$dn_t = rn_t\, dt + \int_0^\infty x \exp\left(rt + x\xi_t - \frac{1}{2}x^2 t\right) p(dx)\, d\xi_t. \tag{4.8}$$

It follows then by use of (4.4) and (4.5) that

$$dn_t = (r + \lambda_t^2)\, n_t\, dt + \lambda_t n_t\, dW_t, \tag{4.9}$$

and therefore that

$$d\pi_t = -r\pi_t\, dt - \lambda_t \pi_t\, dW_t. \tag{4.10}$$

Hence we are led to the conclusion that the volatility of the pricing kernel is (minus) the market price of risk, as it of course should be in the $\{\mathcal{F}_t\}$-dynamics of the pricing kernel, and we can write

$$\pi_t = \exp\left(-rt - \int_0^t \lambda_s\, dW_s - \int_0^t \lambda_s^2\, ds\right). \tag{4.11}$$

Such an expression for the pricing kernel or state price density is often used as the starting point of various investigations in the theory of finance—but note that we have not assumed that $\{\pi_t\}$ takes this form, we have deduced it.

10

rspa.royalsocietypublishing.org Proc R Soc A 469: 20130024

As a model constructed in the spirit of classical mathematical finance, without direct mention of the risk aversion variable X, one thus has the following. We begin with a probability space $(\Omega, \mathcal{F}, \mathbb{P})$, on which a standard Brownian motion $\{W_t\}$ is defined, and we let $\{\mathcal{F}_t\}$ be the associated filtration. The model inputs include the initial price S_0, the interest rate r, the volatility σ, and a measure $p(\mathrm{d}x)$ on $\mathbb{R}^+$. With this data at hand, one defines a smooth function of two variables $\lambda : \mathbb{R} \times \mathbb{R}^+ \to \mathbb{R}^+$ given by $(\xi, t) \to \lambda(\xi, t)$, where

$$\lambda(\xi, t) = \frac{\int_0^\infty x \exp(x\xi - \frac{1}{2}x^2 t) p(\mathrm{d}x)}{\int_0^\infty \exp(x\xi - \frac{1}{2}x^2 t) p(\mathrm{d}x)}. \tag{4.12}$$

One can check that for fixed t the function $\lambda(\xi, t)$ is increasing in the variable ξ. In particular, a calculation shows that $\lambda'(\xi, t) > 0$, where the prime denotes differentiation with respect to ξ. The process $\{\xi_t\}$ is then defined as the solution to the stochastic differential equation

$$\mathrm{d}\xi_t = \lambda(\xi_t, t)\mathrm{d}t + \mathrm{d}W_t, \tag{4.13}$$

with the initial condition $\xi_0 = 0$. Having obtained $\{\xi_t\}$, one defines the process $\{\lambda_t\}$ by setting $\lambda_t = \lambda(\xi_t, t)$. The SDE for the asset price is taken to be (4.6), with the initial condition S_0, and the SDE for the pricing kernel is taken to be given by (4.10), with the initial condition unity. That gives a complete characterization of the dynamics of the asset price and the pricing kernel.

Having constructed the model in the filtration $\{\mathcal{F}_t\}$ without reference to the random variable X, one might ask whether it is possible in some sense to reconstruct X. It turns out that one can. In fact, we can *derive* expressions for the two 'hidden' objects X and $\{B_t\}$ appearing in (2.6) from the ingredients arising in the $\{\mathcal{F}_t\}$ version of the modelling framework. Specifically, let $\{\xi_t\}$ satisfy the stochastic differential equation (4.13), with $\xi_0 = 0$. We can then show (i) that the random variables defined by

$$X = \lim_{T\to\infty} T^{-1}\xi_T \quad \text{and} \quad B_t = \xi_t - Xt \tag{4.14}$$

are independent for all t, (ii) that the distribution of X is given by $p(\mathrm{d}x)$, and (iii) that the process $\{B_t\}$ thus arising is a standard $\mathbb{P}$-Brownian motion. The details of the arguments involved in establishing these facts are summarized in appendix C.

5. Geometric Lévy models

Remarkably, the considerations that we have presented in connection with GBM models generalize very naturally to the context of geometric Lévy models (GLMs). As a consequence, we are able to construct a large and rich family of financial models for asset prices with jump risk in situations where the market exhibits variation among its participants in the excess rate of return required (above the interest rate) as compensation for the assumption of such risk. We assume familiarity with basics of the theory and application of Lévy processes in what follows, as discussed for example in Anderson & Lipton [29], Cont & Tankov [30], Kyprianou [31], Protter [32] or Schoutens [33]. Numerous investigations have been pursued concerning the development of Lévy-based models in finance, and as a consequence the literature is very extensive. We mention, for example, the works of Madan & Senata [34], Madan & Milne [35], Heston [36], Gerber & Shiu [37], Eberlin & Keller [38], Eberlin & Jacod [39], Madan *et al.* [40], Chan [41], Carr *et al.* [42], Kallsen & Shiryaev [43], Hubalek & Sgarra [44], Baxter [45], and Yor [46]. To set the notation, we begin with a few definitions. A Lévy process on a probability space $(\Omega, \mathcal{F}, \mathbb{P})$ is a process $\{X_t\}$ such that $X_0 = 0$, $X_t - X_s$ is independent of $\mathcal{F}_s$ for $t \geq s$ (independent increments), and

$$\mathbb{P}(X_t - X_s \leq y) = \mathbb{P}(X_{t+h} - X_{s+h} \leq y) \tag{5.1}$$

(stationary increments), where $\{\mathcal{F}_t\}$ denotes the augmented filtration generated by $\{X_t\}$. In order for $\{X_t\}$ to give rise to a GLM, we require that it should satisfy

$$\mathbb{E}[\mathrm{e}^{\alpha X_t}] < \infty \tag{5.2}$$

for all $t \geq 0$, for some connected real interval $\alpha \in A$ containing the origin. We consider Lévy processes satisfying such a condition. It follows by the stationary and independent increments property that there exists a function $\psi(\alpha)$, the Lévy exponent, such that

$$\mathbb{E}[e^{\alpha X_t}] = e^{t\psi(\alpha)} \tag{5.3}$$

for $\alpha \in \{w \in \mathbb{C} : \mathrm{Re}(w) \in A\}$, and one can check that the process defined by

$$M_t = e^{\alpha X_t - t\psi(\alpha)} \tag{5.4}$$

is an $\{\mathcal{F}_t\}$-martingale. We call $\{M_t\}$ the geometric Lévy martingale (or Esscher martingale) associated with $\{X_t\}$, with parameter α. For example, in the case of a standard Brownian motion the Lévy exponent is given by

$$\psi(\alpha) = \tfrac{1}{2}\alpha^2, \tag{5.5}$$

which is defined for all real α, and the associated geometric Lévy martingale is a compensated GBM with volatility α. A Lévy process is fully characterized by its exponent. As a consequence, it is useful to define and classify such processes by presentation of their exponents. For example, the Poisson process with rate m is defined by

$$\psi(\alpha) = m(e^{\alpha} - 1). \tag{5.6}$$

The gamma process with rate m and scale unity is given by

$$\psi(\alpha) = -m\ln(1 - \alpha), \tag{5.7}$$

for $\alpha < 1$. The variance-gamma (VG) process is given for $\alpha^2 < 2m$ by

$$\psi(\alpha) = -m\ln\left(1 - \frac{\alpha^2}{2m}\right). \tag{5.8}$$

The theory of Esscher transformations plays an important role in the analysis of the relation between risk and return in Lévy models. We say that two Lévy exponents $\psi(\alpha)$ and $\tilde{\psi}(\alpha)$ are related by an Esscher transformation with parameter λ if

$$\tilde{\psi}(\alpha) = \psi(\alpha + \lambda) - \psi(\lambda). \tag{5.9}$$

The parameter λ must lie in the domain A of $\psi(\alpha)$, and the domain of $\tilde{\psi}(\alpha)$ consists of those values of α such that $\alpha + \lambda \in A$. The operation is reversible in the sense that if $\tilde{\psi}(\alpha)$ is an Esscher transformation of $\psi(\alpha)$ with parameter λ, then $\psi(\alpha)$ is an Esscher transformation of $\tilde{\psi}(\alpha)$ with parameter $-\lambda$. Thus, if $\psi(\alpha) = \frac{1}{2}\alpha^2$ represents a Brownian motion, then $\tilde{\psi}(\alpha) = \frac{1}{2}\alpha^2 + \alpha\lambda$ represents a Brownian motion with drift λ. If $\psi(\alpha) = m(e^{\alpha} - 1)$ represents a Poisson process with rate m, then $\tilde{\psi}(\alpha) = me^{\lambda}(e^{\alpha} - 1)$ represents a Poisson process with rate me^{λ}, and so on. Each example is rather different in character.

With these definitions at hand, we can present a development of the theory of GLMs for asset pricing [20] that is particularly well adapted to the analysis of jump risk aversion. The straightforward approach to GLMs is as follows. First we construct the pricing kernel $\{\pi_t\}_{t\geq 0}$. Let $\{X_t\}$ be a Lévy process with exponent $\psi(\alpha)$ where $\alpha \in A$. Let $\lambda > 0$, $-\lambda \in A$, and set

$$\pi_t = e^{-rt} e^{-\lambda X_t - t\psi(-\lambda)}. \tag{5.10}$$

We require that the product of the pricing kernel and the asset price should be a martingale, which we assume is of the geometric Lévy form

$$\pi_t S_t = S_0 e^{\beta X_t - t\psi(\beta)} \tag{5.11}$$

for some $\beta \in A$, and we deduce that

$$S_t = S_0\, e^{rt}\, e^{\sigma X_t + t\psi(-\lambda) - t\psi(\sigma - \lambda)}, \tag{5.12}$$

where $\sigma = \beta + \lambda$. We shall assume that $\sigma > 0$ and that $\sigma \in A$. It follows that the price can be expressed by the formula

$$S_t = S_0 \, \mathrm{e}^{rt} \, \mathrm{e}^{R(\lambda,\sigma)t} \, \mathrm{e}^{\sigma X_t - t\psi(\sigma)}, \tag{5.13}$$

where

$$R(\lambda,\sigma) = \psi(\sigma) + \psi(-\lambda) - \psi(\sigma - \lambda). \tag{5.14}$$

It is a remarkable fact that the excess rate of return function $R(\lambda,\sigma)$ thus arising is positive and is increasing with respect to both of its arguments.

6. On the aggregation of jump-risk aversion

In our analysis of jump-risk aversion, it will be useful to cast the foregoing formulation of GLMs into a slightly different form which turns out to be well suited for our purpose. Let $\{X_t\}$ and $\psi(\alpha)$ be defined as above, and set

$$\phi(\alpha) = \psi(\alpha - \lambda) - \psi(-\lambda). \tag{6.1}$$

Clearly, we have

$$\psi(\alpha) = \phi(\alpha + \lambda) - \phi(\lambda), \tag{6.2}$$

and we observe that $\psi(\alpha)$ is given by an Esscher transform of $\phi(\alpha)$, with parameter λ. An exercise then shows that the asset price (5.12) can be expressed in the form

$$S_t = S_0 \, \mathrm{e}^{rt} \, \mathrm{e}^{\sigma X_t - t\phi(\sigma)}. \tag{6.3}$$

Thus, we see that given a 'fiducial' Lévy exponent $\phi(\alpha)$, if we let the exponent of the Lévy process $\{X_t\}$ be an Esscher transform of $\phi(\alpha)$, with parameter λ, then the process S_t defined as above by (6.3) will be a submartingale, which we can take to be the asset price process. The associated pricing kernel is then a supermartingale that takes the form

$$\pi_t = \mathrm{e}^{-rt} \mathrm{e}^{-\lambda X_t + t\phi(\lambda)}. \tag{6.4}$$

The advantage of this representation of the GLM (which is entirely equivalent to that of the previous section) is that it readily generalizes to the situation where the risk aversion parameter is uncertain, thus allowing one to generalize the scheme set out in §§1–4 to models with jumps.

To proceed further, it will be expedient to make use of the general filtering theory associated with Lévy noise developed in Brody *et al.* [47]. We recall that, when phrased in the language of signal processing, what amounts to the 'signal' in the present investigation is the unknown level of risk aversion. In the Brownian context, it is natural for the signal to be obscured by an additive noise. However, in the case of general Lévy noise with jumps, the signal is no longer obscured by noise in an additive manner. In fact, each different type of Lévy process, when viewed as a model for noise, 'carries' the signal in its own distinctive manner.

Rather than developing the theory case by case, here we propose to present the theory in such a way that is applicable to the whole category of Lévy models. For this purpose, we introduce the important notion of *Lévy information*. By a Lévy information process $\{\xi_t\}$ with signal X on a probability space $(\Omega, \mathcal{F}, \mathbb{P})$, we mean a process such that conditional on the sigma field $\mathcal{F}^X$ generated by X, $\{\xi_t\}$ is a Lévy process with exponent

$$\psi_X(\alpha) = \phi(\alpha + X) - \phi(X) \tag{6.5}$$

for $\alpha \in \{w \in \mathbb{C} : \mathrm{Re}(w) = 0\}$. That is to say, we have the relation

$$\mathbb{E}[\mathrm{e}^{\alpha\xi_t} \mid \mathcal{F}^X] = \mathrm{e}^{t\psi_X(\alpha)} \tag{6.6}$$

for imaginary values of α. In terms of the Lévy information process $\{\xi_t\}$, the asset price can be expressed in the form

$$S_t = S_0 \mathrm{e}^{rt} \mathrm{e}^{\sigma\xi_t - t\phi(\sigma)}, \tag{6.7}$$

which can be thought of as the general Lévy-based analogue of the price process (2.7). One way of looking at the formula above is to view $\{\xi_t\}$ as the driving Lévy process in the risk-neutral measure

$\mathbb{Q}$, with respect to which the associated Lévy exponent is given by $\phi(\alpha)$. Under $\mathbb{Q}$, however, $\{\xi_t\}$ encodes no information about the level of risk aversion. For this, we need to work with the physical measure $\mathbb{P}$ and identify the pricing kernel. A naive candidate for $\{\pi_t\}$, analogous to (3.2), is given by the formula

$$\pi_t \stackrel{?}{=} \mathrm{e}^{-rt}\mathrm{e}^{-X\xi_t+t\phi(X)}. \tag{6.8}$$

This expression suffers from the fact that it is not measurable with respect to the sigma field $\mathcal{F}_t$ generated by the trajectory of the information process up to time t. It turns out, fortunately, and perhaps surprisingly, that the approach taken in the case of the Brownian example carries through to the general Lévy context, and for the pricing kernel we have

$$\pi_t = \mathbb{E}_t[\exp(-rt - X\xi_t + \phi(X)t)] = \int_0^\infty \exp(-rt - x\xi_t + \phi(x)t)\, p_t(\mathrm{d}x), \tag{6.9}$$

where

$$p_t(\mathrm{d}x) = \frac{\exp(x\xi_t - \phi(x)t)p(\mathrm{d}x)}{\int_0^\infty \exp(z\xi_t - \phi(z)t)p(\mathrm{d}z)} \tag{6.10}$$

is the $\{\mathcal{F}_t\}$-conditional measure for the distribution of X, and $p(\mathrm{d}x)$ is the unconditional measure. Substituting (6.10) in (6.9), we thus deduce that the pricing kernel in a GLM with random risk aversion is given by the following formula:

$$\pi_t = \frac{1}{\int_0^\infty \exp(rt + x\xi_t - \phi(x)t)p(\mathrm{d}x)}. \tag{6.11}$$

Similarly, for the natural numeraire in the case of a Lévy model with random risk aversion we can write

$$n_t = \int_0^\infty \exp(rt + x\xi_t - \phi(x)t)p(\mathrm{d}x). \tag{6.12}$$

Again, as in the Brownian situation, one observes in the Lévy case the key point that the market numeraire asset can be viewed as a portfolio, the elements of which correspond, with appropriate weights, to the numeraire assets of the various investors, each with a volatility given by the risk aversion factor associated with the particular investor.

With the conditional density (6.10) at hand, we are able to determine the optimal estimate (in the sense of least quadratic error) for the level of jump-risk aversion. This is given by

$$\lambda_t = \frac{\int_0^\infty x\exp(x\xi_t - \phi(x)t)p(\mathrm{d}x)}{\int_0^\infty \exp(x\xi_t - \phi(x)t)p(\mathrm{d}x)}. \tag{6.13}$$

Since the asset price (6.7) is a simple invertible function of ξ_t we are thus in a position to obtain an explicit formula for the jump-risk aversion factor λ_t in terms of the price level S_t in the general setting of a geometric Lévy model. Once λ_t has been determined, the excess rate of return associated with jump risk is given by $R(\lambda_t, \sigma)$. It is perhaps remarkable that the analysis presented in the case of the geometric Brownian model extends so straightforwardly to the case of the general geometric Lévy model, even though the powerful tools of the traditional Ito calculus are not directly applicable in the general Lévy context. This can be viewed as a vindication of the usefulness of pricing kernel methods. Indeed, to grasp the relation between risk, risk aversion, and return, the pricing kernel is an indispensable tool, and this is especially clear when prices can jump, as is in any event typically the case in real financial markets. In particular, since optimal investment strategies depend solely for their specification on the pricing kernel and the risk profile of the investor (as given, for example, by an appropriate utility function), we are led by this reasoning to be able to present a clear account of such strategies in the case of markets with price jumps.

The authors are grateful to I. R. C. Buckley, M. R. Grasselli, E. Mackie, X. Yang, J. P. Zubelli, and participants in the 2012 Research in Options conference in Búzios, Rio de Janeiro, where a preliminary version of this work was presented, for helpful comments.

Appendix A. Conditional distribution of the risk aversion factor

In this appendix, we present the details of the calculation leading to the general expression given by equation (2.9) for the conditional distribution of the risk aversion factor in the case of a filtration generated by a Brownian information process.

We consider a probability space $(\Omega, \mathcal{F}, \mathbb{P})$ on which a Brownian motion $\{B_t\}_{t\geq 0}$ is defined along with an independent square-integrable random variable X, and we assume that $X>0$ almost surely. The filtration $\{\mathcal{F}_t\}$ is taken to be generated by the information process $\{\xi_t\}_{t\geq 0}$ defined by $\xi_t = B_t + Xt$. The conditional distribution of X can be worked out as follows.

First, we note (i) that $\{\xi_t\}$ is a Markov process and (ii) that X is $\mathcal{F}_\infty$-measurable. To establish the Markov property, we note the fact that in the case of Brownian motion the random variables B_t and $B_s/s - B_{s_1}/s_1$ are independent for $t>s>s_1>0$ by virtue of the theory of the Brownian bridge. More generally, if $s>s_1>s_2>s_3>0$, we find that $B_s/s - B_{s_1}/s_1$ and $B_{s_2}/s_2 - B_{s_3}/s_3$ are independent. We observe that for any $k\geq 1$ we have

$$\begin{aligned}\mathbb{P}(\xi_t \leq x \mid \xi_s, \xi_{s_1}, \ldots, \xi_{s_k}) &= \mathbb{P}\left(\xi_t \leq x \,\middle|\, \xi_s, \frac{\xi_s}{s} - \frac{\xi_{s_1}}{s_1}, \ldots, \frac{\xi_{s_{k-1}}}{s_{k-1}} - \frac{\xi_{s_k}}{s_k}\right) \\ &= \mathbb{P}\left(\xi_t \leq x \,\middle|\, \xi_s, \frac{B_s}{s} - \frac{B_{s_1}}{s_1}, \ldots, \frac{B_{s_{k-1}}}{s_{k-1}} - \frac{B_{s_k}}{s_k}\right). \end{aligned} \quad \text{(A 1)}$$

Since ξ_t and ξ_s are independent of $B_s/s - B_{s_1}/s_1, \ldots, B_{s_{k-1}}/s_{k-1} - B_{s_k}/s_k$, it follows that

$$\mathbb{P}(\xi_t \leq x \mid \xi_s, \xi_{s_1}, \ldots, \xi_{s_k}) = \mathbb{P}(\xi_t \leq x \mid \xi_s), \quad \text{(A 2)}$$

and that gives us the Markov property. As regards the $\mathcal{F}_\infty$-measurability, this follows from the fact that $\lim_{t\to\infty} t^{-1}\xi_t = X$. In the calculation of the conditional distribution of X given $\mathcal{F}_t$ it thus suffices to determine the conditional distribution of X given ξ_t. By virtue of the relevant version of the Bayes formula, we have

$$p_t(\mathrm{d}x) = \frac{\rho(\xi_t \mid X=x)p(\mathrm{d}x)}{\int_0^\infty \rho(\xi_t \mid X=x)p(\mathrm{d}x)}, \quad \text{(A 3)}$$

where $p(\mathrm{d}x) = \mathbb{P}(X \in \mathrm{d}x)$ is the *a priori* distribution of X, assumed known, and where for each x the function $\rho(\xi|X=x)$, $\xi \in \mathbb{R}$, is the conditional density for the random variable ξ_t given that $X=x$, which in (A 3) is then valued at $\xi=\xi_t(\omega)$ for each outcome of chance $\omega \in \Omega$. Since B_t is a Gaussian random variable with mean 0 and variance t, we deduce that

$$\rho(\xi \mid X=x) = \frac{1}{\sqrt{2\pi t}} \exp\left(-\frac{(\xi - tx)^2}{2t}\right). \quad \text{(A 4)}$$

Inserting this expression into the Bayes formula (A 3), one is then immediately led to (2.9).

Appendix B. Emergence of the Brownian driver

In the conventional modelling framework (and in the absence of jumps apart from those associated directly with dividend payments) it is usually assumed that the market filtration is generated by a Brownian motion of one or more dimensions, and that the associated asset prices are adapted to this filtration. Although well-established and mathematically sound, from a financial perspective this view of the market is unsatisfactory in various respects. One gets a hint of the nature of the problem when on the one hand (a) the Brownian motion $\{W_t\}$ driving the asset is referred to as 'noise', and on the other hand (b) the sigma field $\mathcal{F}_t = \sigma[\{W_s\}_{0\leq s\leq t}]$ is referred to as 'information'. If one presses a finance theorist on this point, the reply will be a shrug of the shoulders and piece of sophistry of the form, 'Well, it is true that $\{W_t\}$ is noise, but $\mathcal{F}_t$ represents the knowledge of the history of the trajectory of that noise, and therefore carries valuable information'. This point of view, ridiculous as it may seem, permeates the whole subject, and is consequently a source of confusion.

Fortunately, there is a resolution of this seemingly paradoxical issue. Prices are driven by the flow of information, and information is usually communicated along noisy channels. The market accepts this as the normal state of affairs, and prices are based on the best estimates of the relevant factors, given the information available, imperfect as it may be. This is perhaps what Norbert Wiener was getting at when he said that 'Economics is a science of communication' [48].

In this appendix, we present details of the calculations in §4 leading to the emergence of the Brownian driver. Starting with the relation $\xi_t = B_t + Xt$, we define the process $\{W_t\}$ as in (4.2). To prove that $\{W_t\}$ is an $\{\mathcal{F}_t\}$-Brownian motion, it suffices by use of the so-called Lévy criterion to show that $\{W_t\}$ is an $\{\mathcal{F}_t\}$-martingale and that $(\mathrm{d}W_t)^2 = \mathrm{d}t$. First, we shall demonstrate that $\{W_t\}$ is an $\{\mathcal{F}_t\}$-martingale. Letting $t \le T$, we deduce that

$$\begin{aligned}\mathbb{E}[W_T \mid \mathcal{F}_t] &= \mathbb{E}[B_T \mid \mathcal{F}_t] + T\mathbb{E}[X \mid \mathcal{F}_t] - \mathbb{E}\left[\int_0^T \lambda_s \mathrm{d}s \middle| \mathcal{F}_t\right] \\ &= \mathbb{E}[B_T|\mathcal{F}_t] + T\mathbb{E}[X \mid \mathcal{F}_t] - \int_0^T \mathbb{E}[\lambda_s \mid \mathcal{F}_t]\mathrm{d}s, \end{aligned} \tag{B 1}$$

by use of Fubini's theorem. Next, we note that

$$\int_0^T \mathbb{E}[\lambda_s \mid \mathcal{F}_t]\mathrm{d}s = \int_0^t \mathbb{E}[\lambda_s \mid \mathcal{F}_t]\mathrm{d}s + \int_t^T \mathbb{E}[\lambda_s \mid \mathcal{F}_t]\mathrm{d}s = \int_0^t \lambda_s \mathrm{d}s + (T-t)\lambda_t. \tag{B 2}$$

Here, we have used the fact that the process $\{\lambda_t\}$ is by construction an $\{\mathcal{F}_t\}$-martingale. Substituting (B 2) in (B 1), we obtain

$$\mathbb{E}[W_T \mid \mathcal{F}_t] = \mathbb{E}[B_T \mid \mathcal{F}_t] + t\mathbb{E}[X \mid \mathcal{F}_t] - \int_0^t \lambda_s \mathrm{d}s. \tag{B 3}$$

Finally, we observe that by the tower property of conditional expectation we have

$$\mathbb{E}[B_T \mid \mathcal{F}_t] = \mathbb{E}[\mathbb{E}[B_T|\mathcal{F}_t^B, X] \mid \mathcal{F}_t] = \mathbb{E}[B_t \mid \mathcal{F}_t], \tag{B 4}$$

where $\{\mathcal{F}_t^B\}$ denotes the filtration generated by $\{B_t\}$. Inserting this in (B 3), we obtain

$$\begin{aligned}\mathbb{E}[W_T|\mathcal{F}_t] &= \mathbb{E}[B_t|\mathcal{F}_t] + t\lambda_t - \int_0^t \lambda_s \mathrm{d}s \\ &= \mathbb{E}[(B_t + tX)|\mathcal{F}_t] - \int_0^t \lambda_s \mathrm{d}s \\ &= \mathbb{E}[\xi_t|\mathcal{F}_t] - \int_0^t \lambda_s \mathrm{d}s = W_t, \end{aligned} \tag{B 5}$$

and this establishes that $\{W_t\}$ is an $\{\mathcal{F}_t\}$-martingale. Next, we observe that since

$$\mathrm{d}W_t = (X - \lambda_t)\mathrm{d}t + \mathrm{d}B_t, \tag{B 6}$$

it follows at once that $(\mathrm{d}W_t)^2 = \mathrm{d}t$. Taking this result together with the fact that $\{W_t\}$ is an $\{\mathcal{F}_t\}$-martingale, we conclude that $\{W_t\}$ is an $\{\mathcal{F}_t\}$-Brownian motion.

Appendix C. Existence and construction of the hidden variables X and B_t

In this appendix, we present details of the arguments allowing one to establish properties (i), (ii) and (iii) of the constructed versions of the random risk aversion variable X and the associated 'pure noise' process $\{B_t\}$ stated at the end of §4, starting from the formulation of the theory in which all quantities under consideration at the outset are 'financial observables', that is to say, suitably adapted to the market filtration. Let us begin by establishing property (i), the independence of the random variables B_t and X. To this end, it suffices to check that the relation

$$\mathbb{E}[e^{aB_t+bX}]=\mathbb{E}[e^{aB_t}]\,\mathbb{E}[e^{bX}] \tag{C1}$$

holds for all $a,b\in\mathbb{C}^{\mathrm{I}}:=\{w\in\mathbb{C}:\mathrm{Re}\,w=0\}$. Verification that the joint characteristic function factorizes proceeds as follows. By the definitions of B_t and X given at (4.14), we have

$$\mathbb{E}[e^{aB_t+bX}]=\lim_{T\to\infty}\mathbb{E}[e^{a(\xi_t-tT^{-1}\xi_T)+bT^{-1}\xi_T}]. \tag{C2}$$

We shall calculate the expectation in (C2) and show that it factorizes for all T. In this connection, it will be useful to construct a solution to the stochastic differential equation (4.13). We begin with a probability space $(\Omega,\mathcal{F},\mathbb{Q})$ on which we introduce a standard Brownian motion $\{\xi_t\}$. Given the measure $p(\mathrm{d}x)$, which we assume to admit a second moment, one can check that the function $\Phi(\xi,t)$ defined for $\xi,t\geq 0$ by

$$\Phi(\xi,t)=\int_0^\infty \exp\left(x\xi-\frac{1}{2}x^2t\right)p(\mathrm{d}x) \tag{C3}$$

is of class C^2 in ξ and class C^1 in t, and has the space–time harmonic property (Yor [49]),

$$\frac{\partial\Phi}{\partial t}=\frac{1}{2}\frac{\partial^2\Phi}{\partial\xi^2}. \tag{C4}$$

As a consequence, we are able to introduce a process $\{\Phi_t\}$ defined by

$$\Phi_t=\Phi(\xi_t,t)=\int_0^\infty \exp\left(x\xi_t-\frac{1}{2}x^2t\right)p(\mathrm{d}x), \tag{C5}$$

and it is straightforward to verify that $\{\Phi_t\}$ is a martingale under $\mathbb{Q}$ with respect to the filtration $\{\mathcal{F}_t\}$ generated by $\{\xi_t\}$. Applying Ito's lemma, and defining the process $\{\lambda_t\}$ as before by $\lambda_t=\lambda(\xi_t,t)$, where the function $\lambda(\xi,t)$ is given by (4.12), one deduces that $\mathrm{d}\Phi_t=\lambda_t\Phi_t\mathrm{d}\xi_t$, and hence by integration we obtain

$$\int_0^\infty \exp\left(x\xi_t-\frac{1}{2}x^2t\right)p(\mathrm{d}x)=\exp\left(\int_0^t\lambda_s\mathrm{d}\xi_s-\frac{1}{2}\int_0^t\lambda_s^2\mathrm{d}s\right), \tag{C6}$$

which expresses $\{\Phi_t\}$ in the form of an exponential martingale. Since $\{\xi_t\}$ is a $\mathbb{Q}$-Brownian motion, one sees by the use of Girsanov's theorem that the process $\{W_t\}$ defined by

$$W_t=\xi_t-\int_0^t\lambda_s\mathrm{d}s \tag{C7}$$

is a Brownian motion under the measure $\mathbb{P}$ defined by

$$\left.\frac{\mathrm{d}\mathbb{P}}{\mathrm{d}\mathbb{Q}}\right|_{\mathcal{F}_t}=\Phi_t, \tag{C8}$$

and one concludes from (C7) that $\{\xi_t\}$ satisfies the stochastic differential equation (4.13). We see moreover that $\mathbb{Q}$ is the risk-neutral measure. The conditional expectations in the probability measures $\mathbb{P}$ and $\mathbb{Q}$ are related for $0\leq t\leq T$ by the scheme

$$\mathbb{E}_t^{\mathbb{P}}[Y_T]=\frac{1}{\Phi_t}\mathbb{E}_t^{\mathbb{Q}}[\Phi_TY_T]\quad\text{and}\quad\mathbb{E}_t^{\mathbb{Q}}[Y_T]=\Phi_t\mathbb{E}_t^{\mathbb{P}}\left[\frac{1}{\Phi_T}Y_T\right] \tag{C9}$$

for any $\mathcal{F}_T$-measurable random variable Y_T.

Equipped with these results, we proceed to work out the expectation (under $\mathbb{P}$) appearing in (C 2). In particular, we need the relation

$$\mathbb{E}^{\mathbb{P}}[Y_T] = \mathbb{E}^{\mathbb{Q}}[\Phi_T Y_T]. \tag{C 10}$$

We thus observe that

$$\begin{aligned} \mathbb{E}[e^{a(\xi_t - tT^{-1}\xi_T) + bT^{-1}\xi_T}] &= \mathbb{E}^{\mathbb{Q}}\left[\left(\int_0^\infty e^{x\xi_T - \frac{1}{2}x^2 T} p(dx)\right) e^{a(\xi_t - tT^{-1}\xi_T) + bT^{-1}\xi_T}\right] \\ &= \int_0^\infty \mathbb{E}^{\mathbb{Q}}[e^{x\xi_T - \frac{1}{2}x^2 T} e^{a(\xi_t - tT^{-1}\xi_T) + bT^{-1}\xi_T}] p(dx). \end{aligned} \tag{C 11}$$

But since $\{\xi_t\}$ is a Brownian motion under $\mathbb{Q}$, the inner expectation can be worked out by the use of standard techniques from the theory of Brownian motion. The result is

$$\mathbb{E}^{\mathbb{Q}}[e^{x\xi_T - \frac{1}{2}x^2 T} e^{a(\xi_t - tT^{-1}\xi_T) + bT^{-1}\xi_T}] = e^{\frac{1}{2}a^2 t(T-t)T^{-1}} e^{bx + \frac{1}{2}b^2 T^{-1}}, \tag{C 12}$$

from which it follows that

$$\mathbb{E}[e^{a(\xi_t - tT^{-1}\xi_T) + bT^{-1}\xi_T}] = e^{\frac{1}{2}a^2 t(T-t)T^{-1}} \left(\int_0^\infty e^{bx + \frac{1}{2}b^2 T^{-1}} p(dx)\right), \tag{C 13}$$

which exhibits the claimed factorization of the characteristic function for all T. In particular, for large T we obtain

$$\mathbb{E}[e^{aB_t + bX}] = e^{\frac{1}{2}a^2 t} \left(\int_0^\infty e^{bx} p(dx)\right), \tag{C 14}$$

which establishes (C 1), showing that random variables X and B_t defined by (4.14) are independent for all t, which is property (i). It follows further that the distribution of X is given by $p(dx)$, which is property (ii), and that B_t is normally distributed with mean zero and variance t, which gives us part of property (iii). To complete the proof of property (iii), that $\{B_t\}$ is a Brownian motion, we must verify that $\{B_t\}$ has independent increments. It will suffice to demonstrate that

$$\mathbb{E}[e^{aB_t + b(B_u - B_t)}] = \mathbb{E}[e^{aB_t}]\,\mathbb{E}[e^{b(B_u - B_t)}] \tag{C 15}$$

holds for $0 \le t \le u$ and $a, b \in \mathbb{C}^{\mathrm{I}}$. Using the definition of $\{B_t\}$, we can write

$$\mathbb{E}[e^{aB_t + b(B_u - B_t)}] = \mathbb{E}^{\mathbb{Q}}[\Phi_T\, e^{a(\xi_t - tX) + b((\xi_u - uX) - (\xi_t - tX))}], \tag{C 16}$$

where $\Phi_T = \Phi(\xi_T, T)$, and it follows from the definition of X that

$$\mathbb{E}[e^{aB_t + b(B_u - B_t)}] = \lim_{T\to\infty} \mathbb{E}^{\mathbb{Q}}[e^{a(\xi_t - tT^{-1}\xi_T) + b((\xi_u - uT^{-1}\xi_T) - (\xi_t - tT^{-1}\xi_T X))}]. \tag{C 17}$$

In obtaining (C 17), we have used the theory of the Brownian bridge to deduce that ξ_T (and hence Φ_T) is independent of $\xi_t - tT^{-1}\xi_T$ and $\xi_u - uT^{-1}\xi_T$ under $\mathbb{Q}$, and we have used the fact that $\mathbb{E}^{\mathbb{Q}}[\Phi_T] = 1$. One is then left with a calculation involving the expectation of an exponentiated sum of Gaussian random variables, which can be simplified by use of the theory of the Brownian bridge, and for large T we obtain the desired result:

$$\mathbb{E}[e^{aB_t + b(B_u - B_t)}] = e^{\frac{1}{2}a^2 t} e^{\frac{1}{2}b^2(u-t)}. \tag{C 18}$$

The same line of argument applies for any number of increments. Thus, we conclude that $\{B_t\}$ is normally distributed with zero mean and variance t, and has independent increments. Therefore, $\{B_t\}$ is a standard Brownian motion under $\mathbb{P}$.

References

1. Cochrane JH. 2005 *Asset pricing*. Princeton, NJ: Princeton University Press.
2. Brown AA, Rogers LCG. 2012 Diverse beliefs. *Stoch. Int. J. Probab. Stoch. Process.* **84**, 683–703. (doi:10.1080/17442508.2012.656125)
3. Duffie D. 2012 *Dark markets: asset pricing and information transmission in over-the-counter markets*. Princeton, NJ: Princeton University Press.

4. Ziegler A. 2003 *Incomplete information and heterogeneous beliefs in continuous-time finance*. Berlin, Germany: Springer Finance.
5. Björk T, Davis MHA, Landén C. 2010 Optimal investment under partial information. *Math. Methods Oper. Res.* **71**, 371–399. (doi:10.1007/s00186-010-0301-x)
6. Brody DC, Hughston LP, Macrina A. 2007 Beyond hazard rates: a new framework for credit-risk modelling. In *Advances in mathematical finance* (eds MC Fu, RA Jarrow, J-Y Yen, RJ Elliot), pp. 231–257. Basel, Switzerland: Birkhäuser. (doi:10.1007/978-0-8176-4545-8_13)
7. Brody DC, Hughston LP, Macrina A. 2008 Information-based asset pricing. *Int. J. Theor. Appl. Finance* **11**, 107–142. (doi:10.1142/S0219024908004749). Reprinted as chapter 5 in *Finance at fields* (eds MR Grasselli, LP Hughston). Singapore: World Scientific Publishing, 2012.
8. Brody DC, Hughston LP, Macrina A. 2008 Dam rain and cumulative gain. *Proc. R. Soc. A* **464**, 1801–1822. (doi:10.1098/rspa.2007.0273)
9. Brody DC, Hughston LP, Macrina A. 2010 Credit risk, market sentiment and randomly-timed default. In *Stochastic analysis* (ed. D Crisan), pp. 267–280. Berlin, Germany: Springer. (doi:10.1007/978-3-642-15358-7_13)
10. Brody DC, Davis MHA, Friedman RL, Hughston LP. 2009 Informed traders. *Proc. R. Soc. A* **465**, 1103–1122. (doi:10.1098/rspa.2008.0465)
11. Brody DC, Friedman RL. 2009 Information of interest. *Risk* (December issue), 101–106.
12. Filipovic D, Hughston LP, Macrina A. 2012 Conditional density models for asset pricing. *Int. J. Theor. Appl. Finance* **15**, 1250002. (doi:10.1142/S0219024912500021). Reprinted as chapter 7 in *Finance at fields* (eds MR Grasselli, LP Hughston). Singapore: World Scientific Publishing, 2012.
13. Hoyle E. 2010 Information-based models for finance and insurance. PhD thesis, Department of Mathematics, Imperial College London, UK. (http://arxiv.org/abs/1010.0829)
14. Hoyle E, Hughston LP, Macrina A. 2011 Lévy random bridges and the modelling of financial information. *Stoch. Process. Appl.* **121**, 856–884. (doi:10.1016/j.spa.2010.12.003)
15. Hughston LP. Macrina A. 2008 Information, interest, and inflation. In *Advances in mathematics of finance* (ed. L Stettner), Banach Center Publications **83**, 117–138. Warsaw, Poland: Polish Academy of Sciences.
16. Hughston LP, Macrina A. 2012 Pricing fixed-income securities in an information based framework. *Appl. Math. Finance* **19**, 361–379. (doi:10.1080/1350486X.2011.631757)
17. Macrina A. 2006 An information-based framework for asset pricing: x-factor theory and its applications. PhD thesis, King's College London, UK. (http://arxiv.org/abs/0807.2124)
18. Macrina A, Parbhoo PA. 2011 Randomised mixture models for pricing kernels. (http://arxiv.org/abs/1112.2059)
19. Rutkowski M, Yu N. 2007 An extension of the Brody–Hughston–Macrina approach to modeling of defaultable bonds. *Int. J. Theor. Appl. Finance* **10**, 557-589. (doi:10.1142/S0219024907004263)
20. Brody DC, Hughston LP, Mackie E. 2012 General theory of geometric Lévy models for dynamic asset pricing. *Proc. R. Soc. A* **468**, 1778–1798. (doi:10.1098/rspa.2011.0670)
21. Mackie E. 2012 Rational term-structure models and geometric Lévy martingales. PhD thesis, Imperial College Business School, UK.
22. Flesaker B, Hughston LP. 1997 International models for interest rates and foreign exchange. *Net Exposure* **3**, 55–79. Reprinted in *The new interest rate models* (ed. LP Hughston). London, UK: Risk Publications, 2000.
23. Long JB. 1990 The numeraire portfolio. *J. Financ. Econ.* **26**, 29–69. (doi:10.1016/0304-405X(90)90012-O)
24. Shefrin H. 2008 *A behavioral approach to asset pricing*, 2nd edn. Burlington, MA: Academic Press.
25. Shefrin H. 2009 Behaviouralizing finance. *Found. Trends Finance* **4**, 1–184. (doi:10.1561/0500000030)
26. Andruszkiewicz G, Brody DC. 2011 Noise, risk premium, and bubble. (http://arxiv.org/abs/1103.3206)
27. Carr P, Yu J. 2012 Risk, return, and Ross recovery. *J. Derivatives* **20**, 38–59. (doi:10.3905/jod.2012.20.1.038)
28. Ross SA. In press. The recovery theorem. *J. Finance*.
29. Anderson L, Lipton A. 2013 Asymptotics for exponential Lévy processes and their volatility smile: a survey. *Int. J. Theor. Appl. Finance* **16**, 1350001 (doi:10.1142/S0219024913500015)

30. Cont R, Tankov P. 2004 *Financial modelling with jump processes*. London, UK: Chapman & Hall.
31. Kyprianou AE. 2006 *Introductory lectures on fluctuations of Lévy processes with applications*. Berlin, Germany: Springer.
32. Protter P. 1990 *Stochastic integration and differential equations*. New York, NY: Springer.
33. Schoutens W. 2004 *Lévy processes in finance: pricing financial derivatives*. New York, NY: Wiley.
34. Madan D, Seneta E. 1990 The variance gamma (V.G.) model for share market returns. *J. Bus.* **63**, 511–524. (doi:10.1086/296519)
35. Madan D, Milne F. 1991 Option pricing with V.G. martingale components. *Math. Finance* **1**, 39–55. (doi:10.1111/j.1467-9965.1991.tb00018.x)
36. Heston SL. 1993 Invisible parameters in option prices. *J. Finance* **48**, 993–947. (doi:10.1111/j.1540-6261.1993.tb04025.x)
37. Gerber HU, Shiu ESW 1994 Option pricing by Esscher transforms (with discussion). *Trans. Soc. Actuaries* **46**, 99–191.
38. Eberlein E, Keller U. 1995 Hyperbolic distributions in finance. *Bernoulli* **1**, 281–299. (doi:10.2307/3318481)
39. Eberlein E, Jacod J. 1997 On the range of option prices. *Finance Stoch.* **1**, 131–140. (doi:10.1007/s007800050019)
40. Madan D, Carr P, Chang EC. 1998 The variance gamma process and option pricing. *Eur. Finance Rev.* **2**, 79–105. (doi:10.1023/A:1009703431535)
41. Chan T. 1999 Pricing contingent claims on stocks driven by Lévy processes. *Ann. Appl. Probab.* **9**, 504–528. (doi:10.1214/aoap/1029962753)
42. Carr P, Geman H, Madan D, Yor M. 2002 The fine structure of asset returns: an empirical investigation. *J. Bus.* **75**, 305–332. (doi:10.1086/338705)
43. Kallsen J, Shiryaev AN. 2002 The cumulant process and Esscher's change of measure. *Finance Stoch.* **6**, 97–428. (doi:10.1007/s007800200069)
44. Hubalek F, Sgarra C. 2006 On the Esscher transform and entropy for exponential Lévy models. *Quant. Finance* **6**, 125–145. (doi:10.1080/14697680600573099)
45. Baxter M. 2007 Lévy simple structural models. *Int. J. Theor. Appl. Finance* **10**, 593–606. (doi:10.1142/S021902490700438X)
46. Yor M. 2007 Some remarkable properties of gamma processes. In *Advances in mathematical finance* (eds MC Fu, RA Jarrow, J-Y Yen, RJ Elliot), pp. 37–47. Basel, Switzerland: Birkhäuser. (doi:10.1007/978-0-8176-4545-8_3)
47. Brody DC, Hughston LP, Yang X. 2013 Signal processing with Lévy information. *Proc. R. Soc. A* **469**, 20120433. (doi:10.1098/rspa.2012.0433)
48. Jerison D, Stroock DW. 1997 Norbert Wiener. In *The legacy of Norbert Wiener: a centennial symposium* (eds D Jerison, IM Singer, DW Stroock). *Proc. Symp. in Pure Mathematics* **60**, 3–19. Providence, RI: American Mathematical Society.
49. Yor M. 1992 *Some aspects of Brownian motion*. Lectures in Mathematics, ETH Zürich. Basel, Switzerland: Birkhäuser.

rspa.royalsocietypublishing.org Proc R Soc A 469: 20130024

Chapter 11

PROCEEDINGS
OF
THE ROYAL SOCIETY A

rspa.royalsocietypublishing.org

Research

Cite this article: Brody DC, Hughston LP, Yang X. 2012 Signal processing with Lévy information. Proc R Soc A 20120433
http://dx.doi.org/10.1098/rspa.2012.0433

Received: 19 July 2012
Accepted: 20 September 2012

Subject Areas:
applied mathematics, electrical engineering

Keywords:
signal processing, Lévy process, Esscher transformation, nonlinear filtering, information process, cybernetics

Author for correspondence:
Dorje C. Brody
e-mail: dorje.brody@brunel.ac.uk

Signal processing with Lévy information*

Dorje C. Brody[1], Lane P. Hughston[2] and Xun Yang[3,4]

[1]Mathematical Sciences, Brunel University, Uxbridge UB8 3PH, UK
[2]Department of Mathematics, University College London, London WC1E 6BT, UK
[3]Department of Mathematics, Imperial College London, London SW7 2BZ, UK
[4]Shell International Limited, Shell Centre, London SE1 7NA, UK

Lévy processes, which have stationary independent increments, are ideal for modelling the various types of noise that can arise in communication channels. If a Lévy process admits exponential moments, then there exists a parametric family of measure changes called Esscher transformations. If the parameter is replaced with an independent random variable, the true value of which represents a 'message', then under the transformed measure the original Lévy process takes on the character of an 'information process'. In this paper we develop a theory of such Lévy information processes. The underlying Lévy process, which we call the fiducial process, represents the 'noise type'. Each such noise type is capable of carrying a message of a certain specification. A number of examples are worked out in detail, including information processes of the Brownian, Poisson, gamma, variance gamma, negative binomial, inverse Gaussian and normal inverse Gaussian type. Although in general there is no additive decomposition of information into signal and noise, one is led nevertheless for each noise type to a well-defined scheme for signal detection and enhancement relevant to a variety of practical situations.

1. Introduction

The idea of filtering the noise out of a noisy message as a way of increasing its information content is illustrated by Norbert Wiener in his book *Cybernetics* [1] by means of the following example. The true message is represented by a variable X which has a known probability distribution. An agent wishes to determine as best as possible the value of X, but owing to the presence of noise the agent can only observe a noisy

*This chapter was originally published as: D. C. Brody, L. P. Hughston & X. Yang (2013) Signal Processing with Lévy Information. *Proceedings of the Royal Society A* **469**, 20120433:1–23. Reprinted with kind permission from The Royal Society.

version of the message of the form $\xi = X + \epsilon$, where ϵ is independent of X. Wiener shows how, given the observed value of the noisy message ξ, the original distribution of X can be transformed into an improved *a posteriori* distribution that has a higher information content. The *a posteriori* distribution can then be used to determine a best estimate for the value of X.

The theory of filtering was developed in the 1940s when the inefficiency of anti-aircraft fire made it imperative to introduce effective filtering-based devices [2,3]. A breakthrough came with the work of Kalman, who reformulated the theory in a manner more well-suited for dynamical state-estimation problems [4,5]. This period coincided with the emergence of the modern control theory of Bellman & Pontryagin [6,7]. Owing to the importance of its applications, much work has been carried out since then. According to an estimate of Kalman [8], over 200 000 articles and monographs have been published on applications of the Kalman filter alone. The theory of stochastic filtering, in its modern form, is not much different conceptually from the elementary example described by Wiener in the 1940s. The message, instead of being represented by a single variable, in the general setup can take the form of a time series (the 'signal' or 'message' process). The information made available to the agent also takes the form of a time series (the 'observation' or 'information' process), typically given by the sum of two terms, the first being a functional of the signal process, and the second being a noise process. The nature of the signal process can be rather general, but in most applications the noise is chosen to be a Wiener process [9–11]. There is no reason, however, why an information process should necessarily be 'additive', or even why it should be given as a functional of a signal process and a noise process. From a mathematical perspective, it seems that the often proposed ansatz of an additive decomposition of the observation process is well adapted to the situation where the noise is Gaussian, but is not so natural when the noise is discontinuous. Thus, while a good deal of recent research has been carried out on the problem of filtering noisy information containing jumps [12–17] such work has usually been pursued under the assumption of an additive relation between signal and noise, and it is not unreasonable to ask whether a more systematic treatment of the problem might be available that involves no presumption of additivity and that is more naturally adapted to the mathematics of the situation.

The purpose of the present paper is to introduce a broad class of information processes suitable for modelling situations involving discontinuous signals, discontinuous noise and discontinuous information. No assumption is made to the effect that information can be expressed as a function of signal and noise. Instead, information processes are classified according to their 'noise type'. Information processes of the same noise type are then distinguished from one another by the messages that they carry. Each noise type is associated to a Lévy process, which we call the *fiducial process*. The fiducial process is the information process that results for a given noise type in the case of a null message, and can be thought of as a 'pure noise' process of that noise type. Information processes can then be classified by the characteristics of the associated fiducial processes. To keep the discussion elementary, we consider the case of a one-dimensional fiducial process and examine the situation where the message is represented by a single random variable. The goal is to construct the optimal filter for the class of information processes that we consider in the form of a map that takes the *a priori* distribution of the message to an *a posteriori* distribution that depends on the information that has been made available. A number of examples will be presented. The results vary remarkably in detail and character for the different types of filters considered, and yet there is an overriding unity in the general scheme, which allows for the construction of a multitude of examples and applications.

A synopsis of the main ideas, which we develop more fully in the remainder of the paper, can be presented as follows. We recall the idea of the Esscher transform as a change of probability measure on a probability space $(\Omega, \mathcal{F}, \mathbb{P}_0)$ that supports a Lévy process $\{\xi_t\}_{t\geq 0}$ that possesses $\mathbb{P}_0$-exponential moments. The space of admissible moments is the set $A = \{w \in \mathbb{R} : \mathbb{E}^{\mathbb{P}_0}[\exp(w\xi_t)] < \infty\}$. The associated Lévy exponent $\psi(\alpha) = t^{-1} \ln \mathbb{E}^{\mathbb{P}_0}[\exp(\alpha\xi_t)]$ then exists for all $\alpha \in A_{\mathbb{C}} := \{w \in \mathbb{C} : \mathrm{Re}\, w \in A\}$, and does not depend on t. A parametric family of measure changes $\mathbb{P}_0 \to \mathbb{P}_\lambda$ commonly called Esscher transformations can be constructed by use of the exponential martingale family $\{\rho_t^\lambda\}_{t\geq 0}$, defined for each $\lambda \in A$ by $\rho_t^\lambda = \exp(\lambda\xi_t - \psi(\lambda)t)$. If

$\{\xi_t\}$ is a $\mathbb{P}_0$-Brownian motion, then $\{\xi_t\}$ is $\mathbb{P}_\lambda$-Brownian with drift λ; if $\{\xi_t\}$ is a $\mathbb{P}_0$-Poisson process with intensity m, then $\{\xi_t\}$ is $\mathbb{P}_\lambda$-Poisson with intensity $e^\lambda m$; if $\{\xi_t\}$ is a $\mathbb{P}_0$-gamma process with rate parameter m and scale parameter κ, then $\{\xi_t\}$ is $\mathbb{P}_\lambda$-gamma with rate parameter m and scale parameter $\kappa/(1-\lambda)$. Each case is different in character. A natural generalization of the Esscher transform results when the parameter λ in the measure change is replaced by a random variable X. From the perspective of the new measure $\mathbb{P}_X$, the process $\{\xi_t\}$ retains the 'noisy' character of its $\mathbb{P}_0$-Lévy origin, but also carries information about X. In particular, if one assumes that X and $\{\xi_t\}$ are $\mathbb{P}_0$-independent, and that the support of X lies in A, then we say that $\{\xi_t\}$ defines a *Lévy information process* under $\mathbb{P}_X$ carrying the message X. Thus, the change of measure inextricably intertwines signal and noise. More abstractly, we say that on a probability space $(\Omega,\mathcal{F},\mathbb{P})$ a random process $\{\xi_t\}$ is a Lévy information process with message (or 'signal') X and noise type (or 'fiducial exponent') $\psi_0(\alpha)$ if $\{\xi_t\}$ is *conditionally* $\mathbb{P}$-Lévy given X, with Lévy exponent $\psi_0(\alpha+X)-\psi_0(X)$ for $\alpha\in\mathbb{C}^{\mathrm{I}}:=\{w\in\mathbb{C}:\mathrm{Re}\,w=0\}$. We are thus able to classify Lévy information processes by their noise type, and for each noise type we can specify the class of random variables that are admissible as signals that can be carried in the environment of such noise. We consider a number of different noise types, and construct explicit representations of the associated information processes. We also derive an expression for the optimal filter in the general situation, which transforms the *a priori* distribution of the signal to the improved *a posteriori* distribution that can be inferred on the basis of received information.

The plan of the paper is as follows. In §2, after recalling some facts about processes with stationary and independent increments, we define Lévy information, and in proposition 2.2 we show that the signal carried by a Lévy information process is effectively 'revealed' after the passage of sufficient time. In §3, we present in proposition 3.1 an explicit construction using a change of measure technique that ensures the existence of Lévy information processes, and in proposition 3.2 we prove a converse to the effect that any Lévy information process can be obtained in this way. In proposition 3.3 we construct the optimal filter for general Lévy information processes, and in proposition 3.4 we show that such processes have the Markov property. In proposition 3.5 we establish a result that indicates in more detail how the information content of the signal is coded into the structure of an information process. Then in proposition 3.6 we present a general construction of the so-called innovations process associated with Lévy information. Finally, in §4, we proceed to examine a number of specific examples of Lévy information processes, for which explicit representations are constructed in propositions 4.1–4.8.

2. Lévy information

We assume that the reader is familiar with the theory of Lévy processes [18–23]. For an overview of some of the specific Lévy processes considered later in this paper, we refer the reader to [24]. A real-valued process $\{\xi_t\}_{t\ge 0}$ on a probability space $(\Omega,\mathcal{F},\mathbb{P})$ is a Lévy process if: (i) $\mathbb{P}(\xi_0=0)=1$, (ii) $\{\xi_t\}$ has stationary and independent increments, (iii) $\lim_{t\to s}\mathbb{P}(|\xi_t-\xi_s|>\epsilon)=0$, and (iv) $\{\xi_t\}$ is almost surely càdlàg. For a Lévy process $\{\xi_t\}$ to give rise to a class of information processes, we require that it should possess exponential moments. Let us consider the set defined for some (equivalently for all) $t>0$ by

$$A=\{w\in\mathbb{R}:\mathbb{E}^{\mathbb{P}}[\exp(w\xi_t)]<\infty\}. \tag{2.1}$$

If A contains points other than $w=0$, then we say that $\{\xi_t\}$ possesses exponential moments. We define a function $\psi:A\to\mathbb{R}$ called the Lévy exponent (or cumulant function), such that

$$\mathbb{E}^{\mathbb{P}}[\exp(\alpha\xi_t)]=\exp(\psi(\alpha)t) \tag{2.2}$$

for $\alpha\in A$. If a Lévy process possesses exponential moments, then an exercise shows that $\psi(\alpha)$ is convex on A, that the mean and variance of ξ_t are given, respectively, by $\psi'(0)\,t$ and $\psi''(0)\,t$, and that as a consequence of the convexity of $\psi(\alpha)$ the marginal exponent $\psi'(\alpha)$ possesses a unique inverse $I(y)$ such that $I(\psi'(\alpha))=\alpha$ for $\alpha\in A$. The Lévy exponent extends to a function

$\psi : A_{\mathbb{C}} \to \mathbb{C}$ where $A_{\mathbb{C}} = \{w \in \mathbb{C} : \mathrm{Re}\, w \in A\}$, and it can be shown [19, Theorem 25.17] that $\psi(\alpha)$ admits a Lévy–Khintchine representation of the form

$$\psi(\alpha) = p\alpha + \frac{1}{2}q\alpha^2 + \int_{\mathbb{R}\backslash\{0\}} (e^{\alpha z} - 1 - \alpha z \mathbb{1}\{|z| < 1\})\nu(dz) \tag{2.3}$$

with the property that (2.2) holds for all $\alpha \in A_{\mathbb{C}}$. Here, $\mathbb{1}\{\cdot\}$ denotes the indicator function, $p \in \mathbb{R}$ and $q \geq 0$ are constants, and the so-called Lévy measure $\nu(dz)$ is a positive measure defined on $\mathbb{R}\backslash\{0\}$ satisfying

$$\int_{\mathbb{R}\backslash\{0\}} (1 \wedge z^2)\nu(dz) < \infty. \tag{2.4}$$

If the Lévy process possesses exponential moments, then for $\alpha \in A$ we also have

$$\int_{\mathbb{R}\backslash\{0\}} e^{\alpha z}\mathbb{1}\{|z| \geq 1\}\nu(dz) < \infty. \tag{2.5}$$

The Lévy measure has the following interpretation: if B is a measurable subset of $\mathbb{R}\backslash\{0\}$, then $\nu(B)$ is the rate at which jumps arrive for which the jump size lies in B. Consider the sets defined for $n \in \mathbb{N}$ by $B_n = \{z \in \mathbb{R} : 1/n \leq |z| \leq 1\}$. If $\nu(B_n)$ tends to infinity for large n, we say that $\{\xi_t\}$ is a process of infinite activity, meaning that the rate of arrival of small jumps is unbounded. If $\nu(\mathbb{R}\backslash\{0\}) < \infty$, one says that $\{\xi_t\}$ has finite activity. We refer to the data $K = (p, q, \nu)$ as the characteristic triplet (or 'characteristic') of the associated Lévy process. Thus, we can classify a Lévy process abstractly by its characteristic K, or equivalently its exponent $\psi(\alpha)$. This means that one can speak of a 'type' of Lévy noise by reference to the associated characteristic or exponent.

Now suppose we fix a measure $\mathbb{P}_0$ on a measurable space $(\Omega, \mathcal{F})$, and let $\{\xi_t\}$ be $\mathbb{P}_0$-Lévy, with exponent $\psi_0(\alpha)$. There exists a parametric family of probability measures $\{\mathbb{P}_\lambda\}_{\lambda \in A}$ on $(\Omega, \mathcal{F})$ such that for each choice of λ the process $\{\xi_t\}$ is $\mathbb{P}_\lambda$-Lévy. The changes of measure arising in this way are called Esscher transformations [25–29]. Under an Esscher transformation, the characteristics of a Lévy process are transformed from one type to another, and one can speak of a family of Lévy processes interrelated by Esscher transformations. The relevant change of measure can be specified by use of the process $\{\rho_t^\lambda\}$ defined for $\lambda \in A$ by

$$\rho_t^\lambda := \left.\frac{d\mathbb{P}_\lambda}{d\mathbb{P}_0}\right|_{\mathcal{F}_t} = \exp(\lambda\xi_t - \psi_0(\lambda)t), \tag{2.6}$$

where $\mathcal{F}_t = \sigma[\{\xi_s\}_{0 \leq s \leq t}]$. One can check that $\{\rho_t^\lambda\}$ is an $(\{\mathcal{F}_t\}, \mathbb{P}_0)$-martingale: indeed, as a consequence of the fact that $\{\xi_t\}$ has stationary and independent increments, we have

$$\mathbb{E}_s^{\mathbb{P}_0}[\rho_t^\lambda] = \mathbb{E}_s^{\mathbb{P}_0}[e^{\lambda(\xi_t - \xi_s)}]\, e^{\lambda\xi_s - t\psi_0(\lambda)} = \rho_s^\lambda \tag{2.7}$$

for $s \leq t$, where $\mathbb{E}_t^{\mathbb{P}_0}[\cdot]$ denotes conditional expectation under $\mathbb{P}_0$ with respect to $\mathcal{F}_t$. It is straightforward to show that $\{\xi_t\}$ has $\mathbb{P}_\lambda$-stationary and independent increments, and that the $\mathbb{P}_\lambda$-exponent of $\{\xi_t\}$, which is defined on the set $A_{\mathbb{C}}^\lambda := \{w \in \mathbb{C} : \mathrm{Re}\, w + \lambda \in A\}$, is given by

$$\psi_\lambda(\alpha) := t^{-1} \ln \mathbb{E}^{\mathbb{P}_\lambda}[\exp(\alpha\xi_t)] = \psi_0(\alpha + \lambda) - \psi_0(\lambda), \tag{2.8}$$

from which by use of the Lévy–Khintchine representation (2.3) one can work out the characteristic triplet K_λ of $\{\xi_t\}$ under $\mathbb{P}_\lambda$. We observe that if the Esscher martingale (2.6) is expanded as a power series in λ, then the resulting coefficients, which are given by polynomials in ξ_t and t, form a so-called Sheffer set [30], each element of which defines an $(\{\mathcal{F}_t\}, \mathbb{P}_0)$-martingale. The first three of these polynomials take the form $Q^1(x,t) = x - \psi' t$, $Q^2(x,t) = \frac{1}{2}[(x - \psi' t)^2 - \psi'' t]$, and $Q^3(x,t) = \frac{1}{6}[(x - \psi' t)^3 - 3\psi'' t(x - \psi' t) - \psi''' t]$, where $\psi' = \psi_0'(0)$, $\psi'' = \psi_0''(0)$, and $\psi''' = \psi_0'''(0)$. The corresponding polynomial Lévy–Sheffer martingales are given by $Q_t^1 = Q^1(\xi_t, t)$, $Q_t^2 = Q^2(\xi_t, t)$, and $Q_t^3 = Q^3(\xi_t, t)$.

In what follows, we use the terms 'signal' and 'message' interchangeably. We write $\mathbb{C}^{\mathrm{I}} = \{w \in \mathbb{C} : \mathrm{Re}\, w = 0\}$. For any random variable Z on $(\Omega, \mathcal{F}, \mathbb{P})$, we write $\mathcal{F}^Z = \sigma[Z]$, and when it is convenient we write $\mathbb{E}^{\mathbb{P}}[\cdot|Z]$ for $\mathbb{E}^{\mathbb{P}}[\cdot|\mathcal{F}^Z]$. For processes, we use both of the notations $\{Z_t\}$ and $\{Z(t)\}$, depending on the context.

With these background remarks in mind, we are in a position to define a *Lévy information process*. We confine the discussion to the case of a 'simple' message, represented by a random variable X. In the situation when the noise is Brownian motion, the information admits a linear decomposition into signal and noise. In the general situation, the relation between signal and noise is more subtle, and has the character of a fibre space, where one thinks of the points of the base space as representing the different noise types, and the points of the fibres as corresponding to the different information processes that one can construct in association with a given noise type. Alternatively, one can think of the base as being the convex space of Lévy characteristics, and the fibre over a given point of the base as the convex space of messages that are compatible with the associated noise type.

We fix a probability space $(\Omega, \mathcal{F}, \mathbb{P})$, and an Esscher family of Lévy characteristics K_λ, $\lambda \in A$, with associated Lévy exponents $\psi_\lambda(\alpha)$, $\alpha \in A_{\mathbb{C}}^{\lambda}$. We refer to K_0 as the fiducial characteristic, and $\psi_0(\alpha)$ as the fiducial exponent. The intuition here is that the abstract Lévy process of characteristic K_0 and exponent $\psi_0(\alpha)$, which we call the 'fiducial' process, represents the noise type of the associated information process. Thus, we can use K_0, or equivalently $\psi_0(\alpha)$, to label the noise type.

Definition 2.1. By a Lévy information process with fiducial characteristic K_0, carrying the message X, we mean a random process $\{\xi_t\}$, together with a random variable X, such that $\{\xi_t\}$ is conditionally K_X-Lévy given $\mathcal{F}^X$.

Thus, given $\mathcal{F}^X$, we require $\{\xi_t\}$ to have conditionally independent and stationary increments under $\mathbb{P}$, and to possess a conditional exponent of the form

$$\psi_X(\alpha) := t^{-1} \ln \mathbb{E}^{\mathbb{P}}[\exp(\alpha \xi_t) | \mathcal{F}^X] = \psi_0(\alpha + X) - \psi_0(X) \tag{2.9}$$

for $\alpha \in \mathbb{C}^{\mathrm{I}}$, where $\psi_0(\alpha)$ is the fiducial exponent of the specified noise type. It is implicit in the statement of definition 2.1 that a certain compatibility condition holds between the message and the noise type. For any random variable X, we define its support S_X to be the smallest closed set F with the property that $\mathbb{P}(X \in F) = 1$. Then we say that X is compatible with the fiducial exponent $\psi_0(\alpha)$ if $S_X \subset A$. Intuitively speaking, the compatibility condition ensures that we can use X to make a random Esscher transformation. In the theory of signal processing, it is advantageous to require that the variables to be estimated should be square integrable. This condition ensures that the conditional expectation exists and admits the interpretation as a best estimate in the sense of least squares. For our purpose, it will suffice to assume throughout the paper that the information process is square integrable under $\mathbb{P}$. This in turn implies that $\psi'(X)$ is square integrable, and that $\psi''(X)$ is integrable. Note that we do not require that the Lévy information process should possess exponential moments under $\mathbb{P}$, but a sufficient condition for this to be the case is that there should exist a nonvanishing real number ϵ such that $\lambda + \epsilon \in A$ for all $\lambda \in S_X$.

To gain a better understanding of the sense in which the information process $\{\xi_t\}$ actually 'carries' the message X, it will be useful to investigate its asymptotic behaviour. We write $I_0(y)$ for the inverse marginal fiducial exponent.

Proposition 2.2. *Let $\{\xi_t\}$ be a Lévy information process with fiducial exponent $\psi_0(\alpha)$ and message X. Then for every $\epsilon > 0$ we have*

$$\lim_{t \to \infty} \mathbb{P}[|I_0(t^{-1}\xi_t) - X| \geq \epsilon] = 0. \tag{2.10}$$

Proof. It follows from (2.9) that $\psi_X'(0) = \psi_0'(X)$, and hence that at any time t the conditional mean of the random variable $t^{-1}\xi_t$ is given by

$$\mathbb{E}^{\mathbb{P}}[t^{-1}\xi_t | \mathcal{F}^X] = \psi_0'(X). \tag{2.11}$$

A calculation then shows that the conditional variance of $t^{-1}\xi_t$ takes the form

$$\mathrm{Var}^{\mathbb{P}}[t^{-1}\xi_t | \mathcal{F}^X] := \mathbb{E}^{\mathbb{P}}[(t^{-1}\xi_t - \psi_0'(X))^2 | \mathcal{F}^X] = \frac{1}{t}\, \psi_0''(X), \tag{2.12}$$

which allows us to conclude that

$$\mathbb{E}^{\mathbb{P}}[(t^{-1}\xi_t - \psi_0'(X))^2] = \frac{1}{t}\, \mathbb{E}^{\mathbb{P}}[\psi_0''(X)], \tag{2.13}$$

and hence that

$$\lim_{t\to\infty} \mathbb{E}^{\mathbb{P}}[(t^{-1}\xi_t - \psi_0'(X))^2] = 0. \tag{2.14}$$

On the other hand, for all $\epsilon > 0$ we have

$$\mathbb{P}[|t^{-1}\xi_t - \psi_0'(X)| \geq \epsilon] \leq \frac{1}{\epsilon^2}\mathbb{E}^{\mathbb{P}}[(t^{-1}\xi_t - \psi_0'(X))^2] \tag{2.15}$$

by Chebychev's inequality, from which we deduce that

$$\lim_{t\to\infty} \mathbb{P}[|t^{-1}\xi_t - \psi_0'(X)| \geq \epsilon] = 0, \tag{2.16}$$

and it follows that $I_0(t^{-1}\xi_t)$ converges to X in probability. ■

Thus, we see that the information process does indeed carry information about the message, and in the long run 'reveals' it. The intuition here is that as more information is gained, we improve our estimate of X to the point that the value of X eventually becomes known with near certainty.

3. Properties of Lévy information

It will be useful if we present a construction that ensures the existence of Lévy information processes. First, we select a noise type by specification of a fiducial characteristic K_0. Next, we introduce a probability space $(\Omega, \mathcal{F}, \mathbb{P}_0)$ that supports the existence of a $\mathbb{P}_0$-Lévy process $\{\xi_t\}$ with the given fiducial characteristic, together with an independent random variable X that is compatible with K_0.

Write $\{\mathcal{F}_t\}$ for the filtration generated by $\{\xi_t\}$, and $\{\mathcal{G}_t\}$ for the filtration generated by $\{\xi_t\}$ and X jointly: $\mathcal{G}_t = \sigma[\{\xi_s\}_{0\leq s\leq t}, X]$. Let $\psi_0(\alpha)$ be the fiducial exponent associated with K_0. One can check that the process $\{\rho_t^X\}$ defined by

$$\rho_t^X = \exp(X\xi_t - \psi_0(X)t) \tag{3.1}$$

is a $(\{\mathcal{G}_t\}, \mathbb{P}_0)$-martingale. We are thus able to introduce a change of measure $\mathbb{P}_0 \to \mathbb{P}_X$ on $(\Omega, \mathcal{F}, \mathbb{P}_0)$ by setting

$$\left.\frac{\mathrm{d}\mathbb{P}_X}{\mathrm{d}\mathbb{P}_0}\right|_{\mathcal{G}_t} = \rho_t^X. \tag{3.2}$$

It should be evident that $\{\xi_t\}$ is conditionally $\mathbb{P}_X$-Lévy given $\mathcal{F}^X$, since for fixed X the measure change is an Esscher transformation. In particular, a calculation shows that the conditional exponent of ξ_t under $\mathbb{P}_X$ is given by

$$t^{-1}\ln \mathbb{E}^{\mathbb{P}_X}\left[\exp(\alpha\xi_t)|\mathcal{F}^X\right] = \psi_0(\alpha + X) - \psi_0(X) \tag{3.3}$$

for $\alpha \in \mathbb{C}^{\mathrm{I}}$, which shows that the conditions of definition 2.1 are satisfied, allowing us to conclude the following:

Proposition 3.1. *The $\mathbb{P}_0$-Lévy process $\{\xi_t\}$ is a $\mathbb{P}_X$-Lévy information process, with message X and noise type $\psi_0(\alpha)$.*

In fact, the converse also holds: if we are given a Lévy information process, then by a change of measure we can find a Lévy process and an independent 'message' variable. Here follows a more precise statement.

Proposition 3.2. *Let $\{\xi_t\}$ be a Lévy information process on a probability space $(\Omega, \mathcal{F}, \mathbb{P})$ with message X and noise type $\psi_0(\alpha)$. Then there exists a change of measure $\mathbb{P} \to \mathbb{P}_0$ such that $\{\xi_t\}$ and X are $\mathbb{P}_0$-independent, $\{\xi_t\}$ is $\mathbb{P}_0$-Lévy with exponent $\psi_0(\alpha)$, and the probability law of X under $\mathbb{P}_0$ is the same as probability law of X under $\mathbb{P}$.*

Proof. First, we establish that the process $\{\tilde{\rho}_t^X\}$ defined by $\tilde{\rho}_t^X = \exp(-X\xi_t + \psi_0(X)t)$ is a $(\{\mathcal{G}_t\}, \mathbb{P})$-martingale. We have

$$\begin{aligned}\mathbb{E}^{\mathbb{P}}[\tilde{\rho}_t^X|\mathcal{G}_s] &= \mathbb{E}^{\mathbb{P}}[\exp(-X\xi_t + \psi_0(X)t)|\mathcal{G}_s] \\ &= \mathbb{E}^{\mathbb{P}}[\exp(-X(\xi_t - \xi_s))|\mathcal{G}_s]\exp(-X\xi_s + \psi_0(X)t) \\ &= \exp(\psi_X(-X)(t-s))\exp(-X\xi_s + \psi_0(X)t) \end{aligned} \tag{3.4}$$

by virtue of the fact that $\{\xi_t\}$ is $\mathcal{F}^X$-conditionally Lévy under $\mathbb{P}$. By use of (2.9), we deduce that $\psi_X(-X) = -\psi_0(X)$, and hence that $\mathbb{E}^{\mathbb{P}}[\tilde{\rho}_t^X|\mathcal{G}_s] = \tilde{\rho}_s^X$, as required. Then we use $\{\tilde{\rho}_t^X\}$ to define a change of measure $\mathbb{P} \to \mathbb{P}_0$ on $(\Omega, \mathcal{F}, \mathbb{P})$ by setting

$$\left.\frac{\mathrm{d}\mathbb{P}_0}{\mathrm{d}\mathbb{P}}\right|_{\mathcal{G}_t} = \tilde{\rho}_t^X. \tag{3.5}$$

To show that ξ_t and X are $\mathbb{P}_0$-independent for all t, it suffices to show that their joint characteristic function under $\mathbb{P}_0$ factorizes. Letting $\alpha, \beta \in \mathbb{C}^{\mathrm{I}}$, we have

$$\begin{aligned}\mathbb{E}^{\mathbb{P}_0}[\exp(\alpha\xi_t + \beta X)] &= \mathbb{E}^{\mathbb{P}}[\exp(-X\xi_t + \psi_0(X)t)\exp(\alpha\xi_t + \beta X)] \\ &= \mathbb{E}^{\mathbb{P}}[\mathbb{E}^{\mathbb{P}}[\exp((-X+\alpha)\xi_t + \psi_0(X)t + \beta X)|\mathcal{F}^X]] \\ &= \mathbb{E}^{\mathbb{P}}[\exp(\psi_X(-X+\alpha)t + \psi_0(X)t + \beta X)] \\ &= \exp(\psi_0(\alpha)t)\mathbb{E}^{\mathbb{P}}[\exp(\beta X)], \end{aligned} \tag{3.6}$$

where the last step follows from (2.9). This argument can be extended to show that $\{\xi_t\}$ and X are $\mathbb{P}_0$-independent. Next we observe that

$$\begin{aligned}\mathbb{E}^{\mathbb{P}_0}[\exp(\alpha(\xi_u - \xi_t) + \beta\xi_t)] &= \mathbb{E}^{\mathbb{P}}[\exp(-X\xi_u + \psi_0(X)u + \alpha(\xi_u - \xi_t) + \beta\xi_t)] \\ &= \mathbb{E}^{\mathbb{P}}[\mathbb{E}^{\mathbb{P}}[\exp(-X\xi_u + \psi_0(X)u + \alpha(\xi_u - \xi_t) + \beta\xi_t)\,|\mathcal{F}^X]] \\ &= \mathbb{E}^{\mathbb{P}}[\mathbb{E}^{\mathbb{P}}[\exp(\psi_0(X)u + (\alpha - X)(\xi_u - \xi_t) + (\beta - X)\xi_t)\,|\mathcal{F}^X]] \\ &= \mathbb{E}^{\mathbb{P}}[\exp(\psi_0(X)u + \psi_X(\alpha - X)(u-t) + \psi_X(\beta - X)t)] \\ &= \exp(\psi_0(\alpha)(u-t))\exp(\psi_0(\beta)t) \end{aligned} \tag{3.7}$$

for $u \geq t \geq 0$, and it follows that $\xi_u - \xi_t$ and ξ_t are independent. This argument can be extended to show that $\{\xi_t\}$ has $\mathbb{P}_0$-independent increments. Finally, if we set $\alpha = 0$ in (3.6), it follows that the probability laws of X under $\mathbb{P}_0$ and $\mathbb{P}$ are identical; if we set $\beta = 0$ in (3.6), it follows that the $\mathbb{P}_0$ exponent of $\{\xi_t\}$ is $\psi_0(\alpha)$; and if we set $\beta = 0$ in (3.7), it follows that $\{\xi_t\}$ is $\mathbb{P}_0$-stationary. ■

Going forward, we adopt the convention that $\mathbb{P}$ always denotes the 'physical' measure in relation to which an information process with message X is defined, and that $\mathbb{P}_0$ denotes the transformed measure with respect to which the information process and the message decouple. Therefore, henceforth we write $\mathbb{P}$ rather than $\mathbb{P}_X$. In addition to establishing the existence of Lévy information processes, the results of proposition 3.2 provide useful tools for calculations, allowing us to work out properties of information processes by referring the calculations back to $\mathbb{P}_0$. We consider as an example the problem of working out the $\mathcal{F}_t$-conditional expectation under $\mathbb{P}$ of a $\mathcal{G}_t$-measurable integrable random variable Z. The $\mathbb{P}$-expectation of Z can be written in terms of $\mathbb{P}_0$-expectations, and is given by a 'generalized Bayes formula' [31] of the form

$$\mathbb{E}^{\mathbb{P}}[Z|\mathcal{F}_t] = \frac{\mathbb{E}^{\mathbb{P}_0}[\rho_t^X Z|\mathcal{F}_t]}{\mathbb{E}^{\mathbb{P}_0}[\rho_t^X|\mathcal{F}_t]}. \tag{3.8}$$

This formula can be used to obtain the $\mathcal{F}_t$-conditional probability distribution function for X, defined for $y \in \mathbb{R}$ by

$$F_t^X(y) = \mathbb{P}(X \leq y|\mathcal{F}_t). \tag{3.9}$$

In the Bayes formula, we set $Z = \mathbb{1}\{X \le y\}$, and the result is

$$F_t^X(y) = \frac{\int \mathbb{1}\{x \le y\} \exp(x\xi_t - \psi_0(x)t)\, \mathrm{d}F^X(x)}{\int \exp(x\xi_t - \psi_0(x)t)\, \mathrm{d}F^X(x)}, \tag{3.10}$$

where $F^X(y) = \mathbb{P}(X < y)$ is the *a priori* distribution function. It is useful for some purposes to work directly with the conditional probability measure $\pi_t(\mathrm{d}x)$ induced on $\mathbb{R}$ defined by $\mathrm{d}F_t^X(x) = \pi_t(\mathrm{d}x)$. In particular, when X is a continuous random variable with a density function $p(x)$, one can write $\pi_t(\mathrm{d}x) = p_t(x)\mathrm{d}x$, where $p_t(x)$ is the conditional density function.

Proposition 3.3. *Let $\{\xi_t\}$ be a Lévy information process under $\mathbb{P}$ with noise type $\psi_0(\alpha)$, and let the* a priori *distribution of the associated message X be $\pi(\mathrm{d}x)$. Then the $\mathcal{F}_t$-conditional* a posteriori *distribution of X is*

$$\pi_t(dx) = \frac{\exp(x\xi_t - \psi_0(x)t)}{\int \exp(x\xi_t - \psi_0(x)t)\pi(\mathrm{d}x)}\, \pi(\mathrm{d}x). \tag{3.11}$$

It is straightforward to establish by use of a variational argument that for any function $f:\mathbb{R} \to \mathbb{R}$ such that the random variable $Y = f(X)$ is square integrable, the best estimate for Y conditional on the information $\mathcal{F}_t$ is given by

$$\hat{Y}_t := \mathbb{E}^{\mathbb{P}}[Y|\mathcal{F}_t] = \int f(x)\pi_t(\mathrm{d}x). \tag{3.12}$$

By the 'best estimate' for Y, we mean the $\mathcal{F}_t$-measurable random variable $\hat{Y}_t$ that minimizes the quadratic error $\mathbb{E}^{\mathbb{P}}[(Y - \hat{Y}_t)^2|\mathcal{F}_t]$.

It will be observed that at any given time t the best estimate can be expressed as a function of ξ_t and t, and does not involve values of the information process at times earlier than t. That this should be the case can be seen as a consequence of the following:

Proposition 3.4. *The Lévy information process $\{\xi_t\}$ has the Markov property.*

Proof. For the Markov property, it suffices to establish that for $a \in \mathbb{R}$ we have

$$\mathbb{P}(\xi_t \le a|\mathcal{F}_s) = \mathbb{P}(\xi_t \le a|\mathcal{F}^{\xi_s}), \tag{3.13}$$

where $\mathcal{F}_t = \sigma[\{\xi_s\}_{0\le s\le t}]$ and $\mathcal{F}^{\xi_t} = \sigma[\,\xi_t\,]$. We write

$$\Phi_t := \mathbb{E}^{\mathbb{P}_0}[\rho_t^X|\mathcal{F}_t] = \int \exp(x\xi_t - \psi_0(x)t)\pi(\mathrm{d}x), \tag{3.14}$$

where ρ_t^X is defined as in equation (3.1). It follows that

$$\begin{aligned}\mathbb{P}(\xi_t \le a|\mathcal{F}_s) = \mathbb{E}^{\mathbb{P}}[\mathbb{1}\{\xi_t \le a\}|\mathcal{F}_s] &= \frac{\mathbb{E}^{\mathbb{P}_0}[\Phi_t \mathbb{1}\{\xi_t \le a\}|\mathcal{F}_s]}{\mathbb{E}^{\mathbb{P}_0}[\Phi_t|\mathcal{F}_s]} \\ &= \frac{\mathbb{E}^{\mathbb{P}_0}[\Phi_t \mathbb{1}\{\xi_t \le a\}|\mathcal{F}^{\xi_s}]}{\mathbb{E}^{\mathbb{P}_0}[\Phi_t|\mathcal{F}^{\xi_s}]} = \mathbb{E}^{\mathbb{P}}[\mathbb{1}\{\xi_t \le a\}|\mathcal{F}^{\xi_s}] = \mathbb{P}(\xi_t \le a|\mathcal{F}^{\xi_s}),\end{aligned} \tag{3.15}$$

since $\{\xi_t\}$ has the Markov property under the transformed measure $\mathbb{P}_0$. ■

We note that since X is $\mathcal{F}_\infty$-measurable, which follows from proposition 2.2, the Markov property implies that if $Y = f(X)$ is integrable, we have

$$\mathbb{E}^{\mathbb{P}}[Y|\mathcal{F}_t] = \mathbb{E}^{\mathbb{P}}[Y|\mathcal{F}^{\xi_t}]. \tag{3.16}$$

This identity allows one to work out the optimal filter for a Lévy information process by direct use of the Bayes formula. It should be apparent that simulation of the dynamics of the filter is readily approachable on account of this property.

We remark briefly on what might appropriately be called a 'time consistency' property satisfied by Lévy information processes. It follows from (3.11) that, given the conditional distribution $\pi_s(\mathrm{d}x)$ at time $s \le t$, we can express $\pi_t(\mathrm{d}x)$ in the form

$$\pi_t(\mathrm{d}x) = \frac{\exp(x(\xi_t - \xi_s) - \psi_0(x)(t-s))}{\int \exp(x(\xi_t - \xi_s) - \psi_0(x)(t-s))\pi_s(\mathrm{d}x)}\pi_s(\mathrm{d}x). \tag{3.17}$$

Then, if for fixed $s \ge 0$, we introduce a new time variable $u := t - s$, and define $\eta_u = \xi_{u+s} - \xi_s$, we find that $\{\eta_u\}_{u\ge 0}$ is an information process with fiducial exponent $\psi_0(\alpha)$ and message X with *a priori* distribution $\pi_s(\mathrm{d}x)$. Thus given up-to-date information, we can 're-start' the information process at that time to produce a new information process of the same type, with an adjusted message distribution.

Further insight into the nature of Lévy information can be gained by examination of expression (2.9) for the conditional exponent of an information process. In particular, as a consequence of the Lévy–Khintchine representation (2.3) we are able to deduce that

$$\psi_0(\alpha + X) - \psi_0(X) = \left(p + qX + \int_{\mathbb{R}\backslash\{0\}} z(\mathrm{e}^{Xz} - 1)\mathbb{1}\{|z|<1\})\nu(\mathrm{d}z)\right)\alpha + \frac{1}{2}q\alpha^2$$
$$+ \int_{\mathbb{R}\backslash\{0\}} (\mathrm{e}^{\alpha z} - 1 - \alpha z\mathbb{1}\{|z|<1\})\mathrm{e}^{Xz}\nu(\mathrm{d}z) \tag{3.18}$$

for $\alpha \in \mathbb{C}^{\mathrm{I}}$, which leads to the following:

Proposition 3.5. *The randomization of the $\mathbb{P}_0$-Lévy process $\{\xi_t\}$ achieved through the change of measure generated by the randomized Esscher martingale $\rho_t = \exp(X\xi_t - \psi_0(X)t)$ induces two effects on the characteristics of the process:* (i) *a random shift in the drift term, given by*

$$p \to p + qX + \int_{\mathbb{R}\backslash\{0\}} z(e^{Xz} - 1)\mathbb{1}\{|z|<1\})\nu(\mathrm{d}z), \tag{3.19}$$

and (ii) *a random rescaling of the Lévy measure, given by $\nu(\mathrm{d}z) \to \mathrm{e}^{Xz}\nu(\mathrm{d}z)$.*

The integral appearing in the shift in the drift term is well defined because the term $z(\mathrm{e}^{Xz} - 1)$ vanishes to second order at the origin. It follows from proposition 3.5 that in sampling an information process an agent is in effect trying to detect a random shift in the drift term, and a random 'tilt' and change of scale in the Lévy measure, altering the overall rate as well as the relative rates at which jumps of various sizes occur. It is from these data, within which the message is encoded, that the agent attempts to estimate the value of X. It is interesting to note that randomized Esscher martingales arise in the construction of pricing kernels in the theory of finance [32,33].

We turn to examine the properties of certain martingales associated with Lévy information. We establish the existence of a so-called innovations representation for Lévy information. In the case of the Brownian filter, the ideas involved are rather well understood [9], and the matter has also been investigated in the case of Poisson information [34]. These examples arise as special cases in the general theory of Lévy information. Throughout the discussion that follows, we fix a probability space $(\Omega, \mathcal{F}, \mathbb{P})$.

Proposition 3.6. *Let $\{\xi_t\}$ be a Lévy information process with fiducial exponent $\psi_0(\alpha)$ and message X, let $\{\mathcal{F}_t\}$ denote the filtration generated by $\{\xi_t\}$, let $Y = \psi_0'(X)$, where $\psi_0'(\alpha)$ is the marginal fiducial exponent, and set $\hat{Y}_t = \mathbb{E}^{\mathbb{P}}[Y|\mathcal{F}_t]$. Then the process $\{M_t\}$ defined by*

$$\xi_t = \int_0^t \hat{Y}_u \,\mathrm{d}u + M_t \tag{3.20}$$

is an $(\{\mathcal{F}_t\}, \mathbb{P})$-martingale.

Proof. We recall that $\{\xi_t\}$ is by definition $\mathcal{F}^X$-conditionally $\mathbb{P}$-Lévy. It follows therefore from (2.11) that $\mathbb{E}^{\mathbb{P}}[\xi_t|X] = Yt$, where $Y = \psi_0'(X)$. As before, we let $\{\mathcal{G}_t\}$ denote the filtration generated jointly by $\{\xi_t\}$ and X. First, we observe that the process defined for $t \ge 0$ by $m_t = \xi_t - Yt$ is a

$(\{\mathcal{G}_t\}, \mathbb{P})$-martingale. This assertion can be checked by consideration of the one-parameter family of $(\{\mathcal{G}_t\}, \mathbb{P}_0)$-martingales defined by

$$\rho_t^{X+\epsilon} = \exp((X+\varepsilon)\xi_t - \psi_0(X+\varepsilon)t) \tag{3.21}$$

for $\epsilon \in \mathbb{C}^{\mathrm{I}}$. Expanding this expression to first order in ϵ, we deduce that the process defined for $t \geq 0$ by $\rho_t^X(\xi_t - \psi_0'(X)t)$ is a $(\{\mathcal{G}_t\}, \mathbb{P}_0)$-martingale. Thus, we have

$$\mathbb{E}^{\mathbb{P}_0}[\rho_t^X(\xi_t - \psi_0'(X)t)|\mathcal{G}_s] = \rho_s^X(\xi_s - \psi_0'(X)s). \tag{3.22}$$

Then using $\{\rho_t^X\}$ to make a change of measure from $\mathbb{P}_0$ to $\mathbb{P}$, we obtain

$$\mathbb{E}^{\mathbb{P}}[\xi_t - \psi_0'(X)t|\mathcal{G}_s] = \xi_s - \psi_0'(X)s, \tag{3.23}$$

and the result follows if we set $Y = \psi_0'(X)$. Next, we introduce the 'projected' process $\{\hat{m}_t\}$ defined by $\hat{m}_t = \mathbb{E}^{\mathbb{P}}[m_t|\mathcal{F}_t]$. We note that since $\{m_t\}$ is a $(\{\mathcal{G}_t\}, \mathbb{P})$-martingale we have

$$\begin{aligned}\mathbb{E}^{\mathbb{P}}[\hat{m}_t|\mathcal{F}_s] &= \mathbb{E}^{\mathbb{P}}[\xi_t - Yt|\mathcal{F}_s] \\ &= \mathbb{E}^{\mathbb{P}}[\mathbb{E}^{\mathbb{P}}[\xi_t - Yt|\mathcal{G}_s]|\mathcal{F}_s] \\ &= \mathbb{E}^{\mathbb{P}}[\xi_s - Ys|\mathcal{F}_s] \\ &= \hat{m}_s,\end{aligned} \tag{3.24}$$

and thus $\{\hat{m}_t\}$ is an $(\{\mathcal{F}_t\}, \mathbb{P})$-martingale. Finally, we observe that

$$\mathbb{E}^{\mathbb{P}}[M_t|\mathcal{F}_s] = \mathbb{E}^{\mathbb{P}}\left[\xi_t - \int_0^t \hat{Y}_u \,\mathrm{d}u|\mathcal{F}_s\right] = \mathbb{E}^{\mathbb{P}}[\xi_t|\mathcal{F}_s] - \mathbb{E}^{\mathbb{P}}\left[\int_s^t \hat{Y}_u \,\mathrm{d}u\,\middle|\,\mathcal{F}_s\right] - \int_0^s \hat{Y}_u \,\mathrm{d}u, \tag{3.25}$$

where we have made use of the fact that the final term is $\mathcal{F}_s$-measurable. The fact that $\{\hat{m}_t\}$ and $\{\hat{Y}_t\}$ are both $(\mathcal{F}_t, \mathbb{P})$-martingales implies that

$$\mathbb{E}^{\mathbb{P}}[\xi_t|\mathcal{F}_s] - \xi_s = (t-s)\hat{Y}_s = \mathbb{E}^{\mathbb{P}}\left[\int_s^t \hat{Y}_u \,\mathrm{d}u\,\middle|\,\mathcal{F}_s\right], \tag{3.26}$$

from which it follows that $\mathbb{E}^{\mathbb{P}}[M_t|\mathcal{F}_s] = M_s$, which is what we set out to prove. ■

Although the general information process does not admit an additive decomposition into signal and noise, it does admit a linear decomposition into terms representing (i) information already received and (ii) new information. The random variable Y entering via its conditional expectation into the first of these terms is itself in general a nonlinear function of the message variable X. It follows on account of the convexity of the fiducial exponent that the marginal fiducial exponent is invertible, which ensures that X can be expressed in terms of Y by the relation $X = I_0(Y)$, which is linear if and only if the information process is Brownian. Thus, signal and noise are deeply intertwined in the case of general Lévy information. Vestiges of linearity remain, and these suffice to provide an overall element of tractability.

4. Examples of Lévy information processes

In a number of situations one can construct explicit examples of information processes, categorized by noise type. The Brownian and Poisson constructions, which are familiar in other contexts, can be seen as belonging to a unified scheme that brings out their differences and similarities. We then proceed to construct information processes of the gamma, the variance gamma, the negative binomial, the inverse Gaussian, and the normal inverse Gaussian type. It is interesting to take note of the diverse nature of noise, and to observe the many different ways in which messages can be conveyed in a noisy environment.

Example 1 (Brownian information). On a probability space $(\Omega, \mathcal{F}, \mathbb{P})$, let $\{B_t\}$ be a Brownian motion, let X be an independent random variable, and set

$$\xi_t = Xt + B_t. \tag{4.1}$$

The random process $\{\xi_t\}$ thereby defined, which we call the Brownian information process, is $\mathcal{F}^X$-conditionally K_X-Lévy, with conditional characteristic $K_X = (X, 1, 0)$ and conditional exponent $\psi_X(\alpha) = X\alpha + \frac{1}{2}\alpha^2$. The fiducial characteristic is $K_0 = (0, 1, 0)$, the fiducial exponent is $\psi_0(\alpha) = \frac{1}{2}\alpha^2$, and the associated fiducial process or 'noise type' is standard Brownian motion. In the case of Brownian information, there is a linear separation of the process into signal and noise. This model, considered by Wonham [35], is perhaps the simplest continuous-time generalization of the example described by Wiener [1]. The message is given by the value of X, but X can only be observed indirectly, through $\{\xi_t\}$. The observations of X are obscured by the noise represented by the Brownian motion $\{B_t\}$. Because the signal term grows linearly in time, whereas $|B_t| \sim \sqrt{t}$, it is intuitively plausible that observations of $\{\xi_t\}$ will asymptotically reveal the value of X, and a direct calculation using properties of the normal distribution function confirms that $t^{-1}\xi_t$ converges in probability to X; this is consistent with proposition 2.2 if we note that $\psi_0'(\alpha) = \alpha$ and $I_0(y) = y$ in the Brownian case.

The best estimate for X conditional on $\mathcal{F}_t$ can be derived by use of the generalized Bayes formula (3.8). In the Brownian case, there is an elementary method leading to the same result, worth mentioning briefly because it is of interest. First, we present an alternative proof of proposition 3.4 in the Brownian case that uses a Brownian bridge argument.

We recall that if $s > s_1 > 0$, then B_s and $s^{-1}B_s - s_1^{-1}B_{s_1}$ are independent. More generally, we observe that if $s > s_1 > s_2$, then B_s, $s^{-1}B_s - s_1^{-1}B_{s_1}$, and $s_1^{-1}B_{s_1} - s_2^{-1}B_{s_2}$ are independent, and that $s^{-1}\xi_s - s_1^{-1}\xi_{s_1} = s^{-1}B_s - s_1^{-1}B_{s_1}$. Extending this line of reasoning, we see that for any $a \in \mathbb{R}$ we have

$$\begin{aligned}\mathbb{P}(\xi_t \le a | \xi_s, \xi_{s_1}, \ldots, \xi_{s_k}) &= \mathbb{P}\left(\xi_t \le a \,\middle|\, \xi_s, \frac{\xi_s}{s} - \frac{\xi_{s_1}}{s_1}, \ldots, \frac{\xi_{s_{k-1}}}{s_{k-1}} - \frac{\xi_{s_k}}{s_k}\right) \\ &= \mathbb{P}(\xi_t \le a | \xi_s),\end{aligned} \tag{4.2}$$

since ξ_t and ξ_s are independent of $s^{-1}B_s - s_1^{-1}B_{s_1}, \ldots, s_{k-1}^{-1}B_{s_{k-1}} - s_k^{-1}B_{s_k}$, and that gives us the Markov property (3.13). Since we have established that X is $\mathcal{F}_\infty$-measurable, it follows that (3.16) holds. As a consequence, the *a posteriori* distribution of X can be worked out by use of the standard Bayes formula, and for the best estimate of X, we obtain

$$\hat{X}_t = \frac{\int x \exp(x\xi_t - x^2 t/2)\, \pi(\mathrm{d}x)}{\int \exp(x\xi_t - x^2 t/2)\, \pi(\mathrm{d}x)}. \tag{4.3}$$

The innovations representation (3.20) in the case of a Brownian information process can be derived by the following argument. We observe that the $(\{\mathcal{F}_t\}, \mathbb{P}_0)$-martingale $\{\Phi_t\}$ defined in (3.14) is a 'space–time' function of the form

$$\Phi_t := \mathbb{E}^{\mathbb{P}_0}[\rho_t | \mathcal{F}_t] = \int \exp\left(x\xi_t - \frac{1}{2}x^2 t\right) \pi(\mathrm{d}x). \tag{4.4}$$

By use of the Ito calculus together with (4.3), we deduce that $\mathrm{d}\Phi_t = \hat{X}_t \Phi_t \,\mathrm{d}\xi_t$, and thus by integration we obtain

$$\Phi_t = \exp\left(\int_0^t \hat{X}_s \mathrm{d}\xi_s - \frac{1}{2}\int_0^t \hat{X}_s^2 \,\mathrm{d}s\right). \tag{4.5}$$

Since $\{\xi_t\}$ is an $(\{\mathcal{F}_t\}, \mathbb{P}_0)$-Brownian motion, it follows from (4.5) by the Girsanov theorem that the process $\{M_t\}$ defined by

$$\xi_t = \int_0^t \hat{X}_s \,\mathrm{d}s + M_t \tag{4.6}$$

is an $(\{\mathcal{F}_t\}, \mathbb{P})$-Brownian motion, which we call the innovations process (see [36]). The increments of $\{M_t\}$ represent the arrival of new information.

12

rspa.royalsocietypublishing.org Proc R Soc A 20120433

We conclude our discussion of Brownian information with the following remarks. In problems involving prediction and valuation, it is not uncommon that the message is revealed after the passage of a finite amount of time. This is often the case in applications to finance, where the message takes the form of a random cash flow at some future date, or, more generally, a random factor that affects such a cash flow. There are also numerous examples coming from the physical sciences, economics, and operations research, where the goal of an agent is to form a view concerning the outcome of a future event by monitoring the flow of information relating to it. How does one handle problems involving the revelation of information over finite time horizons?

One way of modelling finite time horizon scenarios in the present context is by use of a time change. If $\{\xi_t\}$ is a Lévy information process with message X and a specified fiducial exponent, then a generalization of proposition 2.2 shows that the process $\{\xi_{tT}\}$ defined over the time interval $0 \leq t < T$ by

$$\xi_{tT} = \frac{T-t}{T}\,\xi\left(\frac{tT}{T-t}\right) \tag{4.7}$$

reveals the value of X in the limit as $t \to T$, and one can check that

$$\mathrm{Cov}[\xi_{sT}, \xi_{tT} | \mathcal{F}^X] = \frac{s(T-t)}{T}\psi_0''(X), \quad (0 \leq s \leq t < T). \tag{4.8}$$

In the case where $\{\xi_t\}$ is a Brownian information process represented as above in the form $\xi_t = Xt + B_t$, the time-changed process (4.7) takes the form $\xi_{tT} = Xt + \beta_{tT}$, where $\{\beta_{tT}\}$ is a Brownian bridge over the interval $[0, T]$. Such processes have had applications in physics [37–40] and in finance [41–45]. It seems reasonable to conjecture that time-changed Lévy information processes of the more general type proposed above may be similarly applicable.

Example 2 (Poisson information). Consider a situation in which an agent observes a series of events taking place at a random rate, and the agent wishes to determine the rate as best as possible because its value conveys an important piece of information. One can model the information flow in this situation by a modulated Poisson process for which the jump rate is an independent random variable. Such a scenario arises in many real-world situations, and has been investigated in the literature [34,46–49]. The resulting scheme can be seen to emerge naturally as an example of our general model for Lévy information.

As in the Brownian case, one can construct the relevant information process directly. On a probability space $(\Omega, \mathcal{F}, \mathbb{P})$, let $\{N(t)\}_{t\geq 0}$ be a standard Poisson process with jump rate $m > 0$, let X be an independent random variable, and set

$$\xi_t = N(\mathrm{e}^X t). \tag{4.9}$$

Thus, $\{\xi_t\}$ is a time-changed Poisson process, and the effect of the signal is to randomly modulate the rate at which the process jumps. It is evident that $\{\xi_t\}$ is $\mathcal{F}^X$-conditionally Lévy and satisfies the conditions of definition 2.1. In particular,

$$\mathbb{E}[\exp(\alpha N(\mathrm{e}^X t)) | \mathcal{F}^X] = \exp(m\mathrm{e}^X(\mathrm{e}^\alpha - 1)t), \tag{4.10}$$

and for fixed X one obtains a Poisson process with rate $m\mathrm{e}^X$. It follows that (4.9) is an information process. The fiducial characteristic is given by $K_0 = (0, 0, m\delta_1(\mathrm{d}z))$, that of a Poisson process with unit jumps at the rate m, where $\delta_1(\mathrm{d}z)$ is the Dirac measure with unit mass at $z = 1$, and the fiducial exponent is $\psi_0(\alpha) = m(\mathrm{e}^\alpha - 1)$. A calculation using (2.9) shows that $K_X = (0, 0, m\mathrm{e}^X\delta_1(\mathrm{d}z))$, and that $\psi_X(\alpha) = m\mathrm{e}^X(\mathrm{e}^\alpha - 1)$. The relation between signal and noise in the case of Poisson information is rather subtle. The noise is associated with the random fluctuations of the inter-arrival times of the jumps, whereas the message determines the average rate at which the jumps occur.

It will be instructive in this example to work out the conditional distribution of X by elementary methods. Since X is $\mathcal{F}_\infty$-measurable and $\{\xi_t\}$ has the Markov property, we have

$$F_t^X(y) := \mathbb{P}(X \le y|\mathcal{F}_t) = \mathbb{P}(X \le y|\xi_t) \tag{4.11}$$

for $y \in \mathbb{R}$. It follows then from the Bayes law for an information process taking values in $\mathbb{N}_0$ that

$$\mathbb{P}(X \le y|\xi_t = n) = \frac{\int \mathbb{1}\{x \le y\}\mathbb{P}(\xi_t = n|X = x)\,\mathrm{d}F^X(x)}{\int \mathbb{P}(\xi_t = n|X = x)\,\mathrm{d}F^X(x)}. \tag{4.12}$$

In the case of Poisson information, the relevant conditional distribution is

$$\mathbb{P}(\xi_t = n|X = x) = \exp(-mt\mathrm{e}^x)\frac{(mt\mathrm{e}^x)^n}{n!}. \tag{4.13}$$

After some cancellation, we deduce that

$$\mathbb{P}(X \le y|\xi_t = n) = \frac{\int \mathbb{1}\{x \le y\}\exp(xn - m(\mathrm{e}^x - 1)t)\,\mathrm{d}F^X(x)}{\int \exp(xn - m(\mathrm{e}^x - 1)t)\,\mathrm{d}F^X(x)}, \tag{4.14}$$

and hence

$$F_t^X(y) = \frac{\int \mathbb{1}\{x \le y\}\exp(x\xi_t - m(\mathrm{e}^x - 1)t)\,\mathrm{d}F^X(x)}{\int \exp(x\xi_t - m(\mathrm{e}^x - 1)t)\,\mathrm{d}F^X(x)}, \tag{4.15}$$

and thus

$$\pi_t(\mathrm{d}x) = \frac{\exp(x\xi_t - m(\mathrm{e}^x - 1)t)}{\int \exp(x\xi_t - m(\mathrm{e}^x - 1)t)\,\pi(\mathrm{d}x)}\pi(\mathrm{d}x), \tag{4.16}$$

which we can see is consistent with (3.11) if we recall that in the case of noise of the Poisson type the fiducial exponent is given by $\psi_0(\alpha) = m(\mathrm{e}^\alpha - 1)$.

If a Geiger counter is monitored continuously in time, the sound that it produces provides a nice example of a Poisson information process. The crucial message (proximity to radioactivity) carried by the noisy sputter of the instrument is represented by the rate at which the clicks occur.

Example 3 (Gamma information). It will be convenient first to recall a few definitions and conventions [50–52]. Let m and κ be positive numbers. By a gamma process with rate m and scale κ on a probability space $(\Omega, \mathcal{F}, \mathbb{P})$, we mean a Lévy process $\{\gamma_t\}_{t\ge 0}$ with exponent

$$t^{-1}\ln \mathbb{E}^{\mathbb{P}}[\exp(\alpha\gamma_t)] = -m\ln(1 - \kappa\alpha) \tag{4.17}$$

for $\alpha \in A_{\mathbb{C}} = \{w \in \mathbb{C} : \mathrm{Re}\, w < \kappa^{-1}\}$. The probability density for γ_t is

$$\mathbb{P}(\gamma_t \in \mathrm{d}x) = \mathbb{1}\{x > 0\}\frac{\kappa^{-mt}x^{mt-1}\exp(-x/\kappa)}{\Gamma[mt]}\,\mathrm{d}x, \tag{4.18}$$

where $\Gamma[a]$ is the gamma function. A short calculation making use of the functional equation $\Gamma[a+1] = a\Gamma[a]$ shows that $\mathbb{E}^{\mathbb{P}}[\gamma_t] = m\kappa t$ and $\mathrm{Var}^{\mathbb{P}}[\gamma_t] = m\kappa^2 t$. Clearly, the mean and variance determine the rate and scale. If $\kappa = 1$, we say that $\{\gamma_t\}$ is a *standard* gamma process with rate m. If $\kappa \ne 1$, we say that $\{\gamma_t\}$ is a scaled gamma process. The Lévy measure associated with the gamma process is

$$\nu(\mathrm{d}z) = \mathbb{1}\{z > 0\}mz^{-1}\exp(-\kappa z)\,\mathrm{d}z. \tag{4.19}$$

It follows that $\nu(\mathbb{R}\backslash\{0\}) = \infty$ and hence that the gamma process has infinite activity. Now let $\{\xi_t\}$ be a standard gamma process with rate m on a probability space $(\Omega, \mathcal{F}, \mathbb{P}_0)$, and let $\lambda \in \mathbb{R}$ satisfy $\lambda < 1$. Then the process $\{\rho_t^\lambda\}$ defined by

$$\rho_t^\lambda = (1 - \lambda)^{mt}\mathrm{e}^{\lambda\gamma_t} \tag{4.20}$$

is an $(\{\mathcal{F}_t\}, \mathbb{P}_0)$-martingale. If we let $\{\rho_t^\lambda\}$ act as a change of measure density for the transformation $\mathbb{P}_0 \to \mathbb{P}_\lambda$, then we find that $\{\gamma_t\}$ is a *scaled* gamma process under $\mathbb{P}_\lambda$, with rate m and scale $1/(1-\lambda)$. Thus we see that the effect of an Esscher transformation on a gamma process is to alter its scale. With these facts in mind, one can establish the following:

Proposition 4.1. *Let $\{\gamma_t\}$ be a standard gamma process with rate m on a probability space $(\Omega,\mathcal{F},\mathbb{P})$, and let the independent random variable X satisfy $X<1$ almost surely. Then the process $\{\xi_t\}$ defined by*

$$\xi_t = \frac{1}{1-X}\gamma_t \tag{4.21}$$

is a Lévy information process with message X and gamma noise, with fiducial exponent $\psi_0(\alpha) = -m\ln(1-\alpha)$ for $\alpha \in \{w\in\mathbb{C} : \mathrm{Re}\, w<1\}$.

Proof. It is evident that $\{\xi_t\}$ is $\mathcal{F}^X$-conditionally a scaled gamma process. As a consequence of (4.17), we have

$$\frac{1}{t}\ln\mathbb{E}^{\mathbb{P}}\left[\exp(\alpha\xi_t)|X\right] = \frac{1}{t}\ln\mathbb{E}^{\mathbb{P}}\left[\exp\left(\frac{\alpha\gamma_t}{1-X}\right)\middle|X\right] = \ln\left(1-\frac{\alpha}{1-X}\right)^{-m} \tag{4.22}$$

for $\alpha\in\mathbb{C}^{\mathrm{I}}$. Then we note that

$$-m\ln\left(1-\frac{\alpha}{1-X}\right) = -m\ln(1-(X+\alpha)) + m\ln(1-X). \tag{4.23}$$

It follows that the $\mathcal{F}^X$-conditional $\mathbb{P}$ exponent of $\{\xi_t\}$ is $\psi_0(X+\alpha)-\psi_0(X)$. ■

The gamma filter arises as follows. An agent observes a process of accumulation. Typically, there are many small increments, but now and then there are large increments. The unknown factor X appearing in the overall rate $m/(1-X)$ at which the process is growing is the figure that the agent wishes to estimate as accurately as possible. The accumulation can be modelled by gamma information, and the associated filter can be used to estimate X. It has long been recognized that the gamma process is useful in describing phenomena such as the water level of a dam or the totality of the claims made in a large portfolio of insurance contracts [53–55]. Use of the gamma information process and related bridge processes, with applications in finance and insurance, is pursued in Brody *et al.* [51], Hoyle [56] and Hoyle *et al.* [57]. We draw the reader's attention to Yor [50] and references cited therein, where it is shown how certain additive properties of Brownian motion have multiplicative analogues in the case of the gamma process. One notes in particular the remarkable property that γ_t and γ_s/γ_t are independent for $t\geq s\geq 0$. Making use of this relation, it will be instructive if we present an alternative derivation of the optimal filter for gamma noise. We begin by establishing that the process defined by (4.21) has the Markov property. We observe first that for any times $t\geq s\geq s_1\geq s_2\geq\cdots\geq s_k$ the variables $\gamma_{s_1}/\gamma_s, \gamma_{s_2}/\gamma_{s_1}$, and so on, are independent of one another and are independent of γ_s and γ_t. It follows that

$$\begin{aligned}\mathbb{P}(\xi_t<a|\xi_s,\xi_{s_1},\ldots,\xi_{s_k}) &= \mathbb{P}(\xi_t<a|(1-X)^{-1}\gamma_s,\ldots,(1-X)^{-1}\gamma_{s_k})\\ &= \mathbb{P}\left(\xi_t<a\middle|(1-X)^{-1}\gamma_s, \frac{\gamma_{s_1}}{\gamma_s},\frac{\gamma_{s_2}}{\gamma_{s_1}},\ldots,\frac{\gamma_{s_k}}{\gamma_{s_{k-1}}}\right)\\ &= \mathbb{P}(\xi_t<a|\xi_s),\end{aligned} \tag{4.24}$$

since $\{\gamma_t\}$ and X are independent, and this gives us (3.13). In working out the distribution of X given $\mathcal{F}_t$, it suffices therefore to work out the distribution of X given ξ_t. We note that the Bayes formula implies that

$$\pi_t(\mathrm{d}x) = \frac{\rho(\xi_t|X=x)}{\int\rho(\xi_t|X=x)\pi(\mathrm{d}x)}\pi(\mathrm{d}x), \tag{4.25}$$

where $\pi(\mathrm{d}x)$ is the unconditional distribution of X, and $\rho(\xi|X=x)$ is the conditional density for the random variable ξ_t, which can be calculated as follows:

$$\begin{aligned}\rho(\xi|X=x) &= \frac{\mathrm{d}}{\mathrm{d}\xi}\mathbb{P}(\xi_t\leq\xi|X=x) = \frac{\mathrm{d}}{\mathrm{d}\xi}\mathbb{P}((1-X)^{-1}\gamma_t\leq\xi|X=x)\\ &= \frac{\mathrm{d}}{\mathrm{d}\xi}\mathbb{P}(\gamma_t\leq(1-X)\xi|X=x) = \frac{\xi^{mt-1}(1-x)^{mt}\mathrm{e}^{-(1-x)\xi}}{\Gamma[mt]}.\end{aligned} \tag{4.26}$$

It follows that the optimal filter in the case of gamma noise is given by

$$\pi_t(\mathrm{d}x) = \frac{(1-x)^{mt}\exp(x\xi_t)}{\int_{-\infty}^{1}(1-x)^{mt}\exp(x\xi_t)\pi(\mathrm{d}x)}\,\pi(\mathrm{d}x). \tag{4.27}$$

We conclude with the following observation. In the case of Brownian information, it is well known (and implicit in Wiener's example [1]) that if the signal is Gaussian, then the optimal filter is a linear function of the observation ξ_t. One might therefore ask in the case of a gamma information process if some special choice of the signal distribution gives rise to a linear filter. The answer is affirmative. Let U be a gamma-distributed random variable with the distribution

$$\mathbb{P}(U \in \mathrm{d}u) = \mathbb{1}\{u > 0\}\,\frac{\theta^r u^{r-1}\exp(-\theta u)}{\Gamma[r]}\,\mathrm{d}u, \tag{4.28}$$

where $r > 1$ and $\theta > 0$ are parameters, and set $X = 1 - U$. Let $\{\xi_t\}$ be a gamma information process carrying message X, let $Y = \psi_0'(X) = m/(1-X)$, and set $\tau = (r-1)/m$. Then the optimal filter for Y is given by

$$\hat{Y}_t := \mathbb{E}^{\mathbb{P}}[Y|\mathcal{F}_t] = \frac{\xi_t + \theta}{t + \tau}. \tag{4.29}$$

Example 4 (Variance-gamma information). The so-called variance-gamma or VG process [58–60] was introduced in the theory of finance. The relevant definitions and conventions are as follows. By a VG process with drift $\mu \in \mathbb{R}$, volatility $\sigma \geq 0$, and rate $m > 0$, we mean a Lévy process with exponent

$$\psi(\alpha) = -m\ln\left(1 - \frac{\mu}{m}\alpha - \frac{\sigma^2}{2m}\alpha^2\right). \tag{4.30}$$

The VG process admits representations in terms of simpler Lévy processes. Let $\{\gamma_t\}$ be a standard gamma process on $(\Omega, \mathcal{F}, \mathbb{P})$, with rate m, as defined in the previous example, and let $\{B_t\}$ be a standard Brownian motion, independent of $\{\gamma_t\}$. We call the scaled process $\{\Gamma_t\}$ defined by $\Gamma_t = m^{-1}\gamma_t$ a standard gamma subordinator with rate m. Note that Γ_t has dimensions of time and that $\mathbb{E}^{\mathbb{P}}[\Gamma_t] = t$. A calculation shows that the Lévy process $\{V_t\}$ defined by

$$V_t = \mu\Gamma_t + \sigma B_{\Gamma_t} \tag{4.31}$$

has the exponent (4.30). The VG process thus takes the form of a Brownian motion with drift, time-changed by a gamma subordinator. If $\mu = 0$ and $\sigma = 1$, we say that $\{V_t\}$ is a 'standard' VG process, with rate parameter m. If $\mu \neq 0$, we say that $\{V_t\}$ is a 'drifted' VG process. One can always choose units of time such that $m = 1$, but for applications it is better to choose conventional units of time (seconds for physics, years for economics), and treat m as a model parameter. In the limit $\sigma \to 0$ we obtain a gamma process with rate m and scale μ/m. In the limit $m \to \infty$ we obtain a Brownian motion with drift μ and volatility σ.

An alternative representation of the VG process results if we let $\{\gamma_t^1\}$ and $\{\gamma_t^2\}$ be independent standard gamma processes on $(\Omega, \mathcal{F}, \mathbb{P})$, with rate m, and set

$$V_t = \kappa_1\gamma_t^1 - \kappa_2\gamma_t^2, \tag{4.32}$$

where κ_1 and κ_2 are nonnegative constants. A calculation shows that the exponent is of the form (4.30). In particular, we have

$$\psi(\alpha) = -m\ln(1 - (\kappa_1 - \kappa_2)\alpha - \kappa_1\kappa_2\alpha^2), \tag{4.33}$$

where $\mu = m(\kappa_1 - \kappa_2)$ and $\sigma^2 = 2m\kappa_1\kappa_2$, or equivalently

$$\kappa_1 = \frac{1}{2m}\left(\mu + \sqrt{\mu^2 + 2m\sigma^2}\right) \quad \text{and} \quad \kappa_2 = \frac{1}{2m}\left(-\mu + \sqrt{\mu^2 + 2m\sigma^2}\right), \tag{4.34}$$

where $\alpha \in \{w \in \mathbb{C} : -1/\kappa_2 < \mathrm{Re}\, w < 1/\kappa_1\}$. Now let $\{\xi_t\}$ be a standard VG process on $(\Omega, \mathcal{F}, \mathbb{P}_0)$, with exponent $\psi_0(\alpha) = -m\ln(1 - (2m)^{-1}\alpha^2)$ for $\alpha \in \{w \in \mathbb{C} : |\mathrm{Re}\, w| < \sqrt{2m}\}$. Under the transformed measure $\mathbb{P}_\lambda$ defined by the change-of-measure martingale (2.6), one finds that $\{\xi_t\}$ is a drifted VG process, with

$$\mu = \lambda\left(1 - \frac{1}{2m}\lambda^2\right)^{-1} \quad \text{and} \quad \sigma = \left(1 - \frac{1}{2m}\lambda^2\right)^{-1/2} \tag{4.35}$$

for $|\lambda| < \sqrt{2m}$. Thus, in the case of the VG process, an Esscher transformation affects both the drift and the volatility. Note that for large m the effect on the volatility is insignificant, whereas the effect on the drift reduces to that of an ordinary Girsanov transformation.

With these facts in hand, we are now in a position to construct the VG information process. We fix a probability space $(\Omega, \mathcal{F}, \mathbb{P})$ and a number $m > 0$.

Proposition 4.2. *Let $\{\Gamma_t\}$ be a standard gamma subordinator with rate m, let $\{B_t\}$ be an independent Brownian motion, and let the independent random variable X satisfy $|X| < \sqrt{2m}$ almost surely. Then the process $\{\xi_t\}$ defined by*

$$\xi_t = X\left(1 - \frac{1}{2m}X^2\right)^{-1}\Gamma_t + \left(1 - \frac{1}{2m}X^2\right)^{-1/2} B(\Gamma_t) \tag{4.36}$$

is a Lévy information process with message X and VG noise, with fiducial exponent

$$\psi_0(\alpha) = -m\ln\left(1 - \frac{1}{2m}\alpha^2\right) \tag{4.37}$$

for $\alpha \in \{w \in \mathbb{C} : \mathrm{Re}\, w < \sqrt{2m}\}$.

Proof. Observe that $\{\xi_t\}$ is $\mathcal{F}^X$-conditionally a drifted VG process of the form

$$\xi_t = \mu_X \Gamma_t + \sigma_X B(\Gamma_t), \tag{4.38}$$

where the drift and volatility coefficients are

$$\mu_X = X\left(1 - \frac{1}{2m}X^2\right)^{-1} \quad \text{and} \quad \sigma_X = \left(1 - \frac{1}{2m}X^2\right)^{-1/2}. \tag{4.39}$$

The $\mathcal{F}^X$-conditional $\mathbb{P}$-exponent of $\{\xi_t\}$ is by (4.30) thus given for $\alpha \in \mathbb{C}^{\mathrm{I}}$ by

$$\begin{aligned}\psi_X(\alpha) &= -m\ln\left(1 - \frac{1}{m}\mu_X\alpha - \frac{1}{2m}\sigma_X^2\alpha^2\right)\\ &= -m\ln\left(1 - \frac{1}{m}X\left(1 - \frac{1}{2m}X^2\right)^{-1}\alpha - \frac{1}{2m}\left(1 - \frac{1}{2m}X^2\right)^{-1}\alpha^2\right)\\ &= -m\ln\left(1 - \frac{1}{2m}(X+\alpha)^2\right) + m\ln\left(1 - \frac{1}{2m}X^2\right),\end{aligned} \tag{4.40}$$

which is evidently by (4.37) of the form $\psi_0(X+\alpha) - \psi_0(X)$, as required. ∎

An alternative representation for the VG information process can be established by the same method if one randomly rescales the gamma subordinator appearing in the time-changed Brownian motion. The result is as follows.

Proposition 4.3. *Let $\{\Gamma_t\}$ be a gamma subordinator with rate m, let $\{B_t\}$ be an independent standard Brownian motion and let the independent random variable X satisfy $|X| < \sqrt{2m}$ almost surely. Write $\{\Gamma_t^X\}$ for the subordinator:*

$$\Gamma_t^X = \left(1 - \frac{1}{2m}X^2\right)^{-1}\Gamma_t. \tag{4.41}$$

Then the process $\{\xi_t\}$ defined by $\xi_t = X\Gamma_t^X + B(\Gamma_t^X)$ is a VG information process with message X.

A further representation of the VG information process arises as a consequence of the representation of the VG process as the asymmetric difference between two independent standard gamma processes. In particular, we have:

Proposition 4.4. *Let $\{\gamma_t^1\}$ and $\{\gamma_t^2\}$ be independent standard gamma processes, each with rate m, and let the independent random variable X satisfy $|X| < \sqrt{2m}$ almost surely. Then the process $\{\xi_t\}$ defined by*

$$\xi_t = \frac{1}{\sqrt{2m} - X}\gamma_t^1 - \frac{1}{\sqrt{2m} + X}\gamma_t^2 \tag{4.42}$$

is a VG information process with message X.

Example 5 (Negative-binomial information). By a negative binomial process with rate parameter m and probability parameter q, where $m > 0$ and $0 < q < 1$, we mean a Lévy process with exponent

$$\psi_0(\alpha) = m \ln\left(\frac{1-q}{1-q\mathrm{e}^{\alpha}}\right) \tag{4.43}$$

for $\alpha \in \{w \in \mathbb{C} : \mathrm{Re}\, w < -\ln q\}$. There are two representations for the negative binomial process [52,61]. The first of these is a compound Poisson process for which the jump size $J \in \mathbb{N}$ has a logarithmic distribution

$$\mathbb{P}_0(J = n) = -\frac{1}{\ln(1-q)}\frac{1}{n}q^n, \tag{4.44}$$

and the intensity of the Poisson process determining the timing of the jumps is given by $\lambda = -m\ln(1-q)$. One finds that the characteristic function of J is

$$\phi_0(\alpha) := \mathbb{E}^{\mathbb{P}_0}[\exp(\alpha J)] = \frac{\ln(1-q\mathrm{e}^{\alpha})}{\ln(1-q)} \tag{4.45}$$

for $\alpha \in \{w \in \mathbb{C} : \mathrm{Re}\, w < -\ln q\}$. Then if we set

$$n_t = \sum_{k=1}^{\infty} \mathbb{1}\{k \le N_t\} J_k, \tag{4.46}$$

where $\{N_t\}$ is a Poisson process with rate λ, and $\{J_k\}_{k\in\mathbb{N}}$ denotes a collection of independent identical copies of J, representing the jumps, one deduces that

$$\mathbb{P}_0(n_t = k) = \frac{\Gamma(k+mt)}{\Gamma(mt)\Gamma(k+1)}q^k(1-q)^{mt}, \tag{4.47}$$

and that the resulting exponent is given by (4.43). The second representation of the negative binomial process makes use of the method of subordination. We take a Poisson process with rate $\Lambda = mq/(1-q)$, and time-change it using a gamma subordinator $\{\Gamma_t\}$ with rate parameter m. The moment-generating function thus obtained, in agreement with (4.43), is

$$\mathbb{E}^{\mathbb{P}_0}[\exp(\alpha N(\Gamma_t))] = \mathbb{E}^{\mathbb{P}_0}[\exp(\Lambda(\mathrm{e}^{\alpha}-1)\Gamma_t)] = \left(\frac{1-q}{1-q\mathrm{e}^{\alpha}}\right)^{mt}. \tag{4.48}$$

With these results in mind, we fix a probability space $(\Omega, \mathcal{F}, \mathbb{P})$ and find:

Proposition 4.5. *Let $\{\Gamma_t\}$ be a gamma subordinator with rate m, let $\{N_t\}$ be an independent Poisson process with rate m, let the independent random variable X satisfy $X < -\ln q$ almost surely, and set*

$$\Gamma_t^X = \left(\frac{q\mathrm{e}^X}{1-q\mathrm{e}^X}\right)\Gamma_t. \tag{4.49}$$

Then the process $\{\xi_t\}$ defined by

$$\xi_t = N(\Gamma_t^X) \tag{4.50}$$

is a Lévy information process with message X and negative binomial noise, with fiducial exponent (4.43).

Proof. This can be verified by direct calculation. For $\alpha \in \mathbb{C}^{\mathrm{I}}$ we have

$$\mathbb{E}^{\mathbb{P}}[\mathrm{e}^{\alpha\xi_t}|X] = \mathbb{E}^{\mathbb{P}}[\exp(\alpha N(\Gamma_t^X))|X] = \mathbb{E}^{\mathbb{P}}\left[\exp\left(m\frac{q\mathrm{e}^X}{1-q\mathrm{e}^X}(\mathrm{e}^{\alpha}-1)\Gamma_t\right)\Bigg| X\right]$$
$$= \left(1 - \frac{q\mathrm{e}^X(\mathrm{e}^{\alpha}-1)}{1-q\mathrm{e}^X}\right)^{-mt} = \left(\frac{1-q\mathrm{e}^X}{1-q\mathrm{e}^{X+\alpha}}\right)^{mt}, \tag{4.51}$$

which by (4.43) shows that the conditional exponent is $\psi_0(X+\alpha) - \psi_0(X)$. ■

There is also a representation for negative binomial information based on the compound Poisson process. This can be obtained by an application of proposition 3.5, which shows how the Lévy measure transforms under a random Esscher transformation. In the case of a negative binomial process with parameters m and q, the Lévy measure is given by

$$\nu(\mathrm{d}z) = m\sum_{n=1}^{\infty}\frac{1}{n}q^n\delta_n(\mathrm{d}z), \tag{4.52}$$

where $\delta_n(\mathrm{d}z)$ denotes the Dirac measure with unit mass at the point $z=n$. The Lévy measure is finite in this case, and we have $\nu(\mathbb{R}) = -m\ln(1-q)$, which is the overall rate at which the compound Poisson process jumps. If one normalizes the Lévy measure with the overall jump rate, one obtains the probability measure (4.44) for the jump size. With these facts in mind, we fix a probability space $(\Omega,\mathcal{F},\mathbb{P})$ and specify the constants m and q, where $m>1$ and $0<q<1$. Then as a consequence of proposition 3.5 we have the following:

Proposition 4.6. *Let the random variable X satisfy $X < -\ln q$ almost surely, let the random variable J^X have the conditional distribution*

$$\mathbb{P}(J^X = n|X) = -\frac{1}{\ln(1-q\mathrm{e}^X)}\frac{1}{n}(q\mathrm{e}^X)^n, \tag{4.53}$$

let $\{J_k^X\}_{k\in\mathbb{N}}$ be a collection of conditionally independent identical copies of J^X, and let $\{N_t\}$ be an independent Poisson process with rate m. Then the process $\{\xi_t\}$ defined by

$$\xi_t = \sum_{k=1}^{\infty}\mathbb{1}\{k \le N(-\ln(1-q\mathrm{e}^X)t)\}\, J_k^X \tag{4.54}$$

is a Lévy information process with message X and negative binomial noise, with fiducial exponent (4.43).

Example 6 (Inverse Gaussian information). The inverse Gaussian (IG) distribution appears in the study of the first exit time of Brownian motion with drift [62]. The name 'inverse Gaussian' was introduced by Tweedie [63], and a Lévy process whose increments have the IG distribution was introduced by Wasan [64]. By an IG process with parameters $a>0$ and $b>0$, we mean a Lévy process with exponent

$$\psi_0(\alpha) = a\left(b - \sqrt{b^2 - 2\alpha}\right) \tag{4.55}$$

for $\alpha \in \{w \in \mathbb{C} : 0 \le \mathrm{Re}\, w < \frac{1}{2}b^2\}$. Let us write $\{G_t\}$ for the IG process. The probability density function for G_t is

$$\mathbb{P}_0(G_t \in \mathrm{d}x) = \mathbb{1}\{x>0\}\frac{at}{\sqrt{2\pi x^3}}\exp\left(-\frac{(bx-at)^2}{2x}\right)\mathrm{d}x, \tag{4.56}$$

and we find that $\mathbb{E}^{\mathbb{P}_0}[G_t] = at/b$ and that $\mathrm{Var}^{\mathbb{P}_0}[G_t] = at/b^3$. It is straightforward to check that under the Esscher transformation $\mathbb{P}_0 \to \mathbb{P}_\lambda$ induced by (2.6), where $0<\lambda<\frac{1}{2}b^2$, the parameter a is left unchanged, whereas $b \to (b^2-2\lambda)^{1/2}$. With these facts in mind, we are in a position to introduce the associated information process. We fix a probability space $(\Omega,\mathcal{F},\mathbb{P})$ and find the following:

Proposition 4.7. *Let $G(t)$ be an inverse Gaussian process with parameters a and b, let X be an independent random variable satisfying $0 < X < \frac{1}{2}b^2$ almost surely, and set $Z = b^{-1}(b^2 - 2X)^{1/2}$. Then the process $\{\xi_t\}$ defined by*

$$\xi_t = Z^{-2}G(Zt) \tag{4.57}$$

is a Lévy information process with message X and inverse Gaussian noise, with fiducial exponent (4.55).

Proof. It should be evident by inspection that $\{\xi_t\}$ is $\mathcal{F}^X$-conditionally Lévy. Let us therefore work out the conditional exponent. For $\alpha \in \mathbb{C}^{\mathrm{I}}$ we have:

$$\begin{aligned}\mathbb{E}^{\mathbb{P}}[\exp(\alpha\xi_t)|X] &= \mathbb{E}^{\mathbb{P}}\left[\exp\left(\alpha\frac{b^2}{b^2-2X}G(b^{-1}\sqrt{b^2-2X}t)\right)\middle|X\right]\\ &= \exp\left(at\left(\sqrt{b^2-2X}-\sqrt{b^2-2(\alpha+X)}\right)\right)\\ &= \exp\left(at\left(b-\sqrt{b^2-2(\alpha+X)}\right)-at\left(b-\sqrt{b^2-2X}\right)\right),\end{aligned} \tag{4.58}$$

which shows that the conditional exponent is of the form $\psi_0(\alpha+X)-\psi_0(X)$. ■

Example 7 (Normal inverse Gaussian information). By a normal inverse Gaussian (NIG) process [65,66] with parameters a, b and m, such that $a>0$, $|b|<a$ and $m>0$, we mean a Lévy process with an exponent of the form

$$\psi_0(\alpha) = m\left(\sqrt{a^2-b^2}-\sqrt{a^2-(b+\alpha)^2}\right) \tag{4.59}$$

for $\alpha \in \{w \in \mathbb{C} : -a-b < \mathrm{Re}\, w < a-b\}$. Let us write $\{I_t\}$ for the NIG process. The probability density for its value at time t is given by

$$\mathbb{P}_0(I_t \in \mathrm{d}x) = \frac{amtK_1(a\sqrt{m^2t^2+x^2})}{\pi\sqrt{m^2t^2+x^2}}\exp\left(mt\sqrt{a^2-b^2}+bx\right)\mathrm{d}x, \tag{4.60}$$

where K_ν is the modified Bessel function of third kind [67]. The NIG process can be represented as a Brownian motion subordinated by an IG process. In particular, let $\{B_t\}$ be a standard Brownian motion, let $\{G_t\}$ be an independent IG process with parameters a' and b', and set $a'=1$ and $b'=m(a^2-b^2)^{1/2}$. Then the characteristic function of the process $\{I_t\}$ defined by

$$I_t = bm^2G_t + mB(G_t) \tag{4.61}$$

is given by (4.59). The associated information process is constructed as follows. We fix a probability space $(\Omega, \mathcal{F}, \mathbb{P})$ and the parameters a, b and m.

Proposition 4.8. *Let the random variable X satisfy $-a-b < X < a-b$ almost surely, let $\{G_t^X\}$ be $\mathcal{F}^X$-conditionally IG, with parameters $a'=1$ and $b'=m(a^2-(b+X)^2)^{1/2}$, and let $F_t = m^2G_t^X$. Then the process $\{\xi_t\}$ defined by*

$$\xi_t = (b+X)F_t + B(F_t) \tag{4.62}$$

is a Lévy information process with message X and NIG noise, with fiducial exponent (4.59).

Proof. We observe that the condition on $\{G_t^X\}$ is that

$$\frac{1}{t}\ln\mathbb{E}^{\mathbb{P}}[\exp(\alpha G_t^X)|X] = m\sqrt{a^2-(b+X)^2}-\sqrt{m^2(a^2-(b+X)^2)-2\alpha} \tag{4.63}$$

for $\alpha \in \mathbb{C}^{\mathrm{I}}$. Thus, if we set $\psi_X(\alpha) = \mathbb{E}^{\mathbb{P}}[\exp(\alpha\xi_t)|X]$ for $\alpha \in \mathbb{C}^{\mathrm{I}}$ it follows that

$$\begin{aligned}\psi_X(\alpha) &= \mathbb{E}^{\mathbb{P}}[\exp(\alpha(b+X)F_t+\alpha B(F_t))|X]\\ &= \mathbb{E}^{\mathbb{P}}[\exp((\alpha(b+X)+\tfrac{1}{2}\alpha^2)m^2G_t^X)|X]\\ &= \mathbb{E}^{\mathbb{P}}\left[\exp\left(mt\sqrt{a^2-(b+X)^2}-mt\sqrt{a^2-(b+X)^2-2(\alpha(b+X)+\tfrac{1}{2}\alpha^2)}\right)\right],\end{aligned} \tag{4.64}$$

which shows that the conditional exponent is of the required form. ■

Similar arguments lead to the construction of information processes based on various other Lévy processes related to the IG distribution, including for example the generalized hyperbolic process [68], for which the information process can be shown to take the form

$$\xi_t = (b + X)\tilde{G}_t + B(\tilde{G}_t). \tag{4.65}$$

Here, the random variable X is taken to be $\mathbb{P}$-independent of the standard Brownian motion $\{B(t)\}$, and $\{\tilde{G}_t\}$ is $\mathcal{F}^X$-conditionally a generalized inverse Gaussian process with parameters $(\delta, (a^2 - (b + X)^2)^{1/2}, \nu)$. It would be of interest to determine whether models can be found for information processes based on the Meixner process [30] and the CGMY process [69,70].

We conclude this study of Lévy information with the following remarks. Recent developments in the phenomenological representation of physical [38] and economic [42] time series have highlighted the idea that signal-processing techniques may have far-reaching applications to the identification, characterization and categorization of phenomena, both in the natural and in the social sciences, and that beyond the conventional remits of *prediction*, *filtering*, and *smoothing* there is a fourth and important new domain of applicability: the *description* of phenomena in science and in society. It is our hope therefore that the theory of signal processing with Lévy information herein outlined will find a variety of interesting and exciting applications.

The research reported in this paper has been supported in part by Shell Treasury Centre Limited, London, and by the Fields Institute, University of Toronto. The authors are grateful to N. Bingham, M. Davis, E. Hoyle, M. Grasselli, T. Hurd, S. Jaimungal, E. Mackie, A. Macrina, P. Parbhoo and M. Pistorius for helpful comments and discussions.

References

1. Wiener N. 1948 *Cybernetics: or the control and communication in the animal and the machine*. New York, NY: Wiley.
2. Wiener N. 1949 *The extrapolation, interpolation, and smoothing of stationary time series*. New York, NY: Wiley.
3. Wiener N. 1954 *The human use of human beings*. Boston, MA: Houghton Mifflin Co.
4. Kailath T. 1974 A view of three decades of linear filtering theory. *IEEE Trans. Inform. Theory* **20**, 146–181. (doi:10.1109/TIT.1974.1055174)
5. Davis MHA. 1977 *Linear estimation and stochastic control*. London, UK: Chapman & Hall.
6. Bellman RE. 1961 *Adaptive control processes*. Princeton, NJ: Princeton University Press.
7. Pontryagin LS, Boltyanskii VG, Gamkrelidze RV, Mishchenko EF. 1962 *The mathematical theory of optimal processes*. New York, NY: Wiley.
8. Kalman RE. 1994 Randomness reexamined. *Modelling, Ident. Cont.* **15**, 141–151. (doi:10.4173/mic.1994.3.3)
9. Liptser RS, Shiryaev AN. 2000 *Statistics of random processes*, vols. I and II, 2nd edn. Berlin, Germany: Springer.
10. Xiong J. 2008 *An introduction to stochastic filtering theory*. Oxford, UK: Oxford University Press.
11. Bain A, Crisan D. 2010 *Fundamentals of stochastic filtering*. New York, NY: Springer.
12. Rutkowski M. 1994 Optimal linear filtering and smoothing for a discrete time stable linear model. *J. Multivar. Anal.* **50**, 68–92. (doi:10.1006/jmva.1994.1035)
13. Ahn H, Feldman RE. 1999 Optimal filtering of a Gaussian signal in the presence of Lévy noise. *SIAM J. Appl. Math.* **60**, 359–369. (doi:10.1137/S0036139996312004)
14. Meyer-Brandis T, Proske F. 2004 Explicit solution of a nonlinear filtering problem for Lévy processes with application to finance. *Appl. Math. Optim.* **50**, 119–134. (doi:10.1007/s00245-004-0798-6)
15. Poklukar DR. 2006 Nonlinear filtering for jump-diffusions. *J. Comput. Appl. Math.* **197**, 558–567. (doi:10.1016/j.cam.2005.11.014)
16. Popa S, Sritharan SS. 2009 Nonlinear filtering of Ito–Lévy stochastic differential equations with continuous observations. *Commun. Stochast. Anal.* **3**, 313–330. See www.math.lsu.edu/cosa/3-3-01[195].pdf.
17. Grigelionis B, Mikulevicius R. 2011 Nonlinear filtering equations for stochastic processes with jumps. In *The Oxford handbook of nonlinear filtering* (eds D Crisan, B Rozovskii). Oxford, UK: Oxford University Press.

18. Bingham NP. 1975 Fluctuation theory in continuous time. *Adv. Appl. Probab.* **7**, 705–766. See www.jstor.org/stable/10.2307/1426397
19. Sato K. 1999 *Lévy processes and infinitely divisible distributions*. Cambridge, UK: Cambridge University Press.
20. Applebaum D. 2004 *Lévy processes and stochastic calculus*. Cambridge, UK: Cambridge University Press.
21. Bertoin J. 2004 *Lévy processes*. Cambridge, UK: Cambridge University Press.
22. Protter PE. 2005 *Stochastic integration and differential equations*, 2nd edn. New York, NY: Springer.
23. Kyprianou AE. 2006 *Introductory lectures on fluctuations of Lévy processes with applications*. Berlin, Germany: Springer.
24. Schoutens W. 2003 *Lévy processes in finance: pricing financial derivatives*. New York, NY: Wiley.
25. Esscher F. 1932 On the probability function in the collective theory of risk. *Skandinavisk Aktuarietidskrift* **15**, 175–195. (doi:10.1080/03461238.1932.10405883)
26. Gerber HU, Shiu ESW. 1994 Option pricing by Esscher transforms (with discussion). *Trans. Soc. Actuaries* **46**, 99–191.
27. Chan T. 1999 Pricing contingent claims on stocks driven by Lévy processes. *Ann. Appl. Probab.* **9**, 504–528. See www.jstor.org/stable/2667343.
28. Kallsen J, Shiryaev AN. 2002 The cumulant process and Esscher's change of measure. *Fin. Stochast.* **6**, 97–428. (doi:10.1007/s007800200069)
29. Hubalek F, Sgarra C. 2006 Esscher transform and the minimal entropy martingale measure for exponential Lévy models. *Quant. Finance* **6**, 125–145. (doi:10.1080/14697680600573099)
30. Schoutens W, Teugels JL. 1998 Lévy processes, polynomials and martingales. *Commun. Statist. Stochast. Models* **14**, 335–349. (doi:10.1080/15326349808807475)
31. Kallianpur G, Striebel C. 1968 Estimation of stochastic systems: arbitrary system process with additive white noise observation errors. *Ann. Math. Statist.* **39**, 785–801. (doi:10.1214/aoms/1177698311)
32. Shefrin H. 2008 *A behavioral approach to asset pricing*, 2nd edn. Burlington, MA: Academic Press.
33. Macrina A, Parbhoo PA. 2011 Randomized mixture models for pricing kernels. (http://arXiv.org/abs/1112.2059)
34. Segall A, Kailath T. 1975 The modelling of randomly modulated jump processes. *IEEE Trans. Inform. Theory* **21**, 135–143. (doi:10.1109/TIT.1975.1055359)
35. Wonham WM. 1965 Some applications of stochastic differential equations to optimal nonlinear filtering. *J. Soc. Ind. Appl. Math. A* **2**, 347–369. (doi:10.1137/0302028)
36. Heunis AJ. 2011 The innovation problem. In *The Oxford handbook of nonlinear filtering* (eds D Crisan, B Rozovskii). Oxford, UK: Oxford University Press.
37. Brody DC, Hughston LP. 2005 Finite-time stochastic reduction models. *J. Math. Phys.* **46**, 082101. (doi:10.1063/1.1990108)
38. Brody DC, Hughston LP. 2006 Quantum noise and stochastic reduction. *J. Phys. A* **39**, 833–876. (doi:10.1088/0305-4470/39/4/008)
39. Adler SA, Brody DC, Brun TA, Hughston LP. 2001 Martingale models for quantum state reduction. *J. Phys. A* **34**, 8795–8820. (doi:10.1088/0305-4470/34/42/306)
40. Brody DC, Hughston LP. 2002 Efficient simulation of quantum state reduction. *J. Math. Phys.* **43**, 5254–5261. (doi:10.1063/1.1512975)
41. Brody DC, Hughston LP, Macrina A. 2007 Beyond hazard rates: a new framework for credit-risk modelling. In *Advances in mathematical finance: Festschrift volume in honour of Dilip Madan* (eds R Elliot, M Fu, R Jarrow, J-Y Yen). Basel, Switzerland: Birkhäuser.
42. Brody DC, Hughston LP, Macrina A. 2008 Information-based asset pricing. *Int. J. Theoret. Appl. Finance* **11**, 107–142. (doi:10.1142/S0219024908004749) Reprinted as chapter 5 in *Finance at Fields* (eds MR Grasselli, LP Hughston). Singapore: World Scientific Publishing, 2012.
43. Rutkowski M, Yu N. 2007 On the Brody–Hughston–Macrina approach to modelling of defaultable term structure. *Int. J. Theoret. Appl. Finance* **10**, 557–589. (doi:10.1142/S0219024907004263)
44. Brody DC, Davis MHA, Friedman RL, Hughston LP. 2009 Informed traders. *Proc. R. Soc. A* **465**, 1103–1122. (doi:10.1098/rspa.2008.0465)
45. Filipović D, Hughston LP, Macrina A. 2012 Conditional density models for asset pricing. *Int. J. Theoret. Appl. Finance*, **15**, 1250002. (doi:10.1142/S0219024912500021) Reprinted as Chapter 9 in *Finance at Fields* (eds MR Grasselli, LP Hughston). Singapore: World Scientific Publishing, 2012.

46. Segall A, Davis MHA, Kailath T. 1975 Nonlinear filtering with counting observations. *IEEE Trans. Inform. Theory* **21**, 143–149. (doi:10.1109/TIT.1975.1055360)
47. Brémaud P. 1981 *Point processes and queues: martingale dynamics*. New York, NY: Springer.
48. Di Masi GB, Runggaldier WJ. 1983 Non-linear filtering with discontinuous observations and applications to life sciences. *Bull. Math. Biol.* **45**, 571–577. (doi:10.1007/BF02459588)
49. Kailath T, Poor HV. 1998 Detection of stochastic processes. *IEEE Trans. Inform. Theory* **44**, 2230–2259. (doi:10.1109/18.720538)
50. Yor M. 2007 Some remarkable properties of gamma processes. In *Advances in mathematical finance, Festschrift volume in honour of Dilip Madan* (eds R Elliott, M Fu, R Jarrow, J-Y Yen). Basel, Switzerland: Birkhäuser. (doi:10.1007/978-0-8176-4545-8_3)
51. Brody DC, Hughston LP, Macrina A. 2008 Dam rain and cumulative gain. *Proc. R. Soc. A* **464**, 1801–1822. (doi:10.1098/rspa.2007.0273)
52. Brody DC, Hughston LP, Mackie E. 2012 General theory of geometric Lévy models for dynamic asset pricing. *Proc. R. Soc. A* **468**, 1778–1798. (doi:10.1098/rspa.2011.0670)
53. Gani J. 1957 Problems in the probability theory of storage systems. *J. R. Statist. Soc. B* **19**, 181–206. See www.jstor.org/stable/2983814.
54. Kendall DG. 1957 Some problems in the theory of dams. *J. R. Statist. Soc. B* **19**, 207–212. See www.jstor.org/stable/2983815.
55. Gani J, Pyke R. 1960 The content of a dam as the supremum of an infinitely divisible process. *J. Math. Mech. (Indiana Univ. Math. J.)* **9**, 639–651. (doi:10.1512/iumj.1960.9.09038)
56. Hoyle E. 2010 Information-based models for finance and insurance. PhD thesis, Department of Mathematics, Imperial College London. (http://arXiv.org/abs/1010.0829)
57. Hoyle E, Hughston LP, Macrina A. 2011 Lévy random bridges and the modelling of financial information. *Stochast. Process. Appl.* **121**, 856–884. (doi:10.1016/j.spa.2010.12.003)
58. Madan DB, Seneta E. 1990 The variance gamma (V.G.) model for share market returns. *J. Bus.* **63**, 511–524. (doi:10.1086/296519)
59. Madan DB, Milne F. 1991 Option pricing with V.G. martingale components. *Math. Finance* **1**, 39–55. (doi:10.1111/j.1467-9965.1991.tb00018.x)
60. Madan DB, Carr P, Chang EC. 1998 The variance gamma process and option pricing. *Eur. Fin. Rev.* **2**, 79–105. (doi:10.1023/A:1009703431535)
61. Kozubowski TJ, Podgórski K. 2009 Distributional properties of the negative binomial Lévy process. *Probab. Math. Statist.* **29**, 43–71. See www.math.uni.wroc.pl/~pms/files/29.1/Article/29.1.3.pdf.
62. Schrödinger E. 1915 Zur Theorie der Fall- und Steigversuche an Teilchen mit Brownscher Bewegung. *Phys. Z.* **16**, 289–295.
63. Tweedie MCK. 1945 Inverse statistical variates. *Nature* **155**, 453–453. (doi:10.1038/155453a0)
64. Wasan MT. 1968 On an inverse Gaussian process. *Scand. Actuarial J.* **1968**, 69–96. (doi:10.1080/03461238.1968.10413264)
65. Rydberg TH. 1997 The normal inverse Gaussian Lévy process: simulation and approximation. *Commun. Statist. Stochast. Models* **13**, 887–910. (doi:10.1080/15326349708807456)
66. Barndorff-Nielsen OE. 1998 Processes of normal inverse Gaussian type. *Finance Stochast.* **2**, 41–68. (doi:10.1007/s007800050032)
67. Erdélyi A. 1953 *Higher transcendental functions*. Bateman Manuscript Project, vol. 2. New York, NY: McGraw-Hill.
68. Barndorff-Nielsen OE. 1977 Exponentially decreasing distributions for the logarithm of particle size. *Proc. R. Soc. Lond. A* **353**, 401–419. (doi:10.1098/rspa.1977.0041)
69. Carr P, Geman H, Madan D, Yor M. 2002 The fine structure of asset returns: an empirical investigation. *J. Bus.* **75**, 305–332. (doi:10.1086/338705)
70. Madan DB, Yor M. 2008 Representing the CGMY and Meixner Lévy processes as time changed Brownian motion. *J. Comput. Finance* **12**, 27–47.

Chapter 12

HEAT KERNEL MODELS FOR ASSET PRICING*

ANDREA MACRINA

Department of Mathematics
University College London
London WC1E 6BT, United Kingdom

and

Department of Actuarial Science
University of Cape Town
Rondebosch 7701, South Africa
a.macrina@ucl.ac.uk

Received 26 September 2013
Accepted 1 July 2014
Published 21 October 2014

A heat kernel approach is proposed for the development of a novel method for asset pricing over a finite time horizon. We work in an incomplete market setting and assume the existence of a pricing kernel that determines the prices of financial instruments. The pricing kernel is modeled by a weighted heat kernel driven by a multivariate Markov process. The heat kernel is chosen so as to provide enough freedom to ensure that the resulting model can be calibrated to appropriate data, e.g. to the initial term structure of bond prices. A class of models is presented for which the prices of bonds, caplets, and swaptions can be computed in closed form. The dynamical equations for the price processes are derived, and explicit formulae are obtained for the short rate of interest, the risk premium, and for the stochastic volatility of prices. Several of the closed-form models presented are driven by combinations of Markovian jump processes with different probability laws. Such models provide a basis for consistent applications in various market sectors, including equity markets, fixed-income markets, commodity markets, and insurance. The flexible multidimensional and multivariate structure on which the resulting price models are based lends itself well to the modeling of dependence across asset classes. As an illustration, the impact of spiraling debt, a typical feature of a financial crisis, is modeled explicitly, and the contagion effects can be readily observed in the dynamics of the associated asset returns.

Keywords: Asset pricing; pricing kernel; Markov processes; Lévy random bridges; equity; interest rates; debt; spread dynamics; contagion.

1. Introduction

In this paper, we take the view that in a modern asset pricing framework the following three principles should be upheld: (i) pricing models should be coherent across all asset classes traded in a financial market; (ii) the pricing models used in

*This chapter was originally published as: A. Macrina (2014) Heat Kernel Models for Asset Pricing. *International Journal of Theoretical and Applied Finance* **17** (7), 1–34.

the front offices of financial firms should be compatible with the risk management models used by such firms; and (iii) pricing models should be applicable both in the banking industry and in the insurance sector. These requirements imply that pricing models need to be formulated in such a way that they can be consistently used both in applications involving the real probability measure $\mathbb{P}$ (such as forecasting and risk management), and in applications involving the risk-neutral measure $\mathbb{Q}$ (such as derivatives pricing and hedging). At the same time, pricing models used should retain a high degree of flexibility and mathematical tractability, while guaranteeing the coherence of the price system for all financial assets.

In what follows, we propose a method for asset pricing that can be applied, in principle, to all asset classes, and that is sufficiently tractable that Monte Carlo techniques are not necessarily required for scenario simulations of price dynamics. The proposed method allows, in part, for the automatic calibration of the models to market data such as the initial prices of assets. The asset price system will be developed by modeling the pricing kernel (state-price density, stochastic discount factor) first. Once the pricing kernel has been specified and the connection with bond prices has been established, we show how the price processes for other asset classes can be derived in a natural way. We also consider how the situation in which the debt of a sovereign country gets out of control can be modeled.

The general setup in the analysis that follows will be developed in finite time, i.e. for $t \in [0, U]$ for some fixed finite time horizon $U < \infty$. We model a financial market by a filtered complete probability space $(\Omega, \mathcal{F}, \mathbb{P}, \{\mathcal{F}_t\})$ that satisfies the usual hypotheses, where $\mathbb{P}$ denotes the real probability measure and $\{\mathcal{F}_t\}$ is the market filtration. We consider a (multi-dimensional) process $\{X_t\}$ on $(\Omega, \mathcal{F}, \mathbb{P})$ and assume that the market filtration is generated by $\{X_t\}$. We shall assume that $\{X_t\}$ has the Markov property with respect to $\{\mathcal{F}_t\}$. We introduce the pricing kernel process $\{\pi_t\}$ to model the market preferences and the dynamics of interest rates in the economy. We write $\{S_t\}_{0\leq t\leq T<U}$ for the price process of a dividend-paying asset, and let $\{D_t\}_{0\leq t\leq T<U}$ denote the (continuous) dividend stream up until T. Then the price S_t at time t is given by

$$S_t = \frac{1}{\pi_t}\mathbb{E}^{\mathbb{P}}\left[\pi_T S_T + \int_t^T \pi_u D_u \mathrm{d}u \,\middle|\, \mathcal{F}_t\right]. \tag{1.1}$$

In order to calculate asset prices explicitly, the following ingredients need to be specified: (i) The Markov process $\{X_t\}$ that generates the market filtration, (ii) the pricing kernel $\{\pi_t\}$, (iii) the random variable S_T and the process $\{D_t\}$. For in-depth accounts about the theory of pricing kernels, preferences, asset pricing, and interest rate modeling, one may consult, e.g. Back (2010), Björk (2009), Cairns (2004), Cochrane (2005), Duffie (2001), and Brigo & Mercurio (2006).

In the next section, we introduce weighted heat kernels to define the class of pricing kernels treated in this paper. Heat kernel models have been proposed by Akahori *et al.* (2014) in an infinite-time setting, and by Akahori & Macrina (2012) in a finite-time context.

First, we summarize the construction of the pricing kernel presented in Akahori & Macrina (2012), and at the same time, we extend the approach so that automatic partial calibration can be accommodated. Then we write the pricing kernel models and the resulting discount bond price processes in a concise formalism, which remains unchanged if one applies a different probability measure. We provide general formulae for the price processes of discount bonds, caplets and swaptions, and the associated interest rate process. The short rate of interest is by construction nonnegative.

In Sec. 3, we show how the formalism reveals a class of rational asset price models, the structure of which can be decomposed, like the models of Flesaker & Hughston (1996), into a deterministic part and a martingale under an auxiliary measure. Thus we are able to derive closed-form price processes for bonds, caplets, and swaptions. Explicit price models are then obtained by specifying the dynamics of the market information flow and the degrees of freedom in the formulation of the pricing kernel model. The dynamics of certain price processes have time-dependent lower and upper bounds, a feature we not necessarily view as being a shortcoming.

In Sec. 4, we derive the dynamical equation for the bond price processes introduced in the previous section in the case for which the market filtration is generated by a continuous process. The market price of risk process for this class of pricing models incorporates a discernible part that can be identified as the incentive for accepting model risk.

In Sec. 5, we introduce multivariate Lévy random bridges and extend the pricing framework to an incomplete market. A generalized class of asset price models characterized by a Fourier transform is presented, and asset price models with higher-order rational structures are developed. Explicit price processes driven by jump processes are derived.

In Sec. 6, the proposed approach is applied to general asset pricing. We show how asset price models constructed under the P-measure translate into asset price models equipped with stochastic interest rates and stochastic volatility under the Q-measure. The interaction between the bond price process and, e.g. the equity component of the discounted share price process is clearly identifiable. This property makes our method appealing for the construction of hedging strategies against losses due to the exposure of a position in a specific market sector. Additional examples of multivariate asset pricing models driven by jump processes are given.

In Sec. 7, we model the impact of out-of-control sovereign debt on the price dynamics of sovereign bonds. The flexibility of the heat kernel approach allows for the construction of explicit dependence models linking the price evolution of, e.g. bonds issued by several sovereign governments. We show that contagion effects arise endogenously, and illustrate with some graphs the impact of dependent economies and markets on the price dynamics of assets.

A. Macrina

2. Pricing Kernel Models and the Pricing of Bonds, Caplets and Swaptions

The backbone of the pricing approach considered in this paper is the following class of pricing kernel models $\{\pi_t\}_{0\leq t\leq U}$:

$$\pi_t = f_0(t) + f_1(t)\int_0^{U-t} \mathbb{E}[F(t+u, X_{t+u})\,|\,X_t]w(t,u)\,\mathrm{d}u, \tag{2.1}$$

where $\{X_t\}$ is an unspecified Markov process defined for $t\in[0,U]$ such that $t+u\leq U$. Furthermore, $f_0(t)$ and $f_1(t)$ are deterministic, positive, and nonincreasing functions, $F(t,x)$ is a positive measurable function, and $w(t,u)$ is a deterministic, positive and measurable function that satisfies

$$w(t, u-s) \leq w(t-s, u)$$

for $s\leq t\wedge u$. Assuming that $F(t,x)$ and $w(t,u)$ are chosen such that the integral in (2.1) is finite for all t, it can be proven that the considered pricing kernel processes are indeed supermartingales adapted to the filtration generated by $\{X_t\}$. We refer to Akahori & Macrina (2012), Sec. 2, for a proof that can be applied also in the present context.

As a special case of the general pricing formula (1.1), the price process of a discount bond with maturity T, is given by

$$P_{tT} = \frac{1}{\pi_t}\,\mathbb{E}[\pi_T\,|\,X_t], \tag{2.2}$$

where $0\leq t\leq T<U$. We keep in mind that the market filtration is generated by the Markov process $\{X_t\}$, and thus it suffices to take the expectation conditional only on X_t. The conditional expectation of π_T can be computed explicitly to obtain

$$\mathbb{E}[\pi_T\,|\,X_t] = f_0(T) + f_1(T)\int_{T-t}^{U-t} \mathbb{E}[F(t+u, X_{t+u})\,|\,X_t]w(T, u-T+t)\mathrm{d}u,$$

where the tower property is invoked and a variable substitution is applied. We define

$$Y_{tT} = \int_{T-t}^{U-t} \mathbb{E}[F(t+u, X_{t+u})\,|\,X_t]w(T, u-T+t)\mathrm{d}u. \tag{2.3}$$

The bond price process can then be written in the compact form

$$P_{tT} = \frac{f_0(T) + f_1(T)\,Y_{tT}}{f_0(t) + f_1(t)\,Y_{tt}}, \tag{2.4}$$

and the initial term structure is given by

$$P_{0t} = \frac{f_0(t) + f_1(t)\,Y_{0t}}{f_0(0) + f_1(0)\,Y_{00}}.$$

Heat Kernel Models for Asset Pricing

We deduce that

$$f_0(t) = P_{0t}[1 + f_1(0)Y_{00}] - f_1(t)Y_{0t}, \tag{2.5}$$

where we may set $f_0(0) = 1$ with no loss of generality. By inserting (2.5) in (2.4), we obtain

$$P_{tT} = \frac{P_{0T} + y(T)(Y_{tT} - Y_{0T})}{P_{0t} + y(t)(Y_{tt} - Y_{0t})}, \tag{2.6}$$

where

$$y(t) = \frac{f_1(t)}{1 + f_1(0)Y_{00}},$$

for $0 \leq t \leq T$. Similarly, the expression for the pricing kernel can be written in the form

$$\pi_t = \pi_0[P_{0t} + y(t)(Y_{tt} - Y_{0t})], \tag{2.7}$$

where $\pi_0 = 1 + f_1(0)Y_{00}$. We note that the pricing kernel is now calibrated to the initial term structure of discount bonds. Assuming that the bond price function is differentiable with respect to T, the expression for the instantaneous forward rate $\{r_{tT}\}$ is given by

$$\begin{aligned} r_{tT} &= -\partial_T \ln(P_{tT}) \\ &= -\frac{\partial_T P_{0T} + (Y_{tT} - Y_{0T})\partial_T y(T) + y(T)(\partial_T Y_{tT} - \partial_T Y_{0T})}{P_{0T} + y(T)(Y_{tT} - Y_{0T})}. \end{aligned} \tag{2.8}$$

The process $\{r_t\}$ for the short rate of interest can then be deduced by setting $r_t = r_{tT|T=t}$:

$$r_t = -\frac{\partial_t P_{0t} + (Y_{tt} - Y_{0t})\partial_t y(t) + y(t)\{(\partial_T Y_{tT} - \partial_T Y_{0T})\}_{T=t}}{P_{0t} + y(t)(Y_{tt} - Y_{0t})}. \tag{2.9}$$

Once the bond price system is derived, one can calculate the price of fixed-income derivatives such as caplets and swaptions. We consider a t-maturity swaption contract with strike K, which is written on a collection of discount bonds P_{tT_i} with maturities $\{T_i\}_{1,\ldots,n}$. An application of the pricing formula (1.1) shows that the price Swp_{0t} of the swaption at time zero is

$$Swp_{0t} = \frac{1}{\pi_0}\mathbb{E}\left[\pi_t \left(1 - P_{tT_n} - K\sum_{i=1}^{n} P_{tT_i}\right)^+\right], \tag{2.10}$$

where

$$P_{tT_i} = \frac{P_{0T_i} + y(T_i)(Y_{tT_i} - Y_{0T_i})}{P_{0t} + y(t)(Y_{tt} - Y_{0t})}.$$

Here, for simplicity, we consider a swaption written on a payer's interest rate swap with unit notional and unit year fraction. The maturity of the swaption is assumed to coincide with the first of the n reset dates of the underlying swap, that is $t = T_0$.

Then, by use of (2.7), we obtain

$$Swp_{0t} = \mathbb{E}\left[\left(P_{0t} - P_{0T_n} - K\sum_{i}^{n} P_{0T_i} + y(t)(Y_{tt} - Y_{0t})\right.\right.$$
$$\left.\left. - y(T_n)(Y_{tT_n} - Y_{0T_n}) - K\sum_{i=1}^{n} y(T_i)(Y_{tT_i} - Y_{0T_i})\right)^+\right].$$

The price of caplets can be calculated in an analogous way. Further details for the calculation of caplets and swaptions prices follow in the next section.

We may wonder at this stage whether it might be possible to construct a class of discount bond price processes for which the associated prices of interest rate derivatives can be calculated in closed form. We shall present such bond price models in detail in the next section. Before, we prepare the ground by making the following observation.

Proposition 2.1. *Let $\{M_t\}_{0\leq t<U}$ be an $(\{\mathcal{F}_t\},\mathbb{P})$-martingale that induces a change of measure from $\mathbb{P}$ to a measure $\mathbb{M}$ with respect to which the Markov property of $\{X_t\}$ is preserved. Let $f_0(t)$ and $f_1(t)$ be deterministic, positive, nonincreasing functions, let $F(t,x)$ be a measurable positive function, and let $w(t,u)$ be a positive measurable function satisfying*

$$w(t, u-s) \leq w(t-s, u),$$

for $s \leq t\wedge u$. Let $\{Y^{\mathbb{M}}_{tT}\}_{0\leq t\leq T<U}$ be defined by

$$Y^{\mathbb{M}}_{tT} = \int_{T-t}^{U-t} \mathbb{E}^{\mathbb{M}}[F(t+u, X_{t+u}) \,|\, X_t]\, w(T, u-T+t)\,\mathrm{d}u,$$

where $F(t,x)$ and $w(t,u)$ are such that $Y^{\mathbb{M}}_{tT} < \infty$ for all t. Then, the process

$$\pi_t = \frac{\pi_0}{M_0}[P_{0t} + y^{\mathbb{M}}(t)(Y^{\mathbb{M}}_{tt} - Y^{\mathbb{M}}_{0t})]M_t \tag{2.11}$$

is a positive $(\{\mathcal{F}_t\},\mathbb{P})$-supermartingale where $\pi_0 = 1 + f_1(0)Y^{\mathbb{M}}_{00}$,

$$P_{0t} = \frac{f_0(t) + f_1(t)\,Y^{\mathbb{M}}_{0t}}{1 + f_1(0)\,Y^{\mathbb{M}}_{00}}$$

and

$$y^{\mathbb{M}}(t) = \frac{f_1(t)}{1 + f_1(0)Y^{\mathbb{M}}_{00}}.$$

Proof. By inserting the expressions for π_0, P_{0t} and $y^{\mathbb{M}}(t)$ in the model (2.11), we recover $\pi_t = M_t/M_0[f_0(t) + f_1(t)Y^{\mathbb{M}}_{tt}]$. Then, for $0 \leq s \leq t < U$, it follows that

$$\mathbb{E}^{\mathbb{P}}[\pi_t \,|\, \mathcal{F}_s] = \mathbb{E}^{\mathbb{P}}\left[\frac{M_t}{M_0}(f_0(t) + f_1(t)Y^{\mathbb{M}}_{tt}) \,|\, \mathcal{F}_s\right] = \frac{M_s}{M_0}\,\mathbb{E}^{\mathbb{M}}[f_0(t) + f_1(t)Y^{\mathbb{M}}_{tt} \,|\, \mathcal{F}_s]$$
$$\leq \frac{M_s}{M_0}\,\mathbb{E}^{\mathbb{M}}[f_0(s) + f_1(s)Y^{\mathbb{M}}_{ss}] = \pi_s \tag{2.12}$$

since the process $\{f_0(t) + f_1(t)Y^{\mathbb{M}}_{tt}\}$ is an $(\{\mathcal{F}_t\}, \mathbb{M})$-supermartingale; compare with (2.1) via (2.3). □

Taking (2.11) as the model for the pricing kernel, it follows that the price process $\{P_{tT}\}$ of the discount bond is given by

$$P_{tT} = \frac{P_{0T} + y^{\mathbb{M}}(T)(Y^{\mathbb{M}}_{tT} - Y^{\mathbb{M}}_{0T})}{P_{0t} + y^{\mathbb{M}}(t)(Y^{\mathbb{M}}_{tt} - Y^{\mathbb{M}}_{0t})}, \tag{2.13}$$

where P_{0t} is the initial term structure for $0 \le t \le T < U$. To verify the validity of (2.13), the pricing kernel model (2.11) is inserted in (2.2) and the abstract version of the Bayes formula is applied to obtain the discount bond price processes expressed under the $\mathbb{M}$-measure. Thus, if convenient, we can construct pricing kernel models by making use of the $\mathbb{M}$-measure while using the form (2.11). By comparing (2.6) with (2.13), we observe that the form of the asset price formulae remains unchanged.

3. Closed-Form and Explicit Price Models

In this section, we construct a class of pricing kernels for which the price processes of underlying and derivative assets are obtained analytically. We explicitly calculate the price processes of bonds, caplets, and swaptions, and note that some models lead to bounded price processes — a property we not necessarily view as a shortcoming.

In order to obtain explicit pricing models, the following quantities need to be specified in the definition of the pricing kernel (2.1): (i) The finite-time Markov process $\{X_t\}$ that generates the market filtration and drives all prices, (ii) the positive function $F(t+u, x)$ that, to a great extent, characterizes the type of pricing model (the DNA of the model), (iii) the weight function $w(t, u)$, and (iv) the deterministic functions $f_0(t)$ and $f_1(t)$. The particular class of models considered in this paper allows for explicit calibration of $f_0(t)$ to the initial term structure, and for a one-to-one correspondence between the degree of freedom $f_1(t)$ and option data (e.g. caplets and swaptions). Thus we only specify the Markov process $\{X_t\}$, $F(t+u, x)$, and $w(t, u)$.

3.1. *Quadratic and exponential quadratic models*

Two examples are provided in Akahori & Macrina (2012), namely the *quadratic* and the *exponential quadratic classes*. Here, for example, the Markov process $\{X_t\}$, that generates $\{\mathcal{F}_t\}$, is taken to be the Brownian random bridge $\{L_{tU}\}$ defined by

$$L_{tU} = \sigma\, t\, X_U + \beta_{tU}, \tag{3.1}$$

where σ is a constant parameter, X_U is an $\mathcal{F}_U$-measurable random variable with *a priori* density $p(x)$, and $\{\beta_{tU}\}_{0\le t\le U}$ is an independent standard Brownian bridge where U is fixed. In order to obtain the quadratic models, $F(t+u, x) = x^2$ and $w(t, u) = U - t - u$ are chosen and inserted in the pricing kernel model (2.1). By following the steps from (2.2) to (2.4) one arrives at the explicit expression for the discount bond price process within the quadratic class. This is one way. Another way is to realize that there exists a probability measure $\mathbb{M}$, equivalent to $\mathbb{P}$, under which the Markov process (3.1) has the law of a standard Brownian bridge for $t \in [0, U)$. The change of measure from $\mathbb{P}$ to $\mathbb{M}$ is induced by the density martingale $\{M_t\}_{0 \le t < U}$ defined by

$$\mathrm{d}M_t = -\frac{\sigma U}{U-t}\mathbb{E}^{\mathbb{P}}[X_U \mid L_{tU}] M_t \, \mathrm{d}W_t^{\mathbb{P}},$$

where $\{W_t^{\mathbb{P}}\}$ is a Brownian motion process specified by (4.7) in the next section. The expectation $\mathbb{E}^{\mathbb{P}}[X_U \mid L_{tU}]$ can be calculated by the conditional version of Bayes formula as shown for instance in Brody *et al.* (2008). Thus, instead of deriving the explicit model for $\{P_{tT}\}$ by use of the $\mathbb{P}$-measure, we instead apply Proposition 2.1, in particular (2.13), and work with the probability measure $\mathbb{M}$, which simplifies the task of working out conditional expectations. As we shall see in Sec. 5, changing the measure to an auxiliary probability measures has also other advantages. The expression (2.13) for the discount bond then simplifies such that it can be written in the form

$$P_{tT} = \frac{P_{0T} + b(T)\, A_t}{P_{0t} + b(t)\, A_t}, \tag{3.2}$$

where, for the quadratic class, one has

$$\begin{aligned} P_{0t} &= \frac{f_0(t) + \frac{1}{12U}(U-t)^3(U+3t)\, f_1(t)}{1 + \frac{1}{12}U^3 f_1(0)}, \\ b(t) &= \frac{(U-t)^4 f_1(t)}{4U[1 + \frac{1}{12}U^3 f_1(0)]}, \\ A_t &= \frac{U}{(U-t)^2} L_{tU}^2 - \frac{t}{U-t}, \quad 0 \le t \le T < U. \end{aligned} \tag{3.3}$$

An analogous calculation leads to the explicit expression for the discount bond price process within the exponential quadratic class which is characterized by

$$F(t,x) = \exp\left(\frac{x^2}{2\,(U-t)}\right)$$

and $w(t,u) = (U-t-u)^{\eta-1/2}$, $\eta > 1/2$. The explicit bond price process (2.4), or equivalently (2.13), can then also be written in the form (3.2) where

$$\begin{aligned} P_{0t} &= \frac{f_0(t) + \frac{1}{\eta}(U-t)^{\eta} U^{1/2} f_1(t)}{1 + \frac{1}{\eta}U^{\eta+1/2} f_1(0)}, \quad b(t) = \frac{\frac{1}{\eta}(U-t)^{\eta} U^{1/2} f_1(t)}{1 + \frac{1}{\eta}U^{\eta+1/2} f_1(0)}, \\ A_t &= \sqrt{1 - \frac{t}{U}} \exp\left(\frac{L_{tU}^2}{2(U-t)}\right) - 1, \quad 0 \le t \le T < U. \end{aligned} \tag{3.4}$$

It can be proven that the process $\{A_t\}_{0 \le t < U}$, in (3.3) and (3.4), is an $(\{\mathcal{F}_t\}, \mathbb{M})$-martingale by showing $\mathbb{E}^{\mathbb{M}}[|M_t|] < \infty$ and $\mathbb{E}^{\mathbb{M}}[A_t | \mathcal{F}_t] = A_s$ for $0 \le s \le t < U$.

This property makes the representation (3.2) appealing for the construction of further models. We summarize the various observation as follows:

Lemma 3.1. *Given the pricing kernel class* (2.1), *there exist equivalent measures* $\mathbb{M}$, *deterministic functions* $b(t)$ *and* $(\{\mathcal{F}_t\}, \mathbb{M})$*-martingales* $\{A_t\}_{0\le t<U}$ *such that*

$$\pi_t = \frac{\pi_0}{M_0}[P_{0t} + b(t)\, A_t] M_t, \tag{3.5}$$

where $\{M_t\}_{0\le t<U}$ *is the density martingale inducing the change-of-measure* $\mathbb{P} \to \mathbb{M}$, *and* P_{0t} *is the initial term structure of the discount bond system with price process*

$$P_{tT} = \frac{P_{0T} + b(T)\, A_t}{P_{0t} + b(t)\, A_t} \tag{3.6}$$

for $0 \le t \le T < U$. *Assuming that the discount bond system is differentiable with respect to its maturity parameter* T, *the associated short rate of interest process* $\{r_t\}$ *is given by*

$$r_t = -\frac{\partial_t P_{0t} + A_t \partial_t b(t)}{P_{0t} + b(t)\, A_t}. \tag{3.7}$$

Proof. To prove (3.7), we first derive the instantaneous forward rate $\{r_{tT}\}$ as in (2.8), that is by $r_{tT} = -\partial_T \ln(P_{tT})$, and then we set $T = t$ in the resulting process $\{r_{tT}\}$ which gives us the short rate $\{r_t\}$. □

Although written in a less unifying form, and in the case of the quadratic models with fewer useful degrees of freedom, the quadratic and exponential quadratic models were first developed in Akahori & Macrina (2012). The exponential quadratic class appears also in Hughston & Macrina (2012). We also note that interest rate models with a quadratic or exponential quadratic structure have been studied in Jamashidian (1996) and McCloud (2009, 2012), too. More examples of asset price models of the form (3.6), and thus associated with a pricing kernel of the type (3.5), are given in Secs. 5–7. Those models also include jumps in their dynamics.

3.2. *Caplets and swaptions*

We now proceed to calculate the prices of caplets and swaptions when the pricing kernel model is of the form (3.5). At time 0, the price C_{0t} of a caplet with maturity t and strike K can be expressed as the price of a put bond option, that is

$$C_{0t} = \frac{1}{\pi_0}\mathbb{E}^{\mathbb{P}}[\pi_t(K - P_{tT})^+]. \tag{3.8}$$

Expressions (3.5) and (3.6) are plugged in, whereby M_t/M_0 in (3.5) is utilized to change the probability measure from $\mathbb{P}$ to $\mathbb{M}$. Since $P_{0t} + b(t)\, A_t$ is by construction positive, it can be taken inside the *max*-function so to obtain

$$C_{0t} = \mathbb{E}^{\mathbb{M}}[(KP_{0t} - P_{0T} + [Kb(t) - b(T)]A_t)^+]. \tag{3.9}$$

In order for the caplet to be in-the-money, $[Kb(t) - b(T)]\, A_t > P_{0T} - KP_{0t}$ needs to hold. There are three cases: (i) $Kb(t) - b(T) > 0$ leading to $A_t >$

A. Macrina

$(P_{0T} - KP_{0t})/|Kb(t) - b(T)|$, (ii) $Kb(t) - b(T) < 0$ leading to $A_t < -(P_{0T} - KP_{0t})/|Kb(t) - b(T)|$, and (iii) $Kb(t) - b(T) = 0$ resulting in A_t being undetermined, in which case we may set $C_{0t} = 0$. The caplet price can thus be written as follows:

$$C_{0t} = (KP_{0t} - P_{0T}) \int_{a^*} p(a)\mathrm{d}a + [Kb(t) - b(T)] \int_{a^*} a\, p(a)\mathrm{d}a, \tag{3.10}$$

where $p(a)\mathrm{d}a = \mathbb{M}[A_t \in \mathrm{d}a]$. Furthermore, $a^* = \{a : a > a_c \text{ if } Kb(t) - b(T) > 0\}$ or $a^* = \{a : a < -a_c \text{ if } Kb(t) - b(T) < 0\}$, where

$$a_c := \frac{P_{0T} - KP_{0t}}{|Kb(t) - b(T)|}. \tag{3.11}$$

We set $C_{0t} = 0$ for the case $Kb(t) - b(T) = 0$. As an example, we apply the caplet price formula (3.10) in the case that the pricing kernel is modeled by the quadratic class (3.3). The $\mathbb{M}$-density $p(a)$ is quadratic Gaussian in this class, and the critical value κ necessary to calculate the value of the in-the-money option is

$$\kappa = \sqrt{1 + \frac{U-t}{t}\,\frac{P_{0t} - KP_{0T}}{|Kb(t) - b(T)|}}. \tag{3.12}$$

Then, the caplet price, in the quadratic class, can be expressed as follows: For $K\,b(t) - b(T) > 0$, we have

$$C_{0t} = 2(KP_{0t} - P_{0T})N(-\kappa) + \sqrt{\frac{2}{\pi}}\frac{|\,Kb(t) - b(T)|\,t}{U-t}\,\kappa\,\exp\!\left(-\frac{1}{2}\kappa^2\right), \tag{3.13}$$

where $N(x)$ denotes the cumulative normal distribution function. For $K\,b(t) - b(T) < 0$, the caplet price is

$$C_{0t} = (KP_{0t} - P_{0T})(2\,N(\kappa) - 1) + \sqrt{\frac{2}{\pi}}\frac{|\,K\,b(t) - b(T)|\,t}{U-t}\,\kappa\,\exp\left(-\frac{1}{2}\kappa^2\right). \tag{3.14}$$

For $K\,b(t) - b(T) = 0$, we set $C_{0t} = 0$, by definition.

A similar calculation leads to the analytical caplet price in the case one applies the exponential quadratic class (3.4). We shall give the details of an example utilizing the exponential quadratic class when computing the explicit price of a swaption.

We recall that the price Swp_{0t} of a swaption with maturity t and strike K is given by (2.10). Assuming that the pricing kernel model is of the form (3.5), we obtain

$$Swp_{0t} = \mathbb{E}^{\mathbb{M}}\left[\left(P_{0t} - P_{0T_n} - K\sum_{i=1}^{n} P_{0T_i} + \left[b(t) - b(T_n) - K\sum_{i=1}^{n} b(T_i)\right] A_t\right)^{+}\right]. \tag{3.15}$$

The swaption price is nonzero if the argument of the *max*-function is positive. We are lead to three cases that depend on the sign of $b(t) - b(T_n) - K[b(T_1) + \cdots + b(T_n)]$.

Similar to the calculation of the caplet price above, the swaption price can be written in a form that includes the three cases:

$$Swp_{0t} = \left(P_{0t} - P_{0T_n} - K\sum_{i=1}^{n} P_{0T_i}\right)\int_{a^*} p(a)\mathrm{d}a + \left[b(t) - b(T_n) - K\sum_{i=1}^{n} b(T_i)\right]\int_{a^*} a\,p(a)\mathrm{d}a, \tag{3.16}$$

where $p(a)\mathrm{d}a = \mathbb{M}[A_t \in \mathrm{d}a]$. Here, $a^* = \{a : a > a_S$ if $b(t) - b(T_n) - K[b(T_1) + \cdots + b(T_n)] > 0\}$ or $a^* = \{a : a < -a_S$ if $b(t) - b(T_n) - K[b(T_1) + \cdots + b(T_n)] < 0\}$ where

$$a_S := \frac{K\sum_{i=1}^{n} P_{0T_i} + P_{0T_n} - P_{0t}}{|b(t) - b(T_n) - K\sum_{i=1}^{n} b(T_i)|}. \tag{3.17}$$

In the case that $b(t) - b(T_n) - K[b(T_1) + \cdots + b(T_n)] = 0$, we set $Swp_{0t} = 0$. We note here that the strike K, the maturity t and the reset dates T_i, $i = 1, \ldots, n$, are all fixed contractually. This means that the discriminant as to which of the three cases prevails, is essentially predetermined in the swaption contract once a specific pricing model is chosen.

Next, we compute the price of a swaption by use of the exponential quadratic class (3.4). The swaption price is given as follows: We first define

$$\nu = \sqrt{\frac{2U}{t}\ln\left[\left(1 - \frac{t}{U}\right)^{-1/2}\left(\frac{K\sum_{i=1}^{n} P_{0T_i} + P_{0T_n} - P_{0t}}{|b(t) - b(T_n) - K\sum_{i=1}^{n} b(T_i)|} + 1\right)\right]}. \tag{3.18}$$

Then, for $b(t) - b(T_n) - K[b(T_1) + \cdots + b(T_n)] > 0$, we have

$$Swp_{0t} = 2\left(P_{0t} - P_{0T_n} - K\sum_{i=1}^{n} P_{0T_i}\right)N(-\nu) + 2\left[b(t) - b(T_n) - K\sum_{i=1}^{n} b(T_i)\right]\left(N\left(-\sqrt{1 - \frac{t}{U}}\,\nu\right) - N(-\nu)\right). \tag{3.19}$$

For $b(t) - b(T_n) - K[b(T_1) + \cdots + b(T_n)] < 0$, we have

$$Swp_{0t} = \left(P_{0t} - P_{0T_n} - K\sum_{i=1}^{n} P_{0T_i}\right)(2N(\nu) - 1) - 2\left|b(t) - b(T_n) - K\sum_{i=1}^{n} b(T_i)\right|\left(N\left(\sqrt{1 - \frac{t}{U}}\,\nu\right) - N(\nu)\right). \tag{3.20}$$

For the case $b(t) - b(T_n) - K[b(T_1) + \cdots + b(T_n)] = 0$, we have $Swp_{0t} = 0$, by definition. An analogous calculation leads to the explicit price of a swaption when applying the quadratic models (3.3).

3.3. *Boundedness of prices*

Bond prices fluctuate by construction between zero and one, and the associated interest rate is nonnegative. However, the bond price processes produced by the above models, e.g. the quadratic and the exponential quadratic models, have tighter time-dependent bounds, and the same holds for the interest rate and the yield of the bond. One might think that having bounded bond prices and associated interest rates is a shortcoming. Such boundedness is a general feature of so-called rational models (Flesaker & Hughston (1996), Brody & Hughston (2004), Hughston & Rafailidis (2005) and Parbhoo (2013)). On the contrary, we think that such a feature may be advantageous, especially if the time-dependent bounds are wide enough for the interest rate to have sufficient freedom. The bounds may be put in relation with economic policies of which goal is to keep bond prices within a certain range. In turn, this may suggest to use the additional degree of freedom $f_1(t)$, cast inside the deterministic function $b(t)$, to include regulators' policies, for instance. Research regarding bounded asset prices and the relation to regulators' policies and markets might be continued elsewhere. We keep the boundedness property inherent in certain rational asset pricing models in our mind for when we later turn to general asset pricing, Sec. 6, and to the impact on prices by an economy's spiraling deficit, Sec. 7. The higher-order price models presented in Sec. 5 do not necessarily exhibit tighter bounds.

4. Dynamical Equations

We derive the dynamical equation of the bond price for the case that the martingale $\{A_t\}$ introduced in Lemma 3.1 is an Ito process. The expression of the bond price dynamics reveals the market price of risk, which is obtained endogenously. It turns out that the market price of risk process is constituted by two distinct stochastic components. We highlight an example in which the unambiguous interpretation of the two components emerges naturally: One part of the risk premium is associated with the stochasticity of a financial market due to noisy information about the market factors. The second part of the risk premium can be identified as model risk that is directly related to the choice of the class of price models. Furthermore, the Brownian motion that drives the bond price process arises also endogenously, and is identified with the innovations process updating the price process as the quality of market information improves.

Proposition 4.1. *Let $\{W_t^{\mathbb{P}}\}_{0\leq t<U}$ be a standard $(\{\mathcal{F}_t\},\mathbb{P})$-Brownian motion. Let the $(\{\mathcal{F}_t\},\mathbb{M})$-martingale $\{A_t\}_{0\leq t<U}$, considered in Lemma* 3.1, *satisfy*

$$\mathrm{d}A_t = \nu_t(\mathrm{d}W_t^{\mathbb{P}} + \vartheta_t\mathrm{d}t), \quad A_0 = 0, \tag{4.1}$$

where $\{\nu_t\}_{0\leq t<U}$ and $\{\vartheta_t\}_{0\leq t<U}$ are well-defined $\{\mathcal{F}_t\}$-adapted processes. Then, the discount bond price process (3.6) *satisfies*

$$\frac{\mathrm{d}P_{tT}}{P_{tT}} = (r_t + \lambda_t\Omega_{tT})\mathrm{d}t + \Omega_{tT}\mathrm{d}W_t^{\mathbb{P}}, \tag{4.2}$$

where $\{r_t\}$ *is determined by* (3.7) *and*

$$\lambda_t = \vartheta_t - \nu_t \frac{b(t)}{P_{0t} + b(t)\, A_t}, \tag{4.3}$$

$$\Omega_{tT} = \nu_t \left[\frac{b(T)}{P_{0T} + b(T)\, A_t} - \frac{b(t)}{P_{0t} + b(t)\, A_t} \right].$$

We note here that, via the Girsanov Theorem, we have introduced an $(\{\mathcal{F}_t\}, \mathbb{M})$-Brownian motion $\{W_t^{\mathbb{M}}\}$ that satisfies $\mathrm{d}W_t^{\mathbb{M}} = \mathrm{d}W_t^{\mathbb{P}} + \vartheta_t \mathrm{d}t$.

Lemma 4.1. *The instantaneous forward rate* $\{r_{tT}\}$ *of a bond with price dynamics* (4.2) *satisfies the dynamical equation*

$$\frac{\mathrm{d}r_{tT}}{r_{tT}} = -\sigma_{tT}\, \Omega_{tT} \mathrm{d}t + \sigma_{tT} (\mathrm{d}W_t^{\mathbb{P}} + \lambda_t \mathrm{d}t), \tag{4.4}$$

where the instantaneous forward rate volatility $\{\sigma_{tT}\}$ *is defined by*

$$\sigma_{tT} = -\nu_t \left(\frac{b(T)}{P_{0T} + b(T) A_t} - \frac{\partial_T b(T)}{\partial_T P_{0T} + A_t \partial_T b(T)} \right). \tag{4.5}$$

The dynamical equations derived in Proposition 4.1 and in Lemma 4.1 are obtained by applying Ito's differentiation rules to (3.2) given the specification (4.1). The stochastic differential equation for the short rate of interest $\{r_t\}$ is given by

$$\frac{\mathrm{d}r_t}{r_t} = \left(\frac{\partial_{tt} P_{0t} + A_t \partial_{tt} b(t)}{\partial_t P_{0t} + A_t \partial_t b(t)} + r_t \right) \mathrm{d}t + \sigma_t (\mathrm{d}W_t^{\mathbb{P}} + \lambda_t \mathrm{d}t), \tag{4.6}$$

where $\{\lambda_t\}$ is the instantaneous market price of risk (4.3) and the volatility σ_t is obtained by setting $T = t$ in (4.5). Here we implicitly assume that the deterministic function $b(t)$ is twice differentiable. We emphasize that the deduced instantaneous forward rates have the HJM-form, cf. Heath *et al.* (1992) and Filipović (2009). The stochastic differential equations (4.4) and (4.6) can be written with respect to the risk-neutral measure $\mathbb{Q}$, which is associated with the market price of risk $\{\lambda_t\}$, by introducing $(\{\mathcal{F}_t\}, \mathbb{Q})$-Brownian motion $\{W_t^{\mathbb{Q}}\}_{0 \le t < U}$ that satisfies $\mathrm{d}W_t^{\mathbb{Q}} = \mathrm{d}W_t^{\mathbb{P}} + \lambda_t \mathrm{d}t$.

4.1. *Model risk*

The risk premium $\{\lambda_t\}$ in (4.3) is composed by two adapted processes, that is $\{\vartheta_t\}$ and another that incorporates $\{\nu_t\}$. In order to better understand the role these two components play, we consider the bond price processes generated by (3.3) and (3.4) and which are driven by the Markov process (3.1). The dynamical equation satisfied by these bond price models belongs to the class produced in Proposition 4.1, and the Brownian motion $\{W_t^{\mathbb{P}}\}$ satisfies

$$\mathrm{d}W_t^{\mathbb{P}} = \mathrm{d}L_{tU} - \frac{1}{U - t} (\sigma U\, \mathbb{E}^{\mathbb{P}}[X_U \,|\, L_{tU}] - L_{tU}) \mathrm{d}t. \tag{4.7}$$

It can be shown, by Lévy's characterization of Brownian motion, that the process satisfying (4.7) is indeed an $(\{\mathcal{F}_t\}, \mathbb{P})$-Brownian motion for $t \in [0, U)$, see Brody *et al.* (2008). Furthermore, it follows that the process $\{\vartheta_t\}$ is given by

$$\vartheta_t = \frac{\sigma U}{U-t} \mathbb{E}^{\mathbb{P}}[X_U \mid L_{tU}],$$

and that $\{\nu_t\}$ satisfies (i)

$$\nu_t = \frac{2U}{(U-t)^2} L_{tU}$$

in the case of the quadratic models (3.3), and (ii)

$$\nu_t = \frac{L_{tU}}{\sqrt{U(U-t)}} \exp\left[\frac{L_{tU}^2}{2(U-t)}\right]$$

in the case of the exponential quadratic models (3.4). We thus observe that: (i) $\{\vartheta_t\}$ is determined by the filtration model, that is, by the choice of the generating Markov process $\{L_{tU}\}$, and (ii) $\{\nu_t\}$ depends on the selection of the heat kernel models, that is, on the choice for $F(t,x)$ and $w(t,u)$. We can view $\{\vartheta_t\}$ as the risk premium component associated with the uncertainty in the market modeled via the information flow process $\{L_{tU}\}$. The component $\{\nu_t\}$ may however be interpreted as the premium associated with model risk since it is closely related to the choice of the specific asset price model.

5. Incomplete Market Models Driven by LRBs

In this section, we extend the pricing framework to include multi-dimensional risk factors, and we generate asset pricing models in an incomplete market. We consider a class of finite-time Markov processes, the so-called "Lévy random bridges" (LRBs), as constructed in Hoyle *et al.* (2011). An LRB can be interpreted as a Lévy process that is bound to match a prescribed, albeit arbitrary, distribution at a fixed future time. The LRB and the generating Lévy process are linked by an equivalent probability measure with respect to which the LRB has the law of the generating Lévy process. Before we state the multivariate version of this result appearing in Hoyle *et al.* (2011), we first give the definition of a multivariate LRB. This definition also establishes the notation of what follows in the subsequent sections.

Definition 5.1. We say that $\{L_{tU}\}_{0\leq t\leq U}$ is a multivariate LRB on $\mathbb{R}^m$ if the following are satisfied: (i) The random variable L_{UU} on $\mathbb{R}^m$ has marginal law ν. (ii) There exist a multivariate Lévy process $\{L_t\}_{0\leq t\leq U}$ on $\mathbb{R}^m$ such that L_t has multivariate density function $\rho_t(x)$ on $\mathbb{R}^m$ for all $t \in (0, U]$. (iii) The marginal law ν concentrates mass where $\rho_U(z)$ is positive and finite, that is $0 < \rho_U(z) < \infty$ for ν-almost-every $z \in \mathbb{R}^m$. (iv) For every $n \in \mathbb{N}_+$, every $0 < t_1 < \ldots < t_n < U$, every $(x_1, \ldots, x_n) \in \mathbb{R}^m \times \mathbb{R}^n$, and ν-almost-every $z \in \mathbb{R}^m$, we have

$$\mathbb{P}[L_{t_1U} \leq x_1, \ldots, L_{t_nU} \leq x_n \mid L_{UU} = z] = \mathbb{P}[L_{t_1} \leq x_1, \ldots L_{t_n} \leq x_n \mid L_U = z].$$

Heat Kernel Models for Asset Pricing

Proposition 5.1. *Let $\{L_{tU}\}_{0\le t\le U}$ denote a multivariate LRB with marginal law ν. Let the multivariate Lévy process $\{L_t\}_{0\le t\le U}$, which generates the LRB, have density $\rho_t(x)$ for all $t \in (0, U]$. Under the measure $\mathbb{L}$ defined by*

$$\ell_t^{-1} := \left.\frac{\mathrm{d}\mathbb{P}}{\mathrm{d}\mathbb{L}}\right|_{\mathcal{F}_t} = \int_{\mathbb{R}^m} \frac{\rho_{U-t}(z - L_{tU})}{\rho_U(z)}\, \nu(\mathrm{d}z), \tag{5.1}$$

the LRB $\{L_{tU}\}$ has the law of the generating Lévy process for $t \in [0, U)$.

The verification of this proposition follows closely the results leading to Proposition 3.7 in Hoyle *et al.* (2011). The measure $\mathbb{L}$ is rather useful for several calculations as we will see, shortly. LRBs, which have joint marginal law at $t = U$ and which are generated by $\mathbb{L}$-independent Lévy processes, are nevertheless independent under $\mathbb{L}$.

Next, we propose multi-factor pricing kernel models, and thus multi-factor asset price models, in the situation where the driving Markov process is a multivariate LRB. The construction of these models follows the technique presented at the end of Secs. 2 and 3.

5.1. *Exponential linear two-factor model with jumps*

We assume that the market filtration $\{\mathcal{F}_t\}$ is generated by a two-dimensional LRB, of which the first component is a Brownian random bridge,

$$L_{tU}^{(1)} = \sigma X_U^{(1)} t + \beta_{tU},$$

and the second component is a gamma random bridge defined by

$$L_{tU}^{(2)} = X_U^{(2)} \gamma_{tU}.$$

The Brownian bridge $\{\beta_{tU}\}$ and the gamma bridge $\{\gamma_{tU}\}$ are assumed $\mathbb{L}$-independent of each other and also $\mathbb{L}$-independent of the random variables $X_U^{(1)}$ and $X_U^{(2)}$. However, the two X random variables may be dependent and have *a priori* bivariate marginal law ν. Next, we recall the bond pricing formula (2.13) where, this time,

$$\begin{aligned} Y_{tT}^{\mathbb{L}} = &\int_{T-t}^{U-t}\int_{T-t}^{U-t} w(T, u_1 - T + t, u_2 - T + t) \\ &\times \mathbb{E}^{\mathbb{L}}[F(t + u_1, t + u_2, L_{t+u_1,U}^{(1)}, L_{t+u_2,U}^{(2)}) \,|\, L_{tU}^{(1)}, L_{tU}^{(2)}]\mathrm{d}u_1\mathrm{d}u_2. \end{aligned} \tag{5.2}$$

Here we replace $\mathbb{M}$ in (2.13) with $\mathbb{L}$ to emphasize that the measure is changed to the $\mathbb{L}$-measure. Since, for $t \in [0, U)$, the two LRB components each have the $\mathbb{L}$-law of the corresponding underlying Lévy process (Brownian motion and the gamma process, respectively), the conditional expectation simplifies considerably under $\mathbb{L}$.

That is,

$$\begin{aligned}\mathbb{E}^{\mathbb{L}}[F(t+u_1,t+u_2,L^{(1)}_{t+u_1,U},L^{(2)}_{t+u_2,U})\,|\,L^{(1)}_{tU}=x_1,L^{(2)}_{tU}=x_2]\\ =\mathbb{E}^{\mathbb{L}}[F(t+u_1,t+u_2,(L^{(1)}_{t+u_1,U}-L^{(1)}_{tU})+x_1,(L^{(2)}_{t+u_2,U}-L^{(2)}_{tU})+x_2)].\end{aligned}$$

For the LRB components are $\mathbb{L}$-independent, even though $X^{(1)}_U$ and $X^{(2)}_U$ may be assumed dependent, and for the $\mathbb{L}$-laws of the LRB components are known, the probability densities of the increments in the above equation are also known. We thus have:

$$\mathbb{L}[L^{(1)}_{t+u_1,U}-L^{(1)}_{tU}\in\mathrm{d}y_1]=\frac{1}{\sqrt{2\pi\,u_1}}\exp\left(-\frac{y_1^2}{2\,u_1}\right)\mathrm{d}y_1, \tag{5.3}$$

$$\mathbb{L}[L^{(2)}_{t+u_2,U}-L^{(2)}_{tU}\in\mathrm{d}y_2]=\frac{\mathbb{1}\{y_2>0\}}{\Gamma[mu_2]}\,y_2^{mu_2-1}\exp(-y_2)\,\mathrm{d}y_2, \tag{5.4}$$

where $m>0$ and $\Gamma[x]$ is the gamma function. In order to work out an explicit example, we need to specify $F(t,y_1,y_2)$ and the weight function $w(t,u_1,u_2)$. We choose the following:

$$F(t+u_1,t+u_2,y_1+x_1,y_2+x_2)=\exp[a(y_1+x_1)-c(y_2+x_2)], \tag{5.5}$$

$$w(t,u_1,u_2)=\exp\left(-\frac{1}{2}a^2(t+u_1)\right)(c+1)^{m(t+u_2)}, \tag{5.6}$$

where $a\in[-\infty,\infty)$, $c\geq 0$ are constants. We then insert (5.3) and (5.4), together with (5.5) and (5.6), in (5.2) and calculate the integrals over u_1 and u_2. The result is:

$$Y^{\mathbb{L}}_{tT}=(U-T)^2(c+1)^{mt}\exp\left(a\,L^{(1)}_{tU}-c\,L^{(2)}_{tU}-\frac{1}{2}\,a^2t\right). \tag{5.7}$$

The two-factor pricing kernel, jointly driven by a Brownian random bridge and a gamma random bridge, is thus given by a formula similar to (2.11) where the change-of-measure density martingale $\{M_t\}$, in the LRB context denoted $\{\ell_t\}$, is the reciprocal of (5.1) while $Y^{\mathbb{L}}_{tt}$, $Y^{\mathbb{L}}_{0t}$, and $Y^{\mathbb{L}}_{00}$ are deduced from (5.7). As for the quadratic and exponential quadratic models analyzed in Sec. 3, also this class of models for the bond price can be written in the form (3.6). We have:

$$P_{tT}=\frac{P_{0T}+b(T)\,A^{\mathbb{L}}_t}{P_{0t}+b(t)\,A^{\mathbb{L}}_t}, \tag{5.8}$$

where, for $0\leq t\leq T<U$,

$$\begin{aligned}P_{0t}&=\frac{f_0(t)+(U-t)^2f_1(t)}{1+U^2f_1(0)},\quad b(t)=\frac{(U-t)^2f_1(t)}{1+U^2f_1(0)},\\ A^{\mathbb{L}}_t&=(c+1)^{mt}\exp\left(a\,L^{(1)}_{tU}-c\,L^{(2)}_{tU}-\frac{1}{2}\,a^2t\right)-1.\end{aligned} \tag{5.9}$$

One can show that $\{A_t^{\mathbb{L}}\}$ is an $(\{\mathcal{F}_t\},\mathbb{L})$-martingale for $t \in [0,U)$. Then, the process $\{\ell_t A_t^{\mathbb{L}}\}$ is an $(\{\mathcal{F}_t\},\mathbb{P})$-martingale, and the bond price process (5.8) has a representation in terms of $(\{\mathcal{F}_t\},\mathbb{P})$-martingales, that is

$$P_{tT} = \frac{P_{0T}\,\ell_t + b(T)\,A_t^{\mathbb{P}}}{P_{0t}\,\ell_t + b(t)\,A_t^{\mathbb{P}}}, \tag{5.10}$$

where $A_t^{\mathbb{P}} = \ell_t\,A_t^{\mathbb{L}}$. Such models might be regarded as belonging to the finite-time equivalence class of Flesaker & Hughston (1996) bond price models. We note that pricing kernel models over infinite time, as in Flesaker & Hughston (1996), must be potentials of class D, see Rogers (1997) and Meyer (1962). In finite time, pricing kernel processes merely need to be positive $(\{\mathcal{F}_t\},\mathbb{P})$-supermartingales to ensure nonnegative interest rates. Furthermore, the martingale processes underlying the price models arise endogenously from the pricing kernel structure (2.1). Formula (2.1) can be viewed as a "machine" that implicitly produces martingales for pricing formulae with a rational form. In Bermin (2012), the Flesaker–Hughston approach to bond pricing is revisited and it is shown how yield curves may be inverted for any short rate process consistent with bond price processes that have an exponentially-affine structure.

In Sec. 3, explicit pricing models are derived, and one may ask at this point what the connection is between these pricing models and the ones specified in (5.8). The link is a change of probability measure. Let us consider an $(\{\mathcal{F}_t\},\mathbb{L})$-martingale $\{A_t^{\mathbb{L}}\}$ and an $(\{\mathcal{F}_t\},\mathbb{M})$-martingale $\{A_t^{\mathbb{M}}\}$. Furthermore, we introduce an $(\{\mathcal{F}_t\},\mathbb{L})$-density-martingale $\{\eta_t\}_{0\le t<U}$ that changes the probability measure $\mathbb{L}$ to the equivalent measure $\mathbb{M}$. We set $A_t^{\mathbb{L}} = \eta_t\,A_t^{\mathbb{M}}$, and finally observe, for $0 \le s \le t < U$, that

$$\mathbb{E}^{\mathbb{L}}[A_t^{\mathbb{L}} \,|\, \mathcal{F}_s] = \mathbb{E}^{\mathbb{L}}[\eta_t\,A_t^{\mathbb{M}} \,|\, \mathcal{F}_s] = \eta_s\,\mathbb{E}^{\mathbb{M}}[A_t^{\mathbb{M}} \,|\, \mathcal{F}_s] = \eta_s\,A_s^{\mathbb{M}} = A_s^{\mathbb{L}}.$$

This type of relation is also what connects (5.8) and (5.10).

5.2. *Useful formula*

The fact that an LRB has the law of its generating Lévy process under the "Lévy probability measure" $\mathbb{L}$ can be exploited to derive asset price formulae expressed in terms of the characteristic function of a Lévy process and a Fourier transform. We consider again the $\mathbb{L}$-conditional expectation

$$\mathbb{E}^{\mathbb{L}}[F(t+u, L_{t+u,U}) \,|\, L_{tU}],$$

where $\{L_{tU}\}$ is an LRB. We specify $F(t,x)$ by its Fourier transform $\widehat{F}(t,y)$, that is

$$F(t,x) = \frac{1}{2\pi}\int_{\mathbb{R}} \mathrm{e}^{i\,xy}\,\widehat{F}(t,y)\,\mathrm{d}y,$$

where $\widehat{F}(t,y)$ is selected such that $F(t,x)$ is positive and integrable. We then have:

$$\mathbb{E}^{\mathbb{L}}[F(t+u, L_{t+u,U}) \,|\, L_{tU}] = \mathbb{E}^{\mathbb{L}}\left[\frac{1}{2\pi}\int_{\mathbb{R}} \exp(iyL_{t+u,U})\,\widehat{F}(t+u,y)\,\mathrm{d}y \,\middle|\, L_{tU}\right].$$

A. Macrina

Assuming that Fubini's Theorem is herewith satisfied, we swap the expectation with the integral, and obtain

$$\mathbb{E}^{\mathbb{L}}[F(t+u, L_{t+u,U}) \,|\, L_{tU}] = \frac{1}{2\pi}\int_{\mathbb{R}} \mathbb{E}^{\mathbb{L}}[\exp(iyL_{t+u,U}) \,|\, L_{tU}]\widehat{F}(t+u,y)\,\mathrm{d}y.$$

Since, under $\mathbb{L}$, the LRB has the law of the underlying Lévy process for $t \in [0, U)$, we can calculate the conditional expectation by recalling that the increments of a Lévy process are independent and stationary. The result is:

$$\mathbb{E}^{\mathbb{L}}[\exp(iyL_{t+u,U}) \,|\, L_{tU}] = \exp(iyL_{tU})\mathbb{E}^{\mathbb{L}}[\exp(iyL_{uU})].$$

The expectation on the right-hand side of the equation above is the generating function of a Lévy process. We denote the Lévy exponent by $\Psi(y)$, and thus write

$$\mathbb{E}^{\mathbb{L}}[\exp(iyL_{uU})] = \exp[-u\,\Psi(y)],$$

for $u \in [0, U)$. This leads to

$$\mathbb{E}^{\mathbb{L}}[F(t+u, L_{t+u,U}) \,|\, L_{tU}] = \frac{1}{2\pi}\int_{\mathbb{R}} \exp[iyL_{tU} - u\,\Psi(y)]\widehat{F}(t+u,y)\mathrm{d}y,$$

and hence to the useful formula

$$\begin{aligned} Y^{\mathbb{L}}_{tT} &= \int_{T-t}^{U-t} w(T, u-T+t)\,\mathbb{E}^{\mathbb{L}}[F(t+u, L_{t+u,U}) \,|\, L_{tU}]\mathrm{d}u \\ &= \int_{T-t}^{U-t} w(T, u-T+t)\frac{1}{2\pi}\int_{\mathbb{R}} \exp[iyL_{tU} - u\,\Psi(y)]\widehat{F}(t+u,y)\mathrm{d}y\mathrm{d}u. \end{aligned} \tag{5.11}$$

An expression analogous to (5.11) can be derived in the multi-factor case, in which the LRB $\{L_{tU}\}$ is a multi-dimensional vector. The elements of the LRB vector may be dependent through their terminal marginal laws as considered at the beginning of this section. The model (5.7) may be derived as a special case of the formula (5.11). In order to obtain bond price models, (5.11) is inserted in (2.13) to replace $Y^{\mathbb{M}}_{tT}$.

We conclude this section by producing multi-dimensional and multi-factor asset price processes. For the rest of this section, the following process $\{Y^{(i)}_{tT}\}$ is defined under the $\mathbb{L}$-measure. For $i = 1, 2, \ldots, n$, let

$$Y^{(i)}_{tT} = \int_{T-t}^{U-t} \mathbb{E}^{\mathbb{L}}[F_i(t+u, L_{t+u,U}) \,|\, L_{tU}]w_i(T, u-T+t)\,\mathrm{d}u,$$

where $F_i(t, x)$ is a positive and integrable function, and $w_i(t, u)$ is a weight function such that the combination of the two ensure $Y^{(i)}_{tT} < \infty$ for all t. We emphasize that the Markov process $\{L_{tU}\}_{0 \leq t \leq U}$ may be multi-dimensional. Then, the following is a multi-dimensional and multi-factor model for the bond price:

$$P_{tT} = \frac{P_{0T} + \sum_{i=1}^{n} y_i(T)(Y_{tT}^{(i)} - Y_{0T}^{(i)})}{P_{0t} + \sum_{i=1}^{n} y_i(t)(Y_{tt}^{(i)} - Y_{0t}^{(i)})}, \tag{5.12}$$

where

$$y_i(t) = \frac{f_i(t)}{1 + \sum_{i=1}^{n} Y_{00}^{(i)}}.$$

These models can be extended further. Let us assume that the multivariate LRBs generating the market filtration $\{\mathcal{F}_t\}$ are driven by $\mathbb{L}$-independent Lévy processes and may have joint terminal marginal distribution. Then, the product of an $(\{\mathcal{F}_t\}, \mathbb{L})$-supermartingale is again an $(\{\mathcal{F}_t\}, \mathbb{L})$-supermartingale. This leads us to the construction of higher-order asset pricing models, hereunder applied to the pricing of bonds. We generalize the bond price model (5.8): For $0 \le t \le T$ and $N \in \mathbb{N}$,

$$P_{tT} = \frac{P_{0T} + \sum_{i=1}^{N} \Lambda_{tT}^{(i)}}{P_{0t} + \sum_{i=1}^{N} \Lambda_{tt}^{(i)}}, \tag{5.13}$$

where $\Lambda_{tT}^{(i)}$

$$= \sum_{j_{n_i-m_i}=1}^{n_i-m_i} b_{j_{n_i-m_i}}^{(i)}(T)\, A_t^{(i,\, j_{n_i-m_i})} \sum_{j_{n_i-(m_i-1)}=j_{n_i-m_i}+1}^{n_i-(m_i-1)} b_{j_{n_i-(m_i-1)}}^{(i)}(T)\, A_t^{(i,\, j_{n_i-(m_i-1)})}$$

$$\cdots \sum_{j_{n_i-1}=j_{n_i-2}+1}^{n_i-1} b_{j_{n_i-1}}^{(i)}(T)\, A_t^{(i,\, j_{n_i-1})} \sum_{j_{n_i}=j_{n_i-1}+1}^{n} b_{j_{n_i}}^{(i)}(T)\, A_t^{(i,\, j_{n_i})} \tag{5.14}$$

for $n_i \ge m_i \in \mathbb{N}$. By setting $T = t$ in (5.14) one obtains $\{\Lambda_{tt}\}$. The deterministic functions $b_1^{(i)}(t), b_2^{(i)}(t), \ldots, b_n^{(i)}(t)$ are specified such that the pricing kernel underlying the price model is a positive supermartingale. The processes $\{A_t^{(i,j)}\}_{0 \le t < U}$ and $\{A_t^{(i,k)}\}_{0 \le t < U}$ are $(\{\mathcal{F}_t\}, \mathbb{L})$-martingales, and these are $\mathbb{L}$-independent for $j \ne k$. For instance, for $N = 1$, $n_1 = 3$ and $m_1 = 2$, one obtains the third-order model

$$P_{tT} = \frac{P_{0T} + b_{123}(T)\, A_t^{(1)}\, A_t^{(2)}\, A_t^{(3)}}{P_{0t} + b_{123}(t)\, A_t^{(1)}\, A_t^{(2)}\, A_t^{(3)}}, \tag{5.15}$$

where $b_{123}(t) = b_1(t)\, b_2(t)\, b_3(t)$ for $0 \le t \le T$. For $N = 1$, $n_1 = 3$ and $m_1 = 1$, we have the second-order model

$$P_{tT} = \frac{P_{0T} + b_{12}(T)\, A_t^{(1)}\, A_t^{(2)} + b_{13}(T)\, A_t^{(1)}\, A_t^{(3)} + b_{23}(T)\, A_t^{(2)}\, A_t^{(3)}}{P_{0t} + b_{12}(t)\, A_t^{(1)}\, A_t^{(2)} + b_{13}(t)\, A_t^{(1)}\, A_t^{(3)} + b_{23}(t)\, A_t^{(2)}\, A_t^{(3)}}, \tag{5.16}$$

where $b_{ij}(t) = b_j(t) b_k(t)$ for $j \ne k$ and $0 \le t \le T$. In order to lighten the notation, the i-index is suppressed in (5.15) and (5.16) since we have only one type of higher-order term in the sum over i. For $N = 2$, $n_1 = 3$, $m_1 = 2$, $n_2 = 3$ and $m_2 = 1$, a combination of third-order and second-order summands drives the bond price. We note that the construction of higher-order pricing formulae is not limited to models driven by LRBs. The pricing kernel model (2.1) can be used to construct higher-order price models driven by other Markov processes. Higher-order models gain in importance when considering general asset pricing including dependences across several types of asset. For instance, models such as (5.15) and (5.16) might be applied in the pricing of bond portfolios where the portfolio assets share one or more "drivers" in common, be them the A-processes of various types (e.g. quadratic, exponential linear and quadratic, etc.) and/or the underlying Markov processes, perhaps also of various types of probability laws. Another situation in which one can foresee higher-order models to be useful is when a financial instrument is exposed to various sectors of a financial market. We can think of a portfolio of shares, of which prices are discounted and thus certainly linked to the bond market. Then there are dependences across the shares composing the portfolio; perhaps one is also interested to hedge the portfolio with positions in a shares index, and so on. These are all situations where the degrees of freedom of the higher-order models are expected to be useful, in particular for the modeling of portfolio dependences. The next section is devoted to the pricing of general assets, and we shall keep in mind that higher-order models can be constructed also for general financial instruments.

6. Pricing of a Generic Asset

The pricing formula (1.1) implies that the price process of an asset has the martingale property with respect to the market filtration $\{\mathcal{F}_t\}$ and the real probability measure $\mathbb{P}$. There are several ways to construct $(\{\mathcal{F}_t\}, \mathbb{P})$-martingales; we consider however a natural method within the pricing method developed thus far. For some fixed T, we denote by $\{m_{tT}\}_{0\le t\le T}$ an $(\{\mathcal{F}_t\}, \mathbb{P})$-martingale, and write

$$\pi_t S_{tT} = m_{tT}. \tag{6.1}$$

Definition 6.1. Let $\{Z_{tT}\}_{0\le t\le T<U}$ be defined by

$$Z_{tT} = \int_{T-t}^{U-t} \mathbb{E}^{\mathbb{P}}[G(t+u, X_{t+u}) \,|\, X_t]\psi(T, u-T+t)\mathrm{d}u, \tag{6.2}$$

where the deterministic function $G(t,x)$ is measurable, $\psi(t,u)$ is a deterministic and measurable function with the property $\psi(t, u-s) = \psi(t-s, u)$ for $s \le t \wedge u$. The combination $G(t,x)$ and $\psi(t,u)$ is such that it ensures $Z_{tT} < \infty$ for all t.

Proposition 6.1. *Let $0 \le t \le T < U$, and let $g_0(T)$ and $g_1(T)$ be deterministic functions. Then, for each fixed T,*

$$m_{tT} = g_0(T) + g_1(T)Z_{tT} \tag{6.3}$$

is an $(\{\mathcal{F}_t\}, \mathbb{P})$-martingale.

Proof. This proposition can be proven by following the steps in the proof of Proposition 2.2 in Akahori & Macrina (2012). We observe that $\psi(t, u-s) = \psi(t-s, u)$ implies $\psi(t,u) = \psi(t+u)$. □

In contrast to $F(t,x)$ and $w(t,u)$ in (2.1), we require that neither $G(t,x)$ nor $\psi(t,u)$ be positive functions. This is to include the pricing of assets that are not of limited liability and thus do not necessarily have positive prices. We now have the necessary ingredients in order to propose the following class of asset price models.

Lemma 6.1. *Let* $\{\pi_t\}$ *and* $\{m_{tT}\}$ *be the processes* (2.7) *and* (6.3), *respectively. Then the asset price model* (6.1) *takes the form*

$$S_{tT} = \frac{S_{0T} + z(T)(Z_{tT} - Z_{0T})}{P_{0t} + y(t)(Y_{tt} - Y_{0t})}, \tag{6.4}$$

where $z(T) = g_1(T)/\pi_0$.

Proof. The relation (6.4) follows from (6.1) by inserting (2.7) and (6.3). The degree of freedom $g_0(T)$ can be calibrated to the asset price S_{0T} at time 0 via

$$g_0(T) = S_{0T}\pi_0 - g_1(T)Z_{0T},$$

where $\pi_0 = 1 + f_1(0)Y_{00}$. □

Since the martingale family $\{m_{tT}\}$ is not necessarily positive-valued, the price process $\{S_{tT}\}$ is neither. We deliberately keep this level of generality, as opposed to requiring assets to have positive prices, since we might wish to consider also the pricing of portfolios of which value might become negative at times. As at the beginning of Sec. 3, we next derive general asset price models for which semi-explicit (possibly up to numerical root-finding) expressions for derivatives can be computed. Depending on the form of the functions Y_{tt} and Z_{tT}, the "useful formula" (5.11) can be applied to compute option prices. We also apply the results in Proposition 2.1.

Lemma 6.2. *Given the class of asset price models* (6.4), *there exist equivalent measures* $\mathbb{M}$, *induced by a change-of-measure density* $(\{\mathcal{F}_t\},\mathbb{P})$*-martingale* $\{M_t\}_{0\leq t<U}$, $(\{\mathcal{F}_t\},\mathbb{M})$*-martingales* $\{A_t^{(i)}\}_{0\leq t<U}^{i=1,2}$ *with* $A_0^{(i)}=0$, *and deterministic functions* $b_i(t)$ *such that the asset price process* $\{S_{tT}\}_{0\leq t\leq T<U}$ *takes the form*

$$S_{tT} = \frac{S_{0T} + b_1(T)\,A_t^{(1)}}{P_{0t} + b_2(t)\,A_t^{(2)}}. \tag{6.5}$$

The asset price S_{tT} *is the value at time* t *of the cash flow*

$$S_{TT} = \frac{S_{0T} + b_1(T)\,A_T^{(1)}}{P_{0T} + b_2(T)\,A_T^{(2)}} \tag{6.6}$$

at time T, *where* $\{S_{tT}\}$ *is quoted in units of the pricing kernel process*

$$\pi_t = \frac{\pi_0}{M_0}[P_{0t} + b_2(t)\,A_t^{(2)}]M_t. \tag{6.7}$$

A. Macrina

Proof. The expression (6.5) is obtained by computing the expectation in

$$S_{tT} = \frac{1}{\pi_t}\,\mathbb{E}^{\mathbb{P}}[\pi_T\, S_{TT} \,|\, \mathcal{F}_t],$$

where, by use of $\{M_t\}$, the measure $\mathbb{P}$ is first changed to $\mathbb{M}$ in order to exploit the martingale property of $\{A^{(1)}_t\}_{0\le t<U}$ under $\mathbb{M}$. A first example proving existence follows immediately. A second example is given at the end of this section. □

6.1. *Asset price diffusion with stochastic discounting*

Let the market filtration $\{\mathcal{F}_t\}$ be generated by two Brownian random bridges $\{L^{(i)}_{tU}\}$, $i = 1, 2$, which are constructed in terms of possibly dependent random variables $X^{(i)}_U$. We consider the quadratic model (3.3) for the pricing kernel $\{\pi_t\}$ modeled in terms of $\{A^{(2)}_t\}$ and driven by $\{L^{(2)}_{tU}\}$, and the exponential quadratic model (3.4) for the component modeled in terms of $\{A^{(1)}_t\}$ and driven by $\{L^{(1)}_{tU}\}$. In such a case, one obtains an asset price process of the form

$$S_{tT} = \frac{S_{0T} + \frac{\frac{1}{\eta}(U-T)^{\eta}U^{1/2}g_1(T)}{4U[1+(1/12)\,f_1(0)U^3]}\left[\sqrt{1-t/U}\,\exp\left(\frac{L^{(1)\,2}_{tU}}{2(U-t)}\right)-1\right]}{P_{0t} + \frac{(U-t)^4 f_1(t)}{4U[1+(1/12)\,f_1(0)U^3]}\left[\frac{U}{(U-t)^2}\,L^{(2)\,2}_{tU} - \frac{t}{U-t}\right]}, \tag{6.8}$$

where P_{0t} is specified in (3.3) and

$$S_{0T} = \frac{g_0(T) + \frac{1}{\eta}(U-T)^{\eta}U^{1/2}g_1(T)}{1 + \frac{1}{12}U^3 f_1(0)}. \tag{6.9}$$

The price process (6.8), which is simulated in Fig. 1, can be generalized to an incomplete market setup by considering a vector Brownian random bridge $\{\bar{L}^{(1)}_{tU}, \bar{L}^{(2)}_{tU}, \ldots, \bar{L}^{(n)}_{tU}\}$. Then, for instance, we might set $L^{(1)}_{tU} = \{\bar{L}^{(1)}_{tU}, \bar{L}^{(2)}_{tU}, \ldots, \bar{L}^{(m)}_{tU}\}$ and $L^{(2)}_{tU} = \{\bar{L}^{(1)}_{tU}, \bar{L}^{(2)}_{tU}, \ldots, \bar{L}^{(n)}_{tU}\}$, $m \le n$. Another way is proposed in (5.13).

6.2. *Dynamical equations*

We consider price processes of the form (6.5) which are adapted to a filtration $\{\mathcal{F}_t\}$ generated by Brownian random bridges

$$L^{(i)}_{tU} = \sigma_i\, X^{(i)}_U\, t + \beta^{(i)}_{tU}. \tag{6.10}$$

While $X^{(i)}_U$ and $\{\beta^{(i)}_{tU}\}$ are assumed independent and σ_i is constant, we may take the Brownian bridges $\{\beta^{(i)}_{tU}\}$ to be correlated, here. We further assume that the processes $\{A^{(i)}_t\}_{0\le t<U}$ satisfy

$$\mathrm{d}A^{(i)}_t = \nu^{(i)}_t(\mathrm{d}W^{\mathbb{P}(i)}_t + \vartheta^{(i)}_t \mathrm{d}t), \quad A^{(i)}_0 = 0, \tag{6.11}$$

Heat Kernel Models for Asset Pricing

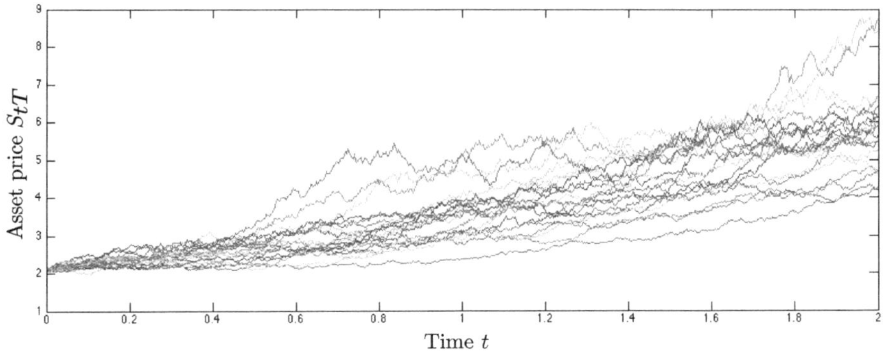

Fig. 1. Simuation of an asset price diffusion with stochastic discounting. A quadratic model is utilized for the pricing kernel that discounts the asset price S_{tT}. The equity-component of the asset price is determined by an exponential quadratic model. Both, the pricing kernel and the equity-component are driven by Brownian random bridges of which marginal distribution is joint. The deterministic degrees of freedom utilized to calibrate to the initial prices are assumed to decay exponentially with a constant damping rate.

where $\{\nu_t^{(i)}\}$ is $\{\mathcal{F}_t\}$-adapted and

$$\begin{aligned}\vartheta_t^{(i)} &= \frac{\sigma_i U}{U-t}\,\mathbb{E}^{\mathbb{P}}[X_U^{(i)} \mid \mathcal{F}_t],\\ \mathrm{d}W_t^{\mathbb{P}(i)} &= \mathrm{d}L_{tU}^{(i)} - \frac{1}{U-t}(\sigma_i U\,\mathbb{E}^{\mathbb{P}}[X_U^{(i)} \mid \mathcal{F}_t] - L_{tU}^{(i)})\mathrm{d}t.\end{aligned} \tag{6.12}$$

It then follows, by the Ito Formula, that, on $0 \le t \le T < U$, the price process (6.5) satisfies the stochastic differential equation

$$\frac{\mathrm{d}S_{tT}}{S_{tT}} = (r_t + \lambda_t \Sigma_{tT})\mathrm{d}t + \Sigma_{tT}\,\mathrm{d}W_t^{\mathbb{P}}, \tag{6.13}$$

where

$$r_t = -\frac{\partial_t P_{0t} + A_t^{(2)}\,\partial_t b_2(t)}{P_{0t} + b_2(t)\,A_t^{(2)}}, \quad \lambda_t = \begin{pmatrix} \vartheta_t^{(1)} - \rho_{ij}\,\nu_t^{(2)}\,\dfrac{b_2(t)}{P_{0t} + b_2(t)\,A_t^{(2)}} \\ \vartheta_t^{(2)} - \nu_t^{(2)}\,\dfrac{b_2(t)}{P_{0t} + b_2(t)\,A_t^{(2)}} \end{pmatrix},$$

$$\Sigma_{tT} = \begin{pmatrix} \dfrac{b_1(T)\nu_t^{(1)}}{S_{0T} + b_1(T)\,A_t^{(1)}} \\ -\dfrac{b_2(t)\nu_t^{(2)}}{P_{0t} + b_2(t)\,A_t^{(2)}} \end{pmatrix}.$$

The process $W_t^{\mathbb{P}} = (W_t^{\mathbb{P}(1)}, W_t^{\mathbb{P}(2)})$ is a two-dimensional $(\{\mathcal{F}_t\}, \mathbb{P})$-Brownian motion where $\mathrm{d}W_t^{\mathbb{P}(i)}\mathrm{d}W_t^{\mathbb{P}(j)} = \rho_{ij}\,\mathrm{d}t$ for $i \neq j$, $\rho_{ij} \in [-1, 1)$, and $\mathrm{d}W_t^{\mathbb{P}(i)}\mathrm{d}W_t^{\mathbb{P}(j)} = \mathrm{d}t$ for $i = j$.

Remark 6.1. The example (6.8) satisfies (6.13) where $A^{(1)}_t$, $b_1(t)$ and S_{0T} are respectively specified in (3.4) and (6.9), and $A^{(2)}_t$, $b_2(t)$ and P_{0t} are determined in (3.3). Furthermore,

$$\nu^{(1)}_t = \frac{(\frac{U-t}{U})^{1/2}}{U-t}\, L^{(1)}_{tU} \exp\left[\frac{L^{(1)\,2}_{tU}}{2(U-t)}\right], \quad \nu^{(2)}_t = \frac{2U}{(U-t)^2}\, L^{(2)}_{tU}.$$

Another example is, of course, where $\{A^{(1)}_t\}$ and $\{A^{(2)}_t\}$ respectively belong to the quadratic and exponential quadratic class, instead. Generalized versions of (6.13) can be obtained in which the driving random Brownian bridges are multidimensional and the price process (6.5) is constructed by higher-dimensional systems as in (5.15) or (5.16). We imagine multidimensional examples being useful when a more refined dependence structure between the "equity component" and the discount factor is necessary, and in particular when modeling portfolio assets. Also, the market filtration might be modeled by different random Gaussian bridges which are likely to suggest different classes of $\{A_t\}$-processes.

Remark 6.2. The processes $\{\nu^{(i)}_t\}$, $i = 1, 2$, are determined by the specific choice of the models at the basis of the processes $\{A^{(i)}_t\}$, and thus are model-specific. Inside the market price of risk vector $\{\lambda_t\}$, one notices the correlation parameter ρ_{ij} that arises from the $\mathrm{d}A^{(i)}_t\mathrm{d}A^{(j)}_t$-term containing $\mathrm{d}W^{\mathbb{P}(i)}_t\mathrm{d}W^{\mathbb{P}\,(j)}_t$ that, following (6.12), yields $\mathrm{d}L^{(i)}_{tU}\,\mathrm{d}L^{(j)}_{tU} = \mathrm{d}\beta^{(i)}_{tU}\,\mathrm{d}\beta^{(j)}_{tU} = \rho_{ij}\mathrm{d}t$.

Remark 6.3. The dynamics (6.13) can be transformed to obtain the risk-neutral dynamical equation of the asset price process $\{S_{tT}\}_{0\le t\le T}$. We have:

$$\frac{\mathrm{d}S_{tT}}{S_{tT}} = r_t\mathrm{d}t + \Sigma_{tT}\,\mathrm{d}W^{\mathbb{Q}}_t, \tag{6.14}$$

where $\mathrm{d}W^{\mathbb{Q}}_t = \mathrm{d}W^{\mathbb{P}}_t + \lambda_t\mathrm{d}t$ is the risk-neutral Brownian motion defined in terms of the $\mathbb{P}$-Brownian motion $\{W^{\mathbb{P}}_t\}$ and the market price of risk process $\{\lambda_t\}$. The solution to the stochastic differential equation (6.14) has the familiar $\mathbb{Q}$-log-normal form

$$S_{tT} = S_{0T}\exp\!\left(\int_0^t \left(r_s - \frac{1}{2}\Sigma^2_{sT}\right)\mathrm{d}s + \int_0^t \Sigma_{sT}\,\mathrm{d}W^{\mathbb{Q}}_s\right). \tag{6.15}$$

How one may obtain "finite-time Black–Scholes-type models" from (6.15) can be deduced by consulting Brody *et al.* (2008), Sec. 9. In addition, appropriate choices for the functions $F(x)$, $G(x)$, and the related weight functions will need to be made.

Remark 6.4. The solution to the stochastic differential equation (6.13) is a positive-valued process, namely (6.15) as written in its risk-neutral form. Recalling Lemma (6.1), or in particular Lemma (6.2), one may wonder what ensures the positivity of the constructed asset price process. The answer is: no such condition is imposed, in general. However, the diffusion price processes (6.13) is based on the Ito-dynamics (6.11), which in combination with the rational form of $\{S_t\}$, results

Heat Kernel Models for Asset Pricing

in a positive price process. It is perhaps surprising that the stochastic differential equation (6.13) is solved by an explicit expression of the form (6.5), for instance by (6.8), which might be hard to guess in its form (6.15) or in the equivalent one under $\mathbb{P}$.

6.3. *Asset price dynamics with heavy tails and stochastic discounting*

We now give one more example of an asset price process (6.5), which is driven by three different types of Lévy random bridges. Let the market filtration be generated by (i) a stable-1/2 random bridge $\{L^{(1)}_{tU}\}$, (ii) two gamma random bridges $\{L^{(2)}_{tU}\}$ and $\{L^{(3)}_{tU}\}$, and (iii) a Brownian random bridge $\{L^{(4)}_{tU}\}$. For details about 1/2-stable random bridges, we refer to Hoyle *et al.* (2014). The four random bridges are assumed to be independent under the "Lévy probability measure" $\mathbb{L}$, which is not to say that the marginals at time $t = U$ of the four LRBs are independent (as explained below Proposition 5.1). Next we make use of Definition 6.1 and Proposition 6.1. It is convenient to take the expectations under an auxiliary probability measure as presented in Proposition 2.1. Given that in this example the market filtration is generated by four LRBs, we choose to compute the expectations under the "Lévy probability measure" $\mathbb{L}$, under which the LRBs have the law of the generating underlying Lévy processes. For the function $G(t+u, X_{t+u})$ in Definition (6.1), we set

$$G(t+u_1, t+u_2, L^{(1)}_{t+u_1,U}, L^{(2)}_{t+u_2,U}) = \exp(-\kappa L^{(1)}_{t+u_1,U} + cL^{(2)}_{t+u_2,U}), \qquad (6.16)$$

where $\kappa \geq 0$, $0 \leq c \leq 1$. The Laplace transform of the stable-1/2 subordinator $\{L_t\}$, which is a Lévy process, is

$$\mathbb{E}[\exp(-\kappa L_t)] = \exp\left(-\frac{\alpha\sqrt{\kappa}}{\sqrt{2}}\, t\right),$$

where $\alpha > 0$ is the activity parameter that features in the subordinator's density function

$$\rho_t(y) = \mathbb{1}\{y > 0\}\frac{\alpha\, t}{\sqrt{2\pi}\, y^{3/2}} \exp\left(-\frac{\alpha^2\, t^2}{2\, y}\right). \qquad (6.17)$$

We now calculate (6.2) with the specification (6.16) and by setting

$$\psi(t+u) = \widetilde{\psi}(t, u_1, u_2) = \exp\left(\frac{\alpha\sqrt{\kappa}}{\sqrt{2}}(t+u_1)\right)(1-c)^{m(t+u_2)},$$

where $m > 0$. The result is:

$$Z_{tT} = (U-T)^2 \exp\left(-\kappa L^{(1)}_{tU} + \frac{\alpha\sqrt{\kappa}}{\sqrt{2}}\, t\right)(1-c)^{mt} \exp(cL^{(2)}_{tU}).$$

In this case, the price process $\{S_{tT}\}$ given in (6.4) can be written in the form (6.5). For the denominator, we choose a discount factor of the kind (5.8). We obtain the

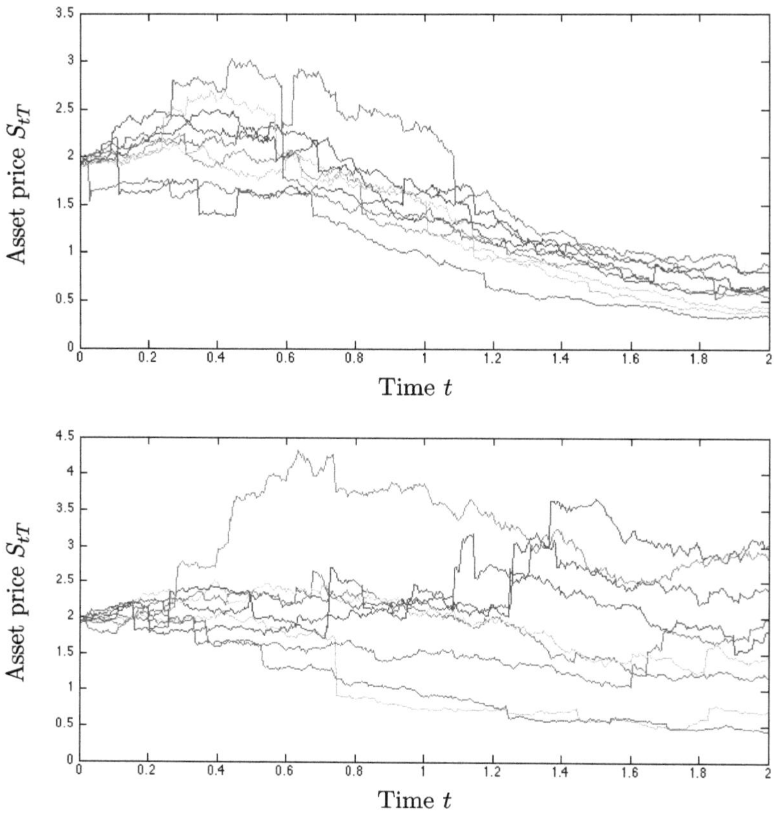

Fig. 2. Two distinct simulations of an asset price process with heavy tails and stochastic discounting. Here the pricing kernel that discounts the price process is modeled by an exponential-linear function of a Brownian random bridge and a gamma random bridge. The equity-component is determined by an exponential-linear function of a stable-1/2 random bridge and a gamma random bridge. The marginal distributions of the four random bridges are joint. The dynamics of the asset price can vary significantly depending on the interaction of the driving factors.

following price process for, e.g. equity:

$$S_{tT} = \frac{S_{0T} + b_1(T)\, A_t^{(1)}}{P_{0t} + b_2(t)\, A_t^{(2)}}, \tag{6.18}$$

where, for $\eta \geq 0$, $a \in [-\infty, \infty)$, $q > 0$, and $0 \leq t \leq T < U$, we have

$$\begin{aligned} S_{0T} &= \frac{g_0(T) + (U-T)^2 g_1(T)}{1 + U^2 f_1(0)}, \quad b_1(T) = \frac{(U-T)^2 g_1(T)}{1 + U^2 f_1(0)}, \\ A_t^{(1)} &= (1-c)^{mt} \exp\left(-\kappa L_{tU}^{(1)} + \frac{\alpha\sqrt{\kappa}}{\sqrt{2}}\, t + cL_{tU}^{(2)}\right) - 1; \end{aligned} \tag{6.19}$$

Heat Kernel Models for Asset Pricing

$$P_{0t} = \frac{f_0(t) + (U-t)^2 f_1(t)}{1 + U^2 f_1(0)}, \quad b_2(t) = \frac{(U-t)^2 f_1(t)}{1 + U^2 f_1(0)},$$
$$A_t^{(2)} = (\eta+1)^{qt} \exp\Big(-\eta L_{tU}^{(3)} + a L_{tU}^{(4)} - \frac{1}{2}a^2 t\Big) - 1. \tag{6.20}$$

Two distinct simulations of the price process (6.18), specified by (6.19) and (6.20), are shown in Fig. 2. The stable-1/2 LRB is simulated as in Hoyle *et al.* (2014). The four LRBs, one stable-1/2, two gamma and one Brownian random bridge, have each four possible outcomes at time U with joint probabilities. The deterministic functions $f_0(t)$, $f_1(t)$, $g_0(T)$ and $g_1(T)$ are chosen to decay exponentially at a constant rate.

Another example could be constructed by generating asset price models driven by "Variance Gamma random bridges" and quoted in units of the natural numeraire at the basis of the model (5.8). In the case that the economic factors modeled by the random variables $L_{UU}^{(i)}$ are dependent, one obtains simple dependence structures between the dynamics of the equity and the associated discount bond system that determines the discount rate in the financial market. The more advanced dependence models introduced in the next section can also be applied to model interactions between different segments of a financial market.

7. Spiraling Debt and Its Impact on International Bond Markets

We now address in more detail the pricing of sovereign bonds. Even though the majority of sovereign bonds pay coupons, we focus on discount bonds, for convenience. This simplification does not affect the view taken or the problem we intend to tackle here. The emphasis is shifted on the value of a sovereign bond that should reflect the level of economic health of the issuing country. News regarding the bond market over the last few years has constantly reminded us that investors frequently balance the capability of a sovereign economy to grow *vis-à-vis* the amount of accumulated debt held at any one time. We choose this point of view, and wonder how to construct asset pricing models, which take into account at least some of this perspective.

We consider a simple model for the economic structure of a country. We assume that a central government has a source of income, for instance taxes and the revenues of state-owned companies. On the other hand it also has expenditures in order, for instance, to finance armed forces, public education, a public health system, and other welfare. While the difference between income and expenditures fluctuates over the course of time, we assume that it is unlikely, at least in a well-run and periodically well-assessed economy, that this difference spikes for the better or for the worse. If it were the case, then we might see an economy's growth rate move from 1% to 10% within a few months, or a drop in the growth rate by a similar amount in the same time span. It is more likely though that a central government has to step-in to cover huge unexpected losses due to, e.g. the unfolding of an international financial crisis, domestic or international wars, natural catastrophes, and other calamities hard to predict and with disastrous impact on the economic health of a country. So, in addition to the "structural" income and outcomes of an economy, we consider the accumulation of significant debt due to severe losses, which may very well make the level of financial stress of an economy "jump". We model the structural part of the various cash flows of an economy by a Brownian random bridge

$$L^{(1)}_{tU} = \sigma t X_U + \beta_{tU},$$

where X_U may represent the economic wealth of a country at a future time U. We model the spiraling cumulative debt amassed by a sovereign country in the time interval $[0, U]$ by a gamma random bridge $\{L^{(2)}_{tU}\}$. The random total (extraordinary) debt amassed by time U is modeled by $L^{(2)}_{UU} = X^{(2)}_U$. Its distribution can be arbitrarily specified. We imagine that the "structural" or "noncrisis" balance $L^{(1)}_{UU}$ is dependent on the total debt (losses) $L^{(2)}_{UU}$ accumulated by time U. For instance, a sovereign government may decide at time U to make substantial cuts to the expenditures for public welfare if the amount of "extraordinary losses (debt)" will have spiraled by time U beyond what is perceived to be manageable. Therefore $L^{(1)}_{UU}$ and $L^{(2)}_{UU}$ are assumed to have a joint marginal distribution, and this means that we are in the same modeling environment as in Sec. 5.

The bond pricing model presented next is one of the simplest, though still rich enough to capture the desiderata within this discussion. One can of course choose to develop more sophisticated models. We choose a class of bond price models similar to (5.8), and follow the steps from (5.2) to (5.9) with one minor change in equation (5.5). We consider

$$F(t+u_1, t+u_2, y_1+x_1, y_2+x_2) = \exp(-a(y_1+x_1) + c(y_2+x_2)),$$

$$w(t, u_1, u_2) = \exp\left(-\frac{a^2}{2}(t+u_1)\right)(1-c)^{m(t+u_2)}.$$

The reason for the change in the sign is that this way the losses will be recognized as downward jumps in the time series of the bond price. We emphasize that expectations are computed under the $\mathbb{L}$-measure, under which LRBs with joint terminal marginals are nevertheless independent and inherit the law of the generating Lévy processes. The bond price is then given by

$$P_{tT} = \frac{P_{0T} + b(T)\,A^{\mathbb{L}}_t}{P_{0t} + b(t)\,A^{\mathbb{L}}_t}, \tag{7.1}$$

where, for $a \geq 0$, $0 \leq c \leq 1$, $m > 0$, we have

$$\begin{aligned} P_{0t} &= \frac{f_0(t) + (U-t)^2 f_1(t)}{1 + U^2 f_1(0)}, \quad b(t) = \frac{(U-t)^2 f_1(t)}{1 + f_1(0) U^2}, \\ A^{\mathbb{L}}_t &= (1-c)^{mt} \exp\left(-a\,L^{(1)}_{tU} - \frac{1}{2}a^2 t + c\,L^{(2)}_{tU}\right) - 1, \quad 0 \leq t \leq T < U. \end{aligned} \tag{7.2}$$

7.1. *Dependence in international markets*

The effects of losses getting out of control are not confined to one's domestic economy. Especially in a global financial market, the deterioration of an economy's health exposes, for instance, foreign creditors holding debt of the distressed economy to higher credit risk. Bond markets are global "debt networks" linking several national economies with one another. The result of such network might be "contagion": an ailing economy may severely damage creditors which, through financial exposure, can be affected by spiraling losses experienced by the debtor. For instance, a foreign investor may see their investments in foreign bonds significantly devalued if the bond price declines due to unexpected losses, or out-of-control debt management. The foreign investor's loss may be commensurate with the percentage investment in an ailing economy compared with their total financial exposure and reserves gained through income. Here size matters, of course, and the discussions about the magnitude of the Greek versus the Italian debt impacting on the Eurozone or world economy come to one's mind. The next example aims at illustrating how contagion effects can be modeled in the present asset pricing approach. We introduce a linear combination of cumulative random bridge processes defined by

$$\widetilde{L}^{(j)}_{tU} = \sum_{i}^{n} w^{(j)}_i \, L^{(i)}_{tU},$$

where $\{L^{(i)}_{tU}\}$ are increasing random bridges, e.g. gamma random bridges with joint terminal distribution and generated by independent gamma processes. The weight parameter $w^{(j)}_i$ measures the level of exposure to each cumulative process $\{L^{(i)}_{tU}\}$. Since the linear combination may not be the same for any creditor exposed to the pool $\{\widetilde{L}^{(j)}_{tU}\}$, further freedom is given through j-indexing the exposed entity (sovereign state, private company, etc.). For instance *Country A* may have a financial exposure of 15% to *Country X* and 8% to *Country Y*. The percentage exposures, which can be collected from various financial intelligence organizations, can be used to determine the weights for *Country A*. On the other hand, *Country B* may be exposed by 34% to *Country Y*'s economic performance and by 65% to *Country Z*'s. One sees that, even though *Country A* and *B* may not hold any of each others financial assets, they are linked to each other through the common exposure to *Country*

Table 1. Illustrative values for the weight parameter $W^{(i)}_i$ governing the financial exposures of Country j's economy to the sovereign debt of countries i.

$w^{(j)}_i$	GER	FRA	ESP	ITA
GER	1	0	0	0
FRA	0	1	0	0
ESP	0.57	0.47	1	0
ITA	0.49	0.25	0	1

Y's economy, albeit to different levels. The bonds of *Country A* and *Country B* are expected to both show the impact of their respective exposures to *Country Y*. The bond price processes,

$$P_{tT}^{(j)} = \frac{P_{0T}^{(j)} + b_j(T)\,A_t^{\mathbb{L}\,(j)}}{P_{0t}^{(j)} + b_j(t)\,A_t^{\mathbb{L}\,(j)}}, \tag{7.3}$$

of the exposed entity j can be modeled, for example, along the lines of (7.1) where

$$P_{0t}^{(j)} = \frac{f_0^{(j)}(t) + (U-t)^{n+1} f_1^{(j)}(t)}{1 + U^{n+1} f_1^{(j)}(0)}, \quad b_j(t) = \frac{(U-t)^{n+1} f_1^{(j)}(t)}{1 + U^{n+1} f_1^{(j)}(0)},$$

$$A_t^{\mathbb{L}\,(j)} = \prod_{i=1}^{n}(1 - w_i^{(j)})^{m_i t} \exp\Big(-a_j\,L_{tU}^{(j)} - \frac{1}{2}a_j^2 t + \widetilde{L}_{tU}^{(j)}\Big) - 1, \quad 0 \le t \le T < U, \tag{7.4}$$

and $0 \le w_i^{(j)} \le 1$, $m_i > 0$. Here, $\{L_{tU}^{(j)}\}$ is taken to be a Brownian random bridge associated with the ordinary budget of the entity j. The level of financial exposure to a specific economy can be measured, at least in part, in terms of debt instruments held. Hereafter, we look at a simulation of contagion due to exposure to sovereign debt of two foreign countries. In particular, we suppose that Germany and France are exposed to the Spanish and Italian economic environment. The level of exposures $w_i^{(j)}$, governing in part the levels of dependence among the debt holders, are selected as follows: In this basic illustration, Germany has no exposure to the French economy, however it has exposure levels 0.57 and 0.49 to Spain and Italy, respectively. The numbers listed in the table are not normalized. Dependence among the four economies is also subject to the joint marginal distribution of the LRBs underlying the dynamics of the yield processes. The closer the time horizon U, the more the joint marginal distribution of the multivariate random variable L_{UU} will govern the dynamics of the dependent yield processes.

7.2. *Simulation of contagion*

The scenario that follows, simulated in Figs. 3 and 4, is based on the contagion model (7.3) and on the debt exposure matrix $w_i^{(j)}$ above. The yield process $\{y_{tT}^{(j)}\}_{0\le t<T}$ and the spread process $\{s_{tT}^{(j)}\}_{0\le t<T}$ are defined by

$$y_{tT}^{(j)} = -\frac{\ln(P_{tT}^{(j)})}{T-t}, \quad s_{tT} = -\frac{\ln(P_{tT}^{(j)})}{T-t} + \frac{\ln(P_{tT}^{GER})}{T-t}, \tag{7.5}$$

where country j's spread is quoted against Germany's yield. The quantities in (7.4) are set as follows: The horizon of the financial market is $U = 5$, and the maturity of bond j is $T = 2$. Germany's and France's bond are both exposed to Spain's and Italy's debt, thus $n = 2$. Furthermore,

$$f_0^{(j)}(t) = \mathrm{e}^{-\alpha_j t}, \quad f_1^{(j)}(t) = \frac{\beta_j}{\ln(\gamma_j + t)}, \tag{7.6}$$

Heat Kernel Models for Asset Pricing

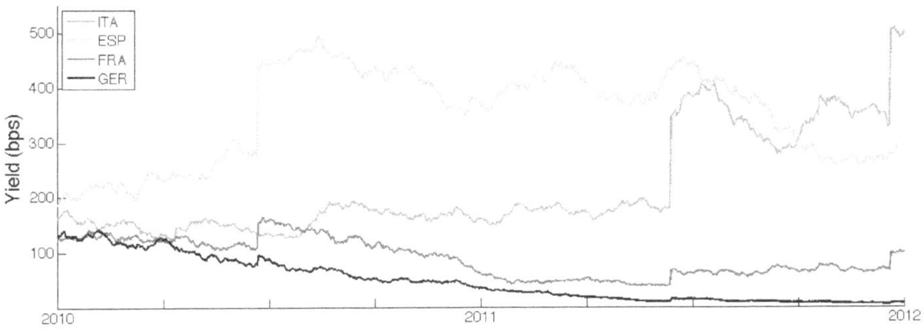

Fig. 3. Simulation of the yield process of the two-year-maturity bonds issued by Germany, France, Italy, and Spain. Contagion effects between each country's yield process are observed in particular when significant jumps occur (in the middle of the years 2010 and 2011).

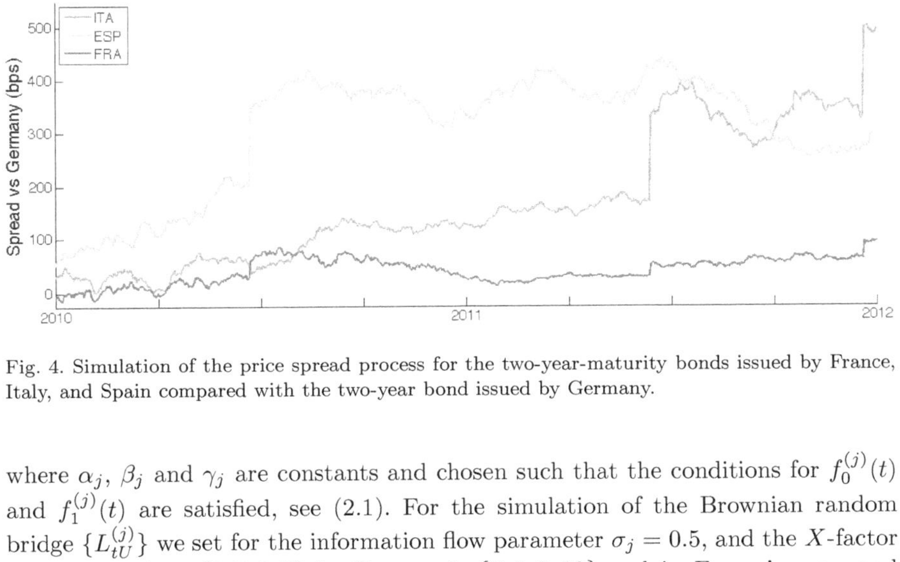

Fig. 4. Simulation of the price spread process for the two-year-maturity bonds issued by France, Italy, and Spain compared with the two-year bond issued by Germany.

where α_j, β_j and γ_j are constants and chosen such that the conditions for $f_0^{(j)}(t)$ and $f_1^{(j)}(t)$ are satisfied, see (2.1). For the simulation of the Brownian random bridge $\{L_{tU}^{(j)}\}$ we set for the information flow parameter $\sigma_j = 0.5$, and the X-factor takes the values $\{0, 5, 6, 7\}$ in Germany's $\{0, 5, 8, 10\}$ and in France's case, and $\{8, 10, 15, 20\}$ in Italy's and Spain's case. In all cases, the *a priori* probabilities for the X-factor's outcome are the same, namely $\{0.7, 0.2, 0.05, 0.05\}$. For the simulation of the gamma random bridge $\{L_{tU}^{(i)}\}$, the X-factor takes the values $\{0, 1, 2, 0\}$ in Germany's and $\{-4, -3, -2, 0\}$ in France's case, and $\{-4, -3, -2, 0\}$ in Italy's and $\{-5, -4, -3, 0\}$ in Spain's case. The *a priori* probabilities for this X-factor's outcomes are $\{0.2, 0.4, 0.4, 0\}$ for all four countries. Moreover, $a_j = 0.5$ and $m_i = 1$. In Fig. 3, we see the impact of spiraling debt on the yield process of sovereign bonds. The significant jumps in the yield processes of Spain and Italy (first and second trajectories from above) are due to unexpected losses (e.g. bank bail-outs, natural disasters) over relatively short periods of time. These spikes then have repercussions on the yield processes of France and Germany to various degrees of severity. The level of repercussion on each exposed country is relative to the health of their own economy. In the simulation above, we see that France's yield process (third trajectory from above) needs more time than Germany's yield trajectory to recover from the shocks. The implication is that although Germany has a higher exposure level to Spain's and Italy's finances, it has a more robust domestic economy — with, e.g. higher growth rate — than France. Thus, Germany is in a position to better weather foreign economic shocks. Contagion effects, due to increased economic stress, are also observed in the behavior of the spread process when comparing the performance of bonds issued by different sovereign states. In Fig. 4, we plot the difference between the yield processes of France, Spain, and Italy when compared with the yield process of the German sovereign bond. We observe the widening of the spread level for Spain and Italy, due to the two upward jumps in economic deficit. France keeps the evolution of the spread between the yield of its bond and the one by Germany in check even though it takes the hit from the exposures to the Spanish and Italian economies.

8. Conclusions

Building on the work of Akahori & Macrina (2012), this paper presents several novel contributions which include: (a) a compact formalism for the weighted heat kernel pricing models in finite time with partial automatic calibration; (b) characterization of a class of versatile and tractable asset pricing models which includes the quadratic and exponential quadratic models constructed in reference Akahori & Macrina (2012); (c) pricing formulae for caplets and swaptions with explicit examples; (d) dynamical equations for price processes driven by continuous Markov processes and derivation of the endogenous interest rate and market price of risk models underlying the dynamics of bond prices; (e) transition to the risk-neutral measure consistent with the interest rate model, and identification of the source of model risk as a component of the risk premium; (f) explicit, multi-factor, incomplete-market price models with jumps and potential application to portfolio assets across dependent market sectors; (g) generalized price models based on Fourier transforms and designed for weighted heat kernels driven by Lévy random bridges; (h) extension of the weighted heat kernel approach to the pricing of general financial assets; (i) explicit examples of price diffusions with stochastic discounting and stochastic volatility, and examples of price processes with heavy-tail distribution; (j) modeling of contagion in financial markets and illustration of indirect credit-risk effects due to spiraling debt accumulation.

The list of investigations connected with the asset pricing approach presented in this paper is by no means complete. The developed theory is applicable to the modeling of foreign exchange rates and the pricing of foreign exchange securities. Inflation-linked bonds and other indexed assets can be priced in a similar way.

Forward rate agreements on LIBOR may be viewed as derivatives discounted by the short-term rate of interest (see Mercurio (2010)). In this paper, the overnight rate of interest (e.g. OIS) is modeled as part of the pricing kernel. How perceived credit risk and changes in liquidity may affect the dynamics of the pricing kernel, or how pricing kernel models could produce multi-curve discounting, is worth further research work. Then there are commodity assets, including energy and agricultural products, which may involve insurance contracts to hedge against substantial losses due to averse weather conditions. Insurance pricing models which include endogenous stochastic interest rate models are likely to be in line with hedge-instruments, e.g. interest rate swaps, traded in a financial market, and thus are more likely to be market-consistent (Solvency II). In Sec. 7, effects on asset prices by perceived insolvency risk are considered in the dynamics of their returns. Further work in this direction, may include the modeling of "costs of funding" arising from shifts in asset prices due to the deterioration of a creditor's economic situation. Although credit risk models remain to be developed within the present pricing method, the material in Sec. 7 can be looked at from the perspective of modeling "credit valuation adjustments". The bounds, within which the dynamics of certain price processes are confined, could be exploited to model the levels of sustainability for the costs of funding, or applied by regulators to impose time-dependent capital requirements. Although treated in this paper, the explicit modeling of dependence structures for asset portfolios remains somewhat in the background. The weighted heat kernel approach, however, offers a versatile basis for the inclusion of manageable dependence models that could be useful for the risk analysis of asset portfolios. One could begin with mean–variance optimization whereby covariance matrices are explicitly modeled, and partial information about the underlying risk factors drives the portfolio. Another investigation may concern models for volatility surfaces, which arise from the selection of particular pricing kernels and their application to specific asset classes. Such an investigation extends to the analysis of the derived option price models and their calibration to data relevant for the pricing of assets.

Acknowledgments

The author is grateful to J. Akahori, D. Brigo, C. Buzzi, S. Crepéy, M. A. Crisafi, D. Filipović, M. Forde, A. E. V. Hoyle, L. P. Hughston, M. Kupper, C. Mainberger, P. McCloud, P. A. Parbhoo, M. Riedle, J. Sekine and D. R. Taylor for their useful discussions, and to conference and seminar participants at the African Institute for Mathematical Science in Cape Town, the Technische Universität Berlin, the Rand Merchant Bank in Johannesburg, the South African Reserve Bank in Pretoria, the SIMC-2013, and the 2014 Bachelier Finance Society 8th World Congress for helpful comments. Part of this work was carried out while the author was a member of the Department of Mathematics, King's College London. Support from the African Collaboration for Quantitative Finance and Risk Research (ACQuFRR), University of Cape Town, is gratefully acknowledged.

A. Macrina

References

J. Akahori, Y. Hishida, J. Teichmann & T. Tsuchiya (2014) A heat kernel approach to interest rate models, *Japan Journal of Industrial and Applied Mathematics* **31**, 419–439.

J. Akahori & A. Macrina (2012) Heat Kernel interest rate models with time-inhomogeneous Markov Processes, *International Journal of Theoretical and Applied Finance* **15**, 1250007-1–15.

K. E. Back (2010) *Asset Pricing and Portfolio Choice Theory*. Oxford: Oxford University Press.

H.-P. Bermin (2012) Bonds and options in exponentially affine bond models, *Applied Mathematical Finance*, i*First* **19**(6), 1–22.

T. Björk (2009) *Arbitrage Theory in Continuous Time*. Oxford: Oxford University Press.

D. Brigo & F. Mercurio (2006) *Interest Rate Models — Theory and Practice: With Smile, Inflation and Credit*. Berlin: Springer-Verlag.

D. C. Brody & L. P. Hughston (2004) Chaos and coherence: A new framework for interest rate modelling, *Proceedings of the Royal Society A* **460**, 85–110.

D. C. Brody, L. P. Hughston & A. Macrina (2008) Information-based asset pricing, *International Journal of Theoretical and Applied Finance* **11**, 107–142.

A. J. G. Cairns (2004) *Interest Rate Models: An Introduction*. Princeton: Princeton University Press.

J. H. Cochrane (2005) *Asset Pricing*. Princeton: Princeton University Press.

D. Duffie (2001) *Dynamic Asset Pricing Theory*. Princeton: Princeton University Press.

D. Filipović (2009) *Term-Structure Models. A Graduate Course*. Berlin: Springer-Verlag.

B. Flesaker & L. P. Hughston (1996) Positive interest, *Risk Magazine* **9**, 46–49.

D. Heath, R. Jarrow & A. Morton (1992) Bond pricing and the term structure of interest rates: A new methodology for contingent claims valuation, *Econometrica* **60**, 77–105.

E. Hoyle, L. P. Hughston & A. Macrina (2011) Lévy random bridges and the modelling of financial information, *Stochastic Processes and Their Applications* **121**, 856–884.

E. Hoyle, L. P. Hughston & A. Macrina (2014) Stable 1/2-bridges and insurance. In: *Advances in Mathematics of Finance* (A. Palczewski & L. Stettner, eds.). Warsaw, Poland: Banach Center Publications.

L. P. Hughston & A. Macrina (2012) Pricing fixed-income securities in an information-based framework, *Applied Mathematical Finance* **19**, 361–379.

L. P. Hughston & A. Rafailidis (2005) A chaotic approach to interest rate modelling, *Finance and Stochastics* **9**, 43–65.

F. Jamashidian (1996) Bond, futures and option evaluation in the quadratic interest rate model, *Applied Mathematical Finance* **3**, 93–115.

P. McCloud (2009) Exponential-quadratic semimartingale models of interest rate and asset volatility. *ssrn.com*.

P. McCloud (2012) Symmetry methods for the quadratic gaussian LIBOR model. *ssrn.com*.

F. Mercurio (2010) Modern LIBOR market models: Using different curves for projecting rates and for discounting, *International Journal of Theoretical and Applied Finance* **13**, 113–137.

P. A. Meyer (1962) A decomposition theorem for supermartingales, *Illinois Journal of Mathematics* **6**, 193–205.

P. A. Parbhoo (2013) Information-driven pricing Kernel models. PhD Thesis, University of the Witwatersrand.

L. C. G. Rogers (1997) The potential approach to the term structure of interest rates and foreign exchange rates, *Mathematical Finance* **7**, 157–176.

Chapter 13

Randomised Mixture Models for Pricing Kernels*

Andrea Macrina · Priyanka A. Parbhoo

Published online: 17 June 2014

Abstract Numerous kinds of uncertainties may affect an economy, e.g. economic, political, and environmental ones. We model the aggregate impact by the uncertainties on an economy and its associated financial market by randomised mixtures of Lévy processes. We assume that market participants observe the randomised mixtures only through best estimates based on noisy market information. The concept of incomplete information introduces an element of stochastic filtering theory in constructing what we term "filtered Esscher martingales". We make use of this family of martingales to develop pricing kernel models. Examples of bond price models are examined, and we show that the choice of the random mixture has a significant effect on the model dynamics and the types of movements observed in the associated yield curves. Parameter sensitivity is analysed and option price processes are derived. We extend the class of pricing kernel models by considering a weighted heat kernel approach, and develop models driven by mixtures of Markov processes.

Keywords Asset pricing · Interest rates · Yield curves · Markov processes · Esscher martingales · Weighted heat kernels

JEL Classification 35K08 · 60G44 · 60G51 · 60J25 · 91B25 · 91G30

A. Macrina (✉)
Department of Mathematics, University College London, London WC1E 6BT, UK
e-mail: a.macrina@ucl.ac.uk

A. Macrina
Department of Actuarial Science, University of Cape Town, Rondebosch 7701, South Africa

P. A. Parbhoo
Global Markets, Standard Bank, 30 Baker Street, Rosebank, Johannesburg 2196, South Africa

*This chapter was originally published as: A. Macrina & P. A. Parbhoo (2014) Randomized Mixture Models for Pricing Kernels. *Asia-Pacific Financial Markets* **21** (4), 281–315. Reprinted with kind permission from Springer.

1 Introduction

In this paper, we develop interest rate models that offer consistent dynamics in the short, medium, and long term. Often interest rate models have valid dynamics in the short term, that is to say, over days or perhaps a few weeks. Such models may be appropriate for the pricing of securities with short time-to-maturity. For financial assets with long-term maturities, one requires interest rate models with plausible long-term dynamics, which retain their validity over years. Thus the question arises as to how one can create interest rate models, which are sensitive to market changes over both short and long time intervals, so that they remain useful for the pricing of securities of various tenors. Ideally, one would have at one's disposal interest rate models that allow for consistent pricing of financial instruments expiring within a range of a few minutes up to years, and if necessary over decades. One can imagine an investor holding a portfolio of securities maturing over various periods of time, perhaps spanning several years. Another situation requiring interest rate models that are valid over short and long terms, is where illiquid long-term fixed-income assets need to be replicated with (rolled-over) liquid shorter-term derivatives. Here it is central that the underlying interest rate model possesses consistent dynamics over all periods of time in order to avoid substantial hedging inaccuracy. Insurance companies, or pension funds, holding liabilities over decades might have no other means but to invest in shorter-term derivatives, possibly with maturities of months or a few years, in order to secure enough collateral for their long-term liabilities reserves. Furthermore, such hedges might in turn need second-order liquid short-term protection, and so forth. Applying different interest rate models validated for the various investment periods, which frequently do not guarantee price and hedging consistency, seems undesirable. Instead, we propose a family of pricing kernel models which may generate interest rate dynamics sufficiently flexible to allow for diverse behaviour over short, medium and long periods of time.

We imagine economies, and their associated financial markets, that are exposed to a variety of uncertainties, such as economic, social, political, environmental, or demographic ones. We model the degree of impact of these underlying factors on an economy (and financial markets) at each point in time by combinations of continuous-time stochastic processes of different probability laws. When designing interest rate models that are sensitive to the states an economy may take, subject to its response to the underlying uncertainty factors, one may wonder a) how many stochastic factor processes ought to be considered, and b) what is the combination, or mixture, of factor processes determining the dynamics of an economy and its associated financial market. It is plausible to assume that the number of stochastic factors and their combined impact on a financial market continuously changes over time, and thus that any interest rate model designed in such a set-up is by nature time-inhomogeneous. The recipe used to construct interest-rate models within the framework proposed in this paper can be summarised as follows:

1. Assume that the response of a financial market to uncertainty is modelled by a family of stochastic processes, e.g. Markov processes.
2. Consider a mixture of such stochastic processes as the basic driver of the resulting interest rate models.

3. In order to explicitly design interest rate models, apply a method for the modelling of the pricing kernel associated with the economy, which underlies the considered financial market.
4. Derive the interest rate dynamics directly from the pricing kernel models, or, if more convenient, deduce the interest rate model from the bond price process associated with the constructed pricing kernel.

The set of stochastic processes chosen to model an economy's response to uncertainty, the particular mixture of those, and the pricing kernel model jointly characterize the dynamics of the derived interest rate model. We welcome these degrees of freedom, for any one of them may abate the shortcoming (or may amplify the virtues) of another. For example, one might be constrained to choose Lévy processes to model the impact of uncertainty on markets. The fact that Lévy processes are time-homogeneous processes with independent increments, might be seen as a disadvantage for modelling interest rates for long time spans. However, a time-dependent pricing kernel function introduces time-inhomogeneity in the resulting interest rate model. The choice of a certain set of stochastic processes implicitly determines a particular joint law of the modelled market response to the uncertainty sources. Although the resulting multivariate law may not coincide well with the law of the combined uncertainty impact, the fact that we can directly model a particular mixture of stochastic processes provides the desirable degree of freedom in order to control the dynamical law of the market's response to uncertainty. In this paper, we consider "randomised mixing functions" for the construction of multivariate interest rate models with distinct response patterns to short-, medium-, and long-term uncertainties. Having a randomised mixing function enables us to introduce the concept of "partially-observable mixtures" of stochastic processes. We take the view that market agents cannot fully observe the actual combination of factor processes underlying the market. Instead they form best estimates of the randomised mixture given the information they possess; these estimates are continuously updated as time elapses. This feature introduces a feedback effect in the constructed pricing models.

The reason why we prefer to propose pricing kernel models in order to generate the dynamics of interest rates, as opposed to modelling the interest rates directly, is that the modelling of the pricing kernel offers an integrated approach to equilibrium asset pricing in general (see Cochrane 2005; Duffie 2001), including risk management and thus the quantification of risk involved in an investment. The pricing kernel includes the quantified total response to the uncertainties affecting an economy or, in other words, the risk premium asked by an investor as an incentive for investing in risky assets. In this work we first consider a particular family of pricing kernel models, namely the Flesaker–Hughston class (see Flesaker and Hughston 1996; Hunt and Kennedy 2004; Cairns 2004; Brigo and Mercurio 2006). Since our goal in this paper is to primarily introduce a framework capable of addressing issues arising in interest rate modelling over short to long term time intervals, we apply our ideas first to the Flesaker–Hughston class of pricing kernels. We conclude the paper by introducing randomised weighted heat kernel models, along the lines of Akahori et al. (2014) and Akahori and Macrina (2012), which extend the class of pricing kernels developed in the first part of this paper.

2 Randomised Esscher Martingales

We begin by introducing the mathematical tools that we shall use to construct pricing kernel models based on randomised mixtures of Lévy processes. We fix a probability space $(\Omega, \mathcal{F}, \mathbb{P})$ where $\mathbb{P}$ denotes the real probability measure.

Definition 2.1 Let $\{L_t\}_{t\geq 0}$ be an n-dimensional Lévy process with independent components, and let $X : \Omega \to \mathbb{R}^m$ be an independent, m-dimensional vector of random variables. For $t, u \in \mathbb{R}_+$, the process $\{M_{tu}(X)\}$ is defined by

$$M_{tu}(X) = \frac{\exp\left(h(u, X)L_t\right)}{\mathbb{E}\left[\exp\left(h(u, X)L_t\right) \mid X\right]}, \tag{2.1}$$

where the function $h : \mathbb{R}_+ \times \mathbb{R}^m \to \mathbb{R}^n$ is chosen such that $\mathbb{E}\left[\,|\, M_{tu}(X)\,|\,\right] < \infty$ for all $t \in \mathbb{R}_+$.

Given that X is an independent vector-random-variable, it is in particular also independent of $\{L_t\}_{0\leq t}$. This property will be applied in Eq. (2.5).

Proposition 2.1 *Let the filtration $\{\mathcal{H}_t\}_{t\geq 0}$ be given by $\mathcal{H}_t = \sigma\left(\{L_s\}_{0\leq s\leq t}, X\right)$. Then the process $\{M_{tu}(X)\}$ is an $(\{\mathcal{H}_t\}, \mathbb{P})$-martingale.*

We note that X is $\mathcal{H}_0$-measurable and therefore, that $\{\mathcal{H}_t\}$ is an initial enlargement of the natural filtration of $\{L_t\}$ by the random variable X. Furthermore, $M_{0u}(X) = 1$ and $M_{tu}(X) > 0$ for all $t, u \in \mathbb{R}_+$.

Proof 2.1 The condition that $\mathbb{E}\left[\,|\, M_{tu}(X)\,|\,\right]$ be finite for all $0 \leq t < \infty$ is ensured by definition. It remains to be shown that

$$\mathbb{E}\left[M_{tu}(X) \mid \mathcal{H}_s\right] = M_{su}(X) \tag{2.2}$$

for all $0 \leq s \leq t < \infty$. We observe that the denominator in (2.1) is $\mathcal{H}_0$-measurable so that we can write

$$\mathbb{E}\left[M_{tu}(X) \mid \mathcal{H}_s\right] = \frac{\mathbb{E}\left[\exp\left(h(u, X)L_t\right) \mid \mathcal{H}_s\right]}{\mathbb{E}\left[\exp\left(h(u, X)L_t\right) \mid X\right]}. \tag{2.3}$$

Next we expand the right-hand-side of the above equation to obtain

$$\frac{\mathbb{E}\left[\exp\left[h(u, X)(L_t - L_s)\right]\exp\left[h(u, X)L_s\right] \mid \mathcal{H}_s\right]}{\mathbb{E}\left[\exp\left[h(u, X)(L_t - L_s)\right]\exp\left[h(u, X)L_s\right] \mid X\right]}. \tag{2.4}$$

Given X, the expectation in the denominator factorizes since $L_t - L_s$ is independent of L_s. In addition, the factor $\exp[h(u, X)L_s]$ is $\mathcal{H}_s$-measurable so that we may write

$$\mathbb{E}\left[M_{tu}(X) \mid \mathcal{H}_s\right] = \frac{\exp\left[h(u, X)L_s\right]}{\mathbb{E}\left[\exp\left[h(u, X)L_s\right] \mid X\right]}\,\frac{\mathbb{E}\left[\exp\left[h(u, X)(L_t - L_s)\right] \mid \mathcal{H}_s\right]}{\mathbb{E}\left[\exp\left[h(u, X)(L_t - L_s)\right] \mid X\right]}. \tag{2.5}$$

Since the increment $L_t - L_s$ and X are independent of L_s, the $\mathcal{H}_s$-conditional expectation reduces to an expectation conditional on X. Thus, Eq. (2.5) simplifies to

$$\mathbb{E}\left[M_{tu}(X) \,|\, \mathcal{H}_s\right] = \frac{\exp\left[h(u, X)L_s\right]}{\mathbb{E}\left[\exp\left[h(u, X)L_s\right] \,|\, X\right]}, \tag{2.6}$$

which is $M_{su}(X)$. □

We call the family of processes $\{M_{tu}(X)\}$ parameterised by $u \in \mathbb{R}_+$ the "randomised Esscher martingales" [see Gerber and Shiu (1994) and Yao (2001) for details on the Esscher transform]. The randomization is produced by $h(u, X)$ which we call the "random mixer".

Example 2.1 Let $\{W_t\}_{t\geq 0}$ be a standard Brownian motion that is independent of X, and set $L_t = W_t$ in Definition 2.1. Then,

$$M_{tu}(X) = \exp\left[h(u, X)W_t - \tfrac{1}{2}h^2(u, X)t\right]. \tag{2.7}$$

Example 2.2 Let $\{\gamma_t\}_{t\geq 0}$ be a gamma process with rate parameter $m > 0$ and scale parameter $\kappa > 0$. Then $\mathbb{E}[\gamma_t] = \kappa m t$ and $\mathrm{Var}[\gamma_t] = \kappa^2 m t$. We assume that $\{\gamma_t\}$ is independent of X. Set $L_t = \gamma_t$ in Definition 2.1. Then, if $h(u, X) < \kappa^{-1}$, we have

$$M_{tu}(X) = \left[1 - \kappa h(u, X)\right]^{mt} \exp\left[h(u, X)\,\gamma_t\right]. \tag{2.8}$$

3 Filtered Esscher Martingales

In this section we construct a projection of the randomised Esscher martingales that can be interpreted as follows. Let us suppose that the exact combination of Lévy processes that forms the stochastic basis of the martingale family $\{M_{tu}(X)\}$ is unknown. That is, we may have little knowledge about how much each of the Lévy processes involved actually contributes to the stochastic evolution of $\{M_{tu}(X)\}$. The random vector $h(u, X)$ however, can naturally be interpreted as the quantity inside $\{M_{tu}(X)\}$ that determines at time u the random mixture of Lévy processes driving the martingale family. Given a certain set of information, the actual mixture might not be fully observable, though. This leads us to the following construction that applies the theory of stochastic filtering. For simplicity, we focus on the case where X is a one-dimensional random variable.

We introduce a standard Brownian motion $\{B_t\}_{t\geq 0}$ on $(\Omega, \mathcal{F}, \mathbb{P})$, and define the filtration $\{\mathcal{G}_t\}$ by

$$\mathcal{G}_t = \sigma\left(\{B_s\}_{0\leq s\leq t}, \{L_s\}_{0\leq s\leq t}, X\right), \tag{3.1}$$

where $\{B_t\}$ is taken to be independent of X and $\{L_t\}$. We consider the pair

$$\mathrm{d}X_t = 0, \tag{3.2}$$

$$\mathrm{d}I_t = \ell(t, X)\mathrm{d}t + \mathrm{d}B_t, \tag{3.3}$$

where $\ell : \mathbb{R}_+ \times \mathbb{R} \to \mathbb{R}$ is a well-defined function. The solution to the signal equation (3.2) is of course the random variable X. In the theory of stochastic filtering, the process $\{I_t\}_{t\geq 0}$ is the so-called observation process. We have

$$I_t = \int_0^t \ell(s, X)\mathrm{d}s + B_t. \tag{3.4}$$

Next, we introduce the filtration $\{\mathcal{F}_t\}_{t\geq 0}$ defined by

$$\mathcal{F}_t = \sigma\left(\{I_s\}_{0\leq s\leq t}, \{L_s\}_{0\leq s\leq t}\right), \tag{3.5}$$

where $\mathcal{F}_t \subset \mathcal{G}_t$. The filtration $\{\mathcal{F}_t\}$ provides full information about the Lévy process $\{L_t\}$, however it only gives partial information about the random variable X. Let us thus consider the stochastic filtering problem defined by

$$\widehat{M}_{tu} = \mathbb{E}\left[M_{tu}(X) \,|\, \mathcal{F}_t\right]. \tag{3.6}$$

We emphasize that X is not $\mathcal{F}_t$-measurable and thus $\{M_{tu}(X)\}$ is not adapted to $\{\mathcal{F}_t\}$. The filtering problem (3.6) is solved in closed form by introducing

$$\mathcal{E}_t := \exp\left(-\int_0^t \ell(s, X)\mathrm{d}B_s - \tfrac{1}{2}\int_0^t \ell^2(s, X)\mathrm{d}s\right), \tag{3.7}$$

where for all $t > 0$

$$\mathbb{E}\left[\int_0^t \ell^2(s, X)\mathrm{d}s\right] < \infty, \tag{3.8}$$

and

$$\mathbb{E}\left[\int_0^t \mathcal{E}_s\, \ell^2(s, X)\mathrm{d}s\right] < \infty. \tag{3.9}$$

The process $\{\mathcal{E}_t\}$ is a $(\{\mathcal{G}_t\}, \mathbb{P})$-martingale (see, e.g., Bain and Crisan 2009), and it may be used to define a change-of-measure density martingale from $\mathbb{P}$ to a new measure $\mathbb{B}$ by setting

$$\left.\frac{\mathrm{d}\mathbb{B}}{\mathrm{d}\mathbb{P}}\right|_{\mathcal{G}_t} = \mathcal{E}_t. \tag{3.10}$$

The $\mathbb{B}$-measure is characterised by the fact that $\{I_t\}$ is a $(\{\mathcal{G}_t\}, \mathbb{B})$-Brownian motion. The Kallianpur–Striebel formula then states that

$$\mathbb{E}\left[M_{tu}(X) \,|\, \mathcal{F}_t\right] = \frac{\mathbb{E}^{\mathbb{B}}\left[\mathcal{E}_t^{-1} M_{tu}(X) \,|\, \mathcal{F}_t\right]}{\mathbb{E}^{\mathbb{B}}\left[\mathcal{E}_t^{-1} \,|\, \mathcal{F}_t\right]}. \tag{3.11}$$

This can be simplified to obtain:

$$\mathbb{E}\left[M_{tu}(X)\,|\,\mathcal{F}_t\right] = \int_{-\infty}^{\infty} M_{tu}(x)\, f_t(x)\mathrm{d}x, \tag{3.12}$$

where the $\mathcal{F}_t$-measurable conditional density $f_t(x)$ of the random variable X is given by

$$f_t(x) = \frac{f_0(x)\, \exp\left(\int_0^t \ell(s,x)\mathrm{d}I_s - \frac{1}{2}\int_0^t \ell^2(s,x)\mathrm{d}s\right)}{\int_{-\infty}^{\infty} f_0(y)\, \exp\left(\int_0^t \ell(s,y)\mathrm{d}I_s - \frac{1}{2}\int_0^t \ell^2(s,y)\mathrm{d}s\right)\mathrm{d}y} \tag{3.13}$$

and $f_0(x)$ is the *a priori* probability density of X. A similar filtering system is presented in a different context in Filipović et al. (2012). In that paper, further conditions are considered on the dynamics of the information process defined in (3.2) and (3.3), which may be necessary from a modelling point of view depending on the situation under consideration.

Proposition 3.1 *Let* $\{\mathcal{F}_t\}$ *be given by* (3.5), *and define the projection* $\widehat{M}_{tu} = \mathbb{E}\left[M_{tu}(X)\,|\,\mathcal{F}_t\right]$, *where* $\{M_{tu}(X)\}$ *is given by* (2.1). *Then, for* $t, u \in \mathbb{R}_+$, $\{\widehat{M}_{tu}\}$ *is an* $(\{\mathcal{F}_t\}, \mathbb{P})$*-martingale family.*

Proof 3.1 Recall that $\mathcal{F}_t \subset \mathcal{G}_t$ for all $t \geq 0$. For $s \leq t$, we have

$$\begin{aligned} \mathbb{E}\left[\widehat{M}_{tu}\,|\,\mathcal{F}_s\right] &= \mathbb{E}\left[\mathbb{E}\left[M_{tu}(X)\,|\,\mathcal{F}_t\right]\,|\,\mathcal{F}_s\right], \\ &= \mathbb{E}\left[M_{tu}(X)\,|\,\mathcal{F}_s\right], \\ &= \mathbb{E}\left[\mathbb{E}\left[M_{tu}(X)\,|\,\mathcal{G}_s\right]\,|\,\mathcal{F}_s\right], \\ &= \mathbb{E}\left[M_{su}(X)\,|\,\mathcal{F}_s\right], \\ &= \widehat{M}_{su}, \end{aligned} \tag{3.14}$$

where we make use of the tower property of the conditional expectation, and the fact that $\{M_{tu}(X)\}$ is a $\{\mathcal{G}_t\}$-martingale—since $\mathcal{H}_t \subset \mathcal{G}_t$ and $\{B_t\}$ is independent of X and $\{L_t\}$. □

3.1 Filtered Brownian Martingales

We consider Example 2.1, in which the total impact of uncertainties is modelled by a Brownian motion $\{W_t\}$. The corresponding filtered Esscher martingale is

$$\widehat{M}_{tu} = \int_{-\infty}^{\infty} f_t(x)\exp\left(h(u,x)W_t - \tfrac{1}{2}h^2(u,x)t\right)\mathrm{d}x, \tag{3.15}$$

where the density process $\{f_t(x)\}$, given in (3.13), is driven by the information process defined by (3.3).

Proposition 3.2 *The filtered Brownian models have dynamics*

$$\mathrm{d}\widehat{M}_{tu} = \int_{-\infty}^{\infty} M_{tu}(x) f_t(x) \left[h(u,x)\mathrm{d}W_t + V_t(x)\mathrm{d}Z_t\right] \mathrm{d}x, \tag{3.16}$$

where

$$M_{tu}(x) = \exp\left[h(u,x)W_t - \tfrac{1}{2}h^2(u,x)t\right], \tag{3.17}$$

$$V_t(x) = \ell(t,x) - \mathbb{E}\left[\ell(t,X) \mid \mathcal{F}_t\right], \tag{3.18}$$

$$Z_t = I_t - \int_0^t \mathbb{E}\left[\ell(s,X) \mid \mathcal{F}_s\right] \mathrm{d}s, \tag{3.19}$$

and $f_t(x)$ *is defined in* (3.13).

Proof 3.2 We first show that

$$\mathrm{d}M_{tu}(x) = h(u,x) M_{tu}(x) \mathrm{d}W_t. \tag{3.20}$$

In Filipović et al. (2012) it is proven that

$$\mathrm{d}f_t(x) = f_t(x)\left(\ell(t,x) - \mathbb{E}\left[\ell(t,X) \mid \mathcal{F}_t\right]\right)\mathrm{d}Z_t, \tag{3.21}$$

where $\{Z_t\}_{t\geq 0}$ is an $(\{\mathcal{F}_t\}, \mathbb{P})$-Brownian motion, defined by (3.19). Thus by the Itô product rule, we get

$$\mathrm{d}[M_{tu}(x) f_t(x)] = f_t(x)\mathrm{d}M_{tu}(x) + M_{tu}(x)\mathrm{d}f_t(x) \tag{3.22}$$

since $\mathrm{d}W_t\,\mathrm{d}Z_t = 0$. This simplifies to

$$\begin{aligned}\mathrm{d}[M_{tu}(x) f_t(x)] = M_{tu}(x) f_t(x) \Bigg[& h(u,x)\mathrm{d}W_t \\ &+ \left(\ell(t,x) - \int_{-\infty}^{\infty} \ell(t,y) f_t(y)\mathrm{d}y\right)\mathrm{d}Z_t\Bigg],\end{aligned} \tag{3.23}$$

and we obtain

$$\mathrm{d}\widehat{M}_{tu} = \int_{-\infty}^{\infty} M_{tu}(x) f_t(x) \left[h(u,x)\mathrm{d}W_t + V_t(x)\mathrm{d}Z_t\right] \mathrm{d}x \tag{3.24}$$

where

$$V_t(x) = \ell(t,x) - \int_{-\infty}^{\infty} \ell(t,y) f_t(y)\,\mathrm{d}y. \tag{3.25}$$

□

Remark 1 The dynamics of $\{\widehat{M}_{tu}\}$ can be written in the following form:

$$\mathrm{d}\widehat{M}_{tu} = \mathbb{E}\left[M_{tu}(X)h(u, X) \mid \mathcal{F}_t\right]\mathrm{d}W_t + \mathbb{E}\left[M_{tu}(X)V_t(X) \mid \mathcal{F}_t\right]\mathrm{d}Z_t. \tag{3.26}$$

3.2 Filtered Gamma Martingales

Let us suppose that the total impact of uncertainties on an economy is modelled by a gamma process $\{\gamma_t\}$ with density

$$\mathbb{P}(\gamma_t \in \mathrm{d}y) = \frac{y^{mt-1}\exp\left(-\frac{y}{\kappa}\right)}{\kappa^{mt}\,\Gamma[mt]}\,\mathrm{d}y, \tag{3.27}$$

where m and κ are the rate and the scale parameter, respectively. The associated randomised Esscher martingale is given in Example 2.2, where $h(u, X) < \kappa^{-1}$. The corresponding filtered process takes the form

$$\widehat{M}_{tu} = \int_{-\infty}^{\infty} f_t(x)\left([1 - \kappa h(u, x)]^{mt}\exp\left[h(u, x)\,\gamma_t\right]\right)\mathrm{d}x \tag{3.28}$$

for $h(u, x) < \kappa^{-1}$, and where the density $f_t(x)$ is given by (3.13).

3.3 Filtered Compound Poisson and Gamma Martingales

We now construct a model based on two independent Lévy processes: a gamma process (as defined previously) and a compound Poisson process. The idea here is to use the infinite activity gamma process to represent small frequently-occurring jumps, and to use the compound Poisson process to model jumps, which are potentially much larger in magnitude, and may occur sporadically. Let $\{C_t\}_{t\geq 0}$ denote a compound Poisson process given by

$$C_t = \sum_{i=1}^{N_t} Y_i \tag{3.29}$$

where $\{N_t\}_{t\geq 0}$ is a Poisson process with rate λ. The independent and identically distributed random variables Y_i are independent of $\{N_t\}$. The moment generating function is given by

$$\mathbb{E}\left[\exp\left(\varrho\, C_t\right)\right] = \exp\left[\lambda t\left(M_Y(\varrho) - 1\right)\right] \tag{3.30}$$

where M_Y is the moment generating function of Y_i. For $h_1(u, X) < \kappa^{-1}$, we have

$$
\begin{aligned}
M_{tu}(X) &= \frac{\exp\left(h_1(u,X)\gamma_t + h_2(u,X)C_t\right)}{\mathbb{E}\left[\exp\left(h_1(u,X)\gamma_t + h_2(u,X)C_t\right) \mid X\right]} \\
&= \frac{\exp\left(h_1(u,X)\gamma_t\right)}{\mathbb{E}\left[\exp\left(h_1(u,X)\gamma_t\right) \mid X\right]} \cdot \frac{\exp\left(h_2(u,X)C_t\right)}{\mathbb{E}\left[\exp\left(h_2(u,X)C_t\right) \mid X\right]} \\
&= M_{tu}^{(\gamma)}(X)\, M_{tu}^{(C)}(X), \qquad (3.31)
\end{aligned}
$$

where, conditional on X, $\exp(h_1(u,X)\gamma_t)$ and $\exp(h_2(u,X)C_t)$ are independent. Furthermore,

$$
M_{tu}^{(\gamma)}(X) = (1 - \kappa\, h_1(u,X))^{mt} \exp\left(h_1(u,X)\gamma_t\right), \qquad (3.32)
$$

$$
M_{tu}^{(C)}(X) = \exp\left[h_2(u,X)C_t - \lambda t\left(M_Y(h_2(u,X)) - 1\right)\right]. \qquad (3.33)
$$

Then, the filtered process takes the form

$$
\begin{aligned}
\widehat{M}_{tu} = \int_{-\infty}^{\infty} & f_t(x)\ [1 - \kappa h_1(u,x)]^{mt} \\
& \times \exp\left[h_1(u,x)\gamma_t + h_2(u,X)C_t - \lambda t\left(M_Y(h_2(u,X)) - 1\right)\right]\mathrm{d}x, \qquad (3.34)
\end{aligned}
$$

where $f_t(x)$ is given by (3.13).

4 Filtered Esscher Martingales with Lévy Information

Up to this point, we have considered a Brownian information process given by Eq. (3.3). However, the noise component in the information process may be modelled by a Lévy process with randomly sized jumps, that is independent of the Lévy process $\{L_t\}$ used to construct the randomised Esscher martingale. In what follows, we give an example of continuously observed information, which is distorted by gamma-distributed pure noise.

Example 4.1 Let $\{\widetilde{\gamma}_t\}_{t\geq 0}$ be a gamma process with rate and scale parameters $\widetilde{m}$ and $\widetilde{\kappa}$, respectively. We define the gamma information process by

$$
I_t = X\widetilde{\gamma}_t. \qquad (4.1)
$$

Brody and Friedman (2009) consider such an observation process in a similar situation. We define the filtration $\{\mathcal{G}_t\}$ by

$$
\mathcal{G}_t = \sigma\left(\{\widetilde{\gamma}_s\}_{0\leq s\leq t}, \{L_s\}_{0\leq s\leq t}, X\right), \qquad (4.2)
$$

and $\{\mathcal{F}_t\}$ by

$$
\mathcal{F}_t = \sigma\left(\{L_s\}_{0\leq s\leq t}, \{I_s\}_{0\leq s\leq t}\right) \qquad (4.3)
$$

where $\{I_t\}$ is given by (4.1). To derive the conditional density of X given $\mathcal{F}_t$, we first show that $\{I_t\}$ is a Markov process with respect to its own filtration. That is, for $a \in \mathbb{R}$,

$$\mathbb{P}\left[I_t < a \mid I_s, I_{s_1}, \ldots, I_{s_n}\right] = \mathbb{P}\left[I_t < a \mid I_s\right] \tag{4.4}$$

for all $t \geq s \geq s_1 \geq \cdots \geq s_n \geq 0$ and for all $n \geq 1$. It follows that

$$\begin{aligned} \mathbb{P}\left[I_t < a \mid I_s, I_{s_1}, \ldots, I_{s_n}\right] &= \mathbb{P}\left[I_t < a \,\middle|\, I_s, \frac{I_{s_1}}{I_s}, \ldots, \frac{I_{s_n}}{I_{s_{n-1}}}\right] \\ &= \mathbb{P}\left[X\,\widetilde{\gamma}_t < a \,\middle|\, X\,\widetilde{\gamma}_s, \frac{\widetilde{\gamma}_{s_1}}{\widetilde{\gamma}_s}, \ldots, \frac{\widetilde{\gamma}_{s_n}}{\widetilde{\gamma}_{s_{n-1}}}\right]. \end{aligned} \tag{4.5}$$

It can be proven that $\widetilde{\gamma}_{s_1}/\widetilde{\gamma}_s, \ldots, \widetilde{\gamma}_{s_n}/\widetilde{\gamma}_{s_{n-1}}$ are independent of $\widetilde{\gamma}_s$ and $\widetilde{\gamma}_t$ (see Brody et al. 2008). Furthermore, $\widetilde{\gamma}_{s_1}/\widetilde{\gamma}_s, \ldots, \widetilde{\gamma}_{s_n}/\widetilde{\gamma}_{s_{n-1}}$ are independent of X. Thus we have

$$\mathbb{P}\left[I_t < a \mid I_s, I_{s_1}, \ldots, I_{s_n}\right] = \mathbb{P}\left[I_t < a \mid I_s\right]. \tag{4.6}$$

We assume that the random variable X has a continuous a priori density $f_0(x)$. Then the conditional density of X,

$$f_t(x) = \frac{\mathrm{d}}{\mathrm{d}x}\mathbb{P}\left[X \leq x \mid I_t\right], \tag{4.7}$$

is given by

$$\begin{aligned} f_t(x) &= \frac{f_0(x)\, p\,(I_t \mid X = x)}{\int_{-\infty}^{\infty} f_0(y)\, p\,(I_t \mid X = y)\, \mathrm{d}y} \\ &= \frac{f_0(x) x^{-\widetilde{m}t} \exp\left[-I_t/(\widetilde{\kappa}x)\right]}{\int_{-\infty}^{\infty} f_0(y) y^{-\widetilde{m}t} \exp\left[-I_t/(\widetilde{\kappa}y)\right]\mathrm{d}y}, \end{aligned} \tag{4.8}$$

where we have used the Bayes formula. The filtered Esscher martingale is thus obtained by

$$\widehat{M}_{tu} = \mathbb{E}\left[M_{tu}(X) \mid \mathcal{F}_t\right]. \tag{4.9}$$

The result is:

$$\widehat{M}_{tu} = \int_{-\infty}^{\infty} M_{tu}(x)\, \frac{f_0(x) x^{-\widetilde{m}t} \exp\left[-I_t/(\widetilde{\kappa}x)\right]}{\int_{-\infty}^{\infty} f_0(y) y^{-\widetilde{m}t} \exp\left[-I_t/(\widetilde{\kappa}y)\right]\mathrm{d}y}\, \mathrm{d}x. \tag{4.10}$$

5 Pricing Kernel Models

The absence of arbitrage in a financial market is ensured by the existence of a pricing kernel $\{\pi_t\}_{t\geq 0}$ satisfying $\pi_t > 0$ almost surely for all $t \geq 0$. We consider, in general, an incomplete market and let $\{S_t\}_{t\geq 0}$ denote the price process of a non-dividend-paying asset. The price of such an asset at time $t \leq T$ is given by the following pricing formula:

$$S_t = \frac{1}{\pi_t} \mathbb{E}[\pi_T S_T \mid \mathcal{F}_t]. \tag{5.1}$$

The price of a discount bond system with price process $\{P_{tT}\}_{0 \leq t \leq T < \infty}$ and payoff $P_{TT} = 1$ is given by

$$P_{tT} = \frac{1}{\pi_t} \mathbb{E}[\pi_T \mid \mathcal{F}_t]. \tag{5.2}$$

The specification of a model for the pricing kernel is equivalent to choosing a model for the discount bond system, and thus also for the term structure of interest rates, and the excess rate of return. A sufficient condition for positive interest rates is that $\{\pi_t\}$ be an $(\{\mathcal{F}_t\}, \mathbb{P})$-supermartingale. If, in addition, the value of a discount bond should vanish in the limit of infinite maturity, then $\{\pi_t\}$ must satisfy

$$\lim_{T \to \infty} \mathbb{E}[\pi_T] = 0. \tag{5.3}$$

A positive right-continuous supermartingale with this property is called a potential. We refer to Meyer (1962) for a presentation of the theory of potentials, and in particular of class (D) potentials. Flesaker and Hughston (1996) provide a framework for constructing positive interest rate models, in which the pricing kernel is a so-called class (D) potential and is modelled by

$$\pi_t = \int_t^\infty \rho(u)\, m_{tu}\, \mathrm{d}u, \tag{5.4}$$

where $\{m_{tu}\}_{0 \leq t \leq u < \infty}$ is a family of positive unit-initialized martingales, and

$$\rho(t) = -\partial_t P_{0t}. \tag{5.5}$$

We emphasize that it suffices to specify a family of positive martingales in order to model such class (D) potentials, see also Hunt and Kennedy (2004). In what follows, we construct explicit Flesaker–Hughston models, which are driven by a randomised mixture of Lévy processes. We develop such a class of pricing kernels by setting

$$\pi_t = \int_t^\infty \rho(u)\, \widehat{M}_{tu}\, \mathrm{d}u \tag{5.6}$$

where the martingale family $\{\widehat{M}_{tu}\}_{0 \leq t \leq u < \infty}$ is defined by (3.6) with $\widehat{M}_{tu} > 0$ and $\widehat{M}_{0u} = 1$. Then, the discount bond system is given by

$$P_{tT} = \frac{\int_T^\infty \rho(u)\, \widehat{M}_{tu}\, \mathrm{d}u}{\int_t^\infty \rho(u)\, \widehat{M}_{tu}\, \mathrm{d}u}. \tag{5.7}$$

The associated instantaneous forward rate $\{r_{tT}\}_{0\le t\le T}$ is defined by $r_{tT} = -\partial_T \ln P_{tT}$. We deduce that

$$r_{tT} = \frac{\rho(T)\,\widehat{M}_{tT}}{\int_T^\infty \rho(u)\,\widehat{M}_{tu}\,\mathrm{d}u}, \tag{5.8}$$

and that the short rate of interest $\{r_t\}_{t\ge 0}$ is given by the formula

$$r_t = \frac{\rho(t)\,\widehat{M}_{tt}}{\int_t^\infty \rho(u)\,\widehat{M}_{tu}\,\mathrm{d}u}, \tag{5.9}$$

where $r_t := r_{tt}$. The interest rate is positive by construction. We note here that the pricing kernel models proposed in Brody et al. (2011) can be recovered by considering a special case of the random mixer, namely $h(u, X) = h(u)$. Takaoka (2006) and Takaoka and Futami (2010) apply weighted averages of geometric Brownian motion for the development of asset price processes. The equilibrium asset price models proposed in particular in Takaoka (2006) could be explored further in future research to find out whether these might be recovered from the pricing kernel models (5.6) or (12.11).

6 Pricing Kernel Models Driven by Filtered Brownian Martingales

In the case where the filtered martingales driving the pricing kernel are Gaussian processes, the dynamics of the discount bond system can be expressed by a diffusion equation of the form (6.2). Inserting the filtered Brownian martingale family (3.15) into (5.7), we obtain the price process of the discount bond in the Brownian set-up:

$$P_{tT} = \frac{\int_T^\infty \rho(u)\int_{-\infty}^\infty f_t(x)\exp\left[h(u,x)W_t - \frac{1}{2}h^2(u,x)t\right]\mathrm{d}x\,\mathrm{d}u}{\int_t^\infty \rho(v)\int_{-\infty}^\infty f_t(y)\exp\left[h(v,y)W_t - \frac{1}{2}h^2(v,y)t\right]\mathrm{d}y\,\mathrm{d}v}. \tag{6.1}$$

A similar expression is obtained for the associated interest rate system by plugging (3.15) into (5.9).

Proposition 6.1 *The dynamical equation of the discount bond process is given by*

$$\frac{\mathrm{d}P_{tT}}{P_{tT}} = [r_t - \theta_{tt}(\theta_{tT} - \theta_{tt}) - \nu_{tt}(\nu_{tT} - \nu_{tt})]\,\mathrm{d}t + (\theta_{tT} - \theta_{tt})\mathrm{d}W_t + (\nu_{tT} - \nu_{tt})\mathrm{d}Z_t \tag{6.2}$$

where

$$\theta_{tT} := \frac{\int_T^\infty \rho(u)\,\mathbb{E}\left[M_{tu}(X)h(u,X)\,|\,\mathcal{F}_t\right]\mathrm{d}u}{\int_T^\infty \rho(u)\,\widehat{M}_{tu}\,\mathrm{d}u}, \tag{6.3}$$

$$\nu_{tT} := \frac{\int_T^\infty \rho(u)\,\mathbb{E}\left[M_{tu}(X)V_t(X)\,|\,\mathcal{F}_t\right]\mathrm{d}u}{\int_T^\infty \rho(u)\,\widehat{M}_{tu}\,\mathrm{d}u}, \tag{6.4}$$

$\theta_{tt} = \theta_{tT}\big|_{T=t}$, *and* $\nu_{tt} = \nu_{tT}\big|_{T=t}$.

Proof 6.1 First we have

$$\mathrm{d}\left[\int_T^\infty \rho(u)\, \widehat{M}_{tu}\, \mathrm{d}u\right] = \int_T^\infty \rho(u)\, \mathrm{d}\widehat{M}_{tu}\, \mathrm{d}u \tag{6.5}$$

where $\mathrm{d}\widehat{M}_{tu}$ is given by (3.26). Also,

$$\mathrm{d}\left[\int_t^\infty \rho(u)\, \widehat{M}_{tu}\, \mathrm{d}u\right] = \int_t^\infty \rho(u)\, \mathrm{d}\widehat{M}_{tu}\, \mathrm{d}u - \rho(t)\, \widehat{M}_{tt}\, \mathrm{d}t. \tag{6.6}$$

We then apply the Itô quotient rule to obtain the dynamics of $\{P_{tT}\}$. We observe that the discount bond volatilities are given by

$$\Omega^{(1)}_{tT} = \theta_{tT} - \theta_{tt}, \tag{6.7}$$

$$\Omega^{(2)}_{tT} = \nu_{tT} - \nu_{tt}. \tag{6.8}$$

The market price of risk associated with $\{W_t\}$ is $\lambda^{(1)}_t := -\theta_{tt}$; the one associated with $\{Z_t\}$ is $\lambda^{(2)}_t := -\nu_{tt}$. The product between the bond volatility vector $\Omega_{tT} = (\Omega^{(1)}_{tT}, \Omega^{(2)}_{tT})$ and the market price of risk vector $\lambda_t = (\lambda^{(1)}_t, \lambda^{(2)}_t)$ gives us the risk premium associated with an investment in the discount bond, that is,

$$\Omega_{tT} \cdot \lambda_t = -\theta_{tt}\, (\theta_{tT} - \theta_{tt}) - \nu_{tt}\, (\nu_{tT} - \nu_{tt}). \tag{6.9}$$

□

Proposition 6.2 *Let $\{M_{tu}(X)\}$ be of the class* (2.7)*, and let $\{\widehat{M}_{tu}\}$ in* (5.8) *be given by the martingale family* (3.15)*. Then the dynamical equation of the forward rate is given by*

$$\mathrm{d}r_{tT} = [\theta_{tT}\, \partial_T\theta_{tT} + \nu_{tT}\, \partial_T\nu_{tT}]\, \mathrm{d}t - \partial_T\theta_{tT}\, \mathrm{d}W_t - \partial_T\nu_{tT}\, \mathrm{d}Z_t \tag{6.10}$$

where

$$\theta_{tT} := \frac{\int_T^\infty \rho(u)\, \mathbb{E}\,[M_{tu}(X)h(u, X)\,|\,\mathcal{F}_t]\, \mathrm{d}u}{\int_T^\infty \rho(u)\, \widehat{M}_{tu}\, \mathrm{d}u}, \tag{6.11}$$

and

$$\nu_{tT} := \frac{\int_T^\infty \rho(u)\, \mathbb{E}\,[M_{tu}(X)V_t(X)\,|\,\mathcal{F}_t]\, \mathrm{d}u}{\int_T^\infty \rho(u)\, \widehat{M}_{tu}\, \mathrm{d}u} \tag{6.12}$$

where $V_t(X)$ is defined by (3.18).

Proof 6.2 We apply the Itô quotient rule to (5.8) to obtain the forward rate dynamics. We make the observations that

$$\partial_T\theta_{tT} = r_{tT}\left(\theta_{tT} - \frac{\mathbb{E}\,[M_{tT}(X)h(T, X)\,|\,\mathcal{F}_t]}{\widehat{M}_{tT}}\right), \tag{6.13}$$

and that

$$\partial_T \nu_{tT} = r_{tT}\left(\nu_{tT} - \frac{\mathbb{E}[M_{tT}(X)V_t(X)\,|\,\mathcal{F}_t]}{\widehat{M}_{tT}}\right). \tag{6.14}$$

□

In particular, if we set

$$\Sigma_{tT} = \theta_{tT} - \theta_{tt}, \tag{6.15}$$
$$\Lambda_{tT} = \nu_{tT} - \nu_{tt}, \tag{6.16}$$

then we can express the risk-neutral dynamics of the forward rate by

$$\mathrm{d}r_{tT} = [\Sigma_{tT}\partial_T\Sigma_{tT} + \Lambda_{tT}\partial_T\Lambda_{tT}]\,\mathrm{d}t - \partial_T\Sigma_{tT}\mathrm{d}\widetilde{W}_t - \partial_T\Lambda_{tT}\mathrm{d}\widetilde{Z}_t, \tag{6.17}$$

where $\{\widetilde{W}_t\}_{t\geq 0}$ and $\{\widetilde{Z}_t\}_{t\geq 0}$ are Brownian motions defined by the Girsanov relations

$$\begin{aligned} \mathrm{d}\widetilde{W}_t &= \mathrm{d}W_t + \lambda_t^{(1)}\,\mathrm{d}t, \\ \mathrm{d}\widetilde{Z}_t &= \mathrm{d}Z_t + \lambda_t^{(2)}\,\mathrm{d}t. \end{aligned} \tag{6.18}$$

The dynamical equation (6.17) has the form of the HJM dynamics for the forward rate under the risk-neutral measure, see Heath et al. (1992).

Example 6.1 As a first illustration, let us now consider the case in which the information process is defined by

$$I_t = \sigma X t + B_t, \tag{6.19}$$

where σ is a positive constant. It can be proven that this is a Markov process (see Brody et al. 2011). Equation (6.19) is a special case of the path-dependent observation process (3.4). Let $\{W_t\}$ be a standard Brownian motion that is independent of X. Then from Example 2.1, we have

$$M_{tu}(X) = \exp\left[h(u,X)W_t - \tfrac{1}{2}h^2(u,X)t\right]. \tag{6.20}$$

We suppose that the a priori distribution of X is uniform over the interval (a, b), where $a \geq 0$ and $b > 0$. We choose to model the random mixer by

$$h(u,X) = c\exp(-uX) \tag{6.21}$$

where $c \in \mathbb{R}$. Here X can be interpreted as the random rate of the exponential decay in $h(u, X)$. We obtain the following expressions for the bond price

$$P_{tT} = \frac{\int_T^\infty \rho(u)\int_a^b \exp\left[\sigma x I_t + c\mathrm{e}^{-ux}W_t - \frac{1}{2}\left(\sigma^2x^2 + c^2\mathrm{e}^{-2ux}\right)t\right]\mathrm{d}x\,\mathrm{d}u}{\int_t^\infty \rho(u)\int_a^b \exp\left[\sigma y I_t + c\mathrm{e}^{-uy}W_t - \frac{1}{2}\left(\sigma^2y^2 + c^2\mathrm{e}^{-2uy}\right)t\right]\mathrm{d}y\,\mathrm{d}u}, \tag{6.22}$$

and the associated interest rate

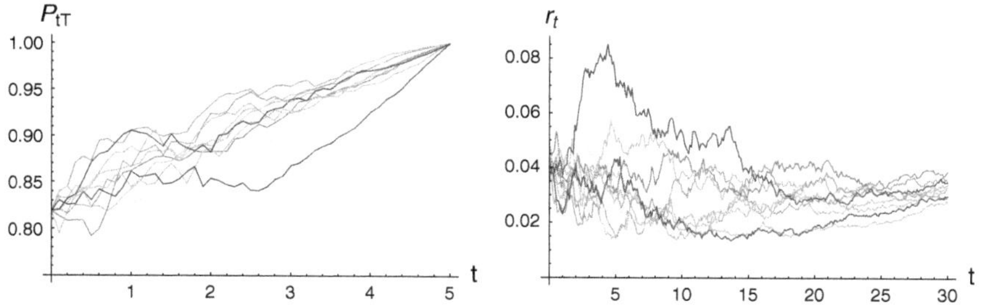

Fig. 1 Sample paths of discount bond with $T = 5$ and short rate. We use the filtered Brownian model with $h(u, X) = c\exp(-uX)$ and $X \sim U(a, b)$. We set $a = 0$, $b = 0.1$, $\sigma = 0.1$, $c = 0.5$ and $P_{0t} = \exp(-0.04t)$

$$r_t = \frac{\rho(t)\int_a^b \exp\left[\sigma x I_t + c\mathrm{e}^{-tx}W_t - \frac{1}{2}\left(\sigma^2x^2 + c^2\mathrm{e}^{-2tx}\right)t\right]\mathrm{d}x}{\int_t^\infty \rho(u)\int_a^b \exp\left[\sigma y I_t + c\mathrm{e}^{-uy}W_t - \frac{1}{2}\left(\sigma^2y^2 + c^2\mathrm{e}^{-2uy}\right)t\right]\mathrm{d}y}. \tag{6.23}$$

Since the model is constructed from a single Lévy process, it is not—strictly speaking—a mixture model as described previously. However, it can be viewed as a kind of two-factor Brownian model owing to the presence of the observation process $\{I_t\}$. The bond price and the associated interest rate are functions of time and the two state variables W_t and I_t. Thus, it is straightforward to generate simulated sample paths (Fig. 1).

The parameters a and b influence the rate at which $\exp(-uX)$ decays, and together with c determine the impact of the Brownian motion $\{W_t\}$ on the bond and interest rate evolution. When c is close to zero, the impact of $\{W_t\}$ is very small. For sufficiently large values of $b-a$, σ or $|c|$, the numerical integration in the calculation of the pricing kernel may fail to converge. For large values of t, we observe that the sample paths of the short rate revert to r_0. Thus, there is built-in reversion to the initial level of the short rate.

Example 6.2 The following model is related to the one in the above example and emphasises the flexibility of the framework presented in this paper. We keep the information process (6.19), but consider $f_0(x) = 1/\sqrt{2\pi}\exp(-1/2x^2)$ for the *a priori* density of X and choose a mixing function of the form $h(u, x) = g(u)x$. Then we obtain

$$\begin{aligned}\widehat{M}_{tu} &= \int M_{tu}(x) f_t(x)\mathrm{d}x,\\ &= \frac{\sqrt{1+\sigma^2 t}}{\sqrt{1+(\sigma^2+g^2(u))t}}\exp\left[\frac{(\sigma I_t + g(u)W_t)^2}{2\left[1+(\sigma^2+g^2(u))t\right]} - \frac{\sigma^2 I_t^2}{2(1+\sigma^2 t)}\right],\end{aligned} \tag{6.24}$$

where (6.20) and

$$f_t(x) = \frac{f_0(x)\exp\left(\sigma x I_t - \frac{1}{2}\sigma^2 x^2 t\right)}{\int f_0(y)\exp\left(\sigma y I_t - \frac{1}{2}\sigma^2 y^2 t\right)\mathrm{d}y}$$

are applied. Assuming that the function $g(u)$ is specified such that the u-integration in the following expression is finite, we obtain a semi-closed-form for the pricing kernel:

$$\pi_t = \sqrt{1+\sigma^2 t}\exp\left[-\frac{\sigma^2 I_t^2}{2(1+\sigma^2 t)}\right]\int_t^{\infty}\frac{\rho(u)}{\sqrt{1+(\sigma^2+g^2(u))t}} \times \exp\left[\frac{(\sigma I_t + g(u)W_t)^2}{2\left[1+(\sigma^2+g^2(u))t\right]}\right]\mathrm{d}u. \tag{6.25}$$

The associated bond price process is then given by

$$P_{tT} = \frac{\int_T^{\infty}\rho(u)\widehat{M}_{tu}\mathrm{d}u}{\int_t^{\infty}\rho(u)\widehat{M}_{tu}\mathrm{d}u}, = \frac{\int_T^{\infty}\frac{\rho(u)}{\sqrt{1+(\sigma^2+g^2(u))t}}\exp\left[\frac{(\sigma I_t+g(u)W_t)^2}{2[1+(\sigma^2+g^2(u))t]}\right]\mathrm{d}u}{\int_t^{\infty}\frac{\rho(u)}{\sqrt{1+(\sigma^2+g^2(u))t}}\exp\left[\frac{(\sigma I_t+g(u)W_t)^2}{2[1+(\sigma^2+g^2(u))t]}\right]\mathrm{d}u}, \tag{6.26}$$

where $\rho(u) = -\partial_u P_{0u}$.

7 Bond Prices Driven by Filtered Gamma Martingales

Let $\{\gamma_t\}$ denote a gamma process with $\mathbb{E}[\gamma_t] = \kappa m t$, and $\mathrm{Var}[\gamma_t] = \kappa^2 m t$. We consider a bond price model based on a pricing kernel that is driven by a family of filtered gamma martingales given by (3.28). Then, Eq. (5.7) for the bond price gives the following expression:

$$P_{tT} = \frac{\int_T^{\infty}\rho(u)\int_{-\infty}^{\infty}f_t(x)\left[1-\kappa h(u,x)\right]^{mt}\exp\left[h(u,x)\gamma_t\right]\mathrm{d}x\,\mathrm{d}u}{\int_t^{\infty}\rho(v)\int_{-\infty}^{\infty}f_t(y)\left[1-\kappa h(v,y)\right]^{mt}\exp\left[h(v,y)\gamma_t\right]\mathrm{d}y\,\mathrm{d}v}. \tag{7.1}$$

We now investigate this bond price model in more detail, and in particular show the effects of the various model components on the behaviour of the bond price.

Example 7.1 Let the information process $\{I_t\}$, driving the conditional density $\{f_t(x)\}$ be of the form

$$I_t = \sigma t X + B_t, \tag{7.2}$$

where X is a binary random variable taking the values $X = 1$ with a priori probability $f_0(1)$, and $X = 0$ with probability $f_0(0)$. We choose the random mixer

$$h(u, X) = c\exp\left[-bu(1-X)\right], \tag{7.3}$$

where $c < \kappa^{-1}$ and $b > 0$. Then the expression for the filtered gamma martingale simplifies to

$$\widehat{M}_{tu} = f_t(0)\exp\left(ce^{-bu}\gamma_t\right)\left(1-\kappa ce^{-bu}\right)^{mt} + f_t(1)\exp\left(c\gamma_t\right)\left(1-\kappa c\right)^{mt}, \quad (7.4)$$

where

$$f_t(0) = \frac{f_0(0)}{f_0(0)+f_0(1)\exp\left(\sigma I_t - \frac{1}{2}\sigma^2 t\right)} \qquad f_t(1) = \frac{f_0(1)\exp\left(\sigma I_t - \frac{1}{2}\sigma^2 t\right)}{f_0(0)+f_0(1)\exp\left(\sigma I_t - \frac{1}{2}\sigma^2 t\right)}. \quad (7.5)$$

There are a number of degrees of freedom in this model which have a significant impact on the behaviour of the trajectories. In what follows, we analyse the degrees of freedom one by one.

A priori probability. When $f_0(1) = 0$, the diffusion $\{I_t\}$ plays no role. The sample paths of the discount bond and the short rate are driven solely by the pure jump process. The size of the jumps decays over time. As $f_0(1)$ increases, there is a greater amount of diffusion in the sample paths. Furthermore, there is a higher likelihood of obtaining sample paths for which the size of the jumps do not decay over time. If $f_0(1) = 1$, then $\{\widehat{M}_{tu}\}$ is no longer u dependent. This yields a stochastic pricing kernel, but flat short rate and deterministic discount bond prices, see Fig. 2.

Information flow rate σ. As the information flow rate increases, the investor becomes more knowledgeable at an earlier stage about whether the random variable may take the value $X = 0$ or $X = 1$, see Fig. 3.

Parameters of the gamma process m and κ. The rate parameter m controls the rate of jump arrivals. The scale parameter κ controls the jump size.

Parameters of the random mixer b and c. The magnitude of c influences the impact of the jumps on the interest rate dynamics. When $c = 0$, the pricing kernel, and thus the short rate of interest, is deterministic. The sign of c affects the direction of the jumps. For $0 < c < \kappa^{-1}$, the short rate (discount bond) sample paths have upward (downward) jumps. The opposite is true for $c < 0$. It should be noted that $\exp\left(c\exp[-bu(1-X)]\gamma_t\right)$, and $(1-\kappa c\exp[-bu(1-X)])^{mt}$ behave antagonistically in c. For large t, one term will eventually dominate the other. Thus, for both $c > 0$ and $c < 0$, the drift of the short rate trajectories is initially negative and then becomes positive for large t, see Fig. 4. The parameter b determines how quickly the jumps are "killed off". Alternatively, b can be viewed as the rate of reversion to the initial level of the interest rate. The interest rate process approaches the initial rate more rapidly for high values of b. When $b = 0$, $\widehat{M}_{tu}$ is no longer u dependent, and we obtain a stochastic pricing kernel, but flat short rate and deterministic discount bond prices, see Fig. 5.

Compared to Example 6.1, this model is more robust to variation in the values of the parameters. An analysis of the sample trajectories suggests that for large t, the short rate reverts to the initial level r_0.

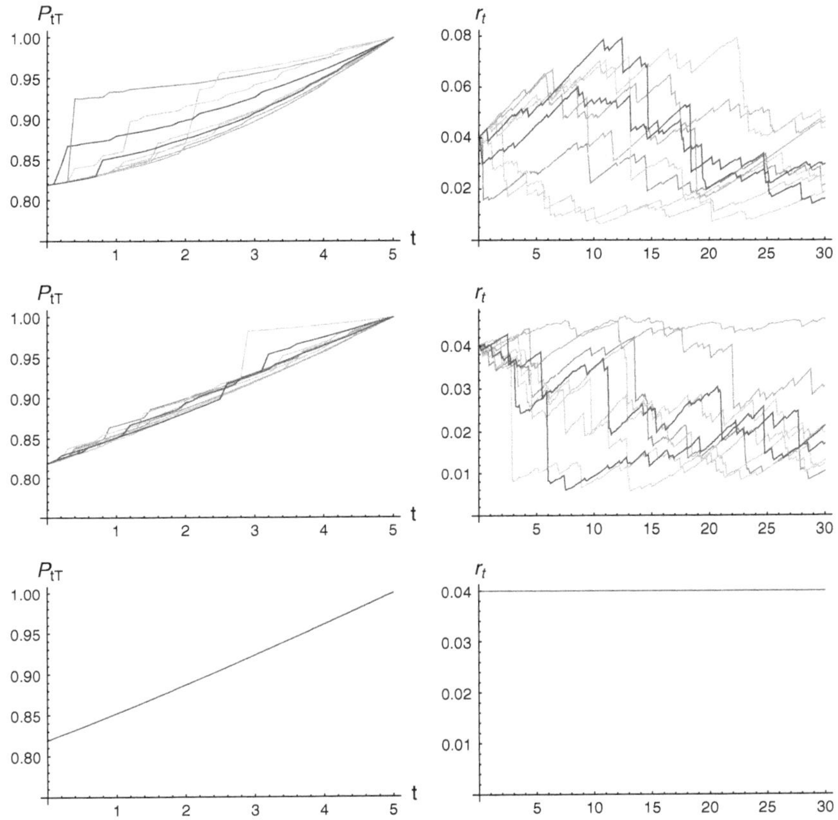

Fig. 2 Sample paths for discount bond with $T = 5$, and associated short rate. We use the Brownian-gamma model with $h(u, X) = c \exp[-bu(1 - X)]$ where $X = \{0, 1\}$ with $m = 0.5$, $\kappa = 0.5$, $\sigma = 0.1$, $c = -2$, $b = 0.03$ and $P_{0t} = \exp(-0.04t)$. We let (i) $f_0(1) = 0$, (ii) $f_0(1) = 0.65$ and (iii) $f_0(1) = 1$

8 Bond Prices Driven by Filtered Variance-Gamma Martingales

We let $\{L_t\}$ denote a variance-gamma process. We define the variance-gamma process as a time-changed Brownian motion with drift (see Carr et al. 1998), that is

$$L_t = \theta \gamma_t + \Sigma B_{\gamma_t} \tag{8.1}$$

with parameters $\theta \in \mathbb{R}$, $\Sigma > 0$ and $\nu > 0$. Here $\{\gamma_t\}$ is a gamma process with rate and scale parameters $m = 1/\nu$ and $\kappa = \nu$, respectively, and $\{B_{\gamma_t}\}$ is a subordinated Brownian motion. The randomised Esscher martingale is expressed by

$$M_{tu}(X) = \exp[h(u, X)L_t] \left(1 - \theta\nu h(u, X) - \tfrac{1}{2}\Sigma^2 \nu h^2(u, X)\right)^{t/\nu}, \tag{8.2}$$

and the associated filtered Esscher martingale is of the form

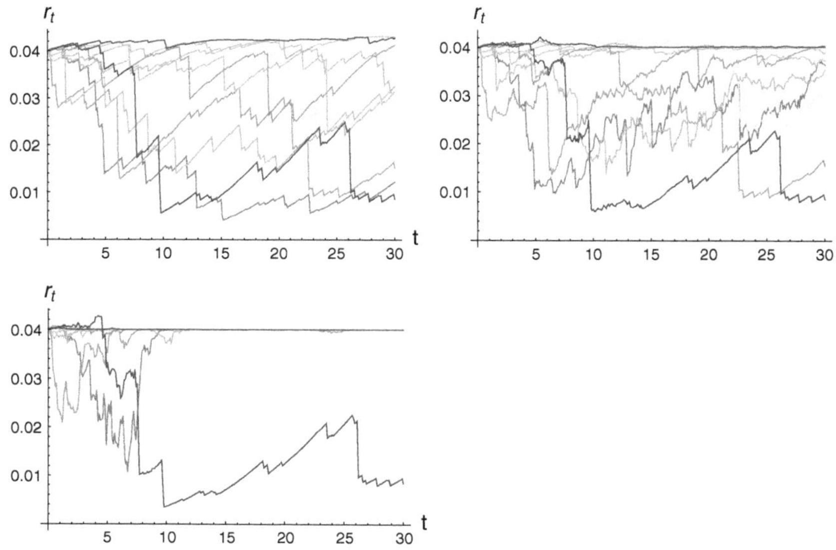

Fig. 3 Short rate sample paths for the Brownian-gamma model with $h(u, X) = c\exp[-bu(1-X)]$ and $X = \{0, 1\}$. We choose $m = 0.5$, $\kappa = 0.5$, $f_0(1) = 0.8$, $c = -2$, $b = 0.03$ and $P_{0t} = \exp(-0.04t)$. We set (i) $\sigma = 0.005$, (ii) $\sigma = 0.4$ and (iii) $\sigma = 1.2$

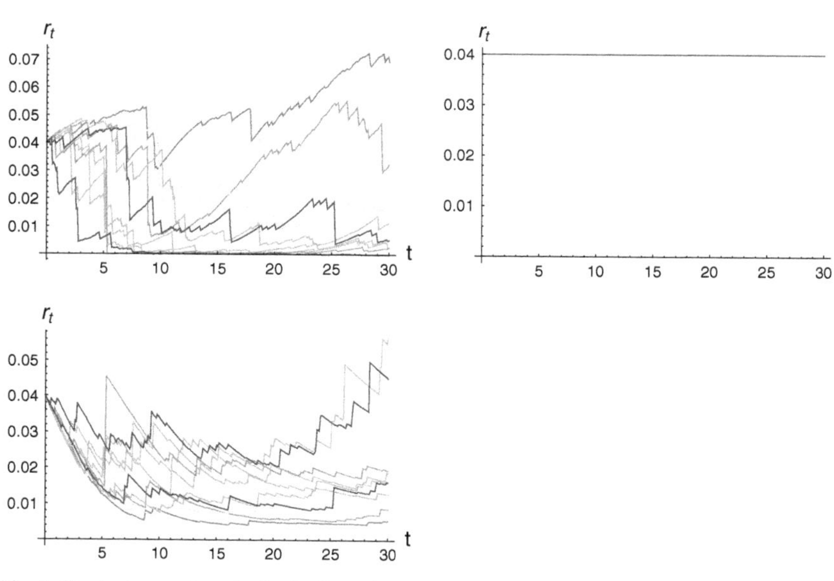

Fig. 4 Short rate sample paths for the Brownian-gamma model with $h(u, X) = c\exp[-bu(1-X)]$ and $X = \{0, 1\}$. We set $m = 0.5$, $\kappa = 0.5$, $f_0(1) = 0.5$, $\sigma = 0.1$, $b = 0.03$ and $P_{0t} = \exp(-0.04t)$. We choose (i) $c = -5$, (ii) $c = 0$ and (iii) $c = 1.5$

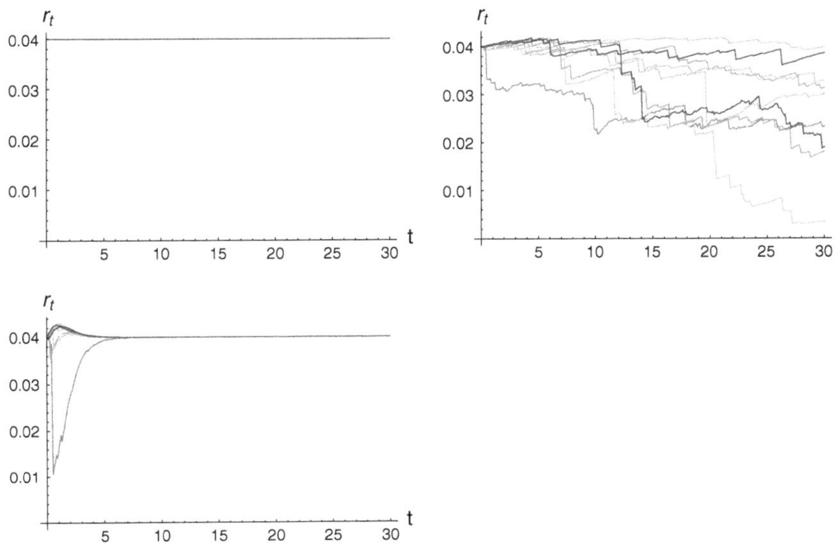

Fig. 5 Short rate sample paths for the Brownian-gamma model with $h(u, X) = c\exp[-bu(1-X)]$ and $X = \{0, 1\}$. We let $m = 0.5$, $\kappa = 0.5$, $f_0(1) = 0.5$, $\sigma = 0.1$, $c = -2$ and $P_{0t} = \exp(-0.04t)$. We choose (i) $b = 0$, (ii) $b = 0.005$ and (iii) $b = 1$

$$\widehat{M}_{tu} = \int_{-\infty}^{\infty} f_t(x) \exp[h(u, x)L_t] \left(1 - \theta \nu h(u, x) - \tfrac{1}{2}\Sigma^2 \nu h^2(u, x)\right)^{t/\nu} \mathrm{d}x, \quad (8.3)$$

where $f_t(x)$ may be given for example by (3.13) or a special case thereof, or by (4.8) depending on the type of information used to filter knowledge about X. This leads to the following expression for the discount bond price process:

$$P_{tT} = \frac{\int_T^{\infty} \rho(u) \int_{-\infty}^{\infty} f_t(x) \exp[h(u, x)L_t] \left(1-\theta\nu h(u, x)-\frac{1}{2}\Sigma^2\nu h^2(u, x)\right)^{t/\nu} \mathrm{d}x\mathrm{d}u}{\int_t^{\infty} \rho(v) \int_{-\infty}^{\infty} f_t(y) \exp[h(v, y)L_t] \left(1-\theta\nu h(v, y)-\frac{1}{2}\Sigma^2\nu h^2(v, y)\right)^{t/\nu} \mathrm{d}y\,\mathrm{d}v}. \quad (8.4)$$

We can also obtain an expression for the short rate of interest by substituting (8.3) into (5.9). We now present another explicit bond pricing model.

Example 8.1 We assume that X is a random time, and hence a positive random variable taking discrete values $\{x_1, \ldots, x_n\}$ with a priori probabilities $\{f_0(x_1), \ldots, f_0(x_n)\}$. We suppose that the information process $\{I_t\}$ is independent of $\{L_t\}$, and that it is defined by $I_t = \sigma X t + B_t$. We take the random mixer to be $h(u, X) = c\exp\left[-b(u-X)^2\right]$ where $b > 0$ and $c \in \mathbb{R}$. We see in Fig. 6 that the random mixer, and thus the weight of the variance-gamma process, increases (in absolute value) until the random time X, and decreases (in absolute value) thereafter.

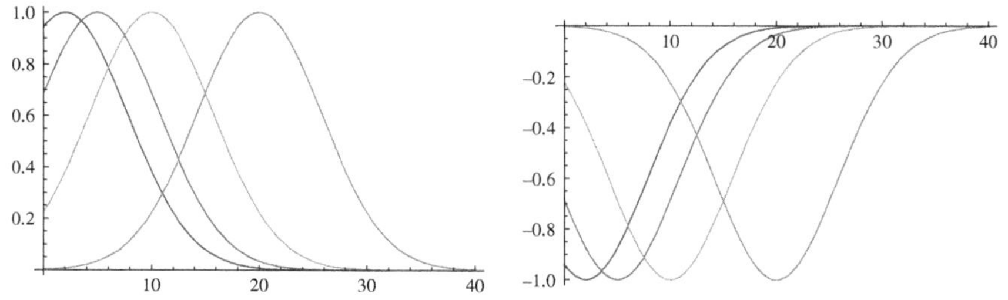

Fig. 6 Plot of $h(u, x_i)$ for $x_1 = 2$, $x_2 = 5$, $x_3 = 10$ and $x_4 = 20$, where $b = 0.015$ and $c = 1$ (*left*) and $c = -1$ (*right*)

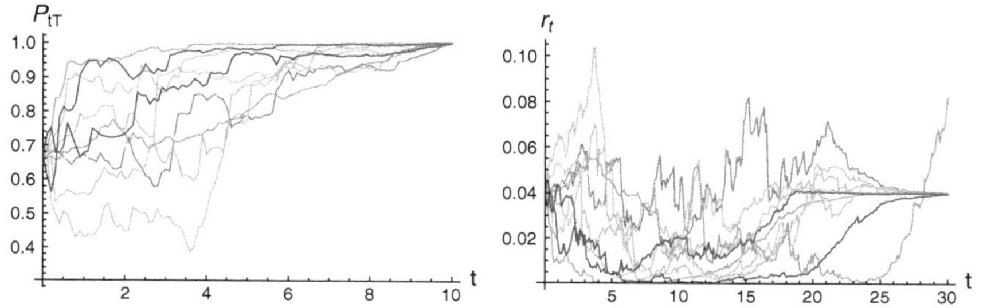

Fig. 7 Sample paths for a discount bond with $T = 10$ and the short rate. We use the variance-gamma model with $h(u, X) = c\exp[-b(u - X)^2]$. We let $\theta = -1.5$, $\Sigma = 2$ and $\nu = 0.25$. We set $f_0(x_1) = 0.2$, $f_0(x_2) = 0.35$, $f_0(x_3) = 0.35$, $f_0(x_4) = 0.1$ and $x_1 = 2$, $x_2 = 5$, $x_3 = 10$, $x_4 = 20$. We choose $\sigma = 0.1$, $c = 0.5$, $b = 0.015$ and the initial term structure is $P_{0t} = \exp(-0.04t)$

The associated bond price and interest rate sample paths are shown in Fig. 7. We observe that over time the sample paths of the interest rate process revert to the initial level r_0. However, some paths may revert to r_0 at a later time than others, depending on the realized value of the random variable X.

9 Chameleon Random Mixers

The functional form of the random mixer $h(u, X)$ strongly influences the interest rate dynamics. The choice of $h(u, X)$ also affects the robustness of the model: there are choices in which the numerical integration in the calculation of the pricing kernel does not converge. So far, we have constructed examples based on an exponential-type random mixer. However, one may wish to introduce other functional forms for $h(u, X)$ for which we can observe different behaviour in the interest rate dynamics, while maintaining robustness. For instance we may consider a random piecewise function of the form

$$h(u, X) = g_1(u)\mathbb{1}_{\{u \leq X\}} + g_2(u)\mathbb{1}_{\{u > X\}} \tag{9.1}$$

where $g_j : \mathbb{R}_+ \to \mathbb{R}$ for $j = 1, 2$. The random mixer now has a "chameleon form": initially appearing to be g_1, and switching its form to g_2 at $X = u$. This results in the martingale $\{\widehat{M}_{tu}\}$, and the resulting interest rate sample paths, exhibiting different hues over time, depending on the choices of g_j $(j = 1, 2)$. We can extend this idea further by considering (i) multiple g_j, or (ii) a multivariate random mixer of the form

$$h(u, X, Y_1, Y_2) = g_1(u, Y_1)\mathbb{1}_{\{u \le X\}} + g_2(u, Y_2)\mathbb{1}_{\{u > X\}}, \tag{9.2}$$

where $X > 0$, Y_1 and Y_2 are independent random variables with associated information processes. In this case, the g_j are themselves random-valued functions. Here X can be regarded as the primary mixer which determines the timing of the regime switch. The variables Y_i $(i = 1, 2)$ can then be interpreted as the secondary mixers determining the weights of the Lévy processes over two distinct time intervals.

Example 9.1 We now present what may be called the "Brownian-gamma chameleon model". We consider the filtered gamma martingale family (3.28) in the situation where the random mixer $h(u, X)$ has the form

$$h(u, X) = c_1 \sin(\alpha_1 u)\mathbb{1}_{\{u \le X\}} + c_2 \exp(-\alpha_2 u)\mathbb{1}_{\{u > X\}} \tag{9.3}$$

where $c_1, c_2 < \kappa^{-1}$ and $\alpha_2 > 0$. The information process $\{I_t\}$ associated with X is taken to be of the form

$$I_t = \sigma t X + B_t. \tag{9.4}$$

We assume that X is a positive discrete random variable taking values $\{x_1, x_2, \ldots, x_n\}$ with a priori probabilities $f_0(x_i)$, $i = 1, 2, \ldots, n$. That is, the function $h(u, X)$ will switch once from sine to exponential behaviour at one of the finitely many random times. Inserting (3.28), with the specification (9.3), in the expression for the bond price (5.7), we obtain

$$P_{tT} = \frac{\int_T^\infty \rho(u) \sum_{i=1}^n f_t(x_i)\,[1 - \kappa\, h(u, x_i)]^{mt} \exp\left[h(u, x_i)\,\gamma_t\right] \mathrm{d}u}{\int_t^\infty \rho(v) \sum_{i=1}^n f_t(y_i)\,[1 - \kappa\, h(v, y_i)]^{mt} \exp\left[h(v, y_i)\,\gamma_t\right] \mathrm{d}v}, \tag{9.5}$$

where $h(u, x_i)$ is given by (9.3) for $X = x_i$, and

$$f_t(x_i) = \frac{f_0(x_i) \exp\left[\sigma x_i I_t - \frac{1}{2}\sigma^2 x_i^2 t\right]}{\sum_{i=1}^n f_0(y_i) \exp\left[\sigma y_i I_t - \frac{1}{2}\sigma^2 y_i^2 t\right]}. \tag{9.6}$$

Since the sine function oscillates periodically within the interval $[-1, 1]$, the integrals in (9.5) may not necessarily converge to one value. However, at some finite random time $u = X$, the sine behaviour is replaced by an exponential decay; this ensures the integrals in the expression for the bond price converge. Such a behaviour may be viewed as a regime switch at a random time. In the simulation below, the analysis of the model parameters is analogous to the one in Example 7.1. It is worth emphasizing nevertheless that (i) the a priori probabilities $f_0(x_i)$, $i = 1, 2, \ldots, n$ have a direct influence on the length of the time span during which the sine function in the chameleon mixer is activated, (ii) the magnitude of α_1 determines the frequency of the sine wave, while α_2 affects the rate at which reversion to the initial interest rate

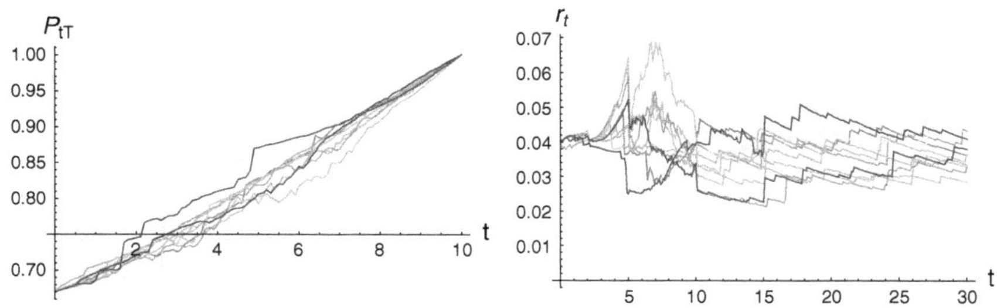

Fig. 8 Sample paths of discount bond with $T = 10$ and short rate trajectories. We use the Brownian-gamma chameleon model with $h(u, X) = c_1 \sin(\alpha_1 u)\mathbb{1}_{\{u \leq X\}} + c_2 \exp(-\alpha_2 u)\mathbb{1}_{\{u > X\}}$. Let X take the values $\{x_1 = 2, x_2 = 5, x_3 = 10, x_4 = 15\}$ with a priori probabilities $\{f_0(x_1) = 0.2, f_0(x_2) = 0.35, f_0(x_3) = 0.35, f_0(x_4) = 0.1\}$. We set $m = 0.5$, $\kappa = 0.5$, $\sigma = 0.1$, $c_1 = 0.2625$, $c_2 = 0.75$, $\alpha_1 = 0.75$, $\alpha_2 = 0.02$ and $P_{0t} = \exp(-0.04t)$

(in the simulation below $r_0 = 4\,\%$) occurs, and (iii) the size of c_1 determines the amplitude of the sine, and it significantly impacts the convergence of the numerical integration. We find that reasonable results are obtained for $-\kappa^{-1} < c_1 < \kappa^{-1}$ (Fig. 8).

10 Model-Generated Yield Curves

The yield curve at any time is defined as the range of yields that investors in sovereign debt can expect to receive on investments over various terms to maturity. For a calendar date t and a time to maturity τ, we let $Y_{t,t+\tau}$ be the continuously compounded zero-coupon spot rate for time to maturity τ, that is, the map $\tau \mapsto Y_{t,t+\tau}$. We write

$$P_{t,t+\tau} = \exp\left(-\tau Y_{t,t+\tau}\right). \tag{10.1}$$

Typically, the following yield curve movements are observed: (i) parallel shifts of the yield curve corresponding to an equal increase in yields across all maturities; (ii) steepening (flattening) of the yield curve, that is the difference between the yields for longer-dated bonds and shorter-dated bonds widens (narrows), and (iii) changes in the curvature and overall shape of the yield curve. The terms "shift", "twist" and "butterfly" are also used to describe these yield curve movements. As shown in Fig. 9 below, the two-factor Brownian-gamma model set-up in Example 7.1 is indeed too rigid to allow for significant changes in the shape of the yield curve. For $f_0(1) = 1$, the yield curve is flat at all times. For $0 \leq f_0(1) < 1$, this model can generate flat, upward sloping yield curves and in certain cases, slightly inverted yield curves. The variance-gamma model (Fig. 10) and the Brownian-gamma chameleon model (Fig. 11) show more flexibility, where changes of slope and different yield curve shapes are observed. These model may generate flat, upward sloping, inverted and humped yield curves. We emphasize that these classes of models are able to capture all three types of yield curve movements.

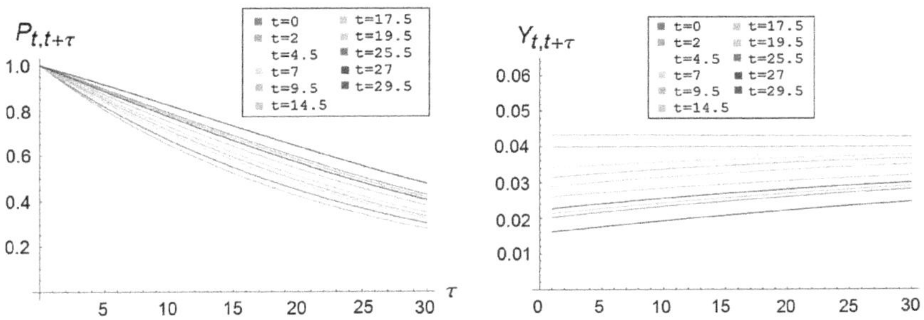

Fig. 9 Discount bond curves for the Brownian-gamma model. We let $X = \{0, 1\}$ with $f_0(1) = 0.3$. We let $m = 2, \kappa = 0.2, \sigma = 0.1, c = -2, b = 0.03, P_{0t} = \exp(-0.04t)$. *Yield curves* for the Brownian-gamma model. We let $X = \{0, 1\}$ with $f_0(1) = 0.3$. We let $m = 2, \kappa = 0.2, \sigma = 0.1, c = -2, b = 0.03$, $P_{0t} = \exp(-0.04t)$

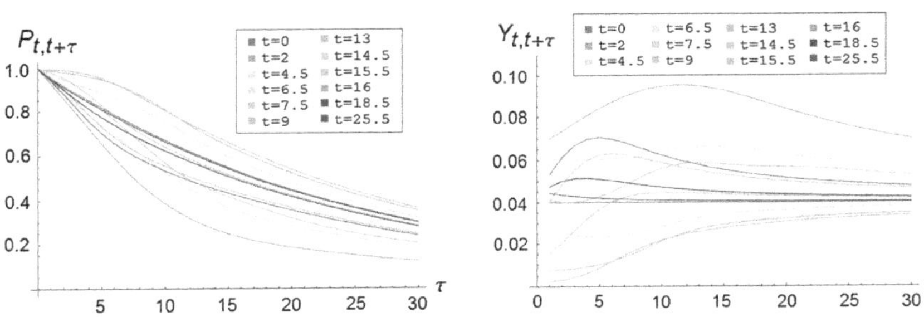

Fig. 10 *Discount bond curves* for the variance-gamma model with $h(u, X) = c\exp[-b(u - X)^2]$. We let $\theta = -1.5$, $\Sigma = 2$ and $\nu = 0.25$. We set $f_0(x_1) = 0.2$, $f_0(x_2) = 0.35$, $f_0(x_3) = 0.35$, $f_0(x_4) = 0.1$ and $x_1 = 2, x_2 = 5, x_3 = 10, x_4 = 20$. We choose $\sigma = 0.1$, $c = 0.5$, $b = 0.015$ and the initial term structure is $P_{0t} = \exp(-0.04t)$. *Yield curves* for the variance-gamma model where $h(u, X) = c\exp[-b(u - X)^2]$. We let $\theta = -1.5$, $\Sigma = 2$ and $\nu = 0.25$. We set $f_0(x_1) = 0.2$, $f_0(x_2) = 0.35$, $f_0(x_3) = 0.35$, $f_0(x_4) = 0.1$ and $x_1 = 2, x_2 = 5, x_3 = 10, x_4 = 20$. We choose $\sigma = 0.1$, $c = 0.5$, $b = 0.015$ and the initial term structure is $P_{0t} = \exp(-0.04t)$

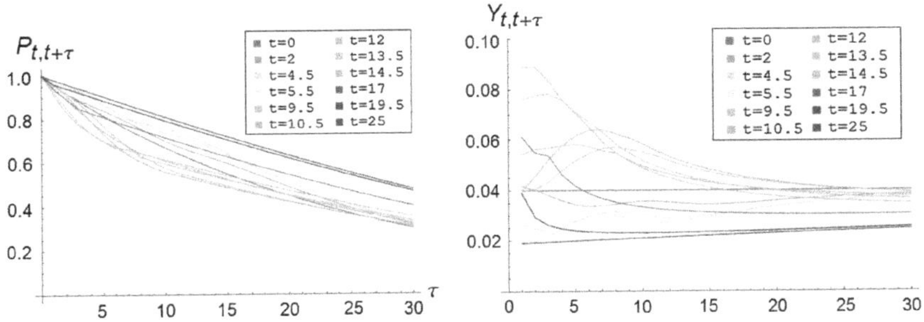

Fig. 11 *Discount bond curves* for the Brownian-gamma chameleon model. We let $X = \{x_1 = 2, x_2 = 5, x_3 = 10, x_4 = 20\}$ with $f_0(x_1) = 0.15$, $f_0(x_2) = 0.35$, $f_0(x_3) = 0.35$, $f_0(x_4) = 0.15$. We let $m = 0.5, \kappa = 0.5, \sigma = 0.1, c_1 = -0.4375, c_2 = -1.25, \alpha_1 = 0.75, \alpha_2 = 0.02, P_{0t} = \exp(-0.04t)$. *Yield curves* for the Brownian-gamma chameleon model. We let $X = \{x_1 = 2, x_2 = 5, x_3 = 10, x_4 = 20\}$ with $f_0(x_1) = 0.15$, $f_0(x_2) = 0.35$, $f_0(x_3) = 0.35$, $f_0(x_4) = 0.15$. We let $m = 0.5, \kappa = 0.5, \sigma = 0.1$, $c_1 = -0.4375, c_2 = -1.25, \alpha_1 = 0.75, \alpha_2 = 0.02, P_{0t} = \exp(-0.04t)$

11 Pricing of European-Style Bond Options

Let $\{C_{st}\}_{0\le s\le t<T}$ be the price process of a European call option with maturity t and strike $0 < K < 1$, written on a discount bond with price process $\{P_{tT}\}_{0\le t\le T}$. The price of the option at time s is given by

$$C_{st} = \frac{1}{\pi_s}\,\mathbb{E}\left[\pi_t(P_{tT} - K)^+ \,|\, \mathcal{F}_s\right]. \tag{11.1}$$

By substituting (5.6) and (5.7) into (11.1), we obtain

$$C_{st} = \frac{1}{\pi_s}\mathbb{E}\left[\left(\int_T^\infty \rho(u)\,\widehat{M}_{tu}\,\mathrm{d}u - K\int_t^\infty \rho(u)\,\widehat{M}_{tu}\,\mathrm{d}u\right)^+ \,\middle|\, \mathcal{F}_s\right]. \tag{11.2}$$

In the single-factor models that we have considered with a Markovian information process $\{I_t\}$, we can define the region $\mathcal{V}$ by

$$\mathcal{V} := \left\{ y, z : \int_T^\infty \rho(u)\,\widehat{M}_{tu}(L_t = y, I_t = z)\,\mathrm{d}u \right.$$
$$\left. -K\int_t^\infty \rho(u)\,\widehat{M}_{tu}(L_t = y, I_t = z)\,\mathrm{d}u > 0 \right\}. \tag{11.3}$$

It follows that the price of the call option is

$$C_{st} = \frac{1}{\pi_s}\iint_{\mathcal{V}} \left(\int_T^\infty \rho(u)\,\widehat{M}_{tu}(y,z)\,\mathrm{d}u \right.$$
$$\left. -K\int_t^\infty \rho(u)\,\widehat{M}_{tu}(y,z)\,\mathrm{d}u \right) q_s(y,z)\,\mathrm{d}y\,\mathrm{d}z \tag{11.4}$$

where

$$q_s(y,z) = \frac{\partial^2}{\partial y\,\partial z}\mathbb{P}\left[L_t \le y, I_t \le z \,|\, \mathcal{F}_s\right]. \tag{11.5}$$

We can use Fubini's theorem to write this more compactly in the form

$$C_{st} = \frac{1}{\pi_s}\left(\int_T^\infty \rho(u)\,\Phi_s(t,u)\,\mathrm{d}u - K\int_t^\infty \rho(u)\,\Phi_s(t,u)\,\mathrm{d}u \right), \tag{11.6}$$

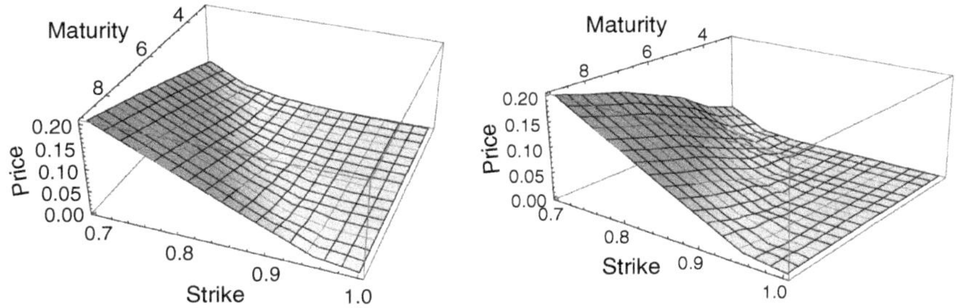

Fig. 12 Option price surface at $s = 2$ of call options on a discount bond with $T = 10$. (i) Simulation based on the Brownian-gamma model. We set $X = \{0, 1\}$ with $f_0(1) = 0.5, m = 0.5, \kappa = 0.5, \sigma = 0.1, c = -2$, $b = 0.03$ and $P_{0t} = \exp(-0.04t)$. (ii) Simulation based on the Brownian-gamma chameleon model. We set $X = \{x_1 = 2, x_2 = 5, x_3 = 10, x_4 = 20\}$ with $f_0(x_1) = 0.15$, $f_0(x_2) = 0.35$, $f_0(x_3) = 0.35$, $f_0(x_4) = 0.15$, $m = 0.5$, $\kappa = 0.5$, $\sigma = 0.1$, $c_1 = 0.35$, $c_2 = 1$, $\alpha_1 = 3$, $\alpha_2 = 0.03$, and $P_{0t} = \exp(-0.04t)$

where

$$\Phi_s(t, u) = \iint_{\mathcal{V}} \widehat{M}_{tu}(y, z)\, q_s(y, z)\, \mathrm{d}y\, \mathrm{d}z. \tag{11.7}$$

We apply Monte Carlo techniques to simulate option price surfaces. A large number of iterations is required to obtain accurate estimates. To increase precision, variance reduction techniques or quasi-Monte Carlo methods can be considered (see Boyle et al. 1997). The choice of the random mixer affects the shape of the resulting option price surface. The simulations in Fig. 12 are based on (i) the Brownian-gamma model constructed in Example 7.1, and (ii) the Brownian-gamma chameleon model in Example 9.1. The wave across the second option price surface is produced by the sine function that defines part of the chameleon random mixer.

In the case of a call option with maturity t which is written on a discount bond with price process (6.26), we can work out a semi-analytical expression for the option price C_{0t} at time 0. We recall the formula (11.6) and calculate (11.7) for $s = 0$. Assuming that $\{I_t\}$ and $\{W_t\}$ are independent, we observe that the density $q_0(y, z)$ is given by

$$\begin{aligned} q_0(y, z)\mathrm{d}y\mathrm{d}z &= \int f_0(x)\mathbb{P}[I_t \in \mathrm{d}z \mid X = x]\mathrm{d}x\, \mathbb{P}[W_t \in \mathrm{d}y], \\ &= \frac{1}{\sqrt{2\pi(1+\sigma^2 t)}} \exp\left[-\frac{z^2}{2(1+\sigma^2 t)t}\right] \mathrm{d}z\, \frac{1}{\sqrt{2\pi t}} \exp\left(-\frac{y^2}{2t}\right) \mathrm{d}y, \end{aligned} \tag{11.8}$$

where $f_0(x) = 1/\sqrt{2\pi} \exp(-1/2x^2)$. Then, it follows that

$$\begin{aligned} \Phi_0(t, u) &= \iint_{\mathcal{V}} \widehat{M}_{tu}(y, z)\, q_0(y, z)\mathrm{d}y\mathrm{d}z = \iint_{\mathcal{V}} \frac{1}{\sqrt{1 + (\sigma^2 + g^2(u))t}} \\ &\quad \times \exp\left[\frac{(\sigma y + g(u)\, z)^2}{2\left[1 + (\sigma^2 + g^2(u))t\right]}\right] \frac{1}{2\pi t} \exp\left[-\frac{y^2 - z^2}{2t}\right] \mathrm{d}y\mathrm{d}z. \end{aligned} \tag{11.9}$$

This is now inserted in (11.6) for $s = 0$ to obtain the price of the option at time 0.

12 Randomised Heat Kernel Interest Rate Models

In Sects. 2 and 3, we constructed martingales based on Lévy processes and an Esscher-type formulation. We recall that the pricing kernel is modelled by

$$\begin{aligned}\pi_t &= \int_t^\infty \rho(u)\, \mathbb{E}\left[M_{tu}(X, L_t) \mid \mathcal{F}_t\right] \mathrm{d}u, \\ &= \int_{-\infty}^\infty \int_t^\infty \rho(u)\, M_{tu}(x, L_t)\, \mathrm{d}u\, f_t(x)\, \mathrm{d}x. \end{aligned} \tag{12.1}$$

The process $\{M_{tu}(X, L_t)\}$ is a unit-initialized positive $\{\mathcal{G}_t\}$-martingale, and the process

$$S_t(X, L_t) := \int_t^\infty \rho(u)\, M_{tu}(X, L_t)\, \mathrm{d}u \tag{12.2}$$

is a positive $\{\mathcal{G}_t\}$-supermartingale. The projection of a positive $\{\mathcal{G}_t\}$-supermartingale onto $\{\mathcal{F}_t\}$, that is

$$\pi_t := \mathbb{E}\left[S_t(X, L_t) \mid \mathcal{F}_t\right], \tag{12.3}$$

is an $\{\mathcal{F}_t\}$-supermartingale (Föllmer and Protter 2011, Theorem 3).

12.1 Weighted Heat Kernel Approach

We now model the impact of uncertainty on a financial market by a process that has the Markov property with respect to its natural filtration, and which we denote $\{Y_t\}_{t\geq 0}$. Of course, the case where $\{Y_t\}$ is a Lévy process, which is a Markov process of Feller type, is included (see Applebaum 2004).

Definition 12.1 Let $\{Y_t\}$ be a Markov process with respect to its natural filtration. A measurable function $p : \mathbb{R}_+ \times \mathbb{R}_+ \times \mathbb{R} \to \mathbb{R}$ is a propagator if it satisfies

$$\mathbb{E}\left[p(t, v, Y_t) \mid Y_s\right] = p(s, v + t - s, Y_s) \tag{12.4}$$

for $(v, t) \in \mathbb{R}_+ \times \mathbb{R}_+$ and $0 \leq s \leq t$.

Next, let $\{n_t\}_{t\geq 0}$ be a pure noise process, and let the filtration $\{\mathcal{G}_t\}$ be generated by

$$\mathcal{G}_t = \sigma\left(\{Y_s\}_{0\leq s\leq t}, \{n_s\}_{0\leq s\leq t}, X\right), \tag{12.5}$$

where $\{Y_t\}$, $\{n_t\}$, and the random variable X are all independent. Let $G(\cdot)$ be a positive bounded function[1], and let $h : \mathbb{R}_+ \times \mathbb{R} \to \mathbb{R}$. Then we set

$$p(t, v, Y_t, X) := \mathbb{E}\left[G\left(h(t+v, X), Y_{t+v}\right) \mid \mathcal{G}_t\right]. \tag{12.6}$$

This is a $\{\mathcal{G}_t\}$-propagator since X is $\mathcal{G}_0$-measurable. It follows that

$$S_t(X, Y_t) := \int_0^\infty w(t, v)\, \mathbb{E}\left[G(h(t+v, X), Y_{t+v}) \mid \mathcal{G}_t\right] \mathrm{d}v \tag{12.7}$$

is a $\{\mathcal{G}_t\}$-supermartingale, see Akahori et al. (2014). Here $w(t, v)$ is a positive function that satisfies

$$w(t, v-s) \leq w(t-s, v) \tag{12.8}$$

for arbitrary $t, v \in \mathbb{R}_+$ and $s \leq t \wedge v$. Now we define the market filtration $\{\mathcal{F}_t\}$ by

$$\mathcal{F}_t = \sigma\left(\{Y_s\}_{0\leq s\leq t}, \{I_s\}_{0\leq s\leq t}\right), \tag{12.9}$$

where $\{I_t\}$ carries information about X, which is distorted by the pure noise $\{n_t\}$. We have that $\mathcal{F}_t \subset \mathcal{G}_t$. Then, by Föllmer and Protter (2011) Theorem 3, the projection

$$\pi_t := \mathbb{E}\left[S_t(X, Y_t) \mid \mathcal{F}_t\right] \tag{12.10}$$

is an $\{\mathcal{F}_t\}$-supermartingale. It follows that

$$\begin{aligned}
\pi_t &= \mathbb{E}\left[\int_0^\infty w(t, v)\, \mathbb{E}\left[G\left(h(t+v, X), Y_{t+v}\right) \mid \mathcal{G}_t\right] \mathrm{d}v \,\middle|\, \mathcal{F}_t\right], \\
&= \int_0^\infty w(t, v)\, \mathbb{E}\left[\mathbb{E}\left[G(h(t+v, X), Y_{t+v}) | \mathcal{G}_t\right] \mid \mathcal{F}_t\right] \mathrm{d}v, \\
&= \int_0^\infty w(t, v)\, \mathbb{E}\left[G(h(t+v, X), Y_{t+v}) \mid \mathcal{F}_t\right] \mathrm{d}v.
\end{aligned} \tag{12.11}$$

We emphasize that in equation (12.11), $\mathbb{E}\left[G(h(t+v, X), Y_{t+v}) \mid \mathcal{F}_t\right]$ is not an $\{\mathcal{F}_t\}$-propagator when $\{I_t\}$ is not a Markov process. Nevertheless, $\{\pi_t\}$ is a valid model for the pricing kernel, subject to regularity conditions.

[1] Once a Markov process $\{Y_t\}$ has been chosen, it may be sufficient to relax the boundedness condition, and choose $G(\cdot)$ to be a positive and integrable function.

12.2 Quadratic Model Driven by the Ornstein–Uhlenbeck Process

We generate term structure models by using Markov processes with dependent increments. We emphasize that such models cannot be constructed based on the filtered Esscher martingales. Let us suppose that $\{Y_t\}$ is an Ornstein–Uhlenbeck (OU) process with dynamics

$$\mathrm{d}Y_t = \delta(\beta - Y_t)\,\mathrm{d}t + \Upsilon\,\mathrm{d}W_t, \tag{12.12}$$

where δ is the speed of reversion, β is the long-run equilibrium value of the process and Υ is the volatility. Then, for $s \le t$, the conditional mean and conditional variance are given by

$$\mathbb{E}\left[Y_t \mid Y_s\right] = Y_s \exp\left[-\delta(t-s)\right] + \beta\left(1 - \exp\left[-\delta(t-s)\right]\right). \tag{12.13}$$

$$\mathrm{Var}\left[Y_t \mid Y_s\right] = \frac{\Upsilon^2}{2\delta}\left(1 - \exp\left[-2\delta(t-s)\right]\right). \tag{12.14}$$

Let us suppose, for a well-defined positive function $h : \mathbb{R}_+ \times \mathbb{R} \to \mathbb{R}_+$, that

$$G(h(v, X), Y_v) = h(v, X)Y_v^2. \tag{12.15}$$

Since X is $\mathcal{G}_0$-measurable, and by applying (12.13) and (12.14), it follows that

$$\begin{aligned} p(u, t, Y_t, X) &= \mathbb{E}\left[h(t+u, X)Y_{t+u}^2 \mid \mathcal{G}_t\right], \\ &= h(t+u, X)\,\mathbb{E}\left[\left(Y_{t+u} - \mathbb{E}\left[Y_{t+u} \mid Y_t\right] + \mathbb{E}\left[Y_{t+u} \mid Y_t\right]\right)^2 \mid Y_t\right], \\ &= h(t+u, X)\left[\mathrm{Var}\left[Y_{t+u} \mid Y_t\right] + \mathbb{E}\left[Y_{t+u} \mid Y_t\right]^2\right], \\ &= h(t+u, X)\left[\frac{\Upsilon^2}{2\delta}\left(1 - \mathrm{e}^{-2\delta u}\right) + \left[Y_t\,\mathrm{e}^{-\delta u} + \beta\left(1 - \mathrm{e}^{-\delta u}\right)\right]^2\right]. \end{aligned} \tag{12.16}$$

The pricing kernel is then given by (12.11), and we obtain

$$\begin{aligned} \pi_t = &\int_0^\infty w(t, u)\left[\frac{\Upsilon^2}{2\delta}\left(1 - \mathrm{e}^{-2\delta u}\right) + \left[Y_t\,\mathrm{e}^{-\delta u} + \beta\left(1 - \mathrm{e}^{-\delta u}\right)\right]^2\right] \\ &\times \int_{-\infty}^{\infty} h(t+u, x) f_t(x)\,\mathrm{d}x\,\mathrm{d}u. \end{aligned} \tag{12.17}$$

It follows that the price of a discount bond is expressed by

$$P_{tT} = \frac{1}{\pi_t}\mathbb{E}\left[\int_0^\infty w(T, v)\,\mathbb{E}\left[G(h(T+v, X), Y_{T+v}) \mid \mathcal{F}_T\right]\mathrm{d}v \,\middle|\, \mathcal{F}_t\right], \tag{12.18}$$

where $\{\pi_t\}$ is given in (12.17), and the conditional expectation can be computed to obtain

$$\int_0^\infty w(T,v)\left[\frac{\Upsilon^2}{2\delta}\left(1-\mathrm{e}^{-2\delta(T+v-t)}\right)+\left[Y_t\,\mathrm{e}^{-\delta(T+v-t)}+\beta\left(1-\mathrm{e}^{-\delta(T+v-t)}\right)\right]^2\right]$$
$$\times\int_{-\infty}^{\infty} h(T+v,x)f_t(x)\,\mathrm{d}x\,\mathrm{d}v. \tag{12.19}$$

Example 12.1 We assume that X is a positive random variable that takes discrete values $\{x_1,\ldots,x_n\}$ with a priori probabilities $\{f_0(x_1),\ldots,f_0(x_n)\}$. We suppose that the information flow $\{I_t\}$ is governed by

$$I_t=\sigma Xt+B_t. \tag{12.20}$$

We choose the random mixer to be

$$h(t+u,X)=c_1\exp[-c_2(t+u-X)](t+u), \tag{12.21}$$

where $c_1>0$ and $c_2>0$, and we assume that the weight function is

$$w(t,u)=\exp[-j(u+t)] \tag{12.22}$$

for $j>0$. Later, we show that this model belongs to the Flesaker–Hughston class. Therefore, the short rate of interest takes the form

$$r_t=\frac{e^{-jt}\,\mathbb{E}[G(h(t,X),Y_t)\,|\,\mathcal{F}_t]}{\int_0^\infty e^{-j(t+v)}\,\mathbb{E}\left[G(h(t+v,X),Y_{t+v})\,|\,\mathcal{F}_t\right]\mathrm{d}v}. \tag{12.23}$$

Next we simulate the trajectories of the discount bond and the short rate process. We refer to Iacus (2008) for the simulation of the OU process using an Euler scheme. We observe oscillations in the sample paths owing to the mean-reversion in the Markov process. The associated model-generated yield curves show changes of slope and shifts. Other changes of shape in the yield curve may be produced by varying the choice of $G(\cdot)$ and $h(\cdot)$ (Figs. 13, 14).

We conclude by looking at some of the links between the classes of models presented in this paper. For example, the pricing kernel models (12.11) can be written in the form (5.4) for a weight function of the form $w(t,v)=\bar{w}(t+v)$, where $\bar{w}:\mathbb{R}_+\to\mathbb{R}_+$ is a bounded, non-increasing function, and $\bar{w}(t)\to 0$ for $t\to\infty$. Let us consider an $\{\mathcal{F}_t\}$-adapted process $\{A_t\}_{t\geq 0}$ with right-continuous and non-decreasing paths where $A_0=0$ almost surely. It is assumed that $\{A_t\}$ is integrable, that is, $\mathbb{E}[A_\infty]<\infty$ where $A_\infty=\lim_{t\to\infty}A_t$. Then, it is stated in Meyer (1962) that any right-continuous version of the supermartingale $\{\zeta_t\}$ defined by

$$\zeta_t=\mathbb{E}[A_\infty\,|\,\mathcal{F}_t]-A_t \tag{12.24}$$

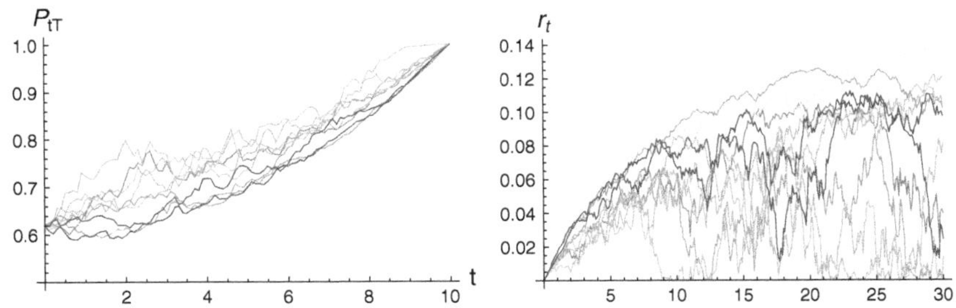

Fig. 13 Sample paths for a discount bond with $T = 10$ and the short rate for the quadratic OU–Brownian model with $h(t+u, X) = c_1 \exp(-c_2(t+u-X))(t+u)$ with $c_1 = 0.02$ and $c_2 = 0.1$. We let $\delta = 0.02$, $\beta = 0.5$, $\Upsilon = 0.2$ and $Y_0 = 1$. We let $x_1 = 1$ and $x_2 = 2$ where $f_0(x_1) = 0.3$ and $f_0(x_2) = 0.7$ and $\sigma = 0.1$. The weight function is given by $w(t, u) = \exp[-0.04(t+u)]$

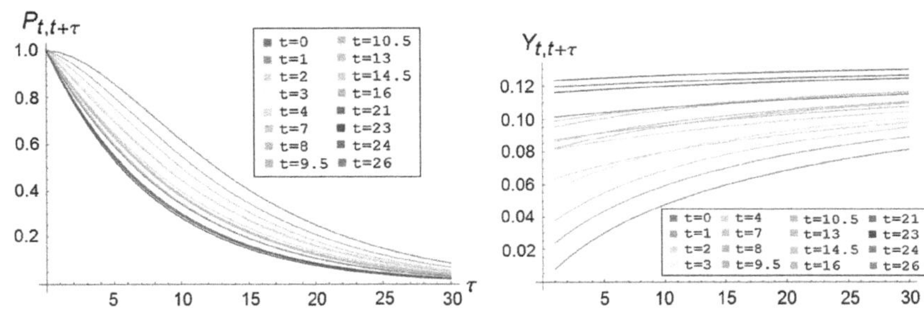

Fig. 14 *Discount bond curves* for the quadratic OU–Brownian model with $h(t+u, X) = c_1 \exp(-c_2(t+u-X))(t+u)$ with $c_1 = 0.01$ and $c_2 = 0.1$. We let $\delta = 0.02$, $\beta = 0.5$, $\Upsilon = 0.2$ and $Y_0 = 1$. We let $x_1 = 1$ and $x_2 = 2$ where $f_0(x_1) = 0.5$ and $f_0(x_2) = 0.5$ and $\sigma = 0.1$. The weight function is given by $w(t, u) = \exp[-0.04(t+u)]$. *Yield curves* for the quadratic OU–Brownian model with $h(t+u, X) = c_1 \exp(-c_2(t+u-X))(t+u)$ with $c_1 = 0.01$ and $c_2 = 0.1$. We let $\delta = 0.02$, $\beta = 0.5$, $\Upsilon = 0.2$ and $Y_0 = 1$. We let $x_1 = 1$ and $x_2 = 2$ where $f_0(x_1) = 0.5$ and $f_0(x_2) = 0.5$ and $\sigma = 0.1$. The weight function is given by $w(t, u) = \exp[-0.04(t+u)]$

is a potential of class (D). It is then proven that a potential belongs to the class (D) if and only if it is generated by the process $\{A_t\}$, the generator of the potential. It turns out that the pricing kernel (5.4) is a potential generated by

$$A_t = \int_0^t \rho(u) m_{uu} \mathrm{d}u \tag{12.25}$$

where we recall that $\{m_{tu}\}_{0 \le t \le u < \infty}$ is a family of positive unit-initialized martingales. Thus the pricing kernel (5.4) is a class (D) potential.

We consider a Markov process $\{Y_t\}$, and let the weight function be given by

$$w(t, v) = \bar{w}(t+v), \tag{12.26}$$

where $\bar{w} : \mathbb{R}_+ \to \mathbb{R}_+$ is a bounded, non-increasing function. We assume that

$$\int_0^\infty \bar{w}(t+v)\,\mathbb{E}\left[G\left(h(t+v,X),Y_{t+v}\right)\right]\mathrm{d}v \;<\; \infty. \tag{12.27}$$

Then, the pricing kernel is given by

$$\pi_t = \int_0^\infty \bar{w}(t+v)\,\mathbb{E}\left[G\left(h(t+v,X),Y_{t+v}\right)\mid\mathcal{F}_t\right]\mathrm{d}v. \tag{12.28}$$

It is sufficient for $\bar{w}(s)\to 0$ as $s\to\infty$ for (12.28) to be a potential. Moreover, (12.28) is a potential generated by

$$A_t = \int_0^t \bar{w}(u)\,\mathbb{E}\left[G\left(h(u,X),Y_u\right)\mid\mathcal{F}_u\right]\mathrm{d}u, \tag{12.29}$$

that is, a potential of class (D). Thus, we can write (12.28) in the Flesaker–Hughston form:

$$\pi_t = \pi_0 \int_t^\infty \rho(u)\,m_{tu}\,\mathrm{d}u, \tag{12.30}$$

where

$$\rho(u) = \frac{\bar{w}(u)\,\mathbb{E}[G(h(u,X),Y_u)]}{\pi_0}, \qquad m_{tu} = \frac{\mathbb{E}[G(h(u,X),Y_u)\mid\mathcal{F}_t]}{\mathbb{E}[G(h(u,X),Y_u)]}, \tag{12.31}$$

and $\{m_{tu}\}$ is a positive unit-initialized $\{\mathcal{F}_t\}$-martingale for each fixed $u \geq t$. The constant π_0 is a scaling factor.

We note that, for instance, the potential models of Rogers (1997) which can be generated by the weighted heat kernel approach with $\bar{w}(t+v) = \exp[-\alpha(t+v)]$ where $\alpha > 0$, are Flesaker–Hughston models. To generate potentials from the weighted heat kernel approach with a general weight $w(t,v)$, the weight function and $G(\cdot)$ should be chosen so that $\mathbb{E}[\pi_t]\to 0$ as $t\to\infty$.

Let us suppose that the Markov process $\{Y_t\}$ is a Lévy process. Then the class of Esscher-type randomised mixture models presented in this paper, for which

$$M_{tu}(X,L_t) = \frac{\exp[h(u,X)L_t]}{\mathbb{E}\left[\exp[h(u,X)L_t]\mid X\right]}, \tag{12.32}$$

cannot be constructed by using the weighted heat kernel approach. We see this by setting

$$G\left(h(v,X),L_{t+v}\right) = \frac{\exp\left[h(v,X)L_{t+v}\right]}{\mathbb{E}\left[\exp\left[h(v,X)L_{t+v}\right]\mid X\right]}, \tag{12.33}$$

and by observing that $\mathbb{E}[G(h(v,X),L_{t+v})\mid\mathcal{G}_t]$ is not a $\{\mathcal{G}_t\}$-propagator. As mentioned earlier, the class of models introduced by Brody et al. (2011) is included in the class of

Esscher-type randomised mixture models. Similarly, models based on kernel functions of the form $G(h(x), Y_t)$ can produce other Esscher-type models by use of the weighted heat kernel approach. The pricing kernel models proposed in this paper are versatile by construction, and potentially allow for many more investigations. For instance, we can think of applications to the modelling of foreign exchange rates where two pricing kernel models are selected—perhaps of different types to reflect idiosyncrasies of the considered domestic and foreign economies. In this context, it might be of particular interest to investigate dependence structures among several pricing kernel models for all the foreign economies involved in a polyhedron of FX rates. We expect the mixing function $h(u, X)$ to play a central role in the construction of dependence models. Furthermore, randomised mixtures models can be applied in a similar way to the pricing of inflation-linked securities. The application of randomised mixtures to a multi-curve interest rate set-up is a natural development of the pricing kernel framework presented in this paper, potentially leading the way to an even more exciting use of the mixing functions to capture the interaction between credit and liquidity risk over various time spans.

Acknowledgments The authors are grateful to J. Akahori, D. Brigo, D. C. Brody, C. Buescu, M. A. Crisafi, M. Grasselli, L. P. Hughston, S. Jaimungal, A. Kohatsu-Higa, O. Menoukeu Pamen, J. Sekine, W. T. Shaw and D. R. Taylor for useful comments. They also like to thank participants at: the Actuarial Science and Mathematical Finance group meetings at the Fields Institute, Toronto, July 2011; the Fourth International MiF Conference, Kruger National Park, South Africa, August 2011; and the Mathematical Finance seminars, Department of Mathematics, Ritsumeikan University, Japan, November 2011, for helpful remarks. P. A. Parbhoo acknowledges financial support from the Commonwealth Scholarship Commission in the United Kingdom (CSC), the National Research Foundation of South Africa (NRF) and the Programme in Advanced Mathematics of Finance at the University of the Witwatersrand. A substantial part of this work was developed while A. Macrina was a member of the Department of Mathematics, King's College London, and P. A. Parbhoo was a member of the School of Computational and Applied Mathematics, University of the Witwatersrand, respectively. A. Macrina acknowledges support from the African Collaboration for Quantitative Finance and Risk Research (ACQuFRR), University of Cape Town.

References

Akahori, J., Hishida, Y., Teichmann, J., & Tsuchiya, T. (2014). A heat kernel approach to interest rate models. *Japan Journal of Industrial and Applied Mathematics*. doi:10.1007/s13160-014-0147-3.

Akahori, J., & Macrina, A. (2012). Heat kernel interest rate models with time-inhomogeneous Markov processes. *International Journal of Theoretical and Applied Finance*, *15*, 1250007–1–1250007-15.

Applebaum, D. (2004). *Lévy processes and stochastic calculus* (1st ed.). Cambridge: Cambridge University Press.

Bain, A., & Crisan, D. (2009). *Fundamentals of stochastic filtering*. New York: Springer.

Boyle, P. P., Broadie, M. N., & Glasserman, P. (1997). Monte Carlo methods for security pricing. *Journal of Economic Dynamics and Control*, *21*, 1267–1321.

Brigo, D., & Mercurio, F. (2006). *Interest rate models: Theory and practice—with smile, inflation and credit* (2nd ed.). Berlin: Springer.

Brody, D. C. & Friedman, R. L. (2009). Information of interest. Risk, pp. 105–110.

Brody, D. C., Hughston, L. P., & Mackie, E. (2011). Rational term structure models with geometric Lévy martingales. *Stochastics: An International Journal of Probability and Stochastic Processes*, *84*, 719–740.

Brody, D. C., Hughston, L. P., & Macrina, A. (2008). Dam rain and cumulative gain. *Proceedings of the Royal Society A*, *464*, 1801–1822.

Brody, D. C., Hughston, L. P., & Macrina, A. (2011). Credit risk, market sentiment and randomly-timed default. In D. Crisan (Ed.), *Stochastic analysis 2010* (pp. 267–280). Berlin: Springer.

Cairns, A. J. G. (2004). *Interest rate models: An introduction*. Princeton: Princeton University Press.

Carr, P. P., Chang, E. C., & Madan, D. B. (1998). The variance gamma process and option pricing. *European Finance Review*, *2*, 79–105.

Cochrane, J. H. (2005). *Asset pricing, revised ed.* Princeton: Princeton University Press.

Duffie, D. (2001). *Dynamic asset pricing theory* (3rd ed.). Princeton: Princeton University Press.

Filipović, D., Hughston, L. P., & Macrina, A. (2012). Conditional density models for asset pricing. *International Journal of Theoretical and Applied Finance*, *15*, 1250002–1–1250002-24.

Flesaker, B. & Hughston, L. P. (1996). Positive interest. Risk, pp. 46–49.

Föllmer, H., & Protter, P. (2011). Local martingales and filtration shrinkage. *ESAIM: Probability and Statistics*, *15*, S25–S38.

Gerber, H. U., & Shiu, E. S. W. (1994). Option pricing by Esscher transforms. *Transactions of the Society of Actuaries*, *46*, 99–191.

Heath, D., Jarrow, R. A., & Morton, A. (1992). Bond pricing and the term structure of interest rates: A new methodology for contingent claims valuation. *Econometrica*, *60*, 77–105.

Hunt, P. J., & Kennedy, J. E. (2004). *Financial derivatives in theory and practice, revised ed.* Chichester: Wiley.

Iacus, S. M. (2008). *Simulation and inference for stochastic differential equations: With R examples*. New York: Springer.

Meyer, P. A. (1962). A decomposition theorem for supermartingales. *Illinois Journal of Mathematics*, *6*, 193–205.

Rogers, L. C. G. (1997). The potential approach to the term structure of interest rates and foreign exchange rates. *Mathematical Finance*, *7*, 157–176.

Takaoka, K. (2006). A complete-market generalization of the Black–Scholes model. *Asia-Pacific Financial Markets*, *11*, 431–444.

Takaoka, K., & Futami, H. (2010). The instantaneous volatility and the implied volatility surface for a generalized black-scholes model. *Asia-Pacific Financial Markets*, 17, 391–436.

Yao, Y. (2001). State price density, Esscher transforms, and pricing options on stocks, bonds, and foreign exchange rates. *North American Actuarial Journal*, *5*, 104–117.

Chapter 14

Stochastic modelling with randomized Markov bridges*

Andrea Macrina[a,b] and Jun Sekine[c]

[a]Department of Mathematics, University College London, London, UK; [b]African Institute for Financial Markets and Risk Management, University of Cape Town, Rondebosch, South Africa; [c]Division of Mathematical Science for Social Systems, Graduate School of Engineering Science, Osaka University, Toyonaka, Osaka, Japan

ABSTRACT
We consider the filtering problem of estimating a hidden random variable X by noisy observations. The noisy observation process is constructed by a randomized Markov bridge (RMB) $(Z_t)_{t\in[0,T]}$ of which terminal value is set to $Z_T = X$. That is, at the terminal time T, the noise of the bridge process vanishes and the hidden random variable X is revealed. We derive the explicit filtering formula, governing the dynamics of the conditional probability process, for a general RMB. It turns out that the conditional probability is given by a function of current time t, the current observation Z_t, the initial observation Z_0, and the *a priori* distribution ν of X at $t = 0$. As an example for an RMB, we explicitly construct the skew-normal randomized diffusion bridge and show how it can be utilized to extend well-known commodity pricing models and how one may propose novel stochastic price models for financial instruments linked to greenhouse gas emissions.

ARTICLE HISTORY
Received 15 September 2017
Accepted 10 December 2019

KEYWORDS
Randomized Markov bridge; hidden random variable; filtering; skew-normal randomized diffusion; commodity pricing; greenhouse gas emission; climate risk management

1. Introduction

Let $E \subset \mathbb{R}^n$ and let $T \in (0, \infty)$. On a probability space $(\Omega, \mathcal{F}, \mathbb{P})$, consider an E-valued (y, T, z)-Markov bridge $Y^{(y,T,z)} := (Y_t^{(y,T,z)})_{t\in[0,T]}$ so that

$$Y_0^{(y,T,z)} = y, \quad Y_T^{(y,T,z)} = z \quad \text{a.s.,} \tag{1}$$

and an E-valued random variable X, which is independent of $Y^{(y,T,z)}$. Here, by a (y, T, z)-Markov bridge, we mean a process obtained by conditioning a Markov process $Y := (Y_t)_{t\geq 0}$ to start in $y \in E$ at time 0 and arrive at $z \in E$ at time $T \in (0, \infty)$. For its construction, we follow Fitzsimmons *et al.* [13]. We define the process $Z := (Z_t)_{t\in[0,T]}$ by

$$Z := Y^{(y,T,X)},$$

which we call *randomized Markov bridge* (RMB). We further define

$$\mathcal{F}_t^Z := \sigma(Z_s; s \in [0, t]), \quad t \in [0, T],$$

and let Z be the noisy observation process of the hidden random variable X. At the terminal time T, the noise in the bridge process $Y^{(y,T,z)}$ vanishes and the hidden variable $X(= Z_T)$

CONTACT Andrea Macrina a.macrina@ucl.ac.uk
This article has been republished with minor changes. These changes do not impact the academic content of the article.

*This chapter was originally published as: A. Macrina & J. Sekine (2019) Stochastic Modelling with Randomized Markov Bridges. *Stochastics: An International Journal of Probability and Stochastic Processes*, doi:10.1080/17442508.2019.1703988. Reprinted with kind permission from Taylor & Francis.

is revealed. We are interested in the stochastic filtering problem of estimating the hidden random variable X through the observation of Z. That is, we are interested in computing the conditional probability,

$$\pi_t(\mathrm{d}x) := \mathbb{P}\left(X \in \mathrm{d}x | \mathcal{F}_t^Z\right), \quad t \in [0, T), \tag{2}$$

and the conditional expectation,

$$\pi_t(f) := \mathbb{E}\left[f(X) | \mathcal{F}_t^Z\right] = \int_E f(x)\pi_t(\mathrm{d}x), \quad t \in [0, T), \tag{3}$$

where $f : E \to \mathbb{R}$ is Borel-measurable so that $f(X)$ is integrable.

Problem (2)–(3) of filtering a hidden random variable X by observing a sub-class of RMB processes Z has been studied in a financial context by, e.g. Brody *et al.* [6], Hoyle *et al.* [16], and Filipović *et al.* [12]. In those financial applications, $f(X)$ represents the cash flow of a financial asset that is paid at the terminal date T, and Z is called the information process. The conditional expectation (3) is used to model the asset price process $(S_t)_{t\in[0,T)}$ by

$$S_t := \mathrm{e}^{-r(T-t)}\pi_t(f) = \mathbb{E}\left[\mathrm{e}^{-r(T-t)}f(X) \mid \mathcal{F}_t^Z\right], \tag{4}$$

where $r \geq 0$ is the constant risk-free interest rate and $\mathbb{P}$ is regarded as being the so-called risk-neutral probability measure. In the above-mentioned works, Brownian random bridges and, more generally, Lévy random bridges (LRB) are employed, and the stochastic dynamics of asset prices are derived.

RMBs generalize the class of information processes which can be applied to develop information-based asset pricing models. Such models describe the stochastic nature of asset prices as the market's price adjustments to the information flow about market factors, modelled by the hidden random variable X, which affect the payoff function of a financial contract. In this setting, the effect of emerging information about market factors is manifested in the conditional probability process underlying the stochastic dynamics of asset prices. By extending the class of information processes with RMBs, the class of information-based asset price models is also extended. The generalized class can now be constructed by starting off with any Markov process, also those that have dependent increments, leading to information processes beyond the LRB class (which are constructed on the basis of Lévy processes). Further work making use of LRBs, that now may be extended by RMBs, includes Macrina [19] on heat kernel asset pricing models, Hoyle *et al.* [17] on insurance claim reserving, and Crépey *et al.* [10] on interest rate modelling.

The main contribution of the present article is to provide the explicit representations of (2) and (3) for a *general* RMB, focusing on its interesting features from a stochastic filtering viewpoint. It is well known that in the general stochastic filtering problem, the conditional probability (2) has an infinite-dimensional structure; it is the solution to the measure-valued Kushner–Stratonovich stochastic differential equation (SDE). In the problem we consider, unlike in the general situation, we obtain the relation

$$\mathbb{P}\left(Z_t \in \mathrm{d}y | \mathcal{F}_s^Z\right) = \mathbb{P}\left(Z_t \in \mathrm{d}y | Z_s, Z_0\right) =: P_{s,t}(Z_s, \mathrm{d}y | Z_0) \tag{5}$$

for $0 \leq s < t \leq T$ (see Propositions 2.1 and 2.2, and Remark 2.3 for details). In words, we can regard Z as satisfying the Markov property with respect to its natural filtration

$(\mathcal{F}_t^Z)_{t\in[0,T)}$, once the initial value Z_0 is fixed (see Proposition 2.2). From the above relation, it follows that:

$$\pi_t(\mathrm{d}y) = \mathbb{P}\left(Z_T \in \mathrm{d}y|\mathcal{F}_t^Z\right) = P_{t,T}(Z_t, \mathrm{d}y|Z_0).$$

We thus observe that the pair of observations (Z_0, Z_t) determines $\pi_t(\mathrm{d}z)$, and the past observation $(Z_s)_{s\in(0,t)}$ is not necessary for the computation of the conditional probability. As a consequence, the dynamics of $(\pi_t(\mathrm{d}z))_{t\in[0,T)}$ can be determined by a finite-dimensional Markovian SDE, see Proposition 2.3.

Remark 1.1: We refer to Baudoin [5] and Çetin and Danilova [8] for related pieces of work: conditioned stochastic differential equations (CSDE) introduced by Baudoin [5], and the weak conditioning of (Markovian) SDEs via h-transforms considered by Çetin and Danilova [8] are directly related with our RMBs (with respect to the filtration $(\mathcal{F}_t^Z)_{t\in[0,T)}$). Although the works by Baudoin [5], Çetin and Danilova [8], and the analysis presented in this article overlap in places, the following viewpoint and motivation appear to be different. For example, (a) we are interested in providing a stochastic filtering interpretation of RMBs, see Propositions 2.1 and 2.3, and (b) we consider general RMBs whereas Baudoin [5] and Çetin and Danilova [8] study SDEs driven by Brownian motions only.

In the following sections, after preparing the setup in detail, we state our results, give additional explanations in the remarks, and provide the proofs. In Section 4, we introduce a new RMB, the *skew-normal randomized diffusion bridge* (SNRDB) which is applied to commodity pricing, and which, in doing so, extends the models by Gibson and Schwarz [14] and Schwarz [21]. In our view, we also find a natural way to apply this class of pricing models to securitize climate risk associated with greenhouse gas (GHG) emissions.

2. Setup and results

Let $E \subset \mathbb{R}^n$ be a Borel state space, and let $T \in (0,\infty)$ be a given constant. For the construction of the E-valued (y, T, z)-Markov bridge $Y^{(y,T,z)} := (Y_t^{(y,T,z)})_{t\in[0,T]}$ which satisfies (1), we follow Section 2 of Fitzsimmons *et al.* [13]. We consider an E-valued strong Markov process $Y := (Y_t)_{t\in[0,T]}$ with càdlàg sample paths, which is realized as the coordinate process Y on Ω_T^1, that is, on the space of right-continuous paths from $[0, T)$ to E that have left limits on $(0, T)$. The law of the Markov process Y that starts from y is denoted by $\tilde{\mathbb{P}}_y^1$, and the natural filtration of Y is denoted by $(\mathcal{F}_t^1)_{t\in[0,T]}$. We assume that the transition probability of the Markov process Y has the density

$$\tilde{P}_t(x, \mathrm{d}y) = \tilde{p}_t(x, y)m(\mathrm{d}y)$$

with respect to a σ-finite measure m on E such that the Chapman–Kolmogorov identity

$$\tilde{p}_{t+s}(x, z) = \int_E \tilde{p}_t(x, y)\tilde{p}_s(y, z)m(\mathrm{d}y)$$

holds true, where $t > 0$ and $s > 0$ $(s + t \le T)$, $x \in E$ and $z \in E$, and $\tilde{p}_t(x, y) > 0$ for all $(t, x, y) \in (0, T] \times E \times E$. Moreover, we assume the following duality: Associated with

$(Y, (\tilde{P}_t)_{t\geq 0})$, there exists $(\hat{Y}, (\hat{P}_t)_{t\geq 0})$, where $\hat{Y}$ is the second Markov process with the state space E and $(\hat{P}_t)_{t\geq 0}$ is the transition probabilities of $\hat{Y}$, which satisfies

$$\int_E (\tilde{P}_t f_1)(x) f_2(x) m(\mathrm{d}x) = \int_E f_1(x)(\hat{P}_t f_2)(x) m(\mathrm{d}x)$$

for $t \geq 0$ and bounded Borel measurable $f_1, f_2 : E \to \mathbb{R}$, where we write $(\tilde{P}_t f_1)(x) := \int_E f_1(y)\tilde{P}_t(x, \mathrm{d}y)$ and $(\hat{P}_t f_2)(x) := \int_E f_2(y)\hat{P}_t(x, \mathrm{d}y)$. Then, by Proposition 1 of Fitzsimmons *et al.* [13], we see the following:

(a) Let $\mathcal{F}^1_{T-} := \sigma(\cup_{0\leq t<T}\mathcal{F}^1_t)$. For each y and $z \in E$, we can construct the probability measure $\mathbb{P}^1_{y,z}$ on $(\Omega^1_T, \mathcal{F}^1_{T-})$ that satisfies

$$\mathrm{d}\mathbb{P}^1_{y,z}\big|_{\mathcal{F}^1_t} = \Lambda^{(y,T,z)}_t \mathrm{d}\tilde{\mathbb{P}}^1_y\big|_{\mathcal{F}^1_t}$$

for all $t \in [0, T)$, where

$$\Lambda^{(y,T,z)}_t := \frac{\tilde{p}_{T-t}(Y_t, z)}{\tilde{p}_T(y, z)}.$$

(b) The law of $(Y_t)_{t\in[0,T)}$ under $\mathbb{P}^1_{y,z}$ is equal to that of the (y, T, z)-Markov bridge. In particular, it holds that

$$\mathbb{P}^1_{y,z}\left(Y_0 = y, Y_{T-} = z\right) = 1.$$

The corresponding transition densities that satisfy

$$p^{(z,T)}(s, y; t, y')m(\mathrm{d}y') := \mathbb{P}^1_{y,z}\left(Y_t \in \mathrm{d}y' | Y_s = y\right)$$

for $y, y', z \in E$ and $0 < s < t < T$ are expressed by

$$p^{(z,T)}(s, y; t, y') = \frac{\tilde{p}_{t-s}(y, y')\tilde{p}_{T-t}(y', z)}{\tilde{p}_{T-s}(y, z)}.$$

Furthermore, we introduce another probability space $(\Omega_2, \mathcal{F}_2, \mathbb{P}_2)$ on which we consider the random variable X with law $\nu := \mathbb{P}_2 \circ X^{-1}$. Let $\Omega := \Omega^1_T \times \Omega_2$, $\mathcal{F}_t := \mathcal{F}^1_t \otimes \mathcal{F}_2$, $\mathcal{F}_{T-} = \mathcal{F}^1_{T-} \otimes \mathcal{F}_2$, and let $\mathbb{P}_y := \mathbb{P}^1_y \otimes \mathbb{P}_2$ such that

$$\mathrm{d}\mathbb{P}_y(\omega_1, \omega_2)\big|_{\mathcal{F}_t} := \Lambda^{(y,T,X)}_t(\omega_1, \omega_2)\mathrm{d}\tilde{\mathbb{P}}^1_y(\omega_1) \otimes \mathrm{d}\mathbb{P}_2(\omega_2)\big|_{\mathcal{F}_t} \tag{6}$$

is satisfied for $t \in [0, T)$ where

$$\Lambda^{(y,T,X)}_t(\omega_1, \omega_2) := \frac{\tilde{p}_{T-t}\left(Y_t(\omega_1), X(\omega_2)\right)}{\tilde{p}_T(y, X(\omega_2))}. \tag{7}$$

Then, on the filtered product space $(\Omega, \mathcal{F}_{T-}, \mathbb{P}_y, (\mathcal{F}_t)_{t\in[0,T)})$, the RMB $(Z_t)_{t\in[0,T]}$ is obtained by setting $Z_t(\omega_1, \omega_2) := Y_t(\omega_1)$ for $t \in [0, T)$ and $Z_T(\omega_1, \omega_2) := X(\omega_2)$.

Remark 2.1: Intuitively, the RMB is constructed as $Z := Y^{(y,T,X)}$, by inserting the random variable X into the terminal value of the Markov bridge $Y^{(y,T,\cdot)}$. For the validity of such a direct approach, the measurability of the function $z \mapsto Y^{(y,T,z)}$ is necessary. The above construction of an RMB avoids this measurability issue. However, there are situations where the measurability issue can be resolved directly: for example, if we consider the SDE for $Y^{(y,T,z)}$, starting from the Markovian SDE (9), then, as we will see in (11), we have

$$\begin{aligned} dY_t^{(y,T,z)} &= \left\{b\left(Y_t^{(y,T,z)}\right) + (\sigma\sigma^\top)\left(Y_t^{(y,T,z)}\right) \nabla \ln \tilde{p}_{T-t}\left(Y_t^{(y,T,z)}, z\right)\right\} dt \\ &\quad + \sigma\left(Y_t^{(y,T,z)}\right) dW_t \quad \left(Y_0^{(y,T,z)} = y\right). \end{aligned}$$

The continuity of $z \mapsto Y^{(y,T,z)}$ can be shown by discussing the continuity of the solution to the above SDE with respect to the parameter z, which is a standard result in SDE theory if we assume the continuity of $z \mapsto \tilde{p}_t(y, z)$.

Remark 2.2: For the construction of Markovian bridges, we follow classical results obtained in Fitzsimmons *et al.* [13]. There are several recent studies, where extended results are discussed: for example, we refer to Chaumont and Uribe Bravo [9], and Çetin and Danilova [8]. Both studies succeed in constructing Markov bridges without assuming the duality condition of the underlying Markov process. The former work derives and utilizes the weak continuity property of a Markov bridge with respect to its terminal value. The latter work is interested in SDE representations of the bridges driven by Brownian motions. Interestingly, the weak conditioning discussed in the latter work directly links to an RMB with respect to its natural filtration $(\mathcal{F}_t^Z)_{t\in[0,T)}$; see Remark 2.6.

2.1. Filtering results

For the filtering problem, we have the following:

Proposition 2.1: *For $t \in [0, T)$, the conditional probability (2) is given by*

$$\pi_t(dz) = \frac{\dfrac{\tilde{p}_{T-t}(Z_t, z)}{\tilde{p}_T(Z_0, z)}\nu(dz)}{\int_E \dfrac{\tilde{p}_{T-t}(Z_t, z')}{\tilde{p}_T(Z_0, z')}\nu(dz')}.$$

Remark 2.3: From a stochastic filtering viewpoint, it is interesting that the conditional probability $\pi_t(dz)$ is expressed by a function of t, Z_t, Z_0, and ν. At each point in time, $\pi_t(dz)$ can be computed by inserting the current observation Z_t and the initial observation Z_0, only. The past information (memory) $(Z_s)_{s\in(0,t)}$ is not necessary.

Proof: By applying the Bayes rule and relations (6) and (7), we have

$$\pi_t(f) := \mathbb{E}_y\left[f(X)|\mathcal{F}_t^Z\right] = \frac{\tilde{\mathbb{E}}_y\left[\Lambda_t^{(y,T,X)} f(X) \mid \mathcal{F}_t^Z\right]}{\tilde{\mathbb{E}}_y\left[\Lambda_t^{(y,T,X)} \mid \mathcal{F}_t^Z\right]},$$

where we use the notation $\tilde{\mathbb{E}}_y[\cdot]$ for the expectation with respect to the probability measure $\mathrm{d}\tilde{\mathbb{P}}^1_y \otimes \mathrm{d}\mathbb{P}_2$. Observing that $\mathcal{F}^Z_t$ and X are independent under $\mathrm{d}\tilde{\mathbb{P}}^1_y \otimes \mathrm{d}\mathbb{P}_2$, we deduce that

$$\pi_t(f) = \frac{\int_E \frac{\tilde{p}_{T-t}(Z_t, z)}{\tilde{p}_T(y, z)} f(z)\nu(\mathrm{d}z)}{\int_E \frac{\tilde{p}_{T-t}(Z_t, z')}{\tilde{p}_T(y, z')}\nu(\mathrm{d}z')}. \tag{8}$$

■

We note that once the initial value Z_0 is fixed, the process $(Z_t)_{t\in[0,T)}$ is 'Markovian' in the following sense:

Proposition 2.2: *For $0 \le s < t < T$, (5) holds where*

$$P_{s,t}(x, \mathrm{d}y|z_0) = q(s, x; t, y|z_0)m(\mathrm{d}y)$$

and

$$q(s, x; t, y|z_0) := \frac{\tilde{p}_{t-s}(x, y)\left\{\int_E \frac{\tilde{p}_{T-t}(y, z)}{\tilde{p}_T(z_0, z)}\nu(\mathrm{d}z)\right\}}{\int_E \frac{\tilde{p}_{T-s}(x, z')}{\tilde{p}_T(z_0, z')}\nu(\mathrm{d}z')}.$$

For a fixed z_0, the transition density $q(s, x; t, y|z_0)$ satisfies the Chapman-Kolmogorov identity:

$$q(s, x; u, z|z_0) = \int_E q(s, x; t, y|z_0)q(t, y; u, z|z_0)m(\mathrm{d}y)$$

for $0 < s < t < u < T$ and $x, y, z \in E$.

Remark 2.4: Let $m(\mathrm{d}x) = \mathrm{d}x$ and $\nu(\mathrm{d}x) = g(x)\mathrm{d}x$. Then, one can check that (a)

$$\lim_{t\uparrow T} \int_E \frac{\tilde{p}_{T-t}(y, z)}{\tilde{p}_T(Z_0, z)}\nu(\mathrm{d}z) = \int_E \frac{\delta_y(z)}{\tilde{p}_T(Z_0, z)} g(z)\mathrm{d}z = \frac{g(y)}{\tilde{p}_T(Z_0, y)},$$

where $\delta_y(\cdot)$ is the Dirac delta function with point mass at y, and (b)

$$\lim_{t\uparrow T} P_{s,t}(Z_s, \mathrm{d}x|Z_0) = \frac{\frac{\tilde{p}_{T-s}(Z_s, y)}{\tilde{p}_T(Z_0, y)}\nu(\mathrm{d}y)}{\int_E \frac{\tilde{p}_{T-s}(Z_s, z')}{\tilde{p}_T(Z_0, z')}\nu(\mathrm{d}z')} = \pi_s(\mathrm{d}x).$$

Proof: The proof is similar to the one for Proposition 2.1. We see that, for $0 \le s \le t < T$,

$$\mathbb{E}_{z_0}\left[f(Z_t)|\mathcal{F}^Z_s\right] = \frac{\tilde{\mathbb{E}}_{z_0}\left[\Lambda^{(y,T,X)}_t f(Z_t) \mid \mathcal{F}^Z_s\right]}{\tilde{\mathbb{E}}_{z_0}\left[\Lambda^{(y,T,X)}_t \mid \mathcal{F}^Z_s\right]},$$

where we use the Bayes rule, (6) and (7). Recalling that $\mathcal{F}^Z_t$ and X are independent under

$\mathrm{d}\tilde{\mathbb{P}}^1_{z_0} \otimes \mathrm{d}\mathbb{P}_2$, the numerator of the right-hand side of the above equation is equal to

$$\int_E \tilde{p}_{t-s}(z_0, y) \left\{ \int_E \frac{\tilde{p}_{T-t}(y,z)}{\tilde{p}_T(z_0,z)} \nu(\mathrm{d}z) \right\} f(y) m(\mathrm{d}y).$$

By computing the denominator in a similar way, we obtain the expression for $P_{s,t}(x, \mathrm{d}y|z_0)$. The Chapman–Kolmogorov identity is seen from

$$\mathbb{E}[f(Z_u)|\mathcal{F}^Z_s] = \mathbb{E}\left[\mathbb{E}\left[f(Z_u)|\mathcal{F}^Z_t\right] \mid \mathcal{F}^Z_s\right], \quad 0 \le s \le t \le u < T,$$

which is the tower property of conditional expectation. ■

Next, we are interested in describing the $(\mathbb{P}, \mathcal{F}^Z_t)$-dynamics of $(\pi_t(f))_{t\in[0,T]}$. To this end, we construct the RMB $(Z_t)_{t\in[0,T]}$, starting with the underlying (unconditioned) Markovian SDE,

$$\mathrm{d}Y_t = b(Y_t)\,\mathrm{d}t + \sigma(Y_t)\,\mathrm{d}\tilde{W}_t, \quad Y_0 = y \tag{9}$$

on $(\Omega^1_T, \mathcal{F}^1_T, \tilde{\mathbb{P}}^1_y, (\mathcal{F}^1_t)_{t\in[0,T]})$. Here, $b : \mathbb{R}^n \to \mathbb{R}^n$ and $\sigma : \mathbb{R}^n \to \mathbb{R}^{n\times d}$ are given functions. Further, $\tilde{W} := (\tilde{W}^1, \ldots, \tilde{W}^d)^\top$, $\tilde{W}^i := (\tilde{W}^i_t)_{t\in[0,T]}$ is a standard d-dimensional $(\tilde{\mathbb{P}}^1_y, \mathcal{F}^1_t)$-Brownian motion. Although assuming the existence (in the sense of its law) of a unique weak solution to (9) is sufficient for constructing an RMB, we assume that there exists a strong, pathwise unique solution to (9) in order to consider the filtering problem with respect to $\mathcal{F}^Z_t$. Moreover, we assume that there exist associated transition densities $\tilde{p}_t(x,y) > 0$ with respect to the Lebesgue measure for $t \in (0,T]$, $x, y \in E$, which are sufficiently smooth with respect to (t,x). We recall that $\tilde{p}_{(\cdot)}(\cdot, y)$ satisfies the Kolmogorov backward equation

$$\begin{aligned}(-\partial_t + \mathcal{L})\,\tilde{p}_t(x,y) &= 0 \quad \text{for } (t,x) \in (0,T] \times E,\\ \tilde{p}_0(x,y) &= \delta_y(x),\end{aligned} \tag{10}$$

where

$$\mathcal{L}(f)(x) := b(x)^\top \nabla f(x) + \frac{1}{2}\mathrm{tr}\left((\sigma\sigma^\top)(x)\nabla\nabla f(x)\right)$$

with $\nabla f := (\partial_{x_1} f, \ldots, \partial_{x_n} f)^\top$ and $\nabla\nabla f := (\partial_{x_i x_j} f)_{1\le i,j\le n}$ being the infinitesimal generator of the Markov process Y. In this case, by using Itô's formula, we see that (7) satisfies

$$\mathrm{d}\Lambda^{(y,T,x)}_t = \Lambda^{(y,T,x)}_t \left[\nabla \ln \tilde{p}_{T-t}(Y_t, x)^\top \sigma(Y_t)\,\mathrm{d}\tilde{W}_t\right],$$

where we denote $\nabla \ln \tilde{p}_t(y,x) := (\partial_{y_1} \ln \tilde{p}_t(y,x), \ldots, \partial_{y_n} \ln \tilde{p}_t(y,x))^\top$. Hence, by Girsanov's theorem, we deduce that

$$W_t := \tilde{W}_t - \int_0^t \sigma(Z_s)^\top \nabla \ln \tilde{p}_{T-s}(Z_s, X)\mathrm{d}s, \quad t \in [0,T)$$

is a $(\mathbb{P}_y, \mathcal{F}_t)$-Brownian motion, and the SDE, defined on $(\Omega, \mathcal{F}_{T-}, \mathbb{P}_y, (\mathcal{F}_t)_{t\in[0,T)})$ and satisfied by $Z := (Z_t)_{t\in[0,T)}$, can be written down as

$$\mathrm{d}Z_t = \left\{b(Z_t) + (\sigma\sigma^\top)(Z_t)\nabla \ln \tilde{p}_{T-t}(Z_t, X)\right\}\mathrm{d}t + \sigma(Z_t)\,\mathrm{d}W_t \quad (Z_0 = y). \tag{11}$$

We deduce that $Z_{T-} := \lim_{t\uparrow T} Z_t = X$, $\mathbb{P}_y$-almost surely. For the calculation of the $(\mathbb{P}_y, \mathcal{F}_t^Z)$-dynamics of Z and $\pi_t(f)$, we prepare the following: (a) We rewrite (12) as

$$\pi_t(f) = \frac{\rho_t(f)}{\rho_t(1)}, \tag{12}$$

where

$$\rho_t(f) := \int_E f(z)\rho_t(\mathrm{d}z) \quad \text{and} \quad \rho_t(\mathrm{d}z) := \frac{\tilde{p}_{T-t}(Z_t, z)}{\tilde{p}_T(y, z)}\nu(\mathrm{d}z).$$

(b) We define

$$R(t, z; f) := \int_E f(z')\frac{\tilde{p}_{T-t}(z, z')}{\tilde{p}_T(y, z')}\nu(\mathrm{d}z') \quad \text{and} \quad \Pi(t, z; f) := \frac{R(t, z; f)}{R(t, z; 1)}, \tag{13}$$

where we fix $Z_0 = y$, recalling the relations

$$\rho_t(f) = R(t, Z_t; f) \quad \text{and} \quad \pi_t(f) = \Pi(t, Z_t; f) = \frac{R(t, Z_t; f)}{R(t, Z_t; 1)}.$$

With this at hand, we obtain the subsequent result.

Proposition 2.3: *Let $f : E \to \mathbb{R}$ be Borel-measurable so that $\int_E |f(x)|\nu(\mathrm{d}x) < \infty$. Assume that $(\sigma\sigma^\top) > 0$ and that*

$$\int_0^t \int_E \left|\sigma^\top(Z_s)\nabla\tilde{p}_{T-s}(Z_s, x)\right|^2 \frac{f(x)}{\tilde{p}_T(Z_0, x)}\nu(\mathrm{d}x)\mathrm{d}s < \infty \tag{14}$$

for any $t \in [0, T)$. For $(s, x) \in (0, T) \times E$, let

$$\ell_s(x) := \ln \tilde{p}_{T-s}(Z_s, x).$$

Then, the following statements hold:

(1) *On the filtered probability space $(\Omega, \mathcal{F}_{T-}, \mathbb{P}_y, (\mathcal{F}_t^Z)_{t\in[0,T)})$, the RMB $Z := (Z_t)_{t\in[0,T)}$ satisfies*

$$\mathrm{d}Z_t = \left\{b(Z_t) + (\sigma\sigma^\top)(Z_t)\pi_t\left(\nabla\ell_t\right)\right\}\mathrm{d}t + (\sigma\sigma^\top)^{1/2}(Z_t)\,\mathrm{d}U_t, \quad (Z_0 = y), \tag{15}$$

and $Z_{T-} := \lim_{t\uparrow T} Z_t = X$ $\mathbb{P}_y$-almost surely. Here,

$$\begin{aligned} U_t &:= \int_0^t (\sigma\sigma^\top)^{-1/2}(Z_s)\left\{\mathrm{d}Z_s - b(Z_s)\,\mathrm{d}s - (\sigma\sigma^\top)(Z_s)\pi_s(\nabla\ell_s)\,\mathrm{d}s\right\} \\ &= \int_0^t (\sigma\sigma^\top)^{-1/2}(Z_s)\left\{\sigma(Z_s)\,\mathrm{d}\tilde{W}_s - (\sigma\sigma^\top)(Z_s)\pi_s(\nabla\ell_s)\,\mathrm{d}s\right\} \end{aligned} \tag{16}$$

is an n-dimensional $(\mathbb{P}_y, \mathcal{F}_t^Z)$-Brownian motion.

(2) *For $t \in [0,T)$, it holds that*

$$\pi_t(f) = \pi_0(f) + \int_0^t \left\{\pi_s\left(f\nabla\ell_s\right) - \pi_s(f)\pi_s\left(\nabla\ell_s\right)\right\}^\top (\sigma\sigma^\top)^{1/2}(Z_s)\,\mathrm{d}U_s. \quad (17)$$

Moreover, we have

$$\nabla\Pi(s,z;f) = \Pi(s,z;f\nabla\ell_s) - \Pi(s,z;f)\Pi(s,z;\nabla\ell_s), \quad (18)$$

where $\nabla\Pi(s,z;f)^\top := (\partial_{z_1}\Pi,\ldots,\partial_{z_n}\Pi)(s,z;f)$, and hence

$$\pi_t(f) = \pi_0(f) + \int_0^t (\nabla\Pi)(s,Z_s;f)^\top(\sigma\sigma^\top)^{1/2}(Z_s)\,\mathrm{d}U_s \quad (19)$$

follows.

Remark 2.5: From a stochastic filtering viewpoint, (17)–(19) are recognized as the Kushner–Stratonovich equations for $(\pi_t(f))_{t\in[0,T)}$, which has the finite-dimensional Markovian 'information state' process Z.

Remark 2.6: Similar SDEs to (15) appear in Section 3 of Baudoin [5] and Theorem 2.1 and 3.1 of Çetin and Danilova [8].

Proof: (1) By the Kolmogorov backward Equation (10) and Itô's formula, we have

$$\tilde{p}_{T-t}(Z_t,x) = \tilde{p}_T(Z_0,x) + \int_0^t \nabla\tilde{p}_{T-s}(Z_s,x)^\top\sigma(Z_s)\,\mathrm{d}\tilde{W}_s.$$

Then, by making use of this relation, we deduce that

$$\begin{aligned}
\rho_t(f) &= \int_E f(x)\frac{\tilde{p}_{T-t}(Z_t,x)}{\tilde{p}_T(Z_0,x)}\nu(\mathrm{d}x)\\
&= \rho_0(f) + \int_E \frac{f(x)}{\tilde{p}_T(Z_0,x)}\left[\int_0^t \tilde{p}_{T-s}(Z_s,x)\nabla\ln\tilde{p}_{T-s}(Z_s,x)^\top\sigma(Z_s)\,\mathrm{d}\tilde{W}_s\right]\nu(\mathrm{d}x)\\
&= \rho_0(f) + \int_0^t\left[\int_E f(x)\nabla\ln\tilde{p}_{T-s}(Z_s,x)^\top\frac{\tilde{p}_{T-s}(Z_s,x)}{\tilde{p}_T(Z_0,x)}\nu(\mathrm{d}x)\right]\sigma(Z_s)\,\mathrm{d}\tilde{W}_s\\
&= \rho_0(f) + \int_0^t \rho_s(f\nabla\ell_s^\top)\sigma(Z_s)\,\mathrm{d}\tilde{W}_s.
\end{aligned}$$

Here, the stochastic version of Fubini's theorem is employed while recalling condition (14), we refer to Theorem 4.65 in Protter [20]. So, we see that

$$\rho_t(1) = \tilde{\mathbb{E}}_y\left[\Lambda_t^{(y,T,X)}\,\middle|\,\mathcal{F}_t^Z\right]$$

satisfies

$$\mathrm{d}\rho_t(1) = \rho_t(\nabla\ell_t^\top)\sigma(Z_t)\,\mathrm{d}\tilde{W}_t = \rho_t(1)\left\{\pi_t(\nabla\ell_t^\top)\sigma(Z_t)\,\mathrm{d}\tilde{W}_t\right\},$$

where we recall (12). Using the above conditional $(\tilde{\mathbb{P}}_y, \mathcal{F}_t^Z)$-martingale density representation, we apply Girsanov's theorem to see that

$$\int_0^t \sigma(Z_u)\left\{\mathrm{d}\tilde{W}_u - \sigma(Z_u)^\top \pi_u(\nabla \ell_u)\,\mathrm{d}u\right\}$$
$$= Z_t - Z_0 - \int_0^t b(Z_u)\,\mathrm{d}u - \int_0^t (\sigma\sigma^\top)(Z_t)\pi_t(\nabla \ell_t)\,\mathrm{d}u, \quad t \in [0,T)$$

is a $(\mathbb{P}_y, \mathcal{F}_t^Z)$ local-martingale. Hence, we deduce that $(U_t)_{t\in[0,T)}$ given by (16) is a $(\mathbb{P}_y, \mathcal{F}_t^Z)$-Brownian motion by using Lévy's characterization. (15) is seen by combining (9) and (16).

(2) By using Itô's formula, (12) and (16), we see that

$$\begin{aligned}
\mathrm{d}\pi_t(f) &= \frac{\mathrm{d}\rho_t(f)}{\rho_t(1)} - \frac{\rho_t(f)\mathrm{d}\rho_t(1)}{\rho_t(1)^2} - \frac{\mathrm{d}\langle\rho(f),\rho(1)\rangle_t}{\rho_t(1)^2} + \frac{\rho(f)\mathrm{d}\langle\rho(1)\rangle_t}{\rho_t(1)^3} \\
&= \frac{\rho_t(f\nabla\ell_t^\top)\sigma(Z_t)\,\mathrm{d}\tilde{W}_t}{\rho_t(1)} - \frac{\rho_t(f)\rho_t(\nabla\ell_t^\top)\sigma(Z_t)\,\mathrm{d}\tilde{W}_t}{\rho_t(1)^2} \\
&\quad - \frac{\rho_t(f\nabla\ell_t^\top)(\sigma\sigma^\top)(Z_t)\rho_t(\nabla\ell_t)}{\rho_t(1)^2}\,\mathrm{d}t + \frac{\rho_t(f)\rho_t(\nabla\ell_t^\top)(\sigma\sigma^\top)(Z_t)\rho_t(\nabla\ell_t)}{\rho_t(1)^3}\,\mathrm{d}t \\
&= \left\{\pi_t(f\nabla\ell_t^\top) - \pi_t(f)\pi_t(\nabla\ell_t^\top)\right\}(\sigma\sigma^\top)^{1/2}(Z_t)\,\mathrm{d}U_t,
\end{aligned}$$

from which (17) follows. Equation (18) can be verified directly, and hence (19) follows. ■

Remark 2.7: If we admit $(t,z) \mapsto \Pi(t,z;f)$ is in $C^{1,2}([0,T) \times E)$, then (19) is obtained from Itô's formula.

The following is a direct interpretation of Proposition 2.3 in a financial context.

Corollary 2.1: *On the filtered probability space $(\Omega, \mathcal{F}_{T-}, \mathbb{P}_y, (\mathcal{F}_t^Z)_{t\in[0,T)})$, the asset price process $(S_t)_{t\in[0,T]}$ given by (4) has the dynamics,*

$$dS_t = rS_t\,\mathrm{d}t + e^{-r(T-t)}\Sigma_t(\sigma\sigma^\top)^{1/2}(Z_t)\,\mathrm{d}U_t, \quad t \in [0,T).$$

Here, $(U_t)_{t\in[0,T)}$ is a $(\mathbb{P}_y, \mathcal{F}_t^Z)$-Brownian motion given by (16),

$$\Sigma_t := \nabla\Pi(t, Z_t; f),$$

where we use (13), and the dynamics of $(Z_t)_{t\in[0,T)}$ is given by (15).

Remark 2.8: As can be seen in Proposition 2.3, the volatility term Σ_t can be rewritten as

$$\Sigma_t = \left\{\pi_t\left(f\nabla\ell_t\right) - \pi_t(f)\pi_t\left(\nabla\ell_t\right)\right\}^\top. \tag{20}$$

In the case of the linear Gaussian diffusion (23) treated in the next section, (20) is simplified to

$$\Sigma_t = \mathrm{Cov}_y\left[f(X), X \mid \mathcal{F}_t^Z\right]^\top V_{T-t}^{-1} e^{(T-t)K}, \tag{21}$$

where we use (25) and (34), and recall that

$$\mathrm{Cov}_y\left[f(X), X \mid \mathcal{F}_t^Z\right] := \mathbb{E}_y\left[f(X)X \mid \mathcal{F}_t^Z\right] - \mathbb{E}_y\left[f(X) \mid \mathcal{F}_t^Z\right]\mathbb{E}_y\left[X|\mathcal{F}_t^Z\right]. \tag{22}$$

We leave it to later to give an economic and financial interpretation to the representation (21) of the volatility process. In Section 4.2, Proposition 4.1, we apply (21) to compute the price sensitivities of a financial security linked to GHG emissions with respect to model parameters.

We end this section by giving a simple example of an RMB, which is introduced in Brody *et al.* [6].

Example 2.1 (Randomized Brownian Bridge): In (9), let $n = 1$ and let $b \equiv 0$ and $\sigma \equiv 1$. That is, we start with

$$Y_t = y + W_t, \quad t \geq 0$$

on the state space $E := \mathbb{R}$, where its transition density with respect to the Lebesgue measure m is written as

$$\tilde{p}_t(y, z) = \frac{1}{\sqrt{2\pi t}} e^{-(|y-z|^2)/2t}.$$

Then, recalling (11) and

$$\nabla\ell_t(x) = \frac{1}{T-t}\left(x - Z_t\right),$$

the SDE for $Z := Y^{(y,T,X)}$ on $(\Omega, \mathcal{F}_{T-}, \mathbb{P}_y, (\mathcal{F}_t)_{t\in[0,T)})$ is given by

$$\mathrm{d}Z_t = \frac{X - Z_t}{T-t}\,\mathrm{d}t + \mathrm{d}W_t, \quad Z_0 = y,$$

whose solution may be written as

$$Z_t = \frac{t}{T}X + \frac{T-t}{T}\left(y + \int_0^t \frac{T}{T-s}\mathrm{d}W_s\right).$$

We see that, in this case, the hidden variable X and the noise part are separated in an additive way. The conditional probability $\pi_t(\mathrm{d}z) = \pi_t(\mathrm{d}z|Z_t, Z_0)$ is represented as a functional of (Z_t, Z_0) as shown in Proposition 6, and the dynamics of Z on $(\Omega, \mathcal{F}_{T-}, \mathbb{P}_y, (\mathcal{F}_t^Z)_{t\in[0,T)})$ is given by

$$\mathrm{d}Z_t = \frac{\pi_t(I) - Z_t}{T-t}\,\mathrm{d}t + \mathrm{d}U_t,$$

where we recall (15), use $I(x) := x$ and the $\mathcal{F}_t^Z$-Brownian motion $(U_t)_{t\in[0,T)}$ defined by (16).

3. Skew-normal randomized diffusion bridge

In this section, we introduce a new example of an RMB, where the conditional probability $\pi_t(\mathrm{d}z)$ given in Proposition 2.1 and the transition density $q(s, x; t, y|z_0)$ given in Proposition 2.2 have explicit representations.

As the underlying Markov process, we employ the linear Gaussian diffusion

$$\mathrm{d}Y_t = (k + KY_t)\,\mathrm{d}t + \Sigma \mathrm{d}W_t, \quad Y_0 \in \mathbb{R}^n, \tag{23}$$

where $k \in \mathbb{R}^n$, K and $\Sigma \in \mathbb{R}^{n\times n}$ so that $\Sigma\Sigma^\top > 0$, and where $(W_t)_{t\geq 0}$ is an n-dimensional $(\mathcal{F}_t)$-Brownian motion. In this case, the transition density $\tilde{p}_t(y, z)$ that satisfies

$$\mathbb{P}\left(Y_t \in \mathrm{d}z | Y_s = y\right) = \tilde{p}_{t-s}(y, z)\mathrm{d}z$$

for $0 \leq s \leq t$, is given by

$$\tilde{p}_t(y, z) = \phi_n\left(z - \mu_t(y), V_t\right) \tag{24}$$

where

$$\phi_n\left(z; V_t\right) := \frac{1}{(2\pi)^{\frac{n}{2}}\sqrt{\det(V_t)}} \exp\left(-\frac{1}{2} z^\top V_t^{-1} z\right)$$

is the probability density function of the n-dimensional normal distribution with the mean vector $\mu_t \in \mathbb{R}^n$ and the covariance matrix $V_t \in \mathbb{S}^n_{++} := \{S \in \mathbb{S}^n | S > 0\}$, and

$$\begin{aligned} \mu_t(y) &:= e^{tK} y + \left(\int_0^t e^{sK} ds\right) k, \\ V_t &:= \int_0^t e^{sK} \Sigma\Sigma^\top e^{sK^\top} \mathrm{d}s. \end{aligned} \tag{25}$$

Next, we set the law of the random variable X as the generalized multivariate skew-normal distribution GMSN(a, b, A, B, C). That is:

$$\nu(\mathrm{d}x) := \mathbb{P}(X \in \mathrm{d}x) := f_{\mathrm{GMSN}}(x; a, b, A, B, C)\mathrm{d}x, \tag{26}$$

where, for $a \in \mathbb{R}^m$, $b \in \mathbb{R}^n$, $A \in \mathbb{S}^m_{++}$, $B \in \mathbb{S}^n_{++}$, $C \in \mathbb{R}^{m\times n}$, $m \in \mathbb{N}$, $n \in \mathbb{N}$, and

$$\Phi_m(x; A) := \int_{\prod_{i=1}^m (-\infty, x_i]} \phi_m(y; A)\,\mathrm{d}y,$$

we have

$$f_{\mathrm{GMSN}}(x; a, b, A, B, C) := \frac{1}{\Phi_m\left(Cb - a, A + CBC^\top\right)} \phi_n(x - b, B)\Phi_m\left(Cx - a, A\right). \tag{27}$$

Remark 3.1: The distribution GMSN(a, b, A, B, C) is introduced in Section 5 of Gupta *et al.* [15]. In the case

$$\begin{pmatrix} X_1 \\ X_2 \end{pmatrix} \sim \mathcal{N}\left(\begin{pmatrix} a \\ b \end{pmatrix}, \begin{pmatrix} A + CBC^\top & -CB \\ -BC^\top & B \end{pmatrix}\right),$$

we see that $X_2 | \{X_1 \leq Cb\} \sim$ GMSN(a, b, A, B, C). Here, noting the relation

$$\mathrm{GMSN}(a, b, A, B, 0) = \mathcal{N}(b, B),$$

we see that the parameter C controls the skewness of the GMSN distribution.

Remark 3.2 (Multivariate Skew-Normal Distribution): Indeed, Gupta *et al.* [15] mainly focus on the multivariate skew-normal distribution (MSN), where $n = m$ and

$$\begin{aligned} f^{(1)}_{\mathrm{MSN}}(x; b, B, C) &:= f_{\mathrm{GMSN}}(x; Cb, b, I_n, B, C) \\ &= \frac{1}{\Phi_n\left(0; I_n + CBC^\top\right)} \phi_n(x-b; B)\Phi_n\left(C(x-b); I_n\right). \end{aligned}$$

Azzalini and Dalla Valle [3] and Azzalini and Capitanio [1,2] focus on yet another MSN distribution, where $m = 1$, $b \in \mathbb{R}^n$, $c \in \mathbb{R}^n$, and

$$\begin{aligned} f^{(2)}_{\mathrm{MSN}}(x; b, c) &:= f_{\mathrm{GMSN}}(x; c^\top b, b, 1, I_n, c^\top) \\ &= 2\phi_n(x-b; I_n)\Phi_1\left(c^\top(x-b); 1\right). \end{aligned}$$

Developments of these MSN families are motivated by modelling the skewness of probabilitistic models. For related studies, we refer to Azzalini and Capitanio [2], for example.

Remark 3.3 (Univariate Skew-Normal Distribution): The univariate skew-normal probability density is given by letting $m = n = 1$ and by setting

$$\begin{aligned} f_{\mathrm{USN}}(x; \mu, \sigma, \alpha) &:= f_{\mathrm{GMSN}}\left(x; \frac{\alpha\mu}{\sigma}, \mu, 1, \sigma, \frac{\alpha}{\sigma}\right) \\ &= \frac{2}{\sigma}\phi_1\left(\frac{y-\mu}{\sigma}; 1\right)\Phi_1\left(\alpha\left(\frac{y-\mu}{\sigma}\right); 1\right). \end{aligned}$$

The parameters $\mu \in \mathbb{R}$, $\sigma > 0$, and $\alpha \in \mathbb{R}$ are called the location parameter, the scale parameter, and the shape parameter, respectively. For various properties and related statistical methodologies of USN, we refer to, e.g. Chapter 1–4 of Azzalini and Capitanio [2].

Proposition 3.1: *For the RMB specified by* (23)–(27), *the conditional probability* $\pi_t(\mathrm{d}z)$ *given in Proposition 2.1 is conditionally GMSN. That is, for* $t \in [0, T)$,

$$\pi_t(\mathrm{d}z) = f_{\mathrm{GMSN}}\left(z; a, \tilde{b}(t, Z_0, Z_t), A, \tilde{B}_t, C\right)\mathrm{d}z,$$

where

$$\begin{aligned} \tilde{b}(t, Z_0, Z_t) &:= \left(V^{-1}_{T-t} - V^{-1}_T + B^{-1}\right)^{-1}\left\{V^{-1}_{T-t}\mu_{T-t}(Z_t) - V^{-1}_T\mu_T(Z_0) + B^{-1}b\right\}, \\ \tilde{B}_t &:= \left(V^{-1}_{T-t} - V^{-1}_T + B^{-1}\right)^{-1}. \end{aligned}$$

The following lemma is useful for proving the proposition.

Lemma 3.1: *Let $P \in \mathbb{S}^n_+ := \{S \in \mathbb{S}^n | S \geq 0\}$ and $p \in \mathbb{R}^n$. For the GMSN density given by (27), it holds that*

$$\begin{aligned}
&\exp\left(-\frac{1}{2}y^\top Py + p^\top y\right) f_{\mathrm{GMSN}}(y; a, b, A, B, C) \\
&= f_{\mathrm{GMSN}}\left(y; a, \tilde{b}, A, \tilde{B}, C\right) \\
&\quad \times \frac{1}{\sqrt{\det(I + BP)}} \frac{\Phi_m\left(C\tilde{b} - a; A + C\tilde{B}C^\top\right)}{\Phi_m\left(Cb - a; A + CBC^\top\right)} \exp\left\{\frac{1}{2}\left(\tilde{b}^\top \tilde{B}^{-1}\tilde{b} - b^\top B^{-1} b\right)\right\},
\end{aligned}$$

where $\tilde{b} := (P + B^{-1})^{-1}(p + B^{-1}b)$ and $\tilde{B} := (P + B^{-1})^{-1}$.

Proof: We see that

$$\begin{aligned}
&\exp\left(-\frac{1}{2}y^\top Py + p^\top y\right) \phi_n(y - b; B) \\
&= \frac{1}{(2\pi)^{\frac{n}{2}}\sqrt{\det(B)}} \exp\left\{-\frac{1}{2}(y - \tilde{b})^\top \tilde{B}^{-1}(y - \tilde{b}) + \frac{1}{2}\left(\tilde{b}^\top \tilde{B}^{-1}\tilde{b} - b^\top B^{-1} b\right)\right\} \\
&= \phi_n\left(y - \tilde{b}; \tilde{B}\right) \frac{1}{\sqrt{\det(I + BP)}} \exp\left\{\frac{1}{2}\left(\tilde{b}^\top \tilde{B}^{-1}\tilde{b} - b^\top B^{-1} b\right)\right\}. \qquad (28)
\end{aligned}$$

Furthermore,

$$\phi_n\left(y - \tilde{b}; \tilde{B}\right) \Phi_m\left(Cy - a; A\right) = \Phi_m\left(C\tilde{b} - a; A + C\tilde{B}C^\top\right) f_{\mathrm{GMSN}}\left(y; a, \tilde{b}, A, \tilde{B}, C\right). \qquad (29)$$

The proof is completed by combining (28) and (29). ■

Next we prove Proposition 3.1:

Proof: We observe that

$$\begin{aligned}
\frac{p_{T-t}(y, z)}{p_T(y_0, z)} &= \sqrt{\frac{\det V_T}{\det V_{T-t}}} \exp\left[-\frac{1}{2}\left\{z - \mu_{T-t}(y)\right\}^\top V_{T-t}^{-1}\left\{z - \mu_{T-t}(y)\right\}\right. \\
&\quad \left. + \frac{1}{2}\left\{z - \mu_T(y_0)\right\}^\top V_T^{-1}\left\{z - \mu_T(y_0)\right\}\right] \\
&= \sqrt{\frac{\det V_T}{\det V_{T-t}}} \exp\left[-\frac{1}{2}z^\top (V_{T-t}^{-1} - V_T^{-1})z\right. \\
&\quad + \left\{V_{T-t}^{-1}\mu_{T-t}(y) - V_T^{-1}\mu_T(y_0)\right\}^\top z \\
&\quad \left. - \frac{1}{2}\mu_{T-t}(y)^\top V_{T-t}^{-1}\mu_{T-t}(y) + \frac{1}{2}\mu_T(y_0)^\top V_T^{-1}\mu_T(y_0)\right].
\end{aligned}$$

We then apply Lemma 3.1 to obtain

$$
\begin{aligned}
J_{t,T}(z;y_0,y) :&= \frac{p_{T-t}(y,z)}{p_T(y_0,z)}\frac{\mathrm{d}\nu}{\mathrm{d}z}(z) \\
&= f_{\mathrm{GMSN}}\left(z;a,\tilde{b}(t,y_0,y),A,\tilde{B}_t,C\right) \\
&\times \frac{1}{\sqrt{\det\left(I+B(V_{T-t}^{-1}-V_T^{-1})\right)}}\frac{\Phi_m\left(C\tilde{b}(t,y_0,y)-a;A+C\tilde{B}_tC^\top\right)}{\Phi_m\left(Cb-a;A+CBC^\top\right)} \\
&\times \sqrt{\frac{\det V_T}{\det V_{T-t}}}\exp\Bigg[\frac{1}{2}\Bigg\{\left(\tilde{b}^\top\tilde{B}_t^{-1}\tilde{b}\right)(t,y_0,y)-b^\top B^{-1}b \\
&- \mu_{T-t}(y)^\top V_{T-t}^{-1}\mu_{T-t}(y)+\mu_T(y_0)^\top V_T^{-1}\mu_T(y_0)\Bigg\}\Bigg].
\end{aligned}
\tag{30}
$$

Hence, the statement of Proposition 3.1 follows by recalling that:

$$
\pi_t(\mathrm{d}z) = \frac{J_{t,T}(z;Z_0,Z_t)\,\mathrm{d}z}{\int_{\mathbb{R}^n} J_{t,T}(z;Z_0,Z_t)\,\mathrm{d}z}.
$$

■

Remark 3.4: By letting $P=0$ in Lemma 3.1, we obtain the explicit expression of the moment generating function of a GMSN-distributed multivariate random variable:

$$
\begin{aligned}
M(p) :&= \int_{\mathbb{R}^n} e^{p^\top y} f_{\mathrm{GMSN}}(y;a,b,A,B,C)\,\mathrm{d}y \\
&= \frac{\Phi_m\left(C(b+Bp)-a;A+CBC^\top\right)}{\Phi_m\left(Cb-a;A+CBC^\top\right)}\exp\left(\frac{1}{2}p^\top Bp+b^\top p\right).
\end{aligned}
$$

From this, we see for example that

$$
\begin{aligned}
\nabla M(0) &= \int_{\mathbb{R}^n} y f_{\mathrm{GMSN}}(y;a,b,A,B,C)\,\mathrm{d}y \\
&= b + BC^\top\left(\frac{\nabla\Phi_m}{\Phi_m}\right)\left(Cb-a;A+CBC^\top\right),
\end{aligned}
\tag{31}
$$

where $\nabla\Phi_m(x) := (\partial_{x_1}\Phi_m(x),\ldots,\partial_{x_m}\Phi_m(x))^\top$.

We introduce the density

$$
\nu(\mathrm{d}x) := \mathbb{P}(X\in\mathrm{d}x) = f_{\mathrm{GMSN}}\left(x;a,\mu_T(Z_0),A,V_T,C\right)\mathrm{d}x, \tag{32}
$$

which is constructed from the marginal law of Y_T, $\mathcal{N}(\mu_T(Z_0),V_T)$, by adding a skewness effect. Then, the expression of the conditional probability $\pi_t(\mathrm{d}z)$ can be simplified as follows:

Corollary 3.1: *For an RMB, consisting of (23)–(25) and (32), it holds that*

$$\pi_t(\mathrm{d}z) = f_{\mathrm{GMSN}}\,(z; a, \mu_{T-t}(Z_t), A, V_{T-t}, C)\,\mathrm{d}z, \quad t \in [0, T).$$

In particular, the conditional probability $\pi_t(\mathrm{d}z)$ is independent of Z_0.

Moreover, we obtain the following:

Proposition 3.2: *For the RMB specified by (23)–(25) and (32), the following holds:*

(1) *The transition density $q(s, x; t, y|Z_0)$, obtained in Proposition 2.2, is expressed by*

$$q(s, x; t, y|Z_0) = q(s, x; t, y) = f_{\mathrm{GMSN}}\left(y; \tilde{a}_t, \mu_{t-s}(x), \tilde{A}_t, V_{t-s}, \tilde{C}_t\right),$$

where

$$\begin{aligned}\tilde{a}_t &:= a - C\left(\int_0^{T-t} e^{uK}\,\mathrm{d}u\right)k,\\ \tilde{A}_t &:= A + CV_{T-t}C^\top,\\ \tilde{C}_t &:= Ce^{(T-t)K},\end{aligned}$$

and is independent of Z_0.

(2) *The dynamical equation of the RMB Z under $(\Omega, \mathcal{F}_{T-}, \mathbb{P}_y, (\mathcal{F}_t^Z)_{t\in[0,T)})$ is given by*

$$\mathrm{d}Z_t = \left\{k + KZ_t - (\Sigma\Sigma^\top)C^\top\left(\frac{\nabla\Phi_m}{\Phi_m}\right)\left(C\mu_{T-t}(Z_t) - a; A + CV_{T-t}C^\top\right)\right\}\mathrm{d}t + (\Sigma\Sigma^\top)^{1/2}\,\mathrm{d}U_t \tag{33}$$

where $Z_0 = y$ and $(U_t)_{t\in[0,T)}$ is the $(\mathcal{F}_t^Z)$-Brownian motion defined by (16) for $b(z) = k + Kz$ and $\sigma(z) = \Sigma$.

Proof: 1. We apply Proposition 2.2 and Formula (30), where $b = \mu_T(z_0)$ and $B = V_T$ and observe that

$$\begin{aligned}q(s, x; t, y|z_0) &= \frac{p_{t-s}(x, y)\int_{\mathbb{R}^n} J_{t,T}(z; z_0, y)\,\mathrm{d}z}{\int_{\mathbb{R}^n} J_{s,T}(z; z_0, x)\,\mathrm{d}z}\\ &= \phi_n\left(y - \mu_{t-s}(x); V_{t-s}\right)\frac{\Phi_m\left(C\mu_{T-t}(y) - a; A + CV_{T-t}C^\top\right)}{\Phi_m\left(C\mu_{T-s}(x) - a; A + CV_{T-s}C^\top\right)}.\end{aligned}$$

By recalling here that

$$\begin{aligned}\Phi_m\left(C\mu_{T-t}(y) - a; A + CV_{T-t}C^\top\right) &= \Phi_m\left(\tilde{C}_t y - \tilde{a}_t; \tilde{A}_t\right),\\ \Phi_m\left(C\mu_{T-s}(x) - a; A + CV_{T-s}C^\top\right) &= \Phi_m\left(\tilde{C}_t\mu_{t-s}(x) - \tilde{a}_t; \tilde{A}_t + \tilde{C}_t V_{t-s}\tilde{C}_t^\top\right),\end{aligned}$$

the assertion follows.

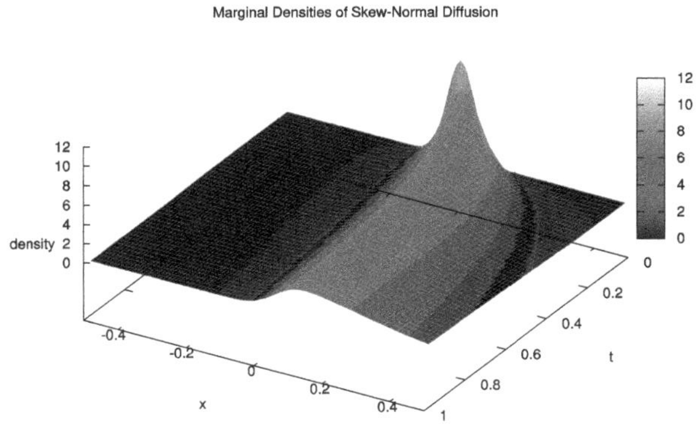

Figure 1. Skew-normal densities $q(0, 0; t, x)$ for $0.01 \leq t \leq 1$.

2. We compute the SDE (15) utilizing the setting of this section. We consider $b(t, z) = k + Kz$, $\sigma(z) = \Sigma$, and

$$\begin{aligned}\ell_t(z) &= \log \tilde{p}_{T-t}(Z_t, z) \\ &= -\frac{1}{2}\left(z - \mu_{T-t}(Z_t)\right)^\top V_{T-t}^{-1}\left(z - \mu_{T-t}(Z_t)\right) - \frac{1}{2}\log\det(V_{T-t}) - \frac{n}{2}\log(2\pi).\end{aligned} \tag{34}$$

By Formula (31) and Corollary 3.1, we deduce that

$$\begin{aligned}\pi_t\left(\nabla \ell_t\right) &= V_{T-t}^{-1}\left\{\mu_{T-t}(Z_t) - \int_{\mathbb{R}^n} z\pi_t(\mathrm{d}z)\right\} \\ &= -C^\top \frac{\nabla \Phi_m}{\Phi_m}\left(C\mu_{T-t}(Z_t) - a; A + CV_{T-t}C^\top\right),\end{aligned}$$

and the assertion follows. ■

In Figures 1 and 2, considering the setting in Proposition 3.2, that is, the skew-normal RMB specified by (23)–(25) and (32), we draw its marginal densities

$$\left\{q(0, x_0; t, x)\right\}_{(t,x)\in[T_0,T]\times\mathbb{R}},$$

where we set $x_0 = 0$, $T_0 = 0.01$, $T = 1$. The parameter values of the RMB are set to $n = 1$, $k = 0$, $K = -0.1$, $\Sigma = 0.3$, $a = 1$, $A = 1$, and $C = 20$.

4. Applications to commodity pricing and securitization of greenhouse gas risk

In this section, we apply the RMBs to construct asset price models following Formula (4). We consider skew-normal randomised diffusion bridges (SNRDB) to price commodity assets and for the securitisation of greenhouse gas (GHG) risk. The applications driven by SNRDB are just an example; the pricing models can be constructed with any

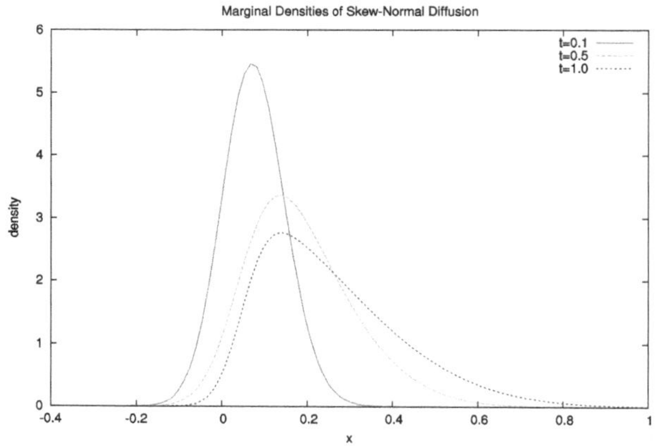

Figure 2. Skew-normal densities $q(0, 0; t, x)$ for $t \in \{0.1, 0.5, 1.0\}$.

RMBs, provided one agrees with the suitability of the implicit statistics for the envisaged application.

It is customary in commodity pricing to assume a spot price process $(S_t)_{0 \le t \le T}$ for the considered commodity and to model the price process $(F_{tT})_{0 \le t \le T}$ of a T-delivery forward contract. The spot price process is $(\mathcal{F}_t)$-measurable and the delivery date T is a fixed date specified in the forward contract. The price F_{tT} at time t of the forward contract with delivery date T is given by

$$F_{tT} = \mathbb{E}\left[S_T \mid \mathcal{F}_t\right], \tag{35}$$

where the expectation is taken under the risk-neutral measure. We assume that the risk-free interest rate is constant, which implies the distribution of S_T under the T-forward measure is unchanged, and we can evaluate the price F_{tT} under the forward measure $\mathbb{P}^T$ by the relation

$$F_{tT} = \mathbb{E}^{\mathbb{P}^T}\left[S_T \mid \mathcal{F}_t\right] = \mathbb{E}\left[S_T \mid \mathcal{F}_t\right]. \tag{36}$$

Next, we construct a commodity pricing model driven by a randomized diffusion bridge with terminal GMSN marginal.

4.1. Commodity pricing

We take the RMB $(Z_t)_{t \in [0,T]}$, specified by (23)–(25) and (32), as the state variable, and define the spot commodity price process by

$$S_t := \exp\left(p^\top Z_t\right) \tag{37}$$

for $t \in [0, T]$ and $p \in \mathbb{R}^n$. This commodity spot price process can be regarded as a flexible extension of the price models proposed in Gibson and Schwartz [14] and Schwartz [21] so to incorporate the skewness of marginal distributions of the log-price process $(\log S_t)_{t \in [0,T]}$. Indeed, the Gibson and Schwartz commodity spot price process is obtained as follows: Let $C = 0$, then $\mathrm{GMSN}(a, \mu_T(Y_0), A, V_T, 0) = \mathcal{N}(\mu_T(Y_0), V_T)$ and $Z_T = X \sim Y_T$, see Remark 3.1. Hence the RMB (Z_t) is equal to the linear Gaussian process (Y_t). For $n = 2$, we consider the parametrization

$$d\begin{pmatrix} Y_t^1 \\ Y_t^2 \end{pmatrix} = \left[\begin{pmatrix} \alpha \\ \kappa\lambda \end{pmatrix} + \begin{pmatrix} 0 & -1 \\ 0 & -\kappa \end{pmatrix}\begin{pmatrix} Y_t^1 \\ Y_t^2 \end{pmatrix}\right] dt + \begin{pmatrix} \sigma_1 & 0 \\ \sigma_2\rho & \sigma_2\sqrt{1-\rho^2} \end{pmatrix} dW_t,$$

where $\alpha, \kappa, \lambda, \sigma_1, \sigma_2 > 0$ and $-1 \le \rho \le 1$. Then, $S_t = e^{p^\top Y_t} = e^{Y_t^1}$ with $p := (1,0)^\top$ is precisely the Gibson and Schwartz [14] model.

By making use of the spot commodity pricing model (37), we now have for the forward price process, delivering at time T

$$F_{tT} := \mathbb{E}\left[S_T \mid \mathcal{F}_t^Z\right] = \mathbb{E}\left[e^{p^\top X} \mid \mathcal{F}_t^Z\right] \tag{38}$$

for $t \in [0, T]$, where the expectation may be taken under the risk-neutral measure, and the filtration $(\mathcal{F}_t^Z)_{t\in[0,T]}$ is generated by the RMB (Z_t). By Corollary 3.1 and Lemma 3.1, we obtain

$$\begin{aligned} F_{tT} &= \int_{\mathbb{R}^n} e^{p^\top x}\pi_t(\mathrm{d}x) \\ &= \int_{\mathbb{R}^n} e^{p^\top x} f_{\mathrm{GMSN}}\left(x; a, \mu_{T-t}(Z_t), A, V_{T-t}, C\right) \mathrm{d}x \\ &= F(t, Z_t), \end{aligned} \tag{39}$$

where

$$\begin{aligned} F(t,z) = {} & \frac{\Phi_m\left(C\left(\mu_{T-t}(z) + V_{T-t}p\right) - a; A + CV_{T-t}C^\top\right)}{\Phi_m\left(C\mu_{T-t}(z) - a; A + CV_{T-t}C^\top\right)} \\ & \exp\left[p^\top \mu_{T-t}(z) + \frac{1}{2}p^\top V_{T-t}p\right]. \end{aligned}$$

On $(\Omega, \mathcal{F}_{T-}, \mathbb{P}_y, (\mathcal{F}_t^Z)_{t\in[0,T)})$, we write down the system in stochastic differential form

$$\begin{aligned} \mathrm{d}F_t &= \nabla_z F(t, Z_t)(\Sigma\Sigma^\top)^{1/2}\,\mathrm{d}U_t, \\ \mathrm{d}Z_t &= \left[k + KZ_t - (\Sigma\Sigma^\top)C^\top\left(\frac{\nabla\Phi_m}{\Phi_m}\right)\left(C\mu_{T-t}(Z_t) - a; A + CV_{T-t}C^\top\right)\right]\mathrm{d}t \\ &\quad + (\Sigma\Sigma^\top)^{1/2}\,\mathrm{d}U_t, \end{aligned}$$

where the SDE determining the dynamics of (Z_t) is given in Proposition 3.2 (2). Furthermore, if we consider the derivative security, whose payoff at the derivative's maturity $T' \le T$ has the form $H := h(F_{T'T})$ with some integrable $h : \mathbb{R}_{++} \to \mathbb{R}$, then its (arbitrage-free)

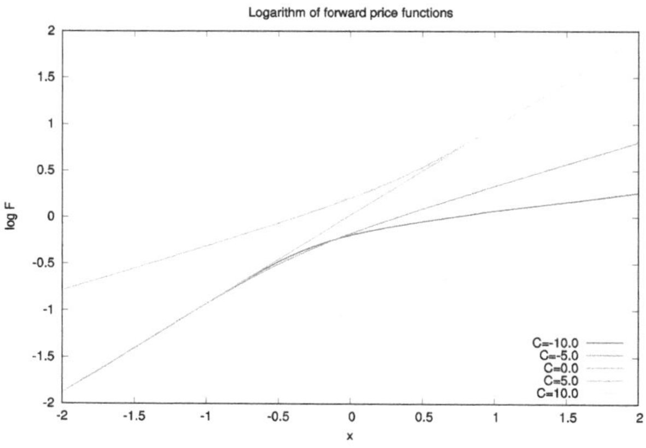

Figure 3. Log-forward functions $L(0.5, x)$.

price at time $t \in [0, T']$ is computed by using Proposition 3.2 (1) as follows:

$$\begin{aligned} V(t, Z_t) &= \mathbb{E}\left[\mathrm{e}^{-r(T'-t)} h\left(F_{T'T}\right) \mid \mathcal{F}_t^Z\right] \\ &= \mathrm{e}^{-r(T'-t)} \int_{\mathbb{R}^n} h\left(F(T', y)\right) q(t, Z_t; T', y)\, \mathrm{d}y \\ &= \mathrm{e}^{-r(T'-t)} \int_{\mathbb{R}^n} h\left(F(T', y)\right) f_{\mathrm{GMSN}}\left(y; \tilde{a}_t, \mu_{T'-t}(Z_t), \tilde{A}_t, V_{T'-t}, \tilde{C}_t\right) \mathrm{d}y, \end{aligned}$$

where r is a constant interest rate. In Figure 3, we consider a one-dimensional SNRDB $(Z_t)_{0 \le t < T}$ given by (23)–(25) and (32) as the state variable, and plot the log-price function $L(t, z) := \log F(t, z)$. The parameter values are set to $n = m = 1, T = 1, k = 0, K = -0.1$, $\Sigma = 0.3, Z_0 = 0, a = 1, A = 1, C = -10, -5, 0, 5, 10, p = 1$, and $t = 0.5$. We note that $L(t, z)$ is affine with respect to z when $C = 0$, that is,

$$\begin{aligned} L(t, z) &= p\mu_{T-t}(z) + \frac{p^2}{2} V_{T-t} \\ &= \left\{\frac{pk}{K} e^{K(T-t)} + \frac{p^2}{4K}\left(e^{K(T-t)} - 1\right)\right\} + pe^{K(T-t)} z. \end{aligned}$$

The RMB (Z_t) is linear-Gaussian when $C = 0$, as we have seen. We draw the non-linear increasing functions $z \to L(t, z)$ for the values $C \in \{-10, -5, 0, 5, 10\}$.

Further, in Figure 4, we draw the marginal probability density functions

$$p_{t,T}(x) := \frac{\mathbb{P}\left(F_{tT} \in \mathrm{d}x\right)}{\mathrm{d}x},$$

for $t \in \{0.25, 0.5, 0.75, 1\}$, by setting the parameters to $n = m = 1$, $T = 1$, $k = 0$, $K = -0.1, \Sigma = 0.3, Z_0 = 0, a = 1, A = 1, C = 5$, and $p = 1$. We see that

$$p_{t,T}(x) = f_{\mathrm{GMSN}}\left(F^{-1}(t, x); \tilde{a}_t, \mu_t(Z_0), \tilde{A}_t, V_t, \tilde{C}_t\right) \frac{1}{\partial_z F\left(t, F^{-1}(t, x)\right)},$$

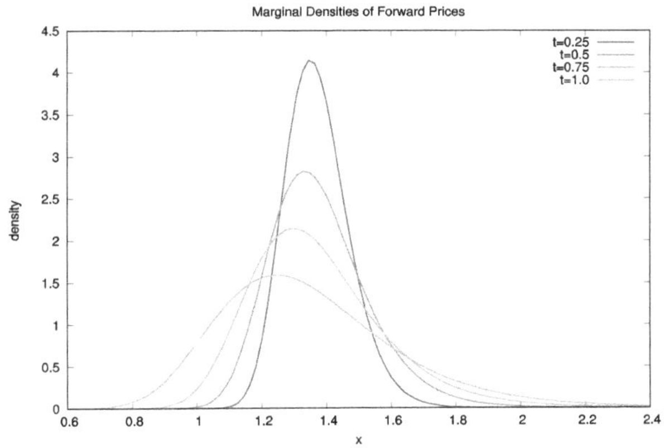

Figure 4. Marginal densities of F_{tT}.

where we use Proposition 3.2 (1), the relation $F_{tT} = F(t, Z_t)$, and the notation $F^{-1}(t, x)$ to denote the inverse function of $F(t, \cdot)$ that satisfies $F(t, F^{-1}(t, x)) = x$, $x \in \mathbb{R}_{++}$.

4.2. GHG risk securitization

In this section, we associate the RMB to GHG emissions. Here we focus on man-made emissions (e.g. burning fossil fuel, farming, etc.), which can be affected by varying collective human activity. We regard the man-made emission as a process that in principle can be controlled or on which one can at least intervene.

We assume that (Z_t) is an RMB with arbitrary marginal distribution at time $t = T$. This RMB is the model for man-made GHG emissions in the environment. The arbitrary distribution of the 'terminal' random variable Z_T is taken to be the target distribution aimed at by, say, an (governmental) emissions policy. Such a target distribution—or indeed the regulatory policy—is specified at $t = 0$, when for instance a new (international) law is ratified. Time T is the date by which the target emission level is to be achieved. Because we believe that it is unreasonable to set a fixed target, we opt for a distribution of possible values. We might like to assume that the mean of the distribution coincides with the agreed target value characterizing a policy. Such environmental policies come with significant financial commitments. We next present an idea on how environmental policies and related costs may sit at the interface with financial markets and the securitization of climate risk.

This is certainly not the first piece of work addressing the question of how financial markets can be involved in reducing GHG emissions. Howison and Schwarz [18] provide—in addition to several references—a useful overview in this area of research. One learns that there are mainly three types of reduction mechanisms: (a) the Clean Development Mechanism, (b) the Joint Implementation, and (c) Emissions Trading. The financial mechanism we present next may be seen closest to Emissions Trading in that financial contracts are traded which are written on emission allowance. Carmona and Hinz [7] use the so-called risk-neutral valuation approach to price such contracts. While we also use a no-arbitrage approach, though we prefer to work under the real-world measure, we think that the design of the here proposed market instruments written on GHG emissions is different. If we were to look for similarities with existing financial instruments, then the GHG-contracts presented next would be related to inflation-linked or possibly insurance-linked securities, see e.g. Dam *et al.* [11] and Barrieu and Albertini [4]. Such contracts provide financial protection against losses due to, for example, currency depreciation or limit financial liabilities beyond a certain amount. Emission allowance certificates have a different nature: the holder of such a note has paid the right to emit a specified amount of GHG-equivalent. Allowance certificates, as exchanged on, e.g. the European Energy Exchange, are not designed to provide financial compensation for potential losses due to (direct or indirect) adverse effects caused by high levels of GHG at a future point in time. While trading emission allowances and the GHG-securities both aim at incentivizing a reduction of future GHG levels, the latter mechanism builds in an additional penalization to the issuer (e.g. a central government)—beyond any specified in international agreements—in a similar way as inflation-linked sovereign bonds result in payments to bond holders by the issuing (governmental) body for failing to keep (future) inflation below a contractually pre-specified level. A governmental GHG policy, as illustrated below, may be viewed as an analogy to a monetary policy and the issuance of GHG-linked securities as an assurance to, e.g. the insurance industry of a central government's plan to reduce GHG levels over a specified time period. We now move one to the stochastic modelling of GHG by use of RMBs and to the no-arbitrage pricing of the proposed GHG-linked securities.

We consider a central government that has agreed to reducing the GHG amount in the atmosphere by a pre-specified future date. We refer to, e.g. The Paris Agreement (2016)[1] whereby the commitment is a reduction of GHG by 80% by 2050 relative to the GHG amount in 1990, see UK Climate Action Following the Paris Agreement (2016) .[2] The target GHG process is modelled by an RMB, where the terminal distribution is a reflection of the uncertainty about the realized target emissions level at time T. We suppose that the governing body needs to raise funds to finance the transition to a lower GHG emissions regime by the fixed future date, and aims at doing business with the financial industry. Here we shall consider the insurance industry, whereby (re)insurance firms have a strong interest in a decarbonized future. It is commonly accepted that climate-driven catastrophes are to become more severe (and thus more costly) if GHG emissions do not decrease (c.f. related increase of average global temperature leading to more severe flooding, droughts, hurricanes, etc.).

We thus consider a governing body that is prepared to sell GHG securities to an insurer where the deal is that (a) if the pre-specified GHG target is met, or even exceeded, then the government retains the funds raised through selling the securities, and (b) if the target is underachieved then the government will have to pay the insurer the difference between the realized GHG amount and the contractually pre-specified target. Such a contract is known as a call option, and in the insurance industry such an instrument may be identified with a stop-loss contract.

We consider the filtered probability space $(\Omega, \mathcal{F}, (\mathcal{F}_t), \mathbb{P})$ where $\mathbb{P}$ is the real probability measure. We take the RMB (Z_t) as a model for the GHG emissions and introduce a $\mathbb{P}$-Brownian motion (B_t). We assume $\mathcal{F}_t = \mathcal{F}_t^B \vee \mathcal{F}_t^Z$, where $\mathcal{F}_t^B$ and $\mathcal{F}_t^Z$ are the filtrations generated by (B_t) and (Z_t), respectively. Further, we introduce a stochastic discount factor

(ζ_t) defined by

$$\zeta_t = \exp\left(-\lambda B_t - \tfrac{1}{2}\lambda^2 t - rt\right).$$

The interest rate r and the market price of risk λ are assumed constant, for simplicity. Next we introduce a random cash flow H_T at the fixed date $T \geq t$ modelled by $H_T = h(Z_T)$. The no-arbitrage price (H_t), $0 \leq t \leq T$, of the GHG-linked security, with cash flow H_T at time T, is given by

$$H_t = \frac{1}{\zeta_t}\mathbb{E}^{\mathbb{P}}\left[\zeta_T\, h(Z_T) \mid \mathcal{F}_t\right]. \tag{40}$$

Unless one has the view that GHG emissions have a direct impact on the dynamics of the stochastic discount factor (ζ_t) (and vice versa), we may assume that ζ_t and Z_t are independent for all $t \in [0, T]$. It then follows that

$$H_t = \frac{1}{\zeta_t}\mathbb{E}^{\mathbb{P}}\left[\zeta_T \mid \mathcal{F}_t^B\right]\mathbb{E}^{\mathbb{P}}\left[h(Z_T) \mid \mathcal{F}_t^Z\right],$$

where it is assumed that $h(Z_T)$ is integrable, and further that

$$H_t = \mathrm{e}^{-r(T-t)}\mathbb{E}\left[h(Z_T) \mid \mathcal{F}_t^Z\right]$$

owing to the fact that $\exp(-\lambda B_t - 1/2\lambda^2 t)$ is an $\{(\mathcal{F}_t), \mathbb{P}\}$-martingale. The conditional expectation is calculated in an analogous way to Formula (39), which gives

$$H_t = \mathrm{e}^{-r(T-t)}\int h(x) f_{\mathrm{GMSN}}\left(x; a, \mu_{T-t}(Z_t), A, V_{T-t}, C\right)\mathrm{d}x. \tag{41}$$

Here, in line with the previous section, we assume that (Z_t) is an SNRDB.

Vanilla option. We next price a stop-loss contract (a call option). We envisage an emissions derivatives market and present price models for GHG emissions options under the said assumptions. We have

$$V_t = \mathrm{e}^{-r(T-t)}\mathbb{E}\left[(H_T - K)^+ \mid \mathcal{F}_t^Z\right] = \mathrm{e}^{-r(T-t)}\mathbb{E}\left[(h(Z_T) - K)^+ \mid \mathcal{F}_t^Z\right], \tag{42}$$

where K is a strike price. This equation boils down to calculating

$$V_t = \mathrm{e}^{-r(T-t)}\int (h(x) - K)^+ f_{\mathrm{GMSN}}\left(x; a, \mu_{T-t}(Z_t), A, V_{T-t}, C\right)\mathrm{d}x. \tag{43}$$

This is a first simple example for a GHG-linked option. One might like to consider a richer market where the option maturities are not necessarily associated with an international GHG reduction treaty and dates agreed therein. In fact, a government could issue GHG options with maturities $T_1 < T_2 < \cdots < T_n$, where $T_n = T$ could coincide with the terminal date (e.g. 2050) by which the GHG reduction must be achieved. The government (and the insurance firms) could then consider holding a basket of GHG options. The policymaker would have goals with shorter terms, which could be more plausible to the buyers in a (financial) insurance market, and the insurers would potentially have access to cash flows after shorter periods of time, which could be used to cover losses. Another type of a contract could be a GHG-linked swap contract, where the insurer exchanges a fixed rate for a floating one that is periodically updated with observations of the realized GHG level. Such a contract gives an opportunity to update the financial liability during a long-dated agreement.

Swap contract. Let $T_1 < T_2 < \cdots < T_i < \cdots < T_n$ be fixed dates. Associated with these dates, we have the cash flows $H_{T_i} = g_i(Z_{T_i})$, $i = 1, \ldots, n$, where Z_{T_i} has the target distribution of the RMB $(Z_t^{(i)})_{0\le t\le T_i}$. The integrable functions g_i may differ for different i's. Here the filtration $(\mathcal{F}_t^Z)_{0\le t}$ is generated by the collection of RMBs $\{(Z_t^{(i)})_{0\le t\le T_i}\}_{i=1,\ldots,n}$. Then we consider the following swap-like structure with price process (Sw_t):

$$Sw_t = \mathbb{E}\left[\sum_i^n \mathrm{e}^{-r(T_i-t)}\left(H_{T_i} - K\right) \mid \mathcal{F}_t^Z\right], \tag{44}$$

where K is a strike value and $(\mathcal{F}_t^Z)$ is generated by the RMBs $\{(Z_t^{(1)}), (Z_t^{(2)}), \ldots, (Z_t^{(n)})\}$. The expression for the price Sw_t at time t can be written as

$$Sw_t = \sum_i^n \mathrm{e}^{-r(T_i-t)}\mathbb{E}\left[g_i(Z_{T_i}) \mid \mathcal{F}_t^Z\right] - K\sum_i^n \mathrm{e}^{-r(T_i-t)}. \tag{45}$$

By setting $Sw_t = 0$, we obtain the so-called *fair swap value* K_t at time t given by

$$\begin{aligned} K_t &= \sum_i^n \mathbb{E}\left[g_i(Z_{T_i}) \mid \mathcal{F}_t\right] \Big/ \sum_i^n \mathrm{e}^{-r(T_i-t)} \\ &= \sum_i^n \int g_i(x_i) f_{\mathrm{GMSN}}\left(x_i; a_i, \mu_{T_i-t}^{(i)}(Z_t^{(i)}), A_i, V_{T_i-t}^{(i)}, C_i\right)\mathrm{d}x_i \Big/ \sum_i^n \mathrm{e}^{-r(T_i-t)}, \end{aligned}$$

where here $\{(Z_t^{(i)})\}_{i=1,\ldots,n}$ are assumed to be SNRDBs. It is K_t that seller (government) and buyer (insurer) trade at. In the case of a swap, the value of K_t is directly related to how likely a government will actually meet the GHG target (or even reduce to below the target). Also, since Sw_t may take positive and negative values, the trade counterparts in principle rebalance their accounts as they go along in contrast to call option contracts where there would be no cashflows for a potentially long period of time.

In Figure 5, we describe how an RMB may be applied to model GHG emission. At T_0, Z_{T_0} denotes the observed initial level of emitted GHG. Also at T_0, the prior distribution of the random GHG level Z_T is specified. The mean $\mathbb{E}[Z_T]$ of the prior distribution is set to match the target GHG level that the guided emissions policy is supposed to meet by the pre-specified date T. The dashed line depicts the GHG emission plan a policymaker commits to and wishes to implement. The stochastic path is one possible realization of the GHG process (Z_t), which is observed as one moves forward in time. The solid line is the implicit drift of the process (Z_t), which in the depicted example does not match the planned GHG policy. At the end of the policy period, that is at T, the terminal GHG level Z_T exceeds the pre-specified target value, which the policymaker had committed to realize. We emphasize that at first the realized GHG level (and in particular the realized drift) is below the dashed GHG policy line, thus indicating, in this particular example, that the implemented emission policy achieved a stronger abatement than intend up to that point in time.

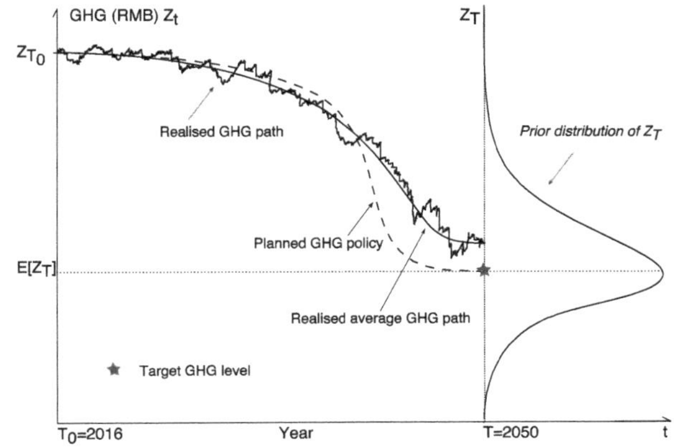

Figure 5. GHG level modelled by an RMB (Z_t).

We conclude the application of RMBs to GHG-risk securitization by taking a closer look at what model parameters a policymaker may influence. In other words, what parameters in the chosen RMB may capture trends a policymaker may wish to control during the planned GHG abatement period. A candidate parameter is k in the linear Gaussian diffusion (23), underlying the dynamics of (Z_t), because it affects the drift of the RMB. This can be seen explicitly via Corollary 3.1 and the set of Equations (25).

The idea is that the GHG level increases or declines depending on what level of k is selected. The parameter k, in turn, affects the price dynamics of a financial security written on (Z_t). Other degrees of freedom, such as the *a priori* target distribution of Z_T, also have an impact, but here we shall focus on the sensitivity of (H_t) on k. As seen in Formula (41), the value (H_t) at time t is impacted by k via μ_{T-t} in the GMSN-density. We express the 'k-sensitivity' of H_t at time $t \in [0, T)$ by $\partial_k H_t$. In the following proposition, we also give an explicit expression for the so-called 'Delta-sensitivity' $\partial_z H_t$. This is the measure of how much the price H_t at time t varies given a change in the underlying value of Z_t at time t. This result is given for the case that the SNRDB is multivariate process.

Proposition 4.1: *Consider the SNRDB, given by* (23)–(25) *and* (32). *Let* $h := (h_1, \ldots, h_d)^\top : \mathbb{R}^n \to \mathbb{R}^d$, *assuming that* $h(X)$ *is integrable. It then holds that*

$$\partial_z \mathbb{E}\left[h(X) \mid \mathcal{F}_t^Z\right] = \mathrm{Cov}\left[h(X), X \mid \mathcal{F}_t^Z\right]^\top V_{T-t}^{-1} e^{(T-t)K}, \tag{46}$$

$$\partial_k \mathbb{E}\left[h(X) \mid \mathcal{F}_t^Z\right] = \mathrm{Cov}\left[h(X), X \mid \mathcal{F}_t^Z\right]^\top V_{T-t}^{-1} \int_0^{T-t} e^{sK} \mathrm{d}s, \tag{47}$$

where we use (22), (13), $\pi_t(h) = \Pi(t, Z_t; h)$, *and write*

$$\partial_z \mathbb{E}\left[h(X) \mid \mathcal{F}_t^Z\right] := \partial_z \Pi(t, Z_t; h) = \left(\partial_{z_j} \Pi(t, Z_t; h_i)\right)_{1 \le i \le d, 1 \le j \le n},$$

$$\partial_k \mathbb{E}\left[h(X) \mid \mathcal{F}_t^Z\right] := \left(\partial_{k_j} \Pi(t, Z_t; h_i)\right)_{1 \le i \le d, 1 \le j \le n}.$$

Proof: Equation (46) is obtained from Proposition 2.3 and (20)–(22) in Remark 2.8. To show (47), we note that, in the right-hand side of the expression

$$\mathbb{E}\left[h(X) \mid \mathcal{F}_t^Z\right] = \int_{\mathbb{R}^n} h(x) f_{\text{GMSN}}\left(x; a, \mu_{T-t}(Z_t), A, V_{T-t}, C\right) \mathrm{d}x, \tag{48}$$

where we use Corollary 3.1, only $\mu_{T-t}(Z_t)$ depends on Z_t and k. We see that

$$\partial_z \mu_{T-t}(Z_t) = e^{(T-t)K}, \tag{49}$$

$$\partial_k \mu_{T-t}(Z_t) = \int_0^{T-t} e^{sK} \mathrm{d}s. \tag{50}$$

From (46), (48), (49) and the chain rule of differentiation, we deduce

$$\partial_b \left\{ \int_{\mathbb{R}^n} h(x) f_{\text{GMSN}}\left(x; a, b, A, V_{T-t}, C\right) \mathrm{d}x \right\} \Big|_{b=\mu_{T-t}(Z_t)} = \text{Cov}\left[h(X), X | \mathcal{F}_t^Z\right] V_{T-t}^{-1}. \tag{51}$$

From (48), (50) and (51), we see that

$$\begin{aligned} \partial_k \mathbb{E}\left[h(X) \mid \mathcal{F}_t^Z\right] &= \partial_b \left\{ \int_{\mathbb{R}^n} h(x) f_{\text{GMSN}}\left(x; a, b, A, V_{T-t}, C\right) \mathrm{d}x \right\} \Big|_{b=\mu_{T-t}(Z_t)} \partial_k \mu_{T-t}(Z_t) \\ &= \text{Cov}\left[h(X), X | \mathcal{F}_t^Z\right] V_{T-t}^{-1} \int_0^{T-t} e^{sK} \mathrm{d}s. \end{aligned}$$

■

Remark 4.1: Letting $h(z) = z$ in Proposition 4.1, we see that

$$\partial_z \mathbb{E}\left[X \mid \mathcal{F}_t^Z\right] = \text{Var}\left[X \mid \mathcal{F}_t^Z\right] V_{T-t}^{-1} e^{(T-t)K} \geq 0,$$

$$\partial_k \mathbb{E}\left[X \mid \mathcal{F}_t^Z\right] = \text{Var}\left[X \mid \mathcal{F}_t^Z\right] V_{T-t}^{-1} \int_0^{T-t} e^{sK} \mathrm{d}s \geq 0.$$

Notes

1. The Paris Agreement (2016), United Nations, Framework Convention on Climate Change, October 2016. http://unfccc.int/paris_agreement/items/9485.php
2. UK Climate Action Following the Paris Agreement (2016), Committee on Climate Change, pp 17-18. https://www.theccc.org.uk/wp-content/uploads/2016/10/UK-climate-action-following-the-Paris-Agreement-Committee-on-Climate-Change-October-2016.pdf

Acknowledgments

A large part of this article was written while J. Sekine was visiting the Department of Mathematics, University College London. UCL is acknowledged for their kind hospitality. The authors are grateful to S. N. Cohen, C. A. Garcia Trillos, M. R. Grasselli and G. W. Peters for interesting discussions and suggestions, and to anonymous reviewers for feedback leading to improvements of this paper. A first version of this work, entitled Filtering with Randomised Markov Bridges, appeared on https://arxiv.org/abs/1411.1214v1.

Disclosure statement

No potential conflict of interest was reported by the authors.

Funding

A. Macrina and J. Sekine acknowledge financial support by The Daiwa Anglo-Japanese Foundation, Small Grant number 3078/12378.

References

[1] A. Azzalini and A. Capitanio, *Statistical applications of the multivariate skew normal distribution*, J. Roy. Statist. Soc. B 61 (1999), pp. 579–602.
[2] A. Azzalini and A. Capitanio, *The Skew-Normal and Related Families*, Institute of Mathematical Statistics Monographs, Cambridge University Press, Cambridge, 2013.
[3] A. Azzalini and A. Dalla Valle, *The multivariate skew-normal distribution*, Biometrika 83(4) (1996), pp. 715–726.
[4] P. Barrieu and L. Albertini, *The Handbook of Insurance-Linked Securities*, Wiley Finance, 2009. https://www.wiley.com/engb/The+Handbook+of+Insurance+Linked+Securities-p-9780470743836
[5] F. Baudoin, *Conditioned stochastic differential equations: theory, examples and application to finance*, Stochastic Process. Appl. 100 (2002), pp. 109–145.
[6] D.C. Brody, L.P. Hughston, A. Macrina, *Information-based asset pricing*. Int. J. Theor. Appl. Finance 11(1) (2008), pp. 107–142.
[7] R. Carmona, J. Hinz, *Risk-neutral models for emission allowance prices and option valuation*. Management Science 57(8) (2011), pp. 1453–1488.
[8] U. Çetin and A. Danilova, *Markov bridges: SDE representation*, Stochastic Process. Appl. 126(3) (2016), pp. 651–679.
[9] L. Chaumont and G. Uribe Bravo, *Markovian bridges: Weak continuity and pathwise constructions*, Ann. Probab. 39(2) (2011), pp. 609–647.
[10] S. Crépey, A. Macrina, M.T. Nguyen, and D. Skovmand, *Rational multi-curve models with counterparty-risk adjustments*, Quant. Finance 16(6) (2016), pp. 847–866.
[11] H. Dam, A. Macrina, D. Sloth, and D. Skovmand, Rational model for inflation-linked derivatives. Available at http://dx.doi.org/10.2139/ssrn.3110835, 2018.
[12] D. Filipović, L.P. Hughston, and A. Macrina, *Conditional density models for asset pricing*, Int. J. Theor. Appl. Finance 15(1) (2012). 1250002, 24 pp.
[13] P. Fitzsimmons, J. Pitman, and M. Yor, *Markovian bridges: Construction, palm interpretation, and splicing*, in *Seminar on Stochastic Processes, 1992. (Progress in Probability)*, Vol. 33, E. Çinlar, K.L. Chung, M.J. Sharpe, R.F. Bass, and K. Burdzy, eds., Birkhäuser, Basel, 1993, pp. 101–134.
[14] R. Gibson and E.S. Schwartz, *Stochastic convenience yield and the pricing of oil contingent claims*, J. Finance 45 (1990), pp. 959–976.
[15] A.K. Gupta, G. González-Farías, and J.A. Domínguez-Molina, *A multivariate skew normal distribution*, J. Multivariate Anal. 89 (2004), pp. 181–190.
[16] E. Hoyle, L.P. Hughston, and A. Macrina, *Lévy random bridges and the modelling of financial information*, Stochastic Process. Appl. 121 (2011), pp. 856–884.
[17] E. Hoyle, L.P. Hughston, and A. Macrina, *Stable-1/2 Bridges and Insurance*. in *Advances in Mathematics of Finance*, Banach Center Publications, Vol. 104, Institute of Mathematics, Polish Academy of Sciences, Warsaw, 2015, pp. 95–120.
[18] S. Howison and D. Schwarz, *Risk-neutral pricing of financial instruments in emission markets: A structural approach*, SIAM Rev. 57(1) (2015), pp. 95–127.
[19] A. Macrina, *Heat Kernel models for asset pricing*, Int. J. Theor. Appl. Finance 17(7) (2014), 1450048, 34 pp.
[20] P Protter, *Stochastic Integration and Differential Equations*. 2nd ed. Springer, Berlin, 2005.
[21] E.S. Schwartz, *The stochastic behavior of commodity prices: Implications for valuation and hedging*, J. Finance 52(3) (1997), pp. 923–973.

Chapter 15

MODULATED INFORMATION FLOWS IN FINANCIAL MARKETS[#]

EDWARD HOYLE

AHL Partners LLP, Man Group plc
London EC4R 3AD, United Kingdom
edward.hoyle@man.com

ANDREA MACRINA[*,†,‡] and LEVENT ALI MENGÜTÜRK[*,§]

[*]*Department of Mathematics, University College London*
London WC1E 6BT, United Kingdom

[†]*African Institute of Financial Markets and Risk Management*
University of Cape Town, Rondebosch 7701, South Africa
[‡]*a.macrina@ucl.ac.uk*
[§]*lmenguturk@gmail.com*

Received 15 April 2020
Revised 10 May 2020
Accepted 11 May 2020
Published 25 June 2020

We model continuous-time information flows generated by a number of information sources that switch on and off at random times. By modulating a multi-dimensional Lévy random bridge over a random point field, our framework relates the discovery of relevant new information sources to jumps in conditional expectation martingales. In the canonical Brownian random bridge case, we show that the underlying measure-valued process follows jump-diffusion dynamics, where the jumps are governed by information switches. The dynamic representation gives rise to a set of stochastically-linked Brownian motions on random time intervals that capture evolving information states, as well as to a state-dependent stochastic volatility evolution with jumps. The nature of information flows usually exhibits complex behavior, however, we maintain analytic tractability by introducing what we term the effective and complementary information processes, which dynamically incorporate active and inactive information, respectively. As an application, we price a financial vanilla option, which we prove is expressed by a weighted sum of option values based on the possible state configurations at expiry. This result may be viewed as an information-based analogue of Merton's option price, but where jump-diffusion arises endogenously. The proposed information flows also lend themselves to the quantification of asymmetric informational advantage among competitive agents, a feature we analyze by notions of information geometry.

Keywords: Information-based theory; jump-diffusion; point processes; stochastic volatility; asymmetric information; f-divergencies.

[‡]Corresponding author.

[#]This chapter was originally published as: E. Hoyle, A. Macrina & L. Mengütürk (2020) Modulated Information Flows in Financial Markets. *International Journal of Theoretical and Applied Finance*, **23** (4) 2050026.

E. Hoyle, A. Macrina & L. A. Mengütürk

1. Introduction

Information flows, especially in social and communication systems, usually exhibit complex structures and behaviors. Through time, not only may new information channels suddenly appear — e.g. following a new politician or a scientist on Twitter — but also some of the existing information sources may cease — e.g. an orbiting satellite stops operating or a national statistical agency stops reporting particular economic data series — and some information may only be temporarily interrupted over random periods of time. In general, if relevant information arrives gradually and continuously in time, then its impact on an observer's inference is small over short time periods. However, if important news arrives sporadically or new information sources appear at discrete points in time (e.g. a relevant data vendor becomes available to the system), then it is reasonable to expect that the impact of new information on the observer's inference is substantial. Such a view was taken in the work of Merton (1976) for financial markets, where we find: "*By its very nature, important information arrives only at discrete points in time. This component is modeled by a jump process reflecting the nonmarginal impact of the information.*" Recent examples of the new information source phenomenon in the financial markets are Elon Musk's tweet about taking Tesla private in 2018, including following announcements and developments, and the fall in the Swatch stock price when the Swiss National Bank stopped defending the EUR-CHF currency floor in January 2015. Another incident of a similar nature is the effect on Snapchat's share price following tweets by Kylie Jenner. A financial example for interrupted information is that of exchanges occasionally halting the trading of securities, following large price moves, with *circuit breakers* for stocks and *limit-up* pricing rules for commodity futures.

The general situation we keep in mind is one where observers or agents in a given system assess a signal on the basis of varying information sets, e.g. various news channels/feeds, accessible to them at any point in time. We develop a stochastic approach for information flows that can dynamically encapsulate information sources switching on and off at random times through a modulated filtration. We show that intelligence, produced on the basis of such information flows, features explicit dependence on the number and the specific information channels that are active or inactive over the course of the inference period. While the approach we develop can be applied broadly in signal processing, stochastic filtering and related fields, our main aim is to systematically and explicitly relate randomly evolving information states to price dynamics, which provides a mathematically rich avenue of possible scenarios. Another area where our framework may offer new insights is the modeling of election dynamics where modulated information flows may impact the outcome of a democratic election. Here, we refer to Brody (2019).

We give an example in financial markets on price formation, which is a complicated mechanism. Market agents will buy or sell a given asset at a given price if suitably incentivized. For market makers, the incentive may not be to profit from anticipated price changes or income, but instead to earn the bid-ask spread or commissions. Although investors often seek to profit from anticipated price changes and income, they may have other incentives to trade that are not directly linked to these, including risk management (to increase, decrease or hedge risk), an evolving mandate (such as a tightening of environmental, social and governance criteria), a change in risk aversion, and a change in wealth. However, it is commonly understood that the price of an asset should reflect the information that the market has about the asset. Consider the situation of a government considering the bailout of a bank or insurance company (the firm). The market may be aware of the firm being in financial difficulty, and this would then be reflected in the prices of the firm's stock and bonds. The market may also anticipate a government bailout. However, due to insider trading legislation, any bailout negotiations between the government and the firm may be held behind closed doors. The market cannot be sure of the bailout until an official government announcement. We can view the government's communication of a bailout with the market as new source of information, which may have certain stylized effects on prices. One such effect is an initial price correction as the market converts a bailout possibility into a certainty; a significant — and immediate — adjustment in the price. The correction is the market absorbing the totality of the private bailout negotiations in one gulp. Salient details for prices would include the bailout's anticipated size and duration. A second effect is a series of small price adjustments as the government regularly reports on the progress of its bailout. This may continue until either the firm recovers and no longer requires government assistance (loans the government has made the firm are repaid, equity the government has bought in the firm is sold), the firm is wholly taken over by the government, or the firm is allowed to fail. At this point the source of market information on the firm ceases.

In order to explicitly model the flow of information, we introduce a multivariate process — each marginal being a Lévy random bridge [LRB, see, Hoyle *et al.* (2011)] — modulated over a random point field dynamically acting on its coordinates. LRBs form a large class of stochastic processes — where Lévy processes are special cases — and the modulation allows for random activation and deactivation of the information flow. Randomized Markov bridges, which are constructed in Macrina & Sekine (2019), form a more general class of stochastic bridge processes. As a canonical subclass, we focus on Brownian random bridges (BRBs) and prove a dynamical representation for the conditional expectation process under the proposed modulated filtration, which offers a new stochastic differential equation to model price dynamics under information switches. Let X denote some square-integrable random variable (e.g. future payoff) and $(\boldsymbol{\xi}_t)_{t\in[0,T]} \in \mathbb{R}^n$ for some finite T where each $(\xi_t^{(i)})$ is an LRB with $\xi_T^{(i)} = X$ for $i = 1, \ldots, n$. Next, we choose some càdlàg jump process $(\tilde{\boldsymbol{J}}_t)_{t\in[0,T]} \in \{0,1\}^n$ associated to some random point field, and define the σ-algebra

$$\mathcal{F}_t = \sigma((\tilde{\boldsymbol{J}}_u \otimes \boldsymbol{\xi}_u)_{0\leq u\leq t}, (\tilde{\boldsymbol{J}}_u)_{0\leq u\leq t}).$$

If we introduce $\mathcal{J}_t = \{i : \tilde{J}_t^{(i)} = 1\}$, $C_t = \sum_{s\leq t} \mathbb{1}\{\tilde{\boldsymbol{J}}_s \neq \tilde{\boldsymbol{J}}_{s-}\}$ and $\pi_j = \inf\{t : C_t = j\}$, we have the following result, which we shall prove later in the paper.

Proposition 1.1. *Let $(\xi_t^{(i)})$ be a BRB for $i = 1, \ldots, n$. Then, the $(\mathcal{F}_t)$-martingale $(X_t)_{[0,T]}$ defined by $X_t := \mathbb{E}[X \mid \mathcal{F}_t]$ admits the dynamic representation*

$$X_t = \mathbb{E}[X] + \sum_{j=1}^{C_t} \left(\int_{\pi_{j-1}}^{\pi_j} \theta_s \, \mathrm{d}W_s^{(j)} \right) \mathbb{1}\{\mathcal{J}_{\pi_{j-1}} \neq \emptyset\}$$
$$+ \left(\int_{\pi_{C_t}}^{t} \theta_s \, \mathrm{d}W_s^{(C_t+1)} \right) \mathbb{1}\{\mathcal{J}_{\pi_{C_t}} \neq \emptyset\} + \sum_{s\leq t} \Delta X_s,$$

for $t < T$, where $(W_t^{(j)})$ for $j = 1, \ldots, C_t + 1$ is a one-dimensional standard $(\mathcal{F}_t)$-Brownian motion between jump times, (θ_t) is an $(\mathcal{F}_t)$-adapted process, and $\Delta X_t \neq 0$ if and only if $\mathcal{J}_t \backslash \mathcal{J}_{t-} \neq \emptyset$.

Thus, a welcome consequence of our approach is an information-based *endogenous* jump-diffusion model with state-dependent stochastic volatility dynamics, arising naturally from the proposed information system. In this sense, we also extend Brody *et al.* (2008a,b, 2009, 2011), Hughston & Macrina (2008) and Rutkowski & Yu (2007), which employ special properties of Brownian bridges [see Emery & Yor (2004) and Fitzsimmons *et al.* (1993)]. We shall also show that the processes $(W_t^{(j)})$ above are stochastically-linked, where their dependence is dynamically controlled by $(\mathcal{J}_t)$.

The modulation framework enables us to derive a Feynman–Kać representation of the conditional expectation, gives an alternative expression for its jump-sizes, and extends Proposition 1.1 to the case of multiple random point fields. We associate these random point fields with projection-valued stochastic processes to construct a more general information system, which may incorporate a wide range of complex behavior, such as what we term *information mixing*. By use of concepts in information geometry, we highlight how the impact of new information sources can be quantified from a geometrical perspective, which later allows for the modeling of information asymmetry. We also provide an analytical expression for the price of a vanilla option under the modulated filtration, as an information-based analogue of the price obtained by Merton (1976) that admits a much broader class of random counting measures dictating price jumps.

We highlight the fact that we do not need to introduce jumps into the information flow by embedding discontinuous noise into individual information processes. In the BRB case, the jumps arise due to the discovery of *new* information sources, even if BRBs have a *continuous* state-space. This has different and rather important implications on the dynamics of (X_t), as opposed to including independent discontinuous noise with no information content on X. First, jumps are caused by random changes in the number of active information sources; hence, jumps carry information about X. Second, the continuous part of (X_t) is driven by different Brownian

Modulated Information Flows in Financial Markets

motions on random time intervals that capture the possible state-configurations of the information flow. Third, since the volatility process also jumps and is state-dependent, the framework offers a link to regime-switching models; see Bollen *et al.* (2000), Hamilton (1989) and Naik (1993). Fourth, the undiscounted price process may remain constant for periods of time if all information sources are "lost", which perhaps could be viewed as a model for certain features arising in illiquid markets or circuit breakers. Fifth, the proposed framework offers links to progressive enlargements of filtrations and stopped filtrations.

2. Modulated Information Processes

Let $(\Omega, \mathcal{G}, (\mathcal{G}_t)_{t\geq 0}, \mathbb{P})$ be a probability space equipped with a filtration $(\mathcal{G}_t)$. All filtrations considered are assumed to be right-continuous and complete. We introduce a random variable $X \in \mathcal{L}^2(\Omega, \mathcal{G}, \mathbb{P})$ with law ν and state-space $(\mathbb{X}, \mathcal{B}(\mathbb{X}))$, where we assume $\mathbb{X} \subseteq \mathbb{R}$. We consider the time interval $\mathbb{T} = [0, 1]$ — and the set $\mathbb{T}_* = [0, 1)$ — though it is straightforward to consider a compact interval $[0, T]$ for $T < \infty$, instead. We let $(\boldsymbol{L}_t)_{t\geq 0}$ be a multivariate Lévy process taking values in $\mathbb{R}^n$ for $n \in \mathbb{N}_+$, with mutually independent coordinates (also independent of X) such that each $\{L_t^{(i)}\}_{i=1,\dots,n}$ has density $0 < f_t < \infty$ for all $t \in (0, 1]$. We assume ν concentrates mass where f_1 is positive and finite ν-a.s. Next, we introduce a $(\mathcal{G}_t)$-adapted multivariate stochastic process $(\boldsymbol{\xi}_t)_{t\in\mathbb{T}}$ taking values in $\mathbb{R}^n$, where each marginal $(\xi_t^{(i)})$ for $i = 1, \dots, n$ is a Lévy random bridge (LRB) satisfying: (i) $\xi_1^{(i)} = X$, (ii) for all $m \in \mathbb{N}_+$, every $0 < t_1 < \cdots < t_m < 1$, every $(y_1, \dots, y_m) \in \mathbb{R}^m$, and ν-a.e. x,

$$\mathbb{P}(\xi_{t_1}^{(i)} \leq y_1^{(i)}, \dots, \xi_{t_m}^{(i)} \leq y_m^{(i)} \,|\, \xi_1^{(i)} = x) = \mathbb{P}(L_{t_1}^{(i)} \leq y_1^{(i)}, \dots, L_{t_m}^{(i)} \leq y_m^{(i)} \,|\, L_1^{(i)} = x),$$

for $i = 1, \dots, n$. We denote the conditional measure as $g(x, y, t)\mathrm{d}y = \mathbb{P}(\xi_t^{(i)} \in \mathrm{d}y \,|\, \xi_1^{(i)} = x)$ when it exists. The finite-dimensional distribution of each $(\xi_t^{(i)})$ is

$$\begin{aligned}
&\mathbb{P}(\xi_{t_1}^{(i)} \in \mathrm{d}y_1, \dots, \xi_{t_m}^{(i)} \in \mathrm{d}y_m, \xi_1^{(i)} \in \mathrm{d}x) \\
&\quad = \prod_{i=1}^{m} (f_{t_i - t_{i-1}}(y_i - y_{i-1})\mathrm{d}y_i) \frac{f_{1-t_m}(x - y_m)}{f_1(x)} \nu(\mathrm{d}x).
\end{aligned}$$

The distributions of LRBs with discrete state-spaces can similarly be written using their probability mass functions. We note that LRBs are constructed in Hoyle *et al.* (2011) where, aside the development of the theory, applications in finance are discussed. In what follows, we use $(\boldsymbol{\xi}_t)$ to model information flows on X. Note that X can be any square-integrable random variable and can be modeled (and simulated) independently from the chosen Lévy process. For example, let $F : \mathcal{D}([0, 1], \mathbb{R}) \to \mathbb{R}$ be a functional from the Skorokhod space $\mathcal{D}([0, 1], \mathbb{R})$ to the real line. Then, for some real-valued semimartingale (S_t) adapted to $(\mathcal{G}_t)$, we can define $X = F((S_u); 0 \leq u \leq 1)$ as a model for a path-dependent signal.

E. Hoyle, A. Macrina & L. A. Mengütürk

Next, we introduce a mechanism for the activation and deactivation of information sources. Let ζ be a random point field (a point process) on $\mathbb{T}^n$, independent of $(\boldsymbol{\xi}_t)$, generating a collection of times $\{\varpi_1^i, \ldots, \varpi_{k_i}^i\}$ for $i \in \{1, \ldots, n\}$ and finite $k_i \in \mathbb{N}_0$. For every i, we associate the random sequence $\{\varpi_1^i, \ldots, \varpi_{k_i}^i\}$ to a coordinate of a $(\mathcal{G}_t)$-adapted càdlàg jump process $(\tilde{\boldsymbol{J}}_t)$ with state space $\mathbb{S} = \{0,1\}^n$. We then define the $\mathbb{R}^{n\times n}$-valued process $(\boldsymbol{J}_t)$ by $J_t^{(i,j)} = \delta_{ij}\tilde{\boldsymbol{J}}_t$. Thus, $(\boldsymbol{J}_t)$ is a diagonal matrix-valued process indicating which coordinates of $(\boldsymbol{\xi}_t)$ are active through the modulated information process $(\boldsymbol{J}_t\,\boldsymbol{\xi}_t)$. When the ith information source is inactive, the ith coordinate of $(\boldsymbol{J}_t\,\boldsymbol{\xi}_t)$ is identically zero. We define a sub-algebra $\mathcal{F}_t \subseteq \mathcal{G}_t$ by

$$\mathcal{F}_t = \sigma((\tilde{\boldsymbol{J}}_u \otimes \boldsymbol{\xi}_u)_{0\le u\le t}, (\tilde{\boldsymbol{J}}_u)_{0\le u\le t}, X\mathbb{1}_{\{t=1\}}),$$

for $t \in \mathbb{T}$. Surely, we can write $\mathcal{F}_t = \sigma((\boldsymbol{J}_u\,\boldsymbol{\xi}_u)_{0\le u\le t}, (\boldsymbol{J}_u)_{0\le u\le t}, X\mathbb{1}_{\{t=1\}})$. The reason why we diagonalize $(\tilde{\boldsymbol{J}}_t)$ will be clear later in Sec. 2.3. Also note that we add $X\mathbb{1}_{\{t=1\}}$ to the filtration to ensure that its value is revealed at $t = 1$, even though all information may be inactive at $t = 1$. This is not a mathematical requirement; if an envisaged application does not need X to be (fully) observed at $t = 1$, then $X\mathbb{1}_{\{t=1\}}$ may be excluded from the algebra $\mathcal{F}_t$. In the remainder of this paper, we shall omit it from the expressions unless necessary.

Remark 2.1. Define $\mathcal{F}_t^* = \sigma((\tilde{\boldsymbol{J}}_u \otimes \boldsymbol{\xi}_u)_{0\le u\le t}, X\mathbb{1}_{\{t=1\}})$, hence, $\mathcal{F}_t^* \subseteq \mathcal{F}_t$. The $(\mathcal{F}_t)$-adapted switching process $(\tilde{\boldsymbol{J}}_t)$ is also $(\mathcal{F}_t^*)$-adapted if and only if $(\boldsymbol{\xi}_t)$ is continuous and $\mathbb{P}[\xi_t^{(i)} = 0] = 0$ for all $i \in \{1, \ldots, n\}$ for $t \in (0, 1]$.

Hence, the individual appearance of $(\tilde{\boldsymbol{J}}_t)$ in the definition of $\mathcal{F}_t$ is not superfluous given that the framework allows the coordinate $(\xi_t^{(i)})$ to be a jump process or such that $0 < \mathbb{P}[\xi_t^{(i)} = 0] < 1$, for some $i \in \{1, \ldots, n\}$ and $t \in \mathbb{T}$. In these cases, it may not be possible to detect the (de)activation of a particular information coordinate if $(\tilde{\boldsymbol{J}}_t)$ is not $(\mathcal{F}_t)$-adapted.

At time $t \in \mathbb{T}$, we denote the last time that the ith information source was active by $\tau_t^{(i)}$. That is, we define

$$\tau_t^{(i)} = 0 \vee \sup\{u : J_u^{(i,i)} = 1, u \in [0,t]\},$$

for $i = 1, \ldots, n$, where we adopt the convention that $\sup\emptyset = -\infty$. Thus, the process $(\tau_t^{(i)})$ is increasing and progressively measurable with respect to $(\mathcal{F}_t)$, and if the ith process has never been active up until time t, then $\tau_t^{(i)} = 0$. Also, by definition, the initial condition is $\tau_0^{(i)} = 0$ whether $J_0^{(i,i)} = 0$ or $J_0^{(i,i)} = 1$.

Proposition 2.1. *The dynamics of* $(\tau_t^{(i)})$ *for* $t \in \mathbb{T}$ *are given by*

$$\mathrm{d}\tau_t^{(i)} = J_t^{(i,i)}\mathrm{d}t + (t - \tau_{t-}^{(i)})\mathrm{d}J_t^{(i,i)}.$$

Proof. Per coordinate i, the dynamics of $(\tau_t^{(i)})$ can be decomposed into its continuous and discontinuous parts, where $\mathrm{d}J_t^{(i,i)} = 0$ or $\mathrm{d}J_t^{(i,i)} = 1$, respectively. Given that $(J_t^{(i,i)})$ has state-space $\{0,1\}$, we have $\tau_t^{(i)} = t$ whenever $J_t^{(i,i)} = 1$ and $\tau_t^{(i)} < t$

Modulated Information Flows in Financial Markets

whenever $J_t^{(i,i)} = 0$. Hence, for the continuous part, when $J_t^{(i)} = 1$, $\mathrm{d}\tau_t^{(i)} = \mathrm{d}t$, and when $J_t^{(i,i)} = 0$, $\mathrm{d}\tau_t^{(i)} = 0$. As for the discontinuous part, just before a jump, if $J_{t-}^{(i,i)} = 1$, then $\mathrm{d}\tau_t^{(i)} = \mathrm{d}t$ since $\tau_{t-}^{(i)} = t$. If just before a jump, $J_{t-}^{(i,i)} = 0$, then $\mathrm{d}\tau_t^{(i)} = (t - t^*)$ given that $\tau_{t-}^{(i)} = t^*$ for some $t^* < t$ and $\tau_t^{(i)} = t$. □

For our purposes, we shall prove that the conditional distribution of X given $\mathcal{F}_t$ can be determined through time-changed LRBs.

Proposition 2.2. *Let $\xi^{(i)}(u)$ be the value of $(\xi_t^{(i)})$ at $u \in \mathbb{T}$.*

(1) *For any $A \in \mathcal{B}(\mathbb{X})$ and $t_i \in \mathbb{T}_*$,*

$$\mathbb{P}[X \in A \,|\, \{(\xi_s^{(i)})_{0\le s\le t_i}\}_{i=1,\ldots,n}] = \mathbb{P}[X \in A \,|\, \{\xi^{(i)}(t_i)\}_{i=1,\ldots,n}].$$

(2) *The sigma-algebra $\mathcal{F}_t$ for any $t \in \mathbb{T}$ is equal to*

$$\mathcal{F}_t = \sigma(\{(\xi^{(i)}(\tau_u^{(i)}))_{0\le u\le t}\}_{i=1,\ldots,n}, (\boldsymbol{J}_u)_{0\le u\le t}, X\mathbb{1}_{\{t=1\}}).$$

Proof. For the first part, for $t < 1$, it is sufficient to show that

$$\begin{aligned}&\mathbb{P}[X \in \mathrm{d}x_0 \,|\, \xi_{t_{1,1}}^{(1)} = x_{1,1}, \ldots, \xi_{t_{1,k_1}}^{(1)} = x_{1,k_1}, \ldots, \xi_{t_{n,1}}^{(n)} = x_{n,1}, \ldots, \xi_{t_{n,k_n}}^{(n)} = x_{n,k_n}]\\ &\quad = \mathbb{P}[X \in \mathrm{d}x_0 \,|\, \xi_{t_{1,k_1}}^{(1)} = x_{1,k_1}, \ldots, \xi_{t_{n,k_n}}^{(n)} = x_{n,k_n}],\end{aligned}$$

for all $k_i \in \mathbb{N}_+$ where $i \in \{1, \ldots, n\}$, all $0 < t_{i,1} < \cdots < t_{i,k_i} < 1$, and all $(x_{i,1}, \ldots, x_{i,k_i}) \in \mathbb{R}^n$. We have

$$\begin{aligned}&\mathbb{P}[X \in \mathrm{d}x_0 \,|\, \xi_{t_{1,1}}^{(1)} = x_{1,1}, \ldots, \xi_{t_{1,k_1}}^{(1)} = x_{1,k_1}, \ldots, \xi_{t_{n,1}}^{(n)} = x_{n,1}, \ldots, \xi_{t_{n,k_n}}^{(n)} = x_{n,k_n}]\\ &\quad = \frac{\mathbb{P}\left[\bigcap_{i=1}^{n}\bigcap_{j=1}^{k_i} \xi_{t_{i,j}}^{(i)} \in \mathrm{d}x_{i,j} \,\middle|\, X = x_0\right]\mathbb{P}[X \in \mathrm{d}x_0]}{\int_{\mathbb{X}} \mathbb{P}\left[\bigcap_{i=1}^{n}\bigcap_{j=1}^{k_i} \xi_{t_{i,j}}^{(i)} \in \mathrm{d}x_{i,j} \,\middle|\, X = x_0\right]\mathbb{P}[X \in \mathrm{d}x_0]}\\ &\quad = \frac{\prod_{i=1}^{n}\mathbb{P}\left[\bigcap_{j=1}^{k_i} \xi_{t_{i,j}}^{(i)} \in \mathrm{d}x_{i,j} \,\middle|\, X = x_0\right]\mathbb{P}[X \in \mathrm{d}x_0]}{\int_{\mathbb{X}} \prod_{i=1}^{n}\mathbb{P}\left[\bigcap_{j=1}^{k_i} \xi_{t_{i,j}}^{(i)} \in \mathrm{d}x_{i,j} \,\middle|\, X = x_0\right]\mathbb{P}[X \in \mathrm{d}x_0]}.\end{aligned}$$

Given X, each coordinate process $(\xi_t^{(i)})$ is a Lévy bridge. It follows that

$$\mathbb{P}\left[\bigcap_{j=1}^{k_i} \xi_{t_{i,j}}^{(i)} \in \mathrm{d}x_{i,j} \,\middle|\, X = x_0\right]$$

$$= \frac{f_{1-t_{i,k_i}}(x_0 - x_{i,k_i})}{f_1(x_0)} \prod_{j=1}^{k_i} f_{t_{i,j}-t_{i,j-1}}(x_{i,j} - x_{i,j-1})\mathrm{d}x_{i,j},$$

where $f_t(x)$ is the marginal density function of the underlying Lévy process.

Hence, we have the following:

$$\mathbb{P}[X \in \mathrm{d}x_0 \,|\, \xi_{t_{1,1}}^{(1)} = x_{1,1}, \ldots, \xi_{t_{1,k_1}}^{(1)} = x_{1,k_1}, \ldots, \xi_{t_{n,1}}^{(n)} = x_{n,1}, \ldots, \xi_{t_{n,k_n}}^{(n)} = x_{n,k_n}]$$

$$= \frac{\displaystyle\prod_{i=1}^{n} \frac{f_{1-t_{i,k_i}}(x_0 - x_{i,k_i})}{f_1(x_0)} f_{t_{i,k_i}}(x_{i,k_i})\,\nu(\mathrm{d}x_0)}{\displaystyle\int_{\mathbb{X}} \prod_{i=1}^{n} \frac{f_{1-t_{i,k_i}}(x_0 - x_{i,k_i})}{f_1(x_0)} f_{t_{i,k_i}}(x_{i,k_i})\,\nu(\mathrm{d}x_0)}$$

$$= \frac{\displaystyle\prod_{i=1}^{n} \mathbb{P}[\xi_{t_{i,k_i}}^{(i)} \in \mathrm{d}x_{i,k_i} \,|\, X = x_0]\mathbb{P}[X \in \mathrm{d}x_0]}{\displaystyle\int_{\mathbb{X}} \prod_{i=1}^{n} \mathbb{P}[\xi_{t_{i,k_i}}^{(i)} \in \mathrm{d}x_{i,k_i} \,|\, X = x_0]\mathbb{P}[X \in \mathrm{d}x_0]}$$

$$= \frac{\mathbb{P}\left[\bigcap_{i=1}^{n} \xi_{t_{i,k_i}}^{(i)} \in \mathrm{d}x_{i,k_i} \,\middle|\, X = x_0\right]\mathbb{P}[X \in \mathrm{d}x_0]}{\displaystyle\int_{\mathbb{X}} \mathbb{P}\left[\bigcap_{i=1}^{n} \xi_{t_{i,k_i}}^{(i)} \in \mathrm{d}x_{i,k_i} \,\middle|\, X = x_0\right]\mathbb{P}[X \in \mathrm{d}x_0]}$$

$$= \mathbb{P}[X \in \mathrm{d}x \,|\, \xi_{t_{1,k_1}}^{(1)} = x_{1,k_1}, \ldots, \xi_{t_{n,k_n}}^{(n)} = x_{n,k_n}].$$

For the second part, if $\mathbb{P}[\xi_t^{(i)} = 0] = 0$ for any $t \in (0,1]$, the coordinate $(J_t^{(i,i)}\xi_t^{(i)})$ and $(\xi^{(i)}(\tau_t^{(i)}))$ differ only when the ith source is inactive, during which the coordinate process is zero, and $(\xi^{(i)}(\tau_t^{(i)}))$ takes the source's last active value. The statement holds directly for the complementary case where $\mathbb{P}[\xi_t^{(i)} = 0] > 0$ for any $t \in (0,1]$. □

Proposition 2.3. *The $\mathcal{F}_t$-conditional distribution of X is given by*

$$\mathbb{P}[X \in \mathrm{d}x \,|\, \mathcal{F}_t] = \frac{\displaystyle\prod_i g(x, \xi^{(i)}(\tau_t^{(i)}), \tau_t^{(i)})\nu(\mathrm{d}x)}{\displaystyle\int_{\mathbb{X}} \prod_i g(x, \xi^{(i)}(\tau_t^{(i)}), \tau_t^{(i)})\nu(\mathrm{d}x)},$$

for $t \in \mathbb{T}_*$ given that $g(x,y,t)$ exists.

Modulated Information Flows in Financial Markets

Proof. First, we note that, for $t_i \in \mathbb{T}_*$ and $i = 1, \ldots, n$, using the mutual independence of $L_t^{(i)}$s for $i = 1, \ldots, n$, we have

$$\mathbb{P}[X \in \mathrm{d}x | \{\xi_{t_i}^{(i)}\}_{i=1,\ldots,n}] = \frac{\prod_{i=1}^{n} g(x, \xi_{t_i}^{(i)}, t_i)\nu(\mathrm{d}x)}{\int_{\mathbb{X}} \prod_{i=1}^{n} g(x, \xi_{t_i}^{(i)}, t_i)\nu(\mathrm{d}x)}. \tag{2.1}$$

For the computation of the conditional distribution $\mathbb{P}[X \in \mathrm{d}x \,|\, \mathcal{F}_t]$, the first step is to use $\{\xi^{(i)}(\tau_t^{(i)})\}_{i=1,\ldots,n}$ to enlarge the information set we are conditioning on, and then to apply the tower property. We here refer to Proposition 2.2.

$$\mathbb{P}[X \in \mathrm{d}x \,|\, \mathcal{F}_t] = \mathbb{E}[\mathbb{P}[X \in \mathrm{d}x | \{(\xi_s^{(i)})_{0 \le s \le \tau_t^{(i)}}\}_{i=1,\ldots,n}, \mathcal{F}_t] \,|\, \mathcal{F}_t].$$

The σ-algebra $\mathcal{F}_t$ contains the history $(\boldsymbol{J}_s)_{0 \le s \le t}$, which tells up to what time t_i the information coordinates $\{\xi^{(i)}(\tau_s^{(i)})_{0 \le s \le t_i}\}_{i=1,\ldots,n}$ have been active. Thus once the stopping times $\{\tau_t^{(i)}\}_{i=1,\ldots,n}$ have occurred, one knows that $(\xi^{(i)}(\tau_t^{(i)})) = (\xi_s^{(i)})_{0 \le s \le t_i}$ for $\tau_t^{(i)} = t_i \le t$. Therefore, we may apply Proposition 2.2 to obtain

$$\begin{aligned}
&\mathbb{E}[\mathbb{P}[X \in \mathrm{d}x \,|\, \{(\xi_s^{(i)})_{0 \le s \le \tau_t^{(i)}}\}_{i=1,\ldots,n}, \mathcal{F}_t] \,|\, \mathcal{F}_t] \\
&\quad = \mathbb{E}[\mathbb{P}[X \in \mathrm{d}x \,|\, \{\xi^{(i)}(\tau_t^{(i)})\}_{i=1,\ldots,n}, \mathcal{F}_t] \,|\, \mathcal{F}_t].
\end{aligned}$$

By use of Eq. (2.1) and $\mathcal{F}_t$-measurability, it follows that

$$\begin{aligned}
\mathbb{P}[X \in \mathrm{d}x \,|\, \mathcal{F}_t] &= \mathbb{E}[\mathbb{P}[X \in \mathrm{d}x \,|\, \{\xi^{(i)}(\tau_t^{(i)})\}_{i=1,\ldots,n}, \mathcal{F}_t] \,|\, \mathcal{F}_t] \\
&= \frac{\prod_{i=1}^{n} g(x, \xi^{(i)}(\tau_t^{(i)}), \tau_t^{(i)})\nu(\mathrm{d}x)}{\int_{\mathbb{X}} \prod_{i=1}^{n} g(x, \xi^{(i)}(\tau_t^{(i)}), \tau_t^{(i)})\nu(\mathrm{d}x)},
\end{aligned}$$

for $t_i \in \mathbb{T}_*$ and $i = 1, \ldots, n$, which gives the statement. □

We can view the appearance of new sources of information from a Hilbert space perspective. We let $\langle \cdot \rangle$ be the inner product on the Hilbert space of square-integrable functions $\mathcal{L}^2(\mathbb{G})$ on a measurable set $\mathbb{G} \subset \mathbb{R}^2$, such that $v, w \in \mathcal{L}^2(\mathbb{G})$ are orthogonal if $\langle v, w \rangle = 0$, and where

$$\mathcal{L}^2(\mathbb{G}) = \bigoplus_{i=1}^{n+1} \mathcal{L}_i^2(\mathbb{G}),$$

where $\mathcal{L}_i^2(\mathbb{G})$ and $\mathcal{L}_j^2(\mathbb{G})$ are mutually orthogonal closed subspaces of $\mathcal{L}^2(\mathbb{G})$ for $i \neq j$, such that any function in $\mathcal{L}^2(\mathbb{G})$ can uniquely be represented by the sum of its projections onto the subspaces $\mathcal{L}_i^2(\mathbb{G})$ for $i = 1, \ldots, n+1$ that span $\mathcal{L}^2(\mathbb{G})$.

As an example, we choose ζ on $\mathbb{T}^n$ such that $k_i = 1$ for all $i = 1, \ldots, n$ and the set of random times is reduced to $\{\varpi_1^i : i = 1, \ldots, n\}$, where we have an

E. Hoyle, A. Macrina & L. A. Mengütürk

ordered collection $0 < \varpi_1^{\pi(1)} < \cdots < \varpi_1^{\pi(i)} < \cdots < \varpi_1^{\pi(n)} < \infty$, given that π is the permutation on the coordinates of $(\tilde{\boldsymbol{J}}_t)$ that produces this order. Letting $H_\alpha(t) = \mathbf{1}(\alpha \le t)$, and denoting $\varpi_1^{\pi(0)} = 0$, we define an $n+1$ vector $\{\boldsymbol{I}\}_{0 \le t \le 1}$ by

$$\boldsymbol{I}_t = [1 - H_{\varpi_1^{\pi(1)}}(t), \ldots, H_{\varpi_1^{\pi(i-1)}}(t)(1 - H_{\varpi_1^{\pi(i)}}(t)), \ldots, H_{\varpi_1^{\pi(n)}}(t)]^\top.$$

We assume that X has a density, where we write $p(x \,|\, \mathcal{F}_t)\mathrm{d}x = \mathbb{P}[X \in \mathrm{d}x \,|\, \mathcal{F}_t]$ for $0 \le t < 1$. Note that if $\hat{p}_t(x) = \sqrt{p(x \,|\, \mathcal{F}_t)}$ for $0 \le t < 1$, then $\hat{p} \in \mathcal{L}^2(\mathbb{X} \times \mathbb{T}_*)$. Also, we let $p_t^{(0)} = \sqrt{p(x)}$ and the sequence

$$p_t^{(i)}(x) = \sqrt{p(x \,|\, \xi_t^{(\pi(1))}, \ldots, \xi_t^{(\pi(i))})},$$

for $i = 1, \ldots, n$. Hence, $p_t^{(1)}(x) = p(x \,|\, \xi_t^{(\pi(1))})^{\frac{1}{2}}$, $p_t^{(2)}(x) = p(x \,|\, \xi_t^{(\pi(1))}, \xi_t^{(\pi(2))})^{\frac{1}{2}}$, etc. and $p^{(i)} \in \mathcal{L}^2(\mathbb{X} \times \mathbb{T}_*)$ for $i = 0, \ldots, n$. We let the disjoint sets $\mathbb{T}_i$, for $i = 0, \ldots, n$ be such that $\mathbb{T}_0 = \{t \in \mathbb{T}_* : t < \varpi_1^{\pi(1)}\}$, $\mathbb{T}_i = \{t \in \mathbb{T}_* : \varpi_1^{\pi(i)} \le t < \varpi_1^{\pi(i+1)}\}$ for $i = 1, \ldots, n-1$, and $\mathbb{T}_n = \{t \in \mathbb{T}_* : \varpi_1^{\pi(n)} \le t\}$. Finally, for the next statement, we define the measurable function $\widehat{\phi}^{(i)} \in \mathcal{L}^2(\mathbb{X} \times \mathbb{T}_*)$ for $i = 0, \ldots, n$ by

$$\widehat{\phi}_t^{(i)}(x) = \begin{cases} p_t^{(i)}(x) & \text{if } t \in \mathbb{T}_i, \\ 0 & \text{otherwise.} \end{cases}$$

Proposition 2.4. *Let $\hat{p}_t(x) = p(x \,|\, \mathcal{F}_t)^{\frac{1}{2}}$ as defined above. Then,*

$$\hat{p} = \widehat{\phi}^{(0)} + \cdots + \widehat{\phi}^{(n)}.$$

Hence, $p(x \,|\, \mathcal{F}_t) = (p_t^{(0)}(x))^2 \boldsymbol{I}_t^{(1)} + \cdots + (p_t^{(n)}(x))^2 \boldsymbol{I}_t^{(n+1)}$.

Proof. Using Propositions 2.2 and 2.3, we can rewrite $\widehat{\phi}^{(i)} \in \mathcal{L}^2(\mathbb{X} \times \mathbb{T}_*)$ as

$$\widehat{\phi}_t^{(i)}(x) = \begin{cases} \sqrt{p(x \,|\, \mathcal{F}_t)} & \text{if } t \in \mathbb{T}_i, \\ 0 & \text{otherwise,} \end{cases}$$

for $i = 0, \ldots, n$. Thus, having $\mathbb{T}_* = \bigcup_{i=0}^n \mathbb{T}_i$, and $\mathbb{G} = \mathbb{X} \times \mathbb{T}_*$ as the domain of the measurable functions $\hat{p}$ and $p^{(i)}$ for $i = 0, \ldots, n$, we can consider the orthogonal decomposition

$$\mathcal{L}^2(\mathbb{X} \times \mathbb{T}_*) = \bigoplus_{i=1}^{n+1} \mathcal{L}_i^2(\mathbb{X} \times \mathbb{T}_*),$$

where $\widehat{\phi}^{(i)} \in \mathcal{L}_{i+1}^2(\mathbb{X} \times \mathbb{T}_*)$ for $i = 0, \ldots, n$. Hence, $\langle \widehat{\phi}^{(i)}, \widehat{\phi}^{(j)} \rangle = 0$ for $i \ne j$ on $\mathbb{X} \times \mathbb{T}_*$, and we have the first part of the statement. The second part follows directly since $\mathbf{I}_t^{(i)} \mathbf{I}_t^{(j)} = 0$ for $i \ne j$ and $\mathbf{I}_t^{(i)} \mathbf{I}_t^{(i)} = \mathbf{I}_t(i)$ for $i = 1, \ldots, n+1$. □

Since each $\phi_t^{(i)}(x)$ takes values in $\mathbb{R}$ for $i = 0, \ldots, n$ and $x \in \mathbb{X}$, we can as well work with any Hilbert space $\mathcal{H}$ isomorphic to $\mathbb{R}^{n+1}$, and canonically represent $\hat{p}$ as

Modulated Information Flows in Financial Markets

an $(n+1)$-tuple in $\mathbb{R}^{n+1}$, and write $\mathbf{I}(i) = e_i = [0, \ldots, 1, \ldots, 0]^\top$ for $i = 1, \ldots, n+1$. Thus, for $\mathcal{H} \cong \mathbb{R}^{n+1}$, since $e_i \in \mathcal{H}$ forms a complete orthonormal sequence for $i = 1, \ldots, n+1$, we have

$$\hat{p} = \sum_{i=1}^{n+1} \langle \hat{p}, e_i \rangle e_i = \sum_{i=1}^{n+1} p^{(i-1)} e_i,$$

and hence, $p^{(i)}$'s for $i = 0, \ldots, n$ are the Fourier coefficients of $\hat{p}$. The insight gained from the Hilbert space brings forth a geometrical interpretation. The function $\hat{p}$ is a nonnegative function, and for a fixed time t, the integral of the square of $\hat{p}_t$ on $\mathbb{X}$ is unity. Thus, $\hat{p}_t$ determines a point on the positive orthant of the unit sphere $\mathcal{S}^+ \subset \mathcal{L}^2$, where the geodesics between $p^{(i)}$s and $p^{(j)}$s for $i \neq j$ are the circles on the Riemannian manifold $(\mathcal{S}^+, \langle \cdot \rangle)$. Note that here, $p^{(i)}$ and $p^{(j)}$ are defined in terms of i and j number of active information sources, respectively.

Remark 2.2. The nonmarginal impact of a new information source can be measured by the spherical distance between the Fourier coefficients $p^{(i)}$ and $p^{(i+1)}$ for $i = 0, \ldots, n-1$ on $\mathcal{S}^+$.

2.1. *Endogenous jump-diffusion*

We focus on a canonical case where $(L_t^{(i)})$ is a Brownian motion such that $L_t^{(i)} \sim \mathcal{N}(0, \sigma_i^2 t)$ for some $\sigma_i > 0$, for $i = 1, \ldots, n$. The reason is two-fold: (i) the Brownian case provides valuable analytical tractability in deriving dynamic representations, (ii) we explicitly show how conditional expectation martingales may exhibit jumps even if $(\boldsymbol{\xi}_t)$ is a continuous process.

Corollary 2.1. *Let $(\boldsymbol{L}_t)_{0 \leq t}$ be a multivariate Brownian motion such that $L_t^{(i)} \sim \mathcal{N}(0, \sigma_i^2 t)$ for $\sigma_i > 0$. Then,*

$$\mathbb{P}[X \in \mathrm{d}x \mid \mathcal{F}_t] = \frac{\prod_i h(x, \xi^{(i)}(\tau_t^{(i)}), \tau_t^{(i)}, \sigma_i) \nu(\mathrm{d}x)}{\int_{\mathbb{X}} \prod_i h(x, \xi^{(i)}(\tau_t^{(i)}), \tau_t^{(i)}, \sigma_i) \nu(\mathrm{d}x)},$$

for $t \in \mathbb{T}_*$, where the transformation $h: \mathbb{R} \times \mathbb{R} \times \mathbb{T}_* \times \mathbb{R}_+ \to \mathbb{R}_+$ is the Gaussian map given by $h(x, y, t, \sigma) = \exp\{(xy - tx^2/2)/(\sigma^2(1-t))\}$.

Proof. Since $L_t^{(i)} \sim \mathcal{N}(0, \sigma_i^2 t)$ is a Brownian motion for some $\sigma_i > 0$, we can write $\xi_t^{(i)} = tX + \sigma_i \beta_t^{(i)}$ for $i = 1, \ldots, n$, where $(\beta_t^{(i)})_{0 \leq t \leq 1}$ is a standard Brownian bridge; a Gaussian process with mean function identically zero, and covariance function $(s, t) \mapsto \min[s, t] - st$, for $s, t \in \mathbb{T}$. This anticipative representation holds since (i) $\xi_1^{(i)}$ has marginal law ν, and (ii) for all $m \in \mathbb{N}_+$, every $0 < t_1 < \cdots < t_m < 1$, every $(y_1, \ldots, y_m) \in \mathbb{R}^m$, and ν-a.e. x, $\mathbb{P}(\xi_{t_1}^{(i)} \in \mathrm{d}y_1^{(i)}, \ldots, \xi_{t_m}^{(i)} \in \mathrm{d}y_m^{(i)} \mid \xi_1^{(i)} = x) = \mathbb{P}(L_{t_1}^{(i)} \in \mathrm{d}y_1^{(i)}, \ldots, L_{t_m}^{(i)} \in \mathrm{d}y_m^{(i)} \mid L_1^{(i)} = x)$. Given that X and the Brownian bridges

E. Hoyle, A. Macrina & L. A. Mengütürk

$\{(\beta_t^{(i)})\}_{i=1,\ldots,n}$, are mutually independent,

$$\mathbb{P}[X \in \mathrm{d}x|\,\{\xi_{t_i}^{(i)}\}_{i=1,\ldots,n}] = \frac{\prod_{i=1}^{n} \exp\left[-\frac{1}{2}\left(\frac{\xi_{t_i}^{(i)} - t_i x}{\sigma_i\sqrt{t_i(1-t_i)}}\right)^2\right]\nu(\mathrm{d}x)}{\int_{\mathbb{X}}\prod_{i=1}^{n} \exp\left[-\frac{1}{2}\left(\frac{\xi_{t_i}^{(i)} - t_i x}{\sigma_i\sqrt{t_i(1-t_i)}}\right)^2\right]\nu(\mathrm{d}x)}$$

$$= \frac{\prod_{i=1}^{n} \exp\left(\frac{x\xi_{t_i}^{(i)} - \frac{t_i x^2}{2}}{\sigma_i^2(1-t_i)}\right)\nu(\mathrm{d}x)}{\int_{\mathbb{X}}\prod_{i=1}^{n} \exp\left(\frac{x\xi_{t_i}^{(i)} - \frac{t_i x^2}{2}}{\sigma_i^2(1-t_i)}\right)\nu(\mathrm{d}x)}.$$

The rest of the proof follows that of Proposition 2.3. □

Accordingly, unless stated otherwise, we shall set $\xi_t^{(i)} = tX + \sigma_i\beta_t^{(i)}$ for $i = 1,\ldots,n$. For $t \in (0,1)$, $\xi_t^{(i)}/t$ is equal to X plus some independent Gaussian noise with variance $\sigma_i^2(1-t)/t$, and $\xi_1^{(i)} = X$, $i = 1,\ldots,n$. This functional form is also natural from the standpoint of stochastic filtering. If there were linear dependence (with nonsingular covariation) between $\{(\beta_t^{(i)})\}_{i=1,\ldots,n}$, then there would exist a linear transformation of $(\boldsymbol{\xi}_t)$ that would fit the framework. Hence, allowing linear dependence between $\{(\beta_t^{(i)})\}_{i=1,\ldots,n}$ does not enrich the model.

Working with $(\tilde{\boldsymbol{J}}_t \otimes \boldsymbol{\xi}_t)$, we maintain analytic tractability by constructing what we term *effective* and *complementary* information processes. For the randomly evolving active coordinates of $(\tilde{\boldsymbol{J}}_t \otimes \boldsymbol{\xi}_t)$, this parametrization allows to reduce the multi-dimensional information system to a dynamically constructed one-dimensional (effective) information process containing all active information at any given time. This idea reduces the complexity of the information flow model substantially without compromising its effectiveness or reducing its richness.

Definition 2.1. Let the set-valued stochastic process $(\mathcal{J}_t)$ be given by $\mathcal{J}_t = \{i : J_t^{(i,i)} = 1\}$. For $\mathcal{J}_t$ nonempty, the effective information process $(\hat{\xi}_t)_{t\in\mathbb{T}}$ on $\mathbb{R}$ is defined by

$$\hat{\xi}_t = \hat{\sigma}_t^2 \sum_{i\in\mathcal{J}_t} \sigma_i^{-2}\xi_t^{(i)}$$

with effective volatility parameter $\hat{\sigma}_t = (\sum_{i\in\mathcal{J}_t}\sigma_i^{-2})^{-1/2}$. For $\mathcal{J}_t = \emptyset$, set $\hat{\xi}_t = 0$ and $\hat{\sigma}_t = 0$.

Adding elements to $\mathcal{J}_t$ decreases the size of $\hat{\sigma}_t$, hence, adding sources of information decreases the effective noise in the system. The dynamics of the effective information process are dependent on the current state $\tilde{\boldsymbol{J}}_t \in \mathbb{S}$. We can make this dependence more explicit by rewriting the effective information as follows:

$$\hat{\xi}_t = \begin{cases} 0 & \text{if } \boldsymbol{J}_t = \boldsymbol{0}, \\ \dfrac{\boldsymbol{\xi}_t^\top \boldsymbol{J}_t \boldsymbol{\rho}}{\boldsymbol{1}^\top \boldsymbol{J}_t \boldsymbol{\rho}} & \text{otherwise,} \end{cases}$$

where $\boldsymbol{\rho} = (\sigma_1^{-2}, \ldots, \sigma_n^{-2})^\top$ and $\boldsymbol{1} = (1, \ldots, 1)^\top$.

Lemma 2.1. *If $\mathcal{J}_t \neq \emptyset$, then the effective information process is given by*

$$\hat{\xi}_t = tX + \hat{\sigma}_t \hat{\beta}_t,$$

where $(\hat{\beta}_t)_{t\in\mathbb{T}}$, defined by $\hat{\beta}_t = \hat{\sigma}_t \sum_{i\in\mathcal{J}_t} \sigma_i^{-1} \beta_t^{(i)}$, is a standard Brownian bridge between the jumps of $(\mathcal{J}_t)$.

Proof. By definition, for $\mathcal{J}_t \neq \emptyset$, the effective information process is $\hat{\xi}_t = tX + \hat{\sigma}_t \sum_{i\in\mathcal{J}_t} \sigma_i^{-1} \beta_t^{(i)}$. A linear combination of independent Brownian bridges is a Brownian bridge. Further, we have

$$\mathbb{E}\left[\hat{\sigma}_t \sum_{i\in\mathcal{J}_t} \sigma_i^{-1} \beta_t^{(i)}\right] = 0, \quad \mathrm{Var}\left[\hat{\sigma}_t \sum_{i\in\mathcal{J}_t} \sigma_i^{-1} \beta_t^{(i)}\right] = t(1-t),$$

hence, $(\hat{\beta}_t)$ is a *standard* Brownian bridge between the jumps of $(\mathcal{J}_t)$. □

The effective information process jumps every time $(\tilde{\boldsymbol{J}}_t)$ changes state. The jump is caused by the change in the number of Brownian bridges defining the effective information process as well as the number of volatility control parameters defining the effective volatility process $(\hat{\sigma}_t)$.

Definition 2.2. Let the set-valued complementary process $(\mathcal{J}_t^{\mathtt{C}})$ be given by $\mathcal{J}_t^{\mathtt{C}} = \{i : J_t^{(i,i)} = 0\}$. The complementary information process $(\eta_t)_{t\in\mathbb{T}}$ is a function-valued process defined by

$$\eta_t : x \mapsto \prod_{i\in\mathcal{J}_t^{\mathtt{C}}} h(x, \xi^{(i)}(\tau_t^{(i)}), \tau_t^{(i)}, \sigma_i),$$

where $\eta_t := 1$ if $\mathcal{J}_t^{\mathtt{C}} = \emptyset$.

The complementary information process is piecewise constant between state changes of $(\tilde{\boldsymbol{J}}_t)$. The next statement on the joint Markov property of effective and complementary information processes will be very useful. For the rest of this work, we define the measure-valued process $(\nu_t)_{t\in\mathbb{T}_*}$ by $\nu_t(A) = \mathbb{P}[X \in A \,|\, \mathcal{F}_t]$ for $A \in \mathcal{B}(\mathbb{X})$.

Proposition 2.5. *The measure $\nu_t(A)$ satisfies*

$$\nu_t(A) = \mathbb{P}[X \in A \,|\, \hat{\xi}_t, \eta_t],$$

for $t \in \mathbb{T}_*$ and for any $A \in \mathcal{B}(\mathbb{X})$.

Proof. Using Proposition 2.3 and noting that $\tau_t^{(i)} = t$ if $i \in \mathcal{J}_t$, we have

$$\mathbb{P}[X \in \mathrm{d}x \,|\, \mathcal{F}_t] = \frac{\prod_{i\in\mathcal{J}_t} h(x, \xi^{(i)}(\tau_t^{(i)}), \tau_t^{(i)}, \sigma_i) \prod_{i\in\mathcal{J}_t^{\complement}} h(x, \xi^{(i)}(\tau_t^{(i)}), \tau_t^{(i)}, \sigma_i)\nu(\mathrm{d}x)}{\int_{\mathbb{X}} \prod_{i\in\mathcal{J}_t} h(x, \xi^{(i)}(\tau_t^{(i)}), \tau_t^{(i)}, \sigma_i) \prod_{i\in\mathcal{J}_t^{\complement}} h(x, \xi^{(i)}(\tau_t^{(i)}), \tau_t^{(i)}, \sigma_i)\nu(\mathrm{d}x)}$$

$$= \frac{\prod_{i\in\mathcal{J}_t} \exp\left\{ \dfrac{x\xi^{(i)}(\tau_t^{(i)}) - \dfrac{\tau_t^{(i)}x^2}{2}}{\sigma_i^2(1-\tau_t^{(i)})} \right\} \eta_t(x)\nu(\mathrm{d}x)}{\int_{\mathbb{X}} \prod_{i\in\mathcal{J}_t} \exp\left\{ \dfrac{x\xi^{(i)}(\tau_t^{(i)}) - \dfrac{\tau_t^{(i)}x^2}{2}}{\sigma_i^2(1-\tau_t^{(i)})} \right\} \eta_t(x)\nu(\mathrm{d}x)}$$

$$= \frac{\exp\left\{ \sum_{i\in\mathcal{J}_t} \dfrac{x\xi_t^{(i)} - \dfrac{tx^2}{2}}{\sigma_i^2(1-t)} \right\} \eta_t(x)\,\nu(\mathrm{d}x)}{\int_{\mathbb{X}} \exp\left\{ \sum_{i\in\mathcal{J}_t} \dfrac{x\xi_t^{(i)} - \dfrac{tx^2}{2}}{\sigma_i^2(1-t)} \right\} \eta_t(x)\nu(\mathrm{d}x)}$$

$$= \frac{h(x, \hat{\xi}_t, t, \hat{\sigma}_t)\eta_t(x)\nu(\mathrm{d}x)}{\int_{\mathbb{X}} h(x, \hat{\xi}_t, t, \hat{\sigma}_t)\eta_t(x)\nu(\mathrm{d}x)},$$

where $h(x, 0, t, 0) := 1$, and where we adopt the convention that a product with an empty index set is equal to one. □

We shall now derive a dynamical equation for the conditional expectation process, which we later use to model asset price dynamics, as an example. The dynamics of the conditional expectation process turn out to be jump-diffusion. The jumps arise from the activation of new sources of information generating the filtration. For the evolution of (ν_t), we introduce two $(\mathcal{F}_t)$-adapted counting processes $(C_t)_{t\in\mathbb{T}}$ and $(N_t)_{t\in\mathbb{T}}$, given by

$$C_t = \sum_{s\leq t} \mathbb{1}\{\tilde{\boldsymbol{J}}_s \neq \tilde{\boldsymbol{J}}_{s-}\}, \quad N_t = \sum_{s\leq t} \delta_s, \quad \text{where } \delta_s = \mathbb{1}\{\mathcal{J}_s \backslash \mathcal{J}_{s-} \neq \emptyset\}.$$

Hence, C_t is the number of times $(\tilde{\boldsymbol{J}}_t)$ has changed state up to and including time t, and N_t is the number of state changes in which at least one inactive information process becomes active. In view of Proposition 2.7, we define the following.

Modulated Information Flows in Financial Markets

Definition 2.3. Let $\pi_j = \inf\{t : C_t = j\}$, with $\pi_0 = 0$. The process $(M_t)_{t\in\mathbb{T}_*}$ is defined by

$$M_t = \sum_{j=1}^{C_t+1} M_t^{(j)} + \int_0^t (\hat{\xi}_s - \hat{\xi}_{s-})\,\mathrm{d}N_s,$$

where $(M_t^{(j)})_{t\in\mathbb{T}_*}$ is given by

$$M_t^{(j)} = \begin{cases} 0, & \text{for } t < \pi_{j-1}, \\ (\hat{\xi}_{t\wedge\pi_j-} - \hat{\xi}_{\pi_{j-1}}) - \displaystyle\int_{\pi_{j-1}}^{t\wedge\pi_j-} \frac{\mathbb{E}[X\,|\,\hat{\xi}_s, \eta_s] - \hat{\xi}_s}{1-s}\,\mathrm{d}s, & \text{for } \mathcal{J}_{\pi_{j-1}} \neq \emptyset, \\ 0, & \text{for } \mathcal{J}_{\pi_{j-1}} = \emptyset. \end{cases}$$

The following statement is important in order to assign a sufficient structure for the dynamics of the continuous part of (M_t), so that the stochastic integrals with respect to the processes $\{(M_t^{(i)})\}_{i=1,\ldots,n}$ are well-defined for the subsequent proposition.

Proposition 2.6. *Let $t \in [\pi_{j-1}, \pi_j \wedge 1)$, where π_{j-1} and π_j are two consecutive jump times of (C_t) where $\mathcal{J}_{\pi_{j-1}} \neq \emptyset$. Then, $(M_t)_{\pi_{j-1}\le t<\pi_j}$ is an $(\mathcal{F}_t)$-martingale.*

Proof. The integrability condition $\mathbb{E}[\,|M_t|\,] < \infty$ for $t \in \mathbb{T}_*$ is satisfied. Next, we show $\mathbb{E}[M_u\,|\,\mathcal{F}_t] = M_t$ for $u \ge t$, where we consider the random interval $(t,u) \in [\pi_{j-1}, \pi_j \wedge 1)$, with $\mathcal{J}_{\pi_{j-1}} \neq \emptyset$, over which (M_t) has no discontinuity. If $\mathcal{J}_{\pi_{j-1}} = \emptyset$, then $(M_t)_{\pi_{j-1}\le t<\pi_j}$ would simply be 0. First, note that we have

$$\begin{aligned} \mathbb{E}[M_u\,|\,\mathcal{F}_t] &= \mathbb{E}[M_u - M_t\,|\,\mathcal{F}_t] + M_t \\ &= M_t + \mathbb{E}[\hat{\xi}_u - \hat{\xi}_t\,|\,\hat{\xi}_t, \eta_t] + \mathbb{E}\left[\int_t^u \frac{\hat{\xi}_s}{1-s}\mathrm{d}s \,\middle|\, \hat{\xi}_t, \eta_t\right] \\ &\quad - \mathbb{E}\left[\int_t^u \frac{\mathbb{E}[X\,|\,\hat{\xi}_s, \eta_s]}{1-s}\mathrm{d}s \,\middle|\, \hat{\xi}_t, \eta_t\right]. \end{aligned}$$

Writing the terms explicitly and using the tower property, we have

$$\begin{aligned} \mathbb{E}[M_u\,|\,\mathcal{F}_t] &= M_t + \mathbb{E}[Xu + \hat{\sigma}_u\hat{\beta}_u\,|\,\hat{\xi}_t, \eta_t] - \mathbb{E}[Xt + \hat{\sigma}_t\hat{\beta}_t\,|\,\hat{\xi}_t, \eta_t] \\ &\quad + \mathbb{E}[X\,|\,\hat{\xi}_t, \eta_t]\int_t^u \frac{s}{1-s}\mathrm{d}s + \mathbb{E}\left[\int_t^u \frac{\hat{\sigma}_s\hat{\beta}_s}{1-s}\mathrm{d}s \,\middle|\, \hat{\xi}_t, \eta_t\right] \\ &\quad - \mathbb{E}[X\,|\,\hat{\xi}_t, \eta_t]\int_t^u \frac{1}{1-s}\mathrm{d}s. \end{aligned}$$

Note that all the terms involving X disappear, and we are left with

$$\begin{aligned} \mathbb{E}[M_u\,|\,\mathcal{F}_t] &= M_t + \mathbb{E}[\hat{\sigma}_u\hat{\beta}_u\,|\,\hat{\xi}_t, \eta_t] - \mathbb{E}[\hat{\sigma}_t\hat{\beta}_t\,|\,\hat{\xi}_t, \eta_t] + \int_t^u \frac{\mathbb{E}[\hat{\sigma}_s\hat{\beta}_s\,|\,\hat{\xi}_t, \eta_t]}{1-s}\mathrm{d}s \\ &= M_t + \hat{\sigma}_t\left(\mathbb{E}[\hat{\beta}_u\,|\,\hat{\xi}_t, \eta_t] - \mathbb{E}[\hat{\beta}_t\,|\,\hat{\xi}_t, \eta_t] + \int_t^u \frac{\mathbb{E}[\hat{\beta}_s\,|\,\hat{\xi}_t, \eta_t]}{1-s}\mathrm{d}s\right), \end{aligned}$$

E. Hoyle, A. Macrina & L. A. Mengütürk

where we used the fact that $(\hat{\sigma}_s)_{t\leq s\leq u} = \hat{\sigma}_t$, since we reside in $[\pi_{j-1}, \pi_j \wedge 1)$, and hence, $\hat{\sigma}_t$ remains constant. By recalling the mutual independence between X and all the $\{(\beta_t^{(i)})\}_{i=1,\dots,n}$, and the tower property, we may write the following:

$$\begin{aligned}\mathbb{E}[\hat{\beta}_u \mid \hat{\xi}_t, \eta_t] &= \mathbb{E}[\mathbb{E}[\hat{\beta}_u \mid X, \hat{\beta}_t, \eta_t] \mid \hat{\xi}_t, \eta_t] = \mathbb{E}[\mathbb{E}[\hat{\beta}_u \mid \hat{\beta}_t] \mid \hat{\xi}_t, \eta_t] \\ &= \frac{1-u}{1-t}\, \mathbb{E}[\hat{\beta}_t \mid \hat{\xi}_t, \eta_t].\end{aligned}$$

With the above expression at hand, we have

$$\mathbb{E}[\hat{\beta}_u \mid \hat{\xi}_t, \eta_t] - \mathbb{E}[\hat{\beta}_t \mid \hat{\xi}_t, \eta_t] + \int_t^u \frac{\mathbb{E}[\hat{\beta}_s \mid \hat{\xi}_t, \eta_t]}{1-s} \mathrm{d}s = 0,$$

which proves $\mathbb{E}[M_u \mid \mathcal{F}_t] = M_t$ for $(t, u) \in [\pi_{j-1}, \pi_j \wedge 1)$. □

Proposition 2.7. *The measure-valued process* (ν_t) *satisfies*

$$\begin{aligned}\nu_t(A) = \nu(A) &+ \sum_{j=1}^{C_t} \left(\int_{\pi_{j-1}}^{\pi_j} \int_A \frac{x - \mathbb{E}[X \mid \hat{\xi}_s, \eta_s]}{\hat{\sigma}_s^2(1-s)} \nu_s(\mathrm{d}x)\, \mathrm{d}M_s^{(j)} \right) \mathbb{1}\{\mathcal{J}_{\pi_{j-1}} \neq \emptyset\} \\ &+ \left(\int_{\pi_{C_t}}^{t} \int_A \frac{x - \mathbb{E}[X \mid \hat{\xi}_s, \eta_s]}{\hat{\sigma}_s^2(1-s)} \nu_s(\mathrm{d}x)\, \mathrm{d}M_s^{(C_t+1)} \right) \mathbb{1}\{\mathcal{J}_{\pi_{C_t}} \neq \emptyset\} \\ &+ \sum_{s\leq t} [\nu_s(A) - \nu_{s-}(A)]\delta_s,\end{aligned}$$

for $t \in \mathbb{T}_*$ *and for any* $A \in \mathcal{B}(\mathbb{X})$.

Proof. Since ζ on $\mathbb{T}^n$ has finite number of jumps, (ν_t) can be represented by the sum of the continuous and the discontinuous components via the decomposition $\nu_t(A) = \nu_t^c(A) + \sum_{s\leq t} \Delta\nu_s(A)$. For the continuous part $\nu_t^c(\mathrm{d}x)$,

$$\nu_t^c(\mathrm{d}x) = \frac{h(x, \hat{\xi}_t^c, t, \hat{\sigma}_t^c)\eta_t^c(x)\nu(\mathrm{d}x)}{\int_{\mathbb{X}} h(x, \hat{\xi}_t^c, t, \hat{\sigma}_t^c)\eta_t^c(x)\nu(\mathrm{d}x)}.$$

If $\mathcal{J}_t = \emptyset$, then $h(x, 0, t, 0) = 1$ and $\mathrm{d}\nu_t^c(\mathrm{d}x) = 0$, thus we consider time periods where $\mathcal{J}_t \neq \emptyset$. As such, the continuous part of volatility $(\hat{\sigma}_t^c)$ is constant between discontinuities and satisfies $(\hat{\sigma}_t^c) > 0$. Then, we define a function of $\hat{\xi}_t^c$, η_t^c and t as

$$g(\hat{\xi}_t^c, t, \eta_t^c; x, \hat{\sigma}_t^c, \mathrm{d}x) = h(x, \hat{\xi}_t^c, t, \hat{\sigma}_t^c)\eta_t^c(x)\nu(\mathrm{d}x),$$

and also its integral over $\mathbb{X}$, where

$$G(\hat{\xi}_t^c, t, \eta_t^c; \hat{\sigma}_t^c) = \int_{\mathbb{X}} g(\hat{\xi}_t^c, t, \eta_t^c; x, \hat{\sigma}_t^c, \mathrm{d}x).$$

Modulated Information Flows in Financial Markets

Using Itô's lemma, we have

$$\begin{aligned}
\mathrm{d}g(\hat{\xi}_t^c, t, \eta_t^c; x, \hat{\sigma}_t^c, \mathrm{d}x) &= \frac{\partial g}{\partial t}\mathrm{d}t + \frac{\partial g}{\partial \hat{\xi}_t^c}\mathrm{d}\hat{\xi}_t^c + \frac{\partial^2 g}{2\partial(\hat{\xi}_t^c)^2}\mathrm{d}(\hat{\xi}_t^c)^2 \\
&\quad + \frac{\partial g}{\partial \eta_t^c}\mathrm{d}\eta_t^c + \frac{\partial^2 g}{2\partial(\eta_t^c)^2}\mathrm{d}(\eta_t^c)^2 + \frac{\partial^2 g}{\partial \hat{\xi}_t^c \eta_t^c}\mathrm{d}\hat{\xi}_t^c \mathrm{d}\eta_t^c \\
&= \frac{\partial g}{\partial t}\mathrm{d}t + \frac{\partial g}{\partial \hat{\xi}_t^c}\mathrm{d}\hat{\xi}_t^c + \frac{\partial^2 g}{2\partial(\hat{\xi}_t^c)^2}(\hat{\sigma}_t^c)^2\mathrm{d}t \\
&= g(\hat{\xi}_t^c, t, \eta_t^c; x, \hat{\sigma}_t^c, \mathrm{d}x)\left(\frac{x\hat{\xi}_t^c}{(\hat{\sigma}_t^c)^2(1-t)^2}\mathrm{d}t + \frac{x}{(\hat{\sigma}_t^c)^2(1-t)}\mathrm{d}\hat{\xi}_t^c\right),
\end{aligned}$$

since the quadratic variation of $(\mathrm{d}\hat{\beta}_t^c)$ is $\mathrm{d}t$ and η_t^c (the continuous part of η_t) is constant between discontinuities. Then using Fubini's theorem, we can write

$$\begin{aligned}
\mathrm{d}G(\hat{\xi}_t^c, t, \eta_t^c; \hat{\sigma}_t^c) &= \int_{\mathbb{X}} g(\hat{\xi}_t^c, t, \eta_t^c; x, \hat{\sigma}_t^c, \mathrm{d}x)\left(\frac{x\hat{\xi}_t^c}{(\hat{\sigma}_t^c)^2(1-t)^2}\mathrm{d}t + \frac{x}{(\hat{\sigma}_t^c)^2(1-t)}\mathrm{d}\hat{\xi}_t^c\right) \\
&= G(\hat{\xi}_t^c, t, \eta_t^c; \hat{\sigma}_t^c)\left(\frac{\mathbb{E}[X \mid \hat{\xi}_t^c, \eta_t^c]\hat{\xi}_t^c}{(\hat{\sigma}_t^c)^2(1-t)^2}\mathrm{d}t + \frac{\mathbb{E}[X \mid \hat{\xi}_t^c, \eta_t^c]}{(\hat{\sigma}_t^c)^2(1-t)}\mathrm{d}\hat{\xi}_t^c\right).
\end{aligned}$$

Finally, for the bracket $\langle G, G\rangle$, we have

$$\mathrm{d}\langle G, G\rangle = G(\hat{\xi}_t^c, t, \eta_t^c; \hat{\sigma}_t^c)^2 \frac{\mathbb{E}[X \mid \hat{\xi}_t^c, \eta_t^c]^2}{(\hat{\sigma}_t^c)^2(1-t)^2}\mathrm{d}t,$$

and the bracket $\langle g, G\rangle$ satisfies

$$\mathrm{d}\langle g, G\rangle = g(\hat{\xi}_t^c, t, \eta_t^c; x, \hat{\sigma}_t^c, \mathrm{d}x)G(\hat{\xi}_t^c, t, \eta_t^c; \hat{\sigma}_t^c)\frac{x\mathbb{E}[X \mid \hat{\xi}_t^c, \eta_t^c]}{(\hat{\sigma}_t^c)^2(1-t)^2}\mathrm{d}t.$$

Using the quotient rule and rearranging terms, we have

$$\mathrm{d}\nu_t^c(\mathrm{d}x) = \frac{x - \mathbb{E}[X \mid \hat{\xi}_t^c, \eta_t^c]}{(\hat{\sigma}_t^c)^2(1-t)}\nu_t^c(\mathrm{d}x)\mathrm{d}M_t^c,$$

for $t \in \mathbb{T}_*$ and $\mathcal{J}_t \neq \emptyset$, where

$$\mathrm{d}M_t^c = \mathrm{d}\hat{\xi}_t^c - \frac{\mathbb{E}[X \mid \hat{\xi}_t^c, \eta_t^c] - \hat{\xi}_t^c}{1-t}\,\mathrm{d}t.$$

The integral in the continuous part of (M_t) is well defined over $[0, t]$ with respect to the Lebesgue measure. That is, having $\pi_j^* \in [0, t)$ for $j = 0, \ldots, m < \infty$ as a subset

E. Hoyle, A. Macrina & L. A. Mengütürk

of π_j's where $\mathcal{J}_{\pi_{j-1}} \neq \emptyset$ for $j \geq 1$, and denoting $u_{m+1} = \pi^*_{m+1}- = t$,

$$\int_0^t \frac{\mathbb{E}[X \,|\, \hat{\xi}_s, \eta_s] - \hat{\xi}_s}{1-s}\, \mathrm{d}s$$

$$= \sum_{j=1}^{m} \lim_{u_{j-1}\to(\pi^*_{j-1})+} \lim_{u_j\to\pi^*_j-} \int_{u_{j-1}}^{u_j} \frac{\mathbb{E}[X \,|\, \hat{\xi}_s, \eta_s] - \hat{\xi}_s}{1-s}\, \mathrm{d}s$$

$$+ \sum_{j=1}^{m} \lim_{u_j\to\pi^*_j+} \lim_{u_{j+1}\to(\pi^*_{j+1})-} \int_{u_j}^{u_{j+1}} \frac{\mathbb{E}[X \,|\, \hat{\xi}_s, \eta_s] - \hat{\xi}_s}{1-s}\, \mathrm{d}s.$$

Finally, the discontinuous part can be rewritten as

$$\sum_{s\leq t} \Delta\nu_s(\mathrm{d}x) = \sum_{s\leq t} (\nu_s(\mathrm{d}x) - \nu_{s-}(\mathrm{d}x))\, \mathbb{1}\{\mathcal{J}_s \backslash \mathcal{J}_{s-} \neq \emptyset\},$$

for $t \in \mathbb{T}_*$. The statement follows by Lebesgue integration over any $A \in \mathcal{B}(\mathbb{X})$. □

The dynamics of $(M_t)_{t\in\mathbb{T}_*}$ are state-dependent, adapting to the system's information configuration at any given time. The process $(\nu_t)_{t\in\mathbb{T}_*}$ evolves continuously when there is no information switch or when an active source becomes inactive. The dynamics exhibit jumps from one state-dependent martingale to another only when an information source becomes active. The process stays constant if all information sources are inactive over a random period of time.

Proposition 2.8. *Let (W_t) be an $(\mathcal{F}_t)$-adapted process defined by $W_t = M_t/\hat{\sigma}_t$ when $\hat{\sigma}_t > 0$.*

(1) *Let $t \in [\pi_{j-1}, \pi_j \wedge 1)$, where π_{j-1} and π_j are two consecutive jump times of (C_t) where $\mathcal{J}_{\pi_{j-1}} \neq \emptyset$. Then $(W_t)_{\pi_{j-1}\leq t<\pi_j}$ is an $(\mathcal{F}_t)$-Brownian motion.*

(2) *Let $(W^{(j)}_t)$ be the Brownian motion given above for $t \in [\pi_{j-1}, \pi_j \wedge 1)$, where $\mathcal{J}_{\pi_{j-1}} \neq \emptyset$. Then, the $(\mathcal{F}_t)$-martingale $(X_t)_{t\in\mathbb{T}}$ defined by $X_t := \mathbb{E}[X \,|\, \mathcal{F}_t]$, satisfies*

$$X_t = \mathbb{E}[X] + \sum_{j=1}^{C_t} \left(\int_{\pi_{j-1}}^{\pi_j} \frac{\Gamma_s}{\hat{\sigma}_s(1-s)}\, \mathrm{d}W^{(j)}_s \right) \mathbb{1}\{\mathcal{J}_{\pi_{j-1}} \neq \emptyset\}$$

$$+ \left(\int_{\pi_{C_t}}^{t} \frac{\Gamma_s}{\hat{\sigma}_s(1-s)}\, \mathrm{d}W^{(C_t+1)}_s \right) \mathbb{1}\{\mathcal{J}_{\pi_{C_t}} \neq \emptyset\} + \sum_{s\leq t} (X_s - X_{s-})\delta_s,$$

for $t \in \mathbb{T}_*$, where $(\Gamma_t)_{t\in\mathbb{T}_*}$ given by $\Gamma_t = \mathrm{Var}[X \,|\, \hat{\xi}_t, \eta_t]$ is an $(\mathcal{F}_t)$-supermartingale.

Modulated Information Flows in Financial Markets

(3) *More generally, the* $(\mathcal{F}_t)$*-martingale* $(X_t^{(k)})_{t\in\mathbb{T}}$ *defined by* $X_t^{(k)} := \mathbb{E}[X^k \mid \mathcal{F}_t]$ *for any* $k \geq 1$ *satisfies*

$$X_t^{(k)} = \mathbb{E}[X^k] + \sum_{j=1}^{C_t} \left(\int_{\pi_{j-1}}^{\pi_j} \frac{X_s^{(k+1)} - X_s^{(k)} X_s}{\hat{\sigma}_s(1-s)} \, \mathrm{d}W_s^{(j)} \right) \mathbb{1}\{\mathcal{J}_{\pi_{j-1}} \neq \emptyset\}$$
$$+ \left(\int_{\pi_{C_t}}^{t} \frac{X_s^{(k+1)} - X_s^{(k)} X_s}{\hat{\sigma}_s(1-s)} \, \mathrm{d}W_s^{(C_t+1)} \right) \mathbb{1}\{\mathcal{J}_{\pi_{C_t}} \neq \emptyset\}$$
$$+ \sum_{s\leq t} (X_s^{(k)} - X_{s-}^{(k)}) \delta_s,$$

for $t \in \mathbb{T}_*$, *given that* $X \in \mathcal{L}^{k+1}(\Omega, \mathcal{G}, \mathbb{P})$.

Proof. The random time π_{j-1} is $(\mathcal{F}_t)$-measurable, $\hat{\sigma}_t > 0$ for $t \in [\pi_{j-1}, \pi_j \wedge 1)$ whenever $\mathcal{J}_{\pi_{j-1}} \neq \emptyset$, $W_{\pi_{j-1}} = 0$ and the subprocess $(\hat{\beta}_t - \hat{\beta}_{\pi_{j-1}})_{\pi_{j-1}\leq t<\pi_j}$ is an $(\mathcal{F}_t)$-Brownian bridge. Thus, the bracket $\mathrm{d}\langle W_t, W_t\rangle$ for $t \in [\pi_{j-1}, \pi_j \wedge 1)$ is $\mathrm{d}t$ given $(\mathcal{F}_t)$. Since the paths $(M_t)_{\pi_{j-1}\leq t<\pi_j}$ and $(\hat{\sigma}_t)_{\pi_{j-1}\leq t<\pi_j}$ are continuous, $(W_t)_{\pi_{j-1}\leq t<\pi_j}$ is an $(\mathcal{F}_t)$-Brownian motion by Lévy's characterization. The dynamics given in the second part follows directly from Proposition 2.7, the $(\hat{\sigma}_t)$-standardization of (M_t) and Lebesgue integration. For the $(\mathcal{F}_t)$-supermartingale property of (Γ_t), define $(S_t)_{0\leq t<1}$ by $S_t = X_t^2$. Using Ito's lemma, (S_t) is an $(\mathcal{F}_t)$-submartingale. Then from Doob–Meyer decomposition,

$$\begin{aligned}\mathbb{E}[\mathbb{E}[X^2 \mid \mathcal{F}_t] - S_t \mid \mathcal{F}_s] &= \mathbb{E}[\mathbb{E}[X^2 \mid \mathcal{F}_t] - (Y_t - I_t) \mid \mathcal{F}_s] \\ &\leq \mathrm{Var}[X \mid \mathcal{F}_s],\end{aligned}$$

where (Y_t) is an $(\mathcal{F}_t)$-martingale and (I_t) is an increasing predictable process. The final part is given by the following:

$$X_t^{(k)} = \mathbb{E}[X^k] + \sum_{j=1}^{C_t} \left(\int_{\pi_{j-1}}^{\pi_j} \frac{\mathbb{E}[X^{k+1} \mid \hat{\xi}_s, \eta_s] - \mathbb{E}[X^k \mid \hat{\xi}_s, \eta_s] X_s}{\hat{\sigma}_s(1-s)} \, \mathrm{d}W_s^{(j)} \right) \mathbb{1}\{\mathcal{J}_{\pi_{j-1}} \neq \emptyset\}$$
$$+ \left(\int_{\pi_{C_t}}^{t} \frac{\mathbb{E}[X^{k+1} \mid \hat{\xi}_s, \eta_s] - \mathbb{E}[X^k \mid \hat{\xi}_s, \eta_s] X_s}{\hat{\sigma}_s(1-s)} \, \mathrm{d}W_s^{(C_t+1)} \right) \mathbb{1}\{\mathcal{J}_{\pi_{C_t}} \neq \emptyset\}$$
$$+ \sum_{s\leq t} (X_s^{(k)} - X_{s-}^{(k)}) \delta_s,$$

which follows from the first two parts and by using Lebesgue integration on Proposition 2.7. □

The endogenous nature of the jump-diffusion, resulting from the modulation of information flow, emerges from the behavior of $(\mathcal{F}_t)$. The jumps are a direct result of the activation of information coordinates determined by $(\tilde{\boldsymbol{J}}_t \otimes \boldsymbol{\xi}_t)$. This is different from generating a jump diffusion by directly specifying the process itself as the sum of drifted Brownian motion and a compound Poisson process, see Cont & Tankov (2004), for example.

Corollary 2.2. *The system of $(\mathcal{F}_t)$-Brownian motions $(W_t^{(j)})$ for $j = 1, \ldots, C_t + 1$ are stochastically-linked through $(\mathcal{J}_t)$.*

Proposition 2.8 proves Proposition 1.1. The diffusion coefficient (θ_t) in Proposition 1.1 can be interpreted as a stochastic volatility process with jumps. This process arises naturally from the system, which is a welcome consequence of the proposed framework without an *a priori* assumption on volatility dynamics. In applications, chiefly in asset pricing and financial risk management, the volatility process — and its dynamical equation — are of crucial importance. Accurate estimates of volatilities are important for measuring the risk of financial assets.

Proposition 2.9. *Let $\mathcal{K}_t = \mathcal{J}_t \backslash \mathcal{J}_{t-}$. The jump size of (X_t) at time t is $X_t - X_{t-} = g(Z) - X_{t-}$, where the conditionally normal random variable Z is given by*

$$Z = \sum_{i \in \mathcal{K}_t} \frac{\xi_t^{(i)}}{\sigma_i^2(1-t)},$$

and the function $g : \mathbb{R} \to \mathbb{R}$, for $t \in \mathbb{T}_*$, is given by

$$g(z) = \frac{\displaystyle\int_{\mathbb{X}} x \exp(xz) \prod_{i \notin \mathcal{K}_t} h(x, \xi^{(i)}(\tau_t^{(i)}), \tau_t^{(i)}, \sigma_i) \prod_{i \in \mathcal{K}_t} \exp\left(\frac{-tx^2}{2\sigma_i^2(1-t)}\right) \nu(\mathrm{d}x)}{\displaystyle\int_{\mathbb{X}} \exp(xz) \prod_{i \notin \mathcal{K}_t} h(x, \xi^{(i)}(\tau_t^{(i)}), \tau_t^{(i)}, \sigma_i) \prod_{i \in \mathcal{K}_t} \exp\left(\frac{-tx^2}{2\sigma_i^2(1-t)}\right) \nu(\mathrm{d}x)}.$$

Proof. For $i \in \mathcal{K}_t$, we have the following:

$$\xi_t^{(i)}|_{X, \mathcal{F}_{t-}} \sim \mathcal{N}(\xi^{(i)}(\tau_{t-}^{(i)}) + (t - \tau_{t-}^{(i)})X, \, \sigma_i^2(t - \tau_{t-}^{(i)})(1-t)).$$

Given X, the variables $\{\xi_t^{(i)}\}_{i=1,\ldots,n}$ are mutually independent. It follows that the conditional distribution of Z is also Gaussian, that is,

$$Z|_{X, \mathcal{F}_{t-}} \sim \mathcal{N}\left(\sum_{i \in \mathcal{K}_t} \frac{\xi^{(i)}(\tau_{t-}^{(i)}) + (t - \tau_{t-}^{(i)})X}{\sigma_i^2(1-t)}, \sum_{i \in \mathcal{K}_t} \frac{t - \tau_{t-}^{(i)}}{\sigma_i^2(1-t)}\right).$$

Hence, the density of Z is given by

$$z \mapsto \frac{1}{\sqrt{2\pi V}} \int_{x \in \mathbb{R}} \exp\left(-\frac{(z - U(x))^2}{2V}\right) \nu_{t-}(\mathrm{d}x),$$

where we have defined the following:

$$U(x) = \sum_{i \in \mathcal{K}_t} \frac{\xi^{(i)}(\tau_{t-}^{(i)}) + (t - \tau_{t-}^{(i)})x}{\sigma_i^2(1-t)}, \quad V = \sum_{i \in \mathcal{K}_t} \frac{t - \tau_{t-}^{(i)}}{\sigma_i^2(1-t)}.$$

Modulated Information Flows in Financial Markets

Note that one can decompose the conditional distribution of X in terms of $\mathcal{K}_t$ and write

$$\mathbb{P}[X \in \mathrm{d}x \,|\, \mathcal{F}_t] = \frac{\exp(xZ) \prod_{i \notin \mathcal{K}_t} h(x, \xi^{(i)}(\tau_t^{(i)}), \tau_t^{(i)}, \sigma_i) \prod_{i \in \mathcal{K}_t} \exp\left(\frac{-tx^2}{2\sigma_i^2(1-t)}\right) \nu(\mathrm{d}x)}{\int_{\mathbb{X}} \exp(xZ) \prod_{i \notin \mathcal{K}_t} h(x, \xi^{(i)}(\tau_t^{(i)}), \tau_t^{(i)}, \sigma_i) \prod_{i \in \mathcal{K}_t} \exp\left(\frac{-tx^2}{2\sigma_i^2(1-t)}\right) \nu(\mathrm{d}x)}.$$

Hence, the statement follows. □

For the next statement, for $t < 1$, we denote $\mu(\hat{\xi}_t, \eta_t, t) = (\mathbb{E}[X \,|\, \hat{\xi}_t, \eta_t] - \hat{\xi}_t)/(1-t)$ when $\mathcal{J}_t \neq \emptyset$, and $\mu(\hat{\xi}_t, \eta_t, t) = 0$ otherwise. We also recall $\hat{\sigma}_t = 0$ when $\mathcal{J}_t = \emptyset$.

Proposition 2.10. *Let (λ_t) be the intensity process of (N_t), and $\psi : \mathbb{R} \to \mathbb{R}$ and $\phi : \mathbb{R} \to \mathbb{R}$ be continuous bounded functions.*

(1) *The functional $\mathbb{E}[\mathrm{e}^{-\int_t^1 \psi(s)\mathrm{d}s}\phi(X) \,|\, \mathcal{F}_t]$, hence,*

$$v(\hat{\xi}_t, \eta_t, t) := \mathbb{E}[\mathrm{e}^{-\int_t^1 \psi(s)\mathrm{d}s}\phi(X) \,|\, \hat{\xi}_t, \eta_t, X\mathbb{1}_{\{t=1\}}],$$

satisfies the partial differential equation (PDE)

$$\frac{\partial v(\hat{\xi}_t, \eta_t, t)}{\partial t} + \mu(\hat{\xi}_t, \eta_t, t)\frac{\partial v(\hat{\xi}_t, \eta_t, t)}{\partial \hat{\xi}_t} + \hat{\sigma}_t^2 \frac{\partial^2 v(\hat{\xi}_t, \eta_t, t)}{2\partial \hat{\xi}_t^2}$$
$$- \psi(t)v(\hat{\xi}_t, \eta_t, t) + (v(\hat{\xi}_t, \eta_t, t) - v(\hat{\xi}_{t-}, \eta_{t-}, t-))\lambda_t = 0,$$

with the boundary condition $v(\hat{\xi}_1, \eta_1, 1) = \phi(X)$.

(2) *Choose the random point field ζ such that $\tilde{J}_t^{(i)} = 1$ implies $\tilde{J}_u^{(i)} = 1$ for $u \geq t$. Let there be at least one active source of information at $t = 0$. Then,*

$$v(\hat{\xi}_t, t) = \mathbb{E}\left[\exp\left(-\int_t^1 \psi(s)\mathrm{d}s\right)\phi(X) \,\middle|\, \hat{\xi}_t\right],$$

satisfies the same PDE as $v(\hat{\xi}_t, \eta_t, t)$ with the boundary condition $v(\hat{\xi}_1, 1) = \phi(X)$.

Proof. For part one, by use of the Doob–Meyer decomposition, we can write $N_t = \hat{N}_t + \Lambda_t$, where $(\hat{N}_t)$ is an $(\mathcal{F}_t)$-adapted martingale and $\Lambda_t = \int_0^t \lambda_s \mathrm{d}s$ is the compensator process. Transforming the conditional expectation $v(\hat{\xi}_t, \eta_t, t)$ by multiplying it with the corresponding exponential function, we define the martingale $\hat{v}(\hat{\xi}_t, \eta_t, t) = \mathrm{e}^{-\int_0^t \psi(s)\mathrm{d}s} v(\hat{\xi}_t, \eta_t, t)$. Then, by applying Ito's lemma to $\hat{v}(\hat{\xi}_t, \eta_t, t)$

E. Hoyle, A. Macrina & L. A. Mengütürk

after decomposing it into continuous and discontinuous parts, we have

$$\frac{\hat{v}(\hat{\xi}_t,\eta_t,t)}{\partial t}\mathrm{d}t+\frac{\hat{v}(\hat{\xi}_t,\eta_t,t)}{\partial\hat{\xi}_t}(\mathrm{d}M_t+\mu(\hat{\xi}_t,\eta_t,t)\mathrm{d}t)$$

$$+\hat{\sigma}_t^2\frac{\partial^2\hat{v}(\hat{\xi}_t,\eta_t,t)}{2\partial\hat{\xi}_t^2}\mathrm{d}t+(\hat{v}(\hat{\xi}_t,\eta_t,t)-\hat{v}(\hat{\xi}_{t-},\eta_{t-},t-))(\mathrm{d}\hat{N}_t+\mathrm{d}\Lambda_t).$$

Note that for the continuous part, we have $\mathrm{d}\eta_t=0$ and $\mathrm{d}\langle\eta_t,\eta_t\rangle=0$. Thus, once the conditional expectation is taken with respect to $\mathcal{F}_t$, the continuous part of (M_t) and the discontinuous part $(\hat{N}_t)$ vanish,

$$\mathrm{e}^{-\int_0^t\psi(s)\mathrm{d}s}\left(\frac{\partial v(\hat{\xi}_t,\eta_t,t)}{\partial t}-\psi(t)v(\hat{\xi}_t,\eta_t,t)+\mu(\hat{\xi}_t,\eta_t,t)\frac{\partial v(\hat{\xi}_t,\eta_t,t)}{\partial\hat{\xi}_t}\right.$$

$$\left.+\hat{\sigma}_t^2\frac{\partial^2 v(\hat{\xi}_t,\eta_t,t)}{2\partial\hat{\xi}_t^2}\right)\mathrm{d}t+\mathrm{e}^{-\int_0^t\psi(s)\mathrm{d}s}(v(\hat{\xi}_t,\eta_t,t)$$

$$-\mathrm{e}^{-\int_0^{t-}\psi(s)\mathrm{d}s}v(\hat{\xi}_{t-},\eta_{t-},t-))\lambda_t\mathrm{d}t=0.$$

Once we divide both sides by $\mathrm{e}^{-\int_0^t\psi(s)\mathrm{d}s}\mathrm{d}t$, the jump part remains to be

$$(v(\hat{\xi}_t,\eta_t,t)-\mathrm{e}^{\int_{t-}^t\psi(s)\mathrm{d}s}v(\hat{\xi}_{t-},\eta_{t-},t-))\lambda_t.$$

However, $\int_{t-}^t\psi(s)\mathrm{d}s=0$ due to continuity, and hence, $\mathrm{e}^{\int_{t-}^t\psi(s)\mathrm{d}s}=1$. Finally, $X\mathbb{1}_{\{t=1\}}$ ensures that the boundary condition is satisfied even if $\mathcal{J}_1=\emptyset$.

For part two, active sources never deactivate. Thus for inactive states $i\in\mathcal{J}_t^c$, the complementary information is $\eta_t=1$ for all $t\in[0,1]$, since $\xi^{(i)}(0)=0$ and $\tau_t^{(i)}=0$ must hold for all $t\in[0,1]$. Therefore, we can write $\mathbb{E}[\exp(-\int_t^1\psi(s)\mathrm{d}s)\phi(X)\,|\,\mathcal{F}_t]=v(\hat{\xi}_t,t)$. The boundary condition follows since at least one coordinate of $(\boldsymbol{J}_t\,\boldsymbol{\xi}_t)$ is always active over $\mathbb{T}$. □

2.2. *Multiple point fields*

As an extension to Brody *et al.* (2008a), we consider a system where the random variable X is given by a function of multiple factors about which observers have differing information. That is, for some $m\in\mathbb{N}_+$, we introduce a vector $\boldsymbol{X}$ of mutually independent random variables $X^\alpha\in\mathcal{L}^2(\Omega,\mathcal{G},\mathbb{P})$ with law ν^α for $\alpha=1,\ldots,m$, respectively, each with the state-space $(\mathbb{X},\mathcal{B}(\mathbb{X}))$, where $\mathbb{X}\subseteq\mathbb{R}$. We treat the case where $X=g(X^1,\ldots,X^m)$ for some bounded measurable function $g:\mathbb{X}^m\to\mathbb{X}$.

Accordingly, we introduce $\mathbb{R}^{n(\alpha)}$-valued $(\mathcal{G}_t)$-adapted multivariate stochastic processes $(\boldsymbol{\xi}_t^\alpha)_{t\in\mathbb{T}}$, for $\alpha=1,\ldots,m$, where $n(\alpha)$ highlights that the dimensions of $(\boldsymbol{\xi}_t^\alpha)$ may be different across α. As before, we define information coordinates by $\xi_t^{\alpha,(i)}\overset{\text{law}}{=}tX^\alpha+\sigma_i^\alpha\beta_t^{\alpha,(i)}$, for $\sigma_i^\alpha>0$ and $i=1,\ldots,n(\alpha)$. For parsimony, we assume that the standard Brownian bridges $\{\beta_t^{\alpha,(i)}\}$s are mutually independent and of X^αs across $i=1,\ldots,n(\alpha)$ and $\alpha=1,\ldots,m$.

Modulated Information Flows in Financial Markets

Next, we introduce a set of mutually independent random point fields ζ^α for $\alpha = 1, \ldots, m$ on $\mathbb{T}^{n(\alpha)}$, which are also independent of $(\boldsymbol{\xi}_t^\alpha)$s, each generating a collection of times $\{\varpi_1^{\alpha,i}, \ldots, \varpi_{k_i}^{\alpha,i}\}$ for $i = 1, \ldots, n(\alpha)$ and finite $k_i \in \mathbb{N}_0$. For every (α, i), we associate the random sequence $\{\varpi_1^{\alpha,i}, \ldots, \varpi_{k_i}^{\alpha,i}\}$ to a coordinate of a $(\mathcal{G}_t)$-adapted càdlàg jump process $(\tilde{\boldsymbol{J}}_t^\alpha)$ with state space $\mathbb{S} = \{0,1\}^{n(\alpha)}$. We then define the $\mathbb{R}^{n(\alpha)\times n(\alpha)}$-valued process $(\boldsymbol{J}_t^\alpha)$ by $J_t^{\alpha,(i,j)} = \delta_{ij}\tilde{\boldsymbol{J}}_t^\alpha$. As before, $(\boldsymbol{J}_t^\alpha)$ is a diagonal matrix-valued process indicating which coordinates of $(\boldsymbol{\xi}_t^\alpha)$ are active through $(\boldsymbol{J_t}^\alpha\, \boldsymbol{\xi}_t^\alpha)$ for $\alpha = 1, \ldots, m$. We define a sub-algebra $\mathcal{H}_t \subseteq \mathcal{G}_t$ by

$$\mathcal{H}_t = \sigma((\tilde{\boldsymbol{J}}_u^\alpha \otimes \boldsymbol{\xi}_u^\alpha)_{0\le u\le t}, (\tilde{\boldsymbol{J}}_u^\alpha)_{0\le u\le t}, \boldsymbol{X}\mathbb{1}_{\{t=1\}}; \alpha = 1, \ldots, m),$$

for $t \in \mathbb{T}$, or equally $\mathcal{H}_t = \sigma((\boldsymbol{J}_u^\alpha\, \boldsymbol{\xi}_u^\alpha)_{0\le u\le t}, (\boldsymbol{J}_u^\alpha)_{0\le u\le t}, \boldsymbol{X}\mathbb{1}_{\{t=1\}}; \alpha = 1, \ldots, m)$.

We define $\mathbb{R}$-valued effective information processes $(\hat{\xi_t^\alpha})_{t\in\mathbb{T}}$ for $\alpha = 1, \ldots, m$ by

$$\hat{\xi_t^\alpha} = (\hat{\sigma_t^\alpha})^2 \sum_{i\in\mathcal{J}_t^\alpha} (\sigma_i^\alpha)^{-2} \xi_t^{\alpha,(i)}, \quad \text{where } \hat{\sigma_t^\alpha} = \left(\sum_{i\in\mathcal{J}_t^\alpha} (\sigma_i^\alpha)^{-2}\right)^{-1/2},$$

where $\mathcal{J}_t^\alpha = \{i : J_t^{\alpha,(i,i)} = 1\}$. We set $\hat{\xi_t^\alpha} = 0$ and $\hat{\sigma_t^\alpha} = 0$ when $\mathcal{J}_t^\alpha = \emptyset$. In a similar fashion, we define function-valued complementary information processes $(\eta_t^\alpha)_{t\in\mathbb{T}}$ for $\alpha = 1, \ldots, m$ by

$$\eta_t^\alpha : x^\alpha \mapsto \prod_{i\in\mathcal{J}_t^{\alpha\complement}} h(x^\alpha, \xi^{\alpha,(i)}(\tau_t^{\alpha,(i)}), \tau_t^{\alpha,(i)}, \sigma_i^\alpha),$$

where $\mathcal{J}_t^{\alpha\complement} = \{i : J_t^{\alpha,(i,i)} = 0\}$ and $\tau_t^{\alpha,(i)} = 0 \vee \sup\{u : J_u^{\alpha,(i,i)} = 1, u \in [0,t]\}$ for $i = 1, \ldots, n(\alpha)$, where by convention $\sup\emptyset = -\infty$. We set $\eta_t^\alpha = 1$ when $\mathcal{J}_t^{\alpha\complement} = \emptyset$.

Proposition 2.11. *The measure* $\nu_t(\mathrm{d}\boldsymbol{x}) = \mathbb{P}[\boldsymbol{X} \in \mathrm{d}\boldsymbol{x} \,|\, \mathcal{H}_t]$ *satisfies*

$$\nu_t(\mathrm{d}\boldsymbol{x}) = \prod_{\alpha=1}^m \mathbb{P}[X^\alpha \in \mathrm{d}x^\alpha \,|\, \hat{\xi}_t^\alpha, \eta_t^\alpha],$$

for $t \in \mathbb{T}_*$, *where* $(\hat{\xi_t^\alpha})$ *and* (η_t^α) *are defined as above for* $\alpha = 1, \ldots, m$.

Proof. Using the independence properties given above, we have

$$\begin{aligned}\nu_t(\mathrm{d}\boldsymbol{x}) &= \prod_{\alpha=1}^m \mathbb{P}[X^\alpha \in \mathrm{d}x^\alpha \,|\, \sigma((\boldsymbol{J}_u^\alpha\, \boldsymbol{\xi}_u^\alpha)_{0\le u\le t}, (\boldsymbol{J}_u^\alpha)_{0\le u\le t}, X^\alpha\mathbb{1}_{\{t=1\}})] \\ &= \prod_{\alpha=1}^m \frac{h(x^\alpha, \hat{\xi}_t^\alpha, t, \hat{\sigma}_t^\alpha)\eta_t^\alpha(x^\alpha)\,\nu^\alpha(\mathrm{d}x^\alpha)}{\int_{\mathbb{X}} h(x^\alpha, \hat{\xi}_t^\alpha, t, \hat{\sigma}_t^\alpha)\eta_t^\alpha(x^\alpha)\,\nu^\alpha(\mathrm{d}x^\alpha)},\end{aligned}$$

by following similar mid-steps as done in Proposition 2.5. □

We define $\pi_j^\alpha = \inf\{t : C_t^\alpha = j\}$, with $\pi_0^\alpha = 0$, where $C_t^\alpha = \sum_{s\le t} \mathbb{1}\{\tilde{\boldsymbol{J}}_s^\alpha \ne \tilde{\boldsymbol{J}}_{s-}^\alpha\}$, and also $N_t^\alpha = \sum_{s\le t} \delta_s^\alpha$, where $\delta_s^\alpha = \mathbb{1}\{\mathcal{J}_s^\alpha \backslash \mathcal{J}_{s-}^\alpha \ne \emptyset\}$ for $\alpha = 1, \ldots, m$.

Proposition 2.12. *Let $(W_t^{\alpha,(j)})$ be mutually independent $(\mathcal{H}_t)$-Brownian motions across $\alpha = 1, \ldots, m$ for $t \in [\pi_{j-1}^\alpha, \pi_j^\alpha \wedge 1)$. The $(\mathcal{H}_t)$-martingale $(X_t)_{t\in\mathbb{T}}$ defined by $X_t := \mathbb{E}[X \,|\, \mathcal{H}_t]$, satisfies*

$$X_t = \mathbb{E}[X] + \sum_{\alpha=1}^{m} \sum_{j=1}^{C_t^\alpha} \left(\int_{\pi_{j-1}^\alpha}^{\pi_j^\alpha} \frac{\Theta_s^\alpha}{\hat{\sigma}_s^\alpha (1-s)} \, \mathrm{d}W_s^{\alpha,(j)} \right) \mathbb{1}\{\mathcal{J}_{\pi_{j-1}^\alpha}^\alpha \neq \emptyset\}$$
$$+ \sum_{\alpha=1}^{m} \left(\int_{\pi_{C_t^\alpha}}^{t} \frac{\Theta_s^\alpha}{\hat{\sigma}_s^\alpha (1-s)} \, \mathrm{d}W_s^{\alpha(C_t+1)} \right) \mathbb{1}\{\mathcal{J}_{\pi_{C_t}^\alpha}^\alpha \neq \emptyset\} + \sum_{\alpha=1}^{m} \sum_{s \le t} (X_s - X_{s-}) \delta_s^\alpha,$$

for $t \in \mathbb{T}_*$, where $(\Theta_t^\alpha)_{t\in\mathbb{T}}$ is given by $\Theta_t^\alpha = \mathrm{Cov}[X, X^\alpha \,|\, \mathcal{H}_t]$ for $\alpha = 1, \ldots, m$.

Proof. Let $\nu_t^\alpha(\mathrm{d}x^\alpha) = \mathbb{P}[X^\alpha \in \mathrm{d}x^\alpha \,|\, \hat{\xi}_t^\alpha, \eta_t^\alpha]$ for $\alpha = 1, \ldots, m$. Then using the independence properties given above, Proposition 2.11 and following similar steps as for Proposition 2.7, there exists a set of $(\mathcal{H}_t)$-Brownian motions $(W_t^{\alpha,(j)})$ over random periods $t \in [\pi_{j-1}^\alpha, \pi_j^\alpha \wedge 1)$, which are mutually independent from each other across $\alpha = 1, \ldots, m$, where the brackets $\langle \mathrm{d}W_t^{a,(j)}, \mathrm{d}W_t^{b,(j)} \rangle = 0$ for $a, b \in \{1, \ldots, m\}$, such that (ν_t) satisfies

$$\nu_t(\mathrm{d}\boldsymbol{x}) \overset{\text{law}}{=} \nu_0(\mathrm{d}\boldsymbol{x}) + \sum_{\alpha=1}^{m} \sum_{j=1}^{C_t^\alpha} \left(\int_{\pi_{j-1}^\alpha}^{\pi_j^\alpha} \frac{x^\alpha - \mathbb{E}[X^\alpha \,|\, \hat{\xi}_s^\alpha, \eta_s^\alpha]}{\hat{\sigma}_s^\alpha (1-s)} \prod_{\alpha=1}^{m} \nu_s^\alpha(\mathrm{d}x^\alpha) \, \mathrm{d}W_s^{\alpha,(j)} \right)$$
$$\times \mathbb{1}\{\mathcal{J}_{\pi_{j-1}^\alpha}^\alpha \neq \emptyset\}$$
$$+ \sum_{\alpha=1}^{m} \left(\int_{\pi_{C_t^\alpha}}^{t} \frac{x^\alpha - \mathbb{E}[X^\alpha \,|\, \hat{\xi}_s^\alpha, \eta_s^\alpha]}{\hat{\sigma}_s^\alpha (1-s)} \prod_{\alpha=1}^{m} \nu_s^\alpha(\mathrm{d}x^\alpha) \, \mathrm{d}W_s^{\alpha,(C_t+1)} \right) \mathbb{1}\{\mathcal{J}_{\pi_{C_t}^\alpha}^\alpha \neq \emptyset\}$$
$$+ \sum_{\alpha=1}^{m} \sum_{s \le t} (\nu_s(\mathrm{d}\boldsymbol{x}) - \nu_{s-}(\mathrm{d}\boldsymbol{x})) \delta_s^\alpha,$$

for $t \in \mathbb{T}_*$. From Proposition 2.11, we have $\nu_t(\mathrm{d}\boldsymbol{x}) = \prod_{\alpha=1}^m \nu_t^\alpha(\mathrm{d}x^\alpha)$. Therefore, since $g : \mathbb{X}^m \to \mathbb{X}$ is a bounded measurable function, we have

$$X_t = \int_{\mathbb{X}^m} g(x^1, \ldots, x^m) \nu_t^1(\mathrm{d}x^\alpha) \ldots \nu_t^m(\mathrm{d}x^\alpha),$$

and the statement follows via Lebesgue integration. □

The diffusion coefficient of (X_t) takes the form of a stochastic covariance process, which itself jumps when any of the information sources switches on. Hence, (X_t) adapts to a new covariance state of the system under a new active information configuration.

The next statement generalizes Proposition 2.10 for the functional $\mathbb{E}[\cdot \,|\, \mathcal{H}_t]$. As before, for $t < 1$, we set $\mu^\alpha(\hat{\xi}_t^\alpha, \eta_t^\alpha, t) = (\mathbb{E}[X^\alpha \,|\, \hat{\xi}_t^\alpha, \eta_t^\alpha] - \hat{\xi}_t^\alpha)/(1-t)$ when $\mathcal{J}_t^\alpha \neq \emptyset$ and $\mu^\alpha(\hat{\xi}_t^\alpha, \eta_t^\alpha, t) = 0$ otherwise, for $\alpha = 1, \ldots, m$.

Proposition 2.13. *Let* $\hat{\boldsymbol{\xi}}_t = [\hat{\xi}_t^1, \ldots, \hat{\xi}_t^m]$, $\boldsymbol{\eta}_t = [\eta_t^1, \ldots, \eta_t^m]$, *and* (λ_t^α) *be the intensity process of* (N_t^α). *Let* $\psi : \mathbb{R} \to \mathbb{R}$ *and* $\phi : \mathbb{R} \to \mathbb{R}$ *be continuous bounded functions. Then the conditional expectation*

$$v(\hat{\boldsymbol{\xi}}_t, \boldsymbol{\eta}_t, t) = \mathbb{E}[\mathrm{e}^{-\int_t^1 \psi(s)\mathrm{d}s}\phi(X)|\hat{\boldsymbol{\xi}}_t, \boldsymbol{\eta}_t, \boldsymbol{X}\mathbb{1}_{\{t=1\}}],$$

satisfies the PDE

$$\frac{\partial v(\hat{\boldsymbol{\xi}}_t, \boldsymbol{\eta}_t, t)}{\partial t} + \sum_{\alpha=1}^{m} \mu^\alpha(\hat{\xi}_t, \eta_t, t)\frac{\partial v(\hat{\boldsymbol{\xi}}_t, \boldsymbol{\eta}_t, t)}{\partial \hat{\xi}_t^\alpha} + \sum_{\alpha=1}^{m} (\hat{\sigma}_t^\alpha)^2 \frac{\partial^2 v(\hat{\boldsymbol{\xi}}_t, \boldsymbol{\eta}_t, t)}{2(\partial \hat{\xi}_t^\alpha)^2}$$

$$- \psi(t)v(\hat{\boldsymbol{\xi}}_t, \boldsymbol{\eta}_t, t) + \sum_{\alpha=1}^{m}(v(\hat{\boldsymbol{\xi}}_t, \boldsymbol{\eta}_t, t) - v(\hat{\boldsymbol{\xi}}_{t-}, \boldsymbol{\eta}_{t-}, t-))\lambda_t^\alpha = 0,$$

with the boundary condition $v(\hat{\boldsymbol{\xi}}_1, \boldsymbol{\eta}_1, 1) = \phi(X)$.

We omit the proof of Proposition 2.13 to avoid repetition, which follows from similar steps as done in Propositions 2.7 and 2.10 by overlaying the independence properties given above, where we see that the brackets $\langle \mathrm{d}\hat{\xi}_t^{a,(j)}, \mathrm{d}\hat{\xi}_t^{b,(j)} \rangle = 0$ for $a \neq b$ and $a, b \in \{1, \ldots, m\}$.

2.3. *Modulation as projection*

For any $t \in \mathbb{T}$ and for any fixed $\alpha = 1, \ldots, m$, $\tilde{\boldsymbol{J}}_t^\alpha \otimes \boldsymbol{\xi}_t^\alpha \mapsto \boldsymbol{J}_t^\alpha \boldsymbol{\xi}_t^\alpha$ defines an orthogonal projection from the space of all available information sources to an information subspace. That is, $(\boldsymbol{J}_t^\alpha)$ is a projection-valued stochastic process acting on $\boldsymbol{\xi}_t^\alpha$, whereas $\boldsymbol{A}_t^\alpha = \boldsymbol{I} - \boldsymbol{J}_t^\alpha$, with $\boldsymbol{I}$ the identity matrix, is an annihilator matrix determining a complementary information subspace. This projection can also be formalized by starting from an enlarged filtration, where

$$\mathcal{Z}_t = \sigma((\boldsymbol{\xi}_u^\alpha)_{0 \le u \le t}, (\boldsymbol{J}_u^\alpha)_{0 \le u \le t}, \boldsymbol{X}\mathbb{1}_{\{t=1\}}; \alpha = 1, \ldots, m),$$

is a subalgebra $\mathcal{Z}_t \subseteq \mathcal{G}_t$ for $t \in \mathbb{T}$. Thus, $\mathcal{H}_t \subseteq \mathcal{Z}_t$ and

$$\mathbb{P}[\boldsymbol{X} \in \mathrm{d}\boldsymbol{x} \,|\, \mathcal{H}_t] = \mathbb{E}[\mathbb{P}[\boldsymbol{X} \in \mathrm{d}\boldsymbol{x}) \,|\, \mathcal{Z}_t] \,|\, \mathcal{H}_t],$$

is a projection. Having $\xi_t^{\alpha,(i)} = tX^\alpha + \sigma_i^\alpha \beta_t^{\alpha,(i)}$, for $\sigma_i^\alpha > 0$ and $i = 1, \ldots, n(\alpha)$, we can define the full effective processes

$$\Psi_t^\alpha = (\epsilon^{\hat{\alpha}})^2 \sum_{i=1}^{n(\alpha)} (\sigma_i^\alpha)^{-2} \xi_t^{\alpha,(i)}, \quad \text{where } \epsilon^{\hat{\alpha}} = \left(\sum_{i=1}^{n(\alpha)} (\sigma_i^\alpha)^{-2} \right)^{-1/2},$$

without the need for any complementary process, and where the $\epsilon^{\hat{\alpha}}$s are constants and $\epsilon^{\hat{\alpha}} > 0$ for $\alpha = 1, \ldots, m$. Accordingly, we can define $(\mathcal{Z}_t)$-martingales $(M_t^\alpha)_{t \in \mathbb{T}_*}$ by

$$M_t^\alpha = \Psi_t^\alpha - \int_0^t \frac{\mathbb{E}[X^\alpha \,|\, \Psi_t^\alpha] - \Psi_t^\alpha}{1-s} \mathrm{d}s,$$

where the martingale property follows as a simple case of Proposition 2.6. Therefore, $(B_t^\alpha)_{t\in\mathbb{T}_*}$ defined by $B_t^\alpha = M_t^\alpha/\epsilon^\alpha$ are $(\mathcal{Z}_t)$-Brownian motions for $\alpha = 1,\ldots,m$. Hence, using Proposition 2.5 and following similar steps to Proposition 2.12, the measure $\hat{\nu}_t(\mathrm{d}\boldsymbol{x}) = \mathbb{P}[\boldsymbol{X} \in \mathrm{d}\boldsymbol{x} \,|\, \mathcal{Z}_t]$ satisfies

$$
\begin{aligned}
\hat{\nu}_t(\mathrm{d}\boldsymbol{x}) &= \mathbb{P}[\boldsymbol{X} \in \mathrm{d}\boldsymbol{x}) \,|\, \{\Psi_t^\alpha : \alpha = 1,\ldots,m\}] \\
&= \hat{\nu}_0(\mathrm{d}\boldsymbol{x}) + \sum_{\alpha=1}^{m} \int_0^t \frac{x^\alpha - \mathbb{E}[X^\alpha \,|\, \Psi_s^\alpha]}{\epsilon^\alpha(1-s)} \hat{\nu}_s(\mathrm{d}\boldsymbol{x})\,\mathrm{d}B_s^\alpha \\
&= \hat{\nu}_0(\mathrm{d}\boldsymbol{x}) + \int_0^t \hat{\nu}_s(\mathrm{d}\boldsymbol{x}) \sum_{\alpha=1}^{m} \Gamma_s^\alpha \,\mathrm{d}B_s^\alpha,
\end{aligned}
$$

where $(\Gamma_s^\alpha)_{0\le t<1}$ is defined correspondingly as above for $\alpha = 1,\ldots,m$. Then, following similar steps to Proposition 2.11 and solving the SDE above, we have

$$
\begin{aligned}
\nu_t(\mathrm{d}\boldsymbol{x}) &= \mathbb{E}[\hat{\nu}_t(\mathrm{d}\boldsymbol{x}) \,|\, \hat{\xi}_t^\alpha, \eta_t^\alpha] \\
&= \mathbb{E}\left[\prod_{\alpha=1}^{m} \mathbb{P}[X^\alpha \in \mathrm{d}x^\alpha \,|\, \{\Psi_t^\alpha : \alpha = 1,\ldots,m\}] \,|\, \hat{\xi}_t^\alpha, \eta_t^\alpha\right] \\
&= \nu_0(\mathrm{d}\boldsymbol{x})\mathbb{E}\left[\exp\left(-\frac{1}{2}\int_0^t \sum_{\alpha=1}^{m} (\Gamma_s^\alpha)^2\,\mathrm{d}s + \int_0^t \sum_{\alpha=1}^{m} \Gamma_s^\alpha\,\mathrm{d}B_s^\alpha\right) \,\middle|\, \hat{\xi}_t^\alpha, \eta_t^\alpha\right],
\end{aligned}
$$

since $\nu_0(\mathrm{d}\boldsymbol{x}) = \hat{\nu}_0(\mathrm{d}\boldsymbol{x})$, the bracket $\langle \mathrm{d}B_t^\alpha, \mathrm{d}B_t^\beta\rangle = 0$ for $\alpha,\beta \in \{1,\ldots,m\}$, and since Novikov's condition holds

$$
\mathbb{E}\left[\exp\left(\frac{1}{2}\int_0^t \left|\sum_{\alpha=1}^{m}\sum_{\beta=1}^{m} \Gamma_s^\alpha \Gamma_s^\beta\right|^2 \mathrm{d}\langle B_s^\alpha, B_s^\beta\rangle\right)\right] < \infty.
$$

This motivates us to ask how far we can push this idea towards its logical limits for modeling information modulation. To maintain generality, we let $(\boldsymbol{\xi}_t^\alpha)_{t\in\mathbb{T}}$ below to be LRBs, not necessarily Brownian bridge information processes, nor even the same class of LRB across $\alpha = 1,\ldots,m$.

Definition 2.4. A *modulated Lévy random bridge information system* is given by the probability space $(\Omega, \mathcal{H}, \mathbb{P})$ equipped with a right-continuous and complete filtration $(\mathcal{H}_t)_{t\in\mathbb{T}}$, where

(1) $\mathcal{H}_t = \sigma((\boldsymbol{P}_u^\alpha\,\boldsymbol{\xi}_u^\alpha)_{0\le u\le t}, (\boldsymbol{P}_u^\alpha)_{0\le u\le t}, \boldsymbol{X}\mathbb{1}_{\{t=T\}}; \alpha = 1,\ldots,m)$.
(2) $(\boldsymbol{\xi}_t^\alpha)_{t\in\mathbb{T}}$ is an $\mathbb{R}^{n(\alpha)}$-valued Lévy random bridge with generating law ν^α for $\alpha = 1,\ldots,m$.
(3) $(\boldsymbol{P}_t^\alpha)_{t\in\mathbb{T}}$ is an $n(\alpha)$-dimensional projection-valued stochastic process with real càdlàg paths for $\alpha = 1,\ldots,m$.

Modulated Information Flows in Financial Markets

(4) $\boldsymbol{X} \in \mathcal{L}^2(\Omega, \mathcal{G}, \mathbb{P})$ is an m-dimensional vector of random variables with law $\boldsymbol{\nu}$ and state-space $(\mathbb{X}^m, \bigotimes_{\alpha=1}^m \mathcal{B}(\mathbb{X}))$, where $\mathbb{X} \subseteq \mathbb{R}$ and $\mathcal{B}(\mathbb{X})$ is the Borel σ-field.
(5) $\mathbb{T} = [0, T]$ is a finite interval for some $T < \infty$.

This definition of the system does not explicitly rely on any random point field. However, one can assign a law to $(\boldsymbol{P}_t^\alpha)_{t\in\mathbb{T}}$ via associating it with a random point field ζ^α. Although we leave a detailed study of such a system for future research, we shall nonetheless provide a simple example to show how — what we call — *information mixing* arises.

Example 2.1. Let $m = 1$, $(\boldsymbol{\xi}_t)_{t\in\mathbb{T}}$ is such that $\xi_t^{(i)} = tX + \sigma_i \beta_t^{(i)}$ for $\sigma_i^\alpha > 0$, and $p_t^{(ij)}$ denote the (i,j)th coordinate of an n-dimensional projection matrix $\boldsymbol{P}_t$. Then at any $t \in \mathbb{T}$, the σ-algebra $\mathcal{H}_t$ allows the mapping $\boldsymbol{P}_t\,\boldsymbol{\xi}_t \mapsto \boldsymbol{\psi}_t$, where

$$\psi_t^{(i)} = \begin{cases} 0 & \text{if } p_t^{(ij)} = 0 \text{ for all } j \in \{1, \ldots, n\}, \\ tX + \hat{p}_t^{(i)} \displaystyle\sum_{j=1}^n p_t^{(ij)} \sigma_j \beta_t^{(j)}, & \text{otherwise} \end{cases}$$

and where $\hat{p}_t^{(i)} = (\sum_{j=1}^n p_t^{(ij)})^{-1}$. Thus, $\psi_t^{(i)} = tX + \alpha_t^{(i)} B_t^{(i)}$ given that $(B_t^{(i)})_{t\in\mathbb{T}}$ is a standard Brownian bridge and the bridge coefficient is

$$\alpha_t^{(i)} = \hat{p}_t^{(i)} \left(\sum_{j=1}^n (p_t^{(ij)})^2 \sigma_j^2 \right)^{\frac{1}{2}}.$$

When $\boldsymbol{P}_t$ is diagonal (e.g. $\boldsymbol{P}_t = \boldsymbol{J}_t$), the observer of $\boldsymbol{P}_t\,\boldsymbol{\xi}_t$ also observes the active coordinates of $\boldsymbol{\xi}_t$, possibly scaled. Generally, the observer may not be able to decouple all the active coordinates of $\boldsymbol{\xi}_t$ from the observed $\boldsymbol{P}_t\,\boldsymbol{\xi}_t$, since $\boldsymbol{P}_t$ is noninvertible, unless $\boldsymbol{P}_t = \boldsymbol{I}$, for it is a projection. Hence, the original information provided from each source may get mixed with another.

3. Applications

Thus far, we have not specified an interpretation for X. Next, we apply the framework to finance in the spirit of Brody *et al.* (2008a). We assume that $\mathbb{P}$ is the pricing measure, $(\mathcal{F}_t)$ is the market information and X is the cash flow of a financial asset at $t = 1$. We let the risk-free system be deterministic and denote the system of discount functions by $(P_{0t})_{0\le t<\infty}$. We assume that P_{0t} is differentiable, strictly decreasing and that it satisfies $0 < P_{0t} \le 1$ and $\lim_{t\to\infty} P_{0t} = 0$. The no-arbitrage condition implies that $P_{t1} = P_{01}/P_{0t}$ for $t \le 1$. We write $\overline{X}_t = P_{t1} X_t = P_{t1}\mathbb{E}[X \mid \mathcal{F}_t]$ for the price at time t. The price process $(\overline{X}_t)$ has jump-diffusion dynamics, see Sec. 2.1.

3.1. *Merton-type jump-diffusion models for vanilla options*

We choose ζ such that $\tilde{J}_t^{(i)} = 1$ implies $\tilde{J}_u^{(i)} = 1$ for $u \ge t$. This removes any path-dependency in the system caused by randomly paused flows of information.

E. Hoyle, A. Macrina & L. A. Mengütürk

We also let there be at least one active source of information at $t = 0$, so that some information about X is always available to market participants. In this setting, if $\xi_t^{(i)} = tX + \sigma_i \beta_t^{(i)}$, Proposition 1.1 reduces down to

$$X_t = \mathbb{E}[X] + \sum_{j=1}^{C_t} \int_{\pi_{j-1}}^{\pi_j} \theta_s \, \mathrm{d}W_s^{(j)} + \int_{\pi_{C_t}}^{t} \theta_s \, \mathrm{d}W_s^{(C_t+1)} + \sum_{s \le t} (X_s - X_{s-}) \delta_s.$$

As an example, we shall price a European-style call option with strike price K and exercisable at a fixed time $t \in (0, 1)$. The price at time zero is given by $C_0 = P_{0t} \mathbb{E}[(\overline{X}_t - K)^+]$ where $0 < t < 1$, and to make the derivation easier to follow, we represent processes explicitly as a function of the state $k \in \mathbb{S}$, e.g. we write $\hat{\xi}_t(k)$ for $\tilde{\boldsymbol{J}}_t = k$.

Proposition 3.1. *The price at time* 0 *of the European-style call option is given by*

$$C_0 = P_{0t} \sum_{k \in \mathbb{S}} \mathbb{P}(\tilde{\boldsymbol{J}}_t = k) \int_{\mathbb{X}} x \mathcal{N}\left(-\hat{z}_t(k) + \frac{x\sqrt{t}}{\hat{\sigma}_t^2(k)\sqrt{(1-t)}} \right) \nu(\mathrm{d}x)$$
$$- P_{0t} \sum_{k \in \mathbb{S}} \mathbb{P}(\tilde{\boldsymbol{J}}_t = k) K \int_{\mathbb{X}} \mathcal{N}\left(-\hat{z}_t(k) + \frac{x\sqrt{t}}{\hat{\sigma}_t^2(k)\sqrt{(1-t)}} \right) \nu(\mathrm{d}x),$$

for $t \in (0, 1)$, *where* $\mathcal{N}(\cdot)$ *is the standard normal distribution and* $\hat{z}_t(k) = \hat{\varsigma}(k)/\sqrt{t(1-t)}$, *where* $\hat{\varsigma}(k)$ *is the unique solution to*

$$\int_{\mathbb{X}} (P_{t1} x - K) \exp\left[\frac{1}{\hat{\sigma}_t^2(k)(1-t)} \left(x \hat{\varsigma}(k) - \frac{t x^2}{2} \right) \right] \nu(\mathrm{d}x) = 0.$$

Proof. Let $\overline{X}_t(k) = P_{t1} \mathbb{E}[X \,|\, \hat{\xi}_t(k)]$, which is the price of the asset given that $\tilde{\boldsymbol{J}}_t$ is in state $k \in \mathbb{S}$. That is, since $\hat{\xi}_t$ has to be in one of the 2^n states at any time, k should be understood as an identifier of the active and inactive coordinates of $\boldsymbol{\xi}_t$. Then, the price of the option is given by the following:

$$C_0 = \sum_{k \in \mathbb{S}} C_0(k) \mathbb{P}(\tilde{\boldsymbol{J}}_t = k),$$

for $t \in (0, 1)$, where $C_0(k) = P_{0t} \mathbb{E}[(\overline{X}_t(k) - K)^+]$. This follows from the law of total expectation, where we have

$$\begin{aligned} \mathbb{E}[(\overline{X}_t - K)^+] &= \mathbb{E}[\mathbb{E}[(\overline{X}_t - K)^+ \,|\, \tilde{\boldsymbol{J}}_t]] \\ &= \sum_{k \in \mathbb{S}} \mathbb{E}[(\overline{X}_t - K)^+ \,|\, \tilde{\boldsymbol{J}}_t = k] \mathbb{P}(\tilde{\boldsymbol{J}}_t = k) \\ &= \sum_{k \in \mathbb{S}} \mathbb{E}[(\overline{X}_t(k) - K)^+] \mathbb{P}(\tilde{\boldsymbol{J}}_t = k), \end{aligned}$$

since $(\boldsymbol{\xi}_t)$ is Markovian and independent of the state process $(\tilde{\boldsymbol{J}}_t)$, and $\eta_t = 1$ for all $t \in \mathbb{T}$. We can write the conditional distribution as an explicit function of $k \in \mathbb{S}$,

$$\nu_t(\mathrm{d}x; k) = \frac{\exp\left[\frac{1}{(1-t)}\hat{\sigma}_t^{-2}(k)\left(x\hat{\xi}_t(k) - \frac{tx^2}{2}\right)\right]\nu(\mathrm{d}x)}{\int_{\mathbb{X}}\exp\left[\frac{1}{(1-t)}\hat{\sigma}_t^{-2}(k)\left(x\hat{\xi}_t(k) - \frac{tx^2}{2}\right)\right]\nu(\mathrm{d}x)},$$

for $t \in (0,1)$. Following similar steps to Brody *et al.* (2008a) while decomposing with respect to the state $k \in \mathbb{S}$, we have

$$C_0(k) = P_{0t}\mathbb{E}\left[\frac{1}{\Phi_t(k)}\left(\int_{\mathbb{X}}(P_{t1}x - K)\chi_t(x;k)\nu(\mathrm{d}x)\right)^+\right],$$

where $\Phi_t(k) = \int_{\mathbb{X}}\chi_t(x;k)\nu(\mathrm{d}x)$ and

$$\chi_t(x;k) = \exp\left(\frac{x\hat{\xi}_t(k) - \frac{tx^2}{2}}{\hat{\sigma}_t^2(k)(1-t)}\right).$$

Then, for $t \in (0,1)$, we can define the measure $\mathbb{B}$ on $(\Omega, \mathcal{G}, \{\mathcal{G}_t\})$ through a sequence of Radon–Nikodym derivatives

$$\left\{\left.\frac{\mathrm{d}\mathbb{B}}{\mathrm{d}\mathbb{P}}\right|_{\sigma((\hat{\xi}_s(k))_{0\le s\le t})}\right\}_{k\in\mathbb{S}} = \left\{\frac{1}{\Phi_t(k)}\right\}_{k\in\mathbb{S}}.$$

This follows because the process $(1/\Phi_t(k))$ is a $\mathbb{P}$-martingale; that is,

$$\mathbb{E}\left[\frac{1}{\Phi_t(k)}\,\middle|\,\hat{\xi}_s(k)\right] = \frac{1}{\Phi_s(k)} \tag{3.1}$$

for $s < t$, and also $\Phi_0(k) = 1$ and $\Phi_t(k) > 0$. In particular,

$$(\Phi_t(k))^{-1} = \exp\left(-\int_0^t \frac{\mathbb{E}[X\,|\,\hat{\xi}_s(k)]}{\hat{\sigma}_s(k)(1-s)}\mathrm{d}W_s(k) - \frac{1}{2}\int_0^t \frac{\mathbb{E}[X\,|\,\hat{\xi}_s(k)]^2}{\hat{\sigma}_s^2(k)(1-s)^2}\mathrm{d}s\right),$$

and the Novikov's condition

$$\mathbb{E}\left[\exp\left(\frac{1}{2}\int_0^t \frac{\mathbb{E}[X\,|\,\hat{\xi}_s(k)]^2}{\hat{\sigma}_s^2(k)(1-s)^2}\mathrm{d}s\right)\right] < \infty,$$

is satisfied. Under the measure $\mathbb{B}$, the random variable $\hat{\xi}_t(k)$ is Gaussian and we have

$$C_0 = P_{0t}\sum_{k\in\mathbb{S}}\mathbb{P}(\tilde{\boldsymbol{J}}_t = k)\mathbb{E}^{\mathbb{B}}\left[\left(\int_{\mathbb{X}}(P_{t1}x - K)\chi_t(x;k)\nu(\mathrm{d}x)\right)^+\right].$$

The statement follows by computing the critical value $\hat{\varsigma}(k)$. □

E. Hoyle, A. Macrina & L. A. Mengütürk

The option price can be represented as the weighted sum of Black–Scholes–Merton prices induced by the various combinations of active information processes. The functional form of the price is very similar to that presented in Merton (1976) where jumps are assumed to be driven by a Poisson process. In our framework, the jump-diffusion dynamics of the price process emerges from the nature of the market information (i.e. *endogenous*), the jump distribution is not specified *a priori* and it corresponds to the much larger class of random counting measures.

Example 3.1. As a special case, we can choose the underlying random point field to generate an independent Poisson process with intensity λ such that we have

$$
\begin{aligned}
C_0 = P_{0t} \sum_{k=1}^{\infty} \frac{\mathrm{e}^{-\lambda t}(\lambda t)^{k-1}}{(k-1)!} \int_{\mathbb{X}} x \mathcal{N}\left(-\hat{z}_t(k) + \frac{x\sqrt{t}}{\hat{\sigma}_t^2(k)\sqrt{(1-t)}}\right) \nu(\mathrm{d}x) \\
- P_{0t} \sum_{k=1}^{\infty} \frac{\mathrm{e}^{-\lambda t}(\lambda t)^{k-1}}{(k-1)!} K \int_{\mathbb{X}} \mathcal{N}\left(-\hat{z}_t(k) + \frac{x\sqrt{t}}{\hat{\sigma}_t^2(k)\sqrt{(1-t)}}\right) \nu(\mathrm{d}x),
\end{aligned}
$$

We refer to Cont & Tankov (2004) and Crandall & Lions (1983) for partial integro-differential equations and viscosity solutions that offer alternative techniques for option pricing with respect to jump-diffusion dynamics.

3.2. *Information asymmetry and market competition*

We consider a setting in which there are two market agents who are unaware of each other's actions and have differing access to a fixed universe of information sources. We here allude to a randomly evolving competition between agents, where some may have an informational advantage over a period of time and suddenly find that the wheel has turned with them having to come to terms with several of their information sources being disabled.

Let $(\tilde{\boldsymbol{J}}_t^{(1)}) \in \mathbb{S}$ and $(\tilde{\boldsymbol{J}}_t^{(2)}) \in \mathbb{S}$, which are $\mathcal{G}_t$-adapted càdlàg jump processes of Agents 1 and 2, respectively. The jump processes are generated by two random point fields $\zeta^{(1)}$ and $\zeta^{(2)}$, both independent of $(\boldsymbol{\xi}_t)$. We define the sub-algebras $\mathcal{F}_t^{(j)} \subseteq \mathcal{G}_t$ by

$$
\mathcal{F}_t^{(j)} = \sigma((\tilde{\boldsymbol{J}}_u^{(j)} \otimes \boldsymbol{\xi}_u)_{0\le u\le t}, (\tilde{\boldsymbol{J}}_u^{(j)})_{0\le u\le t}, X\mathbf{1}_{\{t=T\}}),
$$

for $j = \{1,2\}$. Then we introduce $\nu_t^{(j)}(A) = \mathbb{P}[X \in A \,|\, \mathcal{F}_t^{(j)}]$, where, if we use Proposition 2.5, we have $\nu_t^{(j)}(A) = \mathbb{P}[X \in A \,|\, \hat{\xi}_t^{(j)}, \eta_t^{(j)}]$. We note that $\mathbb{P}[\hat{\xi}_t^{(1)} = \hat{\xi}_t^{(2)}] < 1$ and $\mathbb{P}[\eta_t^{(1)} = \eta_t^{(2)}] < 1$, since the set-valued processes $(\mathcal{J}_t^{(j)})$, which define the effective and complementary information processes of the agents, are different. To model the information asymmetry in a dynamic competition between the agents, we shall use f-divergences; see Amari & Nagaoka (2008), Ali & Silvey (1966) and Csiszar (1967). We can define a symmetric f-divergence between equivalent probability

Modulated Information Flows in Financial Markets

measures $\mathbb{P}^{(1)}$ and $\mathbb{P}^{(2)}$ as

$$\Delta_f[\mathbb{P}^{(1)} \,\|\, \mathbb{P}^{(2)}] = \frac{1}{2}\left[\int_\Omega f\left(\frac{\mathrm{d}\mathbb{P}^{(1)}(\omega)}{\mathrm{d}\mathbb{P}^{(2)}(\omega)}\right)\mathrm{d}\mathbb{P}^{(2)}(\omega) + \int_\Omega f\left(\frac{\mathrm{d}\mathbb{P}^{(2)}(\omega)}{\mathrm{d}\mathbb{P}^{(1)}(\omega)}\right)\mathrm{d}\mathbb{P}^{(1)}(\omega)\right],$$

for $\omega \in \Omega$, where f is a convex function that satisfies $f(1) = 0$, and where $\mathrm{d}\mathbb{P}^{(1)}/\mathrm{d}\mathbb{P}^{(2)}$ is the Radon–Nikodym derivative. Alternatively, a symmetric f-divergence can be defined in terms of probability densities, assuming that they exist. For convenience, we assume that X has a density and write $\nu_t^{(j)}(\mathrm{d}x) = p_t^{(j)}(x)\mathrm{d}x$ such that $p_t^{(j)}(x) > 0$ for $t \in \mathbb{T}_*$ and $x \in \mathbb{X}$.

As an example, we shall utilize Kullback–Leibler divergence (relative entropy), which is not a distance metric on the space of probability distributions, but measures the information gain when moving from a prior distribution to a posterior distribution. For $t \in \mathbb{T}_*$,

$$\Delta_{\mathrm{KL}}[p_t^{(1)} \,\|\, p_t^{(2)}] = \frac{1}{2}\int_{\mathbb{X}}\left[p_t^{(1)}(x)\log\left(\frac{p_t^{(1)}(x)}{p_t^{(2)}(x)}\right) + p_t^{(2)}(x)\log\left(\frac{p_t^{(2)}(x)}{p_t^{(1)}(x)}\right)\right]\mathrm{d}x.$$

We represent the probability density functions explicitly as a function of the state; $p_t^{(j)}(x;k_j)$ for $\tilde{\boldsymbol{J}}_t^{(j)} = k_j$, where $k_j \in \mathbb{S}$ for $j = \{1,2\}$. Thus, if $\xi_t^{(i)} \overset{\text{law}}{=} tX + \sigma_i\beta_t^{(i)}$, we have $p_t^{(j)}(x;k_j)\mathrm{d}x = \mathbb{P}[X \in \mathrm{d}x \,|\, \hat{\xi}_t(k_j), \eta_t^{(j)}(k_j)]$. Then, by defining the processes $(A_t(k_1,k_2))$ and $(B_t(k_1,k_2))$ by

$$A_t(k_1,k_2) = \int_{\mathbb{X}} \log\left(\frac{p_t^{(1)}(x;k_1)}{p_t^{(2)}(x;k_2)}\right)\nu_t^{(j)}(\mathrm{d}x;k_1),$$

$$B_t(k_1,k_2) = \int_{\mathbb{X}} \log\left(\frac{p_t^{(2)}(x;k_2)}{p_t^{(1)}(x;k_1)}\right)\nu_t^{(2)}(\mathrm{d}x;k_2),$$

respectively, we may write

$$2\Delta_{\mathrm{KL}}[p_t^{(1)}||p_t^{(2)}] = \sum_{k_1\in\mathbb{S}}\sum_{k_2\in\mathbb{S}}(A_t(k_1,k_2) + B_t(k_1,k_2))\,\mathbb{1}\{\tilde{\boldsymbol{J}}_t^{(1)} = k_1\}\mathbb{1}\{\tilde{\boldsymbol{J}}_t^{(2)} = k_2\}.$$

As a geometric measure for information asymmetry, since $\sqrt{p_t^{(j)}(x)}$ for $j = \{1,2\}$ determines a point on $\mathcal{S}^+ \in \mathcal{L}^2$, we can define the angle process $\{\Theta_t^{1,2}\}_{0\le t<T}$ by the $\mathcal{L}^2$-inner product,

$$\begin{aligned}\cos\Theta_t^{1,2}(k_1,k_2) &= \frac{\langle\sqrt{p_t^{(1)}(x;k_1)},\sqrt{p_t^{(2)}(x;k_2)}\rangle}{\langle\sqrt{p_t^{(1)}(x;k_1)},\sqrt{p_t^{(1)}(x;k_1)}\rangle^{\frac{1}{2}}\langle\sqrt{p_t^{(2)}(x;k_2)},\sqrt{p_t^{(2)}(x;k_2)}\rangle^{\frac{1}{2}}}\\ &= \int_{\mathbb{X}}\sqrt{p_t^{(1)}(x;k_1)}\sqrt{p_t^{(2)}(x;k_2)}\,\mathrm{d}x\\ &= 1 - \frac{1}{2}\int_{\mathbb{X}}(\sqrt{p_t^{(1)}(x;k_1)} - \sqrt{p_t^{(2)}(x;k_2)})^2\,\mathrm{d}x,\end{aligned}$$

since the $\mathcal{L}^2$-norm of $\sqrt{p_t^{(j)}(x)}$ equals unity, and $\mathcal{S} \in \mathcal{L}^2$ is a Riemannian manifold when equipped with the inner product $\langle \cdot , \cdot \rangle$. Here, $\Theta_t^{1,2}(k_1, k_2) = \Theta_t^{2,1}(k_2, k_1)$ is the Bhattacharyya angle between $p_t^{(1)}$ and $p_t^{(2)}$; the angle from the center of $\mathcal{S}$ subtended to the endpoints on $\mathcal{S}^+$.

$$\cos \Theta_t^{1,2} = \sum_{k_1 \in \mathbb{S}} \sum_{k_2 \in \mathbb{S}} \cos \Theta_t^{1,2}(k_1, k_2) \mathbb{1}\{\tilde{\boldsymbol{J}}_t^{(1)} = k_1\} \mathbb{1}\{\tilde{\boldsymbol{J}}_t^{(2)} = k_2\}.$$

These are useful representations to derive SDEs for the Kullback–Leibler divergence Δ_{KL} and spherical Θ asymmetry processes via Proposition 2.7. These processes jump every time one of the agents gains access to a new source of information. If both agents have the same information at a given time, that is, if $\nu_t^{(1)}(\mathrm{d}x; k_1) = \nu_t^{(2)}(\mathrm{d}x; k_2)$ for some $t \in \mathbb{T}_*$, then the processes are zero at that time. The study of information asymmetry, e.g. in Amendinger *et al.* (1998), Ankirchner *et al.* (2006) and Leon *et al.* (2003), has benefited substantially from the theory of enlargements of filtrations; see Jacod (1980) and Yor (1980).

Proposition 3.2. *The activation and deactivation of new information sources at random times can be understood as a dynamic interplay between enlargements of filtrations and stopped filtrations.*

We leave a formal treatment of this remark and a corresponding rigorous application of information asymmetry to market competition with multiple agents for future research.

3.3. *Conclusions*

In order to model information switches, we have worked in the foregoing with filtrations generated by dynamically modulated multivariate Lévy random bridges. In the case of Brownian random bridges, we have constructed what we call effective and complementary information processes, which provide us with analytical tractability to prove a dynamical representation for the conditional expectation martingale in terms of standard Brownian motions. The effective process is a one-dimensional aggregation of all active information sources and the complementary process reflects the information supplied by now inactive sources. As an application, we have worked out the price of a vanilla option under the modulated information system, and we have highlighted the similarity of its functional form with that obtained by Merton (1976). Our second application addresses information asymmetry between agents whose access to information sources differ. We have concluded by producing an example of modulated information and the associated endogenous jump-diffusion dynamics. In Fig. 1, we show a simulated path of the conditional expectation process (X_t) given in Proposition 2.8. This jump-diffusion process jumps whenever an information coordinate is activated. At each point in time a Markov chain dictates which information coordinates are active. Because of the permanent nature of each

Modulated Information Flows in Financial Markets

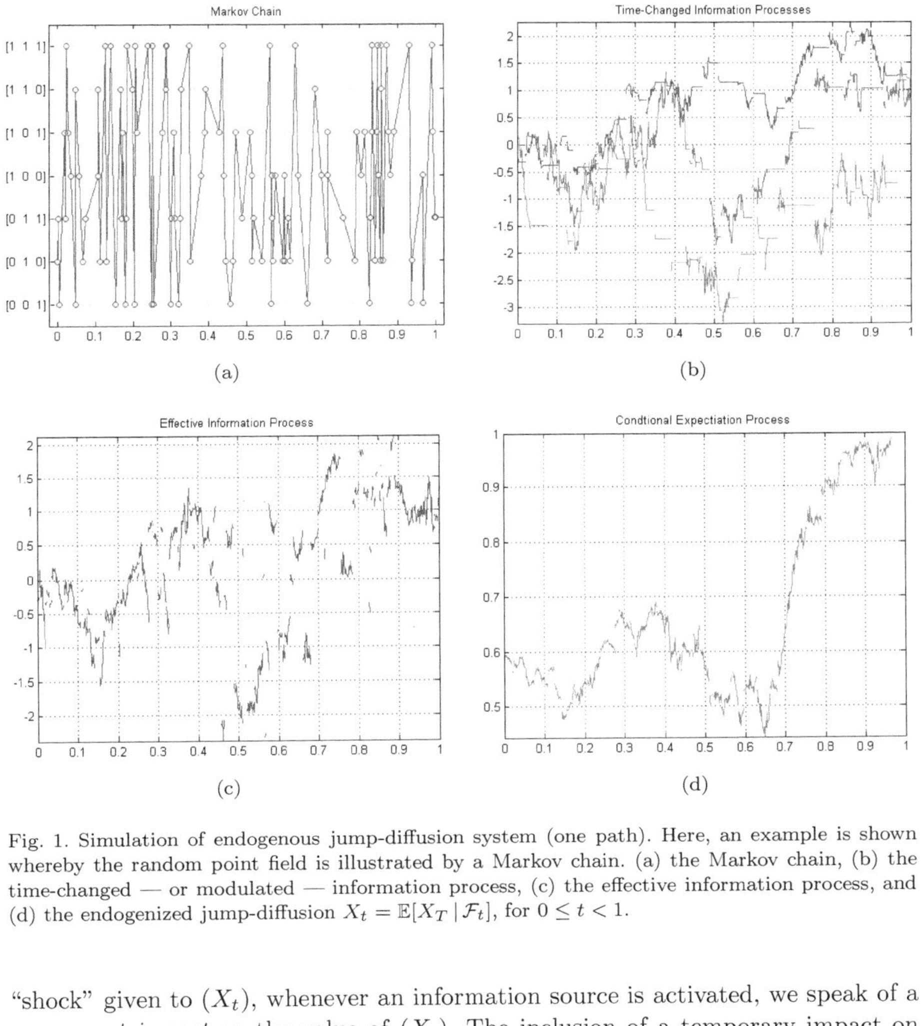

Fig. 1. Simulation of endogenous jump-diffusion system (one path). Here, an example is shown whereby the random point field is illustrated by a Markov chain. (a) the Markov chain, (b) the time-changed — or modulated — information process, (c) the effective information process, and (d) the endogenized jump-diffusion $X_t = \mathbb{E}[X_T \mid \mathcal{F}_t]$, for $0 \leq t < 1$.

"shock" given to (X_t), whenever an information source is activated, we speak of a *permanent impact* on the value of (X_t). The inclusion of a temporary impact on (X_t) is a suggestion for future research, where the informational contribution of a particular information coordinate (source) "fades away" over time once the source is deactivated.

Acknowledgments

The authors thank J. Akahori, G. W. Peters, J. Sekine, peer-reviewers, and participants in the Osaka-UCL Workshop on Stochastics, Numerics and Risk (March 2017), which was co-sponsored by The Daiwa Anglo-Japanese Foundation, participants in the 6th International Conference, Mathematics in Finance, RSA (August

2017), and in the Seminar of the Actuarial Mathematics & Statistics Department, Heriot-Watt University (May 2019), for comments and suggestions.

References

M. S. Ali & S. D. Silvey (1966) A general class of coefficients of divergence of one distribution from another, *Journal of Royal Statistical Society B* **28**, 131–142.

S. Amari & H. Nagaoka (2008) *Methods of Information Geometry*, Providence: American Mathematical Society.

J. Amendinger, P. Imkeller & M. Schweizer (1998) Additional logarithmic utility of an insider, *Stochastic Processes and Their Applications* **75**, 263–286.

S. Ankirchner, S. Dereich & P. Imkeller (2006) The shannon information of filtrations and the additional logarithmic utility of insiders, *The Annals of Probability* **34** (2), 743–778.

N. P. B. Bollen, S. F. Gray & R. E. Whalley (2000) Regime switching in foreign exchange rates: Evidence from currency option prices, *Journal of Econometrics* **94**, 239–276.

D. C. Brody (2019) Modelling election dynamics and the impact of disinformation, *Information Geometry* **2**, 209–230.

D. C. Brody, M. H. A. Davis, R. L. Friedman & L. P. Hughston (2009) Informed traders, *Proceedings of royal society A* **465**, 1103–1122.

D. C. Brody, L. P. Hughston & A. Macrina (2008a) Information-based asset pricing, *International Journal of Theoretical and Applied Finance* **11**, 107–142.

D. C. Brody, L. P. Hughston & A. Macrina (2008b) Dam rain and cumulative gain, *Proceedings of Royal Society A* **464**, 1801–1822.

D. C. Brody, L. P. Hughston & A. Macrina (2011) Modelling information flows in financial markets, In: *Advanced Mathematical Methods for Finance* (G. Di Nunno, B. Oksendal, eds.) Springer, pp. 133–153.

R. Cont & P. Tankov (2004) *Financial Modelling with Jump Processes.* Chapman and Hall/CRC Financial Mathematics Series.

M. G. Crandall & P. L. Lions (1983) Viscosity solutions of Hamilton–Jacobi equations, *Transactions of the American Mathematical Society* **277** (1), 1–42.

I. Csiszar (1967) Information-type measures of difference of probability distributions and indirect observations, *Studia Science and Mathematics* **2**, 299–318.

M. Emery & M. Yor (2004) A parallel between Brownian bridges and gamma bridges, *Publications of the Research Institute for Mathematical Sciences* **40**, 669–688.

P. J. Fitzsimmons, J. Pitman & M. Yor (1993) Markovian bridges: Construction, palm interpretation, and splicing, *Seminar on Stochastic Processes* **33**, 102–133.

J. D. Hamilton (1989) A new approach to the economic analysis of nonstationary time series and the business cycle, *Econometrica* **57**, 357–384.

E. Hoyle, L. P. Hughston & A. Macrina (2011) Lévy random bridges and the modelling of financial information, *Stochastic Processes and Their Applications* **121** (4), 856–884.

L. P. Hughston & A. Macrina (2008) Information, inflation, and interest. Banach. In: *Advances in Mathematics of Finance* (L. Stettner, ed.), Centre Publications, Institute of Mathematics, Polish Academy of Sciences, Vol. 83, pp. 117–138.

J. Jacod (1980) Grossissement initial, hypothese (H') et theoreme de Girsanov. In: *Grossissements de Filtrations: Exemples et Applications* (T. T. Jeulin & M. Yor, eds.), Lecture Notes in Mathematics, Vol. 1118. Berlin: Springer.

J. A. Leon, R. Navarro & D. Nualart (2003) An anticipating calculus approach to the utility maximization of an insider, *Mathematical Finance* **13**, pp. 171–185.

Modulated Information Flows in Financial Markets

A. Macrina & J. Sekine (2019) Stochastic modelling with randomized Markov bridges, *Stochastics*, doi:10.1080/17442508.2019.1703988.

R. C. Merton (1976) Option pricing when underlying returns are discontinuous, *Journal of Financial Economics* **3** (1–2), 125–144.

V. Naik (1993) Option valuation and hedging strategies with jumps in the volatility of assets returns, *Journal of Finance* **48**, 1969–1984.

M. Rutkowski & N. Yu (2007) On the Brody–Hughston–Macrina approach to modelling of defaultable term structure, *International Journal of Theoretical and Applied Finance* **10**, 557–589.

M. Yor (1980) Grossisement de filtration et absolue continuité de noyaux. In: *Grossissements de Filtrations: Exemples et Applications* (T. Jeulin & M. Yor, eds.), Lecture Notes in Mathematics, Vol. 1118. Berlin: Springer.

Chapter 16

Pricing with Variance Gamma Information†

Lane P. Hughston [1,*] **and Leandro Sánchez-Betancourt** [2]

1 Department of Computing, Goldsmiths University of London, New Cross, London SE14 6NW, UK
2 Mathematical Institute, University of Oxford, Oxford OX2 6GG, UK; leandro.sanchezbetancourt@maths.ox.ac.uk
* Correspondence: L.Hughston@gold.ac.uk

Received: 11 September 2020; Accepted: 30 September 2020; Published: 10 October 2020

check for updates

Abstract: In the information-based pricing framework of Brody, Hughston & Macrina, the market filtration $\{\mathcal{F}_t\}_{t\geq 0}$ is generated by an information process $\{\xi_t\}_{t\geq 0}$ defined in such a way that at some fixed time T an $\mathcal{F}_T$-measurable random variable X_T is "revealed". A cash flow H_T is taken to depend on the market factor X_T, and one considers the valuation of a financial asset that delivers H_T at time T. The value of the asset S_t at any time $t \in [0, T)$ is the discounted conditional expectation of H_T with respect to $\mathcal{F}_t$, where the expectation is under the risk neutral measure and the interest rate is constant. Then $S_{T^-} = H_T$, and $S_t = 0$ for $t \geq T$. In the general situation one has a countable number of cash flows, and each cash flow can depend on a vector of market factors, each associated with an information process. In the present work we introduce a new process, which we call the normalized variance-gamma bridge. We show that the normalized variance-gamma bridge and the associated gamma bridge are jointly Markovian. From these processes, together with the specification of a market factor X_T, we construct a so-called variance-gamma information process. The filtration is then taken to be generated by the information process together with the gamma bridge. We show that the resulting extended information process has the Markov property and hence can be used to develop pricing models for a variety of different financial assets, several examples of which are discussed in detail.

Keywords: information-based asset pricing; Lévy processes; gamma processes; variance gamma processes; Brownian bridges; gamma bridges; nonlinear filtering

---

1. Introduction

The theory of information-based asset pricing proposed by Brody et al. (2007, 2008a, 2008b) and Macrina (2006) is concerned with the determination of the price processes of financial assets from first principles. In particular, the market filtration is constructed explicitly, rather than simply assumed, as it is in traditional approaches. The simplest version of the model is as follows. We fix a probability space $(\Omega, \mathscr{F}, \mathbb{P})$. An asset delivers a single random cash flow H_T at some specified time $T > 0$, where time 0 denotes the present. The cash flow is a function of a random variable X_T, which we can think of as a "market factor" that is in some sense revealed at time T. In the general situation there will be many factors and many cash flows, but for the present we assume that there is a single factor $X_T : \Omega \to \mathbb{R}$ such that the sole cash flow at time T is given by $H_T = h(X_T)$ for some Borel function $h : \mathbb{R} \to \mathbb{R}^+$. For simplicity we assume that interest rates are constant and that $\mathbb{P}$ is the risk neutral measure. We require that H_T should be integrable. Under these assumptions, the value of the asset at time 0 is

$$S_0 = \mathrm{e}^{-rT}\,\mathbb{E}\left[h(X_T)\right], \tag{1}$$

Risks **2020**, *8*, 105; doi:10.3390/risks8040105 www.mdpi.com/journal/risks

†This chapter was originally published as: L. P. Hughston & L. Sánchez-Betancourt (2020) Pricing with Variance Gamma Information. *Risks* **8**, 105:1–22. Reprinted with kind permission from MDPI.

where $\mathbb{E}$ denotes expectation under $\mathbb{P}$ and r is the short rate. Since the single "dividend" is paid at time T, the value of the asset at any time $t \geq 0$ is of the form

$$S_t = \mathrm{e}^{-r(T-t)} \mathbb{1}_{\{t<T\}} \mathbb{E}\left[h(X_T) \mid \mathscr{F}_t\right], \tag{2}$$

where $\{\mathscr{F}_t\}_{t\geq 0}$ is the market filtration. The task now is to model the filtration, and this will be done explicitly.

In traditional financial modelling, the filtration is usually taken to be fixed in advance. For example, in the widely-applied Brownian-motion-driven model for financial markets, the filtration is generated by an n-dimensional Brownian motion. A detailed account of the Brownian framework can be found, for example, in Karatzas and Shreve (1998). In the information-based approach, however, we do not assume the filtration to be given *a priori*. Instead, the filtration is constructed in a way that specifically takes into account the structures of the information flows associated with the cash flows of the various assets under consideration.

In the case of a single asset generating a single cash flow, the idea is that the filtration should contain partial or "noisy" information about the market factor X_T, and hence the impending cash flow, in such a way that X_T is $\mathscr{F}_T$-measurable. This can be achieved by allowing $\{\mathscr{F}_t\}$ to be generated by a so-called information process $\{\xi_t\}_{t\geq 0}$ with the property that for each t such that $t \geq T$ the random variable ξ_t is $\sigma\{X_T\}$-measurable. Then by constructing specific examples of cádlàg processes having this property, we are able to formulate a variety of specific models. The resulting models are finely tuned to the structures of the assets that they represent, and therefore offer scope for a useful approach to financial risk management. In previous work on information-based asset pricing, where precise definitions can be found that expand upon the ideas summarized above, such models have been constructed using Brownian bridge information processes (Brody et al. (2007, 2008a, 2009, 2010, 2011), Filipović et al. (2012), Hughston and Macrina (2012), Macrina (2006), Mengütürk (2013), Rutkowski and Yu (2007)), gamma bridge information processes (Brody et al. (2008b)), Lévy random bridge information processes (Hoyle (2010), Hoyle et al. (2011, 2015, 2020), Mengütürk (2018)) and Markov bridge information processes (Macrina (2019)). In what follows we present a new model for the market filtration, based on the variance-gamma process. The idea is to create a two-parameter family of information processes associated with the random market factor X_T. One of the parameters is the information flow-rate σ. The other is an intrinsic parameter m associated with the variance gamma process. In the limit as m tends to infinity, the variance-gamma information process reduces to the type of Brownian bridge information process considered by Brody et al. (2007, 2008a) and Macrina (2006).

The plan of the paper is as follows. In Section 2 we recall properties of the gamma process, introducing the so-called scale parameter $\kappa > 0$ and shape parameter $m > 0$. A standard gamma subordinator is defined to be a gamma process with $\kappa = 1/m$. The mean at time t of a standard gamma subordinator is t. In Theorem 1 we prove that an increase in the shape parameter m results in a transfer of weight from the Lévy measure of any interval $[c, d]$ in the space of jump size to the Lévy measure of any interval $[a, b]$ such that $b - a = d - c$ and $c > a$. Thus, roughly speaking, an increase in m results in an increase in the rate at which small jumps occur relative to the rate at which large jumps occur. This result concerning the interpretation of the shape parameter for a standard gamma subordinator is new as far as we are aware.

In Section 3 we recall properties of the variance-gamma process and the gamma bridge, and in Definition 1 we introduce a new type of process, which we call a normalized variance-gamma bridge. This process plays an important role in the material that follows. In Lemmas 1 and 2 we work out various properties of the normalized variance-gamma bridge. Then in Theorem 2 we show that the normalized variance-gamma bridge and the associated gamma bridge are jointly Markov, a property that turns out to be crucial in our pricing theory. In Section 4, at Definition 2, we introduce the so-called variance-gamma information process. The information process carries noisy information about the value of a market factor X_T that will be revealed to the market at time T, where the noise is represented by the normalized variance-gamma bridge. In Equation (58) we present a formula that relates the values of the information process at different times, and by use of that we establish in Theorem 3 that the information process and the associated gamma bridge are jointly Markov.

In Section 5, we consider a market where the filtration is generated by a variance gamma information process along with the associated gamma bridge. In Lemma 3 we work out a version of the Bayes formula in the form that we need for asset pricing in the present context. Then in Theorem 4 we present a general formula for the price process of a financial asset that at time T pays a single dividend given by a function $h(X_T)$ of the market factor. In particular, the *a priori* distribution of the market factor can be quite arbitrary, specified by a measure $F_{X_T}(\mathrm{d}x)$ on $\mathbb{R}$, the only requirement being that $h(X_T)$ should be integrable. In Section 6 we present a number of examples, based on various choices of the payoff function and the distribution for the market factor, the results being summarized in Propositions 1–4. We conclude with comments on calibration, derivatives, and how one determines the trajectory of the information process from market prices.

2. Gamma Subordinators

We begin with some remarks about the gamma process. Let us as usual write $\mathbb{R}^+$ for the non-negative real numbers. Let κ and m be strictly positive constants. A continuous random variable $G : \Omega \to \mathbb{R}^+$ on a probability space $(\Omega, \mathscr{F}, \mathbb{P})$ will be said to have a gamma distribution with scale parameter κ and shape parameter m if

$$\mathbb{P}\,[G \in \mathrm{d}x] = \mathbb{1}_{\{x>0\}} \frac{1}{\Gamma[m]} \kappa^{-m} x^{m-1} \mathrm{e}^{-x/\kappa} \, \mathrm{d}x \,, \tag{3}$$

where

$$\Gamma[a] = \int_0^\infty x^{a-1} \mathrm{e}^{-x} \, \mathrm{d}x \tag{4}$$

denotes the standard gamma function for $a > 0$, and we recall the relation $\Gamma[a+1] = a\Gamma[a]$. A calculation shows that $\mathbb{E}\,[G] = \kappa\, m$, and $\mathrm{Var}[G] = \kappa^2\, m$. There exists a two-parameter family of gamma processes of the form $\Gamma : \Omega \times \mathbb{R}^+ \to \mathbb{R}^+$ on $(\Omega, \mathscr{F}, \mathbb{P})$. By a gamma process with scale κ and shape m we mean a Lévy process $\{\Gamma_t\}_{t\geq 0}$ such that for each $t > 0$ the random variable Γ_t is gamma distributed with

$$\mathbb{P}\,[\Gamma_t \in \mathrm{d}x] = \mathbb{1}_{\{x>0\}} \frac{1}{\Gamma[m\,t]} \kappa^{-m\,t} x^{m\,t-1} \mathrm{e}^{-x/\kappa} \, \mathrm{d}x \,. \tag{5}$$

If we write $(a)_0 = 1$ and $(a)_k = a(a+1)(a+2)\cdots(a+k-1)$ for the so-called Pochhammer symbol, we find that $\mathbb{E}[\Gamma_t^n] = \kappa^n (mt)_n$. It follows that $\mathbb{E}[\Gamma_t] = \mu\, t$ and $\mathrm{Var}[\Gamma_t] = \nu^2\, t$, where $\mu = \kappa\, m$ and $\nu^2 = \kappa^2\, m$, or equivalently $m = \mu^2/\nu^2$, and $\kappa = \nu^2/\mu$.

The Lévy exponent for such a process is given for $\alpha < 1$ by

$$\psi_\Gamma(\alpha) = \frac{1}{t} \log \mathbb{E}\,[\exp(\alpha\Gamma_t)] = -m \log(1 - \kappa\alpha) \,, \tag{6}$$

and for the corresponding Lévy measure we have

$$\nu_\Gamma(\mathrm{d}x) = \mathbb{1}_{\{x>0\}}\, m \frac{1}{x} \mathrm{e}^{-x/\kappa} \, \mathrm{d}x \,. \tag{7}$$

One can then check that the Lévy-Khinchine relation

$$\psi_\Gamma(\alpha) = \int_{\mathbb{R}} \left(\mathrm{e}^{\alpha x} - 1 - \mathbb{1}_{\{|x|<1\}}\, \alpha x\right)\, \nu_\Gamma(\mathrm{d}x) + p\alpha \tag{8}$$

holds for an appropriate choice of p (Kyprianou 2014, Lemma 1.7).

By a standard gamma subordinator we mean a gamma process $\{\gamma_t\}_{t\geq 0}$ for which $\kappa = 1/m$. This implies that $\mathbb{E}[\gamma_t] = t$ and $\mathrm{Var}[\gamma_t] = m^{-1}\, t$. The standard gamma subordinators thus constitute a one-parameter family of processes labelled by m. An interpretation of the parameter m is given by the following:

Theorem 1. *Let $\{\gamma_t\}_{t\geq 0}$ be a standard gamma subordinator with parameter m. Let $\nu_m[a,b]$ be the Lévy measure of the interval $[a,b]$ for $0 < a < b$. Then for any interval $[c,d]$ such that $c > a$ and $d - c = b - a$ the ratio*

$$R_m(a,b\,;c,d) = \frac{\nu_m[a,b]}{\nu_m[c,d]} \tag{9}$$

is strictly greater than one and strictly increasing as a function of m.

Proof. By the definition of a standard gamma subordinator we have

$$\nu_m[a,b] = \int_a^b m\, \frac{1}{x}\, \mathrm{e}^{-m\,x}\, \mathrm{d}x\,. \tag{10}$$

Let $\delta = c - a > 0$ and note that the integrand in the right hand side of (10) is a decreasing function of the variable of integration. This allows one to conclude that

$$\nu_m[a+\delta, b+\delta] = \int_{a+\delta}^{b+\delta} m\, \frac{1}{x}\, \mathrm{e}^{-m\,x}\, \mathrm{d}x < \int_a^b m\, \frac{1}{x}\, \mathrm{e}^{-m\,x}\, \mathrm{d}x\,, \tag{11}$$

from which it follows that $0 < \nu_m[c,d] < \nu_m[a,b]$ and hence $R_m(a,b\,;c,d) > 1$. To show that $R_m(a,b;c,d)$ is strictly increasing as a function of m we observe that

$$\nu_m[a,b] = m \int_a^\infty \frac{1}{x}\, \mathrm{e}^{-m\,x}\, \mathrm{d}x - m \int_b^\infty \frac{1}{x}\, \mathrm{e}^{-m\,x}\, \mathrm{d}x = m\, \left(E_1[m\,a] - E_1[m\,b]\right), \tag{12}$$

where the so-called exponential integral function $E_1(z)$ is defined for $z > 0$ by

$$E_1(z) = \int_z^\infty \frac{\mathrm{e}^{-x}}{x} \mathrm{d}x\,. \tag{13}$$

See Abramowitz and Stegun (1972), Section 5.1.1, for properties of the exponential integral. Next, we compute the derivative of $R_m(a,b\,;c,d)$, which gives

$$\frac{\partial}{\partial m} R_m(a,b\,;c,d) = \frac{1}{m\, \left(E_1[m\,c] - E_1[m\,d]\right)}\, \mathrm{e}^{-m\,a} \left(1 - \mathrm{e}^{-m\,\Delta}\right) \left(R_m(a,b\,;c,d) - \mathrm{e}^{m(c-a)}\right), \tag{14}$$

where

$$\Delta = d - c = b - a\,. \tag{15}$$

We note that

$$\frac{1}{m\, \left(E_1[m\,c] - E_1[m\,d]\right)}\, \mathrm{e}^{-m\,a} \left(1 - \mathrm{e}^{-m\,\Delta}\right) > 0\,, \tag{16}$$

which shows that the sign of the derivative in (14) is strictly positive if and only if

$$R_m(a,b\,;c,d) > \mathrm{e}^{m(c-a)}. \tag{17}$$

But clearly

$$\int_0^{\Delta m} \frac{e^{-u}}{u + a\,m}\, du > \int_0^{\Delta m} \frac{e^{-u}}{u + c\,m}\, du \tag{18}$$

for $c > a$, which after a change of integration variables and use of (15) implies

$$e^{m\,a} \int_{a\,m}^{b\,m} \frac{e^{-x}}{x}\, dx > e^{m\,c} \int_{c\,m}^{d\,m} \frac{e^{-x}}{x}\, dx, \tag{19}$$

which is equivalent to (17), and that completes the proof. □

We see therefore that the effect of an increase in the value of m is to transfer weight from the Lévy measure of any jump-size interval $[c, d] \subset \mathbb{R}^+$ to any possibly-overlapping smaller-jump-size interval $[a, b] \subset \mathbb{R}^+$ of the same length. The Lévy measure of such an interval is the rate of arrival of jumps for which the jump size lies in that interval.

3. Normalized Variance-Gamma Bridge

Let us fix a standard Brownian motion $\{W_t\}_{t\geq 0}$ on $(\Omega, \mathscr{F}, \mathbb{P})$ and an independent standard gamma subordinator $\{\gamma_t\}_{t\geq 0}$ with parameter m. By a standard variance-gamma process with parameter m we mean a time-changed Brownian motion $\{V_t\}_{t\geq 0}$ of the form

$$V_t = W_{\gamma_t}. \tag{20}$$

It is straightforward to check that $\{V_t\}$ is itself a Lévy process, with Lévy exponent

$$\psi_V(\alpha) = -m \log\left(1 - \frac{\alpha^2}{2\,m}\right). \tag{21}$$

Properties of the variance-gamma process, and financial models based on it, have been investigated extensively in Madan (1990), Madan and Milne (1991), Madan et al. (1998), Carr et al. (2002) and many other works.

The other object we require going forward is the gamma bridge (Brody et al. (2008b), Emery and Yor (2004), Yor (2007)). Let $\{\gamma_t\}$ be a standard gamma subordinator with parameter m. For fixed $T > 0$ the process $\{\gamma_{tT}\}_{t\geq 0}$ defined by

$$\gamma_{tT} = \frac{\gamma_t}{\gamma_T} \tag{22}$$

for $0 \leq t \leq T$ and $\gamma_{tT} = 1$ for $t > T$ will be called a standard gamma bridge, with parameter m, over the interval $[0, T]$. One can check that for $0 < t < T$ the random variable γ_{tT} has a beta distribution (Brody et al. 2008b, pp. 6–9). In particular, one finds that its density is given by

$$\mathbb{P}\left[\gamma_{tT} \in dy\right] = \mathbb{1}_{\{0<y<1\}} \frac{y^{mt-1}(1-y)^{m(T-t)-1}}{B[mt, m(T-t)]}\, dy, \tag{23}$$

where

$$B[a, b] = \frac{\Gamma[a]\,\Gamma[b]}{\Gamma[a+b]}. \tag{24}$$

It follows then by use of the integral formula

$$B[a, b] = \int_0^1 y^{a-1}(1-y)^{b-1} dy \tag{25}$$

that for all $n \in \mathbb{N}$ we have

$$\mathbb{E}\left[\gamma_{tT}^{n}\right] = \frac{B[mt+n, m(T-t)]}{B[mt, m(T-t)]}, \tag{26}$$

and hence

$$\mathbb{E}\left[\gamma_{tT}^{n}\right] = \frac{(mt)_n}{(mT)_n}. \tag{27}$$

Accordingly, one has

$$\mathbb{E}[\gamma_{tT}] = t/T, \quad \mathbb{E}[\gamma_{tT}^2] = t(mt+1)/T(mT+1) \tag{28}$$

and therefore

$$\mathrm{Var}[\gamma_{tT}] = \frac{t(T-t)}{T^2(1+mT)}. \tag{29}$$

One observes, in particular, that the expectation of γ_{tT} does not depend on m, whereas the variance of γ_{tT} decreases as m increases.

Definition 1. *For fixed $T > 0$, the process $\{\Gamma_{tT}\}_{t\geq 0}$ defined by*

$$\Gamma_{tT} = \gamma_T^{-\frac{1}{2}} \left(W_{\gamma_t} - \gamma_{tT}\, W_{\gamma_T}\right) \tag{30}$$

for $0 \leq t \leq T$ and $\Gamma_{tT} = 0$ for $t > T$ will be called a normalized variance gamma bridge.

We proceed to work out various properties of this process. We observe that Γ_{tT} is conditionally Gaussian, from which it follows that $\mathbb{E}\left[\Gamma_{tT} \mid \gamma_t, \gamma_T\right] = 0$ and $\mathbb{E}\left[\Gamma_{tT}^2 \mid \gamma_t, \gamma_T\right] = \gamma_{tT}\,(1-\gamma_{tT})$. Therefore $\mathbb{E}[\Gamma_{tT}] = 0$ and $\mathbb{E}[\Gamma_{tT}^2] = \mathbb{E}[\gamma_{tT}] - \mathbb{E}[\gamma_{tT}^2]$; and thus by use of (28) we have

$$\mathrm{Var}\left[\Gamma_{tT}\right] = \frac{mt\,(T-t)}{T\,(1+mT)}. \tag{31}$$

Now, recall (Yor (2007), Emery and Yor (2004)) that the gamma process and the associated gamma bridge have the following fundamental independence property. Define

$$\mathscr{G}_t^* = \sigma\left\{\gamma_s/\gamma_t,\ s \in [0,t]\right\}, \quad \mathscr{G}_t^+ = \sigma\left\{\gamma_u,\ u \in [t,\infty)\right\}. \tag{32}$$

Then, for every $t \geq 0$ it holds that $\mathscr{G}_t^*$ and $\mathscr{G}_t^+$ are independent. In particular γ_{st} and γ_u are independent for $0 \leq s \leq t \leq u$ and $t > 0$. It also holds that γ_{st} and γ_{uv} are independent for $0 \leq s \leq t \leq u \leq v$ and $t > 0$. Furthermore, we have:

Lemma 1. *If $0 \leq s \leq t \leq u$ and $t > 0$ then Γ_{st} and γ_u are independent.*

Proof. We recall that if a random variable X is normally distributed with mean μ and variance ν^2 then

$$\mathbb{P}\left[X < x\right] = N\left(\frac{x-\mu}{\nu}\right), \tag{33}$$

where $N : \mathbb{R} \to (0,1)$ is defined by

$$N(x) = \frac{1}{\sqrt{2\pi}} \int_{-\infty}^{x} \exp\left(-\frac{1}{2}y^2\right) \mathrm{d}y. \tag{34}$$

Since Γ_{tT} is conditionally Gaussian, by use of the tower property we find that

$$\begin{aligned} F_{\Gamma_{st},\gamma_u}(x,y) &= \mathbb{E}\left[\mathbb{1}_{\{\Gamma_{st}\le x\}}\,\mathbb{1}_{\{\gamma_u\le y\}}\right] \\ &= \mathbb{E}\left[\mathbb{E}\left[\mathbb{1}_{\{\Gamma_{st}\le x\}}\,\mathbb{1}_{\{\gamma_u\le y\}}\,\middle|\,\gamma_s,\gamma_t,\gamma_u\right]\right] \\ &= \mathbb{E}\left[\mathbb{1}_{\{\gamma_u\le y\}}\,\mathbb{E}\left[\mathbb{1}_{\{\Gamma_{st}\le x\}}\,\middle|\,\gamma_s,\gamma_t,\gamma_u\right]\right] \\ &= \mathbb{E}\left[\mathbb{1}_{\{\gamma_u\le y\}}\,N\left(x\left(\gamma_{st}\,(1-\gamma_{st})\right)^{-\frac{1}{2}}\right)\right] \\ &= \mathbb{E}\left[\mathbb{1}_{\{\gamma_u\le y\}}\right]\mathbb{E}\left[N\left(x\left(\gamma_{st}\,(1-\gamma_{st})\right)^{-\frac{1}{2}}\right)\right], \end{aligned} \tag{35}$$

where the last line follows from the independence of γ_{st} and γ_u. □

By a straightforward extension of the argument we deduce that if $0\le s\le t\le u\le v$ and $t>0$ then Γ_{st} and γ_{uv} are independent. Further, we have:

Lemma 2. *If $0\le s\le t\le u\le v$ and $t>0$ then Γ_{st} and Γ_{uv} are independent.*

Proof. We recall that the Brownian bridge $\{\beta_{tT}\}_{0\le t\le T}$ defined by

$$\beta_{tT} = W_t - \frac{t}{T}W_T \tag{36}$$

for $0\le t\le T$ and $\beta_{tT}=0$ for $t>T$ is Gaussian with $\mathbb{E}[\beta_{tT}]=0$, $\mathrm{Var}[\beta_{tT}]=t(T-t)/T$, and $\mathrm{Cov}[\beta_{sT},\beta_{tT}]=s(T-t)/T$ for $0\le s\le t\le T$. Using the tower property we find that

$$\begin{aligned} F_{\Gamma_{st},\Gamma_{uv}}(x,y) &= \mathbb{E}\left[\mathbb{1}_{\{\Gamma_{st}\le x\}}\,\mathbb{1}_{\{\Gamma_{uv}\le y\}}\right] \\ &= \mathbb{E}\left[\mathbb{E}\left[\mathbb{1}_{\{\Gamma_{st}\le x\}}\,\mathbb{1}_{\{\Gamma_{uv}\le y\}}\,\middle|\,\gamma_s,\gamma_t,\gamma_u,\gamma_v\right]\right] \\ &= \mathbb{E}\left[\mathbb{E}\left[\mathbb{1}_{\{\Gamma_{st}\le x\}}\,\middle|\,\gamma_s,\gamma_t,\gamma_u,\gamma_v\right]\mathbb{E}\left[\mathbb{1}_{\{\Gamma_{uv}\le y\}}\,\middle|\,\gamma_s,\gamma_t,\gamma_u,\gamma_v\right]\right] \\ &= \mathbb{E}\left[N\left(x\left((1-\gamma_{st})\,(\gamma_{st})\right)^{-\frac{1}{2}}\right)\right]\mathbb{E}\left[N\left(y\left((1-\gamma_{uv})\,(\gamma_{uv})\right)^{-\frac{1}{2}}\right)\right], \end{aligned} \tag{37}$$

where in the final step we use (30) along with properties of the Brownian bridge. □

A straightforward calculation shows that if $0\le s\le t\le u$ and $t>0$ then

$$\Gamma_{su} = (\gamma_{tu})^{\frac{1}{2}}\,\Gamma_{st} + \gamma_{st}\,\Gamma_{tu}\,. \tag{38}$$

With this result at hand we obtain the following:

Theorem 2. *The processes $\{\Gamma_{tT}\}_{0\le t\le T}$ and $\{\gamma_{tT}\}_{0\le t\le T}$ are jointly Markov.*

Proof. To establish the Markov property it suffices to show that for any bounded measurable function $\phi:\mathbb{R}\times\mathbb{R}\to\mathbb{R}$, any $n\in\mathbb{N}$, and any $0\le t_n\le t_{n-1}\le\,\dots\,\le t_1\le t\le T$, we have

$$\begin{aligned} &\mathbb{E}\left[\phi(\Gamma_{tT},\gamma_{tT})\,\middle|\,\Gamma_{t_1T},\gamma_{t_1T},\Gamma_{t_2T},\gamma_{t_2T},\dots,\Gamma_{t_nT},\gamma_{t_nT}\right] \\ &\quad = \mathbb{E}\left[\phi(\Gamma_{tT},\gamma_{tT})\,\middle|\,\Gamma_{t_1T},\gamma_{t_1T}\right]. \end{aligned} \tag{39}$$

We present the proof for $n = 2$. Thus we need to show that

$$\mathbb{E}\left[\phi(\Gamma_{tT}, \gamma_{tT}) \,\middle|\, \Gamma_{t_1T}, \gamma_{t_1T}, \Gamma_{t_2T}, \gamma_{t_2T}\right] = \mathbb{E}\left[\phi(\Gamma_{tT}, \gamma_{tT}) \,\middle|\, \Gamma_{t_1T}, \gamma_{t_1T}\right]. \tag{40}$$

As a consequence of (38) we have

$$\mathbb{E}\left[\phi(\Gamma_{tT}, \gamma_{tT}) \,\middle|\, \Gamma_{t_1T}, \gamma_{t_1T}, \Gamma_{t_2T}, \gamma_{t_2T}\right] = \mathbb{E}\left[\phi(\Gamma_{tT}, \gamma_{tT}) \,\middle|\, \Gamma_{t_1T}, \gamma_{t_1T}, \Gamma_{t_2t_1}, \gamma_{t_2t_1}\right]. \tag{41}$$

Therefore, it suffices to show that

$$\mathbb{E}\left[\phi(\Gamma_{tT}, \gamma_{tT}) \,\middle|\, \Gamma_{t_1T}, \gamma_{t_1T}, \Gamma_{t_2t_1}, \gamma_{t_2t_1}\right] = \mathbb{E}\left[\phi(\Gamma_{tT}, \gamma_{tT}) \,\middle|\, \Gamma_{t_1T}, \gamma_{t_1T}\right]. \tag{42}$$

Let us write

$$f_{\Gamma_{tT}, \gamma_{tT}, \Gamma_{t_1T}, \gamma_{t_1T}, \Gamma_{t_2t_1}, \gamma_{t_2t_1}}(x, y, a, b, c, d) \tag{43}$$

for the joint density of $\Gamma_{tT}, \gamma_{tT}, \Gamma_{t_1T}, \gamma_{t_1T}, \Gamma_{t_2t_1}, \gamma_{t_2t_1}$. Then for the conditional density of Γ_{tT} and γ_{tT} given $\Gamma_{t_1T} = a,\ \gamma_{t_1T} = b,\ \Gamma_{t_2t_1} = c,\ \gamma_{t_2t_1} = d$ we have

$$g_{\Gamma_{tT}, \gamma_{tT}}(x, y, a, b, c, d) = \frac{f_{\Gamma_{tT}, \gamma_{tT}, \Gamma_{t_1T}, \gamma_{t_1T}, \Gamma_{t_2t_1}, \gamma_{t_2t_1}}(x, y, a, b, c, d)}{f_{\Gamma_{t_1T}, \gamma_{t_1T}, \Gamma_{t_2t_1}, \gamma_{t_2t_1}}(a, b, c, d)}. \tag{44}$$

Thus,

$$\mathbb{E}\left[\phi(\Gamma_{tT}, \gamma_{tT}) \,\middle|\, \Gamma_{t_1T}, \gamma_{t_1T}, \Gamma_{t_2t_1}, \gamma_{t_2t_1}\right] = \int_{\mathbb{R}}\int_{\mathbb{R}} \phi(x,y)\, g_{\Gamma_{tT}, \gamma_{tT}}(x, y, \Gamma_{t_1T}, \gamma_{t_1T}, \Gamma_{t_2t_1}, \gamma_{t_2t_1})\, \mathrm{d}x\, \mathrm{d}y. \tag{45}$$

Similarly,

$$\mathbb{E}\left[\phi(\Gamma_{tT}, \gamma_{tT}) \,\middle|\, \Gamma_{t_1T}, \gamma_{t_1T}\right] = \int_{\mathbb{R}}\int_{\mathbb{R}} \phi(x,y)\, g_{\Gamma_{tT}, \gamma_{tT}}(x, y, \Gamma_{t_1T}, \gamma_{t_1T})\, \mathrm{d}x\, \mathrm{d}y, \tag{46}$$

where for the conditional density of Γ_{tT} and γ_{tT} given $\Gamma_{t_1T} = a,\ \gamma_{t_1T} = b$ we have

$$g_{\Gamma_{tT}, \gamma_{tT}}(x, y, a, b) = \frac{f_{\Gamma_{tT}, \gamma_{tT}, \Gamma_{t_1T}, \gamma_{t_1T}}(x, y, a, b)}{f_{\Gamma_{t_1T}, \gamma_{t_1T}}(a, b)}. \tag{47}$$

Note that the conditional probability densities that we introduce in formulae such as those above are "regular" conditional densities (Williams 1991, p. 91). We shall show that

$$g_{\Gamma_{tT}, \gamma_{tT}}(x, y, \Gamma_{t_1T}, \gamma_{t_1T}, \Gamma_{t_2t_1}, \gamma_{t_2t_1}) = g_{\Gamma_{tT}, \gamma_{tT}}(x, y, \Gamma_{t_1T}, \gamma_{t_1T}). \tag{48}$$

Writing

$$F_{\Gamma_{tT}, \gamma_{tT}, \Gamma_{t_1T}, \gamma_{t_1T}, \Gamma_{t_2t_1}, \gamma_{t_2t_1}}(x, y, a, b, c, d) = \mathbb{E}\left[\mathbb{1}_{\{\Gamma_{tT}<x\}}\mathbb{1}_{\{\gamma_{tT}<y\}}\mathbb{1}_{\{\Gamma_{t_1T}<a\}}\mathbb{1}_{\{\gamma_{t_1T}<b\}}\mathbb{1}_{\{\Gamma_{t_2t_1}<c\}}\mathbb{1}_{\{\gamma_{t_2t_1}<d\}}\right] \tag{49}$$

for the joint distribution function, we see that

$$\begin{aligned}
&F_{\Gamma_{tT},\gamma_{tT},\Gamma_{t_1T},\gamma_{t_1T},\Gamma_{t_2t_1},\gamma_{t_2t_1}}(x,y,a,b,c,d)\\
&=\mathbb{E}\left[\mathbb{1}_{\{\Gamma_{tT}<x\}}\mathbb{1}_{\{\gamma_{tT}<y\}}\mathbb{1}_{\{\Gamma_{t_1T}<a\}}\mathbb{1}_{\{\gamma_{t_1T}<b\}}\mathbb{1}_{\{\Gamma_{t_2t_1}<c\}}\mathbb{1}_{\{\gamma_{t_2t_1}<d\}}\right]\\
&=\mathbb{E}\left[\mathbb{E}\left[\mathbb{1}_{\{\Gamma_{tT}<x\}}\mathbb{1}_{\{\gamma_{tT}<y\}}\mathbb{1}_{\{\Gamma_{t_1T}<a\}}\mathbb{1}_{\{\gamma_{t_1T}<b\}}\mathbb{1}_{\{\Gamma_{t_2t_1}<c\}}\mathbb{1}_{\{\gamma_{t_2t_1}<d\}}\,\middle|\,\gamma_{t_2},\gamma_{t_1},\gamma_t,\gamma_T\right]\right]\\
&=\mathbb{E}\left[\mathbb{1}_{\{\gamma_{tT}<y\}}\mathbb{1}_{\{\gamma_{t_1T}<b\}}\mathbb{1}_{\{\gamma_{t_2t_1}<d\}}\,\mathbb{E}\left[\mathbb{1}_{\{\Gamma_{tT}<x\}}\mathbb{1}_{\{\Gamma_{t_1T}<a\}}\mathbb{1}_{\{\Gamma_{t_2t_1}<c\}}\,\middle|\,\gamma_{t_2},\gamma_{t_1},\gamma_t,\gamma_T\right]\right]\\
&=\mathbb{E}\Bigg[\mathbb{E}\left[\mathbb{1}_{\{\Gamma_{tT}<x\}}\mathbb{1}_{\{\gamma_{tT}<y\}}\mathbb{1}_{\{\Gamma_{t_1T}<a\}}\mathbb{1}_{\{\gamma_{t_1T}<b\}}\,\middle|\,\gamma_{t_1},\gamma_t,\gamma_T\right]\\
&\qquad\qquad\times N\left(\frac{c}{\sqrt{(1-\gamma_{t_2t_1})\,(\gamma_{t_2t_1})}}\right)\mathbb{1}_{\{\gamma_{t_2t_1}<d\}}\Bigg],
\end{aligned}\tag{50}$$

where the last step follows as a consequence of Lemma 2. Thus we have

$$\begin{aligned}
&F_{\Gamma_{tT},\gamma_{tT},\Gamma_{t_1T},\gamma_{t_1T},\Gamma_{t_2t_1},\gamma_{t_2t_1}}(x,y,a,b,c,d)\\
&=\mathbb{E}\left[\mathbb{1}_{\{\Gamma_{tT}<x\}}\mathbb{1}_{\{\gamma_{tT}<y\}}\mathbb{1}_{\{\Gamma_{t_1T}<a\}}\mathbb{1}_{\{\gamma_{t_1T}<b\}}N\left(\frac{c}{\sqrt{(1-\gamma_{t_2t_1})\,(\gamma_{t_2t_1})}}\right)\mathbb{1}_{\{\gamma_{t_2t_1}<d\}}\right]\\
&=\mathbb{E}\left[\mathbb{1}_{\{\Gamma_{tT}<x\}}\mathbb{1}_{\{\gamma_{tT}<y\}}\mathbb{1}_{\{\Gamma_{t_1T}<a\}}\mathbb{1}_{\{\gamma_{t_1T}<b\}}\right]\mathbb{E}\left[N\left(\frac{c}{\sqrt{(1-\gamma_{t_2t_1})\,(\gamma_{t_2t_1})}}\right)\mathbb{1}_{\{\gamma_{t_2t_1}<d\}}\right]\\
&=F_{\Gamma_{tT},\gamma_{tT},\Gamma_{t_1T},\gamma_{t_1T}}(x,y,a,b)\times F_{\Gamma_{t_2t_1},\gamma_{t_2t_1}}(c,d),
\end{aligned}\tag{51}$$

where the next to last step follows by virtue of the fact that Γ_{st} and γ_{uv} are independent for $0\le s\le t\le u\le v$ and $t>0$. Similarly,

$$\begin{aligned}
&F_{\Gamma_{t_1T},\gamma_{t_1T},\Gamma_{t_2t_1},\gamma_{t_2t_1}}(a,b,c,d)\\
&=\mathbb{E}\left[\mathbb{1}_{\{\Gamma_{t_1T}<a\}}\mathbb{1}_{\{\gamma_{t_1T}<b\}}\mathbb{1}_{\{\Gamma_{t_2t_1}<c\}}\mathbb{1}_{\{\gamma_{t_2t_1}<d\}}\right]\\
&=\mathbb{E}\left[\mathbb{E}\left[\mathbb{1}_{\{\Gamma_{t_1T}<a\}}\mathbb{1}_{\{\gamma_{t_1T}<b\}}\mathbb{1}_{\{\Gamma_{t_2t_1}<c\}}\mathbb{1}_{\{\gamma_{t_2t_1}<d\}}\,\middle|\,\gamma_{t_2},\gamma_{t_1},\gamma_T\right]\right]\\
&=\mathbb{E}\left[\mathbb{1}_{\{\gamma_{t_1T}<b\}}\mathbb{1}_{\{\gamma_{t_2t_1}<d\}}\,\mathbb{E}\left[\mathbb{1}_{\{\Gamma_{t_1T}<a\}}\mathbb{1}_{\{\Gamma_{t_2t_1}<c\}}\,\middle|\,\gamma_{t_2},\gamma_{t_1},\gamma_T\right]\right],
\end{aligned}\tag{52}$$

and hence

$$\begin{aligned}
&F_{\Gamma_{t_1T},\gamma_{t_1T},\Gamma_{t_2t_1},\gamma_{t_2t_1}}(a,b,c,d)\\
&=\mathbb{E}\left[N\left(\frac{a}{\sqrt{(1-\gamma_{t_1T})\,(\gamma_{t_1T})}}\right)\mathbb{1}_{\{\gamma_{t_1T}<b\}}N\left(\frac{c}{\sqrt{(1-\gamma_{t_2t_1})\,(\gamma_{t_2t_1})}}\right)\mathbb{1}_{\{\gamma_{t_2t_1}<d\}}\right]\\
&=\mathbb{E}\left[N\left(\frac{a}{\sqrt{(1-\gamma_{t_1T})\,(\gamma_{t_1T})}}\right)\mathbb{1}_{\{\gamma_{t_1T}<b\}}\right]\mathbb{E}\left[N\left(\frac{c}{\sqrt{(1-\gamma_{t_2t_1})\,(\gamma_{t_2t_1})}}\right)\mathbb{1}_{\{\gamma_{t_2t_1}<d\}}\right]\\
&=F_{\Gamma_{t_1T},\gamma_{t_1T}}(a,b)\times F_{\Gamma_{t_2t_1},\gamma_{t_2t_1}}(c,d).
\end{aligned}\tag{53}$$

Thus we deduce that

$$f_{\Gamma_{tT},\gamma_{tT},\Gamma_{t_1T},\gamma_{t_1T},\Gamma_{t_2t_1},\gamma_{t_2t_1}}(x, y, a, b, c, d) \tag{54}$$
$$= f_{\Gamma_{tT},\gamma_{tT},\Gamma_{t_1T},\gamma_{t_1T}}(x, y, a, b) \times f_{\Gamma_{t_2t_1},\gamma_{t_2t_1}}(c, d), \tag{55}$$

and

$$f_{\Gamma_{t_1T},\gamma_{t_1T},\Gamma_{t_2t_1},\gamma_{t_2t_1}}(a, b, c, d) = f_{\Gamma_{t_1T},\gamma_{t_1T}}(a, b) \times f_{\Gamma_{t_2t_1},\gamma_{t_2t_1}}(c, d), \tag{56}$$

and the theorem follows. □

4. Variance Gamma Information

Fix $T > 0$ and let $\{\Gamma_{tT}\}$ be a normalized variance gamma bridge, as defined by (30). Let $\{\gamma_{tT}\}$ be the associated gamma bridge defined by (22). Let X_T be a random variable and assume that X_T, $\{\gamma_t\}_{t\geq 0}$ and $\{W_t\}_{t\geq 0}$ are independent. We are led to the following:

Definition 2. *By a variance-gamma information process carrying the market factor X_T we mean a process $\{\xi_t\}_{t\geq 0}$ that takes the form*

$$\xi_t = \Gamma_{tT} + \sigma\,\gamma_{tT}\,X_T \tag{57}$$

for $0 \leq t \leq T$ and $\xi_t = \sigma X_T$ for $t > T$, where σ is a positive constant.

The market filtration is assumed to be the standard augmented filtration generated jointly by $\{\xi_t\}$ and $\{\gamma_{tT}\}$. A calculation shows that if $0 \leq s \leq t \leq T$ and $t > 0$ then

$$\xi_s = \Gamma_{st}\,(\gamma_{tT})^{\frac{1}{2}} + \xi_t\,\gamma_{st}\,. \tag{58}$$

We are thus led to the following result required for the valuation of assets.

Theorem 3. *The processes $\{\xi_t\}_{0\leq t\leq T}$ and $\{\gamma_{tT}\}_{0\leq t\leq T}$ are jointly Markov.*

Proof. It suffices to show that for any $n \in \mathbb{N}$ and $0 < t_1 < t_2 < \cdots < t_n$ we have

$$\mathbb{E}\left[\phi(\xi_t,\gamma_{tT})\,\middle|\,\xi_{t_1},\xi_{t_2},\ldots,\xi_{t_n},\gamma_{t_1T},\gamma_{t_2T},\ldots,\gamma_{t_nT}\right] = \mathbb{E}\left[\phi(\xi_t,\gamma_{tT})\,\middle|\,\xi_{t_1},\gamma_{t_1T}\right]. \tag{59}$$

We present the proof for $n = 2$. Thus, we propose to show that

$$\mathbb{E}\left[\phi(\xi_t,\gamma_{tT})\,\middle|\,\xi_{t_1},\xi_{t_2},\gamma_{t_1T},\gamma_{t_2T}\right] = \mathbb{E}\left[\phi(\xi_t,\gamma_{tT})\,\middle|\,\xi_{t_1},\gamma_{t_1T}\right]. \tag{60}$$

By (58), we have

$$\begin{aligned}
&\mathbb{E}\left[\phi(\xi_t,\gamma_{tT})\,\middle|\,\xi_{t_1},\xi_{t_2},\gamma_{t_1T},\gamma_{t_2,T}\right] \\
&\quad= \mathbb{E}\left[\phi(\xi_t,\gamma_{tT})\,\middle|\,\xi_{t_1},\xi_{t_2},\gamma_{t_1T},\gamma_{t_2t_1}\right] \\
&\quad= \mathbb{E}\left[\phi(\xi_t,\gamma_{tT})\,\middle|\,\xi_{t_1},\Gamma_{t_2t_1},\gamma_{t_1T},\gamma_{t_2t_1}\right] \\
&\quad= \mathbb{E}\left[\phi(\Gamma_{tT}+\gamma_{tT}\,\sigma\,X_T,\gamma_{tT})\,\middle|\,\Gamma_{t_1T}+\gamma_{t_1T}\,\sigma\,X_T,\Gamma_{t_2t_1},\gamma_{t_1T},\gamma_{t_2t_1}\right].
\end{aligned} \tag{61}$$

Finally, we invoke Lemma 2, and Theorem 2 to conclude that

$$\begin{aligned}&\mathbb{E}\left[\phi(\xi_t,\gamma_{tT})|\xi_{t_1},\,\xi_{t_2},\,\gamma_{t_1T},\,\gamma_{t_2,T}\right]\\&\quad=\mathbb{E}\left[\phi(\Gamma_{tT}+\gamma_{tT}\,\sigma\,X_T,\gamma_{tT})\,\middle|\,\Gamma_{t_1T}+\gamma_{t_1T}\,\sigma\,X_T,\,\gamma_{t_1T}\right]\\&\quad=\mathbb{E}\left[\phi(\xi_t,\gamma_{tT})|\xi_{t_1},\,\gamma_{t_1T}\right].\end{aligned} \tag{62}$$

The generalization to $n > 2$ is straightforward. □

5. Information Based Pricing

Now we are in a position to consider the valuation of a financial asset in the setting just discussed. One recalls that $\mathbb{P}$ is understood to be the risk-neutral measure and that the interest rate is constant. The payoff of the asset at time T is taken to be an integrable random variable of the form $h(X_T)$ for some Borel function h, where X_T is the information revealed at T. The filtration is generated jointly by the variance-gamma information process $\{\xi_t\}$ and the associated gamma bridge $\{\gamma_{tT}\}$. The value of the asset at time $t \in [0, T)$ is then given by the general expression (2), which on account of Theorem 3 reduces in the present context to

$$S_t = \mathrm{e}^{-r\,(T-t)}\,\mathbb{E}\left[h(X_T)\,|\,\xi_t,\,\gamma_{tT}\right], \tag{63}$$

and our goal is to work out this expectation explicitly.

Let us write F_{X_T} for the *a priori* distribution function of X_T. Thus $F_{X_T} : x \in \mathbb{R} \mapsto F_{X_T}(x) \in [0, 1]$ and we have

$$F_{X_T}(x) = \mathbb{P}\left(X_T \le x\right). \tag{64}$$

Occasionally, it will be typographically convenient to write $F^{(x)}_{X_T}$ in place of $F_{X_T}(x)$, and similarly for other distribution functions. To proceed, we require the following:

Lemma 3. *Let X be a random variable with distribution $\{F_X(x)\}_{x\in\mathbb{R}}$ and let Y be a continuous random variable with distribution $\{F_Y(y)\}_{y\in\mathbb{R}}$ and density $\{f_Y(y)\}_{y\in\mathbb{R}}$. Then for all $y \in \mathbb{R}$ for which $f_Y(y) \neq 0$ we have*

$$F^{(x)}_{X|Y=y} = \frac{\int_{u\in(-\infty,x]} f^{(y)}_{Y|X=u}\,\mathrm{d}F^{(u)}_X}{\int_{u\in(-\infty,\infty)} f^{(y)}_{Y|X=u}\,\mathrm{d}F^{(u)}_X}, \tag{65}$$

where $F^{(x)}_{X|Y=y}$ denotes the conditional distribution $\mathbb{P}\left(X \le x \mid Y = y\right)$, and where

$$f^{(y)}_{Y|X=u} = \frac{\mathrm{d}}{\mathrm{d}y}\mathbb{P}\left(Y \le y \mid X = u\right). \tag{66}$$

Proof. For *any* two random variables X and Y it holds that

$$\begin{aligned}\mathbb{P}\left(X \le x,\, Y \le y\right) &= \mathbb{E}\left[\mathbb{1}_{\{X\le x\}}\,\mathbb{1}_{\{Y\le y\}}\right]\\&= \mathbb{E}\left[\mathbb{E}\left[\mathbb{1}_{\{X\le x\}}|Y\right]\mathbb{1}_{\{Y\le y\}}\right]\\&= \mathbb{E}\left[F^{(x)}_{X|Y}\,\mathbb{1}_{\{Y\le y\}}\right].\end{aligned} \tag{67}$$

Here we have used the fact that for each $x \in \mathbb{R}$ there exists a Borel measurable function $P_x : y \in \mathbb{R} \mapsto P_x(y) \in [0,1]$ such that $\mathbb{E}\left[\mathbb{1}_{\{X \le x\}} \middle| Y\right] = P_x(Y)$. Then for $y \in \mathbb{R}$ we define

$$F^{(x)}_{X|Y=y} = P_x(y)\,. \tag{68}$$

Hence

$$\mathbb{P}\,(X \le x,\, Y \le y) = \int_{v \in (-\infty, y]} F^{(x)}_{X|Y=v}\, \mathrm{d}F^{(v)}_Y\,. \tag{69}$$

By symmetry, we have

$$\mathbb{P}\,(X \le x,\, Y \le y) = \int_{u \in (-\infty, x]} F^{(y)}_{Y|X=u}\, \mathrm{d}F^{(u)}_X\,, \tag{70}$$

from which it follows that we have the relation

$$\int_{u \in (-\infty, x]} F^{(y)}_{Y|X=u}\, \mathrm{d}F^{(u)}_X = \int_{v \in (-\infty, y]} F^{(x)}_{X|Y=v}\, \mathrm{d}F^{(v)}_Y\,. \tag{71}$$

Moving ahead, let us consider the measure $F_{X|Y=y}(\mathrm{d}x)$ on $(\mathbb{R}, \mathcal{B})$ defined for each $y \in \mathbb{R}$ by setting

$$F_{X|Y=y}(A) = \mathbb{E}\left[\mathbb{1}_{\{X \in A\}} \middle| Y = y\right] \tag{72}$$

for any $A \in \mathcal{B}$. Then $F_{X|Y=y}(\mathrm{d}x)$ is absolutely continuous with respect to $F_X(\mathrm{d}x)$. Indeed, suppose that $F_X(B) = 0$ for some $B \in \mathcal{B}$. Now, $F_{X|Y=y}(B) = \mathbb{E}\left[\mathbb{1}_{\{X \in B\}} \middle| Y = y\right]$. But if $\mathbb{E}\left[\mathbb{1}_{\{X \in B\}}\right] = 0$, then $\mathbb{E}\left[\mathbb{E}\left[\mathbb{1}_{\{X \in B\}} \middle| Y\right]\right] = 0$, and hence $\mathbb{E}\left[\mathbb{1}_{\{X \in B\}} \middle| Y\right] = 0$, and therefore $\mathbb{E}\left[\mathbb{1}_{\{X \in B\}} \middle| Y = y\right] = 0$. Thus $F_{X|Y=y}(B)$ vanishes for any $B \in \mathcal{B}$ for which $F_X(B)$ vanishes. It follows by the Radon-Nikodym theorem that for each $y \in \mathbb{R}$ there exists a density $\{g_y(x)\}_{x \in \mathbb{R}}$ such that

$$F^{(x)}_{X|Y=y} = \int_{u \in (-\infty, x]} g_y(u)\, \mathrm{d}F^{(u)}_X\,. \tag{73}$$

Note that $\{g_y(x)\}$ is determined uniquely apart from its values on F_X-null sets. Inserting (73) into (71) we obtain

$$\int_{u \in (-\infty, x]} F^{(y)}_{Y|X=u}\, \mathrm{d}F^{(u)}_X = \int_{v \in (-\infty, y]} \int_{u \in (-\infty, x]} g_v(u)\, \mathrm{d}F^{(u)}_X\, \mathrm{d}F^{(v)}_Y\,, \tag{74}$$

and thus by Fubini's theorem we have

$$\int_{u \in (-\infty, x]} F^{(y)}_{Y|X=u}\, \mathrm{d}F^{(u)}_X = \int_{u \in (-\infty, x]} \int_{v \in (-\infty, y]} g_v(u)\, \mathrm{d}F^{(v)}_Y\, \mathrm{d}F^{(u)}_X\,. \tag{75}$$

It follows then that $\{F^{(y)}_{Y|X=x}\}_{x \in \mathbb{R}}$ is determined uniquely apart from its values on F_X-null sets, and we have

$$F^{(y)}_{Y|X=x} = \int_{v \in (-\infty, y]} g_v(x)\, \mathrm{d}F^{(v)}_Y. \tag{76}$$

This relation holds quite generally and is symmetrical between X and Y. Indeed, we have not so far assumed that Y is a continuous random variable. If Y is, in fact, a continuous random variable, then its distribution function is absolutely continuous and admits a density $\{f^{(y)}_Y\}_{y \in \mathbb{R}}$. In that case, (76) can be written in the form

$$F^{(y)}_{Y|X=x} = \int_{v\in(-\infty,y]} g_v(x)\, f^{(v)}_Y\, \mathrm{d}v\,, \tag{77}$$

from which it follows that for each value of x the conditional distribution function $\{F^{(y)}_{Y|X=x}\}_{y\in\mathbb{R}}$ is absolutely continuous and admits a density $\{f^{(y)}_{Y|X=x}\}_{y\in\mathbb{R}}$ such that

$$f^{(y)}_{Y|X=x} = g_y(x)\, f^{(y)}_Y\,. \tag{78}$$

The desired result (65) then follows from (73) and (78) if we observe that

$$f^{(y)}_Y = \int_{u\in(-\infty,\infty)} f^{(y)}_{Y|X=u}\, \mathrm{d}F^{(u)}_X\,, \tag{79}$$

and that concludes the proof. □

Armed with Lemma 3, we are in a position to work out the conditional expectation that leads to the asset price, and we obtain the following:

Theorem 4. *The variance-gamma information-based price of a financial asset with payoff $h(X_T)$ at time T is given for $t < T$ by*

$$S_t = \mathrm{e}^{-r\,(T-t)} \int_{x\in\mathbb{R}} h(x)\, \frac{\mathrm{e}^{\left(\sigma\,\xi_t\,x - \frac{1}{2}\sigma^2 x^2 \gamma_{tT}\right)(1-\gamma_{tT})^{-1}}}{\int_{y\in\mathbb{R}} \mathrm{e}^{\left(\sigma\,\xi_t\,y - \frac{1}{2}\sigma^2 y^2 \gamma_{tT}\right)(1-\gamma_{tT})^{-1}}\, \mathrm{d}F^{(y)}_{X_T}}\, \mathrm{d}F^{(x)}_{X_T}\,. \tag{80}$$

Proof. To calculate the conditional expectation of $h(X_T)$, we observe that

$$\mathbb{E}\left[h(X_T)\,|\,\xi_t,\,\gamma_{tT}\right] = \mathbb{E}\left[\mathbb{E}\left[h(X_T)\,|\,\xi_t,\,\gamma_{tT},\,\gamma_T\right]\,\middle|\,\xi_t,\,\gamma_{tT}\right], \tag{81}$$

by the tower property, where the inner expectation takes the form

$$\mathbb{E}\left[h(X_T)\,|\,\xi_t = \xi,\,\gamma_{tT} = b,\,\gamma_T = g\right] = \int_{x\in\mathbb{R}} h(x)\, \mathrm{d}F^{(x)}_{X_T|\xi_t=\xi,\,\gamma_{tT}=b,\,\gamma_T=g}\,. \tag{82}$$

Here by Lemma 3 the conditional distribution function is

$$\begin{aligned} F^{(x)}_{X_T|\xi_t=\xi,\,\gamma_{tT}=b,\,\gamma_T=g} &= \frac{\int_{u\in(-\infty,x]} f^{(\xi)}_{\xi_t\,|\,X_T=u,\,\gamma_{tT}=b,\,\gamma_T=g}\, \mathrm{d}F^{(u)}_{X_T\,|\,\gamma_{tT}=b,\,\gamma_T=g}}{\int_{u\in\mathbb{R}} f^{(\xi)}_{\xi_t\,|\,X_T=u,\,\gamma_{tT}=b,\,\gamma_T=g}\, \mathrm{d}F^{(u)}_{X_T\,|\,\gamma_{tT}=b,\,\gamma_T=g}} \\ &= \frac{\int_{u\in(-\infty,x]} f^{(\xi)}_{\xi_t\,|\,X_T=u,\,\gamma_{tT}=b,\,\gamma_T=g}\, \mathrm{d}F^{(u)}_{X_T}}{\int_{u\in\mathbb{R}} f^{(\xi)}_{\xi_t\,|\,X_T=u,\,\gamma_{tT}=b,\,\gamma_T=g}\, \mathrm{d}F^{(u)}_{X_T}} \\ &= \frac{\int_{u\in(-\infty,x]} \mathrm{e}^{\left(\sigma\,\xi\,u - \frac{1}{2}\sigma^2 u^2 b\right)(1-b)^{-1}}\, \mathrm{d}F^{(u)}_{X_T}}{\int_{\mathbb{R}} \mathrm{e}^{\left(\sigma\,\xi\,u - \frac{1}{2}\sigma^2 u^2 b\right)(1-b)^{-1}}\, \mathrm{d}F^{(u)}_{X_T}}\,. \end{aligned} \tag{83}$$

Therefore, the inner expectation in Equation (81) is given by

$$\mathbb{E}\left[h(X_T)\,|\,\xi_t,\,\gamma_{tT},\,\gamma_T\right] = \int_{x\in\mathbb{R}} h(x)\,\frac{\mathrm{e}^{\left(\sigma\,\xi_t\,x-\frac{1}{2}\,\sigma^2\,x^2\,\gamma_{tT}\right)\,(1-\gamma_{tT})^{-1}}}{\int_{y\in\mathbb{R}}\mathrm{e}^{\left(\sigma\,\xi_t\,y-\frac{1}{2}\,\sigma^2\,y^2\,\gamma_{tT}\right)\,(1-\gamma_{tT})^{-1}}\,\mathrm{d}F^{(y)}_{X_T}}\,\mathrm{d}F^{(x)}_{X_T}\,. \tag{84}$$

But the right hand side of (84) depends only on ξ_t and γ_{tT}. It follows immediately that

$$\mathbb{E}\left[h(X_T)\,|\,\xi_t,\,\gamma_{tT}\right] = \int_{x\in\mathbb{R}} h(x)\,\frac{\mathrm{e}^{\left(\sigma\,\xi_t\,x-\frac{1}{2}\,\sigma^2\,x^2\,\gamma_{tT}\right)\,(1-\gamma_{tT})^{-1}}}{\int_{y\in\mathbb{R}}\mathrm{e}^{\left(\sigma\,\xi_t\,y-\frac{1}{2}\,\sigma^2\,y^2\,\gamma_{tT}\right)\,(1-\gamma_{tT})^{-1}}\,\mathrm{d}F^{(y)}_{X_T}}\,\mathrm{d}F^{(x)}_{X_T}\,, \tag{85}$$

which translates into Equation (80), and that concludes the proof. □

6. Examples

Going forward, we present some examples of variance-gamma information pricing for specific choices of (a) the payoff function $h:\mathbb{R}\to\mathbb{R}^+$ and (b) the distribution of the market factor X_T. In the figures, we display sample paths for the information processes and the corresponding prices. These paths are generated as follows. First, we simulate outcomes for the market factor X_T. Second, we simulate paths for the gamma process $\{\gamma_t\}_{t\geq 0}$ over the interval $[0,T]$ and an independent Brownian motion $\{W_t\}_{t\geq 0}$. Third, we evaluate the variance gamma process $\{W_{\gamma_t}\}_{t\geq 0}$ over the interval $[0,T]$ by subordinating the Brownian motion with the gamma process, and we evaluate the resulting gamma bridge $\{\gamma_{tT}\}_{0\leq t\leq T}$. Fourth, we use these ingredients to construct sample paths of the information processes, where these processes are given as in Definition 2. Finally, we evaluate the pricing formula in Equation (80) for each of the simulated paths and for each time step.

Example 1: Credit risky bond. We begin with the simplest case, that of a unit-principal credit-risky bond without recovery. We set $h(x)=x$, with $\mathbb{P}(X_T=0)=p_0$ and $\mathbb{P}(X_T=1)=p_1$, where $p_0+p_1=1$. Thus, we have

$$F_{X_T}(x) = p_0\delta_0(x) + p_1\delta_1(x)\,, \tag{86}$$

where

$$\delta_a(x) = \int_{y\in(-\infty,x]}\delta_a(\mathrm{d}y)\,, \tag{87}$$

and $\delta_a(\mathrm{d}x)$ denotes the Dirac measure concentrated at the point a, and we are led to the following:

Proposition 1. *The variance-gamma information-based price of a unit-principal credit-risky discount bond with no recovery is given by*

$$S_t = \mathrm{e}^{-r\,(T-t)}\,\frac{p_1\,\mathrm{e}^{\left(\sigma\,\xi_t-\frac{1}{2}\,\sigma^2\,\gamma_{tT}\right)\,(1-\gamma_{tT})^{-1}}}{p_0+p_1\,\mathrm{e}^{\left(\sigma\,\xi_t-\frac{1}{2}\,\sigma^2\,\gamma_{tT}\right)\,(1-\gamma_{tT})^{-1}}}\,. \tag{88}$$

Now let $\omega\in\Omega$ denote the outcome of chance. By use of Equation (57) one can check rather directly that if $X_T(\omega)=1$, then $\lim_{t\to T}S_t=1$, whereas if $X_T(\omega)=0$, then $\lim_{t\to T}S_t=0$. More explicitly, we find that

$$S_t\Big|_{X_T(w)=0} = \mathrm{e}^{-r(T-t)}\,\frac{p_1\,\exp\left[\sigma\,\left(\gamma_T^{-1/2}\,(W_{\gamma_t}-\gamma_{tT}\,W_{\gamma_T})-\frac{1}{2}\,\sigma\,\gamma_{tT}\right)\,(1-\gamma_{tT})^{-1}\right]}{p_0+p_1\,\exp\left[\sigma\,\left(\gamma_T^{-1/2}\,(W_{\gamma_t}-\gamma_{tT}\,W_{\gamma_T})-\frac{1}{2}\,\sigma\,\gamma_{tT}\right)\,(1-\gamma_{tT})^{-1}\right]}\,, \tag{89}$$

whereas

$$S_t\Big|_{X_T(w)=1} = \mathrm{e}^{-r(T-t)}\,\frac{p_1\,\exp\left[\sigma\left(\gamma_T^{-1/2}\,(W_{\gamma_t}-\gamma_{tT}\,W_{\gamma_T})+\frac{1}{2}\,\sigma\,\gamma_{tT}\right)\,(1-\gamma_{tT})^{-1}\right]}{p_0+p_1\,\exp\left[\sigma\left(\gamma_T^{-1/2}\,(W_{\gamma_t}-\gamma_{tT}\,W_{\gamma_T})+\frac{1}{2}\,\sigma\,\gamma_{tT}\right)\,(1-\gamma_{tT})^{-1}\right]}\,, \tag{90}$$

and the claimed limiting behaviour of the asset price follows by inspection. In Figures 1 and 2 we plot sample paths for the information processes and price processes of credit risky bonds for various values of the information flow-rate parameter. One observes that for $\sigma = 1$ the information processes diverge, thus distinguishing those bonds that default from those that do not, only towards the end of the relevant time frame; whereas for higher values of σ the divergence occurs progressively earlier, and one sees a corresponding effect in the price processes. Thus, when the information flow rate is higher, the final outcome of the bond payment is anticipated earlier, and with greater certainty. Similar conclusions hold for the interpretation of Figures 3 and 4.

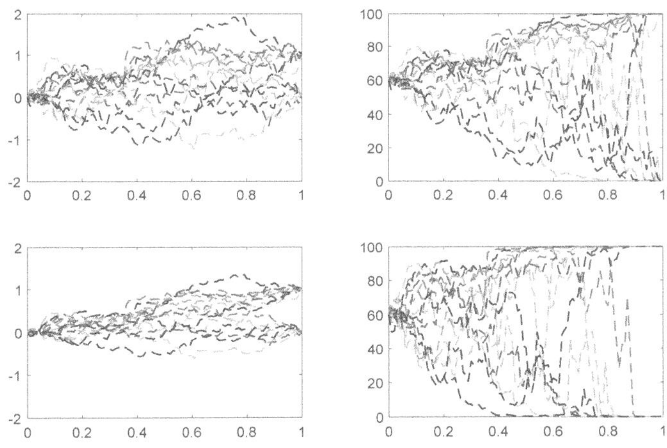

Figure 1. Credit-risky bonds with no recovery. The panels on the left show simulations of trajectories of the variance gamma information process, and the panels on the right show simulations of the corresponding price trajectories. Prices are quoted as percentages of the principal, and the interest rate is taken to be zero. From top to bottom, we show trajectories having $\sigma = 1$, 2, respectively. We take $p_0 = 0.4$ for the probability of default and $p_1 = 0.6$ for the probability of no default. The value of m is 100 in all cases. Fifteen simulated trajectories are shown in each panel.

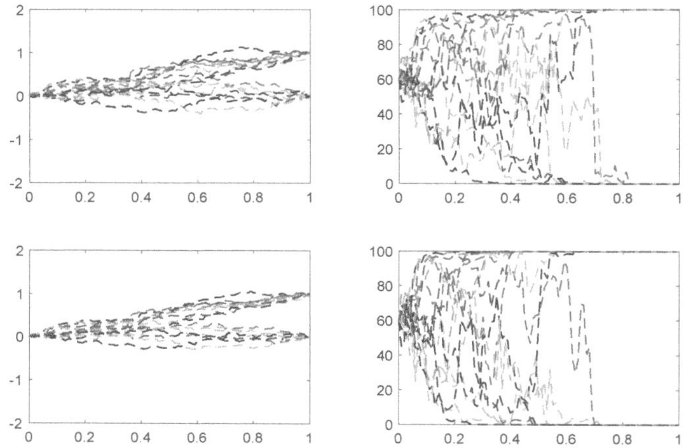

Figure 2. Credit-risky bonds with no recovery. From top to bottom we show trajectories having $\sigma = 3, 4$, respectively. The other parameters are the same as in Figure 1.

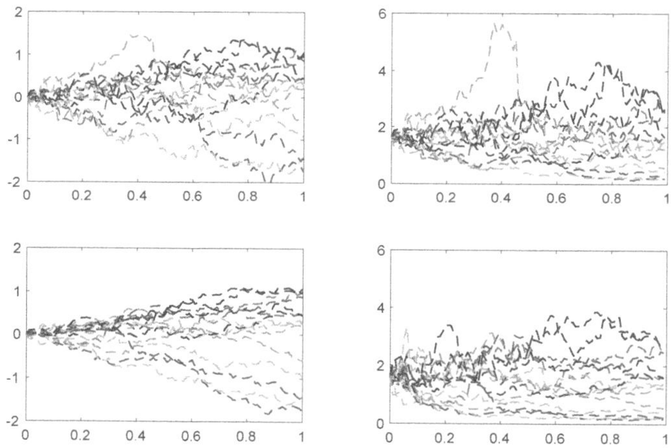

Figure 3. Log-normal payoff. The panels on the left show simulations of the trajectories of the information process, whereas the panels on the right show simulations of the corresponding price process trajectories. From the top to bottom, we show trajectories having $\sigma = 1, 2$, respectively. The value for m is 100. We take $\mu = 0$, $\nu = 1$, and show 15 simulated trajectories in each panel.

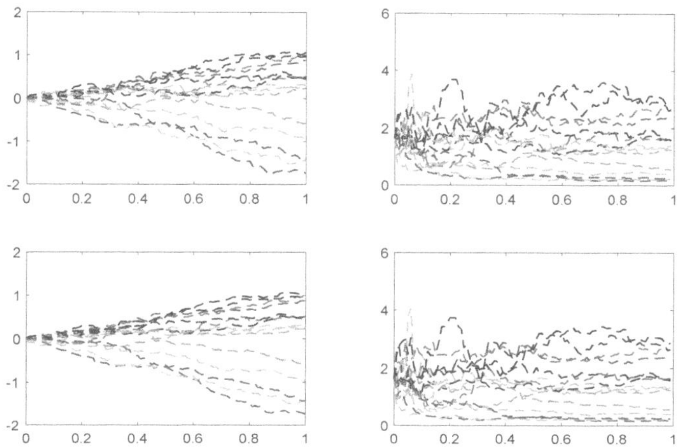

Figure 4. Log-normal payoff. From the top row to the bottom, we show trajectories having $\sigma = 3$, 4, respectively. The other parameters are the same as those in Figure 3.

Example 2: Random recovery. As a somewhat more sophisticated version of the previous example, we consider the case of a defaultable bond with random recovery. We shall work out the case where $h(x) = x$ and the market factor X_T takes the value c with probability p_1 and X_T is uniformly distributed over the interval $[a, b]$ with probability p_0, where $0 \leq a < b \leq c$. Thus, for the probability measure of X_T we have

$$F_{X_T}(\mathrm{d}x) = p_0\, \mathbb{1}_{\{a \leq x < b\}}\, \mathrm{d}x + p_1\, \delta_c(\mathrm{d}x)\,, \tag{91}$$

and for the distribution function we obtain

$$F_{X_T}(x) = p_0\, x\, \mathbb{1}_{\{a \leq x < b\}} + \mathbb{1}_{\{x \geq c\}}\,. \tag{92}$$

The bond price at time t is then obtained by working out the expression

$$S_t = \mathrm{e}^{-r(T-t)}\, \frac{p_0 \int_a^b x\, \mathrm{e}^{\left(\sigma \xi_t x - \frac{1}{2}\sigma^2 x^2 \gamma_{tT}\right)(1-\gamma_{tT})^{-1}}\, \mathrm{d}x + p_1\, c\, \mathrm{e}^{\left(\sigma \xi_t - \frac{1}{2}\sigma^2 \gamma_{tT}\right)(1-\gamma_{tT})^{-1}}}{p_0 \int_a^b \mathrm{e}^{\left(\sigma \xi_t x - \frac{1}{2}\sigma^2 x^2 \gamma_{tT}\right)(1-\gamma_{tT})^{-1}}\, \mathrm{d}x + p_1\, \mathrm{e}^{\left(\sigma \xi_t - \frac{1}{2}\sigma^2 \gamma_{tT}\right)(1-\gamma_{tT})^{-1}}}\,, \tag{93}$$

and it should be evident that one can obtain a closed-form solution. To work this out in detail, it will be convenient to have an expression for the incomplete first moment of a normally-distributed random variable with mean μ and variance ν^2. Thus we set

$$N_1(x, \mu, \nu) = \frac{1}{\sqrt{2\,\pi\,\nu^2}} \int_{-\infty}^{x} y\, \exp\left(-\frac{1}{2}\frac{(y-\mu)^2}{\nu^2}\right) \mathrm{d}y\,, \tag{94}$$

and for convenience we set

$$N_0(x, \mu, \nu) = \frac{1}{\sqrt{2\,\pi\,\nu^2}} \int_{-\infty}^{x} \exp\left(-\frac{1}{2}\frac{(y-\mu)^2}{\nu^2}\right) \mathrm{d}y\,. \tag{95}$$

Then we have

$$N_1(x,\mu,\nu) = \mu\, N\left(\frac{x-\mu}{\nu}\right) - \frac{\nu}{\sqrt{2\pi}}\exp\left(-\frac{1}{2}\frac{(x-\mu)^2}{\nu^2}\right), \tag{96}$$

and of course

$$N_0(x,\mu,\nu) = N\left(\frac{x-\mu}{\nu}\right), \tag{97}$$

where $N(\,\cdot\,)$ is defined by (34). We also set

$$f(x,\mu,\nu) = \frac{1}{\sqrt{2\pi\nu^2}}\exp\left(-\frac{1}{2}\frac{(x-\mu)^2}{\nu^2}\right). \tag{98}$$

Finally, we obtain the following:

Proposition 2. *The variance-gamma information-based price of a defaultable discount bond with a uniformly-distributed fraction of the principal paid on recovery is given by*

$$S_t = \mathrm{e}^{-r(T-t)}\,\frac{p_0\left(N_1(b,\mu,\nu) - N_1(a,\mu,\nu)\right) + p_1\, c\, f(c,\mu,\nu)}{p_0\left(N_0(b,\mu,\nu) - N_0(a,\mu,\nu)\right) + p_1\, f(c,\mu,\nu)}, \tag{99}$$

where

$$\mu = \frac{1}{\sigma}\frac{\xi_t}{\gamma_{tT}}, \qquad \nu = \frac{1}{\sigma}\sqrt{\frac{1-\gamma_{tT}}{\gamma_{tT}}}. \tag{100}$$

Example 3: Lognormal payoff. Next we consider the case when the payoff of an asset at time T is log-normally distributed. This will hold if $h(x) = \mathrm{e}^x$ and $X_T \sim \mathrm{Normal}(\mu,\nu^2)$. It will be convenient to look at the slightly more general payoff obtained by setting $h(x) = \mathrm{e}^{qx}$ with $q \in \mathbb{R}$. If we recall the identity

$$\frac{1}{\sqrt{2\pi}}\int_{-\infty}^{\infty}\exp\left(-\frac{1}{2}Ax^2 + Bx\right)\mathrm{d}x = \frac{1}{\sqrt{A}}\exp\left(\frac{1}{2}\frac{B^2}{A}\right), \tag{101}$$

which holds for $A > 0$ and $B \in \mathbb{R}$, a calculation gives

$$\begin{aligned} I_t(q) &:= \int_{-\infty}^{\infty}\mathrm{e}^{qx}\,\frac{1}{\sqrt{2\pi}\,\nu}\exp\left[-\frac{1}{2}\frac{(x-\mu)^2}{\nu^2} + \frac{1}{1-\gamma_{tT}}\left(\sigma\,\xi_t\,x - \frac{1}{2}\sigma^2x^2\gamma_{tT}\right)\right]\mathrm{d}x \\ &= \frac{1}{\nu\sqrt{A_t}}\exp\left(\frac{1}{2}\frac{B_t^2}{A_t} - C\right), \end{aligned} \tag{102}$$

where

$$A_t = \frac{1-\gamma_{tT}+\nu^2\sigma^2\gamma_{tT}}{\nu^2(1-\gamma_{tT})}, \quad B_t = q + \frac{\mu}{\nu^2} + \frac{\sigma\,\xi_t}{1-\gamma_{tT}}, \quad C = \frac{1}{2}\frac{\mu^2}{\nu^2}. \tag{103}$$

For $q = 1$, the price is thus given in accordance with Theorem 4 by

$$S_t = \mathrm{e}^{-r(T-t)}\,\frac{I_t(1)}{I_t(0)}. \tag{104}$$

Then clearly we have

$$S_0 = \mathrm{e}^{-rT}\exp\left[\mu + \frac{1}{2}\nu^2\right], \tag{105}$$

and a calculation leads to the following:

Proposition 3. *The variance-gamma information-based price of a financial asset with a log-normally distributed payoff such that* $\log(S_{T^-}) \sim \text{Normal}(\mu, \nu^2)$ *is given for* $t \in (0, T)$ *by*

$$S_t = \mathrm{e}^{r\,t}\, S_0 \exp\left[\frac{\nu^2\,\sigma^2\,\gamma_{tT}\,(1-\gamma_{tT})^{-1}}{1+\nu^2\,\sigma^2\,\gamma_{tT}\,(1-\gamma_{tT})^{-1}}\left(\frac{1}{\sigma\,\gamma_{tT}}\,\xi_t - \mu - \frac{1}{2}\,\nu^2\right)\right]. \tag{106}$$

More generally, one can consider the case of a so-called power-payoff derivative for which

$$H_T = (S_{T^-})^q\,, \tag{107}$$

where $S_{T^-} = \lim_{t\to T} S_t$ is the payoff of the asset priced above in Proposition 3. See Bouzianis and Hughston (2019) for aspects of the theory of power-payoff derivatives. In the present case if we write

$$C_t = \mathrm{e}^{-r\,(T-t)}\,\mathbb{E}_t\left[(S_{T^-})^q\right] \tag{108}$$

for the value of the power-payoff derivative at time t, we find that

$$C_t = \mathrm{e}^{r\,t}\, C_0 \exp\left[\frac{\nu^2\,\sigma^2\,\gamma_{tT}\,(1-\gamma_{tT})^{-1}}{1+\nu^2\,\sigma^2\,\gamma_{tT}\,(1-\gamma_{tT})^{-1}}\left(\frac{q}{\sigma\,\gamma_{tT}}\,\xi_t - q\,\mu - \frac{1}{2}\,q^2\,\nu^2\right)\right], \tag{109}$$

where

$$C_0 = \mathrm{e}^{-r\,T}\exp\left[q\,\mu + \frac{1}{2}\,q^2\,\nu^2\right]. \tag{110}$$

Example 4: Exponentially distributed payoff. Next we consider the case where the payoff is exponentially distributed. We let $X_T \sim \exp(\lambda)$, so $\mathbb{P}\left[X_T \in \mathrm{d}x\right] = \lambda\,\mathrm{e}^{-\lambda\,x}\,\mathrm{d}x$, and take $h(x) = x$. A calculation shows that

$$\int_0^\infty x\,\exp\left[-\lambda\,x + \left(\sigma\,\xi_t\,x - \frac{1}{2}\,\sigma^2\,x^2\,\gamma_{tT}\right)(1-\gamma_{tT})^{-1}\right]\mathrm{d}x = \frac{\mu - N_1(0,\mu,\nu)}{f(0,\mu,\nu)}, \tag{111}$$

where we set

$$\mu = \frac{1}{\sigma}\,\frac{\xi_t}{\gamma_{tT}} - \frac{\lambda}{\sigma^2}\,\frac{1-\gamma_{tT}}{\gamma_{tT}}, \quad \nu = \frac{1}{\sigma}\sqrt{\frac{1-\gamma_{tT}}{\gamma_{tT}}}, \tag{112}$$

and

$$\int_0^\infty \exp\left[-\lambda\,x + \left(\sigma\,\xi_t\,x - \frac{1}{2}\,\sigma^2\,x^2\,\gamma_{tT}\right)(1-\gamma_{tT})^{-1}\right]\mathrm{d}x = \frac{1 - N_0(0,\mu,\nu)}{f(0,\mu,\nu)}. \tag{113}$$

As a consequence we obtain:

Proposition 4. *The variance-gamma information-based price of a financial asset with an exponentially distributed payoff is given by*

$$S_t = \frac{\mu - N_1(0,\mu,\nu)}{1 - N_0(0,\mu,\nu)}, \tag{114}$$

where N_0 *and* N_1 *are defined as in Example 2.*

7. Conclusions

In the examples considered in the previous section, we have looked at the situation where there is a single market factor X_T, which is revealed at time T, and where the single cash flow occurring at T depends on the outcome for X_T. The value of a security S_t with that cash flow is determined by the information available at time t. Given the Markov property of the extended information process $\{\xi_t, \gamma_{tT}\}$ it follows that there exists a function of three variables $F : \mathbb{R} \times [0,1] \times \mathbb{R}^+ \to \mathbb{R}^+$ such that $S_t = F(\xi_t, \gamma_{tT}, t)$, and we have worked out this expression explicitly for a number of different cases, given in Examples 1-4. The general valuation formula is presented in Theorem 4.

It should be evident that once we have specified the functional dependence of the resulting asset prices on the extended information process, then we can back out values of the information process and the gamma bridge from the price data. So in that sense the process $\{\xi_t, \gamma_{tT}\}$ is "visible" in the market, and can be inferred directly, at any time, from a suitable collection of prices. This means, in particular, that given the prices of a certain minimal collection of assets in the market, we can then work out the values of other assets in the market, such as derivatives. In the special case we have just been discussing, there is only a single market factor; but one can see at once that the ideas involved readily extend to the situation where there are multiple market factors and multiple cash flows, as one expects for general securities analysis, following the principles laid out in Brody et al. (2007, 2008a), where the merits and limitations of modelling in an information-based framework are discussed in some detail.

The potential advantages of working with the variance-gamma information process, rather than the highly tractable but more limited Brownian information process should be evident—these include the additional parametric freedom in the model, with more flexibility in the distributions of returns, but equally important, the scope for jumps. It comes as a pleasant surprise that the resulting formulae are to a large extent analytically explicit, but this is on account of the remarkable properties of the normalized variance-gamma bridge process that we have exploited in our constructions. Keep in mind that in the limit as the parameter m goes to infinity our model reduces to that of the Brownian bridge information-based model considered in Brody et al. (2007, 2008a), which in turn contains the standard geometric Brownian motion model (and hence the Black-Scholes option pricing model) as a special case. In the case of a single market factor X_T, the distribution of the random variable X_T can be inferred by observing the current prices of derivatives for which the payoff is of the form

$$H_T = \mathrm{e}^{rT} \mathbb{1}_{X_T \le K}, \tag{115}$$

for $K \in \mathbb{R}$. The information flow-rate parameter σ and the shape parameter m can then be inferred from option prices. When multiple factors are involved, similar calibration methodologies are applicable.

Author Contributions: The authors have made equal contributions to the work. Both have read and agreed to the published version of the manuscript.

Funding: This research has received no external funding.

Acknowledgments: The authors wish to thank G. Bouzianis and J. M. Pedraza-Ramírez for useful discussions. LSB acknowledges support from (a) Oriel College, Oxford, (b) the Mathematical Institute, Oxford, (c) Consejo Nacional de Ciencia y Tenconología (CONACyT), Ciudad de México, and (d) LMAX Exchange, London. We are grateful to the anonymous referees for a number of helpful comments and suggestions.

Conflicts of Interest: The authors declare no conflicts of interest.

Risks **2020**, *8*, 105

References

Abramowitz, Milton, and Irene A. Stegun, eds. 1972. *Handbook of Mathematical Functions with Formulas, Graphs, and Mathematical Tables*. United State Department of Commerce, National Bureau of Standards, Applied Mathematics Series 55. Washington: National Bureau of Standards.

Bouzianis, George, and Lane P. Hughston. 2019. Determination of the Lévy Exponent in Asset Pricing Models. *International Journal of Theoretical and Applied Finance* 22: 1950008.

Brody, Dorje C., Lane P. Hughston, and Andrea Macrina. 2007. Beyond Hazard Rates: A New Framework for Credit-Risk Modelling. In *Advances in Mathematical Finance*. Edited by Michael C. Fu, Robert A. Jarrow, Ju-Yi J. Yen and Robert J. Elliot. Basel: Birkhäuser.

Brody, Dorje C., Lane P. Hughston, and Andrea Macrina. 2008a. Information-Based Asset Pricing. *International Journal of Theoretical and Applied Finance* 11: 107–42.

Brody, Dorje C., Lane P. Hughston, and Andrea Macrina. 2008b. Dam Rain and Cumulative Gain. *Proceeding of the Royal Society A* 464: 1801–22.

Brody, Dorje C., Mark H. A. Davis, Robyn L. Friedman, and Lane P. Hughston. 2009. Informed Traders. *Proceedings of the Royal Society A* 465: 1103–22.

Brody, Dorje C., Lane P. Hughston, and Andrea Macrina. 2010. Credit Risk, Market Sentiment and Randomly-Timed Default. In *Stochastic Analysis in 2010*. Edited by Dan Crisan. Berlin: Springer-Verlag.

Brody, Dorje C., Lane P. Hughston, and Andrea Macrina. 2011. Modelling Information Flows in Financial Markets. In *Advanced Mathematical Methods for Finance*. Edited by Giulia Di Nunno and Bernt Øksendal. Berlin: Springer-Verlag.

Carr, Peter, Hélyette Geman, Dilip B. Madan, and Marc Yor. 2002. The Fine Structure of Asset Returns: An Empirical Investigation. *Journal of Business* 75: 305–32.

Émery, Michel, and Marc Yor. 2004. A Parallel between Brownian Bridges and Gamma Bridges. *Publications of the Research Institute for Mathematical Sciences, Kyoto University* 40: 669–88.

Filipović, Damir, Lane P. Hughston, and Andrea Macrina. 2012. Conditional Density Models for Asset Pricing. *International Journal of Theoretical and Applied Finance* 15: 1250002.

Hoyle, Edward. 2010. *Information-Based Models for Finance and Insurance*. Ph.D. thesis, Imperial College London, UK.

Hoyle, Edward, Lane P. Hughston, and Andrea Macrina. 2011. Lévy Random Bridges and the Modelling of Financial Information. *Stochastic Processes and their Applications* 121: 856–84.

Hoyle, Edward, Lane P. Hughston, and Andrea Macrina. 2015. Stable-1/2 Bridges and Insurance. In *Advances in Mathematics of Finance*. Edited by Andrzej Palczewski and Lukasz Stettner. Warsaw: Polish Academy of Sciences.

Hoyle, Edward, Andrea Macrina, and Levent A. Mengütürk. 2020. Modulated Information Flows in Financial Markets. *International Journal of Theoretical and Applied Finance* 23: 2050026.

Hughston, Lane P., and Andrea Macrina. 2012. Pricing Fixed-Income Securities in an Information-Based Framework. *Applied Mathematical Finance* 19: 361–79.

Karatzas, Ioannis, and Steven E. Shreve. 1998. *Methods of Mathematical Finance*. New York: Springer-Verlag.

Kyprianou, Andreas E. 2014. *Fluctuations of Lévy Processes with Applications*, 2nd ed. Berlin: Springer-Verlag.

Macrina, Andrea. 2006. *An Information-based Framework for Asset Pricing: X-factor Theory and its Applications*. Ph.D. thesis, King's College London, UK.

Macrina, Andrea, and Jun Sekine. 2019. Stochastic Modelling with Randomized Markov Bridges. *Stochastics* 19: 1–27.

Madan, Dilip, and Eugene Seneta. 1990. The Variance Gamma (VG) Model for Share Market Returns. *Journal of Business* 63: 511–24.

Madan, Dilip, and Frank Milne. 1991. Option Pricing with VG Martingale Components. *Mathematical Finance* 1: 39–55.

Madan, Dilip, Peter Carr, and Eric C. Chang. 1998. The Variance Gamma Process and Option Pricing. *European Finance Review* 2: 79–105.

Mengütürk, Levent A. 2013. *Information-Based Jumps, Asymmetry and Dependence in Financial Modelling*. Ph.D. thesis, Imperial College London, UK.

Mengütürk, Levent A. 2018. Gaussian Random Bridges and a Geometric Model for Information Equilibrium. *Physica A* 494: 465–83.

Rutkowski, Marek, and Nannan Yu. 2007. An Extension of the Brody-Hughston-Macrina Approach to Modeling of Defaultable Bonds. *International Journal of Theoretical and Applied Finance* 10: 557–89.

Williams, David. 1991. *Probability with Martingales*. Cambridge, United Kingdom: Cambridge University Press.

Yor, Marc. 2007. Some Remarkable Properties of Gamma Processes. In *Advances in Mathematical Finance*. Edited by Michel C. Fu, Robert A. Jarrow, Ju-Yi J. Yen and Robert J. Elliot. Basel: Birkhäuser.

Chapter 17

On the Pricing of Storable Commodities

Dorje C. Brody
Department of Mathematics, University of Surrey
Guildford GU2 7XH, United Kingdom

Lane P. Hughston
Department of Computing, Goldsmiths University of London
New Cross, London SE14 6NW, United Kingdom

Xun Yang
Shell Research Limited, Shell Centre, London SE1 7NA, United Kingdom

This paper introduces an information-based model for the pricing of storable commodities such as crude oil and natural gas. The model uses the concept of market information about future supply and demand as a basis for valuation. Physical ownership of a commodity is taken to provide a stream of convenience dividends equivalent to a continuous cash flow. The market filtration is assumed to be generated jointly by the following: (i) current and past levels of the dividend rate, and (ii) partial information concerning the future of the dividend flow. The price of a commodity is the expectation under a suitable pricing measure of the totality of the discounted risk-adjusted future convenience dividend, conditional on the information provided by the market filtration. In the situation where the dividend rate is modelled by an Ornstein–Uhlenbeck process, the prices of options on commodities can be derived in closed form. The approach that we present can be applied to other assets that yield potentially negative effective cash flows, such as real estate, factories, refineries, mines, and power generating plants.

Keywords: Commodity markets; commodity derivatives; crude oil; natural gas; convenience yield; information-based asset pricing; market microstructure.

1. Introduction

In the extensive literature devoted to the pricing and risk management of commodity derivatives, most investigations take as a starting point the specification of a dynamical model for the price process for the commodity. The outcome of chance in the market in which the commodity is traded is usually represented in such studies with the specification of a fixed probability space equipped with the filtration generated by a Brownian motion of one or more dimensions, and it is typically assumed that the commodity price can be modelled as an Ito process adapted to this filtration. Such an approach to the pricing of commodities and related derivatives is in line with the "standard" modelling framework for asset pricing within which much or even most of modern finance theory has been pursued [1,2].

Nevertheless, there is a fundamental methodological issue in the standard framework: namely, that the market filtration is fixed in an essentially *ad hoc* way, and no indication is provided concerning the nature of the information it purports to convey, or why it is relevant to the price. The information is, in practice, normally no more than that of the price movements themselves, so it can hardly be claimed in any useful way that the price movements are taking place "in response" to "shocks" associated with the arrival of information, for the shocks, as we have said, are no more than the asset price movements themselves.

One knows, however, that in real markets, information concerning the possible future cash flows and other benefits or obligations linked to the physical possession of an asset can be crucial in the determination of trading decisions, even in situations where such information is imperfect. The movement of the price of an asset should thus be regarded as a *derived* concept, induced by the flow of information to market participants. This is the point of view put forward in the information-based asset pricing theory of Brody, Hughston & Macrina [3–5] that forms the analytical basis of the present investigation; see also [6, 7].

The goal of this paper is to incorporate the role played by forward-looking information in commodity markets in such a context and to derive a model for the prices used as underlyings in the valuation of commodity derivatives. Specifically, we make use of the concept of market information about future supply and demand as a basis for the valuation of storable commodities. The theory of commodity pricing from a modern perspective has a long history, starting from the works of Black [8] and Brennan & Schwartz [9]. For a detailed treatment of theory of storage, convenience yield, and related concepts, the reader can refer to Geman [10] and references cited therein. In our approach, we shall assume that the possession of one standard unit of a commodity provides a net "convenience dividend" equivalent to a cash flow $\{X_t\}_{t\geq 0}$. We thus work directly with the actual flow of benefit arising from the possession of the commodity, rather than the percentage convenience yield. The point is that the percentage convenience yield, so often used in commodity modelling, is a secondary notion since it depends on the price, which is what we are trying to determine. In what follows, we present a simple model for the convenience dividend process $\{X_t\}$. Additionally, we introduce a market information process $\{\xi_t\}_{t\geq 0}$ that provides partial or speculative information about the future dividend flow. The market filtration is then assumed to be generated jointly by these two processes. In that sense, we are explicitly constructing the market filtration in such a way that it contains information relevant to the commodity price. Given the market filtration, the price of the commodity is taken to be the risk-adjusted discounted expected value of the totality of the future convenience dividends. We model $\{X_t\}$ by an Ornstein–Uhlenbeck process. We model $\{\xi_t\}$ by a process that consists of two terms: a "signal" term containing information about the future convenience dividend flow, and a "noise" term given by an independent Brownian motion. By use of this information-based model we are able to derive closed-form expressions for both the price of the commodity and the prices of associated derivatives.

The remainder of the paper is organized as follows. In Section 2, we introduce our model for the net convenience dividend and market filtration. In Section 3, various useful facts relating to the Ornstein–Uhlenbeck (OU) process are recalled—in particular, certain features of the OU bridge. These are used in Section 4 to show in Proposition 1 that the information process and the convenience dividend rate are jointly Markovian, and in Section 5 to derive an expression for the commodity price. Finally, in Section 6, we present pricing formulae for call options on the underlying spot price.

2. Information-based commodity pricing

In the information-based approach of Brody, Hughston, and Macrina [3–5], the starting point is the specification of (i) a set of one or more random variables (called "market factors") determining the cash flows associated with a given asset, and (ii) a set of one or more random processes (called "information processes") determining the flow of information to market participants concerning these market factors. The setup, more specifically, is as follows. We model the outcome of chance in a commodity market with the specification of a probability space $(\Omega, \mathcal{F}, \mathbb{Q})$. The market is not assumed to be complete, but we do assume the existence of a preferred pricing measure (or "risk neutral" measure) $\mathbb{Q}$. In more detail, we assume the existence of a physical measure and a pricing kernel that with respect to the physical measure takes the form of a discount factor times a strictly positive martingale. The martingale is used to change the measure to $\mathbb{Q}$, and from that point onward we formulate the details of the theory with reference to that measure. Then, if $\{X_t\}$ represents the net convenience dividend, which is given by the benefits associated with possession of the commodity less storage costs and any other direct costs associated with the said possession, the price of the commodity at time t is given by

$$S_t = \frac{1}{\pi_t}\mathbb{E}\left[\int_t^\infty \pi_u X_u \mathrm{d}u \,\middle|\, \mathcal{F}_t\right], \tag{2.1}$$

where the expectation is taken under $\mathbb{Q}$. Here, the discount factor $\{\pi_t\}_{t\geq 0}$ is given in terms of the short rate $\{r_t\}_{t\geq 0}$ by

$$\pi_t = \exp\left(-\int_0^t r_s \mathrm{d}s\right). \tag{2.2}$$

The associated money-market account process is given by $\{1/\pi_t\}_{t\geq 0}$. For simplicity, we assume that the default-free interest rate system is deterministic. The market filtration $\{\mathcal{F}_t\}$, with respect to which the conditioning is taken in (2.1), is taken to be generated jointly by (a) the convenience dividend process $\{X_t\}_{t\geq 0}$, and (b) a market information process $\{\xi_t\}_{t\geq 0}$ of the form

$$\xi_t = \sigma t \int_t^\infty \pi_u X_u \mathrm{d}u + B_t, \tag{2.3}$$

representing partial or noisy information about the future dividend flow. The parameter σ determines the rate at which information about the future dividend stream is revealed to the market. The $\mathbb{Q}$-Brownian motion $\{B_t\}$ represents noise arising from rumour, baseless speculation, uninformed trading, fake news, and the like, and is assumed to be independent of the dividend process $\{X_t\}$. Therefore, for each $t \geq 0$ we have

$$\mathcal{F}_t = \sigma\left[\{\xi_s\}_{0\leq s\leq t}, \{X_s\}_{0\leq s\leq t}\right]. \tag{2.4}$$

The next step is to specify the form of the dividend process. We consider in this paper the case in which $\{X_t\}$ is an Ornstein–Uhlenbeck (OU) process. It is worth recalling, by way of contrast, that Gibson & Schwartz [11, 12] assume that the percentage convenience yield should follow a mean-reverting process, an approach that has been followed in many subsequent works [13–20]. The idea of the present work, however, is that a mean-reverting absolute convenience dividend reflects the notion that in the long term, there is an equilibrium rate of benefit obtained by storing or holding the commodity. We thus assume that the dividend process satisfies a stochastic equation of the form

$$\mathrm{d}X_t = \kappa(\theta - X_t)\mathrm{d}t + \psi\,\mathrm{d}\beta_t, \tag{2.5}$$

where $\{\beta_t\}$ is a $\mathbb{Q}$-Brownian motion that is independent of $\{B_t\}$. We allow for the possibility that the dividend rate may occasionally be negative. The mean reversion level θ, the reversion rate κ, and the dividend volatility ψ are assumed to be constant in the present discussion, although the results can be readily generalized to the time-dependent case.

3. Properties of the Ornstein–Uhlenbeck process

Before we proceed to work out the conditional expectation (2.1), it will be useful to comment on various properties of the Ornstein–Uhlenbeck process. These properties, some of which will be well known, but others perhaps less so, will help us simplify the calculations. It is an elementary exercise to check that the solution to (2.5) takes the form

$$X_t = \mathrm{e}^{-\kappa t}X_0 + \theta(1 - \mathrm{e}^{-\kappa t}) + \psi\mathrm{e}^{-\kappa t}\int_0^t \mathrm{e}^{\kappa s}\mathrm{d}\beta_s. \tag{3.1}$$

The Ornstein–Uhlenbeck process has the property that if we "reinitialize" the process at time t, then its value at some later time $T > t$ can be expressed as

$$X_T = \mathrm{e}^{-\kappa(T-t)}X_t + \theta(1 - \mathrm{e}^{-\kappa(T-t)}) + \psi\mathrm{e}^{-\kappa T}\int_t^T \mathrm{e}^{\kappa u}\,\mathrm{d}\beta_u. \tag{3.2}$$

Since $\{X_t\}$ is a Gaussian process, one can verify the following by use of covariance relations:

Lemma 3.1. *The random variables X_t and $X_T - \mathrm{e}^{-\kappa(T-t)}X_t$ are independent.*

Proof. The mean of X_t is given by

$$\mathbb{E}[X_t] = \mathrm{e}^{-\kappa t}X_0 + \theta(1 - \mathrm{e}^{-\kappa t}). \tag{3.3}$$

A straightforward calculation using the Ito isometry then shows that

$$\mathrm{Var}[X_t] = \frac{\psi^2}{2\kappa}(1 - \mathrm{e}^{-2\kappa t}) \tag{3.4}$$

and that for $0 \leq t \leq T$ we have

$$\mathrm{Cov}[X_t, X_T] = \frac{\psi^2}{\kappa}\mathrm{e}^{-\kappa T} \sinh \kappa t, \tag{3.5}$$

from which it follows that

$$\mathrm{Cov}[X_t, X_T - \mathrm{e}^{-\kappa(T-t)} X_t] = 0, \tag{3.6}$$

and hence the claimed independence. □

This property of the OU process corresponds to an orthogonal decomposition of the form

$$X_T = (X_T - \mathrm{e}^{-\kappa(T-t)} X_t) + \mathrm{e}^{-\kappa(T-t)} X_t \tag{3.7}$$

for $T > t$. The validity of Lemma 3.1 can also be checked by direct inspection of (3.1) and (3.2). It should be evident that if the reversion rate is set to zero, then (3.7) reduces to the independent-increments decomposition of a Brownian motion.

Interestingly, there is another orthogonal decomposition of the OU process that is somewhat less obvious than (3.7). This is given by the identity

$$X_t = \left(X_t - \frac{\sinh \kappa t}{\sinh \kappa T} X_T \right) + \frac{\sinh \kappa t}{\sinh \kappa T} X_T. \tag{3.8}$$

The process $\{b_{tT}\}_{0 \leq t \leq T}$, defined for fixed T by

$$b_{tT} = X_t - \frac{\sinh \kappa t}{\sinh \kappa T} X_T, \tag{3.9}$$

appearing in (3.8), is an OU bridge. The OU bridge interpolates between the fixed values $b_{0T} = X_0$ and $b_{TT} = 0$, and we are led to another useful result.

In particular, a calculation shows the following:

Lemma 3.2. *The Ornstein–Uhlenbeck bridge $\{b_{tT}\}_{0 \leq t \leq T}$ and the random variable X_U are independent for all T and U such that $0 \leq T \leq U$.*

Proof. Since $\{b_{tT}\}_{0 \leq t \leq T}$ and X_U are jointly Gaussian, it suffices to show that for any choice of t, T, U such that $t \leq T \leq U$ the random variables b_{tT} and X_U are independent. We have

$$\mathrm{Cov}[X_t, X_U] = \frac{\psi^2}{\kappa}\mathrm{e}^{-\kappa U} \sinh \kappa t \tag{3.10}$$

and

$$\mathrm{Cov}[X_T, X_U] = \frac{\psi^2}{\kappa} \mathrm{e}^{-\kappa U} \sinh \kappa T, \tag{3.11}$$

from which it follows that

$$\mathrm{Cov}\left[X_t - \frac{\sinh \kappa t}{\sinh \kappa T} X_T, X_U\right] = 0, \tag{3.12}$$

and hence the claimed independence. □

We note that the mean and variance of the OU bridge are given, respectively, by

$$\mathbb{E}[b_{tT}] = \frac{\sinh \kappa(T-t)}{\sinh \kappa T} X_0 + \left[1 - \frac{\sinh \kappa t + \sinh \kappa(T-t)}{\sinh \kappa T}\right] \theta \tag{3.13}$$

and

$$\mathrm{Var}[b_{tT}] = \frac{\psi^2}{\kappa} \sinh \kappa t \left[\cosh \kappa t - \frac{\sinh \kappa t}{\sinh \kappa T} \cosh \kappa T\right]. \tag{3.14}$$

4. Markov property of market information

When working with conditional expectations, we often use the shorthand $\mathbb{E}[Y|Z]$ in place of $\mathbb{E}[Y|\sigma\{Z\}]$, where $\sigma\{Z\}$ denotes the σ-algebra generated by Z. Keeping in mind this notation, we frequently make use of the following. Let X, Y, and Z be random variables, and we assume that X is integrable. Then, if $\sigma\{X, Y\}$ and $\sigma\{Z\}$ are independent, it holds that

$$\mathbb{E}[X|\, Y, Z] = \mathbb{E}[X|Y]. \tag{4.1}$$

See, for example, Williams [21], Section 9.7. We proceed to work out the conditional expectation in (2.1) to determine the commodity price. The following result will facilitate the calculations:

Proposition 4.1. *The information process $\{\xi_t\}$ and the dividend rate $\{X_t\}$ are jointly Markov.*

Proof. We need to show that for $0 \le t \le u$ it holds that

$$\mathbb{Q}\left[\xi_u < a \cap X_u < b \,|\, \{\xi_s\}_{0\le s\le t}, \{X_s\}_{0\le s\le t}\right] = \mathbb{Q}\left[\xi_u < a \cap X_u < b \,|\, \xi_t, X_t\right]. \tag{4.2}$$

Let us define a process $\{\eta_t\}$ by setting

$$\eta_t = \sigma t \int_0^\infty \pi_u X_u \mathrm{d}u + B_t. \tag{4.3}$$

It should be evident that

$$\sigma[\{\xi_s\}_{0\le s\le t}, \{X_s\}_{0\le s\le t}] = \sigma[\{\eta_s\}_{0\le s\le t}, \{X_s\}_{0\le s\le t}]. \tag{4.4}$$

This follows from the fact that

$$\eta_t = \xi_t + \sigma t \int_0^t \pi_u X_u \mathrm{d}u. \tag{4.5}$$

We observe that $\{\eta_t\}$ is Markov in its own filtration. To see this, it suffices to verify that

$$\mathbb{Q}\left(\eta_t \leq x \,\middle|\, \eta_s, \eta_{s_1}, \eta_{s_2}, \cdots, \eta_{s_k}\right) = \mathbb{Q}\left(\eta_t \leq x \middle| \eta_s\right) \tag{4.6}$$

for any collection of times $t, s, s_1, s_2, \cdots, s_k$ such that $t \geq s \geq s_1 \geq s_2 \geq \cdots \geq s_k > 0$. Now, it is an elementary property of Brownian motion that for any times t, s, s_1 satisfying $t > s > s_1 > 0$, the random variables B_t and $B_s/s - B_{s_1}/s_1$ are independent. More generally, for $s > s_1 > s_2 > s_3 > 0$, we find that $B_s/s - B_{s_1}/s_1$ and $B_{s_2}/s_2 - B_{s_3}/s_3$ are independent. Observing that $\eta_s/s - \eta_{s_1}/s_1 = B_s/s - B_{s_1}/s_1$, we find that

$$\begin{aligned}
\mathbb{Q}\left(\eta_t \leq x \,\middle|\, \eta_s, \eta_{s_1}, \cdots, \eta_{s_k}\right) &= \mathbb{Q}\left(\eta_t \leq x \,\middle|\, \eta_s, \frac{\eta_s}{s} - \frac{\eta_{s_1}}{s_1}, \cdots, \frac{\eta_{s_{k-1}}}{s_{k-1}} - \frac{\eta_{s_k}}{s_k}\right) \\
&= \mathbb{Q}\left(\eta_t \leq x \,\middle|\, \eta_s, \frac{B_s}{s} - \frac{B_{s_1}}{s_1}, \cdots, \frac{B_{s_{k-1}}}{s_{k-1}} - \frac{B_{s_k}}{s_k}\right).
\end{aligned} \tag{4.7}$$

But since η_t and η_s are jointly independent of $B_s/s - B_{s_1}/s_1, \cdots$, the Markov property (4.6) follows for $\{\eta_t\}$. Let us now define

$$\mathcal{G}_t = \sigma\left(\left\{\frac{\eta_t}{t} - \frac{\eta_s}{s}\right\}_{0<s\leq t}\right). \tag{4.8}$$

Then, clearly we have

$$\mathcal{G}_t = \sigma\left(\left\{\frac{B_t}{t} - \frac{B_s}{s}\right\}_{0<s\leq t}\right), \tag{4.9}$$

that is to say, $\mathcal{G}_t$ is generated by the Brownian bridge underlying the noise component of the information process. Note that the σ-algebras $\sigma[\eta_t, \{X_s\}]$ and $\mathcal{G}_t$ are independent. As a consequence, writing

$$F[a, b \,|\, \mathcal{F}_t] = \mathbb{P}\left[\xi_u < a \cap X_u < b \,|\, \mathcal{F}_t\right] \tag{4.10}$$

for the conditional bivariate distribution function, we have

$$\begin{aligned}
F[a, b \,|\, \mathcal{F}_t] &= \mathbb{E}\left[\mathbb{1}(\xi_u < a)\mathbb{1}(X_u < b) \,|\, \mathcal{F}_t\right] \\
&= \mathbb{E}\left[\mathbb{1}(\xi_u < a)\mathbb{1}(X_u < b) \,|\, \{\xi_s\}_{0\leq s\leq t}, \{X_s\}_{0\leq s\leq t}\right] \\
&= \mathbb{E}\left[\mathbb{1}(\xi_u < a)\mathbb{1}(X_u < b) \,|\, \{\eta_s\}_{0\leq s\leq t}, \{X_s\}_{0\leq s\leq t}\right] \\
&= \mathbb{E}\left[\mathbb{1}(\xi_u < a)\mathbb{1}(X_u < b) \,|\, \eta_t, \mathcal{G}_t, \{X_s\}_{0\leq s\leq t}\right] \\
&= \mathbb{E}\left[\mathbb{1}(\xi_u < a)\mathbb{1}(X_u < b) \,|\, \eta_t, \{X_s\}_{0\leq s\leq t}\right] \\
&= \mathbb{E}\left[\mathbb{1}(\xi_u < a)\mathbb{1}(X_u < b) \,|\, \xi_t, \{X_s\}_{0\leq s\leq t}\right].
\end{aligned} \tag{4.11}$$

On the other hand, recalling the definition of the OU bridge given by (3.9), we have

$$\sigma[\xi_t, \{X_s\}_{0\leq s\leq t}] = \sigma[\xi_t, X_t, \{b_{st}\}_{0\leq s\leq t}]. \tag{4.12}$$

Now, it is easy to see that $\{b_{st}\}_{0\leq s\leq t}$ and $\{X_u\}_{u\geq t}$ are independent. It follows that $\sigma[\{b_{st}\}_{0\leq s\leq t}]$ and $\sigma[\xi_t, X_t, \xi_u, X_u]$ are independent, from which we get (4.2). □

5. Commodity pricing formula

The joint Markov property (4.2) implies that

$$\mathbb{E}\left[\int_t^\infty \pi_u X_u \,\mathrm{d}u \,\middle|\, \{\xi_s\}_{0\le s\le t}, \{X_s\}_{0\le s\le t}\right] = \mathbb{E}\left[\int_t^\infty \pi_u X_u \,\mathrm{d}u \,\middle|\, \xi_t, X_t\right], \quad (5.1)$$

which allows one to reduce the problem of working out the commodity price (2.1) to that of calculating

$$S_t = \frac{1}{\pi_t}\mathbb{E}\left[\int_t^\infty \pi_u X_u \,\mathrm{d}u \,\middle|\, \xi_t, X_t\right]. \quad (5.2)$$

One observes that from the orthogonal decomposition (3.7) we can isolate the dependence of the commodity price on the current level of the convenience dividend rate X_t. Remarkably, the dependence turns out to be linear. That is, we have

$$\int_t^\infty \pi_u X_u \,\mathrm{d}u = \int_t^\infty \pi_u \left(X_u - \mathrm{e}^{-\kappa(u-t)}X_t\right)\mathrm{d}u + \left(\int_t^\infty \pi_u \mathrm{e}^{-\kappa(u-t)}\,\mathrm{d}u\right) X_t. \quad (5.3)$$

Substituting this formula in Equation (5.2), we deduce that

$$\begin{aligned} \pi_t S_t &= \mathbb{E}\left[\int_t^\infty \pi_u \left(X_u - \mathrm{e}^{-\kappa(u-t)}X_t\right)\mathrm{d}u \,\middle|\, \xi_t, X_t\right] \\ &\quad + \mathbb{E}\left[\left(\int_t^\infty \pi_u \mathrm{e}^{-\kappa(u-t)}\,\mathrm{d}u\right) X_t \,\middle|\, \xi_t, X_t\right] \\ &= \mathbb{E}\left[A_t \,|\, \xi_t, X_t\right] + \left(\int_t^\infty \pi_u \mathrm{e}^{-\kappa(u-t)}\,\mathrm{d}u\right) X_t, \end{aligned} \quad (5.4)$$

where

$$A_t = \int_t^\infty \pi_u (X_u - \mathrm{e}^{-\kappa(u-t)}X_t)\mathrm{d}u. \quad (5.5)$$

Next, we observe that as a consequence of (2.3) and (5.5), we have

$$\xi_t = \sigma t\left[A_t + \left(\int_t^\infty \pi_u \mathrm{e}^{-\kappa(u-t)}\mathrm{d}u\right) X_t\right] + B_t. \quad (5.6)$$

It follows that

$$\pi_t S_t = \mathbb{E}\left[A_t \,|\, \sigma t A_t + B_t, X_t\right] + \left(\int_t^\infty \pi_u \mathrm{e}^{-\kappa(u-t)}\mathrm{d}u\right) X_t. \quad (5.7)$$

Note that the conditioning with respect to X_t in the first term of the right-hand side of (5.7) drops out since, by Lemma (3.1), the random variables $\{X_u - \mathrm{e}^{-\kappa(u-t)}X_t\}_{u\ge t}$ and X_t are independent, which allows one to deduce that the σ-algebras $\sigma\{X_t\}$ and $\sigma\{A_t, B_t\}$ are independent. Therefore,

$$\pi_t S_t = \mathbb{E}\left[A_t \,|\, \sigma t A_t + B_t\right] + \left(\int_t^\infty \pi_u \mathrm{e}^{-\kappa(u-t)}\mathrm{d}u\right) X_t. \quad (5.8)$$

The problem of determining the commodity price is thus reduced to that of calculating a conditional expectation of the form $\mathbb{E}[A_t|A_t + C_t]$ for $t > 0$, where A_t is given by (5.5) and $C_t = B_t/\sigma t$. We observe that A_t and C_t are independent Gaussian random variables. To compute the conditional expectation, we recall another result concerning orthogonal decompositions of Gaussian random variables:

Lemma 5.1. *If A and C are independent Gaussian random variables, then $A+C$ and $(1-z)A - zC$ are independent if $z = \mathrm{Var}[A]/(\mathrm{Var}[A] + \mathrm{Var}[C])$.*

In view of this observation, let us express A_t in the form

$$A_t = z_t(A_t + C_t) + (1 - z_t)A_t - z_t C_t, \tag{5.9}$$

where

$$z_t = \frac{\mathrm{Var}[A_t]}{\mathrm{Var}[A_t] + \mathrm{Var}[C_t]}. \tag{5.10}$$

Then, we find that

$$\mathbb{E}[A_t|A_t + C_t] = z_t(A_t + C_t) + (1 - z_t)\mathbb{E}[A_t] - z_t\mathbb{E}[C_t]. \tag{5.11}$$

Clearly, we have $\mathbb{E}[C_t] = 0$. Furthermore, if we set $T = u$ in Equation (3.2), we deduce that

$$\begin{aligned}\mathbb{E}[A_t] &= \mathbb{E}\left[\theta \int_t^\infty \pi_u \left(1 - \mathrm{e}^{-\kappa(u-t)}\right) \mathrm{d}u + \psi \int_t^\infty \mathrm{e}^{-\kappa u}\pi_u \int_t^u \mathrm{e}^{\kappa s}\mathrm{d}\beta_s \mathrm{d}u\right] \\ &= \theta \int_t^\infty \pi_u \mathrm{d}u - \theta \int_t^\infty \pi_u \mathrm{e}^{-\kappa(u-t)}\mathrm{d}u. \end{aligned} \tag{5.12}$$

The final step in deriving the commodity price is to determine the variances of A_t and C_t. To simplify the notation, let us write

$$p_t = \int_t^\infty \pi_u \mathrm{d}u, \qquad q_t = \int_t^\infty \pi_u \mathrm{e}^{-\kappa(u-t)}\mathrm{d}u. \tag{5.13}$$

Then, a short calculation shows that

$$\mathrm{Var}[A_t] = \psi^2 \int_t^\infty q_s^2 \mathrm{d}s, \qquad \mathrm{Var}[C_t] = \frac{1}{\sigma^2 t}, \tag{5.14}$$

and hence that

$$z_t = \frac{\sigma^2\psi^2 t \int_t^\infty q_s^2 \mathrm{d}s}{1 + \sigma^2\psi^2 t \int_t^\infty q_s^2 \mathrm{d}s}. \tag{5.15}$$

Putting these results together, we deduce that the price of the commodity at t is given by

$$\pi_t S_t = (1 - z_t)\,[\theta p_t + q_t(X_t - \theta)] + \frac{1}{\sigma t} z_t\, \xi_t. \tag{5.16}$$

Observe that the first term in (5.16) is essentially the annuity valuation of a constant dividend rate set at the reversion level θ, together with a correction term to adjust for the present level of the dividend rate. The second term, on the other hand, represents the contribution from the noisy observation of the future dividend flow.

Several interesting observations can be made regarding the weight factor (5.15), which lies between zero and one for all t. For large ψ and/or large σ, the value of z_t tends to unity; for small ψ and/or small σ, the value of z_t tends to zero. Hence, if the market information has a low noise content, or if the volatility of the convenience dividend is high, then market participants also rely heavily on the information available about the future in their determination of the price, rather than assuming that the current value of the dividend is a good indicator for the future.

Conversely, in the absence of a strong signal concerning the future dividend flow, an annuity valuation based on the current dividend level will dominate the price. We see therefore that important intuitive characteristics are encoded explicitly in the pricing formula (5.16). Indeed, (5.16) captures rather well the idea of information-based asset pricing, showing how varying amounts of information about the future can affect the development of prices, and that prices typically represent a kind of compromise between what we know for sure at some given time and the less trustworthy but nevertheless significant intelligence that we may possess regarding events that lay ahead.

In the special case for which the interest rate is constant, the valuation formula (5.16) simplifies somewhat to give the following:

$$S_t = (1 - z_t)\frac{1}{r}\left[\frac{\kappa}{r+\kappa}\theta + \frac{r}{r+\kappa}X_t\right] + \frac{\mathrm{e}^{rt}}{\sigma t}\, z_t\, \xi_t, \tag{5.17}$$

where the weight factors are

$$z_t = \frac{\sigma^2\psi^2 t}{2r\,(r+\kappa)^2\,\mathrm{e}^{2rt} + \sigma^2\psi^2 t}, \qquad 1 - z_t = \frac{2r\,(r+\kappa)^2\,\mathrm{e}^{2rt}}{2r\,(r+\kappa)^2\,\mathrm{e}^{2rt} + \sigma^2\psi^2 t}. \tag{5.18}$$

We have performed Monte Carlo simulation studies to gain further intuition concerning the dynamical behaviour of the commodity price. Furthermore, we have calibrated the model parameters to the prices of crude oil, and we have compared the resulting simulated sample paths to market data. In the case of the crude oil markets, we are able to estimate the expected long-term future spot price from the historical average of spot prices, since there exists a supply–demand equilibrium price level to which the long-run price tends to converge. The results indicate that even in the constant-parameter model considered above, the model is sufficiently rich to capture elements of the behaviour of market data.

6. Pricing commodity derivatives

We now return to the price process (5.17) in the case of a constant interest rate and work out the value of a European-style call option with strike K and maturity T. Since $\mathbb{Q}$ is the pricing measure, we have

$$C_0 = \mathrm{e}^{-rT}\mathbb{E}[(S_T - K)^+]. \tag{6.1}$$

We observe that S_T consists of a linear combination of three random components, namely X_T, $\int_T^\infty \mathrm{e}^{-ru}X_u\mathrm{d}u$, and B_T, and that all three components are Gaussian.

It follows that S_T is also Gaussian; therefore, we can write

$$C_0 = \mathrm{e}^{-rT} \frac{1}{\sqrt{2\pi \mathrm{Var}[S_T]}} \int_K^\infty (z - K) \exp\left(-\frac{(z - \mathbb{E}[S_T])^2}{2\,\mathrm{Var}[S_T]} \right) \mathrm{d}z. \tag{6.2}$$

Performing this integral, we obtain

$$C_0 = \mathrm{e}^{-rT} \left[\sqrt{\frac{\mathrm{Var}[S_T]}{2\pi}} \exp\left(-\frac{(\mathbb{E}[S_T] - K)^2}{2\mathrm{Var}[S_T]} \right) + (\mathbb{E}[S_T] - K) N\left(\frac{\mathbb{E}[S_T] - K}{\sqrt{\mathrm{Var}[S_T]}} \right) \right], \tag{6.3}$$

where $N(x)$ is the normal distribution function. Thus, the problem reduces to a determination of the mean and variance of S_T. A calculation gives

$$\mathbb{E}[S_T] = \frac{1}{r} \left[\frac{\kappa}{r + \kappa} \theta + \frac{r}{r + \kappa} \left[\mathrm{e}^{-\kappa T} X_0 + \theta(1 - \mathrm{e}^{-\kappa T}) \right] \right] \tag{6.4}$$

and

$$\mathrm{Var}[S_T] = \frac{\psi^2}{2\kappa\,(r + \kappa)^2} (1 - \mathrm{e}^{-2\kappa T}) + z_T^2 \left[\frac{\psi^2}{2r(r + \kappa)^2} + \frac{\mathrm{e}^{2rT}}{\sigma^2 T} \right]. \tag{6.5}$$

Substitution of (6.4) and (6.5) in (6.3) then gives the option price. One can also work out the price processes for options. Similar calculations can be carried out to obtain the prices of futures contracts and futures options.

Although very simple in its structure, the model we have presented captures nicely certain aspects of the pricing of commodities in an information-theoretic framework. Looking ahead, it would be interesting to pursue a similar line of argument in more complex settings, such as those presented by electricity markets. To get a sense of what is involved in that case, see [22]. For an alternative approach to the pricing of commodities in an information-based setting, see [23]. For further discussion of the ideas developed in the present paper, see [24].

Acknowledgments

The authors are grateful for helpful comments made by participants at the AMaMeF (Advanced Mathematical Methods in Finance) conferences in Alesund, Norway (2009) and Bled, Slovenia (2010), the Workshop on Derivatives Pricing and Risk Management at the Fields Institute, Toronto (2010), and meetings at the University at Warwick (2011) and the London School of Economics (2012), where parts of this work were presented. We thank the referee for useful suggestions. XY acknowledges support from Shell International Ltd.

References

[1] I. Karatzas & S. E. Shreve (1998) *Methods of Mathematical Finance.* New York: Springer.

[2] D. Duffie (2001) *Dynamic Asset Pricing Theory,* third edition. Princeton, New Jersey: Princeton University Press.

[3] D. C. Brody, L. P. Hughston & A. Macrina (2007) Beyond hazard rates: A new framework for credit-risk modelling. In: *Advances in Mathematical Finance,* M. Fu, R. Jarrow, Ju-Yi Yen & R. Elliott (eds.), pp. 231–257. Basel: Birkhäuser.
[4] D. C. Brody, L. P. Hughston & A. Macrina (2008) Dam rain and cumulative gain. *Proceedings of the Royal Society A* **464**, 1801–1822.
[5] D. C. Brody, L. P. Hughston & A. Macrina (2008) Information-based asset pricing. *International Journal of Theoretical and Applied Finance* **11**(1), 107–142.
[6] A. Macrina (2006) *An Information-Based Framework for Asset Pricing: X-Factor Theory and its Applications.* PhD thesis, Department of Mathematics, King's College London.
[7] M. Rutkowski & N. Yu (2007) An extension of the Brody–Hughston–Macrina approach to modelling of defaultable bonds. *International Journal of Theoretical and Applied Finance* **10**(3), 557–589.
[8] F. Black (1976) The pricing of commodity contracts. *Journal of Financial Economics* **3**, 167–179.
[9] M. Brennan & E. Schwartz (1985) Evaluating natural resource investments. *Journal of Business* **58**, 135–157.
[10] H. Geman (2005) *Commodities and Commodity Derivatives: Modelling and Pricing for Agriculturals, Metals and Energy.* Hoboken, New Jersey: John Wiley & Sons, Inc.
[11] R. Gibson & E. S. Schwartz (1990) Stochastic convenience yield and the pricing of oil contingent claims. *Journal of Finance* **45**, 959–976.
[12] R. Gibson & E. S. Schwartz (1991) Valuation of long term oil-linked assets. In: *Stochastic Models and Option Values,* D. Lund & B. Øksendal (Eds.), North Holland: Elsevier.
[13] E. S. Schwartz (1997) The stochastic behavior of commodity prices: Implications for valuation and hedging. *Journal of Finance* **52**, 923–973.
[14] J. E. Hilliard & J. Reis (1998) Valuation of commodity futures and options under stochastic convenience yields, interest rates, and jump diffusions in the spot. *Journal of Financial and Quantitative Analysis* **33**, 61–86.
[15] J. E. Hilliard & J. Reis (1999) Jump processes in commodity futures prices and options pricing. *American Journal of Agricultural Economics* **81**, 273–286.
[16] K. Miltersen & E. S. Schwartz (1998) Pricing of options on commodity futures with stochastic term structure of convenience yields and interest rate. *Journal of Financial and Quantitative Analysis* **33**, 33–59.
[17] E. S. Schwartz & J. Smith (2000) Short-term variation and long-term dynamics in commodity prices. *Management Science* **46**, 893–911.
[18] K. Miltersen (2003) Commodity price modelling that matches current observables: A new approach. *Quantitative Finance* **3**, 77–105.
[19] M. Nielsen & E. S. Schwartz (2004) Theory of storage and the pricing of commodity claims. *Review of Derivatives Research* **7**, 5–24.
[20] J. Casassus & P. Collin-Dufresne (2005) Stochastic convenience yield implied from commodity futures and interest rates. *Journal of Finance* **58**, 2283–2331.
[21] D. Williams (1991) *Probability with Martingales.* Cambridge, England: Cambridge University Press.
[22] A. Cartea & M. G. Figueroa (2005) Pricing in electricity markets: a mean reverting jump diffusion model with seasonality. *Applied Mathematical Finance* **12**(4), 313–335.
[23] A. Macrina & J. Sekine (2019) Stochastic modelling with randomized Markov bridges. *Stochastics*, doi: 10.1080/17442508.2019.1703988.
[24] X. Yang (2013) *Information-Based Commodity Pricing and the Theory of Signal Processing with Lévy Information.* PhD thesis, Department of Mathematics, Imperial College London.

Chapter 18

Mathematical Models for Fake News

Dorje C. Brody

Department of Mathematics, University of Surrey, Guildford GU2 7XH, UK

David M. Meier

AXA Switzerland, General-Guisan-Strasse 40, 8400 Winterthur, Switzerland

Over the past decade, it has become evident that intentional disinformation in the political context—so-called fake news—is a danger to democracy. However, until now, there has been no clear understanding of how to define fake news, much less how to model it. This paper addresses both of these issues. A definition of fake news is given, and two approaches for the modelling of fake news and its impact in elections and referendums are introduced. The first approach, based on the idea of a representative voter, is shown to be suitable for obtaining a qualitative understanding of phenomena associated with fake news at a macroscopic level. The second approach, based on the idea of an election microstructure, describes the collective behaviour of the electorate by modelling the preferences of individual voters. It is shown through a simulation study that the mere knowledge that fake news may be in circulation goes a long way towards mitigating the impact of fake news.

1. Introduction

"Our democracy is at risk", summarizes the interim report published in July 2018 by the UK House of Commons Digital, Culture, Media and Sport Committee (Collins *et al.* 2018) on the dissemination of disinformation on social media for the purpose of manipulating the public in election and referendum voting. The prevalence of false stories on the internet has made it difficult for many to distinguish what is true from what is false. The issue that lies at the heart of the current threat to the democratic process in the USA, the UK, and elsewhere, is that, unlike in the physical sciences in which the validity of a claim can be put to the test in a reproducible laboratory experiment, statements about past events are impossible to prove with the same degree of scientific rigour. The existence of Holocaust denialists, for instance, illustrates how doubts about a major historical event can gain traction with certain individuals. To combat the forces of fake news, it is important to view the issue through a scientific lens. Borrowing ideas from communication theory, the present paper aims at developing a mathematical theory for the modelling of fake news.

In a broad sense, the concept of "fake news" has been around for centuries. In ancient China, for instance, the military strategist Kongming famously made use of state-sponsored disinformation to his advantage (as described by C. Shou, c. 290, in the historical text, *Records of the Three Kingdoms*). During the Medieval period in Europe, the spreading of fake news often left violence and death in its wake (Soll 2016). Once the technologies for mass printing had developed, fake news found a new kind of application in the form of sensationalist reporting to increase newspaper circulation. The demand for reliable information sources, however, was high in the twentieth century, especially in the post-war period, which made the running of a newspaper based on honest reporting a viable business model. This quasi-stable configuration of mainstream journalism based predominantly on honest reporting has been thrown out of its apparent equilibrium in the twenty-first century by the rapid growth of social media usage. As Soll (2016) puts it, "It wasn't until the rise of web-generated news that our era's journalistic norms were seriously challenged, and fake news became a powerful force again".

Advances in communication technology have their advantages and disadvantages. While it is undoubtedly true that the internet, for instance, has made it possible to access information that previously would have been difficult to acquire, it is also a matter of fact that the internet serves as a platform for the propagation of irrelevant information or "noise". As noise becomes more pervasive, it becomes increasingly difficult to access reliable information. Ultimately, as Norbert Wiener explained in his insightful book, *The Human Use of Human Beings* (Wiener 1954), one has to face the implications of the Second Law of Thermodynamics, which asserts that over time, noise will dominate (or equivalently, in physicists' terminology, entropy will increase). Just as in any physical system, where entropy can be reduced by means of external inputs (such as energy or force), to combat the domination of noise, concerted efforts have to be made because noise will not disappear spontaneously. This has important implications for policy makers.

Today, fake news, fuelled by its speed of dissemination, has become a serious concern to society—perhaps most importantly because it can endanger the democratic process. In response, academic research into various aspects of fake news has intensified recently, especially after the 2016 US presidential election and the "Brexit" referendum in the UK on membership of the European Union. Broadly speaking, research carried out thus far has been primarily focused on the retrospective analysis of the impact of fake news (Allcott & Gentzkow 2017, Amador *et al.* 2017, Bovet & Makse 2018) and on the detection and prevention of fake news using deep learning and other related techniques (Conroy *et al.* 2015, Shu *et al.* 2017, Khajehnejad & Hajimirza 2018, Yang *et al.* 2018). However, to address the issues surrounding the impact of fake news more generally, to make predictions of the impact of fake news, and to conduct a comprehensive scenario analysis, it is important that a consistent mathematical model should be developed that describes the phenomena resulting from the flow of fake news. For such a model to be useful, it should be intuitive (so that the model can be trusted as a plausible candidate) and tractable (so that model parameters can be calibrated against real data, and so that predictions can be made, either analytically or numerically). The purpose of this paper is to introduce a new framework for the mathematical modelling of fake news that fulfils these requirements. Our theory of fake news is straightforward to simulate and yet allows one to replicate qualitative features of empirical observations, as demonstrated below.

2. Fake news and communication theory

Fake news is information that is inconsistent with factual reality. It is information that originates from the "sender" of fake news, is transmitted through a communication channel, and is then received, typically, by the general public. Hence, any realistic model for fake news has to be built on the successful and well-established framework of communication theory. Indeed, this philosophy was already advocated by Wiener (1954), who wrote:

> It is the thesis of this book that society can only be understood through a study of the messages and the communication facilities which belong to it; and that in the future development of these messages and communication facilities, messages between man and machines, between machines and man, and between machine and machine, are destined to play an ever-increasing part.

The modelling framework we propose in this paper embraces Wiener's philosophy. Specifically, we shall apply and extend techniques of filtering theory—a branch of communication theory that aims at filtering out noise in communication channels—in a novel way to generate models that are well suited for the treatment of fake news.

The traditional applications of filtering theory are threefold: (i) extrapolation or prediction, (ii) filtering, and (iii) interpolation, or smoothing (Wiener 1949, Kailath 1974). Over the past decade, however, a fourth application of filtering theory has been developed, namely, in *phenomenology*—the description and modelling of observed phenomena. Perhaps surprisingly, the domain of applicability of the phenomenological use of filtering techniques ranges from scales as small as elementary particles and atoms in physical systems (Brody & Hughston 2006) to scales as large as human activities in social systems (Brody *et al.* 2007, 2008). In the latter context, to describe the phenomena associated with social systems, it is particularly natural to employ the mathematics of filtering theory because the actions of an individual are ultimately based on the result of filtering the noisy information available to that individual. In other words, it is not the predictive power of filtering theory that is relevant; rather, it is the fact that the behaviour of people is guided by their predictions via filters, and thus *this behaviour is itself susceptible to a filtering description.* These observations have opened up a promising avenue towards new discoveries and novel applications, including the one that we explore here for the modelling of fake news.

The paper is organized as follows. We begin by explaining how the techniques of filtering can be applied in the context of behavioural phenomenology of an individual. We then apply this idea to the modelling of fake news as a modification of noise and introduce our key assumption that, to a good approximation, people are rational inasmuch as they follow Bayesian logic in their decision making. Hence, in our approach, those who are influenced by fake news are not viewed as being irrational as such, but rather, they lack the ability to detect and mitigate the changes caused by the presence of fake news in the structure of the noise they are exposed to. In going from the behavioural model of an individual to that of the electorate, we are in effect introducing the idea of a "representative voter" whose perception of the uncertain world represents the aggregation of the diverse views held by the public at large. We then examine the problem of estimating the release times of fake news, which in turn generates a new type of challenge in communication theory. This estimate is required for characterising a voter who is aware of the potential presence of fake news but is unsure which precise items of information are fake. We show as an illustration the dynamics of the opinion-poll statistics in a referendum in the presence of a single piece of fake news. An application to an election in which multiple pieces of fake news are released at random times is then considered. Illustrative simulation results show that the qualitative behaviour of the dynamics of the opinion-poll statistics, seen for instance during the 2016 USA presidential election (Silver 2016), can be replicated by our model. To deepen the analysis further, we introduce what we call an "election microstructure" model in which we employ the same information-based scheme to describe the dynamical behaviour of individual voters and the resulting collective voting behaviour of the electorate under the influence of fake news. We conclude with a summary and a discussion of future directions.

3. From communication theory to phenomenology

Let us begin by explaining the phenomenological application of filtering techniques. In our decision making, we are typically faced with uncertainties so that the most we can do is to arrive at a "best guess" for what the optimal decision might be. Such situations are commonly encountered in our everyday lives. Suppose, for instance, one wants to travel from one location to another in a city. Should one take the bus or travel by underground? The walk to the bus stop may be shorter, but there might be heavy traffic; on the other hand, signal failures on the underground might result in a delay. From experience, one has an initial view concerning whether travelling by bus or by underground is better. To formalise this notion, we let p denote the *a priori* probability that travelling by bus is the better choice. Correspondingly, $1-p$ will be the *a priori* probability that it would be better to travel by underground. In other words, we have a binary random variable X taking values, say $(0,1)$, with corresponding probabilities $(p, 1-p)$, where $X=0$ represents the bus being the better choice and $X=1$ represents the underground being the better choice.

The initial view, represented by the probability p, however, changes over time. A colleague who has been travelling on the underground might complain about the signal failure he encountered. The traffic news on the radio might suggest a delay on the bus route—and so on. As time progresses, one's knowledge increases but uncertainties remain. We wish to model this type of dynamics. For this purpose, we assume for simplicity that reliable knowledge increases linearly in time at a rate σ. The uncertainty, or noise, is modelled by a Brownian motion, denoted by $\{B_t\}_{t\geq 0}$, which is assumed to be independent of X because otherwise it cannot be viewed as representing pure noise. Hence, the flow of information, which we denote by $\{\xi_t\}_{t\geq 0}$, can be expressed in the form

$$\xi_t = \sigma X t + B_t. \tag{3.1}$$

The quantity of interest is the actual value of X. However, since there are two unknowns, X and $\{B_t\}$, and only one known, $\{\xi_t\}$, a rational individual will consider the probability that $X = 0$ (or $X = 1$) conditional on the information contained in the time series $\{\xi_s\}_{0\leq s\leq t}$ gathered up to time t. In other words, writing $(x_0, x_1) = (0, 1)$, one considers the conditional probability $\mathbb{P}(X = x_i|\{\xi_s\}_{0\leq s\leq t})$. In this simple model the time series $\{\xi_t\}$ is a Markov process, from which it follows that the conditional probability equals $\mathbb{P}(X = x_i|\xi_t)$.

The logical step of converting the prior probabilities $\mathbb{P}(X = x_i)$ into the posterior probabilities $\mathbb{P}(X = x_i|\xi_t)$ is captured by the Bayes formula:

$$\mathbb{P}(X = x_i|\xi_t) = \frac{\mathbb{P}(X = x_i)\rho(\xi_t|X = x_i)}{\sum_j \mathbb{P}(X = x_j)\rho(\xi_t|X = x_j)}. \tag{3.2}$$

Here, the conditional density function $\rho(\xi_t|X = x_i)$ for the random variable ξ_t is defined by the relation

$$\mathbb{P}\left(\xi_t \leq y|X = x_i\right) = \int_{-\infty}^{y} \rho(\xi|X = x_i)\,\mathrm{d}\xi, \tag{3.3}$$

and is given by

$$\rho(\xi|X = x_i) = \frac{1}{\sqrt{2\pi t}} \exp\left(-\frac{(\xi - \sigma x_i t)^2}{2t}\right). \tag{3.4}$$

This follows from the fact that, conditional on $X = x_i$, the random variable ξ_t is normally distributed with mean $\sigma x_i t$ and variance t. Recalling that $(x_0, x_1) = (0, 1)$, we thus obtain

$$\mathbb{P}(X = x_i|\xi_t) = \frac{p_i \exp\left(\sigma x_i \xi_t - \frac{1}{2}\sigma^2 x_i^2 t\right)}{p_0 + p_1 \exp\left(\sigma \xi_t - \frac{1}{2}\sigma^2 t\right)}, \tag{3.5}$$

where $p_0 = p$ and $p_1 = 1 - p$. Inferences based on the use of (3.5) are optimal in the sense that they minimize the uncertainty concerning the value of X, as measured by the variance or entropic measures subject to the information available. Hence, a rational individual will at any given time act in accordance with the changing views expressed in (3.5). In the example mentioned above, for instance, the option to travel by bus would be chosen by a rational individual if at the time t of departure it holds that $\mathbb{P}(X = 0|\xi_t) > \frac{1}{2}$. There are suggestions that people need not act rationally as anticipated by the Bayes rule (Kahneman & Tversky 1974, Grether & Plott 1979), but other studies suggest that the Bayes logic is nevertheless a dominant factor (El-Gamal & Grether 1995). It is our opinion that in the context of signal processing, given the prior, it is reasonable to assume that people intuitively follow a Bayesian line of thinking.

The mathematical framework outlined above is that of nonlinear filtering, familiar from communication theory. In communication theory, the random variable X in the first term of (3.1) represents the "signal" that one wishes to estimate in the presence of ambient noise represented by $\{B_t\}$. The parameter σ then determines the signal-to-noise ratio. More generally, the signal typically changes in time, which can be represented by a time series $\{X_t\}_{t\geq 0}$. The case of a fixed X considered here can thus be viewed as a special case, which was studied by Wonham (1965). It is important to emphasise, however, that in the context of communication theory, there is a "sender" actively transmitting the signal, whereas in our behavioural analysis, we often encounter circumstances where there are receivers but no senders of the signal because the random variable X may represent the outcome of a future real-world event that is not known to anyone and hence cannot be transmitted by anyone. Nevertheless, X does exist, and people make decisions in accordance with their best estimate of X based on partial information available to them. This is the sense in which mathematical techniques in communication theory can be applied to describe observed phenomena in science and in society. In what follows, we shall extend the foregoing ideas to tackle the problem of modelling fake news and its impact.

Before we proceed, we remark, incidentally, that although we have considered here the situation involving two possible alternatives, represented by the binary random variable X, the complexity of the analysis remains largely unchanged when X can take multiple values. Likewise, the assumption that knowledge concerning the value of X is revealed at a constant rate σ can be relaxed without affecting analytical tractability (Wonham 1965). In this case, the first term in (3.1) is replaced by $X\int_0^t \sigma(s)\mathrm{d}s$, where $\sigma(s)$ represents the information flow rate at time s. Circumstances where the value of X is revealed with certainty over a finite time horizon can be modelled by replacing the Brownian noise $\{B_t\}$ in (3.1) with a Brownian bridge over that time horizon (Brody *et al.* 2007). More generally, in situations where Brownian motion is not an appropriate model for uncertainties (if the noise process can have jumps, for instance), then one can model the noise term by a Lévy process, again without affecting analytical tractability (Brody & Hughston 2013).

4. Modelling fake news

When fake news is released, for instance by a malicious individual aiming to mislead the public, the false information is superimposed on other information. However, fake news, by its nature, does not represent true statements about the value of the quantity X that people wish to determine, so it cannot be viewed as forming part of the signal that helps people discover the true value of X. On the other hand, from the point of view of signal processing, anything that is not part of the signal can be viewed as noise. Following this logic, we thus arrive at our model for the information process in the presence of fake news:

$$\eta_t = \sigma X t + B_t + F_t, \tag{4.1}$$

where the time series $\{F_t\}_{t\geq 0}$ represents fake news. The noise term $\{B_t\}$, which has no bias, represents the aggregation of a large number of unsubstantiated rumours and speculations about the value of X. The central limit theorem then suggests the normality of the noise distribution, making Brownian motion a viable candidate for modelling noise. The time series $\{F_t\}$ thus introduces an additional bias. We can now offer a precise mathematical answer to the open issue raised in the UK House of Commons Committee Report on fake news (Collins *et al.* 2018):

> There is no agreed definition of the term 'fake news', which became widely used in 2016. Claire Wardle . . . told us . . . that "when we are talking about this huge spectrum, we cannot start thinking about regulation, and we cannot start talking about interventions, if we are not clear about what we mean".

With this in mind, we propose the following:

Definition (Fake News). *A time series $\{F_t\}$ appearing in the information process (4.1) represents "fake news" if it has a bias so that $\mathbb{E}[F_t] \neq 0$, where $\mathbb{E}$ denotes expectation.*

The existence of bias here is important, for otherwise $\{F_t\}$ would merely represent further noise rather than deliberate misinformation. It is certainly the case that additional unbiased noise is a nuisance, delaying the process of discovering the truth; but it cannot ultimately drive the public away from discovering the truth. That said, in some circumstances, there are advantages in merely delaying the process of truths being uncovered, in which case a release of an unbiased noise with $\mathbb{E}[F_t] = 0$ would suffice, and one could describe this situation as representing a mild form of disinformation. Such a scenario, however, is in effect equivalent to manipulating the information flow rate $\sigma(t)$ and corresponds to the disinformation model proposed in Brody & Law (2015). As regards the statistical dependency between $\{F_t\}$ and X, there are two situations that can arise: one in which no one knows the value of X, in which case $\{F_t\}$ should be independent of X, and one in which the value of X is known to a small number of individuals who may wish to disseminate fake news, in which case $\{F_t\}$ may well be dependent on X.

The idea that information-based models of the kind represented in (3.1) can be extended to model deliberate mis-specifications of the truth has previously been envisaged (Brody & Law 2015). The proposal there was that a malicious individual who wishes to manipulate the public can alter the value of the information flow rate σ. Hence, the public would make their inferences based on a particular value of σ, whereas the actual value of σ is in fact different, and as a consequence, the public is misled. Such a scheme amounts to setting $F_t = \mu X t$ for some μ, which might arise in an election-microstructure model, described below, in which the value of X may be known to the candidate but not to the public, thus allowing the candidate to transmit X-dependent fake news. More generally, taking into account the randomness in the release time, one might consider a fake-news structure of the form $F_t = \mu X(t-\tau)\mathbb{1}\{t > \tau\}$. Here, $\mathbb{1}$ denotes the indicator function so that $\mathbb{1}\{A\} = 1$ if A is true and $\mathbb{1}\{A\} = 0$ otherwise. This is equivalent to having the information process $\xi_t = \hat{\sigma} X t + B_t$ with a random $\hat{\sigma}$, for which analytic expressions for the conditional probabilities can be obtained (Brody & Law 2015).

In order to analyse the effects of fake news, it will be useful to classify members of the public into three categories. We define Category I to indicate those who are unaware of the potential existence of fake elements in the information they see. Nevertheless, they act rationally in the sense that they make their estimates in accordance with formula (3.5), except that η_t is substituted in place of ξ_t. In other words, they "correctly" infer the posterior probability but based on the mistaken belief that the information they are receiving is of the type (3.1), while in reality it is of the type (4.1). As we shall see, the people in this category are most vulnerable to exposure to fake news. We denote by Category II those members of the public who are aware of the potential existence of fake news, but without knowing precisely the times at which the items of fake news in the time series $\{F_t\}$ are released. These individuals face the most technically challenging task because in their estimation they must deal with three unknowns, X, $\{B_t\}$, and $\{F_t\}$, but only one known, $\{\eta_t\}$. As we shall see, although analytic expressions for the conditional probability $\mathbb{P}(X = x_i | \{\eta_s\}_{0 \le s \le t})$ can be obtained, the analysis is rather more involved than the one for Category-I voters. Thus, the people in this category are considerably more aware of the uncertainties in their estimates than those in Category I. Finally, Category III consists of those people who are highly informed, to the extent that they know the values of the time series $\{F_t\}$. Because $\{F_t\}$ contains no information relevant to X, they can simply disregard $\{F_t\}$ from their information $\{\eta_t\}$ and use $\xi_t = \eta_t - F_t$ instead to work out their posterior belief according to (3.5). Like those in Category I, people in Category III would tend to be assertive in their judgements. We note however that a Category-III individual should be regarded to some extent as an idealisation. After all, it is an almost insurmountable task for an individual to identify perfectly which items of news are fake and which ones are not.

5. Estimating the arrival times of fake news

From the point of view of those belonging to Category II of our classification, there are two issues to address: First, one must estimate whether the information source has been contaminated with fake news. Based on this consideration, one must then determine the conditional probability $\mathbb{P}(X = x_i | \{\eta_s\}_{0 \le s \le t})$, which gives the best estimate for the likelihood of the event $X = x_i$. Note that the former issue amounts to working out the conditional probability $f_t(u)\mathrm{d}u = \mathbb{P}(\tau \in \mathrm{d}u|\{\eta_s\}_{0\leq s\leq t})$ that τ takes a value within the small interval $[u, u + \mathrm{d}u]$, which we shall calculate.

Before we proceed, we remark that there is an extensively studied research area within communication theory that is concerned with "change-point detection" or "disorder detection" (Page 1954, Shiryaev 1963a,b). The nature of this problem is as follows. One observes a time series with the property that the structure of the series changes at some random time. In a situation where this transition is not immediately apparent from observed data, the task is to detect whether a "regime change" has occurred, and if so, when it might have occurred. Stated mathematically, a prototype of such a problem is to detect the random time τ at which a Brownian motion acquires a drift (Karatzas 2003), or to detect the random time τ at which the jump rate of a Poisson process changes from one to another (Galchuk & Rozovskii 1971, Davis 1976, Peskir & Shiryaev 2002). In the Brownian context, therefore, the observation is modelled by a process of the form $B_t + \mu(t-\tau)\,\mathbb{1}\{t \geq \tau\}$, which is the same as setting $\sigma = 0$ and $F_t = \mu(t-\tau)\,\mathbb{1}\{t \geq \tau\}$ in our information process $\{\eta_t\}$. Thus, we see that the analysis of fake news introduces a new type of problem in signal detection, where one wishes to detect the unknown signal X in a noisy environment where the structure of the noise switches from one regime to another at a random time. In other words, one is trying to detect the moment of the switch—that is, the time τ at which fake news emerges—while at the same time estimating X. It should be intuitively clear that such a problem will have a wide range of applications beyond fake news analysis.

With this in mind, let us examine the conditional density for τ in the context of at most one piece of fake news. For this purpose, let us consider the model for fake news given by $F_t = m(t-\tau)\,\mathbb{1}\{t \geq \tau\}$, where $m : \mathbb{R} \to \mathbb{R}$ is an arbitrary function which we assume to be at least once differentiable. This is the form of the fake-news model that a Category-II voter *assumes* to be the true model. Then a calculation shows that the conditional density for τ is given by

$$f_t(u) = \frac{f_0(u)\sum_i p_i\, \mathrm{e}^{\int_0^t(\sigma x_i + m'(s-u)\mathbb{1}\{s\geq u\})\mathrm{d}\eta_s - \frac{1}{2}\int_0^t(\sigma x_i + m'(s-u)\mathbb{1}\{s\geq u\})^2\mathrm{d}s}}{\int_0^\infty f_0(w)\sum_i p_i\, \mathrm{e}^{\int_0^t(\sigma x_i + m'(s-w)\mathbb{1}\{s\geq w\})\mathrm{d}\eta_s - \frac{1}{2}\int_0^t(\sigma x_i + m'(s-w)\mathbb{1}\{s\geq w\})^2\mathrm{d}s}\mathrm{d}w}, \tag{5.1}$$

where $m'(u) = \mathrm{d}m(u)/\mathrm{d}u$ and $p_i = \mathbb{P}(X = x_i)$. Note that $f_0(u)$ is the *a priori* density for τ, which reflects the initial view on how the release timing is distributed. Hence, the best estimate for the release time of fake news is given by $\int_0^\infty u f_t(u)\mathrm{d}u$.

With the help of $f_t(u)$, we are now in a position to address the estimation of X for the Category-II public. From the tower property of conditional expectation, we can write

$$\mathbb{E}[X|\{\eta_s\}_{0\leq s\leq t}] = \mathbb{E}[\mathbb{E}[X|\{\eta_s\}_{0\leq s\leq t}, \tau]|\{\eta_s\}_{0\leq s\leq t}]. \tag{5.2}$$

Our strategy is to work out the inner expectation first. Since conditional on τ the information process $\{\eta_t\}$ is Markov, this reduces to $Y(\eta_t, \tau) = \mathbb{E}[X|\eta_t, \tau]$, which on account of the Bayes formula is given by

$$Y(\eta_t, \tau) = \frac{\sum_k x_k p_k \exp\left(\sigma x_k \eta_t - \frac{1}{2}\sigma^2 x_k^2 t - \sigma x_k m(t-\tau)\mathbb{1}\{t \geq \tau\}\right)}{\sum_k p_k \exp\left(\sigma x_k \eta_t - \frac{1}{2}\sigma^2 x_k^2 t - \sigma x_k m(t-\tau)\mathbb{1}(t \geq \tau)\right)}. \tag{5.3}$$

It follows that the best estimate for X is given by $\int_0^\infty Y(\eta_t, u) f_t(u)\mathrm{d}u$. The foregoing analysis shows that although it is possible to deduce a closed-form expression for the best estimate of the quantity X that one wishes to determine, the procedure is somewhat intricate. Note that we have treated the case of a single piece of fake news being released at a random time. However, the mathematical formalism describing Category-II voters can be extended in a straightforward manner to the case where multiple items of fake news are released. We shall see below simulations of this more general setup.

6. Representative voter framework

With the foregoing discussion in mind, the classification arising from our modelling setup is clear: There are those members of the public who are easily misled and manipulated since they ignore, by choice or otherwise, the possible existence of fake news; those who are wary of the potential existence of fake news but cannot be too certain about their judgements; and those who are able to detect and disregard fake news. The characteristics of these three categories can be captured most easily by means of simulation studies. For this purpose, let us consider a yes-or-no referendum scenario with a simple linear model for fake news: $F_t = \mu(t-\tau)\,\mathbb{1}\{t \geq \tau\}$. Here, μ is a constant whose sign corresponds to which way the public will be misled, and τ is an exponentially distributed random variable with density $f(u) = \lambda \mathrm{e}^{-\lambda u}$, $\lambda > 0$ a constant.

We let the realisation $X = 1$ be associated with the "yes" vote and $X = 0$ with the "no" vote. In particular, we interpret the likelihoods for the events $X=1$ and $X = 0$ to represent the aggregate opinion of the public. That is to say, $p = \mathbb{P}(X=1)$ represents the current percentage of the public who intend to vote "yes" and conversely for $1 - p = \mathbb{P}(X = 0)$. Thus, the *a priori* probability p can be calibrated from today's opinion-poll statistics. The public opinion, however, changes over time in accordance with the flow of information, and hence the *a priori* probability will be updated accordingly.

It is worth remarking that whereas in the earlier discussion on the phenomenological application of filtering techniques, we described the modelling of the behaviour of an individual, here we take an ensemble point of view in which the *a priori* probability p refers to the aggregation of the diverse opinions held by the public (see Brody and Hughston (2013) for a similar concept). The idea that we advocate here is that of a "representative voter", in analogy with representative agent models in economics. This is useful for the purpose of obtaining a qualitative understanding of the observed phenomena. We shall later in the paper return to the level of individual behaviour by introducing an alternative "election-microstructure"

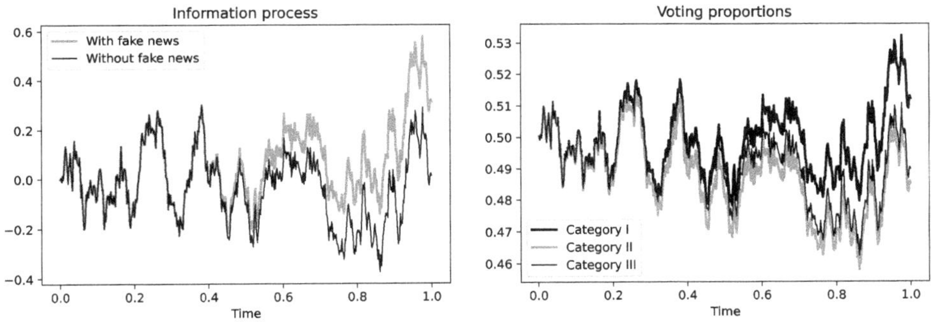

Fig. 1. *Referendum simulation.* A typical sample path associated with the linear fake-news model is sketched. The left panel shows the information processes $\{\xi_t\}$ without fake news and $\{\eta_t\}$ with fake news, released here at time 0.4. The evolution of public opinion over time is shown on the right panel for the following three types of voters: (I) those who are unaware of the existence of fake news; (II) those who are aware of the potential existence of fake news; (III) those who are able to disregard fake news fully. Here, $X = 0$ corresponds to the "no" outcome and $X = 1$ corresponds to the "yes" outcome. We see that in this particular sample path, a majority of Category-III voters will vote for the "no" outcome. However, it is evident that a piece of fake news that attempts to sway the voters in favour of the "yes" outcome has had the effect of moving the percentage figure of Category-I voters by a little over 2%, just enough to change the majority vote to "yes". On the other hand, the relative proximity of Category-II and Category-III curves shows that Category-II voters are able to largely correct for their exposure to fake news. The parameters chosen for the simulation are $\mu = 0.5$, $\sigma = 0.3$, $\lambda = 3$, $p = 0.5$, and for the random variable X, the sample outcome is $X = 0$.

framework in analogy with market microstructure models in economics. This is useful for the purpose of developing countermeasures against fake news and for policy making.

In the ensemble formalism, the event that the random variable X takes the value zero can be interpreted as the situation in which the totality of voters agree that they should be voting for the "no" outcome. If the information flow-rate parameter σ were constant, then indeed the value of X would be revealed asymptotically, and the public opinion would thus eventually converge to one choice or the other, over an infinite time horizon. Of course, this rarely happens in real life because σ will be time dependent and tends to vanish after the election has taken place. Nevertheless, it is not unreasonable in the present context to make the assumption that σ is a constant since we are only interested in the dynamics up to the polling day.

With these preliminary remarks in mind, we have simulated typical sample paths corresponding to the three voter categories for various choices of the model parameters $(\mu, \sigma, \lambda, p)$. The results of the simulation are illustrated in Figure 1. The expected main feature of the simulation paths is that the voters unaware of the existence of fake news are indeed swayed in the intended direction. What is perhaps less obvious is that the Category-II voters, who are aware of the possible existence of fake news but do not know the timing of its release, tend to overcompensate for the possibility that the information they are receiving may be contaminated. As a consequence, their estimates deviate away from the "correct" (Category-III) estimate before fake news is released. However, once the fake news is released, Category-II voters do surprisingly well at removing the effects of fake news from their estimates. One can interpret this as an indication that mere knowledge of the possibility of fake news is already a powerful antidote to its effects. Further evidence of this will be seen below in our discussion of election-microstructure models.

7. Application to opinion-poll statistics in an election

We proceed to model the dynamics for opinion-poll statistics in an election where fake news is present. For simplicity, we shall assume that there are two dominant candidates, represented by a binary random variable X, taking the values 0 and 1 that correspond to the two candidates, with *a priori* probabilities p and $1-p$, respectively. As indicated earlier, in the representative voter framework the *a priori* probability p represents the diverse opinions and mixed views initially held by the public about which value X should take. The opinion of the public, however, evolves over time in accordance with the revelation of information, which we model by the process $\{\eta_t\}$. In the event in which the public at large favours candidate 0, a malicious individual supporting candidate 1 might in response decide to release a false statement about candidate 0. According to our previous model $F_t = \mu(t-\tau)\,\mathbb{1}\{t \geq \tau\}$, the contribution of fake news continues to grow at a rate $\mu > 0$. However, in reality, one might expect that over time the strength of any one fake news item diminishes. Thus, we shall consider here a modification of F_t, whereby the strength of fake news initially grows linearly in time but is then damped exponentially. In other words, we let the contribution to F_t of a single item of fake news released at time τ be given by $m(t-\tau)\,\mathbb{1}\{t \geq \tau\}$, where $m(u) = \mu u \mathrm{e}^{-\alpha u}$ for some damping rate $\alpha > 0$ and τ is distributed according to $f(u) = \lambda \mathrm{e}^{-\lambda u}$. Once the effects of fake news are sufficiently damped, the public support may revert back towards the direction of candidate 0. However, another item of fake news may be released, and so on. The process will be repeated until polling day.

The structure of our model should now be evident. At time τ_1 comes the release of the initial piece of fake news, to be damped gradually; at time τ_2 comes the next release, and so on. The waiting times between fake news releases are modelled by an exponential distribution. In other words, the release times are the jump times of a Poisson process. We are interested in a simulation study of the dynamical evolution of opinion-poll statistics in the presence of various pieces of fake news. For simplicity, we consider fake news to be one sided, i.e., it is released only by the supporters of one of the candidates. For the purpose of simulation, we shall also assume that the damping rates for the various fake news releases are all equal and similarly for the linear growth rates. Typical sample paths resulting from the simulation studies are shown in Figure 2. For clarity, we show only Category-I and Category-III voters. In this way, we can see the full, unmitigated effect of fake news. We see that for this sample path, the candidate who would win the election in the absence of fake news ends up losing it. In fact, based on the parameter choice indicated in the figure

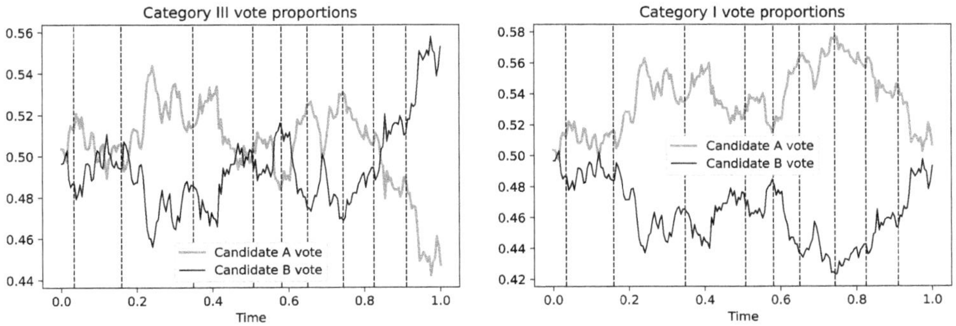

Fig. 2. *Election dynamics without and with fake news.* In this example, in the absence of fake news, Candidate B, who initially struggles somewhat in the opinion poll, nevertheless manages to win the election comfortably (left panel). However, with persistent fake news (released in this example on nine occasions, indicated by the vertical lines), the public is misled sufficiently for Candidate A to secure a narrow victory (right panel). Of the 100,000 simulations we conducted with the same parameter choice, the losing candidate ended up winning the election owing to fake news in about 30% of the cases. The parameters are as follows: $\sigma = 0.3$, $\mu = 2$, $\alpha = 5$, $p = 0.5$, and $\lambda = 10$.

caption, we found that the likelihood of the "losing" candidate (who would have lost the election in the absence of fake news) ending up winning is about 30 %. This number, of course, depends on the choice of model parameters and thus can be increased arbitrarily by increasing the fake news strength or frequency parameters. Thus, while each element of fake news is damped exponentially in time, a persistent attack on democracy can and will succeed if no action is taken against it.

8. Election-microstructure models

The representative voter framework presented above is highly effective in modelling the stylized aspects of fake news and its impact at a phenomenological level. It can also be applied in an efficient scenario analysis by means of simulation studies, for instance, to investigate the parameter dependence of the likelihood of fake news changing the outcome of an election. We shall now turn to an alternative formulation that focuses on the microscopic level of individual voters to deduce the macroscopic behaviour of the general public. While the mathematical ingredients used in this election-microstructure model are essentially the same as those used for the representative voter framework, there is one important conceptual difference, namely, that in the election-microstructure model, the signal in the information process can be transmitted by a sender (e.g., the candidate). What follows is framed in the language of political elections, but the treatment is equally applicable to referendums.

Our model is based on the following idea, which represents a somewhat simplified characterization of the mechanism by which an individual arrives at their preferred choice of candidate: When deciding who to vote for in an election, an individual will attempt to evaluate candidates with respect to a number of issues, or factors. For instance, what are the views of the candidates on taxation, on social welfare, on freedom of the press, on immigration, on abortion, on transport, on gun control, on healthcare, on public spending, and so on? Nonpolitical elements may also be considered, such as the state of health of the candidate, or the level of personal integrity. As we shall outline below, in our model, the positions of the candidates on these factors are then transformed into an overall score, and the voter ultimately picks the candidate with the highest score.

To proceed, let us assume that there are K independent such factors in an election with L candidates and N voters. We let X_k^l denote the lth candidate's position on the kth factor. However, the positions of the candidates on these factors, if they were in office, are not always transparent to voters. Nevertheless, during an election campaign, candidates will attempt to communicate their positions to the electorate. This communication flows through a number of channels: through advertising by the campaigns, through publications by news outlets, through word of mouth, through social media, and so on. The members of the electorate thus obtain partial information, which we shall model as before in the form

$$\eta_t^{k,l} = \sigma_{k,l} X_k^l \, t + B_t^{k,l} + F_t^{k,l} \tag{8.1}$$

for $k = 1, 2, \ldots, K$ and $l = 1, 2, \ldots, L$. In other words, we have a total of KL information processes $\{\eta_t^{k,l}\}$. Some of these may be contaminated by fake news, which can take different forms. For instance, candidates may try to make themselves look more palatable to a wider section of the electorate than they perhaps are (such as by suppressing information about their health, or by downplaying their views on taxation). They may run negative ads to spread untruths or half-truths about their opponents. Or there may be malicious agents spreading entirely fabricated stories supporting one candidate or the other. It is this latter type of fake news that can spread quickly on social media and has thus attracted much attention recently.

A member of the electorate has their own views on how attractive a candidate with a given set of factor values is. We model this by a *score function*, which can differ between individuals and assigns a measure of attractiveness to a candidate with a given factor vector $\boldsymbol{X}^l$. Hence, a member of the electorate will vote for the candidate with the highest score. For the present paper, we consider linear score functions. Thus, the score S_n^l of candidate l determined by voter n is given by

$$S_n^l = \sum_{k=1}^{K} w_n^k X_k^l = \boldsymbol{w}_n \cdot \boldsymbol{X}^l, \tag{8.2}$$

supposing the vector $\boldsymbol{X}^l$ were known. The weights $\{w_n^k\}$ may be positive or negative, with magnitudes that may be large or small depending on how strongly the voter feels about a given issue. Keeping in mind that the factors need to be estimated from the available information, voter n will choose candidate l over candidate l' if and only if

$$\sum_{k=1}^{K} w_n^k \left(\mathbb{E}_t[X_k^l] - \mathbb{E}_t[X_k^{l'}] \right) > 0, \tag{8.3}$$

or, more succinctly, $\boldsymbol{w}_n \cdot (\mathbb{E}_t[\boldsymbol{X}^l] - \mathbb{E}_t[\boldsymbol{X}^{l'}]) > 0$. Here, we let $\mathbb{E}_t[-]$ denote expectation conditional on having observed the information processes $\{\eta_s^{k,l}\}$ up to time t. Each component of the conditional expectations $\mathbb{E}_t[\boldsymbol{X}^l]$ can be worked out by following the methodology described earlier, on account of the independence of policy factors X_k^l and $X_{k'}^l$ for $k \neq k'$. We shall make the reasonable assumption that noise terms for independent factors are independent and make a further simplifying assumption that the release times of fake news associated with independent factors are likewise independent.

A population of voters can be modelled by proposing a distribution over weight vectors $\{\boldsymbol{w}_n\}$. By randomly sampling from this distribution and computing, for each sample, which candidate is preferred, one can build up a population-level picture of voting patterns and investigate, in particular, the effect of fake news. In practice, such a distribution could be obtained by asking randomly chosen voters a series of questions in order to generate an approximation of their weight vectors. Moreover, large internet companies (such as search engines, social networks, and global retailers) possess data that is likely rich enough to reliably estimate these weights for individual users. This places such companies in a position of great responsibility. It should be evident that the knowledge of the weight vectors $\{\boldsymbol{w}_n\}$ is highly valuable in order to implement a targeted campaign. In particular, there is a concern that if such a targeted campaign were carried out by originators of fake news, democracy could be at risk. However, the simulation studies below support the notion that the mere knowledge that there might be fake news in circulation may be sufficient to eliminate to a large degree of the impact of fake news.

9. Opinion polls in the microstructure model

We now present simulation results in the case where candidates are evaluated by three binary independent factors in an election with two candidates. For concreteness, let us suppose that the three factors concern whether the candidate is liberal or conservative, whether the candidate is healthy or not, and whether the candidate is of good or bad character. For the purpose of this simulation, let us assume that the hidden characteristics of the two candidates, labelled here as A and B, are such that $X_1^A = 1$ (candidate A is liberal) and $X_1^B = -1$ (candidate B is conservative), $X_2^A = 1$ (candidate A is in good health) and $X_2^B = -1$ (candidate B is in bad health), and $X_3^A = 1$ (candidate A has good character) and $X_3^B = -1$ (candidate B has bad character), the names and values being chosen for illustration. Voters try to estimate these factor values based on the information available to them.

We take the number of voters to be $N = 1$ million, and we sample the weight vectors according to the following prescription: We draw the weight vectors of 55%

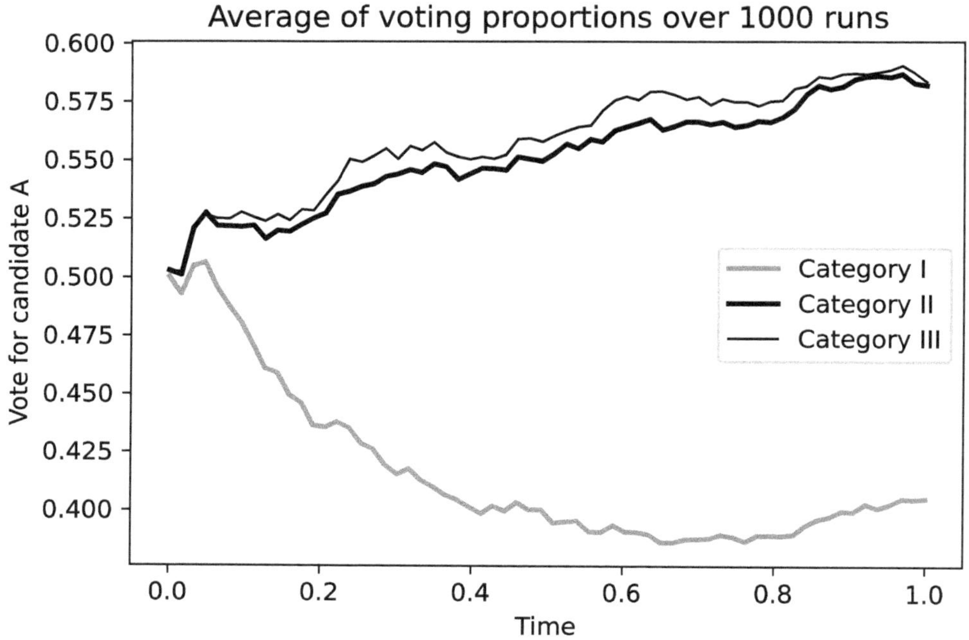

Fig. 3. *Proportion of population voting for candidate A as time passes.* These curves are taken as averages over 1,000 runs. Category-I voters are those that are unaware of the existence of fake news; Category-III voters are those who can fully eliminate fake news and thus represent the "correct" estimates. We see that fake news, which is designed to support candidate B, has the intended effect on average, making an election, which candidate A should win comfortably, more competitive. These effects can be magnified or diminished by varying the parameters of the fake-news terms in the information processes. We also recognize that Category-II voters are successfully correcting for most of the effects of fake news. The parameters used in the simulation are: $\sigma = 0.2$, $|\mu| = 1.5$, $\alpha = 4$, $p = 0.5$, and $N = 1$ million. Waiting times between fake-news releases are drawn at random for each run from an exponential distribution with rate parameter 4. The code used for these simulations is available at github.com/dmmeier/Fake_News.

of voters from a three-dimensional normal distribution with standard deviation 0.4 (Distribution 1), centred at $(1, 1, 1)$, but restricted to the positive values for the second dimension and restricted to the interval $[0, 1]$ for the third dimension. The truncation reflects the fact that voters are unlikely, for instance, to actively prefer candidates in ill health or with bad character. Members of this part of the population tend to prefer liberal, healthy candidates of good character. We then draw the weight vectors of the remaining 45% of the population from the same, truncated normal distribution (Distribution 2), but centred at $(-1, 1, 0)$, representing voters that prefer a conservative, healthy candidate, but who are indifferent in relation to the candidate's character. The distributions are chosen purely for illustration.

It is evident that candidate A, whose factor vector $\boldsymbol{X}^A = (1, 1, 1)$ coincides with the centre of Distribution 1 representing 55% of the population, tends to win the election in the absence of fake news. However, we now assume that in the run-up to the election, various pieces of fake news are released that purport to show that the health and character of candidate A are bad, that the health and character of candidate B are good, that candidate A is more conservative than they seem to be, and that candidate B is more liberal. The intended effect of these elements of fake news is clear: shifting the perceived vector of factors $\boldsymbol{X}^A$ of candidate A out of the centre of Distribution 1, while at the same time, moving candidate B towards it. Clearly, this increases the chances candidate B has of winning the election.

In order to isolate the effect of fake news in our simulations, we take the prior probabilities for all six random variables $\{X_k^A, X_k^B\}_{k=1,2,3}$ to be 0.5 for the value 1 and 0.5 for the value -1. This means that the population starts out in a fully agnostic state. To model fake news, we employ our earlier model in which the effect of a piece of fake news initially grows linearly in time but is then damped exponentially. In Figure 3, we show the average over 1,000 simulations, calculating voting proportions over time for each of the voter categories. The code used for these simulations is available at github.com/dmmeier/Fake_News.

The results show that in the absence of fake news, candidate A on average wins the election quite handsomely—this corresponds to the Category-III curve. Fake news of the type constructed above, however, pushes the relative voting proportions of Category-I voters, who are unaware of the existence of fake news, in favour of candidate B, as we had anticipated. What is perhaps most striking here is the curve showing estimates for Category-II voters. These voters possess the knowledge that there may be fake news in circulation, but they do not know how many pieces of fake news have been released or at what precise time. That is, they only know the statistical distribution of $\{F_t\}$, or equivalently, the prior distribution $f_0(u)$. In spite of this, Category-II voters are able to reduce the effects of fake news significantly by developing a statistical understanding of the nature of fake news and correcting their estimates accordingly. Furthermore, preliminary simulation studies suggest that their performance is robust against modest mis-specifications of the prior distribution.

10. Discussion and outlook

We have presented two approaches for the modelling of fake news in elections and referendums: one based on the idea of a representative voter, useful to obtain a qualitative understanding of the effects of fake news, and one based on the idea of an election microstructure, useful for practical implementation in concrete scenarios. In both cases, the results illustrate rather explicitly the impact of fake news in elections and referendums. We have demonstrated that by merely possessing the knowledge of the possibility that pieces of fake news might be in circulation, a diligent individual (Category II) is able to mitigate the effects of fake news to a significant degree.

The models presented here invite further development in a number of directions. Our simulations, for instance, were based on random draws of waiting times for the release of fake news. However, in reality, a malicious individual trying to influence an election is likely to try to optimize release times to maximize impact (e.g., to maximize the chances of winning the election). It would be interesting to include such optimal release strategies in our models. Furthermore, as indicated above, in our simulations, Category-II voters are assumed to know the parameters of the fake-news terms. This included, in particular, the value of the fake-news drift parameter μ and the damping rate α. A natural extension of the model would allow for these parameters to be themselves random. Finally, the election-microstructure approach could be developed further by allowing dependencies between the various factors or by introducing several different information processes reflecting the news consumption preferences of different sections of society. These generalizations will open up challenging but interesting new directions for research.

At any rate, the performance of Category-II voters, which significantly exceeded the expectations of the present authors, leads to a hopeful conclusion indeed: namely, that by ensuring that members of the electorate are made aware of the possibility and the nature of fake news in the information they consume, policy makers may find success in countering the dark forces of fake news.

Acknowledgments

The authors thank J. Armstrong, A. Macrina, and B. K. Meister for comments, and L. P. Hughston for conversations over the years on the information-based modelling framework.

References

[1] H. Allcott & M. Gentzkow (2017) Social media and fake news in the 2016 election. *Journal of Economic Perspectives*, **31**, 211–236.

[2] J. Amador, A. Oehmichen & M. Molina-Solana (2017) Characterizing political fake news in twitter by its meta-data. arXiv:1712.05999.

[3] M. Beibel (1996) A note on Ritov's Bayes approach to the minimax property of the cusum procedure. *Annals of Statistics* **24**, 1804–1812.

[4] A. Bovet & H. A. Makse (2019) Influence of fake news in Twitter during the 2016 US presidential election. *Nature Communications* **10**, 7.

[5] D. C. Brody & L. P. Hughston (2006) Quantum noise and stochastic reduction. *Journal of Physics* A **39**, 833–876.

[6] D. C. Brody, L. P. Hughston & A. Macrina (2007) Beyond hazard rates: A new framework for credit-risk modelling. In *Advances in Mathematical Finance,* M. Fu, R. Jarrow, Ju-Yi Yen & R. Elliott (Eds.), Basel: Birkhäuser.

[7] D. C. Brody, L. P. Hughston & A. Macrina (2008) Dam rain and cumulative gain. *Proceedings of the Royal Society London* A **464**, 1801–1822.

[8] D. C. Brody, L. P. Hughston & X. Yang (2013) Signal processing with Lévy information. *Proceedings of the Royal Society London* A **469**, 20120433.

[9] D. C. Brody & L. P. Hughston (2013) Lévy information and the aggregation of risk aversion. *Proceedings of the Royal Society London* A **469**, 20130024.

[10] D. C. Brody & Y. T. Law (2015) Pricing of defaultable bonds with random information flow. *Applied Mathematical Finance* **22**, 399–420.

[11] D. Collins, C. Efford, J. Elliott, P. Farrelly, S. Hart, J. Knight, I. C. Lucas, B. O'Hara, R. Pow, J. Stevens & G. Watling (2018) House of Commons Digital, Culture, Media and Sport Committee: *Disinformation and 'Fake News': Interim Report*, Fifth Report of Session 2017–19, www.parliament.uk/dcmscom.

[12] N. J. Conroy, V. L. Rubin & Y. Chen (2015) Automatic deception detection: Methods for finding fake news. *ASIS&T Annual Meeting Proceedings* **52**, 1–4.

[13] M. H. A. Davis (1976) A note on the Poisson disorder problem. *Banach Centre Publications* **1**, 65–72.

[14] M. A. El-Gamal & D. M. Grether (1995) Are people Bayesian? Uncovering behavioral strategies. *Journal of the American Statistical Association* **90**, 1137–1145.

[15] L. I. Galchuk & B. L. Rozovskii (1971) The "disorder" problem for a Poisson process. *Theory of Probability and its Applications* **16**, 712–716.

[16] D. Grether & C. Plott (1979) Economic theory of choice and the preference reversal phenomenon. *American Economic Review* **69**, 623–638.

[17] D. Kahneman & A. Tversky (1974) Judgment under uncertainty: Heuristics and biases. *Science* **185**, 1124–1131.

[18] T. Kailath (1974) A view of three decades of linear filtering theory. *IEEE Transactions of Information Theory* **20**, 146–181.

[19] I. Karatzas (2003) A note on Bayesian detection of change-points with an expected miss criterion. *Statistics and Decisions* **21**, 3–14.

[20] A. Khajehnejad & S. Hajimirza (2018) A Bayesian model for false information belief impact, optimal design, and fake news containment. arXiv:1804.01576.

[21] N. Silver (2016) FiveThirtyEight: Who will win the presidency? https://projects.fivethirtyeight.com/2016-election-forecast/.

[22] E. S. Page (1954) Continuous inspection scheme. *Biometrika* **41**, 100–105.

[23] G. Peskir & A. N. Shiryaev (2002) Solving the Poisson disorder problem. In *Advances in Finance and Stochastics*, essays in honour of Dieter Sondermann, K. Sandmann & P. J. Schönbucher (Eds.), Springer-Verlag.

[24] A. N. Shiryaev (1963a) On optimum methods in quickest detection problems. *Theory of Probability and Its Applications* **8**, 22–46.

[25] A. N. Shiryaev (1963b) On the detection of disorder in a manufacturing process I, II. *Theory of Probability and Its Applications* **8**, 247–265, 402–413.

[26] K. Shu, A. Silva, S. Wang, J. Tang & H. Liu (2017) Fake news detection on social media: A data mining perspective. *ACM SIGKDD Explorations Newsletter* **19**, 22–36.

[27] J. Soll (2016) The long and brutal history of fake news. *Politico Magazine*, 18 December 2016.

[28] N. Wiener (1949) *Extrapolation, Interpolation, and Smoothing of Stationary Time Series,* Boston: The Technology Press of the MIT.

[29] N. Wiener (1954) *The Human Use of Human Beings*, a new and revised edition, Boston: Houghton Mifflin Company.

[30] W. M. Wonham (1965) Some applications of stochastic differential equations to optimal nonlinear filtering. *Journal of the Society for Industrial and Applied Mathematics* A**2**, 347–369.

[31] Y. Yang, L. Zheng, J. Zhang, Q. Cui, Z. Li & P. S. Yu (2018) TI-CNN: Convolutional neural networks for fake news detection. arXiv:1806.00749.

www.ingramcontent.com/pod-product-compliance
Lightning Source LLC
LaVergne TN
LVHW081934200926
848484LV00009B/2432